CAMBRIDGE LATIN AMERICAN STUDIES

GENERAL EDITOR
SIMON COLLIER

ADVISORY COMMITTEE
MARVIN BERNSTEIN, MALCOLM DEAS
CLARK W. REYNOLDS, ARTURO VALENZUELA

52

SUGAR PLANTATIONS IN THE FORMATION OF BRAZILIAN SOCIETY

For a list of books in this series, please turn to page 614.

SUGAR PLANTATIONS
IN THE
FORMATION OF BRAZILIAN SOCIETY

Bahia, 1550–1835

STUART B. SCHWARTZ

Department of History
University of Minnesota

The right of the
University of Cambridge
to print and sell
all manner of books
was granted by
Henry VIII in 1534.
The University has printed
and published continuously
since 1584.

CAMBRIDGE UNIVERSITY PRESS

CAMBRIDGE

LONDON   NEW YORK   NEW ROCHELLE

MELBOURNE   SYDNEY

Published by the Press Syndicate of the University of Cambridge
The Pitt Building, Trumpington Street, Cambridge CB2 1RP
32 East 57th Street, New York, NY 10022, USA
10 Stamford Road, Oakleigh, Melbourne 3166, Australia

First published 1985

Printed in the United States of America

Library of Congress Cataloging in Publication Data
Schwartz, Stuart B.
Sugar plantations in the formation of Brazilian society.
(Cambridge Latin American studies; 52)
Bibliography: p.
Includes index.
1. Sugar trade – Brazil – Bahia (State) – History. 2. Planta-
tions – Brazil – Bahia (State) – History. 3. Slavery – Brazil –
Bahia (State) – History. 4. Bahia (Brazil : State) – Race relatons.
5. Bahia (Brazil : State) – Social conditions. 6. Bahia (Brazil : State) –
Economic conditions. I. Title. II. Series.
HD9114.B7B347   1985   306'.0981'42   85-6716
ISBN 0 521 30934 4 (hard covers)
ISBN 0 521 31399 6 (paperback)

This book is respectfully dedicated to four Bahian intellectuals:
Teodoro Sampaio, born of a slave in Rio Fundo;
Wanderley Pinho, son of a planter family;
Luiz Henrique, from Nazaré das Farinhas on the southern shore;
Katia Mattoso, who came to Bahia from afar.
Their love for their homeland has illumined so many hours of my life.

And to my family: Nancy, Alison, and Lee

CONTENTS

Contents

Appendixes

FIGURES, MAPS, AND TABLES

Figures

PREFACE

Brazil, almost from the moment of its inception as a European colony in 1500 until it finally abolished slavery in 1888 (the last American nation to do so), wove the strands of coerced labor, commercial capitalism, and Iberian seigneurial traditions and attitudes into a complex social fabric. This process resulted in a multiracial, stratified society profoundly influenced by the plantation system and the hierarchies of status inherent in its labor force, as well as by those derived from its juridical and religious codes. This book is an attempt to examine the historical development of that society in Bahia, a major Brazilian plantation zone, over a period of almost three hundred years. It seeks to understand the nature of Bahia's economy and society and to describe in detail the formation and operations of this slave society.

Books about "sugar and slaves" are not uncommon. One need only pick a Caribbean island, and probabilities are high that a study already exists in which sugar and slaves figure in the title or are at least the focus of attention. In Brazil, since the 1930s, books of a similar nature have been published; and many authors have adopted an interpretation in which Brazilian society essentially sprang from the sugar-plantation experience. But despite the popularity of that vision, primary source materials on sugar and slavery are relatively scarce, and authors have long depended on a few colonial chroniclers or travelers from the nineteenth century in order to write about the plantation regime. The result has been a good deal of repetition and analyses that often substitute affirmation or theory for evidence.

In the present study, I have tried to write the history of Bahian plantation society using the traditional sources but adding to them a considerable body of previously little-used or unused materials: wills and testaments, census returns, the few surviving plantation records, notarial and ecclesiastical registers, and more commonly used administrative and private correspondence. I have concentrated my attention on Bahia because it was a major plantation zone and an important terminus of the Atlantic slave trade and because its documentary record, though fragmentary and spotty by antebellum U.S. standards, is better than that of other colonial plantation regions of Brazil. I have been forced to depend heavily on the accounts of ecclesiastical properties, especially the Jesuit plantations of Sergipe and Santana. At one point I was tempted to write a history of only those properties, but I decided instead to attempt a broader study using their records, testing and supporting them with other materials, thus avoiding the tendency to generalize from an atypical case. Although I have limited my analysis to Bahia, I do believe that the process and patterns described here were essentially the same in other sugar-producing areas of Brazil.

Studies of plantation society in Brazil have traditionally been written from the veranda of the "big house," in that the planters produced much of the documentation and the historians were often themselves the descendants of the great planter families. Although planters figure as an important element in my analysis, their genealogies and exploits are not placed at center stage as they usually are. Instead, I have sought to shift the focus of attention to the formation and interaction of the most important social groups and categories within the context of a colonial regime producing a staple for international markets. Obviously, a study of Brazilian plantation society is by definition a study of slavery, and the reader will find that the outpouring of scholarship on slavery in the Americas has informed and stimulated my research and findings. Aspects of slave life – physical conditions, family, demography, culture, resistance – fill the following pages, but this book is not so much about slavery per se as it is about the relationship between plantation production and the overall structure of society. In other words, although slavery lies at the core of the study, I see it as a result of certain economic and cultural features that are themselves influenced by the dynamic relations between slave and master and between slavery and the larger society. In other words, slavery is viewed here as part of a larger structure of social and economic relations.

At the heart of this study I have placed the social aspects of production, the relations between the owners of the means of production and the laborers and between the workers and the productive process. In this I have followed Marx in seeking in those relations the "inner secret" of the society and polity; but unlike some of his followers, I have also taken seriously Marx's admonition to examine empirically the infinite possible variations that can result from these relationships. This, then, is a book that attempts to put work back in its proper place as the most important determinant of a slave society and to understand groups, institutions, and interactions always in the context of the social relations of production on the sugar plantation. The peculiarities of that productive system, its labor organization and requirements, provide an analytical starting point. The reader will discover, however, that although I have kept economic considerations to the fore, I have also sought to give cultural and ideological factors due consideration.

This is not a book of "Marxist" analysis; but I have given serious attention to the insights that Marx and some of his followers have provided about societies, and especially about the historical development of early modern European ones.

To some extent, the origins of this book lie in the growth of a comparative approach to the study of slavery and race relations. I have made comparisons at various points in the text when these were directly applicable, but I decided not to overload the notes with references to publications that deal with the same topic elsewhere in the Americas. Instead, I think that the best contribution that this book can make to the literature on comparative slavery is to present a detailed and accurate account of the Bahian society and economy. Brazil has often been used as a point of comparison for authors who write on the United States or the Caribbean, but in fact the materials available for these comparisons are often misleading, scanty, or wrong. I hope that this volume will partially rectify that situation.

Brazilian scholarship on slavery and slave society owes much to Gilberto Freyre's classic *Casa grande e senzala* (Rio de Janeiro, 1933), which revalidated the African and Indian contributions to Brazilian culture by examining the interior life of the patriarchal planter families of the Northeast. Freyre's emphasis on the adaptability of the Portuguese colonists and the integration of the races in the plantation house led to a somewhat rosy view of slavery and race relations, which a group of Brazilian historians and sociologists, mostly from São Paulo, began to attack vigorously in studies concentrated on the South of Brazil, sometimes on areas in which slavery was a secondary form of labor; but they brought a committed and informed theoretical structure and a good deal of hard evidence to bear in their new vision of Brazilian slavery. This book owes much of its origin to both Freyre and the São Paulo school. I set out to write in the São Paulo tradition but to focus on the Northeast's plantation economy, where slavery had been dominant, and to concentrate on the colonial era rather than the nineteenth century. Although I had originally embarked on a program of proving Freyre wrong, I abandoned that approach as sterile and wrongheaded. His was a book about the formation of a Brazilian mentality, and although it might be criticized on the grounds of evidence or methodology, it provided insights into the creation of plantation society that more than compensated for its faults. As a foreigner and one who had rarely set foot in the *massapé*, I could not hope to write that kind of book or to use social science to replace the perception or knowledge that comes from living totally within, and as part of, a culture. Elie Halévy, the great French historian of England, once wrote of his feelings of insufficiency as he sat in the British Museum watching the Union Jack through the window and thinking of his struggle to understand what any English child in the street knew as a matter of course. I have often felt the same way as I read with jealousy the dedications of books by authors who had grown up in rural Brazil and learned about that world directly from those who lived it.

And so I have tried to write a study based on archival and printed sources, to apply the techniques and methods of modern historical scholarship, to inform myself on social theory, and to attempt, within my limitations, to understand the motives and actions of the people and groups I am studying. Although many quantitative data are found in these pages, I have sought to avoid the pitfalls of Dickens's character Dr. Gradgrind, in whose charmed apartment

. . . the most complicated social questions were cast up, got into exact totals, and finally settled. . . . As if an astronomical observatory should be made without any windows, and the astronomer within should arrange the starry universe solely by pen, ink, and paper, so Mr. Gradgrind, in his Observatory (and there are many like it), had no need to cast an eye upon the teeming myriads of human beings around him, but could settle all their destinies on a slate, and wipe out all their tears with one dirty bit of sponge.

My aim throughout has been not to allow the quantitative data to become an end in themselves but to use them to understand better the historical process and the people within it.

This study is divided into four parts. The first, "Formations, 1500–1600," deals with the origins of the Brazilian plantation system and the early experience with American Indians as workers and slaves. It suggests how and why Indians were replaced by Africans. Part II, "The Bahian Engenhos and Their World," provides a detailed analysis of life and work on the sugar plantations of Bahia by discussing the region, the history of the sugar economy, the process of sugar making, and the finances of plantership. Part III, "Sugar Society," attempts in six chapters to discuss the general organizational principles of this plantation society and then to analyze each of its principal groups. Included here are two somewhat technical chapters on slave demography and family. Finally, in Part IV, "Reorientation and Persistence, 1750–1835," the general political and economic trends of the late colonial and early national periods are discussed as background for an examination of slaveholding in Bahian society. The last chapter gives the slaves the final word, discussing slave resistance and particularly the series of Bahian rebellions in the early nineteenth century that paralleled the political unrest of the struggle for Brazilian independence. In their cumulative effect, these rebellions were an unsuccessful war against slavery.

Throughout the book, I have adopted a number of conventions of which the reader should be aware. Portuguese orthography is a confusing matter because attempts to standardize it in the twentieth century have failed and at times the accepted rules have changed. Thus, some authors have spelled their name differently at various points in their life (e.g., Gonsalves/Gonçalves; Vianna/Viana). For consistency, I have tried to use the most recent usage. I have also preferred contemporary Brazilian rather than Portuguese orthography (e.g., Antônio rather than António). Let any English-speaking reader who is confused take heart from the confusion that has sometimes resulted from this situation in the Lusophone world. In the book, I have also attempted to avoid gender bias in the use of language. Thus, references to a "kettleman" or a "boatman" are in fact historically accurate. In translating a number of important terms I have been forced to make some arbitrary decisions. The word *engenho* was used in Portuguese to refer to what today we call in English a sugar plantation, by which I mean a relatively large tropical or semitropical agricultural estate, cultivated by enslaved or coerced workers, producing for the market. The word *plantation* was never used in its modern sense by the Portuguese in the period studied here. I have used "plantation," however, as a synonym for "engenho," although at some points I have also used "engenho" in its more restricted meaning of a mill for pressing sugarcane. In a similar fashion, I have used *planters* as a synonym for "engenho owners" (*senhores de engenho*) but have not employed it for those who grew cane but did not possess their own mill. These and other foreign terms used repeatedly in the book are defined in the Glossary, near the end of the book.

The basic unit of Portuguese currency was the *real* (plural *réis*). This was actually only a money of account. The *milréis* or 1,000 réis normally written 1$, with fractions carried out to three places (e.g., 1$460). Various Portuguese weights and measures have been defined in a list that follows and in the Glossary. All weights and measures given are metric unless otherwise noted.

Ten years of research and writing have produced a quantity of intellectual debts that are simply impossible to satisfy fully here. The directors and staffs of nearly thirty archives and libraries in six different countries, which are cited in the notes to this book, extended the facilities and services of those institutions; and many of them offered me hospitality and friendship that went far beyond the normal responsibilities of their offices.

Some friends and colleagues devoted their time and expertise to reviewing chapters of the book, making suggestions, and often providing me with frank and fearless criticism. At the time, their frankness was not always appreciated; but I see now how much it has improved the final result. Here, I want to mention particularly those who took on the task more than once. Dauril Alden, Stanley Engerman, Eugene Genovese, Richard Graham, and Herbert Klein all gave me the benefit of their knowledge and time. Fathers Charles Ronan and Matias Kieman and Professor Manoel Cardoso kindly answered my queries about Catholicism. My colleagues at the University of Minnesota Russell Menard and Robert McCaa were especially helpful with the demographic aspects of the manuscript and suffered my incessant questions with patience and goodwill. Ward Barrett shared his knowledge of the history of sugar. Anthropologist Stephen Gudeman collaborated with me on a project involving godparentage among slaves, some of the results of which appear in these pages. Both in Brazil and at Minnesota, various students contributed by helping with archival research or with the computer-related aspects of the project. João Reis, Lowell Gudmundson, Patricia Aufderheide, Robert Ferry, Rosa Maria Peterson, and Steve Burmeister at various times and in various ways contributed to the completion of the book.

In Brazil, conversations with Fernando Novais, Antônio Barros de Castro, José Antônio Gonsalves de Mello, Katia M. de Queirós Mattoso, Luiz Henrique Dias Tavares, Neusa Esteves, José Gabriel Costa Pinto, and José Honório Rodrigues broadened my understanding of Brazil and sometimes led directly to important research materials. I shall never forget the kindness of the late Senhor Luiz Tavares, who took me to see an operating sugar mill and guided me through back roads of the southern Recôncavo, or that of agronomist João Francisco Costa Pinto, whose jeep carried me to canefields and towns in Bahia and who walked 3 kilometers through saltwater swamps with me to visit the ruins of Engenho Sergipe. I was adopted in Cachoeira by Luiz Carlos and "Gaivota," two children who waited outside the town hall for the "professor" who shared his lunch with them, in return for which they shared with me a wisdom far beyond their years. They, and others like them in Brazil whose names I never knew, taught me much I could never have learned by study alone.

Over the years, I have been fortunate to receive the financial support of various institutions for various aspects of the research and writing of this book. I should mention first my own University of Minnesota, which provided research and travel funds through its Office of International Programs and its Graduate School. Additionally, I received research grants from the American Council of Learned Societies (1974–5) and the John Simon Guggenheim Memorial Foundation (1979–80). The University of California, Los Angeles, provided excellent facilities and hospitality when, as a resident scholar, I initiated the writing of the book in 1975. The Newberry Library Program in Quantitative and Social History allowed me to begin in 1974 to acquire a knowledge of the methods of the "new" social history. Most of all, however, I wish to express my gratitude and debt to the Institute for Advanced Study at Princeton, where as a fellow in 1982–3 I spent one of the most stimulating academic years of my life.

In the final preparation of the book, Suzanne Cave and Peg van

Sandt assumed the task of typing the manuscript in its various avatars. They suffered my revisions and changes without complaint. Editor Frank Smith at Cambridge University Press provided encouragement, suggestions, and help in getting the book to press in its present form.

As a writing strategy in a project that covers almost three hundred years of a society's development, I decided to publish detailed articles on some aspects of the research as a way of identifying and answering some of the more interesting themes and questions. At various places in the book, I summarize the conclusions of articles that were published earlier. These are cited in the notes. The reader should be aware, however, that I have incorporated new material in some places and have, in a few instances, changed my conclusions. Two chapters are modified versions of articles originally published in the *American Historical Review* ("Indian Labor and New World Plantations: European Demands and Indian Responses in Northeastern Brazil," *American Historical Review* 83; no. 1 [Feb. 1978]: 43–79; "Patterns of Slaveholding in the Americas: New Evidence From Brazil," *American Historical Review* 87, no. 1 [Feb. 1982]: 55–86). I wish to thank the editor of that journal for permission to reprint portions of those articles.

ABBREVIATIONS AND SPECIAL TERMS

Archives

ACMS	Arquivo da Curia Metropolitana do Salvador
ACS	Arquivo da Câmara Municipal do Salvador
ADB/CSB	Arquivo Distrital de Braga/Coleção São Bento
AGS	Archivo General de Simancas
AHNM	Archivo Historico Nacional de Madrid
AHU	Arquivo Histórico Ultramarino (Lisbon)
ANRJ	Arquivo Nacional do Rio de Janeiro
ANTT	Arquivo Nacional do Torre do Tombo (Lisbon)
APB	Arquivo Público do Estado da Bahia (Salvador)
APMC	Arquivo da Prefeitura Municipal da Cachoeira
ARSI	Archivum Romanum Societatis Iesu (Rome)
ASCMB	Arquivo da Santa Casa da Misericórdia da Bahia
BA	Biblioteca da Ajuda (Lisbon)
BGUC	Biblioteca Geral da Universidade de Coimbra
BI	Biblioteca da Itamaraty (Rio de Janeiro)
BM	British Museum (London)
BNL	Biblioteca Nacional de Lisboa
BNM	Biblioteca Nacional de Madrid
BNRJ	Biblioteca Nacional de Rio de Janeiro
CEB	Centro de Estudos Brasileiros (Universidade de São Paulo)
IHGAP	Instituto Histórico, Geográfico e Arqueológico de Pernambuco (Recife)
IHGB	Instituto Histórico e Geográfico Brasileiro (Rio de Janeiro)
IHGBa	Instituto Histórico e Geográfico da Bahia
LC/Port. Mss.	Library of Congress/Portuguese Manuscripts
MHN/CWP	Museu Histórico Nacional (Rio de Janeiro)/Coleção Wanderley Pinho

NL/GC	Newberry Library (Chicago)/Greenlee Collection
PRO	Public Record Office (London)
SGL	Sociedade de Geografia de Lisboa
StL/VFL	Saint Louis University/Vatican Film Library

Collections

Bras.	Brasilia
Con. Ultra.	Conselho Ultramarino
Corp. cron.	Corpo cronológico
CSJ	Cartório dos Jesuitas
Ord. reg.	Ordens régias
pap. avul.	papéis avulsos
Pres. da Prov.	Presidência da Provincia
sec. jud.	secção judiciária
sec. prov.	secretarias provinciales

Terms for describing archival and documentary materials

alvará	royal decree
assento	council decision
caixa	box
cap. (capítulo)	chapter
consulta	discussion
f., fs.	folio, folios
liv. (livro)	book
maço	bundle
n., ns.	number, numbers
pacote	package
v. (verso)	obverse

Printed works and journals

AAPB	*Anais do Arquivo Público do Estado da Bahia*
ABNR	*Anais da Biblioteca Nacional de Rio de Janeiro*
ACB	*Atas da câmara. Documentos históricos do Arquivo Municipal*, 6 vols. (Salvador, 1944–5?)
ACCBTSGB	*Anais do Congresso Comemorativo do Bicentenário da Transferência da Sede do Govêrno do Brasil*, 4 vols. (Rio de Janeiro, 1963)
AH	*Anais da História* (Assis, São Paulo)
AHR	*American Historical Review*
AMP	*Anais do Museu Paulista*
CHLA	*Cambridge History of Latin America*, ed. Leslie Bethell; 2 vols. to date (Cambridge, 1984–)

Col. chron.	*Collecção chronologica da legislação portugueza,* ed. José Justino de Andrade e Silva; 10 vols. (Lisbon, 1854–9)
CPSNWS	*Comparative Perspectives on Slavery in New World Plantation Societies,* ed. Vera Rubin and Arthur Tuden (New York, 1977)
CSPS	*Calendar of State Papers, Spain*
DH	*Documentos históricos. Biblioteca Nacional de Rio de Janeiro* (1928–)
DHA	*Documentos para a história do açucar,* 3 vols. (Rio de Janeiro, 1954–63)
DUP	*Documentação Ultramarina Portuguesa,* 7 vols. (Lisbon, 1960–75)
EHR	*Economic History Review*
EXEH	*Explorations in Economic History*
HAHR	*Hispanic American Historical Review*
HCJB	*História da Companhia de Jesus no Brasil,* by Serafim Leite; 10 vols. (Lisbon, 1938–50)
HCPB	*História da colonização portuguesa do Brasil,* ed. Carlos Malheiro Dias; 3 vols. (Oporto, 1924–6)
HGB	*História geral do Brasil,* by Francisco Adolfo de Varnhagen; 5 vols. in 3; 7th complete ed. (São Paulo, 1962)
HR/RH	*Historical Reflections/Reflexions Historiques*
JGSWGLA	*Jahrbüch für Geschichte von Staat, Wirtschaft und Gesellschaft Lateinamerikas* (Berlin)
JIH	*Journal of Interdisciplinary History*
JSH	*Journal of Social History*
LBR	*Luso-Brazilian Review*
MAN	*Mensário do Arquivo Nacional* (Rio de Janeiro)
MB	*Monumenta Brasiliae,* ed. Serafim Leite; 5 vols. (Rome, 1956–60)
NCMH	*New Cambridge Modern History,* 14 vols. (Cambridge, 1957–79)
PVCB	*Primeira visitação do Santo Oficio às partes do Brasil. Confissões Bahia 1591–92,* ed. João Capistrano de Abreu (Rio de Janeiro, 1935)
RH	*Revista de História* (São Paulo)
RIAHGP	*Revista do Instituto Arqueológico, Histórico, e Geográfico Pernambucano*
RIEB	*Revista do Instituto de Estudos Brasileiros*
RIHGB	*Revista do Instituto Histórico e Geográfico Brasileiro*
WMQ	*William and Mary Quarterly*

WEIGHTS AND MEASURES

Weight

arroba	14.7 kilograms (approximately 32 pounds)

Dry measure

alqueire	36.3 kilograms (approximately 1 English bushel; 8 gallons)
moio	2,178 kilograms (a measure equal to 60 alqueires)
sirio	a measure that varied in Bahia from 1.75 to 2 alqueires

Length and area

braça	2.20 meters (corresponds to the English fathom)
légua	between 5,555 and 6,000 meters
palmo	0.22 meter (corresponds to the English span)
pé	0.33 meter (corresponds to the English foot)
tarefa	in Bahia, 30 square *braças* or 4,352 square meters
vara	1.10 meters (corresponds to the English yard)

It is always the direct relationship of the owners of the conditions of production to the direct producers – a relationship always naturally corresponding to a definite stage in the development of the methods of labor and thereby its social productivity – which reveals the innermost secret, the hidden basis of the entire social structure, and with it the political form of the relation of sovereignty and dependence, in short the corresponding specific form of the state. This does not prevent the same economic basis – the same from the standpoint of its main conditions – due to innumerable different empirical circumstances, natural environment, racial relations, external historical influences, etc., from showing infinite variations and gradations of appearance, which can be ascertained only by analysis of the empirically given circumstances.

Karl Marx, Capital

PART I

FORMATIONS, 1500–1600

CHAPTER 1

THE SUGAR PLANTATION:
FROM THE OLD WORLD TO THE NEW

> . . . wondrous reeds called by the inhabitants, honey canes, from the sweetness of the juice they contain. The juice of these canes when boiled with care to the proper point converts itself to a kind of honey; if, on the other hand, it is subjected to a more complete and perfect boiling, it becomes condensed into the substance of sugar.
>
> Hugo Falcundus (Sicily, ca. 1170)

The production of sugar and the origins of the American colonial economies were intimately tied. Sugarcane cultivation had been moving westward for centuries before the Spanish and Portuguese introduced it to the New World, and its arrival in the Caribbean and Brazil was a logical extension of the long historical process.[1] From its original home in the lowlands of Bengal or in Southeast Asia, the manufacture of cane sugar had spread to Persia and from there was carried by the Arab conquerors to the shores of the eastern Mediterranean. Estates growing sugarcane, remarkably similar to the later plantations of the Americas, emerged in the crusader kingdoms of twelfth- and thirteenth-century Palestine. By the fourteenth century, Cyprus had become a major producer. On the southern shore of that island, sugar-producing estates were created and exploited by the Hospitalers and by Catalan and Venetian families. Syrian and Arab slaves labored in these fields alongside local peasants. But just as Cyprus had replaced the Levant as the major supplier of the European market, it in turn was overshadowed by a new rival to the west.[2]

As in Cyprus, Crete, and North Africa, sugar had been introduced to Sicily during the westward movement of Islam. The crop flourished on the island, especially in the area around Palermo, even after the Norman invasion of the twelfth century.[3] The little evidence that survives on the internal organization of the Sicilian sugar economy suggests that familiar pattern of enslaved or coerced labor, relatively large land units, and well-developed long-range commerce. Historians, particularly

3

Noel Deerr and Edmund von Lippmann, the two great scholars of sugar, both believed that about 1499 a new type of mill was introduced in Sicily; but recent evidence indicates that they were mistaken. Wherever the innovation was made, however, it was important.[4]

Traditionally, the mill had been composed of a large circular stone that was rolled over pieces of cut cane. Somewhere in the Mediterranean region or on the Atlantic islands in the fifteenth century, a new form of press was introduced. It consisted of two rollers cogged together in such a way that the cane could be passed between them. When powered by oxen, water, or humans, this machine could squeeze a higher proportion of juice from the cane, and it also eliminated the need to cut the cane into pieces.[5] Although it thus reduced the time and labor needed to prepare the cane, it also apparently increased the mill's capacity. The heavy horizontal cylinders created certain problems because all the weight rested on the bottom roller and a great deal of power was needed to drive the mill. Still, the concept of a roller mill represented a great advance, and for the next three hundred years there was no innovation to equal its impact on sugar making, except perhaps for the introduction of the vertical three-roller mill in the seventeenth century. With this technology and the organization of production developed in the eastern Mediterranean, the American plantations simply constitute another chapter in the westward movement of sugar. The innovation of Brazil and the Caribbean was an expansion of scale both of the individual producing units and of the industry as a whole. But between Sicily and the humid coasts of Brazil another and, indeed, crucial chapter was still to be written on the Atlantic islands held by Spain and Portugal.

Sugarcane had been cultivated in the Iberian peninsula since the time of the Moorish conquest, and as early as 1300 sugar from Muslim Malaga was available for sale in Bruges. By the fifteenth century, the irrigated vegas of Valencia and the Portuguese Algarve were marketing sugar as far away as southern Germany, the Low Countries, and England.[6] Although some question has been raised about Sicilian priority in the use of the cylindrical-roller mill, it is quite clear that the Portuguese looked to Sicily as a model to be followed. In the 1420s, Prince Henry sent to Sicily for cane plantings and probably for experienced sugar technicians as well. Both the Portuguese and the Spanish depended on the eastern Mediterranean not only for technical and organizational models but also for capital and commercial know-how.

Charles Verlinden and others have emphasized the crucial role played by the Italians, and especially the Genoese, in the introduction and commercialization of sugar in Portugal. As early as 1404, Giovanni della Palma received a royal grant to construct a sugar mill (*engenho*) in the Algarve, and by the fifteenth century a flourishing industry provided enough surplus to permit Genoese merchants to carry on a brisk trade with Italy and Northern Europe. Genoese merchants and capitalists with a firm base in Castile and Portugal were not lax in exploiting new zones of investment with the expansion of European activity on the islands of the Atlantic. In a sense, the Italians provided the human links in a chain that transferred the techniques, estate management, and commercial organization of sugar production from the eastern to the western Mediterranean and then beyond the Pillars of Hercules to the Atlantic basin. They supplied, and in some sense created, a taste for sugar in Western Europe that the Americas would eventually fill. To be sure, sugar remained in the fifteenth century a "spice," used mostly as a remedy or an exotic seasoning, but sixteenth-century cooking manuals indicate that it was already finding its way into the diet of the European aristocracy.[7]

Expansion: slavery and commerce

The introduction of sugar to southern Iberia stimulated the resurgence of an institution already an aspect of daily life there. Slavery, of course, was not peculiar to the Iberian peninsula. Throughout medieval Europe, various forms of slavery had persisted after the fall of the Roman Empire in the West, but by the thirteenth century they had been replaced on much of the continent by other forms of servitude or coerced labor. It was mainly on the periphery of Europe, in those areas where Europeans came into contact with peoples who were culturally and often ethnically distinct, that the institution of slavery continued to have some importance. In the regions of the Caspian and Black seas, the eastern Mediterranean, and the Iberian peninsula, a cultural and ethnic border was superimposed on a military frontier, and it was exactly in these regions that slavery continued as a viable institution.[8]

The intermittent but continual warfare between Muslims and Christians in Iberia created prisoners and captives for both sides, and thus a constant source of bondsmen. In the central kingdom of Castile, this contact continued until the fall of Granada in 1492, but the earlier reconquest of the Christian kingdoms on the peninsula's eastern and western seaboards effectively interrupted traditional sources of slaves. From the close of the thirteenth century, Aragon-Catalonia and Portugal had to look to other suppliers. The Aragonese called upon their traditional trading areas in the eastern Mediterranean, drawing servants and laborers from the Caspian region and the Levant. In Portugal, the institution of slavery "vegetated" for a century. A small trickle of Moors and Islamized Africans continued to arrive as slaves from North Africa, especially after the Portuguese conquest of Ceuta in 1415; but it was not until the 1440s that slavery began to have an impact on Portugal's economy.

Portuguese expansion down the West African coast in search of gold and spices eventually led to the initiation of an African slave trade. The first shipment of Africans arrived in Lisbon in 1441, and within three years a company had been formed in the Algarve to exploit this trade. By 1448, more than a thousand Africans had been imported to Portugal. The level of importation increased during the remainder of the century, probably averaging some 800 to 900 Africans a year.[9] The crown created a special clearinghouse (Casa dos Escravos) in Lisbon just to handle this trade, but Lisbon was not the only point of entry. Between 1490 and 1496, Lagos in the Algarve received more than 700 African slaves, a number equal to 10 percent of its total population. The economic and demographic impact of this trade was great. By 1551, Lisbon alone had 9,950 slaves in a total population of 100,000, to say nothing of the slaves in the rest of the country or of the freedmen in Lisbon and elsewhere. By this date, black religious brotherhoods were operating in both Lisbon and Lagos, and slaves had become an integral part of the Portuguese social structure.[10]

Until the fifteenth century, slavery in Portugal had been primarily a form of servitude associated with domestic service and urban occupations. This tradition of slavery could be traced to the era of Roman Lusitania, tempered, of course, by subsequent Christian thought. The place of slaves in society, their position before the law, their access to freedom, and even the terms used to describe them all grew from a soil of Roman precedents and urban-domestic situations. The fifteenth-century conjunction of a new source for slaves in West Africa and a new demand for them in the burgeoning canefields of the Algarve and eventually Madeira altered the nature of Portuguese slavery. The urban-domestic tradition continued, but it was now joined by a more demanding form of labor associated with the sugar estate or plantation, a basic productive unit in the commercial capitalism that characterized Europe's expanding economy. Significantly, this plantation slavery was associated almost exclusively with Africans. The two traditions, or rather tendencies, in Iberian slavery coexisted and interacted, fusing eventually in the late fifteenth century into a single institution filled with contradictions born of the persistence of the earlier form in the face of the demands of the other. It was on the Atlantic islands, however, and not the Iberian peninsula, that the anomalies and accommodations of Iberian plantation slavery came most clearly into focus; but it must be emphasized that the union of black slavery and sugarcane had a European origin.

The transfer of sugar cultivation from Iberia to the Atlantic islands was a natural process that accompanied the fifteenth-century maritime expansion of Castile and Portugal. Not surprisingly, the Mediterranean techniques of sugar making and the commercial patterns for distributing that product reestablished themselves in this new area of European activity (see Figure 1-1). By 1498, Genoese and Portuguese merchants were selling Madeiran sugar not only in Portugal but also as far east as

Figure 1-1. Sugar production in the sixteenth century. This view, although based on reports from the Caribbean, probably represents Mediterranean practices. Note the use of a millstone rather than a roller press.

Constantinople and as far north as England.[11] Along with the extension of these traditional commercial and technical methods, the Iberians also transferred to the Atlantic islands the employment of coerced or enslaved labor as a logical, and in fact necessary, feature of the sugar industry. A controlled and usually ethnically distinct labor force associated with sugar agriculture had emerged in the Mediterranean phase of the history of sugar, but it was on the Atlantic islands that this form of labor organization in support of a highly capitalized and commercialized product crystallized into the system that became the plantation complex.

Atlantic-island precedents

Throughout the fifteenth and sixteenth centuries, almost all the Atlantic island groups exported some sugar to European markets, and even today most produce small amounts of sugar for local consumption. The Azores, the Canaries, the Cape Verde Islands, São Tomé, and Madeira all experienced sugar booms to a greater or lesser extent during this period. In the Azores, uninhabited when the Portuguese began settlement in 1439, sugar was quickly introduced; and the islands, especially São Miguel, exported small amounts in the fifteenth century. Lying in the North Atlantic roughly between 37° and 40° north latitude, the Azores had a variable climate that was not particularly suited to cane cultivation; and Azorean agriculturists soon found that wheat, always in demand in Portugal, provided a better-suited and more dependable economic base. This crop, along with pastel (dyestuff) and wine, became one of the mainstays of the Azorean economy.[12]

The situation on Madeira was quite another matter. Portuguese colonization of this uninhabited island began in earnest under the auspices of Prince Henry in 1425. During the next forty years, two parallel systems of agriculture competed for dominance of the island's economy. Traditional wheat farming attracted considerable numbers of humble Portuguese peasants to Madeira, where the opportunity to own land provided a stimulus to colonization. At the same time, sugarcane cultivation initiated, and to some extent promoted, by Genoese and Jewish merchants and commercial agents competed for the available land on the island. It was in some ways a struggle between the freeman's crop, wheat, and the slave crop, sugar. The highly commercialized and more lucrative product eventually gained control of the island's economy.[13] Madeira became a grain importer and a sugar exporter. A royal attempt in the 1460s to establish a virtual monopoly of sugar production was unsuccessful, and the crown had to be content with the revenues generated by sugar taxes.[14] By the late fifteenth century, Madeira had become the largest single producer of sugar in the Western world.

Agriculture on Madeira was difficult. Lacking broad expanses of suitable and easily cultivated fields, the Portuguese constructed a series of mountain terraces that depended on water brought down from higher elevations.[15] The Portuguese, using to some extent Guanche slaves acquired from the neighboring Canary Islands, constructed a complex system of small agricultural-irrigation trenches. These made sugar production not only possible but highly successful. Italians, especially the Genoese, had been associated with the Madeiran enterprise from the outset and were probably responsible for the introduction of sugar to the island. Production at first was limited by the use of hand-operated presses (*alçapremas*), but a major change occurred in 1452 when Diogo de Teive received permission to construct a water-powered engenho.[16] These mills had a far greater productive capacity. By 1456, sugar from Madeira could be bought on the London market. From this point expansion was rapid. In the early 1470s, the island produced some 20,000 arrobas, and by the first decade of the sixteenth century the amount had soared to more than 177,000 arrobas of white sugar and some 230,000 arrobas when *muscavado* (brown sugar) and the other inferior grades were included. This was the zenith of Madeiran production, and annual output never rose beyond the levels attained in the first decade of the century.[17] The decline of sugar production on Madeira was as precipitous as its rise, and by the 1530s the island had returned to fifteenth-century levels of production. The reasons for this decline are claimed to lie both in local matters, such as soil exhaustion, crop failure, and labor problems, and in difficulties brought about by the international commercial aspects of sugar agriculture.[18] The entry of competing suppliers, São Tomé and then Brazil, on the European market also contributed to the decline of the Madeiran sugar industry. By 1613, the fortunes of Madeira had fallen so low that sugar growers on the island sought the importation of Brazilian sugar as the only means of attracting buyers for the local crop.[19]

These production figures also seem to indicate that the individual mills on Madeira were small when compared to those later found in the Northeast of Brazil. In 1493, the eighty engenhos on the island produced about 100,000 arrobas, or an average of 18 tons per mill.[20] The largest engenho of the 1590s was that owned by the Genoese João Esmeraldo. It drew on the labor of eighty male and female slaves, including Africans, mulattoes, and Guanches (inhabitants of the Canary Islands).[21] The Guanches, in fact, had provided much of the Madeiran labor force in the fifteenth century until royal legislation in 1490, repeated in 1505, prevented their continued use.[22] At the end of the sixteenth century, they (or their descendants) were still laboring in the island's canefields along with more recently imported Africans. But Madeiran engenhos seem small because eighty slaves would constitute only a medium-sized engenho by Brazilian standards of the late sixteenth century.

Reconstruction of the production and price history of Madeiran sugar provides an excellent picture of the rise and decline of that crop and its importance in the island's economy. We are less fortunate in regard to the internal organization of the Madeiran sugar economy during its period of florescence. For this reason, the *Livro do almoxarifado das partes de Funchal* (1494) is especially valuable. This tax listing of the sugarcane growers of the captaincy of Funchal and the size of their holdings provides a glimpse into the sugar economy, and, used in conjunction with other sources, it enables us to draw some tentative conclusions about the plantation economy of Madeira.

The *Livro do almoxarifado* lists 221 cane growers in the captaincy of Funchal whose total holdings were capable of producing more than 80,000 arrobas. Because Funchal produced three-fourths of Madeira's sugar, the island's total production at this time must have been close to 100,000 arrobas. Although only sixteen engenhos are mentioned in the *Livro do almoxarifado*, other sources indicate that there were perhaps about eighty on Madeira at this period. These figures suggest that many cane growers did not process their own crop but depended on a nearby engenho for this service. Thus, the island's sugar industry comprised a large number of small and medium-sized cane growers, as well as a small number of wealthy and sometimes not so wealthy engenho owners.

Who were these small and medium-sized sugar producers, and how did they operate? A few bore ranks of nobility, but there were more who were of artisan background or served in some minor administrative position. Holding a piece of caneland appears to have been a suitable enterprise for men whose occupational training and perhaps interests lay in other directions. Not surprisingly, family ties played an important role in the development of the sugar-producing sector, and the listing makes repeated references to links of blood or marriage between the producers. It is also clear that the vast majority of the men and women listed have Portuguese names. Flemings and Italians were present in small numbers as producers, but they concentrated their activity on the commercialization of the crop – a situation that drew the opprobrium of the Portuguese.[23]

The editors of the *Livro do almoxarifado* ably pointed out that document's implications for the existence of small property within the plantation economy of Madeira. They erred, however, in contrasting this situation to the subsequent history of the Brazilian Northeast, dominated, so they believed, following Gilberto Freyre, by a few great "industrial" engenhos.[24] As we shall see, the system of a few mills and a large number of cane growers, both dependent on a coerced labor force, not only emerges clearly from the historical record of Madeira and the Canary Islands but was also exactly the form of organization introduced to the Northeast in the sixteenth century. It was a reasonable social and economic response to a situation in which land was relatively cheap but capital was scarce.

The Spanish were no less interested than the Portuguese in making their Atlantic possessions profitable. The Canary Islands had fallen to Castile by treaty with Portugal in 1479, although Castilian presence in the archipelago dated from the beginning of the century. At the beginning of the sixteenth century, representatives of the island of Tenerife wrote that "sugar estates are the most important thing on the island [*lo principal de la isla*]."[25] Lacking the abundant water and wood to be found on Madeira, the colonists on Tenerife and Gran Canaria established sugar mills on the humid coasts. The sugar industry took root, and throughout the sixteenth century the Canaries exported sugar to Europe, holding their own in competition with the Spanish Caribbean until the seventeenth century.[26] Eventually, like Madeira, the Canaries turned from sugar to wine when faced with the stiff competition of New World producers.

In 1526, Thomas Nichols, an English visitor to the Canary Islands, wrote a description of the sugar-making process he observed there.[27] The techniques he described differed little from those employed earlier in Madeira or to be used later in Brazil. A good-sized Canarian *ingenio* could produce about 50 tons of sugar a year. Gran Canaria had some twenty mills at the height of its sugar boom and a maximum annual output of about 1,000 tons (70,000 arrobas). The competition with

American rivals gradually forced many producers to abandon sugar cultivation, and by the early seventeenth century only five mills remained active.[28]

This familiar story of rise and then decline in the face of fresh competitors to the west is paralleled in the Canaries by the also familiar recapitulation of the internal structure of the sugar industry. Large capital investments needed to establish an ingenio came from Castilian nobles, Catalans, and once again from active Genoese merchant-capitalists like Mateo Viña and Cristóbal d'Aponte. Canarian sugar reached European markets in the hands of Portuguese, Catalan, Castilian, and especially Genoese commercial houses, many of which were represented by resident agents in the Canaries.[29]

Fortunately, in the case of the Canary Islands enough evidence has survived to reconstruct the sugar economy's internal organization. Many of the phenomena suggested by the historical records of Madeira can be securely documented in the Spanish archipelago. The owners of the ingenios were those men who possessed, or had borrowed, enough capital to make the expensive initial outlay. The will and testament of one such man, Cristóbal García del Castillo, filed on Gran Canaria in 1518 lists among his property a water-powered ingenio or mill, a millhouse, a residence, a building for the kettles and furnaces, a corral, a shed for firewood, slave quarters, and a residence for paid workers. García del Castillo also owned three teams of horses (twelve in all) and twenty male and two female slaves. With the exception of scale, such a description (even including the imbalanced sex ratio of the slaves) could have been made of most sugar mills in Brazil throughout the colonial era.[30]

Mill owners like García del Castillo depended on free men, often Portuguese from Madeira, to direct the mill's technical operations. *Cañavereros* directed planting and cutting the cane, *espumeiros* watched the boiling process, and *mestres de azúcar* directed and coordinated all operations. These employees received a wage and sometimes a percentage of the sugar produced. Here, as in Madeira, slaves did the work. At first the island's original inhabitants, the Guanches, provided the necessary labor force, but by the sixteenth century they had been almost entirely replaced on Gran Canaria by Africans. Only on Tenerife did Guanches continue to form part of the slave gangs.[31] Colonists on that island soon discovered that the management of slaves was no easy matter. By 1513 African, Morisco, and Guanche slaves had deserted the ingenios in numbers sufficient to ruin some planters and drive others to the use of wage laborers.[32] Nevertheless, slavery remained the dominant form of labor organization on the Canarian plantations.

The foreign merchants, wealthy millowners, technical specialists, and a captive, ethnically distinct work force are all recognizable characters in the scene that sugar set throughout the Western world. As on Madeira, but far more clearly delineated by the historical record in the Canaries, there was still another social category. Not all colonists could afford the investment needed to establish a mill. Those of more modest resources simply planted sugarcane and then contracted to have it pressed at a neighboring ingenio. The relationship between these *labradores* and the millowners was regulated by legislation.[33] The labrador had to divide the product of his cane equally with the millowner, but if the latter provided transport or assumed other costs he was entitled to all by-products such as molasses. Each labrador made his or her own contract, and these often provided a source of tension between millowners and their dependents. As early as 1508, the *cabildo* (Span., town council) of Tenerife appointed special officers to regulate the milling order at the ingenios in order to avoid arbitrary decisions by the millowners.[34] The *Livro do almoxarifado* from Madeira strongly suggests the existence of this class on that island, but the milling arrangements (*contratos de molienda*) that survive from the Canary Islands demonstrate beyond question the use on Atlantic islands of this system of plantation organization. It was an arrangement that would have great importance in the subsequent history of the Brazilian sugar-plantation economy.

And so in the Atlantic islands of Portugal and Spain, the commercial, technical, and social organization of an economic system came together to form a highly successful and easily transferable complex known as the sugar ingenio. In America, this system would reach new levels of efficiency and success. But before making the Atlantic crossing, there was one last step to be made: the expansion of scale by the continuous addition of large numbers of servile laborers.

The Cape Verde Islands, lying some three to four hundred miles off the African coast, appeared at first as though they might emerge as a large-scale plantation colony. Discovered and in part settled in the 1460s by Italians sailing under the banner of Portugal, the islands, and especially the largest, Santiago, seemed at first to follow the precedent of Madeira. Genoese capital was once again invested in the sugar industry, and an attempt was made to stimulate the creation of a plantation economy. A number of historical and natural factors prevented the realization of this scheme. First, Portuguese colonists were simply unwilling to make the long and difficult journey unless guaranteed support and eventual success. The aridity of the climate and the undependability of the rainfall made large-scale cane cultivation difficult and thus provided little security to the prospective colonists. Moreover, during the period 1475–9 an undeclared but bitter war flared between the Portuguese and the Castilians, who had never surrendered their own claims to the Guinea seas.[35] The Castilians sacked Santiago in 1476 and took most of its inhabitants captive. Such events and the unfavorable climate prohibited the development of a large-scale cash crop. By the first decade of the sixteenth century, the Cape Verdes exported only 4,000 arrobas of sugar a year. During the course of that century, their economy became increasingly dependent on their advantageous position as a way station in the Atlantic slave trade. The islands became provisioning grounds and a port of call for the slave ships, and the local sugar production was utilized to make rum, an item traded on the African coast.

It was not in the Cape Verde Islands but on the island of São Tomé that the Atlantic plantation system achieved its characteristic form. The Portuguese had discovered São Tomé in 1471, but their settlement of the island dated only from the 1480s. Of the four principal islands in the Gulf of Guinea, the Portuguese preferred to concentrate their activity on São Tomé and Principe rather than on Fernando Po, which, though closer to the African coast, was already inhabited by African peoples and less climatically favorable to European settlement. On uninhabited São Tomé the crown apparently intended a colony modeled on Madeira and the Azores. The original colonists included a large number of Jewish children torn from their parents and sent to the island in an attempt at forced proselytization. What emerged on São Tomé, however, was not the European peasant society of the Azores, but rather the closest Old World equivalent to a multiracial plantation economy.[36]

From the outset, the island's settlement was associated with sugar. The original charter (doação) of colonization had urged the planting of sugarcane, and colonists were quick to respond to the suggestion. Taking advantage of the island's numerous rivers, which provided inexpensive power, and employing Madeiran and Genoese sugar experts, the industry grew rapidly. In 1529, the crown issued an order to construct twelve new engenhos, and by the 1550s sixty mills were producing an annual total of 150,000 arrobas.[37] By the beginning of the seventeenth century, the number of mills had doubled but production had not kept pace, and in 1635 the island probably exported fewer than 25,000 arrobas.[38] Crop failures, overexpansion, competition from the better-quality sugars of Madeira and Brazil, European raiders, and the internal unrest caused by marauding fugitive slaves all combined to cause a serious decline in the island's sugar exports.[39]

In the early sixteenth century, São Tomé brought together the technical skills and organization of the Mediterranean sugar complex and combined them with a constant labor source on a scale formerly impossible. The island's advantage in this process was its location. Quite unlike Madeira or the Azores, São Tomé's proximity to the West African coast, especially the trading forts at São Jorge de Mina and Axim, made it an entrepôt in the Atlantic slave trade to Europe and America. In 1516 alone, more than 4,000 slaves were unloaded in the island's slave pens; by 1519, the crown had established regulations for the slave trade to São Tomé.[40] By 1554, the resident population consisted of some 600 whites, perhaps an equal number of mulattoes, and 2,000 plantation slaves. These inhabitants were overshadowed by between five and six thousand slaves in transit held in the baracoons.[41] Eventually, provisioning the slaves became a major aspect of the island's economy, and when the sugar industry fell on hard times in the seventeenth century, the economy of São Tomé shifted markedly toward this activity.[42]

Able to depend on a constant supply of African workers, the engenhos of São Tomé could afford to employ slaves on a scale not yet known in the Atlantic. Valentim Fernandes's description of the island in 1554 reported plantations with one hundred and fifty to three hundred slaves. Although an estate with the latter number of laborers was surely an exception, it demonstrates how the factors of sugar production could be enlarged. Although one author has argued that the labor regime of the São Tomé engenhos was more akin to serfdom than slavery, the conditions of servitude appear quite similar to forms of American plantation slavery. The slaves came from Benin, Angola, and the Senegambia. Their work regime apparently called for a five-day labor week, with Saturdays and four other days each month devoted to growing provisions in their own gardens, a system much like that used in Jamaica in the eighteenth century. It is unclear whether children born to slave mothers on the island were considered free or slave. If they were considered free, this situation would constitute the only significant departure from the outlines of the slave regime as it operated in tropical America.[43]

The use of large numbers of enslaved Africans on the sugar plantations made São Tomé a precursor of subsequent developments in Northeast Brazil, but this was not the only preview that São Tomé provided. Lacking a large European population, a situation was created that fostered the growth of a significant class of free people of color, the mulattoes. They filled many vital positions on the island. Free Africans and mulattoes often crewed the slave ships that traded between Guiné and São Tomé, and during the sixteenth century they increasingly assumed other positions on the island.[44] But as their situation improved, they clashed politically with royal administrators. The crown was never quite sure of its policy toward them. In 1539, "honorable and married" mulattoes were granted royal permission to hold municipal offices and dignities.[45] From such positions, they fought to protect local interests against the programs of often venal governors. This feuding and insubordination eventually moved the crown in 1620 to send female convicts from Portugal to São Tomé and the Cape Verde Islands "to extinguish as far as possible the caste of mulattoes."[46] This policy was crowned with notable failure, and throughout the seventeenth and eighteenth centuries disputes between Lisbon-appointed governors, the church, and local mulattoes caused political anarchy.[47]

São Tomé had still another lesson to teach the plantation colonies of America. With a small European population, a large number of enslaved Africans, and suitable terrain, the opportunities for slave resistance were great. The origins of the fugitive bands on São Tomé apparently lay with a group of Angolan slaves who had been shipwrecked on the island in 1544 and had fled to the interior. These Angolares attracted plantation slaves, and eventually a large settlement of fugitives developed on Mount Cambumbé (Pico do Mocambo) in the highly settled southern portion of the island. In 1574, the Angolares unleashed a series of attacks against the Portuguese, burning plantations and raiding for food and arms. The colonists responded with a series of successful punitive expeditions but were unable to eliminate the fugitives. Their raids intensified in 1595–6 under the able leadership of a man named Amador, but his eventual capture diminished angolar activity. Still, as late as 1690, when the sugar economy was long dead, the Angolares staged occasional raids.[48]

The history of sugar cultivation not only recapitulated the history of that crop in the Mediterranean and Atlantic but also previewed many features of what was to come in the Caribbean and Brazil. The techniques of production, the internal organization of the industry, the transfer of technology from older sugar-producing regions, and the commercial-financial role of foreigners, especially the Genoese, were all present in São Tomé. But there were also particular features that made the island distinctive and foreshadowed what was to come in the New World. Its tropical climate, a demographic pattern of a small number of colonists, many black slaves, eventually a significant mulatto population, and ultimately a seemingly endless supply of African muscle comprised new physical and social conditions and economic possibilities. All the elements of the capitalist plantation system – an economic system oriented toward producing a highly commercialized crop yet capable of marshaling an archaic social form, chattel slavery, to provide its labor – were present in São Tomé. The plantation system or engenho regime had been seasoned in the southern latitudes, and it could now cross the Atlantic with tragic ease.

Brazilian beginnings

The opening of the New World to European settlement and exploitation created new and seemingly endless opportunities for the expansion of large-scale export agriculture, for which sugar was the most logical and probably most lucrative crop. Columbus, who had lived and married on Madeira and worked for a Genoese firm in the sugar trade, brought sugarcane plantings to the Caribbean in his second voyage of 1493.[49] Sugar cultivation suffered the same vicissitudes as the colony as a whole, and it was not until the early years of the sixteenth century that the industry began to thrive on Santo Domingo. A major turning point came when a Spanish physician set up a mill and brought sugar technicians from the Canary Islands at his own expense. By 1530, the island had thirty-four mills, a number that held steady until the 1570s, after which it declined.[50] Cuba, destined to become a great sugar producer in the nineteenth century, was slow to develop a sugar industry; even in the seventeenth century it was producing small amounts, mostly for local consumption. Puerto Rico had more success with mills in operation by the 1520s, but its export of sugar was minimal.[51]

In general, development of a sugar industry in the sixteenth-century Caribbean was hindered by the constant drain of people and financial resources to the mainland, where gold and silver seemed far more glamorous than sugar. Then, too, commercial restrictions, heavy excise taxes, competition from Granada, and a catastrophic decline of the indigenous populations also contributed to the industry's modest beginnings.[52] In Brazil, a different set of historical circumstances produced quite different results.

The exact date when the Portuguese introduced sugarcane to Brazil is uncertain. Most royal and private economic interest between the discovery of 1500 and the establishment of the proprietary captaincies in 1533–4 was directed toward the commerce in brazilwood, valued in Europe for its dye-making qualities. As early as 1516, however, the Casa da India (Colonial Office) ordered that a sugar technician be sent to Brazil and that he be supplied with the materials and resources necessary to build a sugar mill.[53] The Spanish chronicler Antonio de Herrera later wrote that an engenho was in operation in Brazil by 1518, and although some scholars have doubted this assertion, there is now evidence of Brazilian sugar on the market in Antwerp in 1519.[54] In 1526, the Lisbon Customs House (Alfândega) received sugar from the Northeast coast. There a small mill had been established by Cristóvão Jacques, a Portuguese captain, on Itamaracá; but the mill was short-lived and was destroyed by the French in 1530. Before this date, the Brazilian sugar industry was minute, with only a few small mills of limited and sporadic production. At best, a few crates a year found their way to the wharves of Lisbon or Antwerp; Brazilian sugar could have had little influence on the decline of Madeiran production in the first decades of the sixteenth century.

It was during the 1530s and 1540s that sugar agriculture was established in Brazil on a firm basis. The expedition captained by Martim Afonso de Sousa that was sent to Brazil in 1532 to clear the coast of French shipping and to colonize as well carried cane plantings. A skilled sugar expert was among the colonists, as were a number of Portuguese, Italians, and Flemings experienced in the sugar industry in Madeira.[55] The pulse of Portuguese mercantilism was beginning to surge even while this expedition proceeded on its mission. In 1533, King Dom João III initiated the captaincy system. He divided the Brazilian coastline into fifteen parcels, which he ceded to twelve Portuguese noblemen (*fidalgos*) to hold as lord proprietors. Each was granted certain rights and privileges of dominion in return for accepted obligations to colonize, populate, and develop the economy of their territory.[56] The overall results of the system were disappointing. Some of the captaincies were never settled, and others were plagued by donatarial neglect, internecine squabbling, and Indian wars. The few regions that experienced some success owed it to a fortunate combination of sugar agriculture and a reasonably peaceful relationship with the local Indian peoples.

Actually, sugarcane was planted in all the captaincies from São Vicente in the south to Pernambuco in the north. Plantings were brought from Madeira or São Tomé, but it also appears that some donataries obtained them from their neighbors in other captaincies.[57] Engenhos were constructed in Porto Seguro, Ilhéus, and Bahia. In Paraíba do Sul, the donatary Pero de Góes, already responsible for the construction of mills in São Vicente, built two small, animal-powered mills and at least one water-powered engenho with capital from Portugal.[58] Vasco Fernandes Coutinho, donatary of Espírito Santo, proved especially active, and by 1545 his captaincy had seven mills and three more under construction.[59] But in Espírito Santo, as elsewhere, Indian hostility and other difficulties eventually resulted in burned or abandoned mills and the sporadic or discontinuous development of a sugar industry.[60]

Two captaincies proved to be an exception to this general pattern. In both cases active donatarial interest, sufficient capital investment from European sources, and resolution of the relationship with the Indian population all proved to be key factors in the establishment of a sugar industry. The captaincy of São Vicente had been ceded to Martim Afonso de Sousa. Early relations with the Indians there were peaceful due in large part to the role of a number of Portuguese castaways who had lived and married among the peoples of the coast and those of the interior plateau. A number of engenhos were constructed there near the coastal settlement of Santos.[61] Martim Afonso had taken an active interest in stimulating sugar production and was a partowner of a large mill, originally called Engenho do Governador. Among his partners were a number of Portuguese and foreign companions, all of whom were eventually bought out by Erasmo Schetz (or Schecter), a German who established himself and his family's interests in Antwerp. The engenho came to be known as the Engenho São Jorge dos Erasmos, and it was probably the largest in southern Brazil.[62] It was administered for many years by German and Flemish overseers sent from Antwerp by the absentee owners. In many ways, the history of Engenho São Jorge dos Erasmos repeated that of some of the larger mills on Madeira, being primarily a commercial venture on Portuguese lands financed by foreign merchants for a wider European market.

São Vicente was not destined to become a major sugar-producing region in the colonial era, and it was not until the nineteenth century that this region of Brazil (present-day São Paulo) began to produce large amounts of sugar.[63] Still, until the early seventeenth century sugar was a locally important crop for the production of rum and especially as a means of exchange.[64] Father Luís de Grã reported in 1556 that sugar and hardware were used in the captaincy in place of currency.[65] Occasionally ships calling at Santos could find a few crates to carry, and a number of engenhos such as São Jorge dos Erasmos continued production, but by the middle decades of the sixteenth century the locus of Brazilian sugar agriculture was the Northeast coast.[66]

Of all the donatarial captaincies, Pernambuco on the Northeast coast proved to be the most successful.[67] The donatary, Duarte Coelho, came to the colony with his family and personally directed the settlement and development of the colony. Relations with the local Indians were facilitated by a number of unions between Indian women and colonists, among whom was Jerônimo de Albuquerque, the donatary's brother-in-law. These personal connections later proved invaluable when the Portuguese had to stave off concerted Indian resistance. Duarte Coelho actively pursued and protected his proprietary interests and in so doing paid particular attention to the economic foundations of his domain. His letters to Portugal allow us to trace the progress of the sugar industry in Pernambuco.

In 1542, Duarte Coelho reported that a large number of canes had been planted and that he was aiding colonists in these efforts. Predicting that a large engenho would soon be completed, he also petitioned for the right to import African slaves.[68] The first mill completed, Nossa Senhora da Ajuda, belonged to Jerónimo de Albuquerque, brother-in-law to the donatary.[69] By 1550, Duarte Coelho could report five mills in operation. These provided a firm foundation for a steady expansion of the sugar economy.[70] By the 1580s, Pernambuco boasted sixty-six engenhos and was the leading sugar-producing region in Brazil.[71]

Duarte Coelho's ardent defense of his interests also reveals the nature of his efforts to initiate sugar agriculture. In his complaints against colonists who were reluctant to pay him his rents and perquisites, Duarte Coelho pointed out that he had brought artisans and specialists from Portugal, Galicia, and the Canary Islands at his own expense.[72] Once again, we can see the transference of information, skills, and personnel from the older sugar-producing zones to the new areas as a result of intentional effort. Duarte Coelho sought investors in Lisbon, and commercialization of Pernambucan sugar in the early years appears to have been primarily in the hands of the Portuguese, although the brothers Cibaldo and Cristóvão Lins, lusified Germans who represented the Fuggers of Augsburg, arrived in the 1540s and quickly became involved in producing and marketing sugar.[73] Much of the sugar was carried in Dutch bottoms by the beginning of the seventeenth century and was destined for northern ports.[74]

With the basis of sugar production established in the middle decades of the sixteenth century, the economic geography of Brazilian sugar began to take shape. By 1570, the industry was firmly concentrated in the Northeast. At that date, Pero de Magalhães Gandavo reported 60 engenhos in Brazil, of which 50 were in the captaincies from Ilhéus north. A series of reports by various observers made between 1583 and 1585 placed the total number between 108 and 128, but the discrepancies in number did not affect agreement on the preponderance of Northeast captaincies. Pernambuco overshadowed all other regions, with more than half the engenhos of Brazil within its borders. The only other captaincy that could rival it was Bahia, which by the 1580s had some 40-odd sugar mills.[75] Together, these two captaincies probably accounted for some three-quarters of Brazil's total sugar output.

Bahia presented a peculiar case, sharing many of the physical advantages of Pernambuco but suffering from a false start in colonization and development like some of the southern captaincies. The tropical coast of Bahia was well suited to sugarcane cultivation, but the heart of the sugar-growing area was in the Recôncavo, those lands surrounding the Bay of All Saints, a great natural arm of the sea that cut some thirty miles into the coast, forming a bay of spectacular beauty. The shelter that this great body of water provided made the bay a common stopping place for early French and Portuguese vessels and dyewood traders. One castaway, Diogo Alvares Caramurú, had lived successfully among the Indians of the region and fathered a large number of children, who formed a de facto semi-European presence on the bay.[76]

Under the donatarial system, the area of the Bay of All Saints was made part of the captaincy of Bahia and granted to Francisco Pereira Coutinho, a nobleman who had served the crown well in India. He arrived in Brazil in 1536, but despite the advantages secured through cooperation with Caramurú, Pereira Coutinho proved a poor administrator whose weak leadership failed to control the greed and passions of the colonists. Their depredations provoked an Indian siege of the tiny settlement, which led to factional quarrels among the Portuguese. Pereira Coutinho and his supporters were forced to seek refuge in Porto Seguro, and when they attempted to return to the Bay of All Saints the following year, a shipwreck resulted in their death at the hands of Indians on Itaparica Island.[77]

During the nine years of Pereira Coutinho's rule as donatary, little was done to exploit the sugar-growing potential of the region. Two engenhos were constructed. One owned by João de Velosa was built near the inlet of Pirajá. Both mills were razed by the Indians during fighting in the 1540s. Yet, despite this inauspicious beginning, the area of the Recôncavo offered excellent geographical and climatic conditions for growing sugarcane. The area of the Bay of All Saints received adequate rainfall each year, and excellent soils, especially the black-clay *massapé*, were plentiful along its northern and western margins.[78] The bay itself provided an easy and inexpensive means of transportation and communication for engenhos on its shores and offered a safe harbor for the ships needed to transport sugar to Europe. These advantages were appreciated by the crown.

The disaster of Francisco Pereira Coutinho and the general failure of the captaincy system led the Portuguese crown to seek a new program to secure its American possession against the continued threat of foreign rivals. In 1548, Dom João III decided to establish direct royal control through the office of a resident governor and other royal officials. A large expedition under Governor Tomé de Sousa occupied the semideserted captaincy of Bahia in 1549 and began immediately to construct a colonial capital on the shores of the Bay of All Saints. The city, Salvador da Bahia de Todos os Santos, remained the capital of Brazil until 1763 and was the seat of the governor, the high court (*relação*), and the chief fiscal officers of the colony. It also became one of the colony's most active commercial ports. The creation of a royal capital and of the institutions of colonial government did not immediately replace the previous donatarial system. The crown hoped to reclaim gradually the rights of lordship that it had granted to the donataries. In prosperous Pernambuco, it had little immediate success, but there is no doubt that the creation of Salvador was a major step in the process of increased royal control.[79]

From the outset of royal control in Bahia, it was clear that the creation of a sugar industry was a primary concern. The instruction (*regimento*) carried by Tomé de Sousa included specific directives concerning the establishment and regulation of sugar mills.[80] He was instructed to grant land for engenhos to those men who could raise a mill within three years. These individuals were required to reside on their land or in the city of Salvador and to forego any sale of their property for at least three years. They were responsible for the development of their land and for the protection of its residents. Not only were the grant holders to stimulate settlement, but they were also obliged to build a fortified tower and provide arms for the defense of their residents.[81] Moreover, each mill-owner had to process the cane of the lavradores who lived on or near his property. To stimulate the investment and responsibility involved in the erection of an engenho, the crown offered certain tax benefits, for example, temporary exemption from the tithe.[82] The royal treasurer's

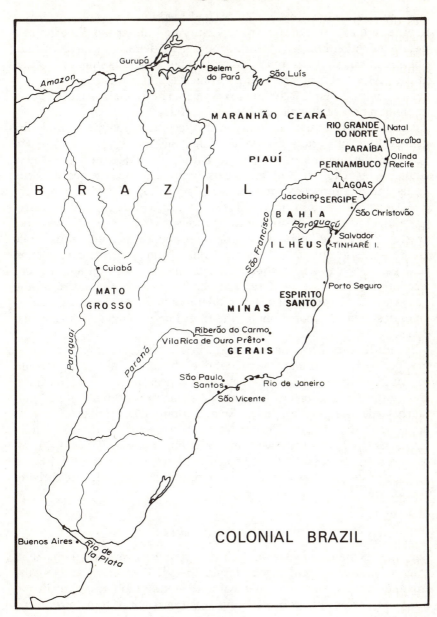

Map 1. Colonial Brazil.

instructions included orders to establish quality inspectors in each captaincy to ensure the proper grading of sugar destined for Europe.[83]

By these plans, the crown hoped to profit from the taxes levied on the sugar produced by the private sector. But Tomé de Sousa was also instructed to build an engenho to be owned directly by the crown. On lands in Pirajá where João de Velosa had tried to raise a mill, the crown now, at the expense of the royal treasury and under the direction of a mestre de engenhos sent from Europe or Madeira, built its own mill. This engenho, although rented to private persons, was still in operation in the 1580s.[84] Its construction by Tomé de Sousa was important as a symbol of the crown's intention to turn Bahia into a major sugar-producing region and perhaps a rival to Pernambuco.

The growth of a sugar industry in the Recôncavo followed closely the general lines of Portuguese political and military expansion at the expense of the Indians of the region. During the 1560s and 1570s, new lands were acquired and engenhos built. This was especially true under the vigorous governorship of Mem de Sá (1558–72), who subdued most of the Recôncavo tribes and carried out a program of regrouping Indians in Jesuit-controlled villages.[85] Mem de Sá was not averse to profiting personally from his political actions, and, while granting a large number of sesmarias (land grants) for the construction of engenhos in newly conquered lands, he also secured an excellent location for his own mill on the Rio Sergipe in the heart of the Recôncavo.[86] There he constructed a large mill known as Engenho Sergipe, destined to become one of the most famous engenhos in colonial Brazil.

By the time of Mem de Sá's death in 1572, the geography of sugar production in Bahia had taken definite shape. Although mills could be found all around the bay, they were concentrated on the northern and western coasts or on the numerous small rivers that emptied into the bay. The larger Paraguaçu River supported a number of engenhos, but south of it the Recôncavo lands were too sandy or too hilly for canes. In 1570, there were eighteen engenhos in Bahia. By 1590, however, the total had almost tripled to between forty and fifty. Bahia had taken its place as a major sugar producer alongside still-thriving Pernambuco.[87]

Engenhos and society

The arrangements of capital, technology, and organization that had emerged as the engenho complex in the Mediterranean and on the Atlantic islands came virtually without modification to Brazil in the early sixteenth century. In part, this was the result of human contacts, the intentional use of people and techniques already proved in Iberia, the Canaries, or Madeira, but to some extent this was also inherent in the nature of sugar production, which imposed its own logic of organization. Since I shall subsequently argue in the specific case of Bahia that this organization determined aspects of the general social structure of the colony, there is some advantage at this point in reviewing the few remaining materials from the inception of the industry in terms of the human and physical structure of the engenho complex.

The first Brazilian engenhos were small. Most were the *trapiche* type powered by oxen or horses. A few water-powered mills were built, usually by the donataries themselves, but the costs of constructing a large waterwheel and a sluice system (*levada*) to bring the water to the proper location were too great for most colonists, despite the economies of scale that the faster and more efficient water-powered engenhos could produce. Some idea of the scale of production is provided by the fact that the mills of Paraíba do Sul could produce in the 1540s only about 1,000 arrobas each per year, an amount equal to less than 15 tons.[88] Even the famous Engenho São Jorge dos Erasmos produced only 1,000 arrobas a year at the end of the sixteenth century.[89] But by that time in the Northeast, a number of factors began to bring about a change in the levels of production. The availability of capital generated from early profits or secured from European investors, expansion of land under cultivation, improved managerial skills, and a higher level of worker productivity brought about by a change in the nature of the labor force all contributed to improvements in the individual performance of engenhos. Added to this in the early seventeenth century was the introduction of technical improvements, which also increased overall production. By that time, an average mill produced some 6,000 arrobas annually, whereas the largest mills were capable of 8,000 to 10,000 arrobas.[90]

Each of the donataries had distributed land to colonists for use as *roças* (truck farms), *fazendas* (larger estates usually devoted to sugarcane, cattle, or other exports such as ginger and cotton), and finally engenhos. The usual instrument of ownership was the *carta de sesmaria*, a medieval Portuguese land title that had developed as a means of distributing newly conquered or reclaimed lands.[91] In the donatarial period, those who acquired sesmarias with the intention of building engenhos were generally the richest colonists in the region. The donataries themselves usually constructed a mill, and often their immediate relatives did the same. As we have seen, Portuguese and foreigners with access to European credit were also among the first millowners. The heavy demands of capital investment, in fact, led to partnerships and joint ownership of a number of the first engenhos, as in the case of Engenho São Jorge. The first five engenhos in Pernambuco give us some idea of the social and economic position of the first Brazilian planters. The owners of these mills included Duarte Coelho, the donatary; Jerônimo de Albuquerque, his brother-in-law; Vasco Lucena, the *almoxarife* (customs officer) of Olinda; and Afonso Gonçalves, captain and founder of the town of Igaracú. The fifth mill, Santiago de Camaragibe, was built by a converted Jew named Diogo Fernandes, along with "other companions from Viana, poor folk."[92]

The correspondence of Duarte Coelho and other contemporaneous documents also makes clear the existence of the lavrador system of tenancy, sharecropping, and other forms of association between the engenhos and those who simply grew cane but did not convert it to sugar themselves. Already present on the Atlantic islands, this form of organization provided an effective way of stimulating colonization and growth of the sugar economy by attracting persons who lacked the financial resources to set up an engenho. The engenho built by Duarte Coelho in 1542 was in part or perhaps totally supplied with cane from lavradores.[93] The letters of Pero de Góes from Paraíba do Sul are suggestive but not conclusive on this problem, speaking as they do of fazendas and *moradores* (settlers) but not specifically of the lavrador arrangement. He did state, however, that one engenho had been built specifically to grind the cane of the moradores.[94]

In this connection, an unsigned letter from a Flemish representative of the Schetz family recently arrived in Brazil who reported on the state of the Engenho São Jorge dos Erasmos in 1548 is particularly instructive. The engenho was making a great deal of sugar for both the estate and the moradores. The moradores had bought or encroached on the lands of the engenho because of the laxity on the part of past managers. The anonymous reporter suggested that it was a disadvantage to maintain these cane farmers because of the high cost of fuel and salaries paid by the engenho. He suggested that the engenho instead mill only its own cane and dispense with cane suppliers. To this end, force and extortion were used to drive the settlers off.[95] As we have already seen, lavradores were an assumed part of the sugar economy that Tomé de Sousa was ordered to establish in Bahia after 1548. In that captaincy, they remained important socially and economically.[96]

Although there appear to have been enough colonists willing to plant cane in the various captaincies, skilled sugar technicians and, in fact, artisans of any kind were at a premium in the sixteenth century. This had been true on the Atlantic islands as well. On Madeira when Canary islanders were expelled in 1505, only sugar masters (*mestres de açúcar*) were allowed to remain; subsequent Portuguese legislation also prohibited the emigration to North Africa of men who knew how to build engenhos.[97] Duarte Coelho had solved the problem by bringing specialists from Iberia and the Canary Islands at his own expense. But, even in Pernambuco, a shortage of skilled labor continued. One Jesuit complained in 1551 that the Jesuits were forced to do everything themselves because of the lack of artisans.[98] In Bahia, the situation was somewhat better after the arrival of Tomé de Sousa in 1549. His expedition included a large number of artisans who set to work building the city of Salvador and presumably then found employment constructing engenhos in the surrounding countryside.[99] Even so, at the beginning of the seventeenth century, the Brotherhood of Artisans (Ofícios mecânicos) established in the Jesuit College of Bahia had only eighty members.[100] The crown sought various ways to remedy this shortage. In July 1551 and then again in 1554, artisans who went to Brazil were offered the same five-year exemption from the tithe that was given to those who set up engenhos.[101]

Artisan skills were needed in both town and country. Masons, boat caulkers, coopers, blacksmiths, sawyers, carters, carpenters, and others all had skills of use to the ports and towns as well as the engenhos. At the end of the sixteenth century, it was estimated that any engenho had some twenty whites employed in various capacities.[102] Engenhos, of course, also had their own peculiar needs related to the production of sugar. Specialists who knew how to build mills and waterwheels were in high demand, as were sugar masters who could direct operations at both field and mill. Men who could perform the tasks of boiling, drying, and crating sugars were also greatly valued, as were managers and overseers.

Donataries and millowners sometimes went to great lengths to obtain these specialists. Pero de Góes, donatary of Paraíba do Sul, brought sugar technicians and artisans from other captaincies. A man was brought to build an engenho at a salary of one cruzado a day. Overseers were also hired and a sugar master was employed on a three-year contract for 60$ a year. Góes was so anxious to keep this man at hand that he paid him in the first year even though the mill was not in operation; he also sought ways of legally binding the sugar master to his contract.[103]

The sugar masters bear special attention. In the early years of the Brazilian sugar industry, men from Madeira were prized in this capacity. High salaries were paid to attract them.[104] The annual salary of a Madeiran sugar master was some 30$, but, as we have just seen, Pero de Góes was willing to pay twice that amount. By the end of the sixteenth century, such men were paid 100$ or more in addition to room and board.[105] In the words of Father Cardim, the sugar masters were the real senhores de engenho, "for in their hands was the production and fame of the engenho, and because of this they are treated with much pampering."[106]

We will have subsequent opportunities to discuss the tasks and activities of sugar production, but two points should be emphasized here. First, the industrial and technological needs of sugar agriculture created a demand for skilled and semiskilled laborers that was difficult to satisfy during the incipient stages of the sugar industry. This was especially true because many of the same skills were required in other aspects of the settlement process. The number of European artisans available for these tasks was limited, and so the early sugar industry was faced with an important question: Could an alternate source of skilled labor be found to meet the demands of export agriculture?

Second, the demands of sugar agriculture and the peculiarities of its organization contributed in no small way to the ordering of society. The Portuguese, like other colonists in the New World, brought with them not only an idealized concept of social hierarchy, hallowed and buttressed by theology, but also a practical understanding of social relationships and positions as these functioned in Portugal. Such concepts and experiences set limitations on the manner in which society took form in Brazil, and at the very least defined the terminology of social organization. Wealthy sugar planters in Brazil aspired to the titles, privileges, and regalia of the traditional nobility, and most groups sought some form of recognition and legitimation of their status through time-honored means.

The creation of a plantation society in Brazil was already under way by the middle of the sixteenth century. In 1549, Duarte Coelho described the occupations of his colonists, and in so doing he also unconsciously began to define the social hierarchy of his captaincy:

Some build engenhos because they are powerful enough to do so, others plant cane, and others cotton, and others foodcrops which are the principal and most important thing in the land; others fish which is also very necessary; others have boats to seek provisions. . . . Others are master engenho builders, sugar masters, carpenters, blacksmiths, masons, potters, the makers of sugar forms and other trades.[107]

This description, though not arranged in a conscious social hierarchy, contained the elements of ordering natural in an economy based on commercial agriculture. The sugar-mill owners, holders of the principal means of production, were mentioned first. They were followed by those linked to export agriculture. The men engaged in the production of food for local consumption were listed in last place, but their occupations received special mention (just as the role of the peasants in Europe was usually singled out as crucial for the maintenance of all else). With only a scant mention of shipping and merchants, Duarte Coelho then turned to the artisans, listing them in roughly the order of their importance to the sugar-making process, or, put another way, in order of the annual salary that each could expect to make.

Although absent from Duarte Coelho's description, the bulk of the colony's population comprised those who provided the necessary labor to make sugar a profitable venture. Sufficient initial capital and experienced and skilled managers were crucial to success. But nothing could be done without laborers, both skilled and unskilled, who provided the broad platform on which the society of the colony was structured. As every schoolchild knows, African slaves eventually filled this role throughout the tropical zones of the Americas, and their presence created the permutations of color that complicated social structures. But in Brazil, they were preceded by the indigenous inhabitants, the Indians, who left few traces in the areas of sugar production but who were the basis of the industry's beginnings. Their role and why they were eventually replaced by imported Africans must be discussed before we can initiate a detailed discussion of the mature society of sugar.

CHAPTER 2

A WASTED GENERATION: COMMERCIAL AGRICULTURE AND INDIAN LABORERS

> . . . for one never believed that so many people would ever be used up, let alone in such a short time.
>
> Father José de Anchieta (Bahia, 1564)

The early Brazilian sugar economy was tragically related to the history of Portuguese–Indian contacts along the coast. Indian enslavement and their work in canefield and mill proved to be a transitory stage in the sugar industry's development, the use of a relatively inexpensive and readily available labor force during a period before the industry was fully capitalized. Eventually, other workers would fill the ranks of the engenhos' labor force as African slaves, cargo in a voluminous branch of the Atlantic trade, replaced Indians in the late sixteenth and early seventeenth centuries.[1] But the process was gradual and never inevitable. Indian slavery withered away because of the cultural perceptions and limitations of both Indians and Europeans, the susceptibility of native Americans to Old World diseases, and the course of historical events. In Bahia, Indians constituted the main labor source for nearly a century, and even after their replacement by African slaves, Indians could be found on plantations and around them as coerced workers, peasants, or wage earners.

This chapter will trace the history of the relationship between Indians and the Bahian plantation economy. The story is essential for an understanding of the Bahian sugar economy's origins, but it is also interesting in a broader perspective because it casts some light on notions that particular labor forms that developed in colonial areas were, in a sense, predetermined by the logic of European capitalist development.[2] This view leaves little historical role for the objective physical conditions and cultural traditions of the peoples in the "colonial areas," and it tends toward a new form of Eurocentrism. By a close examination of Indian slavery, we can address these theories directly. The attempt to use Indians as a coerced labor force cannot simply be dismissed as a "false start." The complex interplay of European and

Indian perceptions and actions set the ways in which Indians did – and did not – become integrated within colonial society. In Brazil, Indian slavery had a short history in legal terms (roughly 1500–70), but various forms of coercion were used well after those dates to acquire indigenous laborers. Even after the large-scale introduction of Africans, Indians could still be found on the engenhos of Northeast Brazil.

The Indians

Our starting point must be the Indians themselves, but we cannot assume here the task of presenting a full ethnography of the indigenous peoples of Brazil, or even of Bahia, on the eve of European contact. Instead, there is some advantage in introducing at this point a discussion of the major groups encountered by the Portuguese on the Brazilian coast, especially in regard to those aspects of indigenous life that help to explain and clarify the process of their absorption into the sugar society of the coastal Northeast.

The most numerous and widely dispersed of the Indian peoples who came into contact with the Europeans in the first two centuries of Brazilian history were the speakers of Tupí-guaraní languages who, at the moment of first contact, were in control of much of the littoral from Maranhão to São Vicente in the south.[3] The major Tupí-speaking group in the region that became the captaincy of Bahia was the Tupinambá, a powerful people who occupied the coast from Sergipe southward to Camamú in a strip twenty to fifty miles wide. South of Camamú, another group of Tupí speakers, the Tupiniquin, controlled the coastal margin southward to Espírito Santo, but their position was precarious because of the pressure and incursions of various non-Tupí peoples, particularly the Aimoré (Botocudos). There were other Tupí speakers scattered in the interior of the captaincy. The Tupinae (Tobajara), for example, had lived in the area of the Bay of All Saints, but at the time of European arrival, they were no longer on the littoral in any numbers, having been pushed inland by the Tupinambá. By the sixteenth century, there were only a few villages left, and those were under constant pressure from the non–Tupí speakers who dominated the sertão (backlands).

The Tupinambá lived in villages of four hundred to eight hundred individuals organized into large family units that shared some four to eight long houses. Patrilineal kinship was an important organizational aspect of their society, but divisions of sex and age were also used to define responsibility and privilege.[4] Warfare, the capture of enemies, and their eventual death as victims in a feast of ritual cannibalism were integrative aspects of Tupinambá society because the acquisition of status, the choice of marriage partners, and progress through the age ranks depended on these manly activities.[5] This need for captives impelled the Tupinambá villages into a constant state of warfare with their immediate neighbors. Needless to say, ritual cannibalism was particularly abhorred by the Portuguese, and it became a principal excuse for the enslavement of the Tupinambá and other peoples. Even after 1570, when the Portuguese crown forbade the enslavement of Indians, cannibalism still provided a "just cause" for slavery.

Although the martial arts and ritual cannibalism were perhaps the aspects of Tupinambá life that provided the underpinnings of their view of the universe and their social organization, there were other features of Tupinambá culture important for understanding their relations to the Portuguese. Unlike some of their neighbors, the Tupinambá practiced agriculture. It was well suited to their habitat and needs and formed an essential part of Tupinambá life. One of the principal obligations of the shamans (pagés) was to ensure sufficient rainfall for the crops.[6]

The Tupinambá economy was basically one of subsistence and autoconsumption. Each village produced what it needed, and there was little trade in foodstuffs with others.[7] Agriculture was always combined with hunting, fishing, and gathering, with seasonal variations in the relative importance of each source of nourishment. The Tupinambá grew a number of crops, such as beans, maize, a variety of tubers, and squash, but by far the most essential part of their food supply was manioc. This root crop grew in a wide range of soils, was resistant to the ravages of most insects, and provided a high number of calories in relation to the area planted. Made into a flour, manioc became the principal food of both native and European Brazilians. It was, along with maize and the potato, one of the principal contributions of the Indian to the world's diet.

Although we know little of the proprietorship of the fields and the distribution of their produce, we do have a fairly complete understanding of the techniques used in Tupinambá agriculture and the sexual division of labor associated with them. The Tupinambá employed a form of slash-and-burn agriculture (coivara) still in use in parts of Brazil today. Men undertook the heavy labor of opening a field by felling the large trees. Fires were then set to clear the underbrush, the ashes providing a natural fertilizer. To the village's women fell the tasks of planting, harvesting, and food preparation. Men hunted and fished. Agriculture was almost exclusively women's work. It was only in the heavy communal labor of clearing timber that Tupinambá men entered the agricultural cycle.

Europeans were often struck by Indians' lack of concern for surplus, profit, and certain forms of property.[8] The Tupinambá and many of their neighbors lived by an economy of use rather than one of exchange, providing for their needs without concern for profit in the European sense of that term. There was no need to produce to the capacity of time or technology, but only to assure a sufficient liveli-hood. In such an economy, the tempo of work, of production, was intermittent and discontinuous.[9] Energy was expended to meet needs, but time was always left for leisure, ceremony, warfare, and other "unproductive" activities. The Jesuit Martim da Rocha later com-mented, "These Indians maintain the time of the Apostles. . . . They have nothing of their own; everything is common among them." Father Nóbrega made the same observation and added that goods "that one has must be divided with the rest, principally if they be foodstuffs."[10]

The habitat of coastal Brazil facilitated such attitudes because an ade-quate food supply could be obtained without extraordinary effort. Game was plentiful, there were many edible plants and insects, the shores and rivers were full of delicious crustaceans, and manioc, won-derful plant that it is, provided nourishment while requiring little care after its planting. This relatively secure food supply made it quite easy for the Portuguese in Bahia to obtain manioc flour (*farinha*) and other food by trade in the period of early contact. During the 1550s, large amounts of farinha were purchased from villages in Bahia and else-where along the coast.[11] The Tupinambá, having satisfied their own needs, attached little importance to their surplus and were willing to trade it for useful goods on a limited basis. But, unlike the Europeans, the Tupinambá's willingness was finite; thus they were an undepend-able source of food and, later, labor.

A communal or reciprocal attitude toward production and consump-tion, the domestic mode of production, a society in which status was not derived from economic ability, and subordination of the economy to other forms of social organization determined Indian responses to European demands. The divergent outlooks of Portuguese and Indians toward the nature and goals of labor and production lie beneath the change in Portuguese–Indian relations and help to explain the subse-quent history of Indians in the plantation regime.

Seeming prodigality, lack of interest in profit, and unconcern with surplus and saving grated upon the European sensibility, and more than once such attitudes were offered as proof of Indian irrationality and thus evidence of their lack of "humanity." Wrote Governor Diogo de Meneses in 1610, "These Indians, Sir, are a very barbarous people having no government and being unable to govern themselves, and they are so lacking in this regard that even in their sustenance they will not save for tomorrow that which is in excess today."[12] Even among the agricultural Tupinambá, the Portuguese were aghast at the "idle-ness" of the villages, where the men seemed to loll about smoking and preparing for battle.[13] It was the confrontation of two peoples whose economic systems and visions of the universe could not have been farther apart. Portuguese attitudes toward the "barbarism" of the

Tupinambá, a people whose practice of agriculture had already brought about at least a partial transition to a neolithic culture, were intensified when confronted by others who had not made that transition. Observers, especially the Jesuits, were sometimes perceptive reporters of Indian life. Unfortunately, much of their understanding of what they saw was screened not only by their own cultural bias but that of their principal informants, the Tupinambá, as well. As a result, our image of the other tribal groups has been doubly distorted by refraction through two cultural prisms.

The early Portuguese colonists adopted the Tupinambá practice of calling all non–Tupí speakers by the general term "Tapuya," or "speakers of twisted tongues." Anthropologists believed for many years that these peoples belonged to the great linguistic family of Gê speakers, and surely some of them did. Recent research has established that the Tapuya belonged to a variety of cultural and linguistic trunks that included, in Bahia, the Gê, Caraíba, and Cariri.[14] Because of Tupinambá occupation of the coast, most of these other peoples inhabited the interior and thus were in far less contact with the Portuguese during the first century of colonization. Nevertheless, European attacks into the sertão, migration, and intertribal warfare sometimes resulted in Tapuya captives in the canefields of the Recôncavo. Because the majority of these people lived entirely by hunting and gathering, our observations about Tupinambá economic attitudes and practices could be repeated and intensified for them. Their conception of an economy of direct utility and of a meager material culture that allowed for great mobility made them particularly unsuited to peaceful contact with the Portuguese. Agricultural slavery weighed perhaps even harder on these peoples than on the Tupinambá.

Although the very diversity of Tapuya peoples precludes a more detailed general discussion, there is one group whose importance in the historical record merits particular attention. No people offered more continual or effective opposition to the Portuguese than the Aimoré, who inhabited Espirito Santo, Ilhéus, and the southern marches of Bahia.[15] Their military effectiveness and determination bear comparison to the Araucanian resistance in Chile. For over two centuries, the Aimoré terrorized the region south of Bahia and even raided the southern margins of the Recôncavo. Settlement in these regions was hazardous, and more than once colonists and sugar planters complained that neither agriculture nor life were secure so long as the Aimoré continued undefeated. The Portuguese sometimes called these people "Botocudos," a name that in Bahia became like "Bugre" in southern Brazil, an epithet for any hostile Indian people.[16]

Because of Aimoré effectiveness and intransigence, the Portuguese had a much dimmer understanding of their life and customs than of those of the Tupinambá. The Aimoré were apparently a Gê-speaking

people. Their material culture was simpler than that of the Tupinambá
or Tupiniquin. They did not practice agriculture but lived solely by
hunting and gathering. Various Portuguese observers claimed that the
Aimoré had no dwellings but lived in the forest like beasts; but, given
the Portuguese dislike of the Aimoré, such statements must be taken
with skepticism.[17] It is probable that the Aimoré social structure, like
that of many Gê peoples, was highly complex, based on a division of
each local group into moities. Warfare, which seems to have been a
major activity before the arrival of the Portuguese, intensified after it.
Aimoré hostility provoked an almost paranoiac response from settlers,
Jesuits, and royal officials, and their accounts of these people are un-
animously mixed with fear, admiration, and disgust. Other Amerindians lived in houses like men; the Aimoré lived in the forest; the
Tupinambá ate their enemies for vengeance; the Aimoré, because they
enjoyed human flesh; and so on. When in 1570 the first royal law
against Indian slavery was promulgated, only the Aimoré were specifically excluded from its protection.[18]

The Aimoré and the Tupinambá were the two major cultural traditions encountered by the Portuguese in Bahia. Both would undergo
considerable modification when confronted by the demands of a colonial export economy. Portuguese attitudes toward Indian "barbarism"
expressed about agricultural peoples were even more intense when
confronted by hunters and gatherers. Such encounters brought together peoples whose economic systems and visions of life were
worlds apart.

Responses to the European economy

In Bahia, as elsewhere along the coast, the nature of European–Indian
relations was determined in large part by the nature of the Portuguese
presence, their economic goals, and European concern in three major
areas: food, defense, and labor. The earliest European commercial activities on the coast were the cutting and exporting of dyewood logs
from the famous brazilwood trees. As early as 1502, contracts for the
export of this commodity were granted to private individuals, and over
the next thirty years both the Portuguese and their French rivals established trading posts on the coast.

Brazilwood did not grow in large stands but was scattered throughout the forest. As the trees along the coast were depleted, the Europeans turned increasingly to the Indians to supply the logs. We should
recall that communal labor, especially the felling of trees, was a characteristic masculine activity of Tupinambá society, and as such it could be
easily integrated into the traditional patterns of indigenous life. Indians
seemed quite willing to cut the trees and drag the heavy logs to the
coastal posts, where they could be traded for trinkets and other trade

goods. Between 1500 and 1535, the Portuguese used barter as the principal means to obtain brazilwood and, secondarily, manioc flour from the Indians. Indirectly, it was also a method for obtaining labor. We do not know whether the Tupinambá and others traded logs, manioc flour, and labor individually or communally during this period, but purchases made in the 1540s imply the latter. If so, then the barter system was functioning within the perimeters of community activity and was, therefore, easily adaptable to traditional patterns of life.

All this began to change radically in the 1530s with the introduction of the donatary system. This plan to grant proprietary rights to Portuguese noblemen – who would in turn develop their grants by settling colonists and establishing a secure economic basis – now made new demands on the Indian inhabitants. Although donataries and colonists continued to barter for brazilwood, food, and even labor needed on a short-term basis for town building, the demands of the new crop of settlement, sugar, could not be met by barter. In Bahia, Pernambuco, and elsewhere along the coast, the Portuguese increasingly turned to chattel slavery as a means to secure labor for the canefields and mills. They moved, as Alexander Marchant put it so ably in the title of his important book, *From Barter to Slavery.*

Marchant argued that the barter system began to collapse because of a series of economic decisions made by the Portuguese and, to some extent, by the Indians as well. First, there was a glut on the trinket market. As Indian demands shifted to more expensive ironware and firearms, the Portuguese costs of supply rose markedly. Moreover, the increased number of colonists and the presence of royal brazilwood contractors created a situation of competition for labor.

This interpretation, though correct in its broad outlines, disregarded two aspects of the problem crucial for our understanding of the interplay of cultural and economic forces that shaped the forms of Indian labor in Brazil. First, not only did the value of the goods cause a crisis in the barter relationship but so did the nature of the goods. Axes and firearms must have had a profound impact on the nature of the Indian economy by transforming two of the most difficult and time-consuming tasks, tree felling and hunting.[19] Iron tools increased productivity and reduced the time expended on certain activities. By enabling Indians to satisfy their material needs more quickly, these tools left them more free time to engage in ceremonies and to make war. Such a hypothesis makes the Indians appear less than "rational" in terms of economic maximization, and this is exactly the problem that underlies Marchant's explanation. Second, Marchant assumes that the Indians were "economic men" involved in a self-regulating labor market, ready to make decisions on the basis of personal or communal economic self-interest. But in many primitive "economies," production and distribution of goods are part of, and usually subordinate to, other considerations of social organization like kinship.[20]

Marshall Sahlins has stated this position with a precision worth quoting: "Even to speak of *the* economy in a primitive society is an exercise in unreality. Structurally, 'the economy' does not exist. . . . Economy is rather a function of the society than a structure."[21] Barter fitted, quite simply, with traditional patterns of culture, even when what was traded was the communal labor for short-term building. Plantation labor did not. Of course, Indian cultures had the capacity to adapt, but what the Portuguese demanded struck at fundamental aspects of Indian life and thought. To the Indians, agriculture was "women's work." Once a man had enough to eat and a few new tools and weapons, why should he want or work for more? Here was a common colonial situation, noted and commented upon in so many places. The natives – obviously capable of great exertion – were seen as congenitally lazy and undependable.[22] Placed on plantations, they would not work; they were given instead to sulky absenteeism or simply running away. For the Indians refused to respond to the objective conditions of the market created by the Portuguese. Thus, the modes of production established were not simply a matter of European choice but were influenced by the nature of Indian society and the internal dynamics of Indian perceptions and needs. Gandavo stated, "If the Indians were not so fickle and given to flight, the wealth of Brazil would be incomparable."[23]

Slaves, peasants, or proletarians

Left alone, Indians refused to respond in predictable ways to the objective conditions of the market. To make them useful to the colonial economy either as food suppliers or sugarcane workers, the Portuguese turned to three different techniques. The first, employed by the colonists, consisted of outright coercion in the form of chattel slavery. The second, attempted by the Jesuits and eventually by other religious orders, was the creation of an indigenous peasantry made pliable to European demands by acculturation and detribalization. The third technique was used by both laymen and ecclesiastics. It consisted of slowly integrating the Indians into a capitalistic self-regulating market as individual wage laborers. The three techniques were in some ways stages in the history of Portuguese–Indian relations during the colonial era, but the divisions were never clearly marked nor was the process always in the same direction at all times in all places. During the sixteenth and early seventeenth centuries in the Northeast, the Portuguese tried all three techniques simultaneously. In a sense, the struggle between the Jesuits and the colonists was a clash between two differing strategies with the same goal: the Europeanization of the native American. In economic terms, it was a polemic between the imposition of a colonial slave regime or the creation of an indigenous peasantry capable of becoming an agricultural proletariat.

The contest between Jesuits and colonists has already been the subject of intensive historical interest, and there is no need to repeat that story in detail here.[24] It should be made clear, however, that this confrontation took place within a specific economic and theological context, which placed limitations on both positions and on the crown's response to them. On one hand, the Portuguese monarchs, both Aviz and Hapsburg, were impelled by moral and theological considerations to recognize the "humanity" of the Indians, to take seriously the crown's obligation to convert them to the Roman Catholic faith, and, as subjects of the Lusitanian scepter, to prohibit their illegal enslavement. With the advocacy of the Jesuits, the crown began to legislate against the enslavement of Indians in 1570, and under the Hapsburgs, restrictive legislation followed in 1595 and 1609. At each juncture, however, the crown was also faced with the economic realities of Brazil, which imposed a logic of their own. The colony's value lay in sugar production – a point that the colonists never tired of making – and sugar demanded a large labor force. The sugar planters did not yet have the capital and credit necessary to supply their needs fully through the expensive transatlantic slave trade with Africa, and thus they were dependent on indigenous workers. As we have seen, for a variety of cultural reasons the Indians, left to their own decisions, would not meet the colony's needs. The crown was thus forced to reconcile its conscience with its treasury receipts.

The crown solved this problem by allowing loopholes in the legislation that permitted the colonists to obtain slaves taken in "just war." Distinctions were made, in effect, between "good" Indians and "bad" ones, and, even though the colonists sometimes could not recognize the difference, the crown was able to live with this situation. Royal support of Jesuit-controlled *aldeias* (villages) was yet another way of resolving the theological and economic problems presented by Brazil. If the Fathers could convert the Indians and make them available for useful activities such as growing food or working in the canefields while still preserving their freedom, so much the better. What is striking in the resolution of the problem is the strength of the colonists and especially the sugar sector in having its way. As long as sugar was Brazil and the major economic inputs for its production came from the colonists themselves, the crown was unwilling to endanger their interests unreasonably. The effectiveness of the sugar planters in countering the moral arguments of the Jesuits with pragmatic defenses of their own and in forcing the crown to listen simply underlines the raison d'être of the colony. From the Indian point of view, both the Jesuits' and colonists' strategies were physically and culturally destructive, albeit in different ways.

The period between 1540 and 1570 saw the apogee of Indian slavery on the engenhos of coastal Brazil in general and of Bahia in particular. By 1545, the southern captaincy of São Vicente had six engenhos and three thousand slaves, the vast majority of whom were Indians.[25] At this date, Indian slaves could also be found on the engenhos of Pernambuco, Bahia, and Porto Seguro. During the 1550s and 1560s, the sugar industry of the Northeast entered a phase of rapid expansion accompanied by a similar increase in the number of captive laborers. By 1570, Pernambuco had twenty-three sugar mills and so many Indian slaves that the surplus could be exported to other captaincies.[26] By 1583, Pernambuco had sixty-six engenhos and some two thousand African slaves. Since an engenho probably drew on the labor of one hundred slaves, Indians still accounted for two-thirds of Pernambuco's engenho work force even during a period of transition to African labor.[27]

In Bahia, the expansion of the sugar economy had received considerable impetus from the establishment of royal government in 1549. Enslavement of the local tribal groups accompanied this expansion. In the 1550s, several military campaigns were carried out in the Recôncavo. Under Dom Duarte da Costa and especially under his successor, Mem de Sá, established engenhos were protected, land was secured for new mills, and captives were obtained by a series of punitive expeditions carried out by the Portuguese and their "domesticated" Indian allies.[28] (See Figure 2-1). In Pernambuco and Bahia, as in other captaincies, the moradores obtained Indian slaves by "ransoming" them (*resgate*) from other Indians who had already taken them as war captives. More common, however, were Portuguese raids made for the specific purpose of obtaining slaves. These incursions (*saltos*) were denounced by the Jesuits and the crown as unlawful. The regimento of Tomé de Sousa prohibited them, but this and subsequent edicts remained a dead letter. As one Jesuit put it, "Only miraculously does one find here a slave not taken by assault."[29]

Unfortunately, our principal traditional source on plantation conditions during the era of Indian slavery are the reports and observations of the Jesuits. Their concerns were naturally as much spiritual and moral as physical, and thus their perceptions are biased in those directions. According to the Jesuit observers, the major problems on the *fazendas* (farms, ranches) of the Northeast captaincies were enslavement by illegal means and the lack of sexual morality among both masters and slaves. The organization of Indian life under slavery, the nature of the labor regime, and the conditions under which these people lived received virtually no detailed attention from them.

The intensive nature of sugar agriculture and perhaps the seemingly

Figure 2-1. The tower adjoining this plantation house emphasizes the defensive function of the early engenhos. The living quarters of the planter were often placed in a second story.

inexhaustible numbers of potential laborers contributed to the hard captivity borne by the native peoples of Brazil. The constant and demanding work regime required on the cane farms and engenhos left little time for leisure. Father Belchior Cordeiro complained that in Pernambuco the Indians could not be indoctrinated since no master would free them from their heavy weekly labors.[30] On Sundays, when the pressure of the church and the beliefs of the slaveowners sometimes released the slaves from the normal round of efforts, the Indians preferred resting, or hunting and fishing to supplement their diet, to attending mass. Father Cordeiro blamed the slaveowners for this state of affairs because they cared only for labor and used the Indians "as if they were brute animals."[31] It was the same observation that Father Manoel da Nóbrega had made almost twenty years before when he wrote that the colonists of Brazil concerned themselves only with engenhos and wealth "though it be with the loss of all their souls."[32] Father Cordeiro, who visited the sugar zones in 1577, believed that conditions in Bahia at that time were better than those in Pernambuco. He claimed that these slaveowners were more concerned with the spiritual welfare of their people, that less sugar was produced and thus the labor demands were not so strenuous, and, finally, that the presence of Christians in the Jesuit-controlled aldeas provided a good example to the slaves on the engenhos.[33] In the Recôncavo, the access of water-borne transport to the engenhos also made it easier for the Jesuits to visit the enslaved Indians and minister to their needs. But in 1591, senhor de engenho João Remirão stated before the Inquisition that most planters in Bahia ignored Sundays and holy days and continued operations.[34]

Although visiting clerics were met on the engenhos with lavish hospitality and demonstrations of piety and devotion, slaveowners resented the Jesuits' meddling in the daily round of engenho life.[35] The Fathers asked uncomfortable questions. Many colonists had expanded their labor force and secured workers by encouraging free Indians (forros) to marry or live with those already enslaved.[36] This tactic enlarged the colonists' labor supply but was against the wishes and edicts of both crown and clergy. Once attached to the estates or households of the Portuguese, there seems to have been little distinction made between forros and escravos. In Bahia, forros were sometimes listed alongside slaves, as was the case in the 1574–8 inventories of Engenhos Sergipe and Santana.[37] Early seventeenth-century wills in São Paulo passed indios forros along to heirs as though they were hardly different from other property.[38] The Jesuits complained bitterly about this practice, and eventually in 1566 they were able, with the aid of Governor Mem de Sá, to establish laws against it.[39] Legislation unfortunately did not eliminate the practice.

If there is any distinction to be made between the phase of Indian slavery in Pernambuco and Bahia, the two major sugar regions, its basis is the relative strength and success of the Jesuits. In the more northern captaincy, the enterprising donatary Duarte Coelho had stimulated the expansion of the sugar economy and had favored his colonists in this activity well before the Jesuits began operations in his territory. Significantly, there were no Jesuit aldeias in the immediate vicinity of Olinda, for here the colonists had their way.[40] In Bahia, the seat of royal authority and Jesuit activities after 1549, the followers of Loyola had far more success in implementing their policy of Indian protection. Twelve aldeias were created in the 1550s and 1560s, the smallest of which, Santo Antônio, contained 2,000 souls. Between 1559 and 1583, 5,000 people were baptized in Aldeia Santo Antônio, a figure that multiplied by twelve yields a total of 60,000 Indians baptized in these villages. Around 1590, when plague and dislocation had already taken a ghastly toll of the aldeias, there were still 3,500 to 5,000 persons in the Bahian villages, twice the number to be found in Pernambuco.[41]

Despite differing levels of success from captaincy to captaincy, the basic policy of the Jesuits was the same throughout the Northeast. In opposition to the enslavement of the Indians, they carried out a program of missionary activity within hamlets or aldeias where both local tribal groups and those brought in from the sertão could receive instruction and guidance. The Indians received an education in how to

live a Christian life, a concept that included not only European morality but work habits as well. Since the Jesuits basically agreed with the
colonists that Indian culture was barbaric, little attempt was made to
accommodate indigenous life or preserve it. Aspects of Tupí culture
that facilitated conversion were utilized by the Fathers but, unlike their
actions in China and India, there was little cultural relativism in their
actions in Brazil.[42] As far as possible, a full Catholic religious life was
created in the aldeias. The Indians selectively accepted the new faith.
Lay brotherhoods and certain religious festivals such as Palm Sunday
were readily accepted, or at least so it would seem from the sometimes
idyllic accounts of the Jesuits themselves.[43] For the Indians, however,
the forced acculturation of the aldeias was simply the better of two
evils.

Although the choice between the rigors of plantation slavery and the
protection of the Jesuit aldeias seems to us hardly a choice at all, the
Indians were less sure. The aldeias, despite the noble intentions of the
crown, the Jesuits, and eventually other missionary orders, were in
their own way as destructive to indigenous life as the engenhos, and in
some ways perhaps even more so. The attention of the Fathers to
moral and spiritual matters interfered more directly and proved more
disruptive to Indian life than the colonists' control of their labor and
regulation of the work regime. The aldeias seem at first glance to provide a communal village existence parallel to the pre-European organization of life. The analogy, however, is deceptive; the Christian
communalism of the ecclesiastics bore little resemblance to indigenous
patterns, especially when major integrative features were eliminated or
transformed. It is easy enough to understand why the Fathers would
seek to exterminate such fundamental features of Tupinambá life as
polygamy, cousin marriages, ritual cannibalism, and warfare; it is just
as easy to perceive the effects of this policy on traditional life. For
reasons of missionary convenience, the villages very quickly lost their
cultural integrity as peoples of various tribal groups and tongues were
mixed together. The Lingua geral, a simplified form of Tupí, was used
by the Jesuits as a lingua franca in the aldeias, providing one more step
in the reduction of Indian culture to a common base that could be
controlled and manipulated by the Fathers. Such methods made
preaching and conversion easier, but in doing so increased the pace of
detribalization.

Indian cultures, like others, had the capacity to adapt and survive in
new situations, but the conditions and regulations imposed by the
Europeans were so inamicable to the persistence of Indian life that
adjustment within a traditional context was virtually unthinkable. The
Indians by their actions commented upon this situation. Despite the
rosy glow of missionary zeal that pervades much of the Jesuit comments on the aldeias, Father Inácio de Azevedo wrote in 1566, "Many

Indians wish to go with them [colonists] and serve them rather than live in the aldeias."[44]

Although the effect of intentional European interference in traditional practices is clear enough, the aldeias were also disruptive in more subtle ways. Let us take, for example, their physical plan. The Jesuit aldeias were physically organized according to European norms, with a central plaza, a church, and rows of house units flanking the open space.[45] Tupinambá village organization, with its layout of four to eight long houses shared by many related families, was quite different; and the complex organization of the Gê speakers, with the village divided into moities and clans and with separate residences for certain age and sex groups, was even farther from the European plan. The village and residence patterns were representations of the social and religious cosmos. To change them was to change the security of the traditional universe and to disorient them in the literal meaning of the word. As Claude Lévi-Strauss has pointed out in another context, "All feeling for their traditions would desert them, as if their social and religious systems . . . were so complex that they could not exist without the schema made visible in their ground-plans and reaffirmed to them in the daily rhythm of their lives."[46]

Of course, from the Jesuit viewpoint the destruction of Indian culture symbolized the success of the aldeias and the Jesuit-sponsored policy of the crown. The Jesuits argued that the aldeias not only protected the Indians from slavery and facilitated their conversion but provided an auxiliary military force for use against hostile tribes, foreign interlopers, and restive slaves as well. "And work for the Jesuits for nothing," muttered the colonists. The Fathers of the Society answered this charge by claiming that the aldeias also provided labor to the estates of the colonists. By 1600, the Jesuits claimed to have 50,000 Indians in the aldeias of Brazil available to both crown and colonists. What disappears relatively early from the Jesuit defense of their Indian policy is that it is an attempt to create an indigenous peasantry.

As Portuguese colonization became increasingly based on agricultural exploitation, conflict with the Indians over land became a central problem. In Bahia, force and deceit were used to eliminate Indians from land capable of sugar production, especially in the northern and western sections of the Recôncavo. Jesuit defenders of the Indians who were also strong advocates of the Indians as independent peasants pleaded for the protection of village lands and even restoration of property seized illegally. Sesmarias were given to aldeias to ensure the Indians against starvation, but these lands were not in the sugar-producing massapé. Even the Jesuits realized that it was difficult to make headway against the economic current represented by sugar. In 1558, Father Nóbrega sought a grant of land to the aldeia São Paulo (in present-day Brotas). He felt that the owner of the land, the count of Castanheira, would cede the property because, lacking water for an engenho, it served for very little.[47] Not even Nóbrega would have tried to secure lands for the Indians that could be used for sugarcane cultivation.

To create an indigenous peasantry in Brazil, the Portuguese were forced to start from scratch. In Brazil, unlike Mexico, the Yucatán, or the Andean highlands, there was no pre-Columbian tradition of communal agriculture linked to a larger state system. As in Paraguay, the Jesuit aldeias of the Brazilian Northeast were an attempt to create peasant communities where none had existed before, at least not in ways that would serve the interests of the colony. The Jesuits were not only the defenders of the Indian communities; they were also their creators.[48]

With the support of the crown and of sympathetic administrators such as Mem de Sá, the Jesuits were able to secure lands for their Indian charges, but the Jesuit attempt to create a peasantry that was not only self-supporting but also a supplier of the colony's needs was never realized. The first royal governor, Tomé de Sousa, had arrived in 1549 with specific instructions to create a weekly market where Portuguese and Indian could conduct business. This system was designed to supply the food requirements of the Portuguese while protecting the Indians from the worst aspects of extortion and fraud by prohibiting the colonists from entering villages at will. But even here at the outset concessions were made to the planter class, for only they and their people were allowed to trade with the Indians for food whenever it was convenient. The system of voluntary supply failed, as we have seen, in part because the Indians would not respond to the market. Aside from the regimento of Tomé de Sousa, there are almost no other references to the weekly feira he was supposed to have established. Lands were given to the Indians primarily to ensure their livelihood and therefore their availability to the colony. Mem de Sá stated this position clearly in his grant of a sesmaria to the Aldeia de Espirito Santo in Bahia, "seeing how beneficial and necessary they are to this Bahia and that they cannot sustain themselves without lands to farm."[49]

Neither the sugar planters nor the crown was anxious to recognize the failure to create an indigenous peasantry. In the ideal mental landscape of the sugar producers, the engenhos would be ringed by canefields as far as possible. Then, at the outer limits, there would be villages of "domesticated Indians," who would keep out the unreduced tribes of the interior while growing large quantities of manioc and other foods. Of course, if the Indians worked at the engenho on occasion that was all the better. Even at the end of the sixteenth century, the crown still made reference to the benefits of having Indians farming close by the engenhos of the Portuguese.[50] Certainly, the engenho population sometimes acquired foodstuffs from Indian growers, but on an intermittent and haphazard basis. Eventually, what emerged in the Recôncavo was a geographical division between the export crop, sugar, and the locally consumed food crops. Large-scale production of manioc was pushed to the southern shores of the Recôncavo and even farther southward to Cairú, Camamú, and Ilhéus. The peasantry that developed in association with this crop was not Indian but a predominantly mixed population of *mestiços* (mestizos; offspring of Indian–white unions) and mulattoes.[51]

Having failed to create an indigenous peasantry, the Jesuits justified their continued control of the villages by emphasizing the military and labor services that their charges provided. In Bahia during the early 1580s, the Jesuit aldeias supplied some four hundred to five hundred workers to the colonists under a system of contract labor. The Indians received a meager wage of four hundred réis per month, scarcely a third of a common boatman's salary, but even this sum was often never paid.[52] Still, the planters were uncomfortable with Jesuit control of their laborers.

Sugar planters were certainly not averse to hiring wage laborers if they could obtain them in sufficient quantities and under favorable conditions. As early as 1561, settlers in Bahia had sought to hire Indians for wages (*soldada*), and the accounts of Engenho Sergipe indicate that Indians did provide services for pay, although usually at a rate far below that of whites, free blacks, or mulattoes.[53] The royal Indian legislation of 1596 is a clear demonstration of the crown's attempt to integrate the domesticated Indians (*índios mansos*) into the colony as wage laborers.[54] At the same time, this law is also indicative of certain other patterns in formation. It was clearly stated that Indian laborers were not to remain for more than two months of continual service on the engenhos and that no advance payments were to be made to them. This is a hint that planters may have been turning to a form of debt peonage as an answer to their labor needs. The crown forbade either jesuits' or colonists' use of Indians unless they were paid "like free men and treated as such."[55] We will never know whether aldeia residents or other Indians within the radius of Portuguese control could have filled the labor demands of the sugar industry as free laborers. The wages the planters were willing to pay were far too low to create an adequate wage labor market so long as an alternate type of cheap labor was available in the form of Indian slaves.[56]

The disaster of contact: Portuguese and Indian readjustments

Portuguese dependence on Indians either as slaves or as wards of the Jesuits was subject to other limitations. Brought into close contact with Europeans in the aldeias and on the plantations, the Indians became increasingly susceptible to European diseases. As early as 1559, plague was reported on the Brazilian coast.[57] The disease, probably smallpox (*bexigas*), spread northward. In 1559 or 1560, it killed over six hundred enslaved Indians in Espirito Santo in such a short space of time that the bodies had to be buried two in a grave.[58] No one had any idea of the number of dead among the free Indians. By 1561, the Recôncavo was suffering the effects of increased mortality. Father Leonardo do Valle reported that he was called on every day to treat the sick slaves, sometimes at two and three different places simultaneously.[59] The epidemic reached its height in 1562. Thousands perished. Estimates placed the figure at thirty thousand dead among the Indians under Portuguese control, to say nothing of countless more in the sertão, where the disease spread as Indians fled the deadly conditions on the coast. Father do Valle wrote of children who died on their mother's breast for lack of milk, of people so debilitated that they could not dig graves for the dead or even draw water for the living. One third of all the Indians in the Jesuit aldeias died. On the sugar plantations, the effects were just as virulent. On some estates, ninety to one hundred slaves perished.[60] The following year brought no respite. In 1563, a second epidemic, this time measles (*sarampo*), struck an already weakened population. Perhaps another thirty thousand died.[61] Not surprisingly, measles proved far more lethal to the Indians than to the Portuguese. The overall effect on the Europeans was one of wonder, as is evidenced by this statement so reminiscent of declarations made in sixteenth-century Mexico in the face of a similar disaster: "The population that was in these parts twenty years ago is wasted in this Bahia, and it seems an incredible thing for one never believed that so many people would ever be used up, let alone in such a short time."[62]

The effects of the epidemics of 1562–3 were disruptive to the social and economic fabric of the colony. Portuguese concentration on the export crop of sugar and their dependence on indigenous supplies of foodstuffs had, even in the best of times, created an unstable situation. Now, with the decimation of the Indians, the main sources of food were completely disrupted, and famine set in. The Portuguese went hungry, and the Indians starved to death. Some, faced with starvation, sold themselves into bondage rather than perish. Those who took this course may have believed that their servitude was to be temporary, but they discovered eventually that this was not the case.[63]

Although in some ways these vital crises of the 1560s facilitated the enslavement of Indians still within the range of Portuguese operations, they also made clear the dangers inherent in dependence on Indian labor.[64] The colonists were not yet ready to abandon this source of labor for the now growing number of sugar mills, but the uncertainty of Indian health and life expectancy made them an investment of great risk. This situation helps to explain why Indian slaves were priced far below Africans, why Africans were more likely to receive training for the skilled tasks at the sugar mills, and why the colonists were not completely against the development of a wage-labor system. The 1570s and 1580s witnessed a number of schemes designed to bring still unreduced Indians from the interior to meet the labor needs of the engenhos. But, faced with the increasing opposition of the crown to enslavement, the growing demands of the sugar economy, and the disastrous example of the 1560s, the colonists turned toward the supply of labor to be found in the Atlantic slave trade. It was no accident that the importation of large numbers of Africans began in the 1570s following the peculiar conjunction of demographic, economic, and political factors that demonstrated the risks of an economy based on captive or coerced indigenous labor.

Still, the colonists persisted. When the local inhabitants had been eliminated by war, disease, or overwork or had been so reduced in numbers that they could no longer fill the colonists' labor requirements, Indians from other regions were imported. An implicit but common policy throughout the colonial period was the forced movement of Indians from region to region. This policy brought at least three obvious benefits to the Portuguese. First, it allowed the Europeans to take advantage of the military skills of their Indian allies by using them against peoples not yet subject to Portuguese rule. Second, it removed potentially dangerous peoples from their native environment and placed them in unfamiliar surroundings where they would present less of a threat. Finally, it allowed the colonists to tap an ever widening labor pool.

Petitions to bring down (*descer*) peoples from the interior to the zone of sugar agriculture were common in the late sixteenth and seventeenth centuries, the period of transition from indigenous to imported labor. The antislavery law of 1570 undoubtedly served as a stimulus in the search for new sources of labor. Both the Jesuits and the colonists participated in the gathering of tribal groups, their reasons being either quite different or else very similar, according to which side of the debate one believes. In 1571, five to six hundred people came into the Bahian aldeias. The conquest of Sergipe de El-Rey in 1575–6 resulted in four thousand more being brought into the Recôncavo. Military operations in the sertão of Orobó reduced another twenty thousand Indians to Portuguese control.[65]

A specific case illustrates how the policy of forced migration helped the Portuguese to both maintain and serve the sugar industry. In Ilhéus, the incessant raids of the Aimoré had brought sugar production to a standstill, a situation that was further complicated by the lack of any other tribes who might provide labor to the engenhos. The solution sought was to bring in friendly Indians as a protective force. As the chronicler Frei Vicente do Salvador put it, war against the Aimoré could only be effected by "other gentiles, forest creatures like themselves."[66] The people chosen for this task were the Potiguar, a

Tupí-speaking group from Paraíba and Pernambuco who could field some sixty thousand warriors and who had aided the Portuguese on other occasions. It was not lost on the Portuguese that the Potiguar "occupied with this and taken from their homeland could not themselves turn to rebellion."[67]

The Potiguar were reluctant to undertake this mission, and it was only through the intercession of the Jesuits that 800 warriors finally agreed to go, on condition that they could return as soon as hostilities had ended. By the time of their arrival in Bahia, sometime in 1601, the Aimoré threat had subsided. But the Portuguese now proved reluctant to let their "allies" depart. One group of 80 bowmen were sent to Ilhéus, while the rest were placed at the disposal of the Recôncavo engenhos. The Potiguar realized that they had been duped and threatened to rebel, but Jesuit intervention once again averted bloodshed. As a result, the Potiguar remained in Bahia in guard positions near the engenhos but surely as laborers as well.

Those who had been sent to Ilhéus did not fulfill the hopes of that captaincy's colonists. The *câmara* (municipal council; in full, *senado da câmara*) of São Jorge complained that the warriors did not come with their wives and families and were not really sufficient to meet the needs of the sugar industry. Although they admitted having received some Indians from Espirito Santo, they felt that the Jesuits could bring a thousand bowmen and their families to serve the labor and defensive needs of the engenhos.[68] Such hopes were never satisfied, and in fact the Potiguar proved a mixed blessing. In 1603, Domingos Fernandes da Cunha, manager of Engenho Santana, complained that Potiguar settled in a nearby village, provided no protection from hostile tribes, and ate all the sugarcane they could lay their hands on.[69] Still he, like so many others in the sugar industry, felt that with the help of God and the use of the Indians there was still profit to be made.

Thus the colonists throughout the late sixteenth and seventeenth centuries viewed the Jesuits' control of Indians with the jealous eyes of men who could see easy profit just beyond their grasp. Gaspar da Cunha, overseer of Engenho Sergipe, wrote in 1585 to his absentee patron, the count of Linhares, that villages placed nearby would protect its margins as well as serve its operations.[70] He recommended that a petition to this end be made. The count of Linhares, the duke of Aveiro, and a few others were successful in obtaining permits to have Indians placed near their holdings.[71] The crown was neither blind to their predicament nor to its own fiscal interests. An *alvará* (royal decree) recognizing the benefits that villages of sertão Indians would provide to the "fazendas and engenhos of my vassals," was issued in 1587, but the eventual control of these settlements by the Jesuits placed restrictions on their use that the colonists were unwilling to accept.[72] Still, their petitions persisted into the seventeenth century, and occasionally they were able to make headway under sympathetic governors such as Diogo de Meneses (1608–12).[73]

Santidade *and resistance*

While colonists, clergymen, and the crown debated the relative merits of various policies, the Indians attempted to decide their own fate. Groups resisted Portuguese rule at the outset by flight or arms, methods that the Portuguese used as excuses to enslave Indians under the "just war" clauses of royal law. Once brought under European control, many Indians proved restive. Opportunities for individual flight were many, and as long as the Indians were operating in their native lands with a "home-court advantage" they proved to be difficult to control. Collective efforts at resistance were also made. In 1567, a general rebellion swept the Recôncavo. Masters were killed in some places as slaves abandoned the canefields in large numbers. Only the intercession of the Jesuit-led aldeia inhabitants brought the situation under control by returning the slaves to their owners.[74] Such large-scale movements were rare, but one in southern Bahia was so long-lived and so indicative of the clash of Indian and European cultures and economies that it deserves special attention.

The Portuguese called the phenomena *santidade*. It was a classic "religion of the oppressed"; a syncretic, messianic cult whose goal was to bring a golden age by lifting the yoke of slavery imposed by Portuguese rule and culture. The movement was first noted in 1551 in São Vicente, but it eventually took hold and flourished in Ilhéus and the southern Recôncavo of Bahia.[75]

In general, the santidade cult appears to have been a combination of the Tupinambá belief in an earthly paradise with the hierarchy and symbols of Roman Catholicism. At the heart of the cult were idols made from gourds or stone that were said to have holy powers. Although the idols had various shapes, their functions and attributes seem to have been the same. They endowed their followers with strength against the whites, and their victories would bring the millennium of Tupinambá paradise. The hoes would go to the fields by themselves, and arrows would speed through the forest in search of game while the hunters rested in the village. The aged would be young again, all could have many wives, and all enemies would be destroyed or captured and eaten. To honor the "saints," new chants and songs were sung, ceremonies of celebration might last for days, and large amounts of alcoholic drink and infusions of tobacco were taken. Apparently, these ceremonies were designed to induce catatonic trances in the celebrants.[76]

It is clear that the movement grew among Indians who had been exposed to the Portuguese. The principal leaders were former slaves, although residents of the aldeias also joined. At least one leader was an Indian who had been raised by the Jesuits. At different places and at different times, followers of santidade emerged into the historical record. Despite some diversity in the detail of their religious life, it is plain that they were considerably influenced by their contact with Catholicism. The symbols and hierarchy of the church were adopted. Leaders proclaimed themselves "pope" and named bishops.[77] "Missionaries" were dispatched to spread the cult and advocate resistance to the Portuguese. Fernão Cabral de Atayde, who in 1585 or 1586 allowed a group to live on the lands of his fazenda, later reported to the Inquisition that they had set up an idol called Mary in a "church" on his property. They prayed using a rosary and had even hung some boards with symbols on them in the church as holy prayers.[78]

The religion of the Europeans, which had aided them in their conquest of the land and destruction of the old ways, would now be turned against the oppressors. The movement was not a retreat into mysticism but the basis of opposition to the Portuguese. By the 1560s, engenhos and fazendas were being raided. The Jesuits were forced to suspend their activities south of the Paraguaçu River, and the fact that the great plague of 1563 began in the region of the santidade was taken by them as a sign of God's displeasure at this heresy.[79] Portuguese retaliation and the plague seemed to combine to bring the movement to a halt by the close of the decade.

The revivalist resistance of santidade did not disappear with the Portuguese repressions of the 1560s. The movement did not bring the millennium to its followers, but its ideology and political goals had developed to a point sufficient for its maintenance in the face of colonial hostility. The historical record of the movement, fragmentary at best, indicates that throughout the period 1560 to 1627 the santidade cult survived in southern Bahia as a syncretic religious movement in which first Indians and eventually runaway African or crioulo (Brazilian-born black) slaves joined in military operations against Portuguese settlements, and especially against the cane farms and engenhos of the southern Recôncavo.[80]

Time and time again, it seemed as though the colonial officials or the Jesuits had exterminated the cult. In 1585, the "pope" of a santidade was captured by colonial authorities when a group of acculturated Indians who had run off to join the cult decided to buy their pardon by betraying him. The governor repaid this favor by allowing the turncoats to determine his punishment. In their Jesuit-administered aldeia, they dragged him about, ripped out his tongue, and then hanged him.[81] The movement was obviously not dependent on the charisma of one man, for only three years later, the instructions of governance issued to Francisco Giraldes noted the continuing threat presented by groups of runaway slaves and hostile Indians in Jaguaripe, the region of the santidade.[82]

By the first decade of the seventeenth century, the growth of the sugar industry and the swelling of the slave population made the continuing existence of santidade more troublesome and more ominous. The increasing number of runaway African slaves who joined the santidade villages seemed to create an especially dangerous situation. In 1610, Governor Diogo de Meneses reported that there were more than twenty thousand Indians and escaped slaves in the santidade villages, where the naming of "bishops and popes" continued. Although Diogo de Meneses, a strong advocate of Indian slavery, may have inflated his figures to better convince the crown of the need for military action, there is no doubt that the santidade continued.[83] In 1613, the crown was finally moved to take direct action against Indians and escaped Africans who "live in idolatry calling their settlements Santidade, sallying forth from them often to rob and kill in the aldeias and engenhos."[84] Because of the Indians' religious errors, and even more because of their effect on the sugar industry and thus on the royal treasury, the crown advocated a war of extermination in which the villages would be destroyed, the runaways returned to their rightful owners, and the Indians sold as slaves to other captaincies. The crown also expressed a fear that, because the runaway slaves were acculturated (ladinos), they might lead these villages to cooperate with foreign enemies as escaped slaves had done in Panama and the Caribbean. In May of 1613, a second royal communiqué to Governor Gaspar de Sousa made it clear that sugar planters in Jaguaripe had taken advantage of the crown's concerns to plead for the return of villages of índios mansos, who not only could protect the frontier against the followers of santidade and secure the coast against foreign interlopers but could also aid in building fortifications, public works, and "other things."[85] The idea of free, indigenous labor had not yet been abandoned.

Jaguaripe and the marches of southern Bahia remained into the eighteenth century an area of continuous warfare with the indigenous peoples. The last specific reference made to santidade came in 1627. In that year, a raiding party fell on the engenho of Nicolau Soares, killing four slaves and a carpenter and mortally wounding three white men. They sacked the engenho, carrying off an Indian woman and her child as well as all the "hardware necessary for the engenho's operations." This tactic may have been more than a simple desire for iron, for on other occasions runaways sometimes stole machinery needed for sugar production. It was an assault on the plantation economy, in this case by a people who had particularly suffered from its growth and expansion. Significantly, the colonial response was also made with reference to the sugar economy. Governor Diogo Luís de Oliveira organized

military operations against the santidade, not only because the Jaguaripe region was an entrance to the sertão but also because it supplied
firewood needed by the engenhos of the Recôncavo for making sugar.[86]

The employment of Indian labor was subject to a variety of constraints and limitations. The deadly triad of warfare, disease, and famine that followed in the train of conquest limited the nature and availability of an indigenous labor force. The competing strategies of the
Jesuits and the colonists over the form and control of this labor system
determined much of the history of Portuguese–Indian relations, but
this rivalry should not mask the basic agreement of planters and missionaries alike that Indian labor was vital to the colony's success. Each
side justified its position to the crown by arguing that its control would
more rapidly lead the Indian to European standards of religion, morality, and habit, including integration of the Indian into a wage-labor
market. But most Indians refused to respond to either: They refused to
be shaped at will by alien policies and historical processes, no matter
how seemingly inexorable. Indian actions and responses varying from
armed resistance to accommodation and acculturation limited and defined the nature of the colonial regime. By examining the inner structure of these processes in relation to the establishment of the plantation
regime, in relation to the formation and definition of the colony's
dominant mode of production, it is possible to define that regime and
suggest the reasons for the abandonment of Indian slavery in the New
World's first successful plantation colony.

CHAPTER 3

FIRST SLAVERY:
FROM INDIAN TO AFRICAN

Since the gentiles of Brazil unlike those of the African coast do not have the custom of daily labor and farm only when in need, relaxing when they have enough to eat; they thus greatly suffer the new life, working by obligation rather than out of desire, as they had in the state of freedom; and in its loss and in their repugnance to, and thought of, captivity so many die that even at the lowest price they are expensive.

Sebastião da Rocha Pitta (1720)

The Brazilian sugar-plantation colony began with the extensive use of Indian labor. From the vantage point of the present, Indian slavery appears to have been a passing moment in this history of colonial export agriculture in Northeast Brazil – and so it was. But to leave this formative stage with only a systemic account of its position within the process of European expansion, or to see it as simply a preview of what was to follow, is to tell only a part of the story. To the people who lived in these times, the inevitability of the transition was far less apparent. The Indians who underwent this experience inhabited a world whose perimeters were often defined by others, and the Indians were forced to accommodate themselves to new modes of behavior. From the viewpoint of the Portuguese, the period of Indian slavery was one in which the system of labor relations was worked out in detail. It was also a time when the contact between Europeans and Indians began to create social and racial categories and definitions that would continually mark the colonial experience. Finally, in the transition from Indian to African labor we can see reflected attitudes, perceptions, and realities that eventually underlay the engenho regime throughout its subsequent history.

Although the stage of Indian slavery has been recognized by other historians in the past, they have rarely been able to examine the actual conditions of life and labor on the engenhos during this period. Indians left no written records in Brazil, and Jesuit observers generally commented on abuses rather than the specific conditions of plantation labor. Extant but little-used plantation records and parish registers offer another option.[1] Using them, this chapter will examine the forms, usages, and structures of Indian labor on the Bahian engenhos during a period when slave labor became essential to this tropical-plantation economy.

Indian labor: terminology, acquisition, and types

The terminology of Indian labor is in itself revealing of its position within the plans and perceptions of the Portuguese. I must emphasize here two points. First, there was a European tendency to reduce all Indians, and to some extent Africans, to a common terminology, which tended to obscure individual cultural distinctions. The Portuguese did recognize differences between Congos and Minas or between Tamoio and Tupinambá but these were secondary to more general classifications. These less precise terms like *negro de Guiné* (black from Guinea), *índio* (Indian), *gentio da terra* (gentile of the land) were, after all, expressions of European perceptions. Second, the categories of social definition and of social structure in Brazil were created to a great extent by the nature of the agricultural enterprise and by the previous continental and overseas experience of the Portuguese. Whatever the philosophical and theological problems provoked in Europe by the discovery of a new "race" of men, the Portuguese on the scene in Brazil tended to draw upon familiar models, especially the recent past of African contacts and Atlantic plantations.

This is made clear by the term *negro da terra*, used often by both Jesuits and colonists to describe Indians. "Negros da terra" was a phrase parallel to the description of Africans as "negros de Guiné." The word "negro" itself had in medieval Portugal become almost a synonym for slave, and certainly by the sixteenth century it carried implications of servility. Its use to describe Indians is revealing of Portuguese perceptions of both Africans and Indians, not so much as to skin color, as to relative social and cultural position vis-à-vis the Portuguese. Over the course of the sixteenth century, "negro da terra" slowly disappeared from common usage as more and more Africans were introduced into the colony. It disappeared, in fact, as Indian slavery itself disappeared.[2]

For those Indians not enslaved but still under Portuguese control and direction, a variety of terms were used. Such people were called *índios aldeados* (village Indians), *índios sob a administração* (Indians under the control of . . .) or, most commonly, *forros*. This last term is somewhat confusing since it was also used to describe a slave who had gained his freedom through manumission (*alforria*), but in sixteenth-century Brazil it was not used exclusively in this way. Instead, *índios forros* were not only freedmen, but also Indians who were not enslaved but under Portuguese control, especially, though not exclusively, that of the Jesuits. The engenhos of Bahia made use of all three categories of Indians during the sixteenth century.

The engenhos of the Recôncavo acquired Indian labor by three principal methods – enslavement, barter, and wages. The law of 1570 had prohibited the illegal enslavement of indigenous people but allowed the acquisition of captives by ransoming them through trade with their captors. This trade, called *resgate*, was theoretically designed to save those already destined for a cruel death at the hands of their traditional enemies. Thus rescue was a favor, which the captive was then required to repay with labor. The practice was open to many abuses, but it was decided in 1574 to proceed with caution in limiting resgate "because of the necessity that the estates have for Indians."[3] A special junta of civil administrators, the senior judge, and the Jesuits decided on this course of moderation because "in Brazil there would be no estates or commerce without the Indians." Thus resgate continued, along with "just wars" carried out against those who refused to accept Portuguese sovereignty or to receive Catholic missionaries. In 1574, Engenho Sergipe had over fifty Indians recently brought in by a resgate expedition, and an inventory of the property made at about that time contained references to axes, cloth, and knives intended for the resgate trade.[4] Resgate enabled the Portuguese settlers to obtain Indian slaves without having to call them slaves, and it permitted the continuance of a type of coerced labor.

Indians already enslaved might be passed from one owner to another and, following traditional practice, the children of slave mothers remained slaves. Natural increase was another element in the acquisition of Indian labor, but it was more than offset by population losses due to intermittent warfare and epidemic disease. In 1582, a plague struck Ilhéus and caused so many deaths that for five months the mills did not operate. Combined with attacks by the Aimoré, depopulation caused a considerable disruption of the sugar economy in that region.[5]

As labor and disease decimated the engenho populations, natural disaster and Portuguese pressure brought in new workers from the interior. In 1599, a group of Tapuyas driven by hunger appeared at Engenho Santana in Ilhéus and were put to work.[6] In 1603, with labor again in short supply, a group of eighteen Indians were brought in from the sertão, and it was during these years that Potiguar from Pernambuco were brought to Ilhéus.[7]

By the 1580s, royal legislation and the increasing effectiveness of the Jesuits had begun to create problems for those who had wished to obtain Indian labor by resgate and "just war." After a visit to the captaincy of Bahia in 1588–9, the Jesuit Cristóvão de Gouvea recommended that the sacrament of confession be refused to anyone involved in the resgate of Indians.[8] Moreover, Jesuit effectiveness in overseeing the activities of free Indians within the Portuguese sphere of influence began to create difficulties for the colonists. In 1589, Ruy Teixeira, administrator of Engenho Sergipe, complained to his absentee employer, the count of Linhares, that new legislation had made the Jesuits "masters of the land and of the Indians who with the title of 'forros' serve them, being in reality more captive than the Guiné slaves." He lamented that no Indians remained for resgate, but he realized that nothing could be done. "I will speak no more of this for these are matters that have no remedy–may God grant us His mercy."[9]

Faced with increasing difficulties in obtaining unencumbered Indian labor, the count of Linhares and others began to seek royal permission to establish Indian villages in the vicinity of the engenhos. A few of these grants were awarded, usually in exceptional cases when the petitioners were powerful nobles with much political leverage at court. Thus the success of the count of Linhares in being allowed to bring Indians from the sertão and place them in villages under his protection makes the situation at Engenhos Santana and Sergipe somewhat atypical. Still, other engenhos made use of aldeia Indians under Jesuit tutelage or hired Indians directly, so that the use of free or forro Indians was not strange to the sugar planters of the Recôncavo. In fact, one is struck in reading the records of the Inquisition in Bahia in 1591–2 by the presence of Indians in the everyday life of the captaincy, of their participation in expeditions into the sertão, and of their role in the Recôncavo.[10]

Free Indians were employed at specific tasks on the plantations. At Engenho Sergipe, they were used primarily as an auxiliary workforce and put to tasks of maintenance or service peripheral to the business of sugar production. They were used to clean and repair the water system, work in the boats, fish, hunt, and cut firewood.[11] Access to aldeia Indians allowed the engenho owners to concentrate their slaves on the central tasks of sugar making, where the returns on investment were highest. The owner of Engenho Sergipe paid the tithe for the aldeia on its boundary and probably felt that the expense was worthwhile.[12] Other free Indians were also employed. In the sixteenth century, the principal labor arrangement was an exchange of trade goods for the completion of a specific task: thus the inventory entries of a corral built at Engenho Sergipe in return for some knife blades, or of a canefield cut by a group of Tupiniquins at Engenho Santana who were then paid with iron hatchets.[13] Similar references are found in the account books of the seventeenth century.[14] By that time, however, Indians worked for wages (although under certain limitations). Slavery, aldeia labor, barter, and the wage system all existed simultaneously on the Bahian engenhos. The relative importance of predominance of each form varied from place to place and time to time, although the general trend was from enslave-

Table 3-1. *Etymology of selected Tupí personal names, Engenho Sergipe, 1572–4*

Name	Probable derivation
Pejuira	peju = to blow; ira = to detach (interrogative)
Pedro rari	rari = to be born
Itaoca	Ita = stone; oka = house
Ocaparana	Oka = house; parana = sea
Mandionaem	Mandio = manioc; nhaẽ = pan
Antonio Jaguare	Jaguare = iâguara = jaguar
Francisco Tapira	Tapira = tapiira = ox
Birapipo	Bira = ybyra = wood; pipó is an interrogative
Cunhamocumarava	kunhãmuku = a girl of marriageable age; marava = marabá = child of an Indian and a stranger
Ubatiba	Uba = port, thighs, fish roe tyba is a plural ending

Source: DHA, III, 89–103.

ment to forms of remunerated voluntary labor. Access to free Indian labor allowed the planters to concentrate the capital invested in slaves in those aspects of production that were crucial and where the continuous labor justified the fixed capital that slaves represented.

The ethnic composition of the Indian slave force

The listing by name of Indian slaves in engenho inventories allows us to draw some tentative conclusions about the composition of the Indian slave force of Bahia in the late sixteenth century. As expected, many people recorded in the Sergipe and Santana inventories of 1572–4 were Tupinambá, native to the coastal area of Bahia. Some were further identified by location references such as *taparique* (Itaparica Island), Tamamaripe, *tapecuru* (Itapicuru River) and *Peroaçu* (Paraguaçu River), or by common Tupí-guaraní descriptive terms such as *açu* (big) or *merim* (small). Other names seem to be clearly of Tupinambá origin. Table 3-1 presents some of the more obvious Tupí names.

Etymological analysis is made uncertain by a variety of problems, some of which are themselves revealing of engenho life. Aside from the usual difficulty of parallel words in more than one language, the Portuguese who recorded these names transformed them into sounds and an orthography suitable to a Romance language. What remains is what a Portuguese heard, not what an Indian said. The Portuguese were themselves sometimes puzzled by the Indian languages and were not always sure of the tribal origins of their slaves. Phrases such as *"pela lingua que não he cristão"* (by his language not a Christian) indicate that the Portuguese were unsure of the linguistic stock of some slaves.[15] At Engenho Sergipe, one of the field observers, Tristão Pacheco, also served as translator (*lingoa do gentio*).[16] Portuguese and mestiços, lay people and clerics, who spoke Indian languages were usually proud of this accomplishment and never failed to point it out to the crown or other authorities since it was a necessary and valuable skill in the sixteenth and early seventeenth centuries.[17]

Locational and ethnographic identification make clear that the plantations drew their Indian slaves from a wide range of geographical and cultural backgrounds. Engenho Sergipe counted among its slaves not only local Tupinambá, but peoples brought from Sergipe de El-Rey to the north, Rio das Contas to the south, and the sertão of the São Francisco River to the west, as well as a large contingent brought from Pernambuco. Also listed are Carijó, Tamoio, and Cayté, all of them Tupí speakers and all from regions hundreds of miles from Bahia.[18] Although the large number of southern Indians on the Sergipe do Conde and Santana plantations may have been extraordinary, Indian laborers were not. The Nossa Senhora da Purificação Church at Engenho Sergipe listed over twenty-five holders of Indian slaves or forros in the period 1595–1626. Indians were the primary element of the Bahian labor force during this period.[19]

Not all the engenho Indians were Tupians. Tapuya names are often encountered in the Engenhos Sergipe and Santana registers of the 1570s and 1591. Here and there, other ethnic references are made. For example, a few Nãmbipiras appear. Also, both inventories of the 1570s contain many identifications that appear to be of ethnic or tribal origins, although they cannot be positively identified (Tingua, Tarabe, Taipe). The conclusion that must be drawn is that Engenhos Sergipe and Santana in particular, and probably all the Bahian mills that depended on Indian labor, made use of a heterogeneous Indian labor force. Whether this policy was intentional – designed, as it was later to be for African slaves, to prevent their close cooperation and forestall rebellion – or was simply a response to the shortage of local laborers is a moot question. Planters seemed to realize the advantage of having slaves who were "strangers" because this made flight more difficult. Although some Indian captives from the South could be found on the Bahian plantations, the interior of the Northeast seems to have been a more common source.[20]

At Engenho Sergipe, the Indians and African slaves lived in separate buildings. There is reason to believe that the over two hundred Indian slaves did not live in a row-house arrangement (*senzala*) so common on the seventeenth-century engenhos, but rather in Tupinambá-style long houses. The inventory mentions "two great houses of straw in which the negros [Indians] are kept."[21] Tupinambá multifamily long houses could hold, according to some observers, over two hundred people, so

Table 3-2. *Sex distribution, Engenhos Sergipe and Santana, 1572–91*

Engenho	Married males	Unmarried males	(% male)	Married females	Unmarried females	(% female)
Sergipe, 1572	51	41	(61%)	51	8	(39%)
Santana, 1572	18	47	(60%)	18	26	(40%)
Sergipe, 1591	17	19	(58%)	17	9	(42%)

that it is quite possible that similar arrangements were made at the engenhos.[22]

The sex distribution of the Indian slave force was remarkably similar to that encountered later among black slaves. Usually, about 60 percent of the slaves were male, and naturally there was a tendency for the men to be young adults. The marital status of Indian slaves and their ability to maintain family ties is difficult to determine from the Engenho Sergipe and Santana inventories because these offer conflicting pictures (See Table 3-2). At Engenho Santana, only 18 married men were listed in an adult population of 109 (65 men, 44 women). At Engenho Sergipe, closer to Salvador and perhaps to ecclesiastical observation, the number of married men was much higher. There, of the 92 men, 51 were married. Whether this difference is explained by variant notarial procedures of recording slave conjugal units or by a different composition of the slave force is impossible to establish. Perhaps more revealing is that among Engenho Sergipe's regular work force there were only 8 unmarried women, and of these 3 were widows and 2 were relatives of other slaves at the mill. This figure underlines the expected preference of slaveowners for young males.

Despite this preference, the nature of Indian slavery resulted in the presence of family units on the plantation. Men were often accompanied into slavery by wife, children, siblings, or other relatives. This pattern placed many people on or near the sugar mills and cane farms whose contribution to the process of sugar making was only marginal. The great Schetz engenho in São Vicente had in 1548 130 slaves, half of whom were children or old people and thus of little use to the owners. Nevertheless, a contemporary observer called this slave force the best in the region.[23] The lists of Engenhos Sergipe and Santana also suggest a high ratio of semi- or unproductive slaves. At Engenho Santana, some 25 percent of the total work force was too old, too young, or too sick to contribute very much to the mill's activity. Obviously, this percentage greatly increased in the years of epidemic disease.

Women like the one depicted in Figure 3-1 made up a significant part of the Indian labor force, but they were not as a rule considered to have skills that contributed directly to sugar making. Female slaves in

Figure 3-1. An Indian worker: A "domesticated" Tupí woman and her child with a plantation house in the background.

the sixteenth-century inventories are invariably listed without occupation, and their values result from combinations of age and health more than anything else. Surely, the susceptibility of Indians to disease diminished their reproductive value. Thus women appear as an omnipresent but not particularly skilled sector of an engenho's primary operations. There is some evidence from Engenho Sergipe that suggests recognition of the traditional role of Indian women in subsistence agriculture: A separate *roça* (farm) was maintained to supply the engenho's food needs, and a group of fifty slaves was assigned there. Two-thirds of these slaves were women – a proportion quite unlike the general sex ratio of the total population of the engenho. This implies a recognition of Indian women's roles in certain kinds of agriculture.[24]

Even when epidemic disease was not important, mortality rates were high. In 1572, a relatively plague-free year, five slaves died at Engenho Santana – a crude mortality rate of forty-three per thousand. In 1606, the chapel of Engenho Sergipe recorded thirty-two Indian deaths and only thirty-five baptisms. Because in this period accurate statistics for compiling general mortality rates are unavailable, there is some advantage in comparing figures with data from other regions of a similar social or economic composition. The crude mortality rate in Pernambuco in 1774 was almost thirty-three per thousand, and it remained at about that level until the late nineteenth century.[25] In Maranhão, the crude mortality rate for Indians in 1798 was close to twenty-two per thousand, whereas that for black slaves was just over twenty-seven per thousand.[26] Thus, the figure from Engenho Santana seems high, although it does not approach the rate of seventy per thousand experienced by African slaves in Jamaica and Barbados in the late seventeenth century.[27]

Acculturation and interaction

For those Indians who survived and for their Portuguese masters and employers, the major problems that remained were introduction to the regime of large-scale export agriculture and adoption of cultural patterns acceptable to Portuguese religious and social sensitivities. The rate and intensity of acculturation are difficult if not impossible to estimate. Indians were not able to select those aspects of European culture that they found best suited to their needs; instead, they were often forced to adopt or accommodate material and mental elements of culture on which the Portuguese placed a high priority. The increasing use of wages to secure Indian labor in the early seventeenth century was to some extent a symbol of their integration into Portuguese society. The fact that even at the end of this period such payments were often made in kind or were a mixture of money and goods should caution us about the completeness of the process.

The difficulties of bending Indians to the work regime of a sugar plantation was discussed in Chapter 2. When possible, the Portuguese employed Indians in activities with which they were already familiar, but some had to be "seasoned" to sugar production. At Engenho Sergipe, the manioc garden seems to have served this purpose. Among the Indian slaves assigned to this activity were a large number of people from other regions of Brazil as well as non-Tupinambá.[28] This diversity of backgrounds suggests that the manioc farm served as an introduction to the engenho regime, a place where new slaves could acquire a knowledge of the rules and expectations of plantation slavery.

The first superficial sign of acculturation was the adoption of a Portuguese name. The inventories of 1572–4 list many Indians who were still using their indigenous names exclusively, even though the tendency of the Portuguese was to assign easily recognizable and, for them, pronounceable names. Of the 191 Indians at Engenho Sergipe, 50 still used only their original names. The inventory of Engenho Santana demonstrates that a period of transition existed during which the Portuguese used one name and the Indians another. This situation is demonstrated by entries such as "by her tongue Capea and by ours, Domingas," or "Salvador, by his tongue Itacaraiba."[29] The assignment of Portuguese names and their eventual recognition and acceptance constituted steps toward integration into the engenho community. When possible, this process was formalized by baptism of the formerly pagan Indians. The assumption of new names had been an important part in Tupí life and had marked changes in social status. Indians could easily comprehend the importance and significance of the baptismal ceremony and the relationship between a new name and a new status.

The trend if not the rate of acculturation is suggested by a comparison of the Engenho Sergipe inventories of 1572–4 and 1591. Whereas the former contained some fifty slaves using only their Indian name, the latter had none. This comparison probably documents the fact that Indians were conforming to Portuguese patterns and that newly captured peoples were relatively rare on the Bahian engenhos by the end of the century.[30] Instead, their places were being filled by Indians born in captivity and baptized at that time, by free Indians, and by increasing numbers of African slaves.

Religion, of course, provided a major avenue of acculturation. The willingness of slaves to participate in church ritual or to accept the sacraments of the Catholic religion is a rough measure of their integration into the framework of Portuguese society. For this reason, the chapel register of Engenho Sergipe is a valuable document despite its incomplete and fragmentary condition. In its record of marriages (1600–26), burials (1598–1627), and especially baptisms (1595–1608), the basic patterns of sexual interaction and ritually defined responsibilities among the three principal racial groups are apparent.[31] The period

Table 3-3. *Racial/ethnic designations of parents and godparents, Engenho Sergipe, 1595–1608*

	White	Indian	African	Negro/ crioulo	Mulatto	Unknown[a]
Father	61	42	27	6	0	98
Mother	43	54	33	8	3	93
Godfather	132	9	6	7	0	70
Godmother	59	21	8	7	7	114

[a]The many unknowns (98) in the case of the fathers result from illegitimate unions and no father present at baptism. In the cases of mothers, godfathers, and godmothers, unknowns are due to failure to report this information or gaps in the documentation.

covered is interesting because between 1570 and 1630 the Bahian plantations crystallized into the distinctive social structure that characterized the area for the next two hundred years.

The chapel register contains 234 complete adolescent baptisms for the period 1595 to 1608, or about 75 percent of the total baptismal entries. Of the 234 baptized, 171 (74 percent) were the children of slave mothers and, therefore, slaves. The racial origins of the 234 mothers (for whom a racial designation has been determined) can be used as a rough gauge of the ethnic proportions of the population. It results in the following distribution: whites, 32 percent; Indians, 40 percent; Afro-Brazilians, 28 percent. Given the predominance of men in the Atlantic slave trade, the sex ratio of Afro-Brazilians would be distorted, and thus these figures probably underestimate this segment of the population. Still, it would appear that Indians continued to be an important part of the plantations' population at the beginning of the seventeenth century, equaling if not outnumbering the Africans and their descendants. Each register of baptism followed a formula such as: "5 August Joana young daughter of Thome de Sousa, single, and of Luiza, an Indian of Domingos Ribeiro; godparents, Bras Dias and Antonia [slaves] of the same Domingos Ribeiro." This formula allows us to examine the relationships between five individuals–the baptized, father, mother, godfather, and godmother. The pattern of these relationships reveals additional information about social organization and contact. Table 3-3 presents a distribution by racial/ethnic group of the four categories.

It is clear that baptism for slaves was a somewhat less formal matter than it was for free people and especially for whites. Whereas a godmother and godfather were always present when the child of a white couple was baptized, this was not always the case for slave children. There were some twenty-five instances (13%) when the godmother or godfather or both were omitted (or unregistered) at the ceremony. On one occasion, a group of slaves served as *padrinhos* (godparents), and on another there were two godfathers and no godmother. Such asymmetry and irregularity were never found among the Portuguese baptisms of Engenho Sergipe. When adult pagans received baptism, they usually did so in small groups of three or four at a time. On these occasions, one set of godparents might sponsor all the baptized individuals.

Among the three principal racial groups, there was a strong tendency toward endogamy, at least in formal, church-sanctioned unions. Between 1601 and 1626 in thirty slave marriages in which the origins of the partners could be determined, all were between individuals of the same racial category, although not of the same ethnic or linguistic group.[32]

Despite this tendency toward endogamy, sexual interaction across the color lines did take place. White males were most easily able to take advantage of their dominant role to select sexual partners from among the slave and free populations. White men fathered over 11 percent of all children born to Indian mothers and 8 percent of those born to African women registered at Engenho Sergipe. If these figures are adjusted to include those cases in which no father was reported, a sign of illegitimacy and unstable or secret relationship, then the percentages rise sharply to 18.5 percent for Indians and almost 30 percent for Afro-Brazilian women.

Opportunities for contact between Africans and Indians also existed in the slave quarters. The Engenho Sergipe inventories list a number of cases in which Africans and Indians had formed permanent family units. Such was the case of Domingos Valente, a sugar master who had married Luiza, *gentio da terra*, and fathered two children, or of Marcos, a Guiné slave who married Martha, an Indian.[33] More impressive, however, is the relative lack of such unions in the chapel register. Only two cases were recorded of children born to such couples, and both of these, unlike those just mentioned, were between Indian men and African women. It appears, therefore, that in the period of transition from Indian to African slavery, the majority of Indians married or had sexual relations with other Indians and maintained themselves to a large extent sexually separate from others. The miscegenation that did take place occurred most frequently between whites and Indians or whites and Africans.[34] It is interesting to note that in sixteenth-century Bahia no distinctive descriptive term was used for the offspring of Indians and Africans. The term *mameluco* was used for any person of mixed parentage in which one parent was an Indian.[35] It was not until the eighteenth century that *cafuso* or *curiboca* was used to describe the children of Indian–African unions.

According to Roman Catholic doctrine and practice, the roles of godfather and godmother were vital to the child's guidance. The relationship between godchild (*afilhado*) and godparents (*padrinhos*) was as

Table 3-4. *Index of godparentage prestige*

	Parents	Godparents	Ratio
Whites	104	191	1.84
Indians	96	30	.31
Afro-Brazilians	64	13	.20

Source: ACMS, Conceição da Praia (Engenho Sergipe) bautismos.

binding as that between child and parents. The parallel set of ties between the parents and godparents established a set of mutual obligations and dependencies. By examining these, we can observe some of the ways in which slaves and masters interacted.

The padrinho or godfather exercised an important function as baptismal sponsor and possible eventual guardian and protector of the child. The role of godfather placed very real obligations on those holding it, and it was not uncommon for godchildren to eventually depend on their padrinhos for economic assistance or protection. Also, at the time of the baptism the godfather usually assumed the expenses. The position of the godfather, therefore, was one of status and prestige. It is not surprising to find a very high percentage of whites in the godfather role in the baptisms examined. Not only did white parents always choose a white godfather, but Indians and Africans also sought out whites to assume this role. In more than 80 percent of the baptisms of the children of Indian mothers, white men served as godfather. Indian men served as godfathers in only nine cases, and in the six in which the ethnic origins of the parents can be identified, all were Indian couples. African men were in a somewhat similar position and like the Indians continually looked to whites (or had to accept them) as godfathers for their children. The predominance of whites can be seen in Table 3-4.

The most pronounced pattern to emerge from data concerning godparents is a marked difference between the godfathers and godmothers: The selection of godmother seems to have been based on different criteria than that of godfather, because it was much more common to find Indians and Afro-Brazilians in the female sponsorship role. White women rarely presented slave children for baptism. Instead, Indian mothers sought Indian godmothers. The godfather could be white, for as protector and benefactor whites were best equipped to aid the child, but the godmother was considered an auxiliary to the child's upbringing and a surrogate parent in the case of the death of the biological mother. Although there were a few instances in which Indian women served as godmothers for children born to African women or of mulatto women who were godmothers to the children of

Indian mothers, the vast majority of the cases indicate that Indians, Africans, and whites selected women of the same racial category as *comadres* (co-mothers). Usually, the *madrinha* (godmother) was a slave of the same master as either or both of the parents.

A few statistics make this situation clear. Whereas male slaves comprised fewer than 12 percent of all godfathers registered, female slaves were more than 30 percent of the godmothers. If only slave and forro baptisms are considered, then the percentage of slave and forro madrinhas rises to more than 80 percent of the total. The ties among the Indians were strong, and in more than 60 percent of the baptisms of children born to Indians, Indian women were in the godmother's role. When both parents were Indians, this figure rose to 90 percent.

Only on rare occasions did a slaveowner or his close relative serve as a baptismal sponsor for the child of his slave. In these early baptisms, a case such as that of Antônio Gonçalves and his daughter, who stood for the child of their Indian slaves in 1604, does appear from time to time.[36] But in truth such occasions were rare, and in fewer than 4 percent of the slave baptisms did the owner, or more frequently his relative, serve as godparent for his own slaves. Even so, such sponsorship seems to have been more characteristic of the period of Indian slavery. As Chapter 14 will show, by the eighteenth century masters never sponsored their black and mulatto slaves. Paternalism did not commonly find expression through godparent ties. Instead, what appears to be the dominant pattern was the selection of a white man who might intercede with the master in case of some future difficulty.

Finally, the use of materials such as a parish register is perhaps somewhat misleading, underlining the process of acculturation because it is set in the framework of Portuguese institutions and culture. There was always a reverse side in this story. The santidade cult demonstrated that acculturation was often shallow or incomplete and that sentiments of resistance often lay close to the surface of life.[37] Indian resistance to enslavement was constant, and runaways from the plantations were a chronic problem, although the Portuguese often turned to free or aldeia Indians to hunt down the fugitives.[38] Moreover, acculturation always had a potential to move in the other direction. Indian cultures offered, or seemed to offer, to some Europeans or to mestiços certain freedoms of thought and behavior.[39] The farther they were from the densely colonized areas or the coastal cities, the more likely were colonists and their descendants to adapt Indian ways. This was especially true in the period before 1600, when the matrix of social norms and structures was still relatively fluid. The interaction of port, engenhos, and sertão and the mixing of populations created geographical and human conditions in Bahia that contributed to the adoption of many features of Indian culture and life.

In this connection, the depositions of a number of mamelucos before the Inquisition in 1591–2 are most revealing. Many admitted that while in the sertão in search of Indians for the fazendas, they had joined the Indians in dances, smoking, drinking the "sacred herb," and generally comporting themselves like pagans.[40] Some painted their bodies like the Indians, and a number admitted to having undergone scarification or tattooing of their arms, legs, and buttocks. Such was the case with Manoel Branco, Thomas Ferreira, Francisco Afonso Capara, and Antônio Dias, a mestre de açúcar.[41] In a number of instances, mamelucos and Portuguese adolescents were converted to santidade. Gonçalo Fernandes, a mameluco subsistence farmer from Paripe, underwent such a conversion brought about by an Indian who had preached to him in an Indian language that "he understood very well."[42] Luisa Barbosa, a Portuguese woman, admitted to such a conversion in 1566 when she was a young girl of twelve and easily misled, she claimed, by the Indians with whom she spoke.[43]

The pattern is perhaps summarized in the epic of Domingos Fernandes Nobre, called Tomacauna. The son of a Portuguese man and an Indian woman, himself married to a white woman, he nevertheless lived from age eighteen to thirty-six more like an Indian than a Portuguese. He abandoned Catholicism and confessed only when necessary to avoid detection. He went often into the sertão and on expeditions to Pernambuco, Porto Seguro, and Paraíba. He lived with the Indians, taking many wives, tattooing his body, putting feathers in his hair, and generally living like an Indian. It was he who was sent to make contact with the main village of santidade in the 1580s, and while there he paid homage to an idol and to the leaders of the religion. Eventually, he brought a number of these people to the plantation of Fernão Cabral de Atayde. The case of Tomacauna is surely exceptional, but it does indicate that the interchange between Europeans and Indians in Northeast Brazil could move in both directions.

From Indian to African

The transition from a predominantly indigenous slave force to one composed mainly of Africans occurred gradually over the course of approximately half a century. As individual engenho owners acquired sufficient financial resources, they bought a few African slaves, and they added more as capital and credit became available. By the end of the sixteenth century, engenho labor forces were racially mixed, and the proportion increasingly changed in favor of imported Africans and their offspring. In the 1550s and 1560s, there were virtually no African slaves at the Northeast sugar mills.[44] By the mid-1580s, Pernambuco had sixty-six engenhos and a reported 2,000 African slaves. If we estimate an average of 100 slaves per engenho, then Africans composed one-third of the captaincy's slaves. In 1577, Engenho São Panteleão do Monteiro near

Olinda had 40 slaves, of whom two-thirds were Indians and the rest Africans. This was apparently an average distribution.[45]

In Bahia, the change can be observed in the transformation of a single engenho's population over time. In 1572, Engenho Sergipe had 280 adult slaves, of whom only 20 (7 percent) were African. In 1591, the engenho had a slave population of 103, of whom 38 (37%) came from Africa. When, in 1638, Engenho Sergipe was rented to Pedro Gonçalves de Mattos, it had 81 slaves, all of whom were African or Afro-Brazilian.[46] The transition to an African labor force was made in the first two decades of the seventeenth century at a time when the sugar industry experienced rapid expansion and considerable internal growth arising from high international sugar prices, a growing European market, and, perhaps, the peaceful maritime conditions brought about by the twelve-year truce between Spain and the Netherlands (1609–21). A comparison of the positions and roles of Indian and African slaves should help explain why the transition to African labor took place.

The shift to African labor depended in part on Portuguese perceptions of the relative abilities of Africans and Indians. With a long history of black slavery in Iberia, which had intensified during the expansion of the sugar industry in the Atlantic, the Portuguese were well acquainted with Africans and their skills. By the end of the sixteenth century, Africans had already impressed the Portuguese with their ability to master the techniques of sugar production on Madeira and São Tomé. The Portuguese in Brazil, long familiar with the use of blacks as servants, urban artisans, and skilled slaves in Portugal and the Atlantic islands, began to look toward Africa as a logical source for these skills. The first black slaves in Brazil came as body servants or skilled laborers, not as field hands. The three extant engenho slave lists from the sixteenth century indicate a high percentage of Africans with various skills, and invariably the most complicated tasks assigned to slaves were given to Africans. In 1548, Engenho São Jorge dos Erasmos in São Vicente had 130 slaves "of the land" as well as seven or eight Africans. All the Africans were *oficiais*, that is, skilled at various tasks, and one was sugar master, the most important managerial position on any engenho. The director of Engenho São Jorge's operations proudly wrote to the absentee owners, the Schetz family of Antwerp, that sugar masters on Madeira usually received 30$ a year, a sum that their engenho now saved by using this skilled black slave.[47] Three other Africans were employed in positions requiring skilled judgment, one as purger (*purgador*) and two as kettleman (*caldereiro*).

A similar situation is found in the inventory lists of Engenhos Sergipe and Santana of the late sixteenth century. At Engenho Sergipe, Indians and Africans were used in different ways during the period of transition. Because the engenho could afford Portuguese technicians and

Table 3-5. *Occupational structure, Engenho Sergipe, 1572, 1591*

	1572		1591	
	Africans	Indians	Africans	Indians
Sugar-making skills				
Mestre de açúcar (sugar master)			1	
Ajuda do mestre (assistant sugar master)			1	
Purgador (purger)			2	1
Ajuda do purgador (assistant purger)	1	2	1	
Tacherio (small kettleman)	1	2	3	
Escumeiro (skimmer)	1			
Ajuda do escumeiro (assistant skimmer)		3		
Caldereiro (kettleman)		6		
Moedor (mill tender)		3	2	
Premseiro (presser)	1	1		
Virador de bagaço (bagasse feeder)		1	1	
Caixeiro (crater)		2	1	1
Dos melles (molasses maker)	1	1		
Artisan skills				
Carapina (carpenter)		1		
Ferreiro (blacksmith)			1	
Calafate (boat caulker)		1		
Falleiro (?)	1	1		
Auxiliary skills				
Vaqueiro (cowboy)	1	1	2	1
Carreiro (carter)	1	1		
Boieiro (herdsman)				3
Pescador (fisherman)		11		
Serrador (sawyer)		7		
Lenadeiro (firewood cutter)				1
Porqueiro/ovelheiro (pig/sheep tender)		2		
"Barcas" (boatman)	1	4		
Management				
Feitor (overseer)		1		
Totals	9 (19)[a]	51 (115)	15 (30)	7 (65)

[a]Number in parentheses is total number of that ethnic category.

managers, the occupational pyramid of the slaves was truncated. The work force was heavily indigenous; of 134 male slaves, 115 were Indians. The same proportions of Africans and Indians were listed with a specific occupation; but, when certain jobs such as fishermen, hunters, and boatmen are not included, the proportion of Indians with special occupations drops considerably. Table 3-5 shows these differences.

The inventory of 1572 – taken when Indians were still plentiful and relatively inexpensive to obtain, when Africans were still not available in large numbers, and when the legislation against Indian slavery was not yet effectively in force – represents a specific period in the history of Indian slavery. Twenty years later, the situation had changed considerably. By 1591, the sugar economy of the Northeast was expanding rapidly to supply a growing European demand. The Atlantic slave trade had been regularized to the extent that the supply, though not yet great, was at least dependable. The majority of Engenho Sergipe's slave force was still Indian, but Africans and Afro-Brazilians now filled almost all the skilled occupations on the estate. Angolan and Guinean men were employed as sugar master, purger, assistant purger, blacksmith, kettleman, and sugar crater. Others were employed in the milling operations of the engenho and a few as cowhands. The Indian occupations were far more rudimentary, and aside from one sugar crater, only three were listed with occupations, one woodcutter and two herdsmen. In other words, when possible, the Portuguese turned to Africans to provide skilled slave labor. Figure 3-2 appears to represent the division of labor among Indians and Africans.

This policy, like the relative price of Indians and Africans, is to some extent explained by demographic and cultural features of both peoples. Many West Africans came from cultures where ironworking, cattle herding, and other activities of value to sugar agriculture were practiced.[48] These skills and a familiarity with long-term agriculture made them more valuable to the Portuguese for the specific slavery of sugar. Africans were certainly no more "predisposed" to slavery than were Indians, Portuguese, Englishmen, or any other people taken from their homes and bent to the will of others by force, but the similiarity of their cultural heritage to European traditions made them more valuable in European eyes. The Indian susceptibility to European disease at all ages made riskier the investment of time and capital in training them as artisans or managers. Africans, of course, also suffered in the environment of Brazil, but the highest rate of black mortality was always found among the newly arrived (boçal) and among infants. Thus, once a slave was "seasoned" and had passed through infancy and childhood, the chances of survival and therefore of safe investment in skill were very good.

African health and skill, as well as lack of resistance, may explain the reluctance of planters to invest in the training of Indian slaves, but it does not respond to the question why, even in cases where Indians were free workers earning a wage, the value of their labor was considered unequal to that of whites, mulattoes, and free blacks. At Engenho Sergipe, an Indian carpenter received only 20 percent of the wages paid to whites for the same task. During the seventeenth century, Indian workers received only 20 réis a day, and skilled artisans averaged 30 réis. In the 1630s, the municipal council of Salvador paid Indian laborers a daily wage of 30 réis, and Paraíba Indians could be paid in manioc and cloth a daily wage of about 15 réis. Black slaves, by contrast, could earn an average of 240 réis per day.[49]

Figure 3-2. The division of agricultural tasks shows darker workers (Africans?) laboring on a sugar plantation while lighter-colored "Indians" cultivate manioc at the top of the picture.

The wage-labor system, therefore, constantly proposed as the ideal way to integrate the Indian into colonial society, was a failure. Indians were often reluctant to participate in the labor market; and the Portuguese, furthermore, did not really allow that market to operate freely: The wages paid to Indians were always below existing rates.[50] The colonists placed Indian wage earners on a scale of reward and labor different from that of other workers. At Engenho Sergipe, they were usually paid by the month rather than by the day, or even more commonly by the task. Their work did not usually require completion at a specific time, and often they received payment in kind rather than in cash. Manioc flour, trade cloth (*pano*), and alcohol were the common "wages" for Indians from Maranhão to São Paulo.[51] Obviously, the Portuguese seemed to believe, for whatever reasons, that Indian workers could not be treated like others.

There was, in fact, a remarkable similarity among all the colonial regimes in the New World in the low value placed on Indian laborers in comparison with Africans. In times and places as widely different as sixteenth-century Mexico, seventeenth-century Brazil, and eighteenth-century Carolina, Spaniards, Portuguese, and Englishmen held similar opinions of Indian and African laborers. The colonists in each situation usually valued Africans three to five times higher than the Indians.[52] Certainly, market availability, demographic patterns, opportunities for flight or resistance (management costs), and European prejudices entered into these calculations. Still, despite the racist implications of arguments about the relative adaptability to tropical labor of one people over another, the similarity of opinion among all the New World slaveholding regimes suggests that there was a comparative advantage, especially in the formative period of slaveholding, in the use of African rather than Indian slaves and that this advantage was based on productivity in terms of return on investment. The statement of one observer in the Carolinas in 1740 that "with them [Indians] one cannot accomplish as much as with Negroes" was echoed everywhere in the Americas.[53]

In Brazil, the relative position of Indian and African slaves within the sugar labor force can be seen in its simplest and crudest form in the comparative prices of the two peoples. The average price of an African slave listed with occupation in 1572 was 25$, whereas Indians with the same skills averaged only 9$. The only skilled Indians whose prices equaled, or even approached, those of African slaves were those who were truly practicing skilled crafts – carpenters, sugar craters, and boat caulkers, for example, or those engaged in the specialized positions of a sugar mill. The vast majority of Indians listed with some occupation, but not an artisan skill, were priced far below the average value of unskilled Africans. The price difference between skilled and unskilled Indians was greater, moreover, than that among Africans.

There is evidence that these values represent real differences in the productivity of Indian and African labor. Production figures from Bahia at the close of the sixteenth century support this interpretation. Although there is some discrepancy in the reported total of engenhos, a number of accounts list fifty mills operating in the captaincy of Bahia by 1590.[54] For 1589, Father Francisco Soares reported that there were fifty engenhos, eighteen thousand slaves, and thirty-six thousand aldeia Indians.[55] If we assume that two-thirds of the slave force was involved in sugar agriculture, then the ratio of slaves to engenhos was

240 to 1. This figure – which does not include any of the settled Indians that also provided labor to the engenhos – is extremely high. It represents not only slaves owned directly by the mills, but those owned by tenants, sharecroppers, and others as well. Father Soares estimated an annual production per mill of four thousand arrobas or fifty-eight tons. Thus, each slave produced at the time almost seventeen arrobas (over five hundred pounds) a year – a very low level of productivity, since the later calculation in Brazil based on black slaves was forty to seventy arrobas annually.[56] Even allowing for technological changes and inexact information, the only conclusion that can be drawn from such figures is that Indian labor was characterized by low productivity.[57]

At the time Father Soares made his estimates, Bahia had between three and four thousand African slaves; thus, three-fourths of its slave force was still Indian in the last decade of the sixteenth century.[58] With the low level of Indian productivity, the price differential between African and Indian slaves becomes readily understandable. In the inventories of 1572–4, African slaves were valued at an average price of 20$, whereas adult Indians averaged about 7$.[59] This ratio of roughly three to one is also the ratio between the estimates of African and Indian productivity in sugar agriculture. It would appear that the Portuguese made a reasonable economic calculation of the comparative profitability of their two alternate work forces. Africans surely cost more to obtain, but in the long run they were a more profitable investment.

We can speculate that the early presence of large numbers of Indians allowed the mills to begin production with a small original outlay in slaves. The expansion of the sugar economy in the 1550s and 1560s depended on the availability of this source of "cheap" labor. During the 1570s, however, resistance, plague, and antienslavement legislation reduced the availability – and profitability – of Indians. Plantation owners now found that the cost differential between Indian and African laborers no longer outweighed differences in productivity between the two labor forces. This disparity in overall productivity also helps to explain why the Portuguese preferred imported Africans to coerced but "free" Indians. Although there were occasional proponents of the Spanish-American-style grants of Indian labor (encomienda), or of peonage in Brazil, the colonists believed that, given the high mortality and low productivity of Indians, Africans were a better investment. The Bahian historian and planter Sebastião da Rocha Pitta probably summarized majority opinion when he observed that Indians suffered from "working by obligation rather than out of desire, as they had in the state of freedom; and in its loss and in their repugnance to, and thought of, captivity so many die that even at the lowest price they are expensive."[60]

A discussion of profitability in strictly neoclassical economic terms will not suffice as an explanation of the transition of the labor force. There were always cultural and political determinants as well. Not everyone in Brazil was convinced of the wisdom of the shift. Portuguese colonists were generally unwilling to surrender control of Indians, especially when they could be obtained for nothing. The colonists demonstrated their reluctance by political remonstrance and demonstration – most notably in 1609 and 1640. Gaspar da Cunha, overseer of Engenho Sergipe, wrote to the count of Linhares in 1585 that Africans "cost too much and are prejudicial to the plantation and to the neighborhood; they are neither as necessary nor as beneficial as the Indians of this land."[61] He then petitioned for more free Indians to be brought to the engenho. By the early seventeenth century, such requests and sentiments were far less frequent.[62] The shift to African labor was well on its way, especially in the Northeast sugar region, where capital had accumulated and the patterns of international commerce were securely established. Colonial slavery had emerged as the dominant mode of production, and the process of its emergence was not dictated by the market so much as by the organization of production. The system of labor and the nature of the labor force were determined not only in the court at Lisbon or in the countinghouses of Amsterdam and London but also in the forests and canefields of America.

PART II

THE BAHIAN ENGENHOS
AND THEIR WORLD

CHAPTER 4

THE RECONCAVO

... it is certain that this captaincy is an agricultural colony and it is convenient that it is so since its products are so valuable.

Miguel Antônio de Melo (1797)

About eleven o'clock we entered the Bay of All Saints, on the northern side of which is situated the town of Bahia or San Salvador. It would be difficult [to] imagine before seeing this view anything so magnificent. It requires, however, the reality of nature to make it so. If faithfully represented in a picture, a feeling of distrust would be raised in the mind.

Charles Darwin (1832)

Maria Graham, an aristocratic Englishwoman later to become Lady Calcott, was an acute observer with a sprightly literary style. As she sailed into the Bay of All Saints in 1824, she was enthralled by the scene, and she and her shipboard companions amused themselves by speculating as to on which shore before them Robinson Crusoe had established his plantation, for Defoe's hero was supposed to have lived here too.[1] No traveler who crossed the bar of Santo Antônio and sailed beneath the fort of that name that guarded it remained unimpressed by the beauty of the prospect that greeted their eyes. At latitude 13 degrees south, longitude 37–9 degrees west, the sea cuts a great arm into the tropical coastline, forming a magnificent bay or inland sea some fifty miles in length. The Portuguese had known this place from the early years of the sixteenth century as the Bay of All Saints. It was, one observer noted, large enough to harbor "not only all the ships of Your Majesty, but all the navies of the monarchs of Europe."

The scene was and is magnificent. On a high bluff at the northern entrance to the bay, the Portuguese had built the city of Salvador, head of the royal captaincy of Bahia and capital of the whole Brazilian colony from its foundation in 1549 until 1763, when Rio de Janeiro assumed that role. Always a place of great commerce, Salvador remained, even after the loss of its prime status, among the most populous cities of the New World. By 1800, it had 50,000 inhabitants. The city commanded the bay but depended on the surrounding lands, its source of food and supplies and of the agricultural products that made Salvador a hub of transatlantic commerce.

Green islands dotted the bay's blue waters. Somewhere between ninety and one hundred were usually reported in the eighteenth century, the discrepancy due to miscounting or submergence. Itaparica, lying directly across the bay from Salvador, was the largest island, some thirty kilometers long. A small town, a few engenhos, and a whaling station were located on it by 1700. Ilha dos Frades, Ilha de Maré, and Cajaíba Island at the mouth of the Sergipe River (sometimes called the Sergimirim or the Sergi) were other islands of some size. Along the southern margins of the bay were dozens of small, low-lying islets where the sea had submerged the coast. The larger islands were integrated with the shore, serving as sources of firewood, cane, and foodstuffs. Small boats moved continually from islands to shore and from both to the city of Salvador and back. A survey made in 1775 reported 2,148 sailing craft of various types and over 4,000 sailors and fishermen, half of whom were slaves, working in Bahian waters.[2] Larger ships could find a haven not only in the roadstead before Salvador, but in the smaller inlets, bays within the bay. The mouth of the Matoim River, sheltered by the Ilha de Maré, was one, and the entrance to the Paraguaçu River provided another. The Bay of All Saints, with its islands and bays, its ports and shores, was a Mediterranean Sea that made profitable and possible an intimacy between the port of Salvador and its agricultural hinterland.

But if the bay provided shelter from storm and a secure port for the active commerce that Bahia's sugar, tobacco, and hides promoted, it was a curse as well. The access from the Atlantic was simply too wide, too open to be adequately defended. The bar between the Ponta do Padrão and Itaparica Island was some thirty kilometers across, and despite a continual fortification of Salvador and the placement of defenses and artillery at strategic locations, Bahia was always subject to attack. Unwelcome visitors were not rare. French privateers were there in the 1520s; three English ships raided shipping in the bay in 1586; for almost two months in 1599, two Dutch vessels patrolled in and around the bay taking prizes; the Dutchman, Van Caarden, attacked in 1604. In 1614, French pirates took merchantmen in the bay and caused a disaster when a hastily armed relief ship sank with great loss of life.[3] The Dutch seized Salvador in 1624 and destroyed engenhos in the Recôncavo. Although the Hollanders were forced to leave in the following year, they returned in 1627. Bahia became a prime target in the Luso–Dutch struggle. Punitive expeditions entered the bay in 1634 and again in 1648, capturing ships, burning engenhos, and causing panic in the countryside. Suggestions for improved defenses were constant, but money for these plans was always in short supply and the geographical difficulties insurmountable. The gift of the Bay of All Saints was not without its price.

In geological and geographical terms, the Bay of All Saints and its surrounding lands or Recôncavo were a large trench in which tertiary and cretaceous soils had developed over the essentially crystalline base of the coast.[4] The lands around the bay were humid and low lying, rising slowly into *tabuleiros,* or bluffs. The whole area generally lies below 200 meters elevation, and the image to the modern traveler is one of low, gently rolling fields undulating into tabuleiros but occasionally broken into a sharper topography by the many rivers that flow into the bay. The predominantly southeastern winds bring abundant rains; modern calculations place the annual average at 1,800 to 2,000 millimeters, with the months of April, May, and June particularly wet. When the Portuguese first arrived, the Recôncavo like most of the Northeast coast was heavily forested, but by the mid–seventeenth century the original forest cover around the bay had been destroyed by agriculture. Only in the southern Recôncavo near Jaguaripe did great timber stands remain, and this region, like the humid coast extending southward toward Ilhéus, became the main supply source for timber and firewood. Modern figures for the size of the Recôncavo vary between 10,000 and 13,000 square kilometers because now, as in colonial times, its extent is undefined.

Water dominated this land. Everywhere it penetrated and controlled the rhythm and organization of human activity. The Recôncavo was lacerated by streams of various sizes ranging from the great Paraguaçu, subject to periodic flooding, and moderately large rivers like the Sergipe, Açu, Pericoara, and Subae to smaller streams like the Cotegipe, Jacarancanga, and Pitanga. None of these, great or small, was navigable by large oceangoing vessels, and at the mouth of each amost invariably a small town (*povoação*) of fisherfolk and boatmen developed. Across the northern interior of the Recôncavo, another series of rivers like the Jacuipe, Joannes, and Pojuca ran eastward, emptying not into the Bay of All Saints but into the sea along the coast north of Salvador. These streams, rising in dry uplands of the sertão, occasionally dried up in the summer. The sugar plantations were, when at all possible, located on the margins of the bay or along the rivers, which provided avenues of transportation and sometimes the power source as well.

The sea exercised its influence in other ways as well. All the lands on the margins of the bay were subject to the *maré* or tides, which could rise as much as four or five miles up the rivers. Lands along the coast were often *mangues* or saltwater swamps, a problem for the planters anxious to appropriate every inch of possible canelands, but salvation for the slaves who depended on the crabs, the *siri,* the blue *guaiamu,* and other crustaceans. Planters took the maré into consideration when setting up their estates. For example, at Engenho Cajaíba, on the island of the same name, steps were built from the great house to the water's edge in such a way that at high tide the visitor could alight at the main door without ever muddying his or her shoes. Small boats or sailing canoes were indispensable equipment for most of the Bahian engenhos, which depended on the bay and the rivers for their supply of cane, firewood, and provisions. "All the activity of this people is by water," wrote Diogo de Campos Moreno in 1612.[5]

Standing at the mouth of this inland sea was the city of Salvador. Throughout its history, it has been intimately linked to its hinterland, dependent on the Recôncavo for food and fuel and serving it as the port for the export of sugar, tobacco, and hides. Despite its intimate association with the Recôncavo and the fact that the planters often transacted their business in the city, maintained homes there, and dominated its civil and religious institutions, distinctions were maintained. Even today, a resident of Salvador going to visit São Francisco or Santo Amaro speaks of going to the interior, as though these places lay far inland instead of on the shores of the bay or just beyond. Salvador represented urban, cosmopolitan life; the interior was perceptibly different: rustic, removed, but also aristocratic, at least in colonial times. In truth, however, most of the Recôncavo lands were within a day's travel from Salvador. This was the gift of the inland sea, and it created an intimacy between plantation and port that served both well.

By the close of the sixteenth century, the city's essential form and functions were already well established.[6] As capital of the colony, Salvador was the seat of the governor-general (the office was elevated to viceroy in the seventeenth century) and of the senior treasury and judicial officers of the colony. A high court or relação staffed by royal judges began to operate in the city in 1609, and despite a suspension of its operations (1626–52) it fulfilled a number of bureaucratic and administrative functions in addition to its judicial ones. In 1551, Salvador became the seat of the bishop of Brazil, and it retained its primate status throughout the colonial era. The city became the archepiscopal see in 1676. Salvador's religious life was enriched by the presence of religious orders. A Jesuit college was established in 1549, and there were monasteries of the Franciscans, Benedictines, and Carmelites by the close of the sixteenth century. The first convent, an establishment of Poor Clares, came much later – in 1677. The brotherhood of the Holy House of Mercy (Misericórdia) maintained a church and provided charitable service to the poor, the sick, and the abandoned. Members of the most distinguished families, royal administrators, planters, and overseas merchants were counted among the Misericórdia's brothers. Local government was in the hands of the senado da câmara or municipal council, as in all Portuguese cities. In Bahia, this body was dominated by sugar planters and merchants and tended to represent the interests of those involved in commercial agriculture and overseas trade.

The major churches and monasteries and the centers of government were concentrated in the upper city, on the top of a steep escarpment, but the pulse of the city was set by life along the waterfront. At the foot of the bluff, the docks bustled with activity. Merchants maintained their shops here within the shadow of the Church of Nossa Senhora da Conceição da Praia, and by the seventeenth century large warehouses and the customs office also operated close by. Although the offices of wealthier merchants engaged in transatlantic shipping could also be found in the upper city, the docks and streets of Conceição da Praia parish in the lower city were the arteries of Salvador's commercial life blood. Like many a colonial port, Salvador was a city of bureaucrats and stevedores, merchants and prostitutes. Its inhabitants moved the papers of government and the crates of sugar and rolls of tobacco – they did not produce goods. Aside from a few distilleries, tanneries, and a handful of artisan shops, this was a city without industry. As late as 1810, the existence of two factories, one for glass and one for rope, was seen as a major result of the opening of the ports to foreign commerce two years before.[7] Foreign visitors such as William Dampier, who visited the city in 1699, spoke admiringly of the governor's palace, the municipal hall, and the thirteen churches, convents, and chapels; but by that year the *alfandega* (royal customshouse) and the trapiches (the warehouses of Maciel, Grande, Julião, Bruçanes, and others), where the agricultural produce of the captaincy was gathered, were the city's most important if less distinguished edifices.[8] In 1587, this modest port was reported to have 800 *vizinhos*, or permanent householders, a figure that probably indicates a population of about 4,000. By 1681, the vizinhos were counted at 3,000. In 1724, Salvador had 5,000 households and a population of just under 25,000.[9]

A modern observer might see Salvador as a commercial and administrative base from which the occupation of the Recôncavo took place. And so it was. But rather than measuring that occupation in terms of population growth, colonial cartographers and ecclesiastics used other criteria; early maps and descriptions make it seem that sugar mills and saints took occupancy of the captaincy, for it was the location of engenhos and the creation of parishes that preoccupied them. The lands of the Recôncavo had been distributed in large grants or sesmarias in the mid–sixteenth century, and a few private captaincies had been created. The whole southern coast had been assigned to Alvaro da Costa in 1566, and the island of Itaparica to the count of Castanheira in 1556. The extensive sugar lands near present-day Santo Amaro (like those in Figure 4-1) belonged to the count of Linhares, a situation that we will discuss in detail shortly. Eventually, by sale, transfer, and alienation, these private captaincies within the Recôncavo were eliminated, and (although in legal form a few lasted until the eighteenth century) they had little effect on the region's development after 1600.

Figure 4-1. Caneland in the Recôncavo. Upland tabuleiros in the distance and smoke rising into the June sky from an old field being cleared.

From the base at Salvador, saints and sugar mills marked the captaincy's settlement. The first parish of the city, Our Lady of Victory (Vitória) was created in 1549 and was followed shortly thereafter by the see parish in 1552. Far down the coast at Ilhéus, the parish of São Jorge was created in 1556, and Nossa Senhora da Assumpção was erected at Camamú in 1560. As small towns began to develop in the Recôncavo and a settled population developed around the sugar mills in the 1560s, the church took cognizance of this reality by creating distinct parishes. Santa Cruz on Itaparica, Santiago on the Paraguaçu (later to be called Santiago de Iguape), and Santo Amaro de Pitanga all dated from 1563. Three more parishes – Nossa Senhora da Purificação of Santo Amaro, São Bartolomeu of Pirajá, and Nossa Senhora do O of Paripe) – were created in 1578. Another spate of foundings were made in 1610 with the creation of São Miguel de Cotegipe, Nossa Senhora do Socorro, São Sebastião do Passé, Nossa Senhora do Monte, and Nossa Senhora da Piedade of Matoim. The last of these did not have resident priests until the 1630s. The final area of the Recôncavo to be organized was the extreme south, where the parish of Nossa Senhora da Ajuda was created, centered on the town of Jaguaripe but encompassing the whole southern margin of the bay.[10] By 1587, there were sixteen parishes in Bahia, nine of which were supported by a royal stipend.[11]

The parish divisions did not remain fixed, and new ones were created to meet the growth or shift of the population. Creating a new parish by subdividing older ones was usually accompanied by grumbling and complaining on the part of the affected units. The citizens of Nossa Senhora do Passé complained when a district containing five engenhos and 2,500 souls was lost in the creation of the new parish of São Sebastião do Passé in 1729.[12] By 1724, there were six parishes in Salvador and nine in the Recôncavo. These varied in size, the larger ones including 5,000 to 60,000 people and the smallest ones such as Pirajá with fewer than 1,000; but the average size seems to have been 2,000 to 4,000. At the close of the eighteenth century, in 1792, Bahia had ninety-two parishes: sixteen in Salvador and its suburbs; seventeen in the Recôncavo; another seventeen in the southern towns, which in fact included a few such as Jaguaripe and Pirajuhia that were physically part of the Recôncavo; and the remainder in the interior sertão or in the northern subcaptaincy of Sergipe de El-Rey.[13]

The parishes of the church provided the basic form of organization for two hundred years in the Recôncavo, but by the close of the seventeenth century a system of secular organization around municipalities also began to take form. In 1698, São Francisco do Conde, Cachoeira, and Jaguaripe townships were created in the Recôncavo; Santo Amaro was established in 1727. Jaguaripe was subdivided in 1724 with the creation of the township of Maragogipe, but not without the usual complaint from the original municipality.[14] These towns were small places. In the 1720s, Santo Amaro had only 400 permanent free male residents.[15] The secondary towns of the Recôncavo simply provided an administrative skeleton, port facilities, and services to the agricultural lands in which they were set. Government in them was loose and often informal. Until the beginning of the nineteenth century, the câmara of Santo Amaro did not meet on a regular basis but was summoned only when important correspondence arrived from Salvador.[16] Still, these towns provided the framework of government. Salvador continued, however, to dominate in population, wealth, and political power. Some idea of Salvador's primate position can be seen in the tax levied on each town to help defray the costs of rebuilding Lisbon after the earthquake of 1755. The contribution of Salvador was assessed at almost three times the amount of all the other towns of Bahia and Sergipe de El-Rey together. At 29,200$, Salvador's assessment was more than fifteen times greater than the wealthiest Recôncavo town – Cachoeira.[17]

During Brazil's colonial era, many observers and travelers commented on or described the Recôncavo. We are fortunate to have detailed if incomplete descriptions from 1587, circa 1724, and 1757 that provide an excellent view of the demographic and economic contours of this region. We can start with Gabriel Soares de Sousa's description, written before 1587. Soares de Sousa was a sugar planter and a promoter of exploration who wrote his account while seeking royal favors in Madrid, but he was also an acute observer. His *Tratado discretivo* has been used extensively by historians since the nineteenth century, but its few pages on the Recôncavo are still the best description of the area in the sixteenth century.[18] Soares de Sousa reported that there were approximately two thousand families (Portuguese) in the Recôncavo. His detailed descriptions of the lands and islands around the bay were primarily concerned with the location and number of the engenhos, the suitability of lands for growing sugar, and the possibilities for further growth. Soares de Sousa identified thirty-six operating engenhos and another four under construction. Twenty-one of the operating mills were the larger water-powered *engenhos reais*. In addition, there were eight *casas de melles*, smaller producers devoted to making treacle and rum. At this time, the Recôncavo mills produced about 1,750 tons of sugar annually for sale.[19]

Soares de Sousa's description moved in an orderly fashion around the bay, highlighting the local geography, identifying the engenhos and their owners, and detailing peculiar features of each subregion. It is clear that most of the mills were located on the shores of the bay or on the rivers that flowed into it. About half the existing engenhos were located in the zone of Pirajá, Matoim, Paripe, and Cotegipe, an area that lay within a few miles of Salvador, just to the north, and that by the mid–seventeenth century would be considered a region of the municipality of Salvador. This area had been cleared of Indians shortly after Salvador's foundation, and it was the most intensely settled part of the Recôncavo at the end of the sixteenth century. Interspersed among the engenhos here were many farms growing European and American fruits and vegetables and others devoted to sugarcane. The mouths of the Pirajá and Matoim rivers also provided shelter for ships and were heavily fished.

The next-largest concentration of engenhos lay in the islands that Soares de Sousa called Marapé, which would eventually become the parishes of the town of São Francisco do Conde. This was the heart of the sugar zone, the "cradle of massapé," but in Soares de Sousa's time these lands were only beginning to be intensively exploited. Just beyond on the Rio Sergipe were the lands of the count of Linhares and his famous Engenho Sergipe that had once belonged to the governor of Brazil, Mem de Sá. The engenho stood about nine kilometers from the river's mouth, and it controlled all the lands between it and the sea. On the other bank, however, were many farms and a Benedictine church. Engenho Sergipe dominated this region (see Appendix A). Much of the land around it was owned by the count of Linhares, who refused to allow others to buy it and set up their own mills, a fact underlined by Soares de Sousa as a barrier to development. The whole area came to be known as the "lands of Sergipe do Conde."

The lands lying to the south of the Sergipe River were almost unpopulated because the land was "weak," that is, it was not good for sugarcane. This region that would later become the areas of Acupe, Itapema, and Saubara was devoted to livestock grazing and the production of manioc.[20] It was not until the banks of the Paraguaçu, the largest river emptying into the Bay of All Saints, that good caneland was again to be found. The Paraguaçu cuts inland above its mouth forming the peninsula of Iguape (called Uguape by Soares de Sousa). Along the shores of the peninsula were farms and engenhos. Soares de Sousa does not mention tobacco in this region, but the lands along the Paraguaçu with their sandier soils became the core of the extensive Bahian tobacco industry.

South of the Paraguaçu were the lands that had been ceded to Alvaro da Costa as a private captaincy. They were not well populated and were generally not very good for sugarcane. In the sixteenth century, however, there were a number of mills located on this side of the bay, especially near the Pirajuhia and Jaguaripe rivers. Soares de Sousa himself owned an engenho here, as did Fernão Cabral de Atayde, who later ran afoul of the Inquisition for permitting his Indian workers to conduct pagan rites.[21] Despite the existence of eight or nine mills on the southern margins of the bay, this region, later known as Jaguaripe and Maragogipe, never produced much sugar and primarily specialized in manioc farming and in supplying firewood and timber to Salvador and the rest of the Recôncavo.

Soares de Sousa's description is clearly promotional in nature. It is infused with ebullience and probably overstatement. It is doubtful that the lowliest peasant in Bahia wore trousers and gibbet of damask or that the lands were quite so pleasant as Soares implies if the insects and summer heat of today were present then, but from his report the essential outlines of the Recôncavo can be seen. A great variety of American and European cultigens were grown, from oranges to beans, peppers, and mustard. There was clearly a hierarchy of cultivation. The best lands were devoted to sugar whenever possible, and other export crops might also be planted in the better lands. Poorer soils were given to vegetables or manioc, and the least productive lands were used for grazing cattle. Although the Recôncavo deserved its reputation as sugar country, in fact the region was never entirely devoted to that agriculture. Soil type, topography, and weather determined the distribution of cultivation around the bay. Essentially, three zones developed. Sugar was concentrated on the northern shores extending to the Sergipe River and the adjacent lands on the bay. The higher, sandier soils of Cachoeira on the Paraguaçu became the center of tobacco growing. And the southern Recôncavo was given to subsistence farming.

Although sugar always remained the leading export crop of the Recôncavo, local planters and the crown sought from time to time to find other sources of revenue in the lands of the Recôncavo. In the

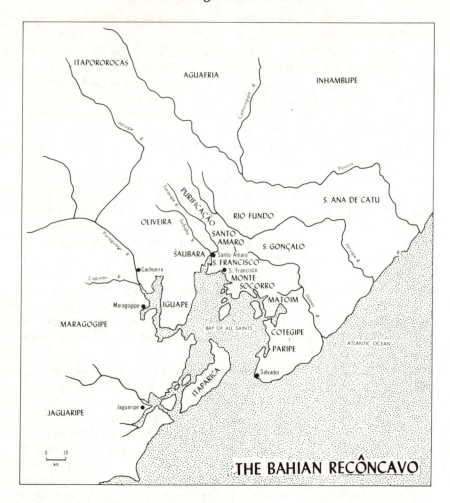

Map 2. The Bahian Recôncavo: towns and parishes.

sixteenth century, both ginger and rice were introduced. Ginger thrived in Bahia, and although it was not as good as that produced in India, by 1573 Bahia produced almost sixty tons for export.[22] The competition was too much for the merchants in the India trade, and their pressure led in 1577 to a prohibition of ginger production in Brazil. The law was in large part ignored, and contraband production continued. Eventually, in 1604, the crown extended the right of Brazilian planters to grow ginger under strict regulation and heavy taxes. Competition from India and from Hispaniola probably led to the demise of this crop in Bahia around 1620.[23] Rice was introduced from Cabo Verde, but it did not become an important foodstuff in Bahia until the eighteenth century.

The Portuguese sought to introduce other tropical crops that might become staples. In 1665, a governor of Bahia who greatly appreciated the taste of chocolate wrote to his counterpart in Pará and sought to have cacao plantings sent to Bahia. Nothing much came of this attempt, and the great cacao plantations of southern Bahia came only in the nineteenth century.[24] Both pepper and cinnamon were introduced into Bahia from India, and in the case of the latter spice two Canarins (Indians from Goa) were also sent to Brazil to advise in the cultivation. Neither of these crops was grown commercially, although cinnamon and Goans were sent again in the early nineteenth century in another attempt to diversify Bahia's agricultural exports.[25]

Despite these halfhearted attempts to find another profitable staple, only tobacco succeeded in joining sugar in the Recôncavo. The *areia* (sandy) soils were considered inappropriate for sugarcane, but with proper cultivation, especially the use of cattle manure, these could be made to produce tobacco. In the fields around the confluence of the Paraguaçú and Jacuipe rivers, and then beyond the edge of the Recôncavo in what was to become the parishes of Agua Fria, Santo Estevão de Jacuipe, and São Pedro do Monte de Muritiba, small growers began to produce tobacco around the second decade of the seventeenth century.[26] The industry began to center on the town of Nossa Senhora do Rosario do Porto de Cachoeira, a few kilometers from the mouth of the Paraguaçu, just above the limits of the tides. Our Lady of the Rosary of the Port of Cachoeira had begun as a staging area for penetration of the interior, a gateway to the sertão, but by the 1670s its importance was as the port for the tobacco producers. In 1697, there were four warehouses in Cachoeira to handle the incoming tobacco rolls, which were then taken in small boats across the bay to the wharves of Salvador.[27] Production by the beginning of the eighteenth century had reached about 2,400 tons, almost all of which went to Portugal. But Bahian tobacco increasingly found a market in West Africa, and by mid-century about 3,000 tons were also going to the Bight of Benin.[28]

Tobacco cultivation gave Cachoeira and its surrounding region, and to some extent Maragogipe, a distinctive social and economic organization within the Recôncavo. Tobacco needed intensive care as seedlings, protection from pests and weeds, and then picking by hand. It could be grown efficiently on small family farms of a few hectares, as well as on larger units with twenty to forty slaves. The use of *esterco* (cattle manure) was essential for producing better grades, and thus mixed cattle and tobacco farms (*sítios*) were common. Most Bahian tobacco was twisted into ropes and wound into rolls of 8 arrobas (256 pounds) for the Lisbon trade and 3 arrobas (96 pounds) for the coast of Africa. The rolls were placed in leather casings for shipping. The twisting process, difficult and precise, was usually carried out by skilled slaves. Poorer growers did not have their own rollers but, rather, paid to have this done. Tobacco could be produced on a small scale, and its processing was less complicated than sugar and less costly as well. Thus it attracted humble farmers who hoped to find a way into the export market. "This agriculture is among the least expensive," said the superintendent of tobacco in 1714, "and thus the least costly for those who practice it."[29] Their abandonment of food crops caused consternation in the government, which issued occasional legislation to limit tobacco farming, with little apparent effect. There were social distinctions among the tobacco growers. In the region of Cachoeira, there were a few families who raised sugar in Iguape and combined this activity with tobacco growing in the Cachoeira fields and ranching in the interior. These were the region's elite. Their sítios might produce fifty to sixty tons a year. At the same time, there were many growers with an annual output of one to two tons. At the beginning of the eighteenth century, there were about two thousand growers.

Tobacco was a less prestigious and less expensive staple, open to more humble cultivators, but it was not a "poor man's crop." Tobacco agriculture rested firmly on the backs of slaves, and in parishes around Cachoeira in the eighteenth century half the population was slave, a percentage lower than in the sugar parishes but large enough to dispel ideas of a yeoman husbandry. Although sugar and tobacco both depended on slave labor and both shared the holds of the merchantmen sailing from Salvador, to a large extent the two crops were geographically and socially separated. The major sugar-planter families did not, for the most part, engage in tobacco farming, and vice versa. The tobacco-growing region was distinct from the sugar-producing areas.

During the course of the seventeenth century, the population of Salvador and the Recôncavo grew, the area that was effectively occupied increased, and the number of engenhos multiplied. The problem is that in this prestatistical age no accurate accounting of this progress was made, or at least none survived. Between 1584 and 1612, the annual rate of engenho increase was 1 percent in Bahia. Fifty mills in 1612 had become 80 by 1629.[30] We know that in 1663 the crown ordered a census of the Recôncavo engenhos, but if there was one, the document has not survived. In 1676, there were 130 engenhos in the Recôncavo.[31] It is really not until the beginning of the eighteenth century that the documentary record begins to improve. In 1710, Bahia was reported to have 146 sugar mills. In an eccelesiastical census, Salvador's six parishes were recorded with 21,601 persons able to confess or above seven years of age, which probably meant about 24,193 people, including children and recently arrived slaves.[32] According to the city council, the urban population had tripled between 1647 and 1717. As to the Recôncavo and the rest of the captaincy, the record for the seventeenth century does not exist.[33] A general census was ordered in 1726 and sent to Portugal the following year, but it has not survived.[34] Fortunately, however, between 1718 and 1724 an ecclesiastical census was made that provides an excellent view of the population of Bahia and the state of the sugar industry at that time.[35]

According to a dissertation presented by Father Gonçalo Soares de França to the Academia dos Esquecidos, a Bahian intellectual society, the captaincy in 1724 had a population of about 80,000, most of which was concentrated in Salvador and the Recôncavo. Despite a movement of people toward the interior during the seventeenth century, the settlements along the São Francisco River and in the mining zone near Jacobina still contained less than 10 percent of the captaincy's inhabitants. The areas to the south – Cairú, Camamú, and Ilhéus – were long settled but remained sparsely populated. There was at least one engenho in this region – Engenho Santana, on the river of that name near the town of Sao Jorge de Ilhéus – but the South was a zone of small farms producing manioc. Camamú and its region was a breadbasket. It sent so much manioc flour to Salvador and the Recôncavo that it was known as "the Sicily of Bahia." Despite the small-farm tradition in southern Bahia, about half the population was slave. Intimately linked with the export trade, slavery was also an essential part of other sectors of the Bahian economy.

The vast majority of the Bahian population continued to reside in Salvador and in the Recôncavo. More than 80 percent of the inhabitants of the captaincy could be found there. Salvador had a population of 25,000, of which just under half were slaves (see Table 4-1). Foreign visitors to Salvador sometimes claimed that slaves greatly outnumbered the free in the city, but the 1724 count indicates that this was an exaggeration. More than likely, travelers confused the numerous free colored population with slaves and thus exaggerated the size of the servile class. The free population had a normal sex ratio, and the 5,209 *fogos*, or households, averaged just under five persons in each.

The parishes of the Recôncavo recorded by Father Soares de França contained just under 40,000 residents, or about half the population of the captaincy. The proportion of slaves in the Recôncavo exceeded 60 percent, and in parishes like Matoim, Santiago de Iguape, and Santo Amaro da Purificação slaves were more than 70 percent of the residents. This was to be expected, for these parishes were the heart of the sugar-producing areas of the Recôncavo. Soares de França listed 106 engenhos in the Recôncavo, but his count is probably incomplete. If we add the 32 engenhos he reported for the subcaptaincy of Sergipe de El-Rey to the north and Engenho Santana that he failed to mention in Ilhéus, the Bahia had a minimum of 139 engenhos in 1724, a figure close to the 146 reported by Antonil in 1710.

Soares de França's description of Bahia is probably incomplete. He seems to have forgotten to mention some engenhos, and at least two parishes are mentioned (Nossa Senhora do Rosario de Cachoeira and

Table 4-1. *The Population of Bahia, circa 1724*

Parish	Date of foundation	Free men	Free women	Criados[a]	Slaves	Total	Engenhos
Salvador							
Sé	1552	2,121	1,537	186	3,992	7,836	
Vitória	1549	348	241		338	927	
Conceição	1623	1,399	640	79	2,820	4,938	
S. Antônio	1648	941	1,023		1,675	3,639	
Desterro	1679	714	1,116	8	1,278	3,116	
S. Pedro	1679	1,088	1,420		2,029	4,537	
Totals		6,611	5,977	273	12,132	24,993	
Recôncavo							
Pirajá	1578	133	164		381	678	
Paripe	1578	187	118		551	856	1
Cotegipe	1606	190	282	20	898	1,390	5
Matoim	1606	234	241	32	1,220	1,727	6
Passé	1606	713	648	122	2,677	4,160	8
Socorro	1606	289	315		1,442	2,046	12
Purificação	1578	950	850	72	4,152	6,024	39
Monte	1606	895	807	4	3,835	5,541	19
Santiago de Iguape	1563	362	430	39	2,212	3,043	16
Pitanga	1563	1,225	1,234	24	2,568	5,051	
S. Cruz Itaparica	1563	640	666	8	1,390	2,704	
S. Amaro Itaparica	1681	160	137	5	407	709	
Maragogipe	1676	955	920	38	1,388	3,301	
Jaguaripe	1625	720	626	16	1,096	2,458	
Totals		7,653	7,438	380	24,217	39,688	106
South coast							
Ilhéus	1556	550	388		893	1,831	(1)
Boipeba	1616	323	327	25	552	1,227	
Camamú	1560	448	250		1,032	2,230	
Cairú	1610	525	406		1,190	2,121	
Totals		1,846	1,371	25	3,667	7,409	
Sertão							
Rio S. Francisco	1682	725	727	56	1,266	2,774	
Jacobina						(5,000)	
Sergipe de El-Rey	1617	1,600	1,856	20	4,200	7,676	32
All Bahia – Totals		18,435	17,369	754	45,482	79,864	139

[a]The term *criados* probably means resident dependents or servants.

São Domingos Saubara) that are not discussed. Still, whatever the deficiencies in the total numbers, the regional distribution and relative concentration of the population seems accurate and provides us a vision of the Recôncavo at the beginning of the eighteenth century.

By the mid–eighteenth century, census taking had become common in Bahia, but the method and form used to record the results were so flawed that not much trust can be placed in the numbers generated.[36]

The customs of excluding children under age seven and of using different age categories for men and women complicate any detailed analysis of these early counts. The discrepancies are apparent in two censuses made in 1757. In one, the city of Salvador had 4,814 households with 34,472 persons over the age of seven. The second, made by a local official, reported 6,821 hearths with 37,323 people. A 1759 census made by the governor reported Salvador with 40,263, the Recôncavo with 72,833, and the whole captaincy with 215,142. This count, however, did not include Indians, clerics and their servants, and children under seven years old. If the total is increased by 12 percent to compensate for the omissions, the Bahian population at that time can be estimated at about 241,000.[37] The Recôncavo population at that time made up only about a third of the captaincy's total, a result of the Recôncavo's stagnation and the expansion of mining and ranching in the interior. Both these processes deserve some comment.

As we shall see, the mid–eighteenth century was a period of stagnation in the Bahian sugar economy. This is reflected demographically by a slower rate of population increase. By comparing populations in those parishes that remained geographically unchanged between 1724 and 1757, this rate can be determined. In Maragogipe, for example, the increase between the two dates from 3,301 to 5,040 is 1.2 percent per year; in Purificação in the heart of sugar country the rate is 1.1 percent. In the suburban parishes such as Cotegipe and Paripe, the population was actually slightly lower in 1757 than it had been in 1724.

It would appear that the annual rate of growth between the 39,688 recorded for 1724 and the Recôncavo population of 72,833 for 1759 would be 1.7 percent, but this figure is probably inflated because of incomplete returns for 1724. In the 1770s, the Recôncavo population and the export economy began to expand. In 1774, the regional population was 85,591. But by 1780, it had grown to 102,853, an increase of about 3.1 percent a year, or almost twice the rate of growth of the earlier period.[38] To a large extent, the expansion of the Recôncavo population must have been due to increased slave importations, although the highest rates of increase were found in the nonsugar parishes of Jaguaripe and Maragogipe. The increases in these marginal zones paralleled the growth in population and economic importance of the interior that lay beyond the Recôncavo.

There had always been a frontier beyond the Recôncavo. In Bahia, the zone of transition or *agreste* between the humid coast and the drier and higher interior was relatively narrow and quickly shaded into the scrub brush and cactus of the sertão. Penetration of the sertão had begun in the 1570s, but a series of Indian campaigns in the mid- and late seventeenth century had opened up vast areas to settlement. In this Bahian outback, the major activity was cattle ranching. The Recôncavo planters had fought to have livestock raising prohibited from the agricultural areas because of the damage they did to canefields, and legislation to that end was finally issued in 1700. Long before that, however, Bahian herds had pushed along the rivers into the sertão, especially along the São Francisco, Itapicuru, and the Paraguaçu. Small ranches of 1,000 to 3,000 head were common, but great ranching families like the Garcia d'Avilas with extensive lands to the north of Salvador or the merchant-turned-rancher João Peixoto Viegas with herds on the upper Paraguaçu might have more than 20,000 head. The religious orders also had ranches. In 1703, the Benedictines of Bahia had a herd of about 3,000 on the São Francisco, but the Jesuit College of Salvador owned about 15,000 head in that decade.[39] In 1710, Antonil estimated that the northeastern sertão contained more than 1,300,000 head of cattle to supply the cities and plantations of the coast and the newly developing mines of southern Bahia and Minas Gerais.

Both Salvador and the Recôncavo depended on the sertão. Salvador needed the sertão for meat. Meat, hides, and tallow were used in town and country, and in addition the engenhos needed oxen for transport and at many mills to provide the power source. Great trail drives sometimes covering forty miles a day brought the herds down to fair towns on the margins of the Recôncavo, where an active trade took place. The first of these was Capoame, established by Francisco Dias d'Avila in 1614. Located in the parish of Santo Amaro de Pitanga, near present-day Camacari, its Wednesday cattle fair flourished. It remained the major fair until the rise of Feira de Santana, "Princess of the Sertão," in the 1820s.[40] By the 1720s, hides became a major item of export from Bahia. The fleet of 1735, for example, carried 180,861 *meios de sola* (shoe leathers) and over 11,000 crude hides.[41] Moreover, the tobacco industry of Cachoeira depended on hides for the wrapping of tobacco rolls, and thus there was also a constant demand within the captaincy for the hides of the sertão.

Beef was the most commonly consumed meat in Salvador and the Recôncavo. In Salvador, meat was sold in municipally licensed butcher shops, and the supply was dependent on the trail drives that brought cattle in from the sertão. When the mining region of Minas Gerais developed in the beginning of the eighteenth century, the officials of Bahia worried that the new demand for meat at the mines would leave Bahia without food. In 1716, the câmara of Salvador sought to have the sertão divided into zones so that the coast would be assured a constant supply of meat from the interior.[42] Despite price fixing and attempts to prohibit speculation, the beef price doubled and tripled in the 1720s and 1730s until Minas Gerais developed its own local supply. Even after this, periodic droughts in the interior caused short-term shortages and high prices on the coast.[43]

The ecclesiastical count of 1724 had listed only about 8,000 people in the sertão, probably an underestimate. By 1759, however, more than

75,000 inhabitants were recorded in the two administrative districts of the interior; the lower sertão (*sertão de baixo*) south of the Itapicuru and the upper sertão (*sertão de cima*) north of that river in the valley of the São Francisco.[44] The great ranchers were truly the masters of men and cattle. Land grants of hundreds of square kilometers were not rare and the arm of royal justice infrequently reached beyond the coast. Although the social and economic organization of the sertão falls outside the aims of this book, the dependence of the sugar industry on the cattle of the interior make it an essential part of our story.

After all is said, it was the production of sugar that gave Bahia, and especially the Recôncavo, its raison d'être and created its distinctive society. From modest beginnings in the sixteenth century, Bahia became the second sugar region of Brazil, behind only Pernambuco; after the eclipse of that captaincy's leadership following the Dutch invasion (1630–54), Bahia took the lead for most of the eighteenth century. It is difficult to estimate the number of mills in operation in any given year because censuses and counts were usually incomplete and because mills often became *fogo morto* or temporarily inactive due to debt, poor management, or other calamity. During the century from 1670 to 1770, the Recôncavo usually had between 130 and 150 engenhos, and its total production fell between 350,000 and 500,000 arrobas (between 5,000 and 7,300 metric tons). This level seems quite small by today's standards but was large for the time. Bahia's production was larger or about the same as Jamaica's until the 1730s and led or equaled Barbados, the major Caribbean producer of the time, until the beginning of the eighteenth century.[45]

As we have seen, the physical formation of the industry in Bahia took place in stages. The lands just outside Salvador, the parishes of Paripe, Pirajá, Cotegipe, and Matoim, witnessed the first growth of the sugar economy in the 1560s. Some of the engenhos in this subregion had been set up on sesmarias distributed by Tomé de Sousa in the 1550s, and as the area was cleared of hostile Indians, the canefields began to expand.[46] Engenho Freguesia in Matoim is a good example of a mill established in the sixteenth century that continued to operate throughout the colonial era. The campaigns of Mem de Sá, the so-called war of the Paraguaçu, cleared more of the Recôncavo in the 1570s, and by the following decade engenhos could be found in Marapé, along the Paraguaçu, and in the southern Recôncavo. These last, however, were subject to Indian attack as late as the 1610s. This threat, in addition to the poorer soils, caused the virtual abandonment of Jaguaripe and Maragogipe to sugarcane agriculture, except for a few small mills on the rivers.

The second area to develop, the core of the sugar Recôncavo, were the zones lying around the Sergipe and Subae rivers, the eventual townships of Santo Amaro and São Francisco. Mem de Sá had distrib-

Figure 4-2. A sugar town. São Francisco do Conde on the Bay of All Saints developed as a warehousing and administrative center for the engenhos that surrounded it.

uted much of this area in sesmarias and took for himself a large grant of three and one-half leagues of coast by four leagues toward the interior, on which he built a large engenho. By 1587, this region had fourteen mills. In the 1620s, the Franciscans constructed a chapel and convent on a hill at the edge of the bay, and it became the nucleus of a small village that slowly began to acquire military, commercial, and administrative functions. In 1698, with the growth of the population and the sugar economy, the town of São Francisco do Conde (see Figure 4-2) was created to serve the needs of both.[47]

São Francisco's predominance was short-lived. About two hours by horseback along the Sergipe River, a small settlement had begun in 1608. Colonists found excellent soil and plentiful firewood in this area, and as the threat of Indian attack was eliminated and the seashore sugar lands were saturated with plantations, this area farther inland became increasingly valued. The settlement became the township of Santo Amaro in 1727, and its location in the midst of good sugar lands and at the point of furthest inland navigation on the Sergipe River gave it peculiar advantages. By 1757, its central parish of Purificação included three distinct plantation zones. Patatiba, which lay along the southern margin of the Sergipe River, contained nine engenhos, of which the Jesuits' Petinga and Engenho Sergipe do Conde were good examples (see Figure 4-3). On the other side of the river in the Subae district were another five mills. Further inland near the Tararipe River

Figure 4-3. All that remains of Engenho Sergipe do Conde, "Queen of the Recôncavo." (The chimney was a nineteenth-century addition that accompanied the introduction of steam-powered mills.)

were another twelve engenhos. These were newer and in many cases smaller engenhos that developed in the eighteenth century as the sugar industry moved inland. This development could also be seen in the parish of São Pedro de Tararipe e Rio Fundo further to the interior.[48] It had been created in 1718 by taking parts of Purificação and Nossa Senhora do Monte in São Francisco township, and by 1757 it had fifteen engenhos. By the beginning of the nineteenth century, São Francisco township included five parishes with eighty engenhos, and Santo Amaro contained four with eighty-five mills.[49] With the exception of Iguape in the Cachoeira region, São Francisco, Santo Amaro, and the suburban parishes were the heart of the sugar Recôncavo and the birthplace of plantation society.

Not all the sugar that Bahia shipped to Europe came from the Recôncavo. In the sixteenth century, a few mills existed along the southern coast near Cairú and then at Ilhéus. These mills suffered from continual Indian attacks from the Aimoré (as we have already seen in Chapter 2), and most were abandoned. The large Engenho Santana on the river of that name not far from São Jorge de Ilhéus continued to produce sugar throughout the colonial period. Estimates of Bahian production usually included small amounts coming from Ilhéus and sometimes from Porto Seguro, but far more important was the sugar produced by the area of Sergipe de El-Rey to the north that also composed part of the Bahian total.

Attempts at the conquest of Sergipe de El-Rey had been made by Bahians as early as the 1570s, but it was not really until the 1590s that effective penetration of the area took place. The settlement of São Cristóvão was established in 1595 and was shortly moved to another more advantageous site at the mouth of the Vasabarris River. Bahian ranchers like the Garcia d'Avila family opened up the interior of Sergipe by moving cattle herds out along the São Francisco and other rivers into the sertão. At the mouth of those rivers – especially the Contenguiba, Sergipe, and Japarantuba – engenhos eventually developed. When the Dutch seized the area in 1637, there were eight operating sugar works in the captaincy. Caught up in the Luso–Dutch war, Sergipe eventually returned to Portuguese control in 1648. The number of mills began to grow in the late seventeenth century – there were twenty-five by the 1720s. Quantities of sugar were continually shipped for sale to Salvador.[50] Sergipe de El-Rey remained through the period of this study a subordinate captaincy ruled by a captain-major under the authority of the governor-general of Bahia and part of the captaincy-general of Bahia.

The sugar production and tithe of Sergipe de El-Rey were usually calculated as part of the Bahian total. Sergipe was, in effect, an extension of the Bahian economy, but there were some differences. The size of engenhos there tended to be smaller. A 1785 listing of slave-worked property in the parishes around São Cristóvão revealed that the engenhos owned an average of 24 slaves and none owned more than 100.[51] There were, however, an average of four lavradores de cana for each mill, and each of the cane farmers owned an average of 6 slaves. In 1798, there were 140 mills in Sergipe, many of them near the mouth of the Cotinguiba River.[52] By the early nineteenth century, 163 engenhos had been registered in Sergipe de El-Rey, and their production made up about 25 percent of the Bahian total. By 1834, Sergipe had a population of 160,452, of whom more than 90 percent were people of color and 30 percent were slaves. In general terms, Sergipe de El-Rey had fewer whites, a higher proportion of free colored, and about the same proportion of slaves as Bahia.[53]

Although Ilhéus and Sergipe de El-Rey must be counted in Bahia's sugar production, the mills of the Recôncavo produced most of the sugar and set the patterns of plantation life. As the engenhos occupied the countryside, especially in the Recôncavo, they developed an existence that transcended ownership or time; or at least they had the potential to do so. In the sixteenth century, the engenhos were the cutting edge of the frontier, pioneer plantations at the rim of European occupancy often subject to Indian attack. Before there were towns and parishes there were engenhos, and in much of the Recôncavo the first church of the parish was the chapel of some engenho. Once established, the engenhos gave identity to their location. Places in the Recôncavo today like Jacú, Terra Boa, and Inhatá had their origins as engenhos, although only ruins remain, and the memory of the mills has long since faded. Once established, engenhos had a tendency to persist for long periods of time, often under the same name. Of ninety-two mills listed in 1757, only seven had disappeared sixty years later in 1817.[54] Owners came and went, sons squandered fortunes, inheritance divided properties, poor management or bad times caused ruin, and sometimes the mill might become inactive, fogo morto, but it is not uncommon to find an engenho appearing on lists separated by two centuries. There are many examples. Engenho Jacarancanga with its Church of Santo Antônio was owned by Cristóvão de Barros in the time of Gabriel Soares de Sousa. About a century later, it became the property of Desembargador Antônio Rodrigues Banha; in 1798, when it was the property of Antônio Feliciano de Sá Carneiro, it appeared on the map of the Recôncavo in the work of Luís dos Santos Vilhena.[55] The historian José Wanderley Araújo Pinho traced the story of Engenho Freguesia in Matoim over the course of four centuries, and others, such as Santana in Ilhéus and Petinga in the Recôncavo, displayed a remarkable longevity.[56]

Engenhos were classified in a number of ways. The earliest mills tended to be located right on the coast or on a river quite close to the mouth. These were generally referred to as seaside mills (a beira mar); they tended to be older and larger and somewhat more aristocratic in the sense that by the late eighteenth century the principal families of Bahia owned a relatively large proportion (35 percent) of these estates.[57] As the sugar industry grew, new mills were constructed further inland, away from the coast. These engenhos "in the woods" (da matta) or "inland" (terra a dentro) were in general smaller and less well capitalized, and they suffered from the higher transportation costs that their location demanded. In addition to location, engenhos were always described in terms of power source. The water-driven mills called engenhos reais were larger, whereas mills powered by horses or (more commonly) oxen moved more slowly and tended to have a lower productive capacity. These animal-powered engenhos were called trapiches, engenhocas, or molinotes, the last two terms being somewhat deprecatory.

Finally, engenhos could be classified by three types of ownership: state, corporate, or private. When sugar was first introduced into Brazil, there were a few mills built with royal funds. The one that operated in Pirajá provided milling facilities to cane growers. By the late sixteenth century, this engenho was rented to private individuals and the crown had essentially abandoned direct investment in favor of stimulating the industry by granting sesmarias and offering tax incentives or other economic benefits to private investors who wished to build their own sugar works. In Bahia, as elsewhere in Brazil, a number of mills were owned by religious corporations. The Carmelites owned Engenho do Carmo and another mill, named Terra Nova in Passé, as well as canefields that produced sugar at other mills. The Benedictines at first brought canes to Engenho Sergipe, but by 1656 they had begun to develop Engenho São Bento dos Lages. Between 1720 and 1723, the order constructed a second mill, São Caetano de Itaporocas, further inland, and a small mill operated at Inhatá in Rio Fundo in the early nineteenth century. The profits of these mills were used to support the activities of their respective orders. In Bahia, about 30 to 40 percent of the Benedictine annual income was derived from their sugar plantations.[58]

Of the religious corporations, the Jesuits were the greatest sugar planters. Six mills in Bahia were at one time or another the property of the Jesuits. The Jesuit College of Salvador built its first mill, Mamo, in Passé about 1601. It operated until the mid–seventeenth century, when they acquired a nearby property, Pitanga, which they enlarged and turned into a profitable enterprise. The Jesuits of Bahia also built an engenho in Camamú around 1607, but it was destroyed by the Dutch in 1640. The Jesuit College of Santo Antão of Lisbon eventually acquired Engenho Sergipe in the Recôncavo and Engenho Santana in Ilhéus after a long legal battle in the seventeenth century. To these, the Lisbon Jesuits added Engenho Petinga, close by the Sergipe mill, in 1745. When the Jesuits were expelled from Brazil in 1757, their engenhos were auctioned to private individuals.[59] Differing in the structure of ownership, the corporately owned mills produced sugar in the same way as their secular counterparts and depended on the same labor force and the same world markets.

The great majority of Bahian plantations were privately owned. Although partnerships existed, they were not common. Mills were actively bought and sold, and, because they enjoyed legal protection as indivisible properties after 1663, they were passed on as units in inheritance dispositions. It was not unusual, however, to find engenhos temporarily administered by the herdeiros (heirs) of a deceased owner, until a settlement could be reached among them over ownership. Multiple ownership was common. Planters who held three or even four mills were not unknown and proprietorship of two not uncommon. In 1798, twenty-three owners held 52 of the 215 engenhos in the Recôncavo.[60] To some extent, technological bottlenecks caused the phenomenon of multiple ownership. When the capacity of a mill was reached and the expenses of bringing cane from long distances became too great, then a planter might simply set up a second mill. The names of sugar works like Engenho Novo (new mill), Engenho Velho (old mill), or Engenho Baixo, Engenho do Meio, or Engenho de Cima (lower, middle, or upper mill) that dot the Brazilian landscape are an artifact of the process of fission.

Socially, a few great planter lineages eventually controlled a large number of the mills. Historian F. W. O. Morton estimates that 92 out of 316 (29 percent) of the Bahian engenhos in 1818 were owned by twenty great families, among them the Góis, Calmon, Fiuza, Costa Pinto, Doria, and Rocha Pitta. These families not only owned many mills but also tended to hold the largest and best-located ones. Of 151 engenhos on the coast or within two leagues of it, the aristocratic planter families owned 66 (43 percent).[61] Because many of these families dominated local politics and social life into the nineteenth and even the twentieth century, it is not surprising that the interest of historians and genealogists has focused on them, but placing them at the center of the canvas has created some false images. For every family like the Calmons or the Costa Pintos who built, maintained, and conserved their properties and social position, there were five or ten who failed or enjoyed only momentary success. Engenhos changed hands rapidly – a bad harvest, a late fleet arrival, a European war could all spell disaster. The sugar industry was not a sure investment, and overreaching aspirant *senhores* (planters) were never lacking. Rather than the stability symbolized by the great planter families, a much more fluid pattern seems to have been characteristic of Bahia's colonial sugar economy.

Yet, despite insecurity and turnover in mill ownership, once the Bahian Recôncavo became established as a region of sugar agriculture in the sixteenth century, it never abandoned that activity. Other crops, most notably tobacco, were also produced in the Recôncavo, but none ever exceeded the value or importance of sugar. The market for that commodity might experience wide fluctuations, and the captaincy sometimes suffered long periods of hardship because of weak demand or low prices for its major agricultural products, but Bahia remained through good times and bad a major producer of sugar and tobacco. The Recôncavo gave Salvador its economic life, it stimulated the settlement and development of the sertão, and its planters dominated the political and social life of the captaincy throughout its history. To say "Bahia" was to say "the Recôncavo," and the Recôncavo was always engenhos, sugar, and slaves.

CHAPTER 5

SAFRA: THE WAYS OF SUGAR MAKING

Agriculture . . . is easier and prettier to write about than to practice. Dependent on the rude and unbearable work of industry, the
cultivation of sugarcane, despite its advantages, is very detrimental
and full of a thousand inconveniences.

José da Silva Lisboa (1781)

The techniques of sugar production in all of the American colonies were
essentially the same, as the classic and roughly contemporaneous descriptions of Père Labat for the French Antilles, Richard Ligon for Barbados, and André João Antonil for Brazil make clear. But details differed in
response to regional distinctions and local conditions. In Brazil, the
techniques of sugar making and the structure of production defined the
colony's social and economic structure for almost one hundred years to
about 1650 and thereafter exercised considerable influence in sugar-
producing regions such as Bahia and Pernambuco, despite the growth of
other economic activities.[1] The foundation on which the Brazilian colony
rested was the relationship of masters to slaves, and this was inherent in
the relations of production engendered by the plantation economy. To
understand the nature of sugar production, then, is to perceive the
needs and desires of the class that controlled the essential property,
lands, and slaves and to grasp the conditions and constraints under
which those who produced the sugar labored.

The sugar industry, Bahia's predominant economic activity, defined
the political and economic concerns of its administrators and leading
citizens. Taxes, tariffs, government limitations on growth, food supply,
slave prices, technological improvements, and commercial restrictions
and conditions – all relating to sugar or the other agricultural products – are themes that run consistently through the documentation of
Bahian history. In a thousand ways, sugar created the context of Bahian life. The existence of the cane farmers as a social category, the
relationship between planters and their merchant creditors, the role of
the state in promoting the interests of local producers, the activities of
the clergy dependent on tithes – all were determined by the sugar econ-

omy. And above all, the requirements and conditions of plantation labor defined the daily life of the majority of the Bahian population, the people for whom the sugar harvest or *safra* had a special meaning. This chapter will examine the specific processes, practices, and rhythms of Bahian sugar production.

The safra

Botou o engenho a moer. (The mill was set in motion.) With these words, the great event of the year, the beginning of the safra, was recorded. In the Recôncavo, about the first or second week of August each year, the engenhos placed everything in readiness. Machinery was repaired, kettles replaced, contracts for cane and firewood reviewed, and oxen brought in from the pastures. All that humans could do was completed, and now only divine help was needed. On the appointed day, the parish priest or the resident chaplain officiated at the blessing of the mill. The owner and his family or the resident administrator was in attendance, along with many free persons from the surrounding area. Christ or the engenho's particular patron saint was invoked to guard from harm all those who labored on the estate and to assure a successful harvest. At the mill itself, slaves and free persons gathered to hear the prayers and observe the sprinkling of holy water on the mill. With a signal, the mill was set in motion, and the priest and the owner passed the first canes through the rollers. The slaves took the matter no less seriously than their masters. Slaves refused to work if the mill was not blessed, and during the ceremony they often pressed forward to receive some drops of holy water on their bodies. The kettles and the workers at them also received a benediction, and the oxcarts arriving from the canefields decorated with pennants made from long sugarcanes tied with colored ribbons were also blessed at the insistence of their drivers. Later in the day, there was often a banquet in the big house, and slaves could look forward to rewards of *garapa* or cane brandy.[2] The safra had begun.

This was a time of great activity, of comings and goings: slaves heading out to the canefields, oxcarts piled high with cut cane creaking their way to the mill, boats arriving with cane or firewood at the docks of the riverine engenhos and those on the bay, kettles boiling above constant fires, shifts of slaves changing in the mill and the purging house, lavradores de cana coming in to arrange for the processing of their cane. And behind it all, there was the constant whirring of the mill as it pressed from the cane the liquid that cost so much bitter sweat and that would crystallize into not only sweet sugar but wealth, prestige, and power as well.

Although the beginning of the safra was a time of expectation and excitement for masters and slaves, those emotions were soon replaced

Figure 5-1. A water-driven engenho real (royal mill) in the seventeenth century. Note the "big house" and chapel on the high ground. This scene, painted by Frans Post (a Dutch landscape artist who spent some years in Northeast Brazil), provides, as does his other Brazilian work, accurate eyewitness testimony not available in Portuguese iconography.

for the latter by weariness and even exhaustion. After a few weeks, said Henry Koster (who managed an engenho in Pernambuco in the 1810s), the constant labor caused them to fall asleep wherever they could lay their heads. "Sleepy like a sugar-mill slave" was a common expression.[3] The labor on a sugar plantation in Brazil continued around the clock, with field tasks done during the day and the mill grinding through the night. Eighteen to twenty hours was the normal milling day, with only a few hours taken to clean the machinery. In the seventeenth century, the Bahian engenhos, like that in Figure 5-1, began to mill at four o'clock in the afternoon and continued through the night until ten o'clock the following morning. The kettles and mill were then cleaned, and at 4:00 p.m. the mill began again.[4] During the few hours of rest, the slaves tried to sleep, but sometimes they spent these moments looking for shellfish or other food. As we shall see, field hands also served on shifts in the mill during the safra, and often an engenho did not have enough workers, so slaves did double shifts. The work of the slaves was "incredible" and so great that "one of these engenhos could be called an inferno."[5]

The unrelenting pace of labor continued in Bahia for about eight to nine months, during which cane was cut and milled and sugar made. The length of the safra varied according to region in Brazil, but in Bahia

Table 5-1. *The Bahian sugar safra: opening and closing dates based on livros de safra of Engenho Sergipe*

Year	Safra begins (botou a moer)	Safra ends (peijou o engenho)	Year	Safra begins (botou a moer)	Safra ends (peijou o engenho)
1611–2	28 July	29 May	1636–7	25 Aug.	
1612–3	21 Aug.	19 May	1637–8	27 July	
1622–3	21 July	19 May	1643–4	13 Aug.	13 May
1624–5[a]			1644–5	11 Aug.	16 May
1625–6	15 Aug		1645–6	30 July	4 May
1626–7	23 July		1646–7	6 Aug.	8 Feb.[b]
1628–9	21 Aug.		1650–1	1 Aug.	10 May
1629–30	27 July		1651–2	30 July	6 May
1630–1	25 July		1654–5	5 Aug.	29 April
1633–4	30 July		1668–9[c]	21 Aug.	
1634–5	26 July				
1635–6	1 Aug.				

[a]Safra interrupted by Dutch invasion. [b]Safra interrupted by Dutch attack. [c]From Engenho Santana Ilhéus.
Source: All dates from livros de safra, Engenho Sergipe except 1654–5: ANTT, CSJ, maço 56, n. 19; and 168–9: ANTT, CSJ, maço 68, n. 123.

it was common to begin in late July or August and end in May of the following year. Table 5-1 presents the opening and closing dates of the Engenho Sergipe safras. This pattern meant that the safra extended over a period of 270 to 300 days and was limited only by the arrival of the heavy winter rains that made cane cutting and transportation particularly difficult.[6] The extended safra gave Bahia a comparative advantage in competition with Caribbean sugar producers, whose harvest season in the eighteenth century lasted an average of 120 to 180 days. The long safra season when the productivity of workers was stretched to their physical limits also created conditions particularly favorable to the use of slaves. Virtually without a "dead time" when slaves could not be usefully employed in preparing or harvesting the main staple, the Bahian sugar cycle was well-adapted to the profitable use of slave labor.[7]

From the records of Engenho Sergipe, it is possible to reconstruct the milling season of a Bahian engenho for four safras (1612, 1643, 1650, and 1651) on a day-to-day basis.[8] In these four harvests, the mill averaged a season of 291 days from the beginning of milling until completion. During these seasons, an average of 78 days (28 percent) a year were lost to various causes. Breakdowns and repairs accounted for about 9 percent of the lost days. The most common problem was a failure of the aqueduct (*levada*) to supply the water needed for the mill's power. Repairing kettles also cost some days from time to time.

Table 5-2. *Holy days observed at Engenho Sergipe, safras of 1612–13, 1622–3, 1643–4, 1644–5, 1645–6, 1650–1, 1651–2*

Aug.		*Jan.*	
5	Our Lady of the Snows[a]	1	Name of Jesus
10	St. Lawrence	6	Epiphany (dos Reis)
15	Assumption	20	St. Sebastian [g]
24	St. Bartholomew[b]	*Feb.*	
Sept.		2	Purification (Candlemas)
8	Nativity (anunciação)	24	Our Lady of the Incarnation
14	(unspecified)	25	St. Matthias[h]
21	St. Matthew	*March*	
29	St. Michael	25	Annunciation
Oct.		*April*	
28	St. Simon and St. Jude	4	Our Lady of Pleasures
Nov.			Holy Thursday (movable)
1	All Saints		Good Friday (movable)
21	Presentation[c]		Easter and three octaves[i] (movable)
30	St. Andrew	*May*	
Dec.		1	St. Philip and St. James
2	St. Francis Xavier[d]	3	Holy Cross
8	Immaculate Conception		
18	Our Lady of O[e]		
21	St. Thomas		
25-8	Christmas and three octaves		
31	St. Silvester[f]		

[a]Not observed after 1650. [b]Not observed after 1645–6. [c]Not observed after 1650. [d]Observed only 1650–1. [e]Not observed after 1650. [f]Observed only after 1650. [g]Not observed 1650–1. [h]Some variation between 24 Feb. and 25 Feb. [i]Easter not observed in 1612–13.

Cane could not be cut and hauled in the rain, and so rainy weather resulted in a lack of cane and no milling. In the safra of 1643, Engenho Sergipe lost 17 days to rainy weather and a lack of cane, but this was a particularly bad year. On the average, the shortage of cane cost the mill about 6 days of milling time or 8 percent of the lost days. The supply of firewood was another major concern. Shortages were due to the inability of the engenho to find adequate suppliers at various times during the safra. About five days a year were lost to the shortage of wood.

Repairs, breakdowns, and shortages, however, together accounted for only one-quarter of the time lost during the safra. Far more important were the losses due to the religious calendar: to Sundays and saints' days. The daily entries at Engenho Sergipe enable us to establish the cycle of religious observance. Table 5-2 lists the holy days regularly observed at Sergipe in the mid–seventeenth century.

The harvest records of Engenho Sergipe recorded daily operations only during the safra and thus do not present a full annual religious calendar. Moreover, only feasts of precept (*festa fori*), which had the double obligation of hearing Mass and rest from labor, were recorded by the engenho's administrator. Although in many places local events and custom influenced the calendar of observance, the feasts of the church kept at Engenho Sergipe were essentially those of the universal church and the Roman Breviary. The obligatory Marian feasts (Assumption, Nativity, Conception, Purification, and Annunciation) were all regularly observed.[9] Our Lady of Purification was particularly important, since she was guardian saint of the chapel of Engenho Sergipe. The feasts of the Apostles were always celebrated, as were Easter, Christmas, and Epiphany. Under Jesuit administration, work at Engenho Sergipe stopped from 25 December to 2 January in recognition both of Christmas and its first three octaves, considered to be days of precept, and also for the feast of the Name of Jesus (1 January). For the days in between, some reason such as poor weather or needed repairs was found to excuse labor. The only specifically Jesuit feast was that of Saint Francis Xavier (2 December), which was celebrated only in one of the recorded safras (1650–1). After 1689, this feast was regularly observed in Salvador itself with a major procession.[10]

Some reorganization of the calendar of observance took place sometime between the harvests of 1646 and 1650, so that the feasts of the years after the latter date differed somewhat from those observed in earlier years. This change was probably a result of the reduction of feasts made by Pope Urban VIII (*Universa per orbem*) in 1642.[11] For example, Our Lady of the Snows was no longer considered a day of precept, nor was the feast of Our Lady of O. (This last was a popular devotion in Iberia, where eight days before Christmas the breviary contains special antiphons for vespers, all beginning with O. Our Lady of Expectation, or O, was thus a particular devotion of pregnant women.)

The question of typicality immediately arises because of Engenho Sergipe's ownership by the Jesuit College of Santo Antão of Lisbon. Certainly, there must have ben some slight variation in the religious calendar from engenho to engenho. The patron saint of each engenho's chapel was probably honored, and other local variations may have occurred. But the safra record of 1612–13, when Engenho Sergipe was still owned by the count of Linhares and not by the Jesuits, indicates with only slight differences that a similar schedule of feasts was observed. The only major departure from this pattern was no observation of Easter and its octaves in that year, but I can suspect that this is a bookkeeping error. Still, we can use the Engenho Sergipe records as the extreme case and assume that it was stricter in its observance of Sundays and feast days of precept than other plantations.

During the four safras for which the records are complete, an average of 35 Sundays and 26 feasts or holy days were observed. Thus, more than 75 percent of the days lost in a safra were due to the religious calendar. We may take these figures as representative of rigid

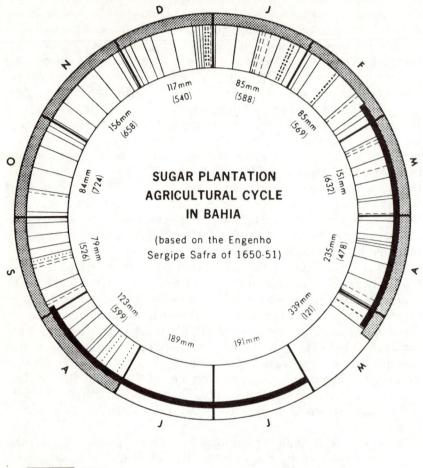

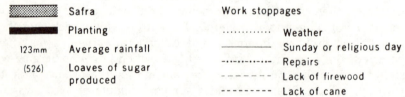

Figure 5-2.

observance, and therefore of maximum work stoppage at a Bahian mill, assuming that shortages and breakdowns were roughly the same at lay-owned engenhos. The loss to religious observance of about 28 percent of the days in a safra can be taken as an upper limit. Given these stoppages, the average milling season on the Bahian engenhos would have between 200 and 220 days.

Figure 5-2 represents the Engenho Sergipe productive year 1650–1.

The figure indicates the days of stoppage by type and also shows the number of sugar forms produced each month. In addition, modern annual rainfall statistics from the Recôncavo have been recorded. The integration of the planting and harvesting activities becomes clear in this cyclical presentation, and it is obvious that only with the arrival of torrential rains in May did work really slacken. Even then, there were forms to be purged and sugar to be carted from the preceding month's milling. Seen in this fashion, the significance of the festivities of June, still so important in the tempo of Bahian life, come sharply into focus. The festivals of Saint John (24 June), Saint Anthony (13 June), and Saint Peter (28 June) all fall in the month that coincides with the end of the sugar safra – reason for both masters and slaves to celebrate. Even today, Bahians believe that nowhere is Saint John's Day gayer and more festive than in the countryside.

The conflict between the religious calendar and its obligations and the desire for profit associated with plantation management placed an inherent contradiction starkly in focus. Ecclesiastical observers complained that too often lay plantation owners did not observe the sabbath or the other days of observance and forced their slaves to labor throughout the week. The practice seems to have been common and was commented upon by observers from the sixteenth to the eighteenth centuries.[12] In contrast, Jesuit administrators at Engenho Sergipe were instructed in 1692 to observe the religious obligations, even if it meant considerable loss to the engenho.[13] The lay planters argued that giving time off to slaves encouraged them in bad habits, drinking, and lascivious dances; a sort of "idleness is the devil's workshop" argument. More importantly, planters held that necessity forced them to violate the restrictions on work. Their position was most cogently and eruditely put forward by Domingos Loreto Couto, a Benedictine, who wrote in the mid–eighteenth century. Since the cane could only be cut and milled effectively in the summer, he said, all efforts had to be made to complete the harvest before the winter rains. Moreover, once the cane was cut, it had to be milled within a day or else the liquid would sour. If work stopped on Sunday, then cane cut on Saturday would be jeopardized, and there would be no cane ready to mill on Monday. Loreto Couto claimed that in fact most planters did observe their obligations, stopping various parts of the operation at different times of the day. The mill itself ceased at midnight, but then the kettles had to continue until 9:00 a.m. Sunday to complete the batch.[14] Milling began again about 4:00 p.m. on Sunday, and the kettles resumed operations about 7:00 p.m. Thus one portion of the engenho worked while the other rested. Religion and necessity were both served. The Jesuit Jorge Benci responded to this old and disingenuous argument that the necessity of saving one's soul came before all else – for slaves as well as freemen.[15]

Strict observance of religious obligations undoubtedly reduced the demands of work, but the continual complaints of various reformers indicate that full observance was the exception and not the rule.[16] Still, the Catholic calendar seemed to mitigate the rigors of slavery. The German travelers Johann von Spix and Karl von Martius who visited the Recôncavo in 1819 believed that the Sundays, thirty-five saints' days, and eighteen other holidays declared by the government made rural slavery not as bad as many Europeans believed it to be. Their comments, however, that although the labor was intense the safra did not last very long, that slaves did not lack for food, and that slaves were rarely overburdened with work, betray a lack of familiarity with the engenhos of the Recôncavo and an acceptance of their hosts' opinions. Their brief stay at Engenho da Ponta in Cachoeira and short visit to Engenho Santana in Ilhéus (which they later named incorrectly) provided little basis for accurate reporting.[17]

During the safra cycle, sugarcane was harvested and then immediately processed into sugar. The combination of agriculture and processing necessary to make sugar made each engenho a factory in the field and gave the mills a distinctive industrial character. The inputs of capital, technology, and labor made engenhos costly and large estates by contemporary standards, and the complexity of the operations made them peculiarly "modern."

From cane to crate

Curiously, in comparison to the many and detailed descriptions of the industrial phases of sugar making left by contemporary observers, the agricultural aspects received comparatively little attention. Perhaps it was a matter of preindustrial men, impressed by the complex technical process in the mill, being less concerned with the more mundane and familiar agrarian stage.[18] In any case, the available information on the cultivation of sugar cane and the labor associated with it is not extensive, despite the fact that this was the most arduous and continual set of tasks and employed more laborers than any other.

In Brazil, the cultivation of sugarcane was a relatively simple but backbreaking and time-consuming activity. It consisted of clearing the fields and then planting, weeding, and cutting the cane with very simple tools and techniques. The complex irrigation system used in Mexican sugarcane farming was unknown in Brazil. Manuring, though used in tobacco growing in the sandy soils of the southern Recôncavo, was not employed in cane farming. The plow was not employed regularly in Bahian sugarcane agriculture until the end of the eighteenth century. Axes, hoes, and mattocks were used to clear the land and prepare the soil for planting, and then a *fouce de cortar cana* (a short-bladed, heavy scythe) was used to cut the cane. These tools, the sweat of slaves, and the whip raised the cane for the Bahian engenhos.

The available land type had much to do with the productivity and preparation of the canefield. The Bahian Recôncavo was sometimes called the "birthplace of the massapé," referring to the heavy dark marl, rich in organic substances, that planters preferred for planting sugarcane. The massapé resulted from the decomposition of cretaceous sediments, and it formed a thick, claylike soil that conserved moisture well – too well, in fact: With heavy rains, massapé turned into a thick mud that impeded the carting of cane or sugar in the oxcarts that were used. Planters continually complained of the death of oxen caused by the labor of working in the massapé. This quality also probably lay behind the lack of the plow in cane agriculture, since the heavy and sticky mud was difficult to furrow using ox-drawn ploughs. On the other hand, massapé was thought to have its advantages. Sugarcane was a perennial plant, and a field once planted could yield four or six good harvests before replanting was necessary. Planters took a certain pride in the fact that with only yearly weedings so many crops could be taken from a field, and there are reports of massapé soils yielding twenty harvests without replanting or the use of fertilizers. Tradition had it that if you could stamp your boot up to the ankle in the massapé, it was ideal for sugarcane.

In addition to massapé, other soils in the Recôncavo were also planted in sugarcane. The reddish *salão* soils that resulted from the decomposition of crystalline deposits were sandier and held less moisture than the massapé but were also suitable for cane. In wet years, cane planted in these soils did better than in massapé, but planters felt that salões were "weaker" in that they did not yield as many good harvests from a single planting and tended to become exhausted more quickly. Ideally, an engenho would have a mixture of the two soil types. The third type of soil found in the Recôncavo was *areia*, a sandy, light-colored soil that was considered unsuitable for sugarcane cultivation and was usually given over to the growing of manioc or other food crops.

Virgin land with first growth, *mata*, on it, was cleared first by use of the ax and the hoe and then by burning. In Bahia, stumps and other obstacles were removed from the field, although elsewhere this was not the case. The field was then ready for planting, which in Bahia was done at two different times. Uplands were planted from the arrival of the rains in late February or early March until late May. Low-lying areas, especially the *várzeas*, or floodplains of the rivers, which conserved moisture well, were planted between June and September.[19] Cane could be planted upright in holes and sometimes was, but more common was the planting of cane pieces twelve to eighteen inches long in trenches. Usually, two pieces were laid side by side so that stronger roots would develop and the cane would be less susceptible to damage from the wind. The upright planting of cane was disliked because it left too much room between the canes and allowed weeds to invade the field. If a cane piece rotted or did not grow, it was quickly replaced to keep weeds from catching hold. The cane used as seed was usually older ratoons, later cuttings with lower yields, or it was *cana brava*, that is, first-growth cane from a virgin field that often grew long and narrow and was considered unsuitable for milling. It was estimated that one cartload of seed cane would produce five carts of cut cane.[20] In Brazil, newly cleared fields were sometimes planted first in vegetables or manioc to "soften" (*amassar*) the soil and prepare it for cane cultivation. Thus, the practice of letting slaves or poorer folk on the margins of the plantations plant food crops had a practical purpose from the plantation owners' point of view.[21]

Within two weeks, the shoots began to appear, and by two months the cane had reached a height of two feet or so. At this point, the most laborious part of the cultivation began in earnest. Canefields were weeded at least three times, and some were weeded even more. The first weeding was the most important because once the cane was well developed it would tend to suppress weeds itself and also because the blades of the mature cane were rough and sharp and made later weedings very unpleasant. The weeding of the canefields was continual, and whenever slaves had completed other tasks they were sent to clean the fields again. Extreme cold or lack of rain were destructive to the cane, as were the foraging of cattle, goats, and pigs. Planters also complained of passers-by who thought nothing of cutting a few canes for refreshment. In 1700, planters succeeded in obtaining legislation allowing them to kill any animal found in their fields and, although cattle raising was limited to areas at least fifty miles from the coast, the need for oxen in the sugar industry and the proximity of plantations caused continual squabbles. Some fencing of canefields was done, but the practice does not seem to have been common.[22]

Information on the size and shape of fields in Bahia is very sparse. Despite many paintings dating from the period of the Dutch occupation of the Brazilian Northeast (1630–54) that show the mills in detail, there is only one crude drawing of an engenho in which the cane fields are also represented. Thus we lack both detailed descriptions and iconography.[23]

Land in Bahia was measured in *tarefas*, a unit of thirty square *braças*. The *braça* was a measure equal to 2.2 meters, so the tarefa was an area of 4,352 square meters and was thus slightly larger than an acre.[24] There was, and is, a good deal of confusion about the tarefa because the term also means "task" and can be applied to piecework or daily quotas. It is often said that the areal tarefa was simply the amount of land needed to grow enough cane to keep the mill operating for one day. This would be an equivalence between the mill's task and the areal measurement. This equivalence may indeed have existed, but the origins of the areal measurement are much older and are bound to be found on the Iberian peninsula. Various measures of eastern Spain such as the *jornal* of Catalonia (4,351 sq.m.) or the jornal of Lerida (4,358 sq.m.), approximate the size of the Bahian tarefa.[25] The differences are inconsequential and indicate a presugar origin of this measure. The tarefa as a land measurement also varied regionally in Brazil. Thus, what the exact relationship of the areal tarefa was to the milling day remains problematical, but making the milling day equivalent to a land area made ratios and calculations of capacity easier for those who harvested and processed the sugarcane. Inventories of sugar properties indicate that fields were planted in units or tabuleiros of one to ten acres as a rule. The fields were usually separated by paths about five to six meters wide that served as firebreaks and allowed the carts to pass through the fields. Poor folk sometimes planted food crops in these spaces and harvested them before the cane cutting began.[26]

Newly planted cane needed fourteen to eighteen months to mature to a state at which it was ready to cut to make sugar. If it survived the dangers of wind, fire, weather, and foraging animals, the cane grew to a height of between five and a half and seven feet and was ready to be cut. Gangs of slaves, usually two or four dozen at a time, composed of men and women, were placed in the canefield. The men cut the cane using a fouce de cortar cana, chopping the tops from the cane, taking off the leaves, and cutting the stalk close to the ground. Women then bound the cane in bundles, which were placed in oxcarts that carried it to the mill or, if the canefield was located on a river or on the bay, to small boats that transported it there. Once cut, the cane would produce a new growth or ratoon about every twelve months, although the amount of liquid that could be extracted declined after the third or fourth cutting. The growth after the first cutting was called *soca*, after the second *resoca*, then *terceira soca* and so forth. Planters and cane farmers paid careful attention to the age, condition, and status of the canefields. Estate inventories reflect the differential value of the types of cane. In 1741, for example, a tarefa of soca was valued unweeded at 7$, with one weeding at 8$, and with two weedings at 10$. In 1816, the value of newly planted cane was placed at one-third higher than that of soca.

The harvesting schedule of an engenho was a complex process about which little information remains but which was a matter of central importance to engenho owners and to the cane farmers who brought their cane to be milled at the engenho. Antonil reported that old cane had to be cut first, and he lamented poetically that unfortunately the fouce of death did not follow the same rule in the harvest of men.[27] The cutting of cane actually depended on its age, the weather, and the type of land in which it was planted. Given the differing maturation periods for newly planted and ratoon cane, the trick was to arrange the planting so that fields would come to maturity in succession, thus allowing for consecutive cutting and a steady flow of cane to the rollers of the mill. Cane left standing too long in the field became dry and brittle and did not make good sugar. Once cut, the cane had to be milled in a day or two or else the liquid in it would dry or become sour. The need to process the cane immediately after cutting and to harvest it at a specific time placed great pressure on those who labored in the fields and on those who scheduled the engenho's operations. This pressure gave the whole safra a certain frenetic rhythm.

The engenho's milling schedule was also a crucial point of collaboration or dispute between the senhores de engenho and their dependent lavradores de cana. Most engenhos had at least two or three dependent cane farmers, and some had many more. Engenho Sergipe sometimes depended on the cane of as many as thirty when in the early seventeenth century it grew no cane of its own. This policy was denounced in 1660 as the principle cause of that estate's lack of profitability. Moreover, it was considered to be poor slave mangement since during the nonsafra months engenho slaves could be fully employed in growing cane.[28] Millowners or their administrators, then, had to project not only the maturation period of the estate's own cane but that of prospective cane farmers as well. An engenho that failed to mill a cane farmer's crop immediately after cutting or failed to cut it at the proper time could ruin it entirely. Thus the milling schedule became a central issue. Francisco de Negreiros, who administered Engenho Sergipe for the count of Linhares, complained that the only thing people sought him for was to make sure that their cane was milled before someone else's.[29] During the safra, it was common for slaves from the engenho to help dependent lavradores bring in their crop or for lavradores' slaves to do service for the engenho.[30]

The complex meshing of field management and milling operations – the knowledge of where and when to plant, of the time when cane was to be cut, of how many slaves were needed in a field, and of how many carts of cane a tarefa would yield – was, in effect, an artisan skill learned only with practice. As Antonil put it, the "counsel of old men whom time and experience had taught" was essential to operate an engenho.[31] The senhor do engenho, if he was resident, took responsibility for general oversight and organization; but, as a governor of Rio de Janeiro noted in 1694, there were often millowners who did not understand the first thing about making good sugar.[32] The *feitor-mor*, or general overseer, took over management in these circumstances, but he then depended on the knowledge and experience of the *feitores* (overseers) who worked in the canefields.[33]

The lack of scientific methods, the dependence on experience, means that estimates of the productivity of land and labor varied widely. Everything in Brazil, said Henry Koster, "is done by the eye."[34] Koster, an Englishman hired to manage a plantation in Pernambuco in the early nineteenth century who was imbued with a certain scientific spirit of the times that provoked him to much criticism of Brazilian agricultural methods, perhaps missed the point. The traditional methods of developing rough ratios between land, labor, and productivities could be learned by experience, and prior to scientific measurement these methods proved to be a relatively effective means of husbandry. The rule of thumb might change from place to place or be altered by a new piece of equipment, but the ratios could always be adjusted and relearned. These ratios, in fact, became essential to the successful operation of the plantation. From field to finished product, the making of sugar was a process or system of routines in which inputs were defined by area, number, and time. Created as an integrated system, based on roughly standardized units like the size of oxcarts, or the daily quota of cane a slave could cut, and dependent to some extent on the capacities of the technology like the speed of the mill or the size of the largest kettle, managers and workers could tell at a glance if the flow of work and production was moving along at the proper pace. The rhythms and dimensions were, in fact, a systematic means of labor organization, imperfect to be sure and dependent on the skill or art of the practitioner, but an integrated and useful system all the same.[35] As Bryan Edwards put it in describing Jamaican sugar estates, "A plantation . . . ought to be considered as a well-constructed machine, compounded of various wheels turning different ways, yet all contributing to the great end proposed; but if any one part runs too fast or too slow, in proportion to the rest, the main purpose is defeated."[36] So it was on the Bahian engenhos.

The dependence on estimate and experience coupled with the normal variations in productivity according to weather, soil, and skill in management led to widely varying estimates and expectations in the relationship of labor to production and of the various units of production to each other. Since we do not have continuous field-management data from a single engenho or group of engenhos, the variation in estimates made at different times cannot be used as an index of changing productivity because calculations varied widely among planters. Still, part of the process of sugarmaking was the ability of planters and their managers to make reasonable estimates of the work capacities of the slaves and the ratio of field units to amounts of sugar produced.

In Bahia, planters calculated the productivity of the tarefa in the number of boatloads or cartloads of cane it could produce. The Benedictine administrators at the Engenho São Bento dos Lages reported in 1656 that eight boatloads of cane had been planted in a new field.[37] Although this measurement appeared from time to time in Bahia,

Table 5-3. *Ratios of units used in Brazilian sugar production, 1584–1862*

Source	Date	Place	No. of canes/ carts	Type of mill	Tarefas	Cart Loads	Forms	Arrobas/ forms	lb.
A	1584	Bahia			1		65	0.5	1,040
B	1624	Pern.– Bahia			1				2,240
C	1639	Pern.		Oxen	1	30*	25	1–1.5	800– 1,200
				Water	1	45*	50	1–1.5	1,600– 2,400
D	1668	Bahia					3,575	6.690	
							1	1.9	
E	1689	Bahia	1,800			1			
			44,200	Water	1	24			
F	1733	Bahia					1	3.4	
G	1751	Bahia			1	30	15	3.0	1,440
						1	1.5		
H	1752	Bahia		Oxen	1		15		1,200
							1	2.5	
I	1781	Bahia			1	18	18		2,016
							1	3.5	
J	1798	Rio				1	1	2.2	
K	1798	Rio	c900– 1,200		1	9–10			
						1			
L	1798	Bahia	1,800–		1	1	1	3.7	
			2,100		1	12	12	(45)	1,440
M	1801	Bahia				600	715		
							1	1.2	4.9
N	1816	Bahia		Oxen	1	18	13	(33)	
							1	2.5	1,056
				Water	1	22	18	(63)	
								3.5	2,016
O	1865	Bahia			1				
P	1862	Rio	c600			1	1	2.5	
Q		Bahia				1		3.5	

Sources: A: Fernão Cardim, *Tratados da terra e gente do Brasil (1583),* 3rd ed. (São Paulo, 1978), 193. B: Joseph Israel da Costa, "Memorial," Algemein Rijksarchief (Hague) Staten Generaal, West Indische Compagnie loketkas 6. C: Adriaen van der Dussen, *Relatório sobre as capitanais conquistadas no Brasil pelos holandeses (1639),* ed. José Antônio Gonçalves de Mello (Rio de Janeiro, 1947), 80,93–6. D: ADB/CSB, 136,f. 71; data are from Engenho de Lages, safra 1667–8. E: André João Antonil, *Cultura e opulência do Brasil por suas drogas e minas,* ed. Andrée Mansuy (Paris, 1965), liv.2. F: Inventory of Luisa Ramos de Flores (1733), APB, sec. jud.,São Francisco, maço 7749,n.5.G: Câmara of Santo Amaro (3 July 1751), ACMS, Cartas do Senado 28.5. H: "Despeza e custo de hum engenho,"AHU, Bahia pap. avul., caixa 61 (1751). I: José da Silva Lisboa (18 Oct. 1781), *ABNR* 32 (1910): 494–505. J: Fazenda Santa Cruz–Rio de Janeiro, ANRJ, codice 18, fs.60–1. K: José Caetano Gomes, "Memorial sobre a cultura e produtos de cana-de-acucar," *Brasil Açucareiro* (March 1965): 162–75. L: Luís do Santos Vilhena, *A Bahia no século xviii,* 3 vols. (Bahia, 1969), I, 178. M: Engenho Buranhaem (Felix

where water transport was an integral part of engenho operations, measurement by oxcartloads was much more common. Antonil calculated that a cart could carry about 150 faggots of cane or about 1,800 canes and that 24 cartloads was equal to a tarefa (44,200 canes), or a milling day of eighteen to twenty hours.[38] This calculation depended, of course, on the size of the cane and that of the cart. The carts described by Antonil were eight *palmos* (a span; a measure of about 9 inches) by seven palmos (72 by 63 inches) and were apparently roughly standardized, but there was considerable variation in their size from plantation to plantation and between regions.[39] Given Antonil's estimate, a water mill in Bahia milled about 1.2 cartloads or 2,250 canes per hour.

The production from a tarefa of cane was figured in terms of the number of sugar loaves (*pães*) that it would make. Evidence from Engenho Sergipe and from van der Dussen's account of Pernambuco indicate that in the sixteenth and early seventeenth centuries small forms holding 16 to 32 pounds were used to make the loaves, although when particularly good sugar was made forms might hold up to 60 pounds.[40] The Engenho Sergipe records indicate that sometime in the 1660s a shift was made to the use of larger forms that could hold 2 to 4 arrobas (64–128 pounds). These apparently became standard in Bahia. By the eighteenth century, almost all observers believed that a cartload of cane would produce about one loaf of sugar with between 2.5 and 3.5 arrobas of sugar (80–112 pounds). Here, too, there was considerable variation depending on the quality of the cane and other factors. A report by senhores de engenho prepared in 1752 estimated that a tarefa of cane produced 15 loaves of sugar, each with 2.5 arrobas or 1,200 pounds. This estimate for the weight of the loaf and the number produced was on the low side of the range of possibilities. José da Silva Lisboa reported in 1781 that a tarefa produced 18 loaves of 3.5 arrobas or 2,016 pounds.[41] Even higher weights can be found in actual production records. Engenho Buranhaem in the safra of 1801 processed 600 carts of cane, which produced 715 loaves weighing a total of 3,754 arrobas (55 tons). Each cartload then produced 1.2 loaves and each loaf weighed almost 5 arrobas or 160 pounds.[42] As Table 5-3 demonstrates, this size was unusual.

The yield of sugar per tarefa is also difficult to calculate because of

Sources for Table 5-3 (*cont.*)

Betancourt Sá), ANRJ, caixa 406, pacote 1.N: Manoel Jacinto Sampaio e Mello, *Nova methodo de fazer acucar* (Bahia, 1816). O: João Monteiro Carson, *Primeiro relatorio . . . sobre os melhoramentos da cultura da canna* (Bahia, 1854). P: F. L. C. Burlamaque, *Monographia da canna d'assucar* (Rio de Janeiro, 1862), estimate by Gregório de Castro Morais e Sousa, Baron of Piriquara. Q: Ibid., estimate of José Augusto Chaves.

Table 5-4. *Comparison of colonial American sugar-plantation yields per acre*

Date	Place	Acres	Tons[a]	Tons/acre	Lb./acre	Kgs./ hectare[b]
1649	Barbados	198	268	1.35	2,970	3,335
1690	Barbados	40	36	.90	1,980	2,223
1727	St. Kitts	200	102	.51	1,122	1,260
1733	Barbados	200	190	.95	2,090	2,347
1755	Barbados	141	122	.86	1,892	2,124
1774	Jamaica	99	63	.64	1,408	1,581
1776–96	Jamaica	259	227	.88	1,936	2,174
1788	St. Domingue (Haiti)	207	220	1.06	2,332	2,618
1785	St. Domingue	254	197	1.37	3,014	3,485
1792–1808	Morelos	247	266	1.07	2,354	2,643
1822	Morelos	274	339	1.23	2,706	3,038
1584[c]	Bahia				967	1,086
1624	Bahia				2,083	2,339
1639	Pernambuco				1,860	2,088
1751	Bahia				1,339	1,503
1752	Bahia				1,116	1,253
1781	Bahia				1,875	2,105
1816	Bahia				1,875	2,105

[a]Calculated on the basis of 2,200 lb. [b]Calculated by multiplying lb./acre by 2.47 (acres/hectare) and then dividing by 2.2 lb./kg. [c]The Brazilian figures are taken from Table 5-3, but the calculation of lb./tarefa have been reduced by 7 percent to compensate fo the difference in size between tarefa and an acre.

Sources: See Table 5-3 for Brazilian estimates. All non-Brazilian citations are from the table pressented in Ward Barrett, *The Efficient Plantation, and the Inefficient Hacienda* (James Ford Bell Lecture No. 16; Minneapolis, 1979), 22, and the sources cited therein.

the variation in the other ratios estimated and because plant cane and ratoons had different yields per acre. If we assume that a tarefa was about equal to an acre, it is possible to place the Bahian estimates in comparison with the figures collected by Barrett for the Caribbean. When this is done, it is apparent that the Bahian estimates, which vary from 35 percent below to 22 percent above one ton a day, fall within the range of opinions collected by Barrett for the Caribbean. Plant cane yields were estimated at about twice those for ratoons. In Bahia, the estimates of eighteen or twenty-four loaves per tarefa, each with 80 to 112 pounds, produces a range of between 967 and 2,083 pounds per acre. Various observers in the Caribbean gave expected yields ranging from 1,066 to 3,000 pounds.[43] (See Table 5-4.)

In the Recôncavo, the cane was moved from the fields to the mills in small boats or in oxcarts. The oxcarts apparently varied in size, although their basic construction was similar throughout Northeast Brazil. Koster described those in Pernambuco as about six feet long by two and a half feet wide, made of heavy timber on solid wood wheels, and pulled by two or four oxen.[44] These vehicles can still be seen in rural Brazil today. Responsibility for moving the cane to the engenho by land fell on the lavrador entirely, but if boats could be used then the lavrador simply had to cart the cane to the dock where the boats of the Engenho could pick it up.[45] The transportation of cane and firewood was an important part of the sugar-making process, and the skills of slaves employed in it were highly valued. Carters and boatmen appear with regularity as listed occupations in inventories of Recôncavo slaves, and transportation-related activities constituted 8 percent of the declared occupations of slaves.[46]

Transportation problems were important in still another way. The length of the harvest season in Brazil was partially determined by the ability to move cane and sugar crates. The rainy months of May, June, and July were avoided for two reasons: First, the cane became wet, and the liquid acquired a high water content, which made it more difficult to process then. Second, the massapé became a quagmire in the heavy rains, preventing oxen and carts from passing through. João Peixoto Viegas had said in 1689 that the safra of eight months would last the whole year if the rains did not prevent the carting, and many observers commented on the toll that the rainy season took on the oxen.[47] The problem was further complicated by the lack of adequate roads and the fact that planters would not allow a right of way across their lands. Engenhos far from the coast or not on rivers suffered particularly from this situation. The governor of Bahia complained in 1799 that there were engenhos in the interior that produced 100 cases of sugar and were able to send only 18 to the city because of the problem of transport. He, and the merchants of Salvador, ascribed the problem to the avarice of some planters who refused to cede any land to public roads or to pasturage for the oxen at way stations on their land. Attempts to force roads through under a policy of eminent domain were not sucessful before 1830.[48]

The cane was deposited by the carts or boats at the main building in the plantation yard, the millhouse or *casa do engenho*. These were usually large structures that housed the mill rollers and the machinery that powered them; provided space for large amounts of cane; and in the case of animal-powered mills, were big enough to allow the animals to move unimpeded in their track around the rollers. We have excellent images of these large, shedlike buildings from the paintings of the Dutch landscape artist Frans Post, whose views of Brazil in the seventeenth century often included engenhos and whose attention to detail was precise.[49] A building at least 75 feet square was considered essential. The casa do engenho at Engenho Sergipe in the 1680s was one of the largest in Bahia and measured 140 feet in length. Located on the banks of a river to facilitate the arrival of cane and firewood in boats and built up on brick pillars, the Engenho Sergipe building was large enough to hold about eighty cartloads of cane.[50]

At the mill, the cane was fed through the rollers and liquid extracted from it. The cane was passed through in bundles ranging from two or three canes to a dozen. The number of times it was put between the rollers depended on the efficiency of the rollers and the power source.[51] Numerous passes, however, created problems because the bottom canes absorbed some of the liquid squeezed from those above and because the more pressing, the more pieces of stalk fiber and other impurities appeared in the liquid. The mills in Brazil were powered by a variety of means. The largest mills with the greatest capacities were water powered. Both undershot and overshot wheels were used, but the latter seem to have been the most popular. Usually, a large water-storage tank was constructed, and then an aqueduct (levada) was used to bring the water to the wheel. The tank constructed in 1625 by Francisco Vaz da Costa for his engenho on Itaparica Island had a capacity to hold the water for thirty to forty tarefas and cost 4$ – a substantial sum.[52] A water-powered mill was known as engenho real (royal mill), probably owing to its size and productivity, which in the mid-seventeenth century was calculated at about 50 arrobas (1,600 lb. or 73 kg.) a day, or twice that of an animal-powered mill.[53]

Although wind-powered mills known in some parts of the Caribbean were not used in Brazil, various kinds of animal traction were employed. Oxen were the most common in the sixteenth- and seventeenth-century Recôncavo mills. Used in teams of two or four at each end of the two or three sweeps that powered the rollers, oxen moved slowly but provided the force for powerful compression. In the eighteenth century, both horses and mules were also used. Animal-powered mills were less expensive to construct but called for the use of drivers, usually young boys, over each set of animals; these mills also demanded additional pasturage and expense for the animals themselves. It was estimated that an oxen-powered mill needed sixty animals.

The juice (caldo) extracted from the canes was gathered in a wooden trough and then run by means of a wooden pipe or channel into a large vat. From there it was ladled or poured into the first cauldron in the next steps in the process, clarifying and evaporation, which were carried out in the boiling house, or, as the Portuguese called it, the kettle house (casa das caldeiras).[54] Each engenho had a battery of large and small cauldrons (caldeiras), kettles (parões), and teaches (tachas) where heat of various temperatures was applied to the juice, removing the water and nonsaccharine materials so that at the end of the process granulation would occur. The kettles were usually placed in a linear arrangement, decreasing in size as the volume of the liquid was reduced. There was some variation in the number of kettles used, but between five and eight was normal.[55] A large engenho real like Sergipe with a high milling capacity had two batteries of kettles to accommodate the volume of juice extracted. In the largest cauldron, the *caldeira do meio*, the juice was heated to a subboiling temperature, impurities rose to the surface and were skimmed off, and then the remaining liquid was ladled into the next cauldron, the *caldeira de melar*, where it was further clarified by heating and by adding wood ash or lime. The skimmings at this point were used to make garapa (a low-grade alcoholic beverage for the slaves), or later skimmings were used to make a nonalcoholic beverage. The liquid by this time was called *meladura* as it became more purified and was then passed through the parões, where it was heated and strained.

At the last stage of the process, the liquid entered the tachas, where it was subjected to intense heat and "cooked." Unlike the early skimmings from the cauldron, which could be reprocessed, skimmings at this point were saved and used to make lower-grade sugars called *escumas*. Each of the tachas was named, and each had its special role.[56] In the last one, the *tacha de bater*, the liquid, now called *melado*, was stirred with a large wooden spatula that the kettlemen handled with great dexterity, lifting the liquid high in the air to observe its consistency. By sight, smell, and touch, the kettlemen and the sugar master could tell when the striking point had been reached and the liquid was ready to be poured into the molds.

The whole process of clarification and evaporation depended on the application of heat to the liquid extracted from the sugarcane. Thus, associated with the boiling house were the fires or furnaces necessary for heating the kettles. In the simplest form, these could be fires over which the kettles were hung, but in most Bahian engenhos, other, more complicated arrangements were made. Often the battery of kettles was placed along a wall and set in brick casings. The furnace below the kettles was actually in a sort of basement beneath the boiling-house floor, and it could be stoked from outside the building because the mouth of the furnace was placed in the outside wall. This arrangement can be seen in the restored building of Engenho Freguesia, and I observed it in 1973 at Engenho do Meio in Jaguaripe. Antonil spoke of a *casa das fornalhas* (furnace house) at Engenho Sergipe, but it is not clear how it was arranged in relation to the boiling house. Large engenhos usually had six furnaces, each manned by a slave whose job it was to put in the firewood and maintain the proper temperature. The use of the Jamaica train, that is, a single fire and a flue designed to reduce the amount of firewood needed in the process, was not generally practiced in Brazil, probably because the access to firewood never became so acute as to demand it and because of the difficulties in controlling the differences in temperature at the kettles and teaches with this system.[57] The wood ash from the furnaces was used as *deco-*

ada or temper and was added to the kettles at various points to aid in the process of clarification.

The heating process depended on large amounts of firewood, and supply of this item became a central concern and expense for most engenhos. About eight cartloads of well-sorted firewood was needed to process eighteen to twenty cartloads of cane.[58] Thus each furnace was, as many observers commented, a great open and insatiable mouth demanding to be constantly fed at great cost and labor. The fires and heat necessary for the sugar-making process also placed great stress on the kettles themselves. These were usually made of copper, and at least the larger caldeiras and parões were probably constructed in sections. Repair was constant, and as many as half the kettles often had to be replaced at the end of a single safra. The need to purchase copper was therefore another major item of expense for the engenhos. At Engenho Sergipe in the 1690s, the combined weight of the copper in the kettles was 175 arrobas, or more than 2.5 tons, in each of the two series of kettles used at that mill.[59] In a set of instructions given in 1663 to an estate administrator the kettles were called the "most important thing on the engenho."[60]

The melado was taken from the tachas in three stages. At the appropriate moment, the man who tended the tacha (the *tacheiro*), under the direction of the overseer of the kettles (the *banqueiro*) or the sugar master, removed some of the partially cooked liquid and placed it in an unheated kettle for partial cooling. It was then ladled into a group of four to five forms or pots. This was done twice more, with the liquid each time being further cooked. The forms were filled in steps because in Bahia almost all the engenhos made clayed sugar, that is, sugar that was made white by further purging of the forms by percolating water through the crystallizing sugar. Filling the forms with melado at various stages of cooking allowed the water to flow through the forms.

The forms were bell shaped, standing about 77 centimeters high and about 508 centimeters in circumference at the mouth. The bottom had a hole that was plugged with a banana leaf. This was essential in the purging process. Many engenhos had their own pottery works (*olaria*) and produced their own forms. Others bought forms from potteries around the the bay. Those of the southern Recôncavo, especially from Maragogipinho, became famous. The pretty red-clay pots with their white painted designs that grace so many Bahian homes today come from the same red clays of Maragogipinho that made the sugar forms. Engenhos paid between 60 and 200 réis for a form between 1680 and 1710. The lack of forms could be disastrous. The marquis of Lavradio as governor of Bahia complained in 1769 that the great safra of that year was lost because the planters had not prepared enough forms to accommodate the sugar produced.[61]

From the boiling house, the filled forms were carried by slaves to the purging house, the *casa de purgar*. This was normally a large oblong building separated from the millhouse and the kettles. There the forms were placed on boards in long rows. The large purging house at Engenho Sergipe described by Antonil was 98 meters long by 19 meters wide and had the capacity to hold two thousand forms. It was supported by brick pillars and lighted by twenty-six windows. The building also contained a broad space where after purging the crating of the sugar could be done.

The liquid in the forms was allowed to harden for about two weeks before a hole was bored in the sugar. The face of the form was then packed down and smeared with a specially prepared clay moistened with water. The water percolated through the mold, and as it drained it carried off remaining impurities and molasses. The molasses was collected in a wooden trough set beneath the forms and then placed in a large vat. The molasses could be used to make *aguardente* rum or went back to the purging house and was made into *batido* sugar, a lower grade. This percolation process was repeated as many as six times, depending on the quality of the sugar. The sugar at the top of the form became white, that in the middle somewhat darker, and that at the bottom very dark. Was it not a wonder, said Antonil, that the dirty mud turned the sugar white just as the mud of our sins mixed with tears of repentance could cleanse our souls?[62] (See Figure 5-3.)

In about four to six weeks, the sugar had crystallized and was ready to be taken from the molds. This was normally done outside in the sun on a raised platform called the *balcão*. The forms were inverted, and the sugar emerged in its characteristic sugarloaf shape. With a large knife or a hatchet, the bottom of the loaf was removed, and the brownish sugar in the middle was separated from the white sugar of the face of the loaf. The process of separation was called *mascavar*. The brown sugar was referred to as muscavado. The ratio of white to muscavado in a loaf depended on the quality of the sugar and on the skill of the purgers. In Bahia, a ratio of 2:1 was often used as an average, although figures of 3:1 and as low as 4:3 can also be found. The sugar loaves were then placed on cloths on a drying platform, where they were successively broken into smaller and smaller pieces to remove any remaining moisture. After drying, the sugar was ready for weighing and crating.

The engenhos of Bahia produced a variety of sugar grades and types. Brazil was famous and its sugar especially prized in Europe because most of it was "clayed" and thus produced the distinctive white sugar sometimes simply called "Brazil sugar."[63] According to its clarity, it was graded as *fino, redondo,* or *baixo.* In addition, brown or muscavado was also exported in large quantities to Europe. Both these types were considered to be *macho* if made from the first processing of the cane

Figure 5-3. The making of "clayed" sugar. Bahia specialized in the production of white sugar in which a preliminary process of refining was applied at the mill. This series of drawings demonstrates the steps in the purging house: (1) The racks in the purgery with channels beneath the forms are ready to drain the molasses. (2) The forms are pierced to allow the crystallizing sugar to drain. (3) Placed in the racks for two weeks, the forms begin to drain. (4) The tops of the forms are scraped and tapped solid. (5) Moist clay is applied over the faces of the forms. (6) After two or three days, water is gently poured over the clay. This process is repeated as many times as the quality of the sugar demands. (7) In the forms, the clay crystallizes into white sugar (*cara*) at the top, brown (muscavado) in the middle, and dark (*panela*) in the foot, or *cabucho*, of the form. (8) The loaves are taken from the forms. (9) The feet are separated. (10) The faces are separated. (11) The sugar is pounded into bits and prepared for crating.

liquid. As was just mentioned, white and muscavado sugar made from skimmings of the first processing by returning these to the kettles was called batidos and considered a lower grade because of the coarser granulation. Escumas sugars made from later skimmings were considered an even lower grade and were rarely exported. The sugar that had not drained of molasses in the molds was called *panela* or sometimes *panela preta* and was exported in small amounts, especially in the sixteenth and seventeenth centuries. Finally, there was the by-product, molasses.[64] It is difficult to calculate the ratio between arrobas of sugar produced and units of molasses, but in 1781 the value of molasses added about 20 percent to the value of a tarefa of sugar.[65] Eventually, with the growth of population the distillation of molasses into rum became an industry of some importance in Brazil. Some sugar-growing regions like Campos and Parati in Rio de Janeiro specialized in rum production. In Bahia, it was always a secondary activity but an important one. Some observers believed that the engenhos broke even on the production of white and muscavado sugar and that it was the panelas and molasses, which unlike the higer-graded products did not have to be divided with the lavradores, that provided their margin of profit.

From the beginning of the industry, Brazilian sugar was shipped to Europe in large wooden crates (*caixas*). These were usually made of jequitiba or camasari wood and in the late seventeenth century measured about 6 by 2 feet (183 by 61 centimeters). Unless the engenho had its own sawmill, the boards were bought precut and assembled at the engenho. The crates were lined with paper and then filled with the loose sugar, which was tamped into the crate. Each engenho usually employed a crater (*caixeiro*) to oversee the packing of the crates and to keep an accounting of the number of crates prepared, the quality of sugar each contained, the weight of the crate, and the division of sugars between the mill and the lavradores. It was also the task of the caixeiro to subtract the tithe and to collect from the lavradores that portion of their production owed to the mill as ground rent.[66] A number of inventories like that of Manoel Lopes Henriques (1706) mention the caixeiro's account book as evidence of production, and though none of these registers has appeared to date, the keeping of such records seems to have been common. The position of caixeiro was usually filled by free persons, but occasionally slaves served here as well.[67]

The packaging of sugar for shipment might seem a relatively uncomplicated and straightforward matter, but, in fact, it was a continual source of dispute between producers and merchants and often involved the government as well. The problem revolved around two issues: the weight of a crate and the declared quality of its contents.

Throughout the history of the Bahian sugar industry, the problem of standardizing the weight of sugar crates proved difficult. In the sixteenth and early seventeenth centuries, the sugar-crate size varied widely. A number of observers placed the weight at 20 arrobas (640 lb.), but there was considerable variation from crate to crate.[68] In fact, using the shipping records of the merchant Miguel Dias de Santiago (1596–1602) and those of the Engenho Sergipe (1608–18), it is possible to establish with some precision the weight of sugar crates in this period.[69] These records demonstrate that the weight of a crate of white sugar was 14 arrobas (448 pounds), with relatively little variation between crates. Muscavado sugar varied more widely in crate weights, although it, too, averaged about 14 arrobas per crate. The lower-grade panela sugars were crated more erratically, varying from 7 to 17 arrobas per crate. Thus estimates of crate weights depend in this period on the type of sugar being shipped. In general, however, the average weight of a full sugar crate in this period was about 14 to 15 arrobas.[70]

During the seventeenth century, the tendency was for the size of the crate to increase. The Dutch during their occupation of the Northeast seemed to favor crates that held 20 to 24 arrobas. By the end of the century, crates twice that size were sent from Brazil. This caused great problems in the customshouses because workers refused to handle the oversize containers. The crown moved to limit the weight of a crate to 35 arrobas in 1695, but complaints from producers resulted in raising the limit to 40 arrobas three years later.[71] This weight was to include that of the crate itself.[72] Any excess of sugar over the prescribed weight was subject to confiscation by the royal treasury. Antonil spoke of crates weighing between 35 and 40 arrobas, and this seems to have become standardized by the early eighteenth century (although larger crates sometimes were still used). A listing of chests shipped from Bahia to Lisbon in 1741 averaged 39 arrobas of sugar per crate.[73] In addition to these large crates, smaller boxes (fechos) were sent in small numbers on the fleets that moved between Brazil and Portugal. The fechos were about one-third to one-half the size of the larger crates. Finally, caras or small packages of fine white sugar were also sent as gifts in the fleets.

By the mid–eighteenth century, the weight of a caixa seems to have been standardized at 40 arrobas – but not always. Occasional references to heavier crates appear. In 1792, for example, senhores de engenho complained that their slaves had to help the warehouse owners weigh the incoming crates, which held "fifty to sixty or more arrobas."[74] The warehouse owners denied this and said that 40 arrobas was the standard weight, but other references seem to confirm that heavier crates were not unknown.

Related to the problem of the weight of the sugar crates was that of the declared quality of the sugar they contained. From the inception of the sugar trade from Brazil, there had been complaints of falsification of the weight and quality. Low-grade sugars were sometimes declared as white, batidos as machos; white sugar might be placed at the top of the crate and then lower grades beneath it; sometimes, even rocks were placed in the bottom of the crates to increase the weight. Lisbon merchants complained that such practices gave Brazilian sugar a poor reputation and made its sale difficult in the rest of Europe. Planters argued that discrepancies in weight were often due to mishandling on the docks and that the quality also suffered when the crates were allowed to sit too long exposed to the elements. Beginning in the 1650s, the government tried to resolve the problem. In 1657, the governor of Brazil, Francisco Barreto, issued an order (*bando*) that each engenho was to number its crates consecutively, clearly mark the grade, and indicate with a specific mark or brand whether the crate contained sugar belonging to the engenho or to a lavrador.[75] The individual brands were to be registered by the câmara of Salvador. In 1687, this system was made general with the further requirement that the quality (fino, redondo, baixo) also be indicated on the crate. Any misrepresentation would result in a fine for the caixeiro and a sentence of two years penal exile in Portugal.[76]

By the time the Brazilian fleet system was in full operation at the close of the seventeenth century, the marking system in Bahia was standardized. By 1702, the governor of Brazil noted that both sugar and tobacco were appropriately marked and that each warehouse (trapiche) kept separate lists. Some of these have survived, and on them we can see the brands used. Like cattle brands, the marks on the sugar crates often combined the producer's initials in an imaginative way.[77] (See Figure 5-4.)

The standardization of marking did not eliminate the conflict between merchants and planters over this matter. In 1709, the merchants again complained that the crates were not being marked truthfully and that the law of 1687 was usually ignored. The governor at Bahia, Lourenço de Almeida, held an inquest. He reported that the merchants' complaints were self-serving and that discrepancies in quality were due not only to poor handling. He suggested that, because the agents who bought the sugar in Brazil always checked the quality, perhaps it was their fault and not that of the planters if when the crates arrived in Lisbon the quality was lower.[78] Planters continually laid the blame on others; on caixeiros, agents (*comisários*), or the merchants themselves. Merchants sought to place responsibility at the feet of the planters. The argument continued, with the planters generally successful in maintaining the status quo. In 1736, for example, when the Overseas Council inquired whether it might be advantageous to ship sugar in barrels rather than crates, the câmara of Salvador flatly rejected the idea.[79]

To some extent, the creation of boards of inspection at the main Brazilian ports in 1751 was a government attempt to deal with the continuing problem of fraud and mishandling in the shipping of Brazilian sugar and other agricultural products. We shall discuss the board and its purposes in Chapter 15, but its function as a government clearing house and registry for sugar is important for our discussion here. Both merchants and planters ranted against the creation of the

Figure 5-4. Some sugar-crate identification marks from the fleet of 1702: (a) Manoel de Chaves, (b) Padres da Companhia de Jesus da Bahia, (c) Cristóvão de Mello, (d) Pedro Barbosa Leal, (e) Cristóvão Coelho Ferreira, (f) Cristóvão de Burgos, (g) Religiosos de Nossa Senhora do Monte de Carmo da Bahia, (h) Colégio de Santo Antão de Lisboa (Jesuitas), (i) Gregório Soares, (j) Antônio da Rocha Pitta.

boards, though for different reasons. Planters objected particularly to the price-fixing powers of the board, but they also disliked a new and more stringent system of quality control and indentification. Even with this government control, complaints about discrepancies did not appear, and now planters could also bemoan the extra fees charged by the board for weighing the crates. In 1772, the board ordered that crates should be weighed and that the owners of the warehouses could charge 480 réis per crate, a sum almost twice that formerly allowed by the câmara. When, in 1782, the board, to avoid fraud, ordered that the crates be weighed on entering and then again on leaving the warehouse and that handling charges could be made at each weighing, the planters were furious.[80] Merchants in Portugal were no less displeased with the boards of inspection. Between 1798 and 1808, a sugar inspector (confiteiro) examined the sugar crates to check on the quality of their contents.[81] The boards of inspection objected vigorously, claiming that these officials had no legal right to do this. What had once been a matter of planters versus merchants had become by the end of the colonial era a dispute between two government agencies.

The search for improvements

The process we have just traced from canefield to finished crate of sugar remained essentially the same in Brazil from the late sixteenth to the late eighteenth centuries with very few modifications. Undoubtedly, there was an expansion in production in the early stages of the industry as more land or labor was put into use, equipment was improved, and management techniques became more effective. The average production of a mill reported by Gandavo in 1570 (3,000 arrobas), Cardim in 1584 (4,000–5,000), and Brandão in 1618 (5,000–10,000) seems to reflect these improvements.[82] Still, the basic techniques of sugar making remained relatively unchanged throughout the period. The Brazilian system was in the seventeenth century considered the best as was evidenced by the desire of other colonial powers to copy it. Portuguese sugar masters and other specialists were employed in Mexico in the period between 1580 and 1640, and the English in Barbados learned how to make clayed sugar by sending people to Pernambuco to acquire the needed skills.[83] Only in the mid–eighteenth century, when the Brazilian sugar economy was in crisis and Caribbean rivals had developed some new techniques, did the Brazilian sugar industry begin to acquire a reputation for being traditional and backward; even then, the charge was undeserved.

Field management and agricultural techniques remained essentially unchanged throughout the period under discussion. The system of dividing canefields into small squares in the planting process that was used in Antigua, the Danish West Indies, and elsewhere in the Caribbean was not introduced into Brazil. Eighteenth-century critics such as Santos Vilhena complained that the plow was not used for cane agriculture and that planters insisted on using the "backward" system of hoeing. In fact, the plow was used in cane agriculture as early as the second decade of the eighteenth century. Antônio da Fonseca Rego, a lavrador de cana at Engenho Velho in Paraíba prosecuted by the Inquisition in 1729, listed an iron plow among his possessions.[84] The Benedictine Fathers of Rio de Janeiro reported in 1770 that at Engenho Camorim, "a new field of cane was planted that will yield 100 carts of cut cane; two old fields were worked with a plow so that they could be planted anew."[85] Its use was not widely diffused in areas like Bahia, not because of the atavism of the planters, but because the massapé soil – wet, heavy, and sticky – was extremely difficult to work with the oxen-pulled plow. Reformers in the late eighteenth century saw in the absence of the plow and in the continuity of agricultural techniques a cause of Brazil's ills, and as we shall see, they offered many suggestions for change.

Although Brazilian sugar producers seem to have been relatively satisfied with their field methods, there was a continual, if unsuccessful, search for improvements in the more industrial aspects of sugar making. The only major breakthrough came at the beginning of the seventeenth century. Until then, the machinery used to make sugar in Brazil did not differ significantly from that used on the Atlantic islands and in the Mediterranean region. Early mills made use of a large and heavy millstone (mó) that passed over the cane after it had been cut into small pieces.[86] This method did not extract the full amount of liquid from the cane, and the pieces were thus placed in a type of screw press (gangorra), where they were subjected to another pressing. This system in which two presses were needed was expensive and the liquid produced was so filled with impurities from the crushing that it called for further steps in preparation before the process of heating could begin. Also in use in Brazil was the cylindrical mill composed of two large meshed, horizontal cylinders driven by water or animal power. This mill had a distinct advantage in that the cane could be passed directly between the rollers and did not need to be cut into small pieces, but because of the way in which it was contructed, it did not press the cane thoroughly,and the gangorra press was still needed. The two-roller mill was heavy and cumbersome and, when driven by animal power, expensive as well. At least a hundred oxen divided into teams were needed to power this machine with all that this meant in pasture, feed, care, and replacement. Thus, although the two-roller mill was an improvement over other milling arrangements, its costs and perhaps complexity of construction slowed its diffusion in Brazil. As the historian Antônio Barros de Castro has put it, "It was a half-advance, offering a solution that was transitory."[87]

Figure 5-5. The three-roller vertical mill. A reconstruction of an ox-driven moenda at Engenho Freguesia in the Recôncavo.

Sometime between 1608 and 1613, a new type of mill was introduced into Brazil.[88] It, too, was a system of rollers. However, instead of two horizontal ones, the rollers were now placed in a vertical position, and the power source was directly attached to a third roller, which became a sort of drive shaft moving the other two rollers, as can be seen in Figure 5-5. Cane could be passed into the rollers from both directions, thereby increasing the pace of operation. And with the weight of the machinery shifted to a base (rather than resting on one of the rollers, as in the horizontal system), smaller cylinders could be used. Thus the new mill was sometimes called the *moenda de palitos* (mill of little sticks) because of the reduced size of its major components. The new mill offered great advantages: It was easier to construct, pressed the cane better and thus did away with the need for secondary presses, did not demand such great amounts of animal power, and could mill cane at a faster rate. Engenho Sergipe in the Recôncavo first adopted it in 1617, and it quickly spread throughout the colony.[89] The increase in construction of new engenhos noted after 1612 is most certainly due to this technological advance and to the lower costs of the three-roller mill compared to the previous system. The financial and social implications of the new mill for the relationships of sugar producers to the crown and of cane growers to millowners are particularly important and will be discussed in Chapter 11.

Figure 5-6. An engenho in operation as viewed by the Dutch naturalist Willem Piso.

Who was responsible for this technological breakthrough is a still-unanswered question. Frei Vicente do Salvador, Brazil's first historian, wrote in 1627 that a Spanish priest coming from Peru introduced the new mill during the administration of Dom Diogo de Meneses. On the other hand, we have the petitions for reward by Gaspar Lopes Coelho, who claimed to be the "inventor of the *molinete de tres paus.*" Lopes Coelho had lived in Pernambuco, where he earned a living as a *mestre de engenhos,* a builder of mills, and he claimed, among other abilities and accomplishments, that his invention had brought new lands under cultivation and much new revenue to the royal treasury.[90] The resolution of the problem may be that suggested by Antônio Barros de Castro. The priest coming from Peru probably learned of the techniques used for milling ore in the silver-mining process. He then explained these to an engenho builder like Gaspar Lopes Coelho, who in turn put these concepts into practice through his knowledge of mechanical engineering. Thus both Frei Vicente's account and Lopes Coelho's claims are possibly accurate.[91] In any case, the introduction of the three-roller vertical mill was a major technological change, and it was the only one of any real importance for almost the next two centuries. Bahian mills in the 1790s produced sugar in almost exactly the same way it had been produced in the 1640s (See Figure 5-6).

"Inventors" and "new methods" abounded, but none brought about the changes or improvements that they promised. Almost all the innovations suggested prior to the late eighteenth century were designed as cost-saving devices intended to increase the planters' margin of profit rather than the mill's productivity. These innovations tended to concentrate on the power source of the mill itself or on the heating system for cauldrons. The surviving documentation does not permit us to examine in detail what the innovators had in mind exactly, in most cases, but it is possible to surmise the objectives of their proposals.

The first innovation to follow the introduction of the three-roller mill was suggested by Juan Lopes Sierra to the câmara of Bahia about 1656. Sierra, a Spaniard with literary pretensions, claimed to have developed a new method of boiling the sugar syrup that used less firewood.[92] As we have seen, firewood costs sometimes reached over one-third of an engenho's expenses, and thus such claims always found a willing ear. But there is no evidence that Sierra's method was adopted or that it had any effect. Perhaps the most famous "invention" of the seventeenth century was that proposed to the crown in 1663 by a certain Claudio Urrey through the royal representative in Amsterdam.[93] Urrey noted that, given the low price of sugar and the high cost of producing it, his invention would be of great benefit, especially to lavradores de cana, who would no longer need to have their cane milled by others. The invention was apparently a new mill in which the power of two slaves would replace the need for horses and oxen. Whether the Urrey mill was connected to the political flurry that erupted in Bahia over the limitation on new engenho construction is unknown, but certainly his innovation would have upset the social balance between millowners and the lavradores de cana. In any case, there does not seem to be any evidence that his smaller and less expensive mill was widely adopted in Brazil. In fact, in 1694 André Pesanha, a resident of Salvador, claimed to have invented a new mill that ground the cane without the use of horses or oxen but only with "two Negroes," just as the Urrey mill was supposed to have done. Pasanha received what amounted to a patent with the right to collect 50$ from whoever adopted the invention, but the lack of evidence that such payments were made casts doubt that it was in fact used.[94]

The last years of the seventeenth century and the first years of the eighteenth were a time of increasing interest in technological and cost-saving change. Faced with rising operational costs, especially in the price of slaves, sugar planters and the government listened attentively, if futilely, to other schemes such as Pesanha's. In 1693, Diogo Soares Alemão claimed to have introduced a new furnace system into Brazil in the 1680s and wanted to receive compensation from those who adopted it. The crown was interested enough in the project to order the governor of Bahia to set up a commission of sugar masters and planters to examine the innovation. In 1697, the governor informed the crown that the innovation was useful because it allowed the mills to make use of smaller pieces of firewood in the new furnaces.[95] Although the crown was pleased by this innovation, there is no evidence that it was widely adopted or that costs of production were reduced in any significant way.

Petitions for patents and government interest in stimulating the sugar industry continued into the following century. Each inventor usually sought financial compensation from anyone adopting his innovation. The municipal and royal officials usually went along with these requests, although the supposed improvements often proved to be ephemeral. In 1702, Dionísio Pinto Passos suggested a new method for grinding cane. In 1705, a certain Bartolomeu Lorenço at the seminary of Belem developed a way of raising water to be used as power for mills, and he received a patent for it. Neither of these innovations was heard of again.[96] In 1732, Manoel de Almeida Mar, an infantry captain in Bahia, claimed to have invented a mill that could operate with only one horse, so that only six horses a day were needed instead of six teams of four to eight horses. The savings in livestock, pasture, and slaves to guard the horses would be great, he claimed, and he asked for an award of 400$ from any engenho that adopted his system. The governor, the count of Sabugosa, felt that the invention would not live up to Almeida Mar's claims, but given the great expenses faced by the sugar planters anything that might lower costs should be encouraged.[97] This was the position that the colonial officials were forced to take as the ingenuous and the greedy sought continually to break the technological limits of the colonial sugar industry.

It was once again motor power that brought the next group of suggested innovations. Manoel de Abreu recieved support from the câmara of Salvador for a method of driving the mills using only one horse, and he was awarded a patent entitling him to 50$ from each adopting plantation.[98] His proposal was followed in 1766 by that of Francisco Machado de Miranda, who claimed that by using one mule at night and one during the day his new method would bring great savings. Although the câmara of Salvador listened to, and even solicited opinions from, the câmaras of Santo Amaro, Cachoeira, and São Francisco in the Recôncavo, once again there is no evidence of any effect on the industry.[99] The desire for improvement and reform continued, however, and began to intensify in the last decades of the century.

For more than three centuries, the safra cycle set the pace of life in the Recôncavo and in the other regions of sugar production. Although the techniques of cane cultivation and sugar making changed little, the desire for improvements that would reduce costs or facilitate production was always present. Still, with a few notable exceptions, sugar making remained a relatively conservative industry. But it was a complex and costly activity that demanded considerable skills and resources from owners, managers, and workers. Combining as it did large inputs of gang labor in the field with a need for skill and experience in the mill and purgery, the sugar plantation created a socially differentiated labor force. But within a regime of varied forms of labor, slavery held sway, set the parameters of all other labor types and social relations, and tended by its very centrality to devalue them. Plantation slavery in Bahia was not unproductive, nor was it inherently antithetical to technical innovation; but as in classical antiquity, it provided a matrix of social relations and attitudes that debased all labor.

Although the sugar plantation characterized the early formation of the Brazilian economy, eventually slavery proved to be a labor form particularly adaptable to other agricultural activities and to urban settings as well. Salvador and other Brazilian cities depended fully on slave muscle, and no area of the rural economy was without slaves.

It is the adaptability of slavery that makes it so theoretically difficult to characterize and classify. Slavery and freedom may seem to be polar opposites in juridical and social definition, but they never were in Brazilian reality. Thus, although it is possible to argue theoretically about how slaves should behave given the objective situation of their labor and their servitude, they did not always do so because conditions could be created by their masters and sometimes by the slaves themselves that mitigated or modified that situation.

An example of this theoretical difficulty is presented in a statement like that of Immanuel Wallerstein, that "slaves . . . are not useful in large-scale enterprises whenever skill is required." Wallerstein holds this position because he believes that "slaves cannot be expected to do more than they are forced to do. Once skill is involved, it is more economic to find alternative methods of labor control, since the low cost is otherwise matched by very low productivity." Wallerstein's position bears much similarity to that of Max Weber but is also shared by Marxist scholars.[100] For Wallerstein, slavery is possible on sugar plantations because these call for crude gang labor, but a close examination of the sugar-making process indicates a relatively advanced and complex technology and process in which slaves fully participated. The existence of slavery in large-scale skilled enterprises would indeed be theoretically difficult if slavery was simply an unchanging system of brutal labor exploitation in which masters could exact work only by force. Although cruel coercion was always present, the demands of sugar production created the need and opportunity for other methods of extracting labor, even skilled labor. It is certainly true that free workers tended to appear in those occupations on the engenhos that demanded the most skills, but they never completely replaced slaves, and in fact on some estates slaves did everything. Plantation slavery proved less rigid than its interpreters have often made it.

CHAPTER 6

WORKERS IN THE CANE, WORKERS AT THE MILL

> . . . peoples the color of the very night working intensely and moaning together without a moment of peace or rest; who sees all the confused and tumultuous machinery and apparatus of that Babylon can not doubt though they may have seen Vesuvius or Mount Etna that this is the same as Hell.
>
> Padre Antônio Vieira (1633)

The crucial element in the manufacture of sugar was the slaves. The conditions under which they lived and worked are a key to the nature of the society that grew from the sugar economy. The relationships of slaves to engenhos and of slaves to the means and process of production are foci of concern. A great deal has been written about the physical condition of slaves in Brazil, although much of it is contradictory. This chaper will briefly outline these physical conditions, but the fundamental topic here will be the work of sugar making, its nature and requirements, for this above all determined the life of the men and women who labored in field and mill.

In the seventeenth century, many planters seem to have subscribed to the three-p theory of slave management mentioned by Antonil: *pau* (the rod), *pão* (bread), and *pano* (clothing).[1] Foreign observers such as Johan Nieuhoff, who visited Brazil in that century, invariably spoke of the brutality of the slave regime and noted that Brazilian slaves were poorly fed, housed, and clothed.[2] The comments of observers whose nationality or religion made them naturally inclined to criticize the Portuguese might be discounted were it not for similar observations made by Portuguese clerics who also pointed accusingly at inhuman masters. Both the ameliorationist clerics and the foreign observers shared with the planters a low regard for Africans in any case, and both held that discipline, chastisement, and work were the only way to overcome the slaves' superstition, indolence, and lack of civility.

Coercion and material conditions

Physical force or punishment was an integral aspect of plantation slavery and served by its reality and threat as a negative incentive. Among the most hallowed myths of Brazilian slavery is the belief that, despite the sometimes sadistic and capricious punishments meted out by jealous wives or bestial overseers, slaves in general were not subjected to continuous or particularly cruel coercion or punishment.[3] This situation supposedly existed because of the close personal relations between masters and slaves, the intervention of church and state, and finally because of logic of slaveownership that made the mistreatment of valuable property senseless and irrational. Slaveowners, of course, varied greatly as individuals, and some were worse than others; but the whim of a sadist who could make the lives of his bondsmen a living hell is not the matter in question here. The slave regime itself created conditions in which the exercise of dominance that called for extreme physical force or punishment was a logical and in fact necessary element of the regime. A Portuguese refrain of the seventeenth century ran: "Whoever wants to profit from his Blacks must maintain them, make them work well, and beat them even better; without this there will be no service or gain."[4]

Slaves had little recourse from the punishments given them. Unless the punishment resulted in death and someone was willing to bring it to the attention of civil authorities, little or nothing could be done. Engenho owners and overseers ran the slave quarters with very little outside interference. Most commentators on slavery in Bahia at least mentioned the common cruelty of the slave regime. Antonil believed that brutal abuse led slave women to abort themselves rather than bear children to live in bondage.[5] The Bahian author Nuno Marques Pereira commented on the cruelty of many masters. When one slaveowner defended his actions by claiming that the slaves were like devils, Marques Pereira responded, "It is the master that makes the slave, and not the slave the master." He lamented, "Oh, state of Brazil, how I fear . . . a great punishment because of the bad governance that many of your inhabitants have with their slaves and families."[6]

These sentiments were echoed by various ecclesiastics who had an opportunity to observe the institution of slavery at close range in Bahia. The Italian Jesuit Jorge Benci, who lived in Bahia at the beginning of the eighteenth century, wrote and published a small book exhorting masters to treat their bondsmen humanely. His *Economia cristã dos senhores no governo de escravos* dealt with the various types of "treatment," and it instructed slaveowners to feed, clothe, work, and punish their slaves with Christian charity.[7] Never denying the legality of slavery or the inferiority of the slaves, Benci argued nevertheless that the "rudeness" or barbarity of the slaves should excuse them from too severe a judgment of their faults and that punishment should be given with moderation. But the situation he observed was quite different. Slaves were burned or scorched with hot wax, branded on face or chest, tortured with hot irons, had their ears or noses lopped off, or suffered sexually related barbarities as the result of jealousy. Was such behavior, he asked slaveowners of Brazil, rational or humane?[8] Benci was joined in his position by Manoel Ribeiro Rocha, a Portuguese secular priest who also lived in Bahia. His *Ethiope resgatado* (1758) took a similar line of argument and went even further in its denunciation of slavery.[9]

Jesuits and the authors of moralistic tracts might seem unreliable sources on the matter of slave punishment and physical abuse except that there is similar evidence from contemporaneous legal or administrative documents. Masters were occasionally apprehended when their crimes against their slaves became common knowledge. Francisco Jorge was arrested for whipping a slave to death, but his appeal in 1678 – that he was a poor man with a wife and family and that the story was a creation of his enemies – won him a pardon from the relação.[10] A similar case occurred in 1737, when Pedro Pais Machado, senhor of Engenho Capanema, was arrested for killing two slaves and a freedman, one of whom was hung in the engenho by his testicles until he perished. Pais Machado was released after a judicial investigation that noted, among other things, that the defendant was "a noble person with family obligations." In this case, the slaves belonged to another owner, but Pais Machado had apparently felt no reluctance in punishing them to death for the crime of having injured an ox.[11]

The recurrence of such acts led the government to institute regulations that would provide the slaves some legal protection. In 1688, two laws were issued that gave anyone, including the slaves themselves, the right to denounce cruel slaveowners to civil or ecclesiastical authorities. Slaveowners could be forced to sell their slaves to someone else if proof could be given that continued ownership might result in unjust treatment.[12]

A case arose on these grounds soon thereafter when Dona Ana de Cavalcanti, member of one of the most powerful families of Bahia, was forced to sell her female slave, Ursula.[13] Government vigilance in such matters continued for a decade. In 1700, the relação was ordered to investigate reports of mutilation, starvation, and excessive punishments meted out to slaves.[14] Another slave petitioned for state intervention in her case in 1701 when an acrimonious dispute arose over a contested manumission.[15] The crown favored the slave's petition and ordered that the owner be constrained to sell the slave, who feared for her life. The governor of Bahia, Dom João de Lencaste, refused to enact the crown's order. He claimed that this case would set an extremely dangerous precedent, leading slaves to believe that they could obtain their freedom simply by bringing suit against their masters. Such a situation was an obvious danger to the whole ideology on which slavery rested, and although the governor couched his objections in moral terms, fearing a rise in sorcery, theft, and offenses to God caused by freed slaves, his real fear was based on other considerations. He resorted, therefore, to the old formula of the Spanish-American viceroys: "I obey but do not comply."[16] This kind of foot dragging by royal officials who supported the position of the sugar planters and other slaveowners prevented any restructuring of the nature of Brazilian slavery from above.

Rare instances did occur when royal officers or the courts intervened to free slaves endangered by their masters or to punish slaveowners who mistreated or murdered their slaves. João de Argolo e Meneses, a sugar planter, was sentenced to five years of penal exile in 1747 for having killed two of his slaves.[17] More common were instances when freemen were prosecuted for killing or abusing someone else's slaves.[18] In such cases, property rights were involved, and the action thus transcended the relation between a master and his slave. The relação could prosecute such a case to the limit of the law, and in rare instances the death penalty was applied. This is what took place when in 1806 two men were sentenced for killing a *pardo* (light-skinned mulatto) slave.[19] Such situations were the glaring exception. Far more common were instances of freemen and slaveowners who mistreated or abused slaves and were subsequently pardoned or exonerated.[20] The usual defense was that the charges were trumped up by the slaveowner's enemies, and if the master was a person of substance with a family or other obligations, the courts proved lenient. Probably most common of all, however, was an absence of prosecution of any sort when slaves were involved. In a list of people prosecuted in Cachoeira between 1780 and 1838, no masters' names appear for crimes against their bondsmen.[21] Their absence most likely reflects a basic policy of noninterference or an ability to uncover such abuses rather than their nonexistence. This situation was destined to continue as long as slaves were effectively barred from bringing charges against their masters. Despite the suggestions of reformers to permit their testimony, slaves in practice had little opportunity to gain the ear of local judges, who themselves were often closely aligned with the planters' interests. In a mid–eighteenth-century case, Garcia d'Avila Pereira Aragão, heir to the Casa da Torre and one of Bahia's wealthiest residents, was denounced to the Inquisition for a sickening series of sexual and physical extravagances carried out against his slaves. Despite much confirming testimony, the tribunal took no action against him.[22] Physical coercion, mistreatment, and sometimes sadistic cruelty remained very real parts of Bahian slavery throughout the colonial era.

If harsh punishments reflected extraordinary situations, daily living conditions in the main were little better. The creature comforts of engenho slaves were minimal. Senzalas, or slave quarters, were usually composed of separate mud-walled and thatched huts or more characteristically of row houses divided into rooms, each of which was occupied by a family or residence unit. Plantation inventories make it clear that the senzalas were the least substantial of the engenhos' buildings. At Engenho Agua Boa in 1795, there were fourteen senzalas to house thirty-four slaves. Each of these units was valued at 4$, whereas the humble *taipa* (abode) and thatch house of a freeman who resided on the property, which had no door or windows, was valued at 8$ or twice the amount of the slave houses.[23] Occasionally, a planter might provide more substantial buildings. João Lopes Fiuza's Engenho do Baixo in Santo Amaro had one senzala built on brick pillars with a tile roof and another of the row-house type with fifteen units.[24] A review of the relative cost of the slave housing units over time in engenho inventories indicates little change for the better.

Most observers at the end of the colonial era still agreed that slaves were poorly housed. Santos Vilhena's recommendation that masters plant coconut trees and dendé palms around the slave cabins to provide extra sustenance suggests that this was not commonly done.[25] Still, the slaves sometimes could overcome their situation. Maria Graham, who visited a Bahian senzala in 1822, found them "cleaner and more comfortable" than she expected. She was impressed that each building had been divided into four or five rooms, each occupied by a family. "In their huts," she said, "something like the blessings of freedom are enjoyed in the family ties and charities they are not forbidden to enjoy."[26] This was a comment on the slaves, however, and not on their houses.

The clothing issued to slaves was minimal. Seventeenth-century observers often described plantation slaves as "naked" and constantly subjected to the vagaries of the weather.[27] Dutch artists of that century, especially Frans Post, have left an image of how slaves dressed. The men usually wore a pair of drawers that came below the knee, no shirt, and a kerchief or headband wrapped around their brow. The women in these paintings are more fully dressed, with skirt, petticoat, blouse, and bodice, but this costume may have been for marketing and not what was worn in the fields.[28] The general issue to slaves was *pano da serra*, a coarse homespun. At Engenho Santana, the Jesuits usually distributed the cloth at Lent, issuing so many *varas* (vara: a measure equal to 1.1 meters) according to the size of the slave. Some cotton cloth and another coarse variety called *raxeta* was also distributed to the women for skirts. On other estates, the custom varied.[29] A 1751 accounting submitted by Bahian planters claimed that slaves were provided one new outfit every other year.[30] Santos Vilhena claimed that the common issue to slaves was a couple of shirts, pants, or skirts of gross cotton and a few yards of *baeta* (baize) for bedding.[31] By the nineteenth century, the observations and engravings produced by travelers in Brazil make clear that slave clothing reflected the differences of occupation and internal hierarchy of the slave quarters. Field hands were less well dressed than house servants or artisans. Curiously, the turbans, lace, and starched *pano da costa* (a type of linen) cloth today so much associated with African religion in Brazil are not mentioned in the literature about engenho slaves.

The way in which the comforts of housing and clothing could be manipulated as incentives is made clear by Henry Koster, who reported about a planter who bought troublesome slaves at below the market price and then turned them into productive workers. His method was to show them the tools of punishment and threaten them but then provide a hut, clothing, and other articles of comfort, "all of which [were] in a state of greater neatness, and [were] afforded in greater quantities than [were] usually bestowed upon the slaves of other plantations."[32]

Probably in no area was the relationship between the slaves' physical situation and the operation of the slave system by means of incentives more apparent than in the matter of food. The methods worked out by masters and slaves to provide sustenance was a matter of survival and in some ways a key to the engenhos' organization. Evidence is consistent from the beginning of the sugar economy to the end of the colonial era that slaves did not recieve an adequate ration. In 1829, Jacques Guinebaud, French consul in Salvador, wrote that the Brazilians were much less demanding of their slaves than the planters of Saint Domingue had been, but he admitted that the slaves did not receive enough sustenance.[33] His observation was seconded by João Imbert, certainly no admirer or friend of the African's, whose handbook for planters pointed out that slaves were given insufficient food, so coarse that it caused them many stomach disorders.[34]

As early as 1604, there were reports that plantation slaves went hungry. In 1606, the crown ordered masters to provide their slaves with sufficient food. Although some argued that the constant thefts by slaves were due to their innate disposition, the Council of India, which administered Brazil at the time, felt that starvation lay behind the slaves' actions. It ordered masters to plant enough food to support their bondsmen. At the same time, the council discussed the legality of forcing owners to allow the slaves a day each week to work on their own plots.[35] By the close of the seventeenth century, many planters had adopted the policy of providing a day each week, usually Saturday, for the slaves to grow their own food; but others demanded that the slaves use Sundays for this purpose.[36] Clerics objected to this violation of the Sabbath, and in 1701 authorities in Lisbon ordered masters to provide adequate food or allow the slaves a free day to grow their own.[37] The law was not immediately obeyed. In 1703, the black Brotherhood of the Rosary petitioned the High Court of Bahia seeking an injunction to force slaveowners to comply with the law.[38] Although some slaveowners, such as the Benedictines, took the prohibition against forcing slaves to labor on Sundays seriously, others followed the principle that if slaves ate on Sunday, they had to work on Sunday as well.[39]

Slaves ate whatever they could lay their hands on. Besides their issue of rations, slaves cajoled, begged, and stole additional food. At Engenho Santana, thefts of cane and food crops by the slaves were continual. In 1731, Father Pedro Teixeira complained that one field with a capacity of 700 alqueires of manioc would produce only 100 because of theft. His successors made similar complaints.[40] Nothing edible escaped the slaves. The canefields were filled with rats, and all that were caught went into the pot.[41] But the staple for slaves, as well as for the free in Brazil, was manioc flour. Standard issue in the mid–eighteenth century was calculated at about one bushel of manioc flour (farinha) every forty days per slave.[42] Salt meat or fish was also provided, but fresh poultry and meat were considered by many planters to be a special nourishment for the sick slaves. Bananas, easy to tend and highly productive, were consumed as early as the 1600s, and rice was planted in Ilhéus by the 1730s at least.[43] In Bahia, scene of a considerable whaling industry, whale meat was also given to slaves. During the safra, as we have seen, slaves also received rum and sugar by-products to stimulate work, and although some authors argued that the safra was the time of "fat and healthy" blacks and animals, the statistics of mortality tell another story.[44]

We have some idea of a field slave's ration from the planter's handbook published by João Imbert in 1832. He took special pride in the food he provided to his slaves, so we can assume it was better than most. Imbert's slaves received bread and a cup of rum (cachaça) on setting out for the fields. Then, at 9:00 a.m. the slaves stopped for a breakfast of rice, bacon, and coffee. Dinner (jantar) was taken in the field. It consisted of dried meat and vegetables, although fresh meat was occasionally substituted. A supper (cea) of cooked vegetables, manioc flour, and fruit was eaten at nightfall.[45] Despite the existence of a few plantation accounts and many references by observers, we cannot establish the quantity or nutritional value of the food consumed by the slaves; on many plantations they provided for their own subsistence or supplemented what was provided to them, thus their food intake went unrecorded.

Engenhos practiced one of the three methods of maintaining their slaves. On some plantations, slaves depended exclusively or almost exclusively on the rations or tamina provided by the owners. On others, they were allowed to grow their own food, using holy days and the free time provided by masters. A combination of both forms of support existed at some engenhos. As one observer noted, the tamina was usually sparse and unhealthy, and the slaves preferred to work on their own even if the labor was beyond their capacity.[46] Although conditions varied from engenho to engenho and from region to region, Bahia had a particularly nasty reputation. In a comparison with neighboring Sergipe de El-Rey, one observer wrote in 1800,

. . . the slaves of the Bahian Recôncavo are fed the scarce and noxious salt meat of Rio Grande [do Sul]; their little houses are covered with straw and provide little protection against the weather while those of Sergipe are roofed with tile. The slaves [of Sergipe] are dressed in cotton made by the slave women while the Recôncavo slaves, for the most part, seem like mute orangoutans.[47]

Work in field and factory

The physical conditions under which slaves labored set the context of their lives, but it was their labor itself that determined their role in the productive process and the way in which the engenhos functioned. Work in the canefields was the central feature of plantation slavery. The majority of the slaves spent the majority of their time in the field, and although other aspects of sugar production and other aspects of slavery received more attention from contemporary observers, and subsequently from modern historians, it was always the workers in the cane who defined the essence of production. Field labor in Brazil was essentially gang labor. Koster described the holing process: The slaves stood in a row. Each struck the earth in front of him or her, and the hoes formed a small trench. Then the whole row of slaves fell back together and repeated the process until the field was turned up.[48] The labor was sometimes accompanied by song to keep the rhythm of the gang and to "soften the yoke of labor."[49] An English traveler to Brazil in the 1820s left this description of slaves in the field:

In a large fallow, in the midst of this green amphitheater were from eighty to one hundred negroes of both sexes; some with infants strapped on their backs, in a rank, breaking up the ground for fresh crops with hoes. . . . With this [hoe], they all struck with the regularity of soldiers drilling for the manual exercise, and cut the ground into square blocks about twice the size of bricks. Over them presided a tawny-colored driver, in a cotton jacquet and a large straw hat, with a long rod in his hand by which he directed their industry, and punished the idle. The whole scene before me presented such a complete picture of a tropical farm, where both the face of nature and the produce and mode of cultivation were objects so unusual to the eye of the European, that I sat some time on my horse, contemplating it.[50]

Despite the Reverend Walsh's somewhat picturesque description, work in the canefield was arduous and continuous, beginning early and ending late. At Engenho Santana, slaves rose around five o'clock for morning prayers before setting out for the fields. A small breakfast was eaten about nine o'clock, the midday meal three or four hours later was taken in the field, and then work continued until nightfall.[51] A

Figure 6-1. Continuities: Cane cutting is still done by hand in pairs, or fouce. In this picture, a man cuts while a young boy binds the cane into bundles.

nineteenth-century observer stated that the slaves worked from six o'clock in the morning until six o'clock at night, with half an hour for breakfast and two hours for lunch when the mill was not operating. With the safra, work demands increased and slaves at the mill had to eat their midday meal on the run as work continued.[52]

Field preparation, cane holing, especially in the heavy massapé soil, was hard labor. A British parliamentary enquiry in 1832 produced a witness who singled out this work as "frightfully severe" and pointed out that at crop time, when slaves were put on the night turn at the mill, the effects of this task were even worse.[53] Weeding was lighter labor, but it was disagreeable.[54] There was also danger of snakebite when working in the canefields. Weeding, moreover, was continuous labor. Planters often sent slaves to weed after they had completed other tasks. Unlike many jobs required of slaves on the engenhos that were assigned on a quota basis, weeding was a dawn-to-dusk operation.

Cane cutting was done in teams or fouces, a name derived from the cane knife used. Each fouce was usually composed of a man and a woman.[55] The man cut the cane, and his companion bound it into faggots (freixes), using the leaves of the cane itself to tie it, as we see in Figure 6-1. Cane cutting was done on a quota basis. Slaves were assigned a certain number of "hands" of cane to be cut as their tarefa or daily task. At Engenho Sergipe in the late seventeenth century, a slave was required to cut seven hands of cane a day. Each hand had five fingers, each finger had ten faggots (*freixes*), and each faggot had twelve canes. Thus a daily quota was 7 hands times 5 fingers times 10 freixes times 12 canes, or a total of 4,200 canes.[56] The amount varied, however, according to place and time. At Engenho Santana at the end of the eighteenth century, the expected tarefa of a cane cutter was six hands; when the slaves of that engenho sought to have their workload reduced, they petitioned to have the tarefa set at five hands with only 10 canes in a freixe. This would have been a total of only 2,500 canes a day, or about 60 percent of the Engenho Sergipe quota of the century before.[57] At the completion of the *tarefa de corte* (daily cane-cutting quota), the slave was free to spend time as he or she liked. Much of the labor on Bahian plantations was assigned by tarefa, not only in the cutting of cane but in the mill, at the pottery, and elsewhere.

A similar kind of labor on many engenhos and cane farms was the cutting of firewood for use at the furnaces of the plantation's boiling house. Engenhos and lavradores often bought wood from the heavily forested region of the southern Recôncavo, both because they lacked woodlands on their own property and because the labor was hard and dangerous to their own slaves.[58] Most planters and cane farmers, however, did cut some wood on their own, especially *capoeira* or secondary brush. A slave was required to cut a daily quota of firewood a pile that was 63 inches high and 72 inches long, a unit equal to one cart or about 1,600 pounds. Eight cartloads were needed to process a tarefa of cane. Thus eight slaves were needed to supply the daily firewood needs of a large Bahian engenho.

The hours and conditions of labor described thus far, as bad as they may seem, do not fully convey the work required of sugar-plantation slaves. In addition to the "normal" workday of crop-related labor, slaves were assigned to building fences, construction, ditch digging, preparing manioc, and other miscellaneous chores. These extra chores, known as *quingingo*, might extend the workday another four to eight hours.[59] Moreover, on many estates slaves were allowed to grow their own food, a situation that gave them some independence but also demanded what free time was available to them. A slave who had met his or her quota of cane cutting might then spend the rest of the day on his or her own plot. At Engenho Sergipe, each slave was given an ax, mattock, and hoe duly marked with the symbol of the College of Santo Antão and was made responsible for these tools. Finally, at crop time when the mill was operating, slaves were divided into shifts to work on the engenho at night as well as doing their field tasks during the day. Usually, there were two six- to eight-hour shifts. The effect of this work routine was exhausting and, given the machinery of the mill and boiling house, dangerous as well. From the planters' point of view, it was an optimal use of labor.

Planters, in fact, paid careful attention to the labor production of field slaves put at various tasks. It was estimated that one slave could plant five cartloads of cane. In the heavy work of clearing new land, a slave's daily capacity was set at 6.6 square meters.[60] The câmara of Santo Amaro in 1753 calculated that it would take thirty slaves to weed a tarefa in a day and it would take twenty fouces (i.e., forty slaves) to cut a tarefa of cane in a day.[61] Since the daily wage of a field slave at hire was set at 120 réis, the total "cost" of producing a tarefa of cane for delivery to the mill was:

Planting	10$000
Weeding, 3 times 30 slaves times 120 réis	10$800
Cutting, 40 slaves times 120 réis	[b]4$800
Carting, 30 slaves x 200 réis	[b]6$000
Total	31$600

These calculations were to some extent "paper costs," for the slaves were not hired or paid but bought. Once purchased, the owner had to pay for their upkeep and for their control.

Field labor was accompanied by force. The overseer, or feitor, and his whip were an integral part of the work process. This was true of both ecclesiastical and secular estates. One Jesuit at Engenho Santana complained that to manage a slave plantation, words were not enough, feet were necessary, and that he constantly went about with "the devil in his mouth and a rod on the backs of the unfortunates."[62] Joseph Israel da Costa, who had lived in Bahia, claimed that the whip was used to drive the workers and to keep them in a state of fear because the ratio of whites to slaves was low, and that without this planned terror a single white in a canefield could not control the thirty to fifty slaves who labored under him.[63] Although even ecclesiastics who criticized the treatment of slaves in Brazil believed that physical punishment was necessary, they, and many of the foreign observers, commented on the poor physical treatment of plantation slaves. Slaves worked from dawn to dark, were exposed to sun and rain with poor clothing and shelter, and were poorly fed. Plantation labor was brutal. The protagonist of Nuno Marques Pereira's moral tract set in Bahia and published in 1728 claimed that peasants in Portugal treated their oxen better than planters treated their slaves, who in Brazil "worked day and night, broken, naked, and without sustenance."[64]

The labor in the mill was a combination of skilled and semiskilled tasks performed under constant supervision by free or slave managers. At the mill itself, seven to eight slaves were employed. Many of the tasks were often, but not always, assigned to women. Two or four slaves were used to feed the cane into the rollers of the mill. A slave would pass the cane between the center roller and one of the exterior ones. A slave on the other side would then pass it back through the other roller. When four slaves were used, they worked in teams at the two rollers. In addition, according to Antonil, another three slaves were employed to bring in the cane to those who placed it in the rollers (*moedeiras*), and two more were used to carry out the crushed stalks or *bagaço*, which were fed to livestock or thrown away. One woman tended to the fish- or whale-oil lamps, and another (called the *calumbá*) kept the receptacles for the cane liquid clean and also placed water on the cogs of the mill itself to reduce friction. Finally, there was a slave (*guindadeira*) assigned to remove the liquid that had been extracted from the cane and to move it by means of a hoist (*guinda*) to the boiling house. As in other parts of the engenho, the slaves at the mill itself worked in shifts, usually two during the eighteen- to twenty-hour workday. Their labor was supervised during the day by the feitor da moenda and at night by his subordinate, the *guarda*, who by the eighteenth century was often a slave.

Although the work at the rollers was repetitive, it demanded some skill and great attention. The cane had to be placed into the rollers at the right speed and in the right quantity, or else the rollers might break or the cane would not be pressed thoroughly enough. Moreover, work at the rollers demanded great attention because of the distinct possibility of an "industrial accident." The crushing power of the mill was enormous.[65] An inexperienced slave, or one who had become inattentive from overwork or from drinking the garapa distributed to slaves during the safra, could easily have a hand pulled into the rollers along with the cane. If this happened at a large mill, the whole body might follow the arm. This is what happened to a young mulatta at Engenho Musurepe in Pernambuco who was caught and "milled with the very cane."[66] Precautions had to be taken. At water-powered mills, a special board to divert the water away from the wheel was kept ready. In addition, almost all observers who wrote in detail about the Brazilian engenhos noted that a crowbar and a small hatchet were kept near the rollers so that if a slave was caught the rollers could be separated and the hand or arm severed, saving the machinery from further damage.

Still, one-armed slave women were a sadly common sight. At Engenho Santana in the 1730s, it was Marcelina, who having lost her arm at the mill continued to work as the calumbá.[67] The French traveler Tollenare provides a particularly poignant case of a beautiful young woman named Theresa who had been a queen in Cabinda. Falling from favor, she had been sold as a slave and at Engenho Sibiró in Pernambuco had been placed at the mill when the moedeiras were ill. Inexperienced, her hand was caught and while trying to free herself her other hand was also crushed. Both arms were amputated.[68] Ox-driven mills were apparently the safest because they turned slowly and the oxen could be easily brought to a halt. The danger with horse-powered moendas was that the screams of the unfortunate slave caused the horses to run faster. Water-powered mills because of their speed and large size were particularly dangerous to the workers.

The scenes of the boiling house and the work at the furnaces and kettles gave the labor of the engenho its distinctive image in the minds of its preindustrial observers. The roaring furnaces heating boiling kettles, which threw off intense heat and steam, reminded many of hell's landscape. For Antonil, an Italian by birth, the scenes were like those of the volcanoes Etna or Vesuvius, but for Padre Vieira, the image was even more that of the inferno. Although Padre Vieira's description of the work in the engenho has been cited by many, its imagery merits repetition:

And truly who sees in the blackness of night those tremendous furnaces perpetually burning; the flames leaping from the borbotões (appertures) of each through the two mouths or nostrils by which the fire breathes; the Ethiopians or cyclopses, bathed in sweat, as black as they are strong, feeding the hard and heavy fuel to the fire, and the tools they use to mix and stir them; the cauldrons, or boiling lakes, continually stirred and restirred, now vomiting froth, exhaling clouds of steam, more of heat than of smoke. . . . the noise of the wheels and chains, the peoples the color of the very night working intensely and moaning together without a moment of peace or rest; who sees all the confused and tumultuous machinery and apparatus of that Babylon can not doubt though they may have seen Vesuvius or Mount Etna that this is the same as Hell.[69]

The fact that so much of this labor was carried out at night made the image even more striking in the eyes of those who witnessed the workings of a sugar mill and those who worked in it. In many ways, it was a preview of the industrial future, and it shocked those who caught a glimpse of what was to come.

The furnaces and boiling cauldron above all else created the image of an inferno. Usually, a slave stoker (metedor) was assigned to feed each furnace, although Santos Vilhena in the late eighteenth century suggests that sometimes fewer slaves were used.[70] The work at the furnaces was hard, dangerous, and unpleasant. The heat from the flames, combined with the humidity and the heat of the Bahian summer, was exhausting. The slaves stoked the furnaces according to the instructions of the kettlemen, who shouted orders calling for more or less heat. The danger of falling into the furnace was always there, although at some engenhos the furnace mouths were designed to prevent this. Men seem to have been used exclusively in this position. Although slaves do appear from time to time listed in inventories with this occupation, it was not common.[71] Slaves suffering from yaws or venereal diseases (boubas) were assigned to the furnaces in hope that the heat would sweat out the disease from their bodies. In fact, Antonil suggests that the furnaces were a place of punishment. Runaways or recalcitrant slaves were placed at the furnaces in chains to work their resistance out of them. The method did not always produce the desired results. In 1626, the overseer at Engenho Santana bought a runaway and placed him at the furnaces to break him to the mill's discipline. The slave committed suicide by throwing himself in the furnace.[72]

Whereas the tending of the furnaces does not seem to have been considered a skilled occupation, the slaves who worked at the large cauldrons and smaller teaches were thought to possess special knowledge or skill. Inventories distinguished between *caldereiros* (kettlemen) and *tacheiros* (teache-men), and the two occupations were apparently not thought to be interchangeable. In fact, even more discrete descriptions of these occupations sometimes appear. For example, caldereiro de melar, referring to the second kettle in the normal series, appears in a number of inventories and indicates a further specialization among the slaves who worked the boiling house. At a large engenho real like Sergipe do Conde, there were four caldereiros and two tacheiros in each shift. Once again, their labor was defined in terms of the task or quota. Each caldereiro was required to clarify three batches or kettles of liquid. The last was called *de entrega* or surrender because it was turned over to the relief halfway completed. Throughout the workday, the teams of kettlemen worked in these shifts of approximately three to four hours at the steaming kettles. The tacheiros also worked by task. Their quota was to fill four or five forms. Finally, in the boiling house a slave woman called the *calcanha* was responsible for keeping the lamps lit and for taking the skimmings and returning them to the first kettle for further processing.[73]

The slaves used in the boiling room were usually mulattoes or crioulos, native-born slaves, who could be taught their occupation at an early age. Both the comments of Antonil and the engenho inventories indicate the use of Brazilian-born slaves in these occupations. The knowledge and skill needed to maintain the proper temperature at each kettle, when to add lime, ash, or water, and how to skim the liquid were acquired solely by experience. Although there was a foreman in the boiling house (as is seen in Figure 6-2), the mestre de açúcar during the day and the banqueiro at night, kettlemen who could make these decisions were greatly prized. This was an office at which both slaves and freemen could be employed. At Engenho Sergipe, a free calcereiro was usually hired for a substantial salary during the seventeenth century. At Antônio de Sá Dória's engenho on Itaparica Island, both a Guiné slave and freeman were used as caldereiros de melar.[74] In a suit for guardianship in 1804, a resident at Engenho Nazaré claimed that he had raised a young mulatto child, teaching him to read and write and handle the duties of a calcereiro.[75] But despite the fact that the men employed in the boiling house were something of a labor elite, their job was also unpleasant and sometimes dangerous. Antonil re-

Figure 6-2. The sugar-making process: A sugar master directs the heating and skimming of the cane juice in this seventeenth-century view.

ported seeing slaves assigned to the kettles as punishment, moving about their tasks in chains, and occasionally accidents could happen here as well.

The tasks in the purging house and in the separation and crating of the sugar were somewhat lighter and less disagreeable or dangerous than in other parts of the sugar-making process. The carrying of the forms to and from the purging house was usually done by men, but many of the tasks in this stage were performed by women. According to Antonil's account, at Engenho Sergipe four women were *purgadeiras*, employed in applying the moistened clay to the sugar forms to begin the purging process. One of the more unpleasant tasks was the preparation of the mudlike clay, a labor assigned to an unfortunate slave. At the separating and drying platforms, about ten women worked under the direction of two knowledgeable and experienced slave women called the *mães de balcão*, or mothers of the platform. Slaves assembled the crates under the direction of the crater, and the sugar was then packed in solidly by groups of men and women who tamped in the loose sugar, as can be seen in Figure 6-3 (top). Many of these tasks were performed by field hands who, during the safra, also took their shift at the mill.

At each stage of the sugar-making process, there were managers and foremen to oversee the operation of the mill, boiling house, and purging of the sugar. Both free persons and slaves were used in these managerial capacities, and as we shall see in Chapter 12, eventually a broad debate developed over the relative savings and efficiency of free or slave workers in these occupations. In each canefield, slaves worked under the supervision of a driver (feitor), often a slave or a free person of color. At the mill itself, a feitor da moenda watched over the milling of the cane and was responsible for making sure that the cane was

Figure 6-3. From Brazil to Portugal. Top: Slaves on a Brazilian engenho pack large sugar crates. Bottom: In the background of this seventeenth-century view of Lisbon's riverside square, sugar crates are weighed and examined.

pressed properly and that the machinery was stopped in case of accident. When Antonil visited Engenho Sergipe, the feitor was apparently a freeman but this was not always the case. At Engenho Barbado in Passé parish in 1769, there were two slaves who divided this duty by night and day: one a pardo and the other a mulatto.[76] In the boiling house, the mestre de açúcar, or sugar master, directed operations, making sure that the capacity of each kettle was filled, overseeing the skimming process, and generally directing operations. These tasks were considered the most important in the making of sugar and the sugar masters, when freemen, were the highest-paid employees after the administrator, if the engenho had one. The sugar master had an assistant for the night shift, the banqueiro, who did essentially the same tasks, and who in turn was aided by a soto-banqueiro, usually a slave, to help with the work. The slave soto-banqueiro usually received some payment to stimulate him to work well.

In the last stages of the sugar-making process, work was directed by the purger (purgador) and the crater (caixeiro). The purgador controlled the purging process and supervised the work of the purgadeiras. It was also the job of the purgador to collect the molasses and to either send them back to the boiling house to make batido sugars or to save them for the still, if the engenho had one, to make aguardente. The caixeiro not only supervised the packing of the sugar but also was responsible for keeping a record of the sugar produced, dividing it between the lavradores and the engenho and deducting the tithe. It was said that an engenho ran best when the sugar master and the crater were not on good terms, so that they could watch each other.

Clearly, the quality and skill of the supervisors and specialists determined the success of an engenho's operations. A good sugar master or purger could do much to improve the yield and quality of sugar made from poor cane, whereas poor work could ruin a good harvest. The problem of supervisory labor was made explicit by Father Pedro Teixeira, who took over administration of Engenho Santana in 1731. He complained that the sugar master was very old and had little skill but was kept on because there were no others, and even if another could be persuaded to go to Ilhéus, it would cost 100$ in salary. There was no banqueiro to spell the master at night and all the other "officials" were slaves "who did everything like the Devil."[77] There were in fact no positions that slaves could not fill, and the tendency over time was for an increasing use of them in the managerial and skilled occupations. When Jerônimo Rodrigues de Castro sold Engenho Cruz das Torres in 1715, he did so along with slaves serving as banqueiro, purgador, and caixeiro.[78] Father Francisco Ribeiro, complaining of the expenses at Engenho Sergipe, argued in 1660 that crioulo and mulatto slaves could replace the salaried free workers on the engenho with great savings and that this was exactly what Francisco Gil, who owned a neighboring engenho, had done. Gil now paid only three white men, and all the other work was done by his own slaves, whereas Engenho Sergipe had fifteen or sixteen free persons employed.[79] Ribeiro's suggestions were eventually adopted at Engenho Sergipe and many other mills. With the rise of scientific management in the late eighteenth century, however, planters in Brazil began to ascribe their failures to the "rudeness" of the slave managers and artisans that they themselves had created.

Labor force: size and organization

The number of slaves required to operate an engenho varied considerably with the size and type of mill as well as with the number of free workers also employed. The figures given by Antonil are somewhat confusing because Engenho Sergipe maintained two series of kettles operating at once to handle the volume of liquid and because Antonil is not always clear about the division of shifts. From his comment, however, we can calculate that at the minimum a shift called for 7 to 8 slaves in the milling house to carry in cane, put it through the rollers, carry out the *bagasse*, or stalks, care for the lamps and waterwheel, and move the caldo to the kettles; 4 to 6 slaves to stoke the furnaces; 4 caldereiros, 4 tacheiros, and 2 women to care for lamps and move skimmings; in the purging house, 4 purgadeiras, 2 men to move forms, and 1 slave to prepare clay; and about 12 slaves in the crating activities. Thus in the milling and boiling process alone about 20 to 25 slaves were needed in a shift.[80] In addition, slaves also filled managerial roles at times. On the larger engenhos with slave forces of more than 100 adults, three shifts were possible, and some apparently operated by allowing one shift to be off every other night. Smaller mills did not have the labor to allow this. Although there were a few engenhos that operated with fewer than 40 slaves, the majority of Bahian mills had between 60 and 80, a number we can take as the minimum requirement for efficient operation.[81]

The structure of engenho slave forces varied considerably according to the size of the estate, the skills of the masters, and probably the aptitudes of the slaves, although this last element is difficult to assess because of the constraints imposed by slavery itself. Table 6-1 attempts to provide a schematic outline of an engenho labor force. About eighty different occupations or skills were recorded for 1,900 rural slaves in the inventories of 50 engenhos and cane farms covering the period from 1713 to 1826.[82] In about 3 percent of the cases examined, slaves were listed with more than one occupation. By taking the full sample of more than 1,400 slaves employed on sugar-mill properties, it is possible to make some general observations about the relative distribution of tasks on an engenho.

Table 6-1. Organization of a Bahian sugar works (Owner – Senhor do Engenho; General Administrator – Feitor-mor)

Hierarchy of labor	Production process				
	Field	Milling house	Boiling house	Purgery	Crating
Foremen	Feitores da fazenda	Feitor da moenda – day Feitor da moenda or guarda – night	Sugar master/ (mestre de açúcar) Assistant sugar master (banqueiro) Assistant banqueiro (soto-banqueiro)	Purger (purgador)	Crater (caixeiro)
Skilled	Carters (carreiros) Boatmen (barqueiros) Helmsmen (arrais)	Millers (moedoras)	Kettlemen (caldeireiros, caldereiro de melar, caldereiro de escumas, escumeiro) Teache-men (taxeiros)	"Clayers" (purgadeiras)	Separaters (mães de balção)
Semi- and unskilled	Field hands (de enxada) Herdsmen (boieiro)	light-keeper (calumbá) animal driver (tangedor) hoist-keeper (guindadeira) porters of cane (bagasse)	Stokers (metedores de lenha) Light and skimmings (calcanha)	Clay preparer (masador de barro)	Porters

Table 6-2. *Structure and average values of Bahian engenho slave forces*

Occupational group	Prime healthy males			Prime healthy females			All slaves[b]		
	N	%	Av. value[a]	N	%	Av. value[a]	N	%	Av. value[a]
Managerial	3	.8	250	0	0	–	10	1.1	205
Artisan	26	6.9	194	0	0	–	60	6.9	153
House	8	2.1	180	32	24.6	132	96	10.9	121
Engenho	43	11.4	165	14	10.7	119	140	16.0	125
Transportation	61	16.3	177	0	0	–	100	11.4	157
Field hands	234	62.4	150	84	64.6	128	469	53.6	129
Unrecorded	(44)			(52)			(582)		

[a]Average values are expressed in milréis.
[b]"All slaves" includes children and those listed as "older."
Source: Data Set A, Slaves from Inventories.

Field hands were always in the majority and constituted over half of all slaves listed with occupations. If we consider that perhaps half of those slaves listed without an occupation were too young or too old for labor, then the remainder would most likely fall into the field hand category, and its proportion would rise to about two-thirds of all the slaves. This distribution is borne out to some extent by an examination of healthy males between the ages of fourteen and about forty-five (see Table 6-2). The female occupational pyramid was more truncated and less diverse. Almost one-quarter of the women listed with occupations were house servants such as cooks, lace makers, seamstresses, or other domestics, whereas none were listed in managerial, artisanal, or transportation activities.

Table 6-2 also suggests that age played an important role in the distribution of occupations. The discrepancy between the total number of slaves listed in an occupational group and the number of prime-age males and females in that group is to a large extent explained by age. The highest ratios of difference are found in the managerial and engenho categories, where age and experience must have been important assets. The lowest ratios of difference are found in the field-hand and transportation categories, where a premium was surely placed on strength and youth.

Although most historiographical attention has been given to house slaves, artisans, and the few drivers and foremen, these groups made up less than a fifth of the engenhos' slave forces. The relative value of these slaves was high in comparison with field hands. The skilled slaves who worked inside the *fábrica* or sugar works were only about 10 percent of the total, but they too were highly valued and were roughly on a par with house slaves in terms of their average price. Boatmen, canoers, and carters were also valuable, and their average inventory

Table 6-3. *Occupational structure according to place of birth or color at Bahian engenhos in the eighteenth century*

Occupation	Africans		Crioulos		Mulattoes	
	N	%	N	%	N	%
Managerial	2	(.3)	5	(1.0)	3	(4.1)
Artisan	15	(1.9)	15	(3.0)	12	(16.2)
House	33	(4.4)	36	(7.1)	13	(17.6)
Engenho	76	(10.1)	49	(9.7)	1	(1.3)
Transportation	58	(7.7)	25	(5.0)	4	(5.4)
Field hands	569	(75.6)	374	(74.2)	41	(55.4)
Totals	753		504		74	

price was equivalent to that of the artisans. Field hands were re-corded in various ways (*de enxada* [hoe], *de machado*, [ax], *de roça* [farm], *de campo* [field], *lavoura* [labor], etc.). They were the essential element of production and comprised three-fifths to two-thirds of en-genho work forces. The world of sugar was truly a world of workers in the cane.

Finally, place of birth or color influenced the placement of slaves in the occupational order. Mulattoes were favored by being given oppor-tunities to acquire skills or to hold positions in the plantation house. Although mulattoes were only about 6 percent of the engenho slave population in the eighteenth century, they held more than 20 percent of the managerial, artisanal, and household positions. Brazilian-born blacks (crioulos) essentially had the same distribution of occupations as Africans with only a slight advantage in becoming house slaves (see Table 6-3). This quantitative evidence supports the image of mulatto advantage given by observers of the engenho regime.

Work requirements and the slave regime

It is not surprising that contemporaries referred to the engenhos as fábricas, for they were in many ways precursors of the modern fac-tory in their organization. With the possible exceptions of mining and shipbuilding, no other activity in the sixteenth century combined so complex a process by integrating technology, management, and labor under conditions remarkably like the modern assembly line. That this complex process, requiring considerable skill at various points, de-pended on slave labor, which according to Marx and other observers was inherently antithetical to industrial organization and advanced technology, raises a series of questions that deserve discussion.[83]

First, let us examine the nature of engenho labor organization in more general terms. Within both the agricultural and industrial aspects of sugar making, there was a relatively clear sexual division of labor. Men and women were used in both field and factory, but there was a separation of tasks by sex. Heavier field tasks – holing, field clearing, wood cutting – were done by men, but women worked alongside men at weeding and cane cutting.

My foregoing description of labor at an engenho depends heavily, as do all others, on Antonil's account. We must keep in mind that Antonil described conditions as he found them at Engenho Sergipe and that, although he attempted to draw a broader picture, what he saw was not necessarily the situation at all engenhos. Still, comparison of Antonil's account with engenho inventories allows us to gain some insight into the sexual organization of labor. In the milling house, the majority of tasks were performed by women. Men occasionally appear listed as moedor, but rarely. Boys were used to drive the oxen or horses to power the mill. The tasks of milling, carrying out bagasse, and the associated work at the mill were usually assigned to women; not so the labor in the boiling house. The furnaces, kettles, and teaches were exclusively men's, with the exception of the women assigned to keep the lamps lit. In the purging house, once again it was women who did the careful labor of claying the pots and who then separated the sugar. At eight Bahian engenhos in 1739, only women were listed as purgadeiras.[84] Supervision was invariably done by men in Bahia.[85] The sexual division of labor reflected varying needs for strength and precision, tasks requiring the former going to men and the latter to women. It becomes clear, however, that women were an essential part of the work force and were assigned critical tasks within the process. The sexual imbalance in engenho work forces appears to result from the demands of field labor or problems of supply in the slave trade and not from the needs in the mill itself.

A second point to be made here is that at the engenhos field hands and house slaves also took on tasks at the mill, taking their turns in the nighttime shifts. Thus the usual distinctions made between the three sets of tasks – house, field, and factory – are somewhat misleading. Although it is true that the skilled occupations – kettlemen, the women who clayed the forms, and so forth – were not assigned to field slaves, these latter ones also did work at the mill, carrying cane or firewood, moving forms, and working at the separation and crating of the sugars. The same was true of house slaves. In 1736, the town council of Salvador argued that even the household slaves of planters should be exempted from seizure for debt because during the safra their service was needed night and day and because "during the grinding even those of the household often work in the engenhos."[86]

Whether those slaves with skilled occupations were used in planting and weeding when the mill was not operating is a question that cannot yet be answered. It would seem that the safra schedule employed slaves directly in the production of the staple crop for much of the year, utilized their labor for a very long workday, and integrated their labor as fully as possible into all aspects of production.[87]

As in the modern factory, the laborers in the sugar-making process were assigned specific and discrete jobs and were separated from the final product of their labor. These, of course, were exactly the aspects of industrial labor that caught Marx's attention. Organized in this way, as Antônio Barros de Castro has pointed out, slaves did not make sugar, only the "engenho" made sugar, whereas each slave simply repeated over and over the same task in the process.[88] The making of sugar was a complex activity, but each part of the process was simplified for the individual worker into a discrete set of tasks. Only the mestre de açúcar or the feitor-mor had to follow and arrange the whole process from beginning to end. The series of tasks necessary to make sugar were individually performed, but integrated by the process itself, being "consecutive in time and simultaneous in space."[89] The utilization of large numbers of workers in canefields and at the mill in shifts leveled out differences in skill, so the ultimate result was a relatively homogeneous labor product, or, as Marx termed it, "labor of an average social quality."[90] In this aspect, the engenho was the forerunner of the modern factory.

But problems remained, because this early "industrialization" took place with slave labor. Many of the tasks called for attention and care, and the whole process could be ruined at many stages by negligence or sabotage. Moreover, the increasing employment of slaves as technicians or "artisans" and as managers called into question their use in a productive process that separated them from the success of their labor. This contradiction underlies the often cited incompatibility of technology or industrialization with slavery.

As we have seen, physical coercion, the whip, and the threat of worse punishment were an integral part of the field management, but neither Antonil nor any of the other commentators on the engenho's operations speaks of drivers or the whip being used inside the fábrica. There, this kind of physical coercion would have been counterproductive, and although masters might force slaves to do certain disagreeable tasks in the mill, most planters found better and more effective means to ensure adequate performance of labor and to protect against intentional disruption of the productive process.

The assignment of labor on a quota or piecework basis for many aspects of plantation operations appears to have been one way of stimulating labor productivity. In the field and forest, cane was cut or planted and firewood prepared on the basis of quotas, with the understanding that, after completing the assigned unit, the slave could use his or her time for rest or other activities such as gardening. Such a system seved as an incentive against slowdowns and malingering. In the mill, boiling house, and purgery, such quotas were also employed to define the work routine, so many kettles to skim, so many forms to fill, but in reality the eight- to nine-hour shifts were determined not by the speed of the individual worker but by the process of sugar making itself, as controlled by the technology employed and the capacity of the equipment.[91]

A mill wheel moved by oxen made about one turn per minute, one powered by mules a turn and a half, whereas a water mill could make two to four or even more rotations in the same time.[92] The kettles could only hold a specific amount, perhaps two *pipas* (one ton) in the largest, and thus when both the first kettle and the receiving pan at the rollers were full, the rollers stopped operating.[93] Loreto Couto indicates that in eighteenth-century Pernambuco a sufficient quantity of liquid was extracted to fill the kettles if the mill pressed cane for three hours and that from the caldeira do meio to filling the final forms with this liquid took about seven hours.[94] The process, however, was continuous, and the kettles were never allowed to become empty until the workday was completed. The trick in the process for managers was to keep the various activities flowing smoothly and to be able to tell from experience with the ratios of the various elements to each other if any one part was moving too fast or too slow. Clocks did not regulate the work. They rarely appear in engenho inventories and only begin to be mentioned in the middle of the eighteenth century. Engenho Santana acquired its first in 1745, and the Benedictine engenho of Camorim in Rio de Janeiro got its first about 1770.[95] For the slaves, above all else, the pace of work was determined by the process itself.

The pace might be regulated in this way, but what about the quality of labor? This was a particular problem in sugar making because the whole process could easily be ruined at many points. For example, simply putting lemon juice into a kettle of melado would prevent it from ever crystallizing into sugar. Sabotage was all too easy. Recalcitrant, coerced laborers were not suited for the more specialized tasks. Planters had to seek another means to extract the necessary quality for this labor. Incentives provided that means.

Within the operations of the Brazilian sugar plantations and within Brazilian slavery as a whole, positive incentives became a common technique of achieving at least temporary cooperation from the slaves. Incentives could be of various kinds. Antonil emphasized that at various stages in the making of sugar, liquid by-products and alcoholic garapa were distributed to the slaves as rewards for their service. The distribution was regularized, those in the milling house receiving their share on some days, those in the boiling house and furnaces on others. Further distribution was made to boatmen and those who sought out shellfish, and even the slave with the disagreeable job of preparing the clay to drain the forms received some, so that "all who felt the weight of work would have their pot, the measure by which they distribute this, their beloved nectar and ambrosia."[96] The beverage could also be traded to other slaves who did not have access to it in return for other kinds of foodstuffs. That this distribution was important is underlined by the instructions of 1663 given by João Fernandes Vieira to his feitormor, in which this ration was "never to be lacking."[97]

Other incentives to good performance could also be used for slaves as well as for free persons. Whereas the sugar master and other technicians or managers were usually paid a salary, they were sometimes paid a percentage of the production.[98] When Antonil visited Engenho Sergipe, the soto-banqueiro was a slave whose performance was rewarded by the payment of small amounts of sugar that he presumably could sell on his own account. I suspect similar incentives must have been offered to slaves who served in these managerial capacities on many estates. In fact, the use of monetary incentives or other rewards seems to have been common. The account books of Engenho Sergipe are filled with small payments to slaves for various minor chores. In 1743, Father Antônio Fernandes at Engenho Santana wrote to his superior thanking him for the religious medals (veronicas) that were sent to "satisfy the slaves to stimulate them to greater service which now with the new canefields is not lacking."[99]

Within this system of incentives, we must consider finally three other "privileges" extended to plantation slaves in Bahia that reinforced the operations of the engenho. First, the use of slaves in skilled occupations and as foremen in the engenho provided an image of possible social mobility. The fact that a banqueiro, a feitor da moenda, or even a sugar master might be a slave stood as an example to all slaves. These positions did not require special education, only experience, ability, and a willingness to take on supervisory functions. Like the foremen in nineteenth-century factories, these men in managerial or semimanagerial roles were essential steps of the pyramid of labor organization.[100] The opportunity to acquire these positions served as an incentive to slave cooperation and productivity. That all slaves did not respond to such incentives should not surprise us, but that some did should be no less surprising. In this and in other ways, the classical model of slavery as coerced labor showed itself to be far more flexible and adaptable than some of its later interpreters.

Also within the context of incentives, the so-called Brazil system of having slaves grow their own food had a place. Almost all the commentators on Brazilian slavery noted that on many plantations slaves were permitted to maintain their own garden plots and were free to dispose of their produce as they saw fit. The 1663 instructions to an overseer in Pernambuco mention slave plots, and Charles Darwin noted them on a Rio de Janeiro estate in 1832.[101] Accounts varied as to the amount of time slaves were given. Antonil stated that one day a week was common, and other, more critical observers objected to the fact that slaves worked on Sundays and saints' days. That slaves welcomed the "independence" that this system presented them is made clear in a number of documents. It was one of their few opportunities to acquire things they needed or to accumulate money that could eventually be used to buy freedom for themselves or their children. Some have suggested that the participation of slaves in this small-scale agriculture and in local markets constituted a "peasant breach" in the slave system. But slave plots may have had another purpose in the system of incentives.[102] Organizing labor by quota and permitting field hands to use their time freely after certain tasks were completed made sense if the planter could be relatively sure that the slaves would devote this time to productive labor on their own plots. Although the slaves could dispose of the produce themselves, they were in effect laboring for their own maintenance. Moreover, knowing that the slaves were anxious to have the "freedom" implied in these plots provided the masters with another way of stimulating labor. To have extra time for their own gardens, slaves met their quotas and malingering was reduced as a problem. When the slaves of Engenho Santana in Ilhéus submitted a list of desiderata in 1789, many of their concerns centered on their opportunities to grow and market their own crops. In fact, at Engenho Santana it was common for the slaves to sell their produce to the engenho, which bought it at a rate about one-third below the normal market price.[103]

Finally, there was the ultimate incentive of eventual freedom through manumission. As we shall see, this was not exactly "pie in the sky," for Brazilian manumissions were common and were available not only for "good" behavior but by purchase as well; they were thus linked to the slaves' ability to accumulate capital. A mulatto or crioulo slave with a skilled engenho occupation or managerial experience could not only hope for eventual freedom but could also be relatively sure of successful employment thereafter. In a particularly candid remark, a Jesuit administrator at Engenho Sergipe reported in 1623, "The mulattoes and crioulos are all very willing and all with hopes of manumission and God forgive whoever gave them this notion but thanks to God I have them all in good service."[104] The reality of manumission might in numerical terms be relatively slight, probably rarely rising above 1 percent per annum throughout most of the period studied here, but this was apparently enough to produce the desired positive incentive.

The relative value of coercion and positive incentives has provoked a storm of controversy in the context of North American slavery.[105] Accepting the presence of positive incentives within salary does not negate the underlying threat of force, nor does it necessarily turn slaves who respond to them into "Protestant capitalists." But to ignore the use of positive incentives is to miss an essential aspect of Brazilian slavery that was probably of special importance in the more technologically advanced activities of sugar making. The common Brazilian customs of allowing slaves to acquire their own property (*peculium*) and of granting manumission freely or by purchase must have served a purpose in the slave system. Plantation slavery in Brazil was not a "model" but an adaptable and malleable system of labor organization. Planters were neither stupid nor backward, and they were well aware that a mix of positive and negative incentives could be used to achieve their goals. The combination of these elements might vary with the personality of the planter, the demands of the specific labor, the custom of the region, or the state of the market, but the goal of extracting optimum labor from the slaves usually resulted from a mix of the two elements.

The slaves were no less imaginative in attempting to overcome the constraints of the slave system and in trying to manipulate the combination of positive and negative incentives to their best advantage. At Engenho Santana, far from the Recôncavo, there was always a shortage of free persons to do the skilled labor and the sugar master was usually the only white man. By 1670, all the other "officials" in the skilled sugar-making tasks were black slaves considered by the administrator to be "worse than galley slaves." By the 1730s, when Santana lacked a feitor to watch the sugar making at night, the slaves simply took what they wanted.[106] At Santana, the slaves continually pushed the contours of the institution to the limit and constantly bargained for better conditions. The administrator threw up his hands in despair when in the 1750s he wrote:

The time of their service is no more than five hours a day and much less when the work is far off. It is the multitude that gets anything done, just as in an anthill. And when I reprimand them with the examples of whites and their slaves who work well, they answer that the whites work and earn money whereas they get nothing, and the slaves of those whites work because they are given enough food and clothes. . . . God knows what I suffer by not resorting to force to avoid runaways. And when I complain, they point to their stomach and say, "The belly makes the ox go," giving me to understand that I do not feed them. It is my sins that have sent me to such an engenho.[107]

Obviously, the slaves of Santana and of other engenhos learned that there was often room for maneuver within the constraints of plantation slavery.

The slaves of Santana provide us with a final comment on this situation. After the expulsion of the Jesuits in 1759, that plantation was sold to a private individual, and in 1789 it was the property of Manoel da Silva Ferreira. In that year, a group of the slaves (some said 50; others, the majority of the 300 resident on the estate) killed their overseer and ran off under the leadership of a *cabra* (a dark mulatto) named Gregório Luís. They brought the engenho to a standstill for two years, but attacked by military expeditions, they were finally moved to propose a peace treaty giving the conditions under which they would return to servitude. Silva Ferreira feigned acceptance and promised manumission to the leader, but on the rebels' return he had them arrested. The leaders were sold to Maranhão, and Gregório Luís was imprisoned.[108]

The proposed treaty gives us a rare insight into slave wishes and provided an image of their perception of life on a sugar plantation. The greatest part of the treaty is concerned with specific conditions of labor and minimum needs of physical comfort. It seeks limitations on unpleasant tasks, asks for reductions in work quotas, and requests a minimum number of workers at specific jobs. Physical punishment is not mentioned, but rivalry between Brazilian-born and African slaves is apparent. Above all, the slaves' concern is to have their own land, grow their own food, and market the surplus. The slaves of Santana requested Friday and Saturday of each week for their own endeavors, the right to plant rice and cut wood wherever they wished, and to be provided with fishing nets and canoes. Moreover, they demanded that Silva Ferreira build a boat to carry their produce to Salvador so that they would not have to pay freightage costs.

Their demands in many ways resemble those in modern labor negotiation, but in the context of slavery they had others that were profoundly revolutionary. They demanded to choose their own overseers and to remain in control of the plantation's equipment. Such demands would have made slavery a farce; thus the unhappy end the rebels suffered. Finally, in this document so concerned with work, the runaways did not forget other matters. They demanded the right to "play, relax, and sing any time we wish without your hindrance nor will permission be needed." Within the context of plantation slavery, it is not strange to find concerns with cultural freedom linked to the specific conditions of work.

Within the complex relationships inherent in sugar-plantation production, both owners and workers sought to obtain their interests as best they could, constrained by cultural, economic, and political realities. Planters found that in the mix of punishment and reward the desired quantity and quality of labor could best be achieved; slaves realized that in this system there were opportunities for them to improve their lives. If we see this society's social relations of work as its innermost secret, phenomena that may seem unrelated can be explained within a larger context.[109] Manumission, for example, may have religious and social meaning outside the labor context, but its persistence and pervasiveness indicate that those meanings did not conflict with its role within the organization of work. The same could be said of slave plots, the quota system, or advancement in the plantation hierarchy. Slavery's adaptability gave it longevity but also provided at least some hope for the slaves.

CHAPTER 7

THE BAHIAN SUGAR TRADE TO 1750

Heretofore we had all our sugars from Portugal and it is computed that they cost us yearly about £400,000. Now that great leak is stopped; and we hardly buy any Portugal or Brazil sugars.

Groans of the Plantations (London, 1689)

It is notorious, calamitous, and deplorable the state in which the sugar planters and cane farmers of the country find themselves, they who are the nerves of the civil and political body. . . . Everyone feels it, everyone complains, everyone laments that they are lost; but always ill from the same malady, they will not take the medicine or permit reform.

Wenceslão Pereira da Silva (1732)

Sugar became in the sixteenth century the predominant Brazilian export, and until the middle of the nineteenth century it never lost its leading position. Even during the gold rush of the eighteenth century, when Brazilian gold poured into the coffers of Europe and, as Adam Smith noted, helped fuel the industrial revolution, the value of Brazilian sugar exports always exceeded those of any other commodity. But the impression often given in the historiography of the Brazilian economy is that sugar experienced its heyday in the early seventeenth century and then fell into a long period of stagnation or decline, becoming in the process virtually moribund. Although it is true that foreign competition severely reduced the Brazilian share of the world sugar market after the mid–seventeenth century, the subsequent history of the sugar sector was not simply one of decline. There were good periods as well as bad, and although Brazil never regained its relative world position as a sugar supplier, the sugar industry and planter class remained dominant in such places as Bahia and Pernambuco.

The Bahian sugar economy always functioned in relation to the international market for that commodity and the changing patterns of politics and economy within the Atlantic world. To understand the operation of the plantation system in Brazil, how and why planters responded to their situation, and how the region was affected by its role as a producer of tropical staples, it is necessary to trace the story of the rise, decline, and resurgence of the Bahian sugar trade. This is no easy task, since it calls for an economic history of Brazil itself and as such is a subject that spreads far beyond the limited goals of this book. Moreover, many essential elements in the story, such as merchant organization, mechanisms of exchange, and the commercialization of sugar in Europe, have not received detailed study despite an abundance of sources.[1] Still, the commercial dimension of the Bahian sugar industry must be examined as a central part of the region's history; my focus in examining the sugar trade, however, will remain Bahian. I have chosen this approach because I believe that the essential aspects of social development resulted in the main from the relations of production inherent in the organization and operation of the engenhos. Thus, whereas in the preceding chapter the work in the engenho was examined from the perspective of the worker, in this chapter it is from the point of view of the senhores de engenho and lavradores de cana, the sugar sector, that I will trace the history of the sugar economy.

Before discussing the history of the Bahian sugar trade, it is important to note that there are three aspects of this commerce that complicate any analysis of decisions and performance: the complexity and variety of the trade, the lack of a home refining industry, and the production of rum and molasses for local consumption. First, as we have seen, Brazilian sugars began to appear in European markets as early as the 1510s (if not before), but it was not until the middle decades of the century that these reached Europe in any quantity. The main destinations were naturally Lisbon and to a lesser extent Oporto, with smaller Portuguese harbors such as Viana do Castelo and Póvoa de Varzim also receiving sugar cargoes.[2] By the late sixteenth century, most Brazilian sugar went to northern European ports, particularly London, Hamburg, and Antwerp (although Amsterdam replaced Antwerp after 1577, when the latter was sacked by Spanish troops). Although ships trading directly with Brazil needed Portuguese licenses and were usually required to pass through Lisbon to pay duties, vessels from Danzig, the Hansa ports, Ragusa, and Venice all occasionally traded with Brazil in the sixteenth century. Holland, however, predominated. Engel Sluiter has estimated that perhaps as much as two-thirds of the Brazilian sugar trade was carried in Dutch bottoms prior to 1600.[3] By the late eighteenth century, Italy and Hamburg had become major buyers of Brazilian sugar.

The complexity and volume of this trade implies an active mercantile community, and merchants were an important part of the Bahian and Pernambucan social structure by the late sixteenth century. They provided the shipping facilities and organization of the trade and extended credit for the establishment and operation of mills. However, not all planters chose to deal with resident merchants, and some preferred to ship their sugar on their own account. The crown ordered in 1629 that one-third of the cargo space on all the ships sailing from Brazil to Portugal had to be reserved for growers shipping directly.[4] The representatives of the count and countess of Linhares at Engenho Sergipe sent that mill's sugar directly to Europe, dividing cargoes into small lots on a number of ships as a means of insurance.[5] In 1653, Padre Francisco Ribeiro, who reviewed practices at Engenho Sergipe, believed that about 800 réis per arroba was lost to an engenho by selling the sugar to a merchant in Bahia rather than shipping directly to Portugal.[6] This would be a loss of 16$ on a twenty-arroba crate. It is impossible to calculate the volume of the sugar trade carried out directly by senhores de engenho, but the practice of consignment continued well into the eighteenth century, especially among the wealthier planters or those who were engaged in commerce as well as sugar growing.[7]

A peculiar aspect of the Brazilian sugar trade was the total lack of refineries, not only in the colony itself but in the metropolis as well. Brazil became famous for its "clayed" sugar, which resulted in high-quality whites and lower-grade, brown-to-yellow muscavado. Both these types were suitable for immediate consumption. Very coarse sugar still full of molasses, what Brazilians called panelas, was not exported in large amounts. This variety, however, was shipped in large quantities from the Caribbean islands after the mid-seventeenth century under the name *mascavado*. It became the raw material for the refining industries of northern Europe. By 1650, 40 refineries were operating in Amsterdam, and by 1770 that number had risen to 110.[8] London was another center, beginning slowly in the seventeenth century but rapidly expanding in the eighteenth to meet a growing demand. By 1753, 80 of England and Scotland's 120 refineries were located in London.[9] The absence of a home refining industry partially explains why the Brazilians concentrated on producing clayed sugars, although in the sixteenth century the ability to produce clayed sugar probably explains the lack of refineries. In any case, the Lisbon sugar market was always less complex than that of other European cities because of the absence of competition between grocers who wanted marketable high grades and refiners who needed raw material.[10]

Finally, discussion of the international sugar trade misses an essential element of the story, the production of rum and molasses, sugar by-products. It was estimated that 100 pounds of clayed sugar yielded about 6.5 gallons of molasses (*melles*), which could be distilled into rum (aguardente).[11] Sugarcane alcoholic beverages locally called cachaça or garapa were consumed in large quantities in Brazil, but the Portuguese wine interests prohibited their export to the metropolis and on various occasions attempted to limit their production in Brazil.[12] In Rio de Janeiro, cachaça rather than sugar was the main product of the engenhos in the eighteenth century, and much of it was used as an item for the slave trade with Angola. In Bahia, that was much less the case. It is impossible to know how much cachaça was produced by Bahian engenhos, since most of it was sold and consumed locally. As was mentioned, planters occasionally claimed that they broke even on sugar production and that it was the sale of aguardente and melles that gave them a margin of profit. On the Benedictine engenhos in Bahia and Pernambuco, melles and aguardente produced between 7 and 17 percent of annual income. This was a significant proportion, and especially in bad times on the world sugar market, planters could depend on it for their margin of profit. The lack of adequate information on the subjects of individual planter consignment, the role of aguardente in the sugar trade, and the problem of refineries must make our analysis, and any other, incomplete.

From growth to decline to resurgence

The development of the Bahian sugar economy can be summarized briefly. There was a period of rapid growth from 1570 to 1620, marked by an expansion in the number of mills and a sugar price that generally rose and remained well ahead of the general price level. Difficulties for the industry were created in the 1620s by a fall in sugar prices and by warfare, but by the 1630s a recovery had been made. In fact, from 1622 to 1635 sugar prices increased about 120 percent while the prices of local goods rose only about 45 percent. After 1635, however, although sugar prices remained strong, the relationship with the general price level changed, and between that date and 1652 sugar prices fell slightly (7 percent) while the general price level rose by almost 40 percent.[13] Analysis of the period from 1650 to 1680 is complicated by European politics, changing markets for sugar, Portuguese fiscal and commercial policies, and a lack of sources. Despite problems and complaints, the Bahian sugar economy appears to have done relatively well in these years, with sugar prices remaining high enough to offset the cost of replacing slaves, a major item of planter expense.

The 1680s saw a severe slump, in which sugar prices fell while costs were rising. Foreign competition began to have severe effects on Brazilian sugar. European war from 1689 to 1713, however, resuscitated the demand for Brazilian sugar, and despite dislocations caused by the discovery of gold in the interior, the Bahian sugar economy did well in these years. But by the 1720s, when sugar prices began to level, the difficulties of the industry became increasingly apparent. Although the production of sugar and its price had been strong in the early years of the eighteenth century, these gains had been more than offset by a general inflationary trend, beginning before, but accelerated by, the gold rush. This was especially true of slave prices, but it characterized foodstuffs as well. Sugar production diminished in the 1720s and 1730s, and the industry began an era of relative stagnation broken by short periods of increased production and growth during conflicts between the European metropolises of Brazilian competitors in the Caribbean.

Thus, in the period after 1750 there were short-term fluctuations in the sugar industry: Hard times in the early 1750s were followed by expansion in the early 1760s as a result of European conflicts. Then came a decade of stagnation followed once again by expansion, this time fueled by the disruption in the world sugar market caused by the American Revolution after 1776 and the conflict between England and France. With the Haitian Revolution in 1793 and the destruction of that great former French plantation colony, a new stimulus was given to all the other sugar-producing regions, and Bahia like other areas of Brazil experienced a rapid expansion of its sugar economy. With some fluctuation, this phase lasted until Brazilian independence in the early 1820s. During the next decade, world sugar prices fell drastically, as did the Brazilian rate of exchange in London. The result was considerably lower earnings despite large crops. Improvement and stability returned after 1835. But by this time Brazilian sugar filled only about 10 percent of the world market, and its relative proportion in Brazilian exports was also falling.

In broad terms, then, the periodization of the Brazilian sugar economy is not simply a "century of sugar" (1570–1670) followed by stagnation and decline. Rather, it is one in which the defining event is the rise of Caribbean competitors and Brazilian responses to that situation. The period after 1750 is in economic terms little different from the one that preceded it, except that after that date the Portuguese government began attempting to deal with the new competitive situation. These efforts combined with changing political contexts and social unrest to create strains in the colonial relationship and within the social order of the colony itself. For this reason, I will deal with the period after 1750 separately, in Part IV; in this chapter, I will examine the major trends in the sugar economy before that date.

Prices and production

I will now try to detail the summary just given with qualitative and quantitative data, although the latter are difficult to obtain. I shall first examine the growth of the sugar economy in terms of the number of engenhos, the producing units. Then the production output and price of sugar will be examined from the sixteenth through the mid–eighteenth century. These two elements will enable me to estimate the total income generated by the sugar economy from the planters' point of view. Finally, I will try to relate that income to the level of costs and expenses in a general way, using especially the price of slaves as a

Table 7-1. *Number of Brazilian sugar mills, 1570–1629*

Captaincy	1. Gandavo, 1570	2. Cardim, 1583	Growth Rate, 1 to 2	3. Campos Moreno, 1612	Growth Rate, 2 to 3	4. Cadena, 1629	Growth Rate, 3 to 4
Pará, Ceafa, Maranhao, Rio Grande				1			
Paraíba				12		24	(4.3)
Itamaracá	1			10		18	(3.5)
Pernambuco	23	66	(8.4)	90	(1.0)	150	(3.1)
Sergipe				1			
Bahia	18	36	(5.4)	50	(1.1)	80	(2.8)
Ilhéus	8	3		5		4	
Porto Seguro	5	1		1			
Espirito Santo	1	6		(8)[a]		8	
Rio de Janeiro		3		(14)[a]1	(5.8)	60	(7.9)
São Vicente, Santo Amaro	4					2	
Totals	60	115	(5.1)	192	(1.8)	346	(3.6)

[a]Figures from Jácome Monteiro (1610) in Serafim Leite, *HCJB*, VIII, 393–428.
Source: Frédéric Mauro, *Le Portugal et l'Atlantique au xvii siècle* (Paris, 1960), 192–211.

measure of costs. This last element will be examined more closely in Chapter 8, which will cover profitability.

Between 1570 and 1630, various observers wrote descriptions of the colony that usually included estimates of the number of sugar mills in each captaincy. Although these estimates vary and are sometimes inconsistent, it is possible to determine the secular trend of engenho construction from them as an indication of the industry's growth. These figures, presented in Table 7-1, indicate a period of rapid growth from 1570 to about 1585, a slowing from 1585 to 1612, and another less intense period of growth from 1612 to 1630.[14]

In 1570, Pedro Magalhães de Gandavo reported that there were 60 engenhos in Brazil, two-thirds of them in Pernambuco and Bahia. During the next fifteen years, the number of mills appears to have almost doubled, according to reports written between 1583 and 1585. The rate of growth in Pernambuco, 8.4 percent, was considerably more than that of Bahia, but the growth in both captaincies was striking. By 1600, Brazil had between 190 and 200 engenhos producing about 600,000 arrobas, or between 8,000 and 9,000 metric tons, of sugar a year. By 1625, the estimate of annual production was 960,000 arrobas, or close to 14,000 tons.[15] The rising price for sugar in Europe provided a constant incentive to expansion. Capital was available, and it was increasingly Portuguese rather than foreign. In 1551, the crown had granted a ten-year exemption from taxes to all newly constructed mills as an incentive, and this privilege was continually extended.

The industry was able to overcome negative conditions. The first law against the enslavement of Indians was promulgated in 1570 and later supplemented in 1585, but planters successfully circumvented this legislation. When in 1609 the crown tried to enact more effective restrictions, the outcry in Brazil was so strong that the crown was forced to retract them. "Cheap" Indian laborers were, as we have seen, still available in the early seventeenth century, although by this time the flow of black slaves from Angola and Guinea was gaining momentum.

The period between the mid-1580s and 1612 witnessed a less rapid growth in the major sugar-producing captaincies, although formerly undeveloped Rio de Janeiro began to grow as a sugar producer. Brazil's overall rate of engenho construction dropped from about 5 percent a year to less than 2 percent. This slowing was then followed by a second spurt of expansion. The report penned by Diogo de Campos Moreno in 1612 listed ninety mills in Pernambuco and twenty-three in its adjacent captaincies. Although this was a significant increase over the sixty-six mills reported for Pernambuco in 1583, the rate of growth was considerably less than in the previous period. The pace of increase in Bahia was even slower; from thirty-six engenhos in 1583 to fifty in 1612, an annual growth rate of only 1 percent.[16]

In the years following Campos Moreno's report, engenho construction began to speed up again. Expansion in the post-1612 period does not seem to have been led by favorable prices, at least in the 1620s when the market for sugar was poor. Instead, it appears that the technical innovation, the three-roller vertical mill, introduced or developed in Brazil between 1608 and 1612, was largely responsible for the spurt of growth. As we discussed in Chapter 5, the principal advantage of the new mill seems to have been a reduction in the cost of establishing an engenho, although there may have been gains in production as well.[17] The new mill was more efficient in extracting the juice from the cane and thus eliminated some of the formerly needed equipment. Older mills were converted to the cheaper system, and many new ones were built.[18] The less costly mills, sometimes called trapiches, were in fact so much less expensive to build that the crown withdrew its ten-year tax exemption from their operations.[19] This innovation, nevertheless, seems primarily responsible for the rapid expansion of mill construction at the beginning of the seventeenth century.

The effects of the expansion can be seen in the report of Pedro Cadena de Vilhasanti, written in 1629.[20] In it, Vilhasanti noted 150 mills in Pernambuco and 80 in Bahia, or a growth rate of 3.1 percent a year in the former and 2.8 percent in the latter for the period from 1612 to 1629. The effect of the three-roller mill was particularly striking in captaincies like Paraíba, where the number of engenhos doubled to 24, or Rio de Janeiro, which by 1629 had 60 mills in operation, although most of these were small. At the time of the Dutch invasion of Pernambuco in 1630, about 350 mills were operating in Brazil.

By the mid–seventeenth century, it is much more difficult to trace the number of mills in a given year because of bankruptcies, destruction due to war, and the fact that plague, drought, or flood often caused temporary stoppage, abandonment, or sale. In 1702, Bahia sent 507,697 arrobas to Portugal under the marks of 249 different producers, but perhaps 100 of these were lavradores without their own mills. Antonil's account from the list for the first decade of the eighteenth century reported 146 engenhos in Bahia producing roughly the same amount of sugar (507,500 arrobas). By 1755, that number had risen to 172 and by 1758 to 180, although the overall average production per engenho seems to have declined in this period because of the construction of smaller units. The increase of Bahian engenhos in between 1710 and 1758 was less than 1 mill a year, a rate reflecting the difficulties encountered by the Brazilian sugar economy in the eighteenth century.

The average productive capacity of an engenho is uncertain. Estimates made at various points during the colonial period vary widely, from as much as 175 tons to as few as 15. To some extent, the discrepancies reflect faulty information, but they also seem to represent a tendency for average production per mill to decline from the sixteenth to the eighteenth centuries. Moreover, yearly production fluctuated widely, depending on climate, rainfall, management, and international conditions. Ambrósio Fernandes Brandão stated in 1612 that small engenhos produced between 3,000 and 4,000 arrobas, whereas large mills could make 10,000 to 12,000 (145–175 metric tons).[21] This last figure is very high and was reached by only a few. At Engenho Sergipe, production reached 7,000 arrobas in only three safras of the fifty for which accounts survive, and it falls into the high range only if we increase that figure by 60 percent to represent sugar kept by lavradores. In a 1624 list of Pernambucan mills, only one unit, Engenho Magdalena, fell into the 10,000-arroba category.[22] In general after 1660, Bahian engenhos seem to have been larger than those of Rio de Janeiro and Pernambuco. By the late seventeenth century, Bahian mills were usually estimated to have an average productive capacity of about 3,700 arrobas, or about 54 tons. Table 7-2 summarizes some of these estimates.

The changing number of engenhos is an imperfect gauge of the vicissitudes of the industry. Another measure needed to trace the health of the Bahian sugar economy is the price at which planters sold their sugar and its by-products – molasses and rum. Establishing sugar prices is no easy matter for a variety of reasons. Price quotations are rare for most of the sixteenth century and are also lacking for many years in the seventeenth century. At least six grades of sugar were produced in Bahia, and price citations often do not distinguish be-

Table 7-2. *Estimates of sugar production and productivity, 1591–1755*

Source	Date	Place	Number of engenhos	Total Production (arrobas)	Production per engenhos (arrobas)	Production per engenhos (metric tons)
A	1591	Pernambuco	63	378,000	6,000	87
B	1610	Bahia	63	300,000	4,762	69
C	1614	Brazil	(192)[a]	700,000	3,646[a]	53
D	1624	Brazil	(300)	960,000	3,200	47
E	1622	Pernambuco	119	544,072	4,824	70
F	1632	Bahia	84	313,500	3,700	54
G	1637	Brazil	350	900,000	2,571	37
H	1737	Brazil	(350)[b]	937,500	2,678	39
I	1675	Bahia	69[c]		7,500	109
J	1702	Bahia Sergipe	(249)[d]	507,697	2,039	30
K	1710	Brazil	528	1,295,700	2,454	36
		Bahia	146	507,500	3,476	51
		Pernambuco	246	403,500	1,750	26
		Rio de Janeiro	136	357,700	2,630	38
L	1751	Pernambuco	276	240,000	1,034	15
M	1755	Bahia	172	357,115	2,076	30
N	1758	Bahia	180	400,000	2,222	32
O	1786	Bahia	150[e]	400,000	2,667	39

[a]Calculations are based on number of engenhos listed in 1612 account of Diogo de Campos Moreno.
[b]Number of engenhos is taken from account of Pedro Cadena of 1629.
[c]Freyre obviously overestimates production of Bahian engenhos, which he places at from 7,000–8,000 arrobas each. In the same year, Sebastião Cardoso de Sampaio wrote of 130 engenhos in the Recôncavo. See Pinheiro da Silva, "A Capitania da Bahia," *Revista Portuguesa de História* 8: 180–1.
[d]This number represents individual producers and must include lavradores de cana as well as senhores de engenho.
[e]*DUP*, II, 213–23.
Sources:
A: Domingos Abreu e Brito, *Um inquérito a vida administrativa e econômica de Angola do Brasil* (1591), ed. Alfredo de Albuquerque Felner (Coimbra, 1931). B: Jácome Monteiro in Leite, *HCJB*, 8, appendix I, 404. C: André Farto da Costa, AHU, Bahia, caixa 1a. D: See later in this chapter. E: Joseph Israel da Costa in *Revista do Museu do Açúcar* 1 (1968): 25–36. F: Pedro Cadena in F. Mauro, *Le Brésil au xviie siècle* (Coimbra, 1963), 170. G&H: Geraldo de Onizio in Serafim Leite, ed., *Relação diária do cêrco da Bahia* 8 (1941), 110. I: Francisco de Brito Freyre, *História da Guerra Brazilica* (Lisbon, 1678), 75, 163. J: ANTT, Junta do Tobaco, various maços. K: Antonil, *Cultura*, liv.3, cap. 10. L: José Ribeiro, Jr., *Colonização e monopólio no nordeste brasileiro* (São Paulo, 1974), 8. M: José Antônio Caldas, *Notícia geral de toda esta capitania da Bahia* (1759) (Bahia, 1951), 429–38. N: Coelho de Mello in *ABNR*, xxxi, 321. O: "Discurso preliminar," in [Manoel] Pinto de Aguiar, *Aspectos da economia colonial* (Salvador, 1957).

tween the various subgrades of white and muscavado. In any given year, or even on a given day, prices could vary widely. The Benedictine Abbott Frei Antônio da Encarnação Penna stated in 1794, "Sugar many times the same day will have various prices depending on supply, the number of ships for loading, the haste with which one or another must sail, the need for money that the senhor de engenho or seller has, and other similar circumstances."[23] The complexity of the local market, therefore, adds to the already serious deficiencies in the data.

We do not have a consistent price series for Brazilian sugar that reflects the amount received by the planters, and it is therefore difficult to calculate regional or individual income within the sugar industry. It is possible, however, to use a number of series to establish trends; even though there are often lacunae in the series, they can be used to analyze earnings. The most important series for these purposes has been extracted from the accounts of Engenho Sergipe and thus are at the mill price. In addition, another set of prices for 1675 to 1769 has been developed by Dauril Alden based on purchases of sugar made by the Misericórdia hospital of Salvador. For the years 1750 to 1830, Katia M. de Queirós Mattoso studied the cost of living. She developed a series of sugar prices, and although these are not published in a form that makes them readily comparable to other series, her study can be used to analyze the basic trend. Using these various series, the secular trend of sugar prices in Brazil can be established with some security, although with more security for some periods than others (see Appendix B). Lacking adequate local records, most analyses of the Brazilian sugar economy have depended on price series based on the major European markets, usually London or Amsterdam. Although these published series are easily accessible and can indicate long-term trends, they are not particularly helpful in understanding local conditions nor the responses of planters or merchants to short-term fluctuations. In fact, the European price series are often misleading, and their movement was sometimes in opposition to the trend in the colony. A war, for example, often interrupted Atlantic commerce and thus caused a shortage of sugar on the wharves of London or Amsterdam. Prices in those markets rose sharply in response to the meager supply. Meanwhile in Bahia, chests of sugar piled up because there were no ships available to carry them or willing to risk the voyage. Prices fell. The European prices are thus not a satisfactory measure of the state of the Bahian sugar economy or of the planters' position in the short term.

The series of at-the-mill prices for white sugar adjusted to compensate for the currency devaluation of 1688 presented in Figure 7-1 represents the secular trend.[24] Its tendency is mildly upward over the more than two hundred years observed, but the curve is also marked by violent peaks and valleys, with each peak, however, somewhat higher

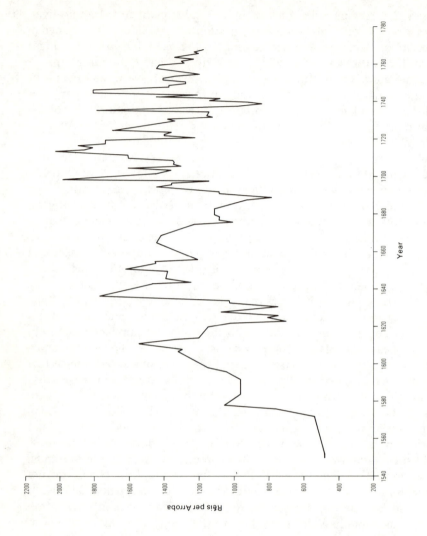

Figure 7-1. Adjusted price of white sugar at the mill in Bahia, 1550–1768.

than that before it. Prices seem to move strongly upward until about 1620, and then there is a serious decline until the mid-1630s. A new peak was reached after 1640, but it was then followed by a period of gradual decline to a new low in the 1680s. Recovery in the 1690s was once again followed by gradual decline, although the early eighteenth century was a period of wide fluctuation. The price series seems to indicate three crises – in the 1620s, the 1680s, and the 1730s – spaced roughly fifty to sixty years apart. From the point of view of the planters, however, the cyclical nature of these crises or the secular trend of the prices was difficult to discern. Their horizons were much more limited, and, so long as the particularly bad years were followed by better ones, hope welled eternally from their breasts and purses.

For the sixteenth century, local prices in Bahia are particularly difficult to obtain. Some scattered observations exist for the 1550s, but these are records of institutional sale or purchase, and their repeated quotation of 400 réis per arroba is not to be fully trusted as the market price.[25] For 1572 to 1579, a short run of prices extracted from the testament of Mem de Sá and the inventory of his two engenhos of Sergipe do Conde and Santana can be made.[26] These prices display a strong upward tendency, with the mean price of white and muscavado sugar rising over 40 percent during these seven years. Prices in Lisbon and London seemed to rise sharply between 1578 and 1582, but there is no way to know if that was the case in Brazil. In fact, the price of 880 réis of 1578 at Engenho Sergipe was higher than the price of 800 réis noted by a visitor to Bahia in 1584.

For the middle 1590s, the account book of Miguel Dias de Santiago, a merchant established in Bahia, provides some sugar prices. These show a steady rise from an average of 865 réis for an arroba of white in 1596 to 910 in 1597 and 950 in 1598, with muscavado and lower-grade panela making similar gains.[27] A decade later, in 1608, Engenho Sergipe received on the average 1$083 for its white sugar, or about 12 percent more than it had received in 1598. Unfortunately, there are no adequate observations for the intervening years.

The first decades of the seventeenth century were apparently a period of boom for the Bahian sugar economy and for that of Brazil in general. A series of good harvests (except for a drought in 1615), the introduction of the three-roller mill, and the conclusion of peace between Spain and the United Provinces of the Netherlands in 1609 all contributed to a climate of peace and expansion. The price of sugar held steady above 1$ until 1620, when it began to drop. That year seems to mark a short downturn or depression in the Atlantic economy, and the price of sugar slipped badly. An arroba of white sugar in 1623 sold for about half its 1613 value. The situation was so bad by 1623 that for six months no one offered to farm the tithe contract because of the "low price and poor reputation of the sugars."[28] Not until 1633 did the price of sugar begin to rise strongly again, finally reaching the level of over 1$ per arroba only in the safra of 1635–6.

What had happened? A Bahian planter watching the final crating of his sugar at the engenho and learning that for the first time in years the price for his product was falling in Europe must have been confused and alarmed. Certainly, observers much closer to the center of the European economy in London and the *arbitristas* or memorialists in Spain were confounded by the same phenomenon and could not agree on the root of the crisis or contraction.[29] In fact, Europe was passing through a period of depression that struck most of the continent between 1619 and 1622. Its causes, effects, and timing are much debated by historians, but it appears that the sixteenth-century expansion of population, urban industries, the stock of money, and the number of entrepreneurs had by 1620 come to an end, and "trade like the moon was on the wane," as one English observer put it.[30]

Specific explanations for the contraction vary from country to country, but some general factors underlay the process. The beginning of the Thirty Years' War in 1618 had thrown the economy of Europe into a period of turmoil as governments sought ways to pay for the fighting. There was a great deal of currency manipulation and devaluation as governments enhanced or debased the relationship of their money of account to silver. The resultant confusion created unfavorable trade balances for some states, such as England, and led to extreme caution in foreign commerce. Added to this monetary crisis was a temporary inventory problem in which stocks had piled up, immobilizing merchant capital and thus reducing orders for more goods.[31] Underlying all this were perhaps more fundamental problems in the basis of Europe's economy, such as a downturn in the flow of silver from Spain's American colonies that had fueled the steady inflation of prices of the late sixteenth century. But the Bahian planter did not perceive these structural problems.[32] What he did know, and know well, was that in 1611 3,000 arrobas of sugar had been worth 3,861$ and that in 1623 those 3,000 arrobas were valued at only 1,740$, a reduction in value of 45 percent.

By 1624, the dislocation of the European markets had been overcome and trade recovered within the context of war. Brazil in general and Bahia in particular were not able to recover so quickly. In 1621, the twelve-year truce between Holland and Spain had expired and the Dutch West India Company had been formed as a partly commercial and partly military organization to carry on the war against Hapsburg Spain. Portugal and its possessions, which had come under Hapsburg control in 1580, were selected as primary targets by the Dutch because they were not well defended, because the ardor of the Portuguese for the Hapsburg cause was doubted, and because the Dutch had traditionally carried much of the Brazilian trade and after 1605 had been excluded from it by Spanish commercial policies. After a propaganda campaign to convince the directors of the company of the advantages of attacking Brazil, an expedition was launched against Bahia.[33] Salvador fell in May 1624, although local resistance continued in the Recôncavo. The following year, a large Luso-Spanish armada retook the city, but the results of the fighting in 1624–5 were disastrous for the sugar economy of the Recôncavo.

We know something of the effects of the Dutch invasion and the subsequent fighting on individual engenhos because of surviving correspondence.[34] Francisco de Abreu da Costa, owner of a mill on Itaparica Island, was in Portugal when the invasion took place. His sons wrote to him from the engenho in July 1625 to report on conditions. The safra of the previous year had been delayed until October because all small boats and canoes needed for transport as well as slaves had been requisitioned by the Luso-Spanish forces. At Engenho Sergipe, everything was in disarray. A report also written in July 1625 noted that the Dutch had seized copper, cloth, and other supplies belonging to the engenho in the city and had taken thirty chests of sugar awaiting shipment.[35] Slaves had run off or died, some chests of sugar hidden in the woods had deteriorated, and Sergipe also had suffered from a lack of boats to transport sugar chests, cane, and firewood. The administrator, Father Simão de Sottomaior, had fled at the news of the Dutch attack, and the mill had lost half the safra of 1623–4 and all that of 1624–5. It was operating again by 1626, but it was "a hospital of despair" (hospital de desemparo), as was the Brazilian economy in general, of which Bahia produced one-third to two-fifths of the total value.[36]

Futher evidence of the severe downturn in the Bahian economy in the 1620s can be seen in the amount paid for the tithe contracts. The tithe was a one-tenth tax on all production owed to the church, but in Brazil it was collected by the monarch in his capacity as grand master of the Order of Christ.[37] In most cases, the state did not actually collect this tax but farmed it out to the highest bidder, who then hoped to collect a certain percentage in excess of his bid. The tithe contract was farmed out in Portugal until 1606, after which it was awarded in Brazil (although there were occasions when bids in Portugal were accepted thereafter).[38]

Some authors have used the tithes as measures of production. This is a misleading use of them. The tithe contracts are best viewed as an educated estimate of the value of production. The contractor had a rough idea of a region's productivity, but he could not foresee droughts, floods, or wars.[39] He probably had a much better ability to estimate the price of the major commodities produced. He knew that if production doubled but the price fell by half, the value of the contract was no greater than it had been before those changes. Thus although the tithe is not a surrogate measure for production, it is an indication of the probable value of production based on an interested observer's best estimate, and as such is a fairly good guide to the health of the economy.[40]

In Bahia in the seventeenth century, the tithe (dizimo) contract was auctioned annually on all production.[41] Usually, the contract included Bahia, Sergipe de El-Rey, Ilhéus, and Porto Seguro. Most products were tithed, but since sugar constituted 90 percent of the value, the tithe is a fair gauge of that industry's progress – with a final caveat, however. Some sugar products, melles and panelas, were not tithed. Then, too, newly constructed or rebuilt mills were often given ten-year exemptions from taxes. Religious corporations such as the Jesuits argued that their estates also enjoyed an exemption, as did property held by knights of the military orders.[42] These exemptions were hotly debated during the colonial era, but they are one more reason why the tithe cannot be used as a direct measure of sugar production. Given these limitations, Figure 7-2 presents the tithe contracts from 1612 to 1657.[43] During the 1610s, the contract was usually farmed for between 60,000 and 70,000 cruzados (a cruzado was a coin equal to 400 réis). The precipitous drop in 1623–4 was due to the collapse of prices and to the Dutch invasion. The slow recovery after that date reflected the disruption of production, interruption of maritime links, and a softening of price on the European markets. Not until 1632–3 was the secular trend of the tithe strongly upward again.[44]

The 1620s were thus a period of depression in the Bahian sugar economy, a situation created by the general economic conditions in Europe but exacerbated by the Dutch invasion and the subsequent fighting in the Recôncavo and on the high seas. The Portuguese estimated that in 1626 and 1627 some eighty ships had been lost with cargoes worth more than 5 million milréis.[45] Maritime losses brought despair in both Portugal and Brazil during the 1620s as various authors sought to identify the problems and suggest remedies for them. These memorials present us an opportunity to examine the outlines of the Bahian sugar economy at the end of its first cycle of expansion.

The first memorial, written in Lisbon about 1627, proposed the creation of a fleet of guard ships to convoy the ships in the Brazil trade.[46] The author estimated that between 1626 and 1627 about 60 of the 300 ships in the Brazil trade had been lost. Each of these had carried 400 to 700 crates of sugar, with each crate averaging 18 arrobas (576 pounds). This amounted to a loss of 540,000 arrobas, and of the tax revenue on this sugar. The author's discussion indicated that about one-quarter of the sugars shipped from Brazil did not pay normal taxes because of the various exemptions. Low sugars (panelas, melles) made up about one-quarter of the total and were not fully taxed, whereas the macho sugar, white and muscavado, paid in various duties an average of 550 réis per

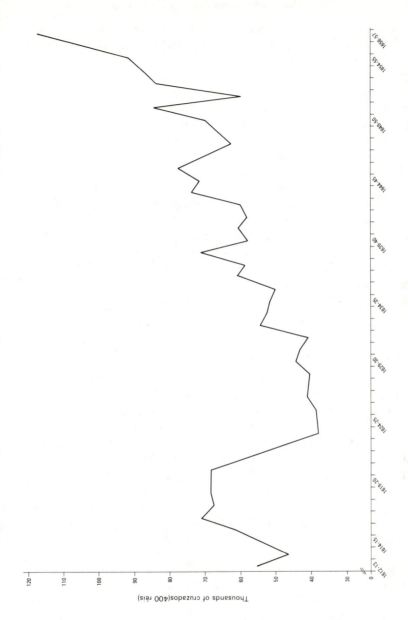

Figure 7-2. Tithes for Bahia, Ilhéus, Porto Seguro, and Sergipe de El-Rey, 1612–57. (Source: 1612–24 Joyce (1974). 1625–56 AHU. Bahia. No. 162 [Fonseca])

arroba.[47] These sugars sold for prices in Lisbon from 40 to 60 percent above the local price in Brazil. Half the 505,000 arrobas sold at the Lisbon market price for white sugar of 1$500 per arroba would be worth 405,000$, and the remaining muscavado at 900 réis and panela at 660 réis would yield another 202,500$ for a total loss of 607,500$ in sugar value, plus an additional 205,000$ in taxes of sugar and on European imports traded for that sugar in Lisbon..

A second memorial penned between 1625 and 1630 spoke in more general terms about the scope and value of Brazil's production and the effects of the war. The Dutch attacks had reduced the colony's value. The tithe contract for all Brazil, which had run at between 135 and 140 cruzados before 1621, now could command only 100 to 110. Brazil's estimated annual production of sugar was about 800,000 arrobas of white and muscavado, the so-called macho sugars, and an additional 150,000 of panelas and lower grades. Of the 800,000 arrobas, two-thirds (534,000) were white sugar. Using the standard Lisbon prices, the memorialist then worked out the value of the sugar crop:

(56%)	534,000 arrobas of white at 1$600	854,400$
(28%)	266,000 arrobas of muscavado at 1$200	319,200$
(16%)	150,000 arrobas of melles at 400 réis	60,000$
Totals	950,000 arrobas	1,233,000$

We know that Bahia and Ilhéus in this period had eighty-four engenhos, and the tithe contracts indicate that Bahia's production was about 33 to 40 percent of the colony's total. Thus, the eighty-four mills produced about 313,500 arrobas, or an average of about 3,700 arrobas per engenho.[48] At the current price in Bahia, using the same percentage distribution of the various grades of sugar, the value of this sugar in 1629 would have been 165,183$982 or 1,966$ per mill. We can compare the effect of the fall of prices at the mills by comparing the figures of 1629 with those of 1612 when prices were high. Table 7-3 presents this comparison, first by assuming a production per mill of 4,700 arrobas in 1612 to allow for the existence of larger units prior to the diffusion of the three-roller mill and then by using the percentage distribution of sugar grades indicated in the memorial. The value of the Bahian sugar crop had declined by more than 20 percent between the two dates, and the average gross income per mill was down by almost half. Even if we assume an average output per mill in 1612 equal to that of 1629, while the value of total output would be about the same, the average income per engenho would still be some 35 percent less at the latter date.

Between 1630 and 1670, the Bahian economy was confronted with a series of short-term gains and losses caused by the struggle between the Dutch and the realms of the Spanish Hapsburgs, which included Portugal and its colonies, and by the responses of European prices to the interruption of colonial trade. Unseen by the Brazilian planters at

Table 7-3. *Estimate of the Bahian sugar crop, 1612 and 1629*

Year	Number of engenhos	Estimated average production per mill (arrobas)	Sugar Type	Arrobas	Price per arroba (réis)	Value (réis)
1612	55	4,700	White	144,760	1,287	186,306$120
			Muscavado	72,380	771	55,804$980
			Panela	41,360	480	19,852$800
			Total	258,500		*Total* 261,963$900
						Average per engenho 4,762$980
1612	55	3,700	White	113,960	1,287	146,666$520
			Muscavado	56,980	771	43,931$800
			Panela	32,560	480	15,628$800
			Total	203,500		*Total* 206,226$900
						Average per engenho 3,749$580
1629–30	84	3,700	White	174,048	714	124,270$270
			Muscavado	87,024	373	32,459$952
			Panela	49,728	170	8,453$760
			Total	310,800		*Total* 165,183$982
						Average per engenho 1,966$476

the time, however, was the development during this same period of a potentially much more serious problem – the rise of new sugar colonies as competitors on the European markets.

Hard times: enemies and competitors

In 1630, the Dutch returned to Brazil and seized Olinda, capital of Pernambuco, Brazil's largest sugar producer. Fighting continued in the interior until 1637, with considerable destruction of canefields and engenhos. In addition to those damaged, sixty-five engenhos were confiscated by the Dutch after they had been abandoned by their Portuguese owners.[49] Although many of these were then sold to other Portuguese residents or to Dutch planters, the overall result of the fighting and confiscation was a sharp decline in Pernambuco's sugar output.[50] The shortage caused by the war in Brazil and the depletion of European stock caused the Amsterdam price for sugar to rise, and by 1633 the situation for Bahian planters looked much improved.[51] Sugar prices at Engenho Sergipe reached a high point in 1637–8, but at no time in the 1640s or 1650s did they fall below a milréi per arroba.

To some extent, Bahia's prosperity was gained through Pernambuco's misfortune. The war seriously damaged the northern captaincy's productive capacity. Pernambuco's potential for sugar production was estimated at 15,000 to 20,000 crates a year, but even during a period of relative peace (1640–5) it barely produced 7,000 crates.[52] Then, too, during the fighting of the 1630s many planters had abandoned Pernambuco for Bahia, bringing with them slaves and capital. Perhaps 7,000 to 8,000 whites and mestiços, and 4,000 or more black slaves left Pernambuco for Bahia or Rio de Janeiro.[53] Some new mills were constructed in Bahia, and slaves were sold or rented out to Bahian planters. Planters in Pernambuco found themselves in need of labor because of the emigration and because of many runaways who took advantage of the disruption to flee. Despite the efforts of the Dutch West India Company to supply credit and slaves, by 1654, when the Dutch were finally expelled from the Northeast, Pernambuco had suffered so much from the fighting, the depletion of labor, and a three-year period of drought that its production of sugar had fallen to only 10 percent of Brazil's total. Even in the period of peace, 1640–5, its share was only about 20 percent; this was a far cry from the late sixteenth century, when Pernambucan sugar had made up some 60 percent of production. During the Dutch period, Bahia overtook Pernambuco as Brazil's leading producer – a position it would maintain for the next century and a half.

Nor was Pernambuco's problem simply one of production. During the Luso-Brazilian revolt (1645–54), which eventually drove the Dutch from Brazil, the military campaigns were essentially supported by taxes levied on sugar. In 1648, more than 80 percent of the taxes were on sugar production and commerce, and by 1649 the sugar tax (donativo de açúcar) alone yielded 36 percent of Pernambuco's total revenue. "The War of Divine Liberation" was, in the words of Brazilian historian Evaldo Cabral de Mello, not only fought over sugar, "but financed by it as well."[54] Whatever profits were being made in sugar growing were being drained by the war, preventing the reinvestment of capital in the industry or in other sectors of the economy. The burning of mills and canefields after 1645 by the rebel troops and the confiscation of plantations by the Dutch added to the disruption. In the subordinate captaincies of Pernambuco (Rio Grande, Itamaraca, and Paraíba), fifty-five engenhos were fogo morto during the period 1646–54. The end of the fighting brought little relief. The rebuilding of Recife was financed by continued taxing of the sugar economy, thereby depleting capital needed for restocking and expansion. A sort of closed circle was created: Because of the disruption of Pernambuco's sugar economy, royal revenues were down, and the funds for rebuilding the captaincy were reduced; the main source of revenue was the sugar industry, and so it was taxed, but that simply reduced its potential for growth and revenue and thus closed the circle.

The Dutch invasion of the Northeast was not without its costs to Bahia as well. As the center of Portuguese government in the colony,

Bahia was a primary target for Dutch military actions.[55] Although the Dutch governor, Johan Maurits of Nassau, had called Bahia "a cat not to be taken without gloves," its defenses did not deter the Hollanders from trying. In March 1627, the Dutch captain Piet Heyn entered the Bay of All Saints and caught a fleet of twenty-six sail at anchor. At least 3,000 crates of sugar were captured. He returned in June and caused further damage. In 1638, Nassau staged a major attack, seizing Itaparica Island in front of Salvador and destroying twenty-seven engenhos in the Recôncavo. In 1646, the Dutch returned to seize Itaparica in an attempt to cut off all commerce to Salvador. They held the island for almost a year, and although the blockade failed, some shipping was lost and shortages of foodstuffs occurred in the city. Again, in late December 1648 (11 December 1648–11 January 1649), the Recôncavo was ravaged. Some twenty-three engenhos were burned, and more than 1,500 crates of sugar were seized.[56]

The Bahian sugar planters suffered not only from the depredations of the Dutch but also from the defensive measures taken by their own government. Small ships and slaves were requisitioned in 1624 for the reconquest of Bahia. This measure was again ordered in 1637, and in addition, since the treasury did not have sufficient funds, senhores de engenho and wealthy lavradores de cana were required, at their own expense, to provide small boats for Bahia's defense. The outcry was so great that the crown rescinded the governor's command in 1639.[57] The crown was forced to balance the advantage of having the fleet supplied with small shipping against the damage that the loss of these boats would cause the safra. The count of Torre, the governor, pointed out to the planters, however, that, if the Dutch simply took control of the entrance to the Bay of All Saints, sugar and other local products would decline in value and imported goods would become extremely expensive. Thus they, too, were faced with a difficult choice – provide for defense and hinder production or fail to do so and perhaps suffer from a drop in prices.[58]

In addition to the disruption of agriculture wrought by foe and friend, Bahian planters suffered from the seizure of their cargoes on the high seas. Although these loses were serious in the 1620s and 1630s, by the following decade they were staggering. In 1647 and 1648, 130 Bahian-laden or -bound vessels were lost.[59] The arrival of these prize cargoes in Amsterdam lowered sugar prices there, while the shortage raised sugar prices in Lisbon. In Bahia, these losses had a negative effect, for the shortage of ships caused stockpiling on the wharves and depressed prices. It was claimed that some planters had actually entirely left sugar agriculture because of the insecurity of commerce.

The vulnerability of Brazilian commerce, in fact, was an old and continual problem. Algerian and Moroccan corsairs sailing between Madeira and Lisbon and French, Dutch, and English privateers working the coasts on either side of the Atlantic had all preyed on the sugar ships. By 1582, a new dimension was added when English privateers sailed under letters of marque from Dom Antônio, the pretender to the Portuguese throne.[60] English attempts to trade peacefully in Brazil had been frustrated by Hapsburg exclusivist policies, and by the 1580s and 1590s "Brazilmen" loaded with sugar and hides were the most common prize taken by these English sea rovers. Thirty-four such vessels were captured in 1588–91.[61]

Nor were the English alone in their depredations on the Portuguese trade with Brazil. The Dutch had been major trading partners with Portugal, carrying Portuguese salt and wines and Brazilian sugar in return for manufactures, cheese, copper, and cloth. Dutch ships, especially the large *urcas*, carried much of the Brazilian trade in the sixteenth century, and as late as 1600 the Dutch sent 124 ships to Lisbon, of which 34 were licensed to sail for Brazil.[62] The 1605 Hapsburg exclusion of the Dutch from trade within Hapsburg dominions, including Portugal and its colonies, upset a long-standing relationship.[63] By 1607, Dutch corsairs were taking large numbers of caravels in the Brazil trade and selling the prize sugars in Germany, Italy, and North Africa, as well as in Holland itself.[64]

Brazilian planters, Lisbon merchants, and the crown were all concerned about these losses. The customshouse of Lisbon was reorganized in 1587, and shipping duties, the *avería* and the *consulado*, were instituted in the 1590s to pay for the costs of providing a coast guard and some protection for the shipping in the trade.[65] In addition, a 20 percent import tax and a 10 percent sales tax were imposed by the crown despite the grumbling of the merchants and the planters, who resented these costs. The crown also began to require that insurance be purchased for Lisbon-bound cargoes.[66] Other taxes on sugar commerce were added in the seventeenth century, and each brought a new complaint from the producers and merchants.

A number of observers perceived the problem to rest at least partially in the nature of the vessels employed in the Brazil trade. The Portuguese had always favored the use of small, light caravels of 80 to 120 tons, which had little or no armament and small crews.[67] These ships were sturdy, and their turnaround time in port was short. A number used by Engenho Sergipe in the early seventeenth century made two and even three voyages a year.[68] Planters and merchants did not find their small capacity a hindrance and often divided cargoes among a number of ships, simply ignoring any other type of insurance against loss. The caravels, however, had their disadvantages. Padre Vieira called them "schools for cowardice," since their only defense was flight; but even that was problematical, as they were often overloaded.[69] Diego Brochado, supervisor of the Lisbon harbor, reported to the Spanish Council of War in 1608 that he had seen these little ships so heavily laden that their decks were virtually awash and their crews of ten or twelve too small to handle a crate of twenty arrobas.[70] In 1632, the crown ordered such overloading to end, but to no effect.[71] Unable to fight or flee, the little ships were easy prizes. Still, the caravels were preferred by many merchants to the urcas or *naos*, the standard larger, better-armed merchant vessels; the capacity of these bigger ships was large enough that, given the limited market in Brazil for European goods, the arrival of two or three vessels in port so lowered the price of imports that the merchants faced a much lower margin of gain.[72] Despite the dangers of commerce in caravels and the pressures of the crown to use larger ships or to alter the manner in which the caravels operated, little change was made. Only with the great losses of the late 1640s did the merchants accede to a change in the nature of shipping to Brazil, but that change was accompanied by an alteration in the nature of trade itself. From a situation of "free trade" to all Portuguese ports, little royal regulation, and no control over the colonial market for imports, a new system of centralized, regulated trade in a convoy system was instituted.

The idea of a convoy or fleet for the Brazil trade had long been discussed. It was suggested as early as 1586, and in 1615 the Spanish ambassador in London renewed the proposal. But its cost and the objections of Portugal's merchants were barriers too great to surmount.[73] The attacks of the Dutch West India Company in the 1620s created renewed interest in the project, but still nothing was done.[74] What the crown had failed to do, the losses of 1647–8 accomplished. With the urging of Salvador de Sá, Father Vieira, and others, the Brazil Company (Companhia geral do estado do Brasil) was created in 1649, mostly with capital raised from New Christians.[75] The company was to maintain a fleet of thirty-six armed ships to convoy a fleet to and from Brazil twice a year, in return for which the company was given a monopoly on the import of wine, flour, olive oil, and codfish to the colony and the right to set prices for these commodities. In addition, it could tax the goods carried back to Portugal. Complaints against the company came from the merchants of smaller ports who resented the control of Lisbon that the new plan implied, from clerics who hated the New Christians, and from many in Brazil who thought, and correctly so, that the monopoly of basic food imports would cause prices to rise. Nevertheless, after 1650 the formerly "open" Brazilian export trade was supplanted by the "closed" economy of the fleet system, centered in Lisbon and able to control the price of imports. With this change, the age of the caravel began to close. Caravels were forbidden to trade with Brazil in 1648, and the fleets were increasingly comprised of larger merchant ships sailing under the protecting guns of Portuguese galleons.[76]

The Brazil Company sent its first fleet to the colony in 1650, and it eventually organized separate fleets that were supposed to sail annu-

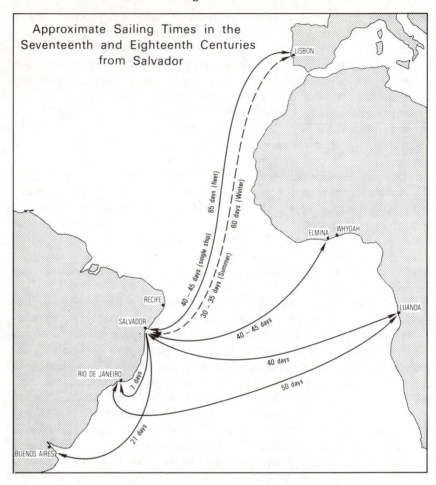

Approximate Sailing Times in the Seventeenth and Eighteenth Centuries from Salvador

LISBON

85 days (fleet)

60 days (Winter)

40 – 45 days (single ship)

30 – 35 days (Summer)

ELMINA   WHYDAH

RECIFE

SALVADOR

40 – 45 days

LUANDA

40 days

RIO DE JANEIRO

7 days

50 days

21 days

BUENOS AIRES

Map 3.

ally to Rio de Janeiro, Recife, Salvador, and the Maranhão. In 1694, the company was transformed into a government agency, the Junta do Comércio, and then in 1720 organization of the fleets became the responsibility of the treasury council.[77] There were continual complaints against the system. Planters suffered especially after those years when there was no fleet and when in the following year the fleet carried two harvests, thus driving prices down. In Bahia at least, the fleets operated with some regularity. Between 1739 and 1763, there were seventeen fleets to Bahia with an annual average of about twenty-three ships in each. The fleet system seemed to provide a partial remedy for the ills of Brazilian commerce, but there were other, more serious problems emerging by the mid-seventeenth century that could not be cured by such measures.

During the three decades of virtually constant warfare on the shores of Brazil and the seas nearby, another process was taking place that ultimately proved even more damaging to the Brazilian sugar economy than the fighting, disruption of production, and maritime losses. The rise of prices in the 1630s for colonial products, especially sugar, created a new series of opportunities for the small Caribbean island colonies of England, France, and Holland, most of which were originally settled in the 1620s and 1630s. Settlers in Barbados, Nevis, and Saint Christopher had done well planting tobacco at first, but as the price of that crop began to fall off in the late 1620s and early 1630s, Caribbean planters experimented with alternative crops like cotton and indigo. The rising price of sugar after 1633 caused by the disruption in Pernambuco made it a possible substitute. Early experiments with sugar in Barbados were unsuccessful, but with the importation of skills and techniques from Pernambuco, Barbadian planters learned the art of sugar making. By 1643, Barbados sugar was for sale in Europe. The French soon followed suit; by 1644, when sugar surpassed indigo in profitability, the English and French planters of the Caribbean were ready to make the transition, supported by high European sugar prices during the revolt in Dutch Brazil. The Caribbean sugar economy received a considerable boost after 1654, when exiles from Dutch Brazil and the Dutch West India Company transferred skills, experience, and capital to the Antilles; but the early growth of that region as a sugar producer and a competitor of Brazil's had predated that shift.[78]

With their own sugar colonies established in the Antilles, the major continental consumers – France and England – began to exclude Brazilian sugar and other products from their shores. Exclusionist policies instituted by Colbert in France and the British navigation acts of 1651, 1660, 1661, and 1673 effectively excluded many Brazilian products from their traditional markets.[79] Between 1650 and 1710, the amount of Brazilian sugar on European markets dropped about 40 percent. Josiah Child, writing in 1669, stated that Portuguese muscavado and panela had been virtually driven out of the European market, and the price of white reduced considerably.[80] In the 1630s, about 80 percent of the sugar sold in London originated in Brazil. By 1670, that figure had fallen to 40 percent; and by 1690, to only 10 percent.[81]

While West Indian planters "groaned" under the heavy taxes and restrictions on trade imposed by their own governments, they were compensated by an assured, and in fact expanding, home market.[82] Portugal with its small population had always depended on reexport as its part of the colonial compact, and by 1670 it could no longer offer either a large home market or receptive allies and neighbors as compensation for the heavy taxes it levied on colonial products.

Finally, the rise of a West Indian sugar economy produced two further long-term negative effects on the Brazilian sugar sector. First, as

Caribbean production increased, so too did those islands' demands for labor. This new and rapidly expanding market for slaves moved the English, Dutch, and French to seek secure slave sources on the African coast. The Dutch, in fact, had seized El Mina in 1638 and Luanda in 1641 in an attempt to supply Dutch Brazil, and although they lost the latter in 1648, their activities in West Africa did not end. Not only did this competition on the African coast disrupt the supply of labor to Portuguese Brazil, which one observer estimated had been 11,000 to 12,000 slaves a year from Angola alone, but the new market for African laborers also tended to increase the price of slaves in Brazil, adding to generally rising costs and driving planter expenses upward.[83]

The second effect of West Indian competition was to set further limits on the possible response of Brazilian planters to their situation. Brazil could still produce more sugar than all its competitors, but it no longer supplied so large a proportion of the market. Thus, because buyers could find other sources of supply, planters increasingly lost the option of dealing with falling prices by suspending production or stockpiling. The alternatives available to Brazilian planters in the face of difficult times were thus more and more limited.

The decades following the expulsion of the Dutch were difficult ones for the Bahian sugar sector and for the Brazilian economy as a whole, owing to both local problems and the international situation. Bahia suffered from a series of natural disasters. In 1665, smallpox caused many slave deaths.[84] In 1667, storms delayed the fleets' arrival and lowered the price at which some planters sold their sugars.[85] The safra of 1668–9 was one of the largest remembered at the time, but hopes for another great harvest the following year were drowned by heavy rains that cut two months off the milling cycle.[86] Droughts occurred in 1671 and 1673, and the captaincy had been hit by a five-year period with little or no rain in the mid-1660s.[87] But production was not the essential problem. Bahia still had the advantages of good soil, easy water transport, and adequate technological and skill levels. Bahia in this period produced more sugar than any other captaincy in Brazil or any competitor in the Caribbean.

Although planters often saw their difficulties as the result of droughts, plagues, or late fleet arrivals, in fact the problems lay deep in the changing political and economic structures of the Atlantic world. Brazilian sugar planters were plagued by both war and peace. The lessening of European tensions after 1648, and especially the end of fighting and a general period of peace after 1675, allowed for the growth of tropical agriculture in the Caribbean and the regularization of the African slave trade. This resulted in both increased international competition for the European sugar trade and, after 1680, a rise in the demand for, and price of, slaves.[88] Because the records for Engenho Sergipe are not available for this period, it is difficult to establish a series of sugar prices in Bahia, but there can be little doubt that these reflected the failing prices on the Lisbon market. Between 1659 and 1668, the Lisbon wholesale price fell by one-third; between 1668 and 1688, it fell by another 11 percent.[89] This same downward trend was noticeable on the London market as well, where, as we have just seen, Caribbean lower grades had all but driven Brazilian sugar from that market. Peace among its competitors was obviously not a blessing to the mills of the Recôncavo.[90]

Attempts at recovery

By 1680 Portugal, like most of Western Europe, was in the grip of a general recession. The underlying causes seem to have been a slowing of population growth, a shortage of capital, and a decline in the flow of bullion from America. Portuguese mercantilist thinkers proposed a variety of remedies, from new crops to industrial development, but by the 1680s Portugal was faced with a chronic public deficit caused by its expenses and by the low price for its colonial products. In 1688, the currency was devalued by 20 percent in an attempt to lessen the debt and create a better trade situation.[91]

In the colonies, the Portuguese crown grasped at any straw. New efforts were made to discover mines in hopes of replacing the specie lost by falling customs revenues. Governor Afonso Furtado de Mendonça arrived at Bahia in 1671 with broad powers to stimulate the search for mineral wealth. He launched a series of campaigns into the Bahia sertão designed to eliminate the Indian threat to the Recôncavo and assure an adequate supply of firewood to the engenhos.[92]

These actions opened new territory for the Bahian ranching and tobacco economies, an important step because hides and tobacco were becoming major items in the Brazil fleets and to some extent can be seen as the captaincy's attempt to develop alternative products. The Bahian tobacco industry, centered in the lands along the Paraguaçu River, had begun to develop in the mid–seventeenth century. As sugar began to experience difficulties, tobacco became an increasingly important export. Bahia came to produce about 90 percent of Brazil's tobacco crop, and the sale of this commodity in Portugal was placed under a government monopoly in 1674. By 1681, Bahia produced more than 18,000 rolls, or about 138,600 arrobas, for the Lisbon market alone.[93] Figure 7-3 demonstrates the growth of the Bahian tobacco trade not only with Lisbon but also with El Mina on the west coast of Africa, where Brazilian tobacco was a welcome item of trade with both the Dutch and Africans.[94]

Peace in Brazil and the south Atlantic had not brought a return to flush times. The expulsion of the Dutch from Angola in 1648 and their final surrender in Brazil in 1654 did not immediately change Brazil's fortunes, although Bahia was better able to benefit than Pernambuco.

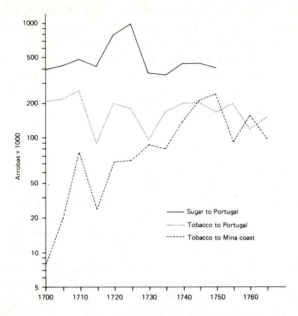

Figure 7-3. Bahian sugar and tobacco exports, 1698–1765, based on five-year averages. (Source: ANTT, Junta do Tabaco, maços 96A–106, passim. Reprinted from Leslie Bethell, ed., *The Cambridge History of Latin America* [Cambridge: Cambridge University Press], II, 459.)

Portugal's restoration of independence in 1640 created a situation of festering warfare with Hapsburg Spain that lasted until 1668. The war effort was expensive, and further costs were incurred in attempts to secure allies. A marriage alliance between Catherine of Bragança, daughter of Dom João IV, and Charles II of England assured Portugal of English support, but the dowry of Tangier, Bombay, and 2 million cruzados was a princely sum.

This money, like the money Portugal agreed to pay Holland as part of the price of peace, was essentially raised by taxing the colonies, and especially colonial products. The *dote da Inglaterra* (dowry of England) was levied on each municipal council in Brazil as an annual tax, and each council then taxed production within its territory. Sugar bore the brunt of these imposts. Bahian planters could complain in 1673 that, aside from the tithe and other taxes on production, they also paid 380 réis on each crate of sugar shipped for the *sustento da infantaria* (infantry support) to maintain the local garrison and then an additional 540 réis in Lisbon to pay for the convoy costs.[95]

Bahia, as Brazil's largest producer in the period, bore the heaviest tax assessment. The câmara of Bahia in 1672 and again in 1673 and 1674 complained of the shortage and cost of slaves, the expense of supplies, the low price of sugar, and the many taxes.[96] In 1691, the câmara lamented that they had already paid 100,000 cruzados for the dowry tax, and two years earlier they had pointedly informed the crown that when tributes were heavy, revenues were few.[97]

This heavy tax burden on the sugar sector might not have been entirely negative had the Portuguese government used this "fiscal linkage" to improve transportation facilities, build warehouses, or stimulate new industries for further processing of the staple. Refining sugar in Brazil, for example, would have added value to Brazilian sugar and improved the colony's trading position, but such activity was not undertaken.[98] The funds Portugal generated from taxing sugar and other colonial products were funneled into the payment of diplomatic debts and war expenses that produced no direct benefit to Brazil.

The construction of refineries in Brazil was, in fact, one of the measures suggested by João Peixoto Viegas in 1687 in his memorial penned at the depths of the crisis of Bahia's sugar economy. Peixoto Viegas was a longtime resident of Bahia with a thorough knowledge of the economy. He had come to Bahia in 1640 and was soon involved in commerce and tax collecting. He served as a municipal councillor three times and eventually, in 1673, purchased the office of secretary of the municipal council. Although he married the daughter of a prominent sugar planter, much of his own interest lay in tobacco farming and ranching, and he therefore understood all aspects of the Bahian economy so that his observations were particularly acute.[99]

The making of sugar, he said, was like the act of procreation because the author never knew the result of his efforts except when these saw the light of day.[100] Brazil's problem lay not in its inability to produce good sugar but in the new sources of supply. Fine Brazilian sugar did not appear on the markets of Europe because the delays of the fleet system often caused the sugar to deteriorate in the crates while in the warehouses or on the docks, and the uncertainties of the fleets caused a constant struggle over the appropriate price of sugar between the merchants and planters in the colony. The continual and heavy taxes placed on Brazilian sugar had so raised the price in Europe that other nations had created their own colonies as sources of supply. Brazil, which had the reputation of being rich, was in fact close to ruin, and yet it bore a heavy burden and contributed more to the empire than any rich province of Portugal itself. Along with alleviating the tax burden, Peixoto Viegas suggested that refineries be created to Brazil to compete with the "nations of the North" and that no muscavado or panela be shipped to Europe, thus depriving these nations of the raw material they needed for refining.

Peixoto Viegas's memorial is important because it demonstrates both the perception of the Brazilian planters and merchants about their situation and their view of the possible solution to it. Planters often were unimaginative in response to their changing fortunes, and they were sometimes misled into believing that their problems were essentially accidental or exogenous, the result of plague or drought, war or taxes, rather than inherent in the structure of their industry. But in fairness to them, slavery and a controlled commercial system also imposed considerable constraints on their opportunities and alternatives.

By the late 1680s, both Portugal and her major colony, Brazil, seemed in the grip of a severe depression. Currency was draining out of Brazil to Portugal to make up the deficit in the balance of trade caused by low prices for sugar, tobacco, and other Brazilian products.[101] Between 1686 and 1691, both Bahia and Pernambuco were swept by yellow fever, which decimated the slave population and thus created new costs for the planters to add to their woes. The crown tried to respond. Some projects aimed at developing an industrial base in Portugal itself were begun in the 1670s in an attempt to free Portugal from dependence on its northern trading partners. After much deliberation, the Portuguese currency was devalued in 1688; the nominal value of gold and silver coinage was increased by 20 percent while the intrinsic value remained the same.[102] This measure immediately raised prices, and it tended for a while to increase the flow of colonial currency to Portugal and exacerbate the shortage. In 1695, a colonial mint was created in Bahia (moved to Rio de Janeiro in 1698).[103] It issued coins for the colony, which were given a value at 10 percent above the rate for similar coins in the metropolis in an attempt to stop the flow of specie to Portugal.

Brazil, like other colonial economies, was temporarily rescued from economic difficulty by the outbreak of European hostilities in 1689. King William's War (1689–97) and the War of the Spanish Succession (1701–13) created a period in which prices fluctuated widely with the vicissitudes of war and the uncertainties of maritime commerce.[104] By 1692, sugar prices were considerably improved in real value, and such forecasters of doom as Peixoto Viegas looked forward to better times. The price of an arroba of white sugar in 1692 rose to 1$200, after having fallen as low as 800 réis per arroba in 1688–9. The trend continued, and in 1699–1700 Engenho Sergipe sold its white sugar for 2$200 per arroba. Although this price fell back, the situation through the 1710s was favorable, with prices holding steady. Another high was reached in 1714–15, when sugar once again sold locally in Bahia for more than 2$. But with the return of peace in Europe, the resuscitation of the sugar economy began to weaken. By the 1720s, sugar prices were falling again, and with the exception of high prices in 1736 due to a shortage caused by a two-year drought, the decline continued into the 1740s.[105]

Meanwhile, other important changes in the Luso-Brazilian economy had taken place. Between 1693 and 1695, large gold deposits were discovered in the interior of Brazil, about two hundred miles inland from the coast of Rio de Janeiro. A gold rush ensued, and within twenty years there were over 20,000 whites and 80,000 black slaves working in the mining zones. In 1701, 1,090 kilograms of gold reached Lisbon, and by 1704 the figure exceeded 4,000 kilograms. The influx of population created an increasing demand in Brazil for European manufactures, local foodstuffs, and slaves. This demand contributed to an inflationary trend already noticeable before the discovery of gold.[106] Not until the 1730s did supply begin to catch up to demand and prices of local and imported commodities begin to level.

From the planters' point of view, the short-term recovery of the 1690s was soon mitigated by a new set of problems associated with the discovery of gold. The price of slaves, already rising due to Caribbean demand, was now sent skyward by the vast new market in the mining zones. Planters complained not only that the prices were high but also that merchants preferred to sell to miners who paid in gold rather than to planters who could only pay in sugar or in the promise on next year's crop. Moreover, the planters believed that the best slaves were sent to Minas Gerais, whereas only the second- or third-quality slaves went to them. Their complaints found sympathetic ears among the governors of Brazil in the first decade of the eighteenth century, and these officials added their voices to those of the planters.[107] The crown was moved to intervene by placing a limit on the number of slaves that could be sold to the mines and by imposing some control over the flow of goods and labor to the rapidly developing mining zone.[108] There was legislation to this end in 1701 and 1704, but as late as 1719 the governor of Brazil reported that the scarcity of slaves and their high price had caused the ruin of agriculture.[109]

By the 1720s, sugar prices were falling again, and the level of planter complaint and anguish was on the rise. In 1723, the câmara of Salvador claimed that the high price of slaves and their shortage had driven twenty-four engenhos into bankruptcy and that safras that ten years ago had produced 18,000 crates of sugar now produced only 5,000 and in a good year 8,000. Merchants charged 200$ for a slave that had formerly cost 40$ to 60$, and only the miners had the money to afford slaves at these prices. Planters simply had to make do with the slaves they already had, who "because of the greatness of the work do not last and are dying."[110] This general complaint was echoed by the administrator of Engenho Sergipe. In 1727, Father Luís Vellozo reported that the safra was so poor that he would hardly cover expenses; the following year, he stated that the engenho would make only 90 or so crates, whereas in the past they had produced 160 to 200. At many engenhos slaves had died, and although the mills on the coast were better off than those inland, many (including some of the best, such as São Bento dos Lages and the engenho of Pedro Marinho) were in trouble. He lamented, "Brazil is reaching its end by every road and not

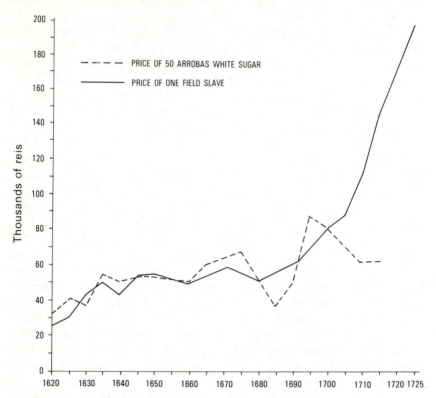

Figure 7-4. Slave and sugar prices, 1620–1720. (Adapted from Schwartz, "Free Farmers in a Slave Economy," in Alden, *Colonial Roots of Modern Brazil*, Slave prices for 1670, 1680, 1688 from Alden, "Commodity Price Movements." Table 2.)

only has this engenho declined but all the others as well – each one feels its illness."[111]

The senhores de engenho, lavradores de cana, and to some extent the tobacco growers were caught in a vise formed by declining prices for their staples and the general inflationary trend, in which the sharply rising price of slaves was a major factor contributing to their costs. Individual engenhos could still produce as much as they had in the past, but that amount at present prices was no longer sufficient to yield acceptable profits. The problem for the sugar industry after the crisis of the 1680s was not an inability to produce, although there were the occasional droughts, or heavy rains, or low sugar prices, but rather the interrelation of those factors with the rising costs of labor and other supplies. This situation characterized the sugar industry in Bahia and in Brazil in general until European wars in the 1750s once again disrupted the supply of Caribbean sugar and created a shortage on European markets. Figure 7-4 demonstrates the relative value of a prime male slave and fifty arrobas of white sugar, and it makes clear the central problem faced by planters in the late seventeenth and eighteenth centuries.[112]

The chronology of Brazilian economic history that I have presented thus far has been accepted generally in the specialized literature for the last two decades.[113] It is clear that the sugar economy was in difficulty by the mid–seventeenth century and even more so in the 1680–90 period, when Brazil, like all the American plantation colonies, suffered from a general depression in the Atlantic commercial system. Brazil was already experiencing rising costs before the gold rush of 1695–1720, and the opening of Minas Gerais simply increased the velocity of that rise. Although some older sources and some general histories still ascribed the problems of staple agriculture to the gold rush, which drained population, capital, and labor away from the coast while driving up prices, most of the monographic literature has demonstrated that the origins of the problems predated the rush by twenty years at least. The war years (1689–1713) brought some relief, but by the late 1710s the sugar sector was once again caught in the deadly embrace of lower staple prices and rising costs, especially the price of slaves.[114]

What, then, was the state of the Bahian sugar economy in the eighteenth century? We can make some attempt to answer that question by estimating the revenue produced by sugar exports carried in the annual fleets. The fleet cargoes were regularly reported to the Junta do Tobaco in Lisbon and were also a matter of concern and report by resident foreign consuls and other observers interested in the sugar trade. When the series of export figures are then combined with at-the-mill prices, it is possible to calculate the annual export earnings of the Bahian sugar sector, to which must be added local sales of sugar, rum, and molasses. There are gaps in the record of the fleet cargoes and discrepancies among the sources for individual years. Moreover, the fleets to Bahia, Pernambuco, and Rio de Janeiro did not sail in some years because of war or because Lisbon merchants had large stocks on hand and did not want any more of the staples. When the next fleet did sail, it often carried very large sugar cargoes, and it is difficult to know whether the large number of crates represented a particularly large harvest from one year or was simply the result of two equal safras.[115] If we use a five-year average to determine annual income, however, as is done in Figure 7-5, it is possible to see the relative changes in the state of the Bahian sugar economy (see Appendix C).

Until 1750, the engenhos of Bahia had a maximum productive capacity of about 17,000 crates of 35 arrobas, or just under 600,000 arrobas, but this level of output was rarely reached in a single year. With the exception of 1701, the first years of the century did not witness a drop in production. But beginning in 1704, the fleets to Bahia sailed only every other year until 1712, when the treaty of Utrecht brought an end

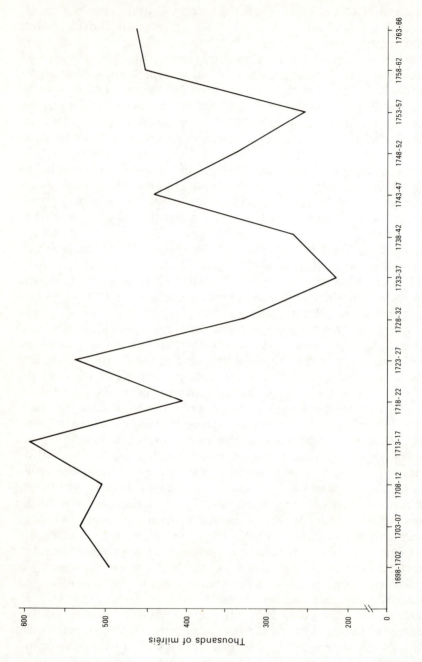

Figure 7-5. Estimated annual average value of Bahian sugar exports during five-year periods, 1698–1766.

to hostilities and allowed for more secure maritime commerce. Beginning in 1714, production began to weaken for Brazilian sugar, but good prices diminished the impact of reduced output. By the 1720s, real problems had set in: Prices dropped, fleets were intermittent, and annual production did not exceed 12,000 crates. This conjuncture remained through the 1730s, but the outbreak of war between England and Spain in 1739 and the widening of that conflict into the War of the Austrian Succession (1740–8) created advantages for neutral Portugal. [116] Brazilian production responded with increased exports when European prices for sugar rose, but at-the-mill prices did not reflect gains, and by 1750 European prices began to decline with the reestablishment of peace. Only the next episode of the struggle for European hegemony, the Seven Years' War (1756–63), brought new opportunities for Brazilian sugar. Bahian production rose from 15,000 crates in 1761 to 23,000 in 1763. Annual Bahian earnings from sugar were 46 percent higher in the period 1763–6 than they had been in 1753–7.

By the 1760s, Portugal and its colonies were in the midst of profound economic and political reforms that prepared a basis for a resurgence of colonial agriculture in the late eighteenth century, but we must leave the details of that development for discussion in Chapter 15. It should be emphasized, however, that, despite a tendency in Brazilian historiography to speak of a sugar cycle followed by a gold cycle, even at the height of the period of gold production, earnings from sugar were always greater than those from gold or any other commodity. In 1760, when Brazil's total exports were valued at 4.8 million milréis, sugar made up 50 percent of that total and gold 46 percent. Although after 1680 to say sugar was no longer to say Brazil, at no time in the colonial era did sugar cease to be Brazil's or Bahia's leading export. [117]

Planter strategies

The commerce in sugar, then, so essential to the health of the Brazilian economy, was a crucial factor in determining the nature of Bahian society. Having traced the history of that commerce, we can now address a final question necessary for understanding the Bahian sugar economy and the society and politics it generated: How did the planters respond to their changing fortunes, and what did they do about their situation?

Faced with unstable or falling sugar prices, rising costs for slaves and equipment, heavy taxes, and intermittent natural disasters, what choices were open to the Bahian planters? A simple response, lowering or withholding production as a way to raise the sugar price, was not really an alternative for two reasons. First, the rise of Caribbean competitors who by the 1660s were themselves major producers meant that any shortage caused by Brazilian stockpiling or lowered production could more than be made up by foreign sugars. There were simply too many competing producers to make such a tactic feasible. Second, the Bahian planters like all sugar producers were captives to their own system of captivity. Agricultural units dependent on a permanent slave labor force that had to be housed, clothed, and fed the year round, in crop time or slack season, whether sugar was produced or not, were constrained to remain in production to meet their fixed costs. The annual cost of upkeep and depreciation figured prominently in planter calculations, along with concern about a need for slave control that might be created by the lack of routine. Then, too, most of the senhores de engenho were indebted, and the servicing of these loans and mortgages called for an annual harvest. Planters might have sought another staple, but the coastal zone of the Northeast did not lend itself to many alternatives, and so much capital was tied up in the equipment of a sugar works that the possibility of making a short-term transition or moving back and forth between sugar and some other crop was limited. The engenhos were tied to slavery and sugar in a complex web of culture and economics that constrained and limited their actions. Whether sugar prices were high or low, planters tended to maximize the output of their laborers.

The engenho was like all business enterprises faced with fixed and variable costs. The planters could continue operations at very low profit margins or even at a loss over some periods, as long as the price of sugar and their production allowed them to cover the variable costs (those that varied with the size of output) and some proportion of the fixed costs (which were going to have to be paid whether the mill produced or not). Stopping production and allowing the mill to go fogo morto was an alternative, but it meant that the slave force had to be sold, and such a sale might entail a loss of status and financial position. It was a last choice. Planters preferred to keep producing even at a loss as long as loans were available to maintain operations. Hope was eternal that next year's harvest would find good prices or that a war in Europe or the Caribbean would create shortages that would make Brazil's sugar more valuable. And such events happened often enough to keep that hope alive.

The senhores de engenho and lavradores de cana, with little ability to control supply and, ultimately, European prices, concentrated their efforts on more immediate goals that seemed to be within their grasp. Their vision of utopia was a world in which government taxes and duties were low or nonexistent; where there were always a great number of vessels to carry the sugar, so that freight costs would be reduced; and where the supply of African labor was constant, of high quality, and of great volume, so that labor costs would remain low. To provide capital and credit, merchants and commercial agents would be allowed in this fantasy world as a necessary evil, but the planters dreamed of a moratorium on debt when times were bad or at least a limitation on the merchants' ability to foreclose on loans in default. Essentially, they dreamed of low costs, low taxes, easy credit with little interest, and high prices for their product. If we understand these goals, then a vast body of documentary evidence falls into place. Planter politics, if we can speak of such a thing, was organized around these themes, and any worsening of the conditions usually brought an intensification of their pleas and demands.

Given the planters' need to borrow capital, especially during periods of low sugar prices, two of their foremost desiderata were a moratorium on debts owed, or, failing this, a recognition that the engenho, its slaves, lands, and equipment, was a unit that could not be attached piecemeal for the payment of debt. As early as 1608 or 1609, Bahian planters had complained against the manipulations of the merchants and their "cruel" foreclosures on mortgages. The planters sought a three-year moratorium on debt and an officially fixed price on sugar so that merchants could not reduce its value when it was used to pay debts to them.[118] To this end, the planters welcomed the arrival of the *tribunal da relação* or royal high court, which arrived in Bahia in 1609 and which they viewed as the crown's response to their pleas. The senhores de engenho and the lavradores de cana did in fact succeed in 1612, when a provision was issued allowing lenders to attach only one-half of an engenho's yearly production and two-thirds that of a lavrador. This measure caused such an uproar among the Lisbon merchants, many of whom had apparently been advancing credit, that the crown rescinded the order in 1614.[119]

Merchant–planter discord emerged, especially in difficult periods. The destruction caused by the Dutch invasion of Bahia and the subsequent fighting in 1625–6 made it impossible for many planters to service their debts. In 1632, rising costs, low sugar prices, and a lack of shipping brought another series of foreclosures at prices that planters felt were well below the market values of the properties. The planters petitioned the câmara of Salvador for relief, citing sixteen engenhos that had been lost by foreclosure and noting that when engenhos stopped operations there was no work for cane farmers, wood cutters, and those who supplied food crops.[120] They petitioned for a law that would allow creditors to attach only the production of an engenho and not its capital stock. They were finally successful in this tactic. In 1636, the governor of Brazil ordered that, if the debt was not roughly equivalent to the value of the whole engenho, it could not be taken by the creditor and a lien could only be placed on production. In any case, slaves, oxen, and equipment could not be sold piecemeal.[121]

At present, it is unknown how long this order remained in force. But by the hard times of the 1660s, the planters and lavradores de cana were again seeking these limitations on their creditors. Once again, the câmara of Salvador carried the case for the sugar sector, and its petition of 1663 found support in Portugal. The law of 1663 prohibiting the piecemeal attachment of parts on an engenho was renewed in 1673, 1681, 1686, 1690, and 1700 in Bahia.[122] The same privilege was extended to planters in other captaincies, despite the grumblings of merchants whose loans were thus limited. By this measure, the crown offered some relief to the planters at little expense to the royal treasury. But it was a privilege not without costs. Merchants, realizing that it might take them "40 or 50 years" to collect on a debt, were reluctant to lend money, or they simply increased their rates to compensate for the risks.[123] The planters' privilege was not entirely a blessing. Their other goal, a moratorium on debt, remained unachieved. An attempt to gain a five-year moratorium in 1745 was flatly rejected.

The privilege remained in force for both senhores de engenho and lavradores de cana in Bahia until 1720, when the high court ruled in favor of Dona Ignácia Cavalcanti, who had loaned money and wished to collect it from a lavrador named Luís de Sousa de Castro. The legal decision caused an uproar. The governor sought opinions from many of the leading citizens, most of whom stated that engenhos and fazendas de canas were all part of the same agriculture and that without the latter engenhos could not exist.[124] They would be "souls without bodies," in the words of one observer. In 1723, the governor ordered that lavradores also be exempt from partial foreclosure and that only their annual production could be taken.[125] Although millowners and lavradores later complained that the law was not always strictly applied, it did remain in force. In 1732, Manoel de Araújo de Aragão, who had inherited the indebted Engenhos da Mata and Tararipe from his father, sought the right to operate without fear of foreclosure according to the law.[126] This protective legislation was not all the planters hoped for, but it was a victory of sorts and a recognition of the sugar sector's ability to influence policy.

The limitation of the industry's growth in Brazil was an even more radical response suggested in the difficult 1660s. Since planters had lost the ability to control the amount of sugar available on the market because of the rise of foreign competitors, there was some attempt to exclude the development of more mills in Bahia itself. Some planters argued that if mills were established too close to each other and if there were too many of them that firewood, pasturage, and cane would be exhausted to the detriment of the common good. In 1660, the *juiz do povo* (people's tribune) in the câmara of Salvador, representing certain planters, petitioned for an injunction against establishment of any new mills, arguing that many rich lavradores became poor senhores de engenho after setting up their own mills and that this led to their ruin and the decline of the industry as a whole. The question was complex, and such limitations could have a profound social effect or disrupt the relations between lavradores de cana and millowners; but throughout the 1660s the issue was debated in Bahia.[127]

The original petition was followed by position papers and memorials in 1662, 1663, and 1665. In 1669, a group of planters wrote to the governor and complained that a large mill capable of producing 7,000 loaves of sugar could hardly produce 2,000 when a small mill had been set up nearby in competition.[128] They pleaded for limitation on construction. Royal officials were reluctant to impose such restrictions on the growth of the industry, but in 1681 a law was passed prohibiting the building of new engenhos within 1,500 braças (33,000 meters) of an established mill.[129] This law remained in effect until the nineteenth century, and although it was sometimes ignored or circumvented, it remained as further evidence both of the sugar sector's power to influence policy and of the nature of its solutions.[130]

The fleet system created another series of problems and opportunities for the planters in their efforts to control their fortunes to some extent. A convoy system had been developed as early as 1593, but it had operated only intermittently.[131] Planters disliked it because it limited competition among shippers or captains. The planters through the câmara of Bahia had strongly opposed a fleet system in 1641, but losses at sea had made it a necessity, and the Brazil Company instituted in 1649 was the result.[132]

The fleet system altered the relationship between merchants and planters, between debtors and creditors, and changed the rules and practices of the sugar business. When the fleet was delayed, local sugar prices fell because no one wished to be caught with too much sugar, the possibility of no ships to carry it, warehouse costs, and wastage in the crates. When the fleet came in, then, since no captain wished to return empty, demand increased and prices rose. Merchants often tried to foreclose on debts long before the fleet's expected arrival because the price of sugar would be low. Since they could only seize production, which was then sold at public auction, it was obviously to their advantage to have it evaluated at low prices. As early as 1652, the planters complained of this practice, and in 1665 they succeeded in obtaining a provision that their sugar could only be auctioned when the fleet arrived. This privilege was renewed various times thereafter.[133]

– Without much ability to influence the price of sugar on European markets, the planters concentrated their efforts on influencing the local price in Bahia. The câmara, or municipal council, played an important role in this policy because it had recognized functions of price and wage control and because it tended to represent the interests of the sugar sector throughout much of its history. The câmara had been involved in fixing freight rates and sugar prices as early as 1626. This practice had continued in the seventeenth century, and after the formation of the Brazil Company the idea of fixing the sugar price in Brazil had become popular among the merchant community as well.[134] Fearing the ability of the planters to hold back their sugars until the last moment and to sell then at high prices, the Brazil Company argued that the "greed of the growers" would drive prices so high that Brazilian sugar would find no outlet in Europe. "Even though fixed prices are usually prejudicial to commerce, which increases with liberty," the representatives of the company argued in 1655, "a fixed price is the only remedy for Brazil."[135] The crown remained undecided. In 1677, it ordered the câmara of Salvador to stop interfering with the sugar price, but later the policy was changed.[136] By 1697, it was fully accepted.[137]

The planters had good reason to want a fixed price. They claimed that the merchants extended them credit for the copper, iron, and other necessary goods on the collateral of the next safra but that the sugar was often undervalued. Thus, even when the price was finally fixed by the câmara, the planters accepted less than half the official price, because "necessity knows no law." This practice had started in the 1660s, and by 1683 a commerce in this discounted "açúcar de damno" (condemned sugar) was carried out by speculators in Salvador. The planters were thus anxious to improve their relative position.[138]

The system of price fixing became regularized. The merchants and sugar producers each elected representatives. These arbiters (louvados) met and negotiated the prices of the various sugar grades. When no agreement could be reached, two judges of the relação acted as final arbiters. That is what happened in 1697 and 1698, and at various times in the eighteenth century.[139] Table 7-4 presents the prices suggested by the two parties at various dates in the first two decades of the eighteenth century. By comparing these suggested prices with the final arbitrated price or the actual price of sugars sold by Engenho Sergipe, it is possible to see how the negotiation worked. The planters generally offered to sell at a price about 30 percent above the real value, and the merchants usually offered to buy at 50 percent below. Both sides had their standard arguments. The growers consistently complained of the high cost of slaves and argued that low prices for their sugar would drive them out of business. The merchants pointed out that if the price was too high in Brazil, Barbados would drive Brazilian sugar from the market.[140] The planters responded by stating that the size of the Bahian safra really determined the price, not the availability of foreign sugars.[141] The price once set was ratified by the câmara and binding on all. In fact, both sides probably gained something from the system, although in a particular year one side or the other felt disadvantaged. Surely the world market price set limits on the negotiation.

The question of price fixing is interesting from a number of angles, not the least of which is the willingness and ability of the planters to act collectively. Sugar production was concentrated in Bahia in the hands of a relatively small number of millowners and their dependent

Table 7-4. *Sugar prices suggested by representatives of planters and merchants in Bahia, 1700–19 (in réis per arroba)*[a]

Year and representatives	Branco macho	Muscavado macho	Branco batido	Muscavado batido
1700				
Planters	3,000	1,600		
Merchants	1,400			
1701				
Planters/merchants	2,560	1,600		
Adjusted	1,800	900		
1703				
Planters	2,000	1,000	1,500	700
Merchants	1,100	600	850	320
1705	1,560	900	1,160	560
1707				
Planters	1,800	900	1,200	600
Merchants	700	450	600	300
1708				
Planters	1,350	950	700	400
Merchants	1,343	640		
1711				
Adjusted	1,600	800	1,028	640
1718	1,920	1,060	1,200	700
1719				
Planters	2,400	1,600	2,000	1,200
Merchants	1,700	900	1,200	600

[a]Adjusted prices were established when the merchants and the planters could not come to an agreement; they were set by the high court.
Sources: ACS, liv. 923, fs. 119–24; fs. 188–92; liv. 924, f. 85; liv. 24, f. 400; CEB, Lamego 45, 25, 26; liv. 9.29, fs. 3v., 33v.–4.

lavradores. Given multiple holdings, at any one time in the seventeenth and eighteenth centuries there were no more than 150 to 250 senhores de engenho and perhaps no more than 1,000 lavradores de cana (and many of the latter were very small producers). Unlike tobacco growing, sugar production was concentrated in the hands of a relatively few people and thus could be controlled to some extent by this closely knit group. As various petitions and the selection of louvados demonstrate, the sugar sector really did function as a self-interested group, able to define and pursue common goals.[142] They possessed a sense of themselves and their interests and a strong desire to achieve those interests. Although the planters might mix socially with merchants, accept them as sons-in-laws, and cooperate with them in governmental institutions, this acceptance did not imply that there was no economic or even political conflict between these two groups.

Planters responded to their costs in other ways as well. There is no doubt that the change in the size of the caixa or crate that we discussed in Chapter 5 was a response to duties levied on each container and to the cost of nails and lumber needed to construct the crates. Over the course of the seventeenth and eighteenth centuries, the crate weights essentially doubled from about twenty to between thirty-five and forty arrobas.[143] Since a number of taxes were levied on each crate, one simple way of lessening the impact of these imposts was to increase the capacity of the containers.[144] In addition, the warehouses in Bahia charged a handling fee per crate, thus making heavier crates even more attractive from the planters' point of view. Larger crates with capacities exceeding a thousand pounds were a planter response to costs.

Still another way in which the Brazilian planters responded to their situation was by continued emphasis on making white clayed sugar. The Portuguese had mastered the technique of claying sugar, and other European nations tried to learn the secrets from them. Although the process was eventually learned by Caribbean planters, the vast majority of Antillean sugar exported to Europe was muscavado or lower grades. This was probably due to both a lack of skill in making clayed sugar in the early years and to the fact that England, France, and Holland developed sugar-refining industries in the metropolis where muscavado was converted into higher grades. Countries like England had both grocers and refiners as purchasers of sugar, and each had its preferences according to color and grain.[145] Portugal, without its own refining industry, had a much smaller home market for muscavado and lower grades. It consumed the clayed sugars of Brazil, and in fact clayed sugar was the one variety that continued to find an outlet in northern European markets. Josiah Childs's above-mentioned statement of 1669 that Brazilian low grades had been driven off the market and the price of Brazilian white had been lowered is evidence that the colony's clayed sugar still had an outlet in the major European cities. The proportion of white to muscavado sugar in Bahia was usually two to one, and the extra processing needed to make clayed sugar was an attempt to add value to the raw material and ensure an adequate European market. The larger engenhos produced even higher proportions of white sugar. At Engenho Sergipe, the white sugar usually constituted between 70 and 85 percent of annual production. Between 1796 and 1811, muscavado made up between 40 and 50 percent of the Bahian sugar exports as Bahian planters responded to new opportunities created by the Atlantic revolutions of the late eighteenth and early nineteenth centuries, but I shall defer a discussion of that period until Chapter 15.[146]

Like any commercial farmers, the Bahian sugar planters paid careful attention to the vagaries of nature, the latest price quotations at home and abroad, news of maritime disaster, and rumors of war or battlefield dispatches. The marquis of Lavradio, who governed Bahia from

1768 to 1769, despaired that conversation in that province was always about sugar, the last harvest or the one to come, a topic far too limited for that urbane gentleman.[147] The senhores de engenho, whatever their status and prestige, operated family businesses and paid careful attention to profit and loss. With a keen sense of themselves as a class with particular interests and goals, they assumed political roles and sought to influence royal and municipal policy. Their search for solutions to their worsening financial situation in the seventeenth and eighteenth centuries demonstrates their ability to influence royal and local government, but also their relative weakness as colonial producers in the Atlantic sugar market. With so little ability to control the international commerce in which they participated, planters turned their attention to the immediate problems they confronted. Their ultimate questions were always: What is our annual income? Will next year be better than last? How can we increase the margin of profit? It is unclear to what extent they were able to make these calculations and estimates, and, as is the case with so much early Brazilian economic history, adequate data are rarely available to permit modern scholars to attempt to answer the question of profitability. But in the following chapter we shall continue our discussion of the sugar economy by moving from the general patterns of the industry to the specific question of capital, costs, and income for an individual engenho.

CHAPTER 8

A NOBLE BUSINESS: PROFITS AND COSTS

> The farming, preparation, and planting of the sweet and domestic canes from which sugar is made is the most onerous and costly activity that has been discovered on earth, and the most difficult, and at the same time, the most ingenious . . . in no way can one begin without a great and considerable expense, in starting and in the infallible replacements in every aspect.
>
> Discurso preliminar (ca. 1789)

Whatever the social and political privileges or status associated with plantership and slaveowning, and we shall see that these were considerable, the business of sugar making was just that, a business. Engenhos and their associated canefields were operated as enterprises, responsive to gain and loss and sensitive to the vagaries of the marketplace. The essential questions we must ask are those the planters asked themselves: What did it cost to set up a sugar mill? From whom could the initial capital be obtained? What was the proper and most profitable mix of productive factors? What did it cost to operate each year, and what was the return on investment? These seem to be rather simple queries, matters of simple accounting, but herein lies the problem. The material needed to answer many of these questions does not exist. Individual estate records are, with a few notable exceptions, lacking. Notarial registers, though more numerous, are scattered, fragmentary, and often silent on important issues. Finally, as a general problem, accounting practices in the period under study consistently mixed current expenses with capital-stock purchases. The result was confusion and a persistent inability to calculate profits. With all these limitations recognized, this chapter will attempt to piece together some answers to the central questions of plantership in colonial Bahia.

To understand the nature of sugar planting in Bahia, two matters can be addressed at the outset. First, as we have seen in Chapter 1, the Brazilian sugar economy from its inception was characterized by a large number of individuals who planted cane but milled it at a nearby engenho. These lavradores de cana were, in essence, proto-planters; although their goal was to own their own mill, not all or even many could realistically hope to achieve it. Still, they constituted an important and numerous class. At some points, Engenho Sergipe had twenty-five dependent lavradores that provided it with cane. But an average of between three and four cane growers per engenho is probably a more realistic figure for most of the colonial period.[1] During the second half of the eighteenth century, there were approximately seven hundred to eight hundred lavradores de cana in the Recôncavo.[2]

Structurally, then, engenhos were composed of the mills, which usually had their own land including some canefields but which also depended on the cane supplied by associated lavradores, some of whom were tenants, sharecroppers, or renters, and others of whom were independent landowners. Senhores de engenho had to calculate the relative costs of dealing with these dependents as part of the mill's operations and balance these against the advantages of spreading the risk and expenses of plantership among other producers. The calamity of a poor harvest or falling prices thus did not fall solely on the shoulders of the millowner but was shared by his lavradores. For their part, the cane growers were willing to bear such risks because sugar planting could be profitable and because they aspired themselves to plantership and the advantages it entailed. The economics of millowning and cane farming were, however, of a somewhat different nature, and they must be examined separately.

The second matter that complicates an analysis of Bahian plantership is the lack of circulating specie in the economy. The problem was both local and imperial. Portugal itself was often deficient in specie, and after the sixteenth century it depended on Spanish supplies of American silver. When that supply began to shrink in the mid–seventeenth century, a serious currency shortage resulted. In Brazil, the situation was even more difficult.[3] Although there was no mint in the colony in the sixteenth century, access to Peruvian silver was obtained through a contraband trade with Buenos Aires. The flow was interrupted in the 1620s and then cut in the 1640s. This interruption combined with a downturn in colonial trade in the 1670s to create an extreme shortage of specie in the colony. Portugal, lacking colonial products to balance its trade deficits, was drained of its specie. By 1675, about one-third of Portugal's foreign trade was paid in currency. Portugal's 20 percent devaluation carried out between 1686 and 1688 was designed to stem the flight of coinage from the empire. In Brazil, the problem was perceived as a lack of blood in the veins of commerce. After 1640, colonials submitted petitions to have the circulating currency of Brazil devalued to halt its flow to Portugal, or, failing this, to have a separate Brazilian currency coined. In 1670, the governor of the colony, responding to local pressure, wrote to the crown, "This country is being lost for lack of money."[4] His solution was trade with Spanish America, and to some extent the creation of Colônia do Sacramento on the banks of the River

Plate was a response to the lack of specie. Government-sponsored expeditions eventually led to the gold strikes of Minas Gerais in the late 1690s, but planters complained that the gold went directly from the miners to the merchants, stimulating inflation and making the agricultural situation even worse.[5]

Cash (*dinheiro de contado*), therefore, was usually in short supply in Brazil, and many transactions were carried out by various forms of credit. Because merchants charged a premium for these arrangements, planters perceived the lack of currency as a major cause of their indebtedness, and they constantly sought ways to alter the conditions that had caused it. Governor Câmara Coutinho wrote from Bahia in 1692, "Brazil is now with a candle in hand and little or no hope of remedy . . . because it lacks the essential, money. All payments are stopped, sugar lies in the warehouses without buyers, and planters owe more than they have, and all cry not knowing why . . . so lacking specie that they can buy nothing."[6] Portuguese devaluation stimulated the flow of Brazilian specie back to Europe and raised the price of imports in the colony. A mint, established temporarily in Bahia (1694–8) but moved to Rio de Janeiro, brought little relief. Throughout the eighteenth century, colonials sought to alleviate their indebtedness by increasing the stock of money.

Capital and credit

Credit, then, underlay the organization of the Brazilian sugar economy, just as it did and was to do in many other export agricultures.[7] Sale and rental contracts usually called for payments over extended time periods, payments in kind, or deferral of payment until the harvest time (when, presumably, the buyer would have cash). Access to credit was more important than cash in hand. It was estimated in 1781 that an individual could acquire an engenho and begin operation with only one-third of the necessary capital, the rest being supplied by merchants or institutional lenders.[8]

Where did the capital and credit for the sugar industry originate? In the sixteenth century, at least some of the funds came from foreign investors, Flemings or Italians, or from Portugal itself. But by the seventeenth century that pattern seems to have diminished in importance if not disappeared. There are no longitudinal studies that would allow us to trace the changes in access to capital, but the work of Rae Flory for the period 1680–1725 provides valuable insights and suggestions when combined with other sources.[9] From the outset, planters had depended on credit to begin operations, meet expenses, and provide for expansion. Loans of 4,000$ or more were not unknown, but the usual amount was more on the order of 400$ to 800$.[10] The loans were often extended for a specific purpose; "to buy a partido" or "to supply an engenho." In return for the money, the debtor usually agreed to repay the principal within a specified period at a predefined rate. Private lenders seemed to prefer short-term loans repayable in a year or two, whereas institutional sources extended credit for longer periods. Co-signers (*fiadores*) were sometimes required to underwrite the contract.

For the period 1680 to 1715, Flory has analyzed 300 loan contracts. Of these, millowners (61) and cane farmers (61) comprised 41 percent of the borrowers and received about 52 percent of the money lent. Merchants or merchant-planters were the other significant group, making up 21 percent of the borrowers and receiving 22 percent of the capital extended.

Loans to the sugar sector were usually secured on realty – an engenho, a cane farm, houses – in such a way that the whole property was in essence mortgaged on the loan. As we have seen, this situation existed because planter political actions obtained laws protecting them from foreclosure on portions of their estates.[11] Since the value of an engenho or cane piece often exceeded the amount of the loan, however, more than one loan was often secured by the same property, and this caused endless difficulties for creditors who tried to collect on bad debts.[12] Church restrictions on usury set the maximum legal interest rate at 6.25 percent; it remained at that level until 1757, when, in an attempt to stimulate the sugar economy and respond to planter complaints, the rate was lowered to 5 percent. Still, although institutional lenders apparently accepted the fixed ceiling, private individuals found ways to increase the rate of return of money at loan. Most popular among the merchants was the technique of extending credit against the planter's next harvest with a price fixed below the anticipated market price. An example of how this worked can be seen in the 1698 contract between the financial magnate João Mattos de Aguiar and Captain Pedro da Silva Daltro. The lender extended 140$ in cash at 4 percent against a lien on a cane farm. The loan was to be repaid in full in sugar at the time of the fleet's arrival in the following year at a discounted rate.[13]

The sources of credit in Bahia were varied. Money was lent by lawyers, clerics, artisans, and millowners, but by far the two chief sources of credit were institutional lenders and merchants. There were no banks in Brazil until 1808, and thus religious institutions of various sorts provided the main credit source. The religious orders lent money. In 1660, about one-sixth of the income of the Benedictines was derived from interest on money on loan. Sodalities such as the Third Order of Saint Francis, the Third Order of Carmo, and others were also creditors. The Convent of Santa Clara do Desterro of the Discalced Carmelites was another source of funds, but by far the most important lending institution in colonial Bahia was the charitable brotherhood of the Misericórdia. It alone accounted for over one-quarter of the credit in the Flory sample. The Misericórdia included among its borrowers some of the wealthiest and most distinguished persons in the captaincy, many of whom were also brothers of the Misericórdia and often members of its governing board.[14] By 1694, the Misericórdia had extended loans totaling over 103,228$, which should have yielded an annual return of 6,452. But many of the loans were in arrears or default. At this time, the Misericórdia carried 171 major loans on its books, 25 mortgaged on engenhos and 42 on cane farms; sugar properties thus secured about 55 percent of the money on loan.[15]

Although most of the Misericórdia loans were small amounts mortgaged on urban property, loans to the sugar sector were larger. The average loan on an engenho was just over 1,000$ and on canefields about 30 percent under that figure. By 1727, when another accounting of the Misericórdia's finances was made, the worsening situation of the sugar economy was reflected in the brotherhood's list of debtors. At that time, 234 debtors, more than half the 303 debtors for whom an occupation could be determined, were millowners or lavradores de cana. The Misericórdia had extended more than 374,000$ in loans, or more than three times the amount in 1694.[16]

The Convent of Santa Clara do Desterro was another institutional source of credit for the sugar industry. Its capital originated in legacies and dowries paid for the entrance of women into the convent. The convent invested these funds, and by 1764 it had made loans totaling almost 128,000$, which yielded close to 6,500$ a year. By the 1790s, the Desterro held liens over twenty engenhos. Even the Jesuits turned to the Poor Clares for money. In 1749, the Jesuits received a large loan of 6,400$ to develop their newly acquired Engenho Pitanga in Santo Amaro.[17]

Institutional creditors favored borrowers who were tied directly to the institution by membership or association. Thus the brothers of the Misericórdia, especially members of its governing board, were favored recipients of loans. In 1694, the largest debt owed to the Misericórdia was that of Gonçalo Ravasco, son of a former *provedor* (president) and himself a brother of that organization. Members of Bahian society's leading families appear with regularity on the lists of those who held loans from Salvador's religious institutions.[18] Status and association were important attributes in establishing a credit rating.

It appears that the Misericórdia and other institutional lenders were often willing to collect only the accrued interest on their loans and were lax in collecting the principal. Given the personal considerations and relationships that underlay these loans, this approach was understandable, but in the long run it led to financial difficulty for the lenders. In 1694, more than half the Misericórdia loans were in arrears, and the brotherhood complained that even when it tried to exercise its legal option of foreclosure the properties were often so encumbered

Table 8-1. *Sources and recipients of credit in colonial Bahia, 1698–1715*

	Creditors			Borrowers		
	Milréis	%	N	Milréis	%	N
Institutions	110,037	45.3	(125)	2,735	1.1	(3)
Merchants	60,277	24.8	(61)	42,167	17.4	(52)
Merchant-planters	3,473	1.4	(6)	12,275	5.0	(11)
Professionals	30,311	12.5	(46)	12,565	5.2	(23)
Senhores de engenho	17,624	7.3	(21)	84,929	35.0	(61)
Artisans	5,820	2.4	(14)	14,916	6.1	(33)
Lavradores de cana, tobacco growers, cattlemen	4,526	1.9	(7)	64,415	26.6	(91)
Privately administered legacies and chaplaincies	3,286	1.4	(9)			
Unknown	7,422	3.0	(11)	8,774	3.6	(26)
Totals of all transactions	242,776	100.0	(300)	242,776	100.0	(300)

Source: Rae Flory, "Bahian Society in the Mid-Colonial Period: "The Sugar Planters, Tobacco Growers, Merchants, and Artisans of Salvador and the Recôncavo, 1680–1725," (Ph.d. thesis, University of Texas, 1978), 73, 75.

with other liens that it was useless to proceed. The Desterro continually turned to the courts for satisfaction of unpaid debts. In 1732, it had twenty cases before the law, and it had to contend with debtors who used every means from bribery to flight to avoid payment.[19] Collection proved to be a difficult and expensive process. If institutions like the Desterro and the Misericórdia, which extended credit to favored borrowers with low-risk, low-yield loans, had difficulty collecting, then the positions of other creditors were probably worse, especially in periods when the sugar economy was in trouble. This situation made credit more expensive and harder to obtain from private lenders, who sought ways to simplify foreclosure to protect themselves. In 1699, João Mattos de Aguiar loaned 250$ to Desembargador Francisco Rodrigues da Silva against the collateral of a cane farm with the provision that the property could not be sold or alienated to a third party while the debt remained unpaid.[20] Such arrangements became a common practice. When in 1817 Soterio de Vieira Barroco sought to borrow 1,000$ to improve his Engenho Aratú in Paripe, he had to offer the mill as collateral and agree not to trade, rent, or alienate it in any way until he had repaid the original debt.[21]

As can be seen in Table 8-1, after the institutional lenders, the merchants resident in Salvador were the most active source of capital and credit. We have already examined that strange symbiosis of merchants and planters that made for a relationship of constant attraction and rejection. Neither side could live with – or without – the other. Although there was social interaction between the two groups that tended to break down firm lines of separation, on issues of economic reality both groups understood remarkably well the nature of their own interests and aims, and these two relatively small groups, perhaps two hundred planter families and one hundred resident merchants, pursued their competitive goals with vigor and insight.[22] That in pursuit of these goals the welfare of crown, colony, empire, and society was often used as a banner to drape class motives should not blind us to underlying intentions and designs.

Merchants were in a particularly advantageous and important position in the financing of the sugar economy. Because of the shortage of specie, many transactions were carried out on an exchange or barter basis with all the difficulties-inherent in such a system. Sugar planters were particularly affected by this situation because of their continual need to purchase operating stock, slaves, and equipment. With currency in short supply, merchants were ideally placed to extend credit rather than cash and to provide the goods desired by the planters on a credit basis. Merchants simply carried standing accounts for mill-owners and cane growers, satisfying their needs for imports and then adjusting accounts at the end of the safra.[23]

The merchants often extracted a fee for the service they rendered by negotiating to receive sugar in payment of debt at a price below the market value. We can take the case of two brothers, Luís and João Ferreira da Rocha, as an example. They borrowed 3,974$377 to purchase a cane farm in Cachoeira in 1794, intending to build an engenho on the property. Their creditor asked for two-thirds of the loan to be repaid at the normal 5 percent interest but for the other third to be paid without interest at 100 réis below the price of sugar at next year's safra. With a markup on imports and such a discount on sugar, merchants could hope to make a good return on their dealings with sugar producers. Planters put up with the arrangement because, as Salvador de Sá had put it, "Necessity knows no law."[24] The capitalization of the sugar industry was thus provided in large part by merchant credit. As José da Silva Lisboa reported in 1781, "This branch of commerce was the surest and the fattest that the merchants have."[25] Merchant loans were probably more important in the late eighteenth century than they had been previously because of the financial decay of major institutional creditors like the Misericórdia. In 1798, the governor of Bahia estimated that each of the leading merchants carried twelve to twenty senhores de engenho and hundreds of lavradores on his books as borrowers.[26]

Only the wealthier and more established planters had alternatives to merchant credit. Institutional loans with their low interest rates were chiefly available to the established planters. Some planters tried to deal directly with Europe and thus avoid the local merchants. Although direct trade with Portugal gave the planters better access to currency, it also meant that other risks and charges had to be assumed by the growers. This was a method of trade not without its own dangers, and it called for skills and contacts not available to many.[27] In fact, during the colonial period most planters were forced to seek credit from the local merchant community, and most merchants, at least those who called themselves businessmen (*homens de negocio*), acted simultaneously as commercial agents and credit resources with the risks inherent in those roles. When the merchant Manoel Gomes Correa died in 1817, he carried seventy-nine debts on account and had twenty-nine actions for collection before the civil courts.[28]

Foreclosures were relatively common but fraught with problems. The laws of 1663 and 1723 were used effectively by planters to keep lenders from seizing an engenho, and creditors often had to be satisfied with a partial payment in each safra. This was the case in 1785 when Engenho Boca do Rio in Paripe parish was attached for debt by the merchant Manoel de O Freire. Previously, Freire had tried to claim the mill, but the governor had prevented foreclosure. It was only when the annual payment had not been made that it had been permitted. But then the owner had brought the case to the courts, where it dragged on for nine years, during which the mill was inactive.[29]

Even when a mill was finally placed at public auction to satisfy debts, problems did not cease. The highest bids were often made without cash in hand on a promise of payments in future installments, and acceptance of these made creditors wait for their money. Conversely, the shortage of cash in the captaincy held down the bids on auctioned property when immediate payment was required. In 1692, Francisco de Estrada complained bitterly against the judge, Antônio Rodrigues Banha, who had forced the sale of Estrada's engenho to satisfy debts and who had insisted on payment in cash, "a thing thus impossible since never has it been done in Brazil."[30] The first bid had been for 18,000$, but because of Banha's insistence the engenho had been finally sold for 8,000$ cash to Banha's mother-in-law. Whatever the motive for Banha's action, the High Court of Bahia in 1709 eventually upheld the principle of payment in cash on auctioned properties so that debts could be satisfied.[31]

Although the senhores de engenho usually portrayed themselves as disadvantaged debtors, they too found ways to use the credit system to their benefit. In the Flory loan sample, about 7 percent of the money lent came from millowners. For these men, the ability to extend capital or credit presented not only the usual advantage of a profitable return on investment but also an opportunity to obtain control of subordinates in the sugar industry. A common pattern was for a senhor de engenho to extend a loan to a lavrador de cana, who in accepting it agreed to mill his cane at the engenho of the lender.[32] In this manner, cane became "obligated" or "captive," and it could not be brought elsewhere, even if better conditions were offered, unless damages were paid to the lender. Senhores de engenho always wanted to be sure of a supply of cane to keep the mill operating at capacity, and by obligating cane the worry, cost, and effort of securing an adequate supply each year could be avoided. Once obligated in this way, any further transactions on the property of the lavrador had to recognize this lien. The results were a complex web of contracts that were often violated and a steady procession of suits that filled the courts. An example is revealing of the problems. João Gonçalves de Azevedo had taken a loan to develop a fazenda de canas in São Francisco parish and had mortgaged that property as security on the loan. The cane was obligated to the nearby engenho of João da Fonseca Vilas Boas. Azevedo, unable to satisfy his debt, was forced to sell the fazenda at public auction, and the property was acquired by Captain Jácome Antônio Merello. The new owner refused to grow sugarcane, and Villas Boas then brought suit claiming that the fazenda was obligated to his engenho. Merello argued that the previous contract only required him to supply cane if he had any, but it did not require him to grow it if he did not want to do so. Merello's death did not bring the matter to a close, and his heirs were forced to continue the battle.[33]

The role of creditor provided millowners with advantages in the competition for cane, and they sought every means to assume this position. The case of Francisco de Brito Freyre, who inherited Engenho Santiago in the 1670s, makes this clear. In 1678, Brito Freyre complained that his engenho, located in Pernamerim, was in disrepair and that he needed at least 600$ to return it to full operation. As a result of its condition, many nearby lavradores had obligated their cane to other mills in return for money, and Brito Freyre believed that the lack of cane would eventually result in the total ruin of his engenho. His only hope was to acquire captive cane in the same way, and to this end he asked that the crown assume a 4,000$ debt owed to him by a third party so that Engenho Santiago could be repaired and money lent to the lavradores under similar conditions.[34] The crown acceded to his request in part, and within three years Brito Freyre was carrying out his program. In 1681, he lent 1,200$ to Captain Antônio de Sousa for a cane farm with the understanding that the cane was obligated and that it would be milled at a rate of one tarefa per week until the debt had been satisfied. For each tarefa of cane that went elsewhere, Sousa was required to pay an amount of 8$ as damages.[35]

Because cash was always in short supply in Bahia, the senhores de engenho, in their search for captive cane, sometimes extended credit in the form of slaves, land, or equipment. Such was the case when

Antônio da Rocha Pitta sold a cane farm to Francisco Machado Passanha. The farm was attached to Rocha Pitta's Engenho Caboto in Matoim parish, and the contract called for its cane to remain obligated "so long as the world may last." A detailed milling schedule was arranged, and payment was to be made by taking one-half the sugar from the share of the lavrador until the debt was satisfied. By such techniques, planters were able to extend loans and capture cane without the necessity of having cash on hand.[36]

Credit then paved the way to plantership. Without it, few people could establish an engenho or a cane farm or conduct affairs once the enterprise had begun. Wills and inventories reveal that few persons connected to the sugar economy died without some active or passive debts, and executors were often admonished in wills to pay or collect some outstanding amount. Although planters bemoaned their indebtedness, the level of debt was also a sign of success. The wealthier the planter and the more valuable his engenho and other assets, the more likely merchants or other lenders would be willing to provide credit. The impression given by the wills and testaments is one in which debts rarely exceeded the value of a year's crop, so that if necessary they could be liquidated quickly. It was when indebtedness went beyond these levels that planters ran into difficulty.

People set out on the course to plantership in a variety of ways. Defoe's hero, Robinson Crusoe, became a sugar planter in Bahia by first raising tobacco and food crops and sending to Africa for a few slaves. After a couple of years, he had amassed enough capital to begin, and with credit from a local merchant he was ready to become a sugar planter.[37] This was the pattern that lavradores de cana hoped to emulate, for of all the crops that promised a profit, sugarcane itself offered the best chance for eventual acquisition of an engenho. With capital or credit, mills could always be begun anew. But by the 1720s much of the best Recôncavo land was already in use, and unless an aspirant planter was willing to pioneer in the outlying parishes, entrance into the planter class usually meant the acquisition of an existing engenho. Often this was done through inheritance or marriage as heirs and spouses assumed responsibility for family properties. Outright purchase of an existing mill was also common. Merchants often financed such purchases, which were almost invariably made in installments. There were also occasional foreclosures that led to public auction (en praça pública) and purchase by open bidding.

The industry had its good times and bad, and individual mills sometimes failed owing to poor management, low prices, or slave recalcitrance. There were always risks, and all it took was "the Devil to get into the head of one of the Blacks for him to ruin all the sugar made without the master or anyone else able to do anything until it was too late."[38] What is important, however, is that there was always someone willing, at the right price, to buy an engenho, take the risks, and produce sugar.

Not everyone who operated an engenho actually owned one. Rental contracts (*arrendamentos*) of varying lengths were common, although three- and nine-year leases were the most popular. In 1817, about 6 percent of the mills of the Recôncavo were in the hands of renters, although engenhos held by them tended to be smaller than average. Contracts usually called on the lessee to make annual payments in sugar or money under a variety of arrangements. In the late eighteenth and early nineteenth centuries, when because of the expansion of the sugar industry such contracts were popular, the rental fee usually fell between 800$ and 1,400$ a year.[39] Higher or lower rents could be found according to the state of the property, the number of slaves on it, or the mill's potential capacity. From the owner's perspective, rental provided a steady income with little risk and trouble. For the renter, the chance to profit from the industry and acquire the status of a senhor without a large initial investment was appealing. Occasionally, owners would continue to reside on their property while it was under the control of a renter, and special agreements had to be made for housing and living arrangements.[40] Contracts normally called for the lessee to quit the property at the termination of the contract unless renewal was mutually agreeable. The common practice in Brazil was for all improvements made on a rural estate to become the property of the owner, but other arrangements were sometimes made.[41]

Property values

For those who did choose to buy their own property, the costs of establishing an engenho varied over time and reflected the general inflationary trend in the colony as well as the differences in scale among producing units. Engenho Sergipe, perhaps the Recôncavo's largest mill in the seventeenth century, was valued in 1635 at about 47,000$, but this figure included lands rented to lavradores and considerable woodlands as well.[42] At the other extreme were mills like those auctioned by the Dutch in Pernambuco in the 1640s. Their average price was only 8,000$, a figure that probably reflects disrepair.[43] Still, that same figure of 8,000$ was also cited as an average price in 1660 by the people's tribune on the town council of Salvador.[44] A 1751 estimate from Pernambuco placed the startup cost for a medium-sized engenho that could produce about 3,500 arrobas of sugar at 12,000$ to 16,000$.[45] From a series of sales and other property transfers made between 1684 and 1725, historian Rae Flory calculated the average value of a Bahian engenho.[46] The seventeen mills examined had an average value of 15,200$, but that figure did not include a slave force. Flory then adjusted the average value upward to

20,000$ to compensate for a minimum of thirty slaves at current prices. We can add some other information to this estimate for the beginning of the eighteenth century. In public auctions of five sequestered engenhos made between 1724 and 1757, the average purchase price was 10,435$ without slaves. Adding forty slaves at 80$ each would raise the average value to 13,635$.[47] This figure is low, and it probably represents the fact that these mills were in disrepair and had been placed on the block to satisfy outstanding debts. But it may also reflect the poor market for sugar properties in the middle decades of the eighteenth century. In another group of ten mills evaluated in wills between 1794 and 1827, the average value was 43,567$, although there were some engenhos evaluated at over 100,000$.[48] Silva Lisboa's estimate in 1781 was an average value of 24,000$ for an animal-powered mill with eighty slaves. The estimate of 40,000$ for an average engenho made a decade later reflects the rising price of sugar properties at the end of the century.[49]

Cane farms owned or rented by lavradores de cana were worth considerably less than engenhos. Cane growers did not need the expensive copper utensils, buildings, and machinery of a mill, nor did they employ the more highly valued skilled slaves of the sugar works. Flory's study reveals that the value of an average fazenda de canas without slaves was 2,560$, and addition of a slave labor force raised the average value to 4,000$, or about one-fifth the value of an engenho.[50] In 1620, a lavrador de cana with twenty slaves but no land of his own would have needed 1,144$ to begin his husbandry, but by 1720 that figure had increased to 3,256$. Much of that increase can be attributed to a rise in slave prices.[51]

Taking the value of engenhos and cane farms together, we can make a rough estimate of the capital invested in the Bahian sugar industry. In 1758, there were 180 engenhos in Bahia. These were supported by an average of four cane growers per mill. Thus at 24,000$ per mill, the 180 units were worth 4,320,000$, to which must be added 2,880,000$ for about 720 lavradores at 4,000$ each.[52] The total capital value was thus approximately 7,200,000$. In the second half of the 1750s, the sugar shipped from Bahia averaged about 450,000$ a year. This would provide a gross annual return of 6.25 percent on exports, from which expenses then had to be deducted. The gross rate of return was equal to the official interest rate, but the net rate fell below and provided only a modest return of perhaps 3 percent to the industry as a whole. Of course, the return was not shared equally. About one-third of the lavrador earnings were appropriated as rent or charges by the mill-owners. Still, these figures indicate that the planters were in hard straits during the 1750s.

What is missing from these calculations, however, is the income generated by the sale of molasses and rum, most of which was sold locally in Bahia. These untithed sugar by-products were not divided with the lavradores and remained the property of the engenhos. Export sales, then, were augmented by this local commerce, which perhaps added another 1 or 2 percent to the return on investment. As the planters sometimes put it, sugar allowed them to break even, cachaça provided the profit.

The money invested in an engenho was distributed among certain essential elements: buildings, the mill, "coppers" (kettles), livestock, carts and boats, pasture, caneland, and slaves. To this necessary equipment were sometimes added features that turned these properties into comfortable symbols of a patriarchal and aristocratic life: a well-furnished chapel, imported furniture, richly tooled saddles, spirited horses, and occasionally a small library. Although the value of engenhos varied widely, so did the relative distribution of investment in their component parts. It is not easy to reconstruct the common pattern of this investment. Notarial records are often incomplete, slave sales were often made separately, and land values or measurements were rarely given with precision prior to the eighteenth century. By that time, however, the relative value of land was so great a proportion of the capital invested in an engenho that any estimates made without it for earlier periods become very suspect.

From a group of ten engenhos that were evaluated between 1716 and 1816 and for which the records are relatively complete, it is possible to derive some idea of the relative distribution of capital on a Bahian sugar mill. The results can be seen in Table 8-2. Clearly, the major item of capital expense was land, which in a number of cases comprised over half the total value of the estate. When the value of the cane growing on that land is added to the total, then the proportion devoted to realty rises even higher. These figures refute the claims of some scholars that labor not land was the crucial factor of production. These historians have argued that since land was relatively abundant and undervalued, Brazilian society could in no way be termed a "feudal regime." Whatever the dubious merits of such reasoning in any case, the evidence from Bahia indicates that, given the relative importance of land, it is based on a false premise.[53] Slaves, however, were not unimportant. The proportion of investment in them ran from 7 to as much as 37 percent, with the usual figure above 20 percent. This is a proportion remarkably similar to that found on plantations in the British Caribbean.[54] The relatively large proportion of capital invested in slaves made planters particularly sensitive to changes in slave prices, but in terms of actual value, land consistently outweighed slaves.

The equipment and tools needed to operate a sugar works were, with a few exceptions, not expensive in unit costs. But the depreciation rate of these items was high. Axes, hoes, cane knives, and the various implements of sugar making were small expenses. Oxcarts or boats, however, were another matter. Even old and worn ones were valued

Table 8-2. *Distribution of capital at some Bahian engenhos, 1716–1816 (in milréis)*

Year	Owner/engenho	Land	Cane	Slaves	Livestock	Buildings	Equipment	Total
1716	Manoel Martins de Almeida	5,200		6,731	2,338	2,862	1,467	18,598
1741	Engenho do Baixo	2,029	400	5,105	896	762	1,428	10,620
1741	S. Pedro de Tararipe	5,350	676	5,155	586	762	1,415	13,944
1769	Engenho Barbado	17,240	856	14,310	3,144	2,800	1,672	40,022
1773	Engenho Santo Antônio	10,750	228	4,427	941	3,805	359	20,510
1779	Engenho Pitanga	7,200	1,128	4,705	1,262	10,220	894	25,409
1795	Engenho Agoa Boa	22,000	1,163	2,590	1,964	6,473	3,219	37,409
1816	Engenhos Trinidade, Buraco, Caboçu	100,254	4,034	35,813	5,364	33,498	9,653	188,616 (av. 62,872)

Source: APB, sec., jud., inventários.

from 6$ to 10$ each. Above all, the coppers, or train of kettles and pans, were the most expensive item of equipment. In the eighteenth century, the value of a mill's coppers usually ran between 1,000$ and 2,000$, and Father Estevão Pereira wrote that hardly a safra passed when the bottoms of the kettles did not need replacement at least once under the constant heat of the furnaces. Replacement costs of copper and iron were especially bothersome and expensive because all Brazil's supply was imported from Europe.

Although our present image of the plantation house is formed by the surviving mansions of the nineteenth-century Bahian aristocracy, in reality few of the "big houses" reached such grandiose proportions. Constructions of taipa were common, as were thatched roofs, at least in the seventeenth century. Two-storied construction for safety and comfort was popular, as the paintings of Frans Post from the Dutch period show. By the eighteenth century, substantial estate houses had been built, as the still-standing examples such as Engenho Cajaíba, Engenho da Ponta, and Engenho Freguesia attest. But these shoreline estates were paralleled by more modest buildings in the newer parishes of the Recôncavo. Lavrador homes were even more modest. Engenhos, in addition, also required other buildings: a millhouse, purging and drying sheds, perhaps a pottery, slave quarters. Even when the great house was a mansion, the total value of buildings on a sugar estate rarely reached 20 percent of the property's total worth.

Livestock were essential for operation but usually constituted a relatively small proportion of capital investment. Saddle horses, milk cows, goats, and sheep appear with regularity in inventory lists (pigs do not), but these animals comprised only a tiny fraction of the estate's value. Far more important were the oxen or horses needed to power the mill or the cart oxen necessary to move the cane from field to mill. Oxen were bought at cattle fairs on the edge of the Recôncavo after being driven in from the interior. Some planters maintained their own herds and brought in fresh animals when needed. All engenhos, however, required some pasturage within their boundaries. Cart oxen were highly valued and worth about 30 percent more than untrained animals. The value of all the livestock of an engenho rarely exceeded 10 percent of the invested capital.

In addition to capital (defined as "the stock of assets capable of generating a flow of economic output"), planters also had a portion of their assets in consumer goods.[55] Jewelry, table silver, furniture, clothing, religious objects, and books regularly appear in estate inventories. In only a few cases did the value of such items exceed 10 percent of all property. Surviving sugar-mill and cane-farm inventories do not create an impression of profligate luxury or a wasteful use of resources. For every rich sugar baron, lord of men and land, with a taste for fine wine

Table 8-3. *Distribution of capital on lavrador de cana estates, 1713–1813 (in milréis)*

Year	Land	Cane	Slaves	(N)	Livestock	Buildings	Equipment	Total	Personal wealth	Debts owed
1713	800	60	2,090	(24)	342	200	34	3,526	49	
1714	1,677		1,651	(16)	186	150	15	3,679	61	808
1722	300	314	2,430	(19)			42			
		400	3,285	(26)				6,771		
1733			250	4,115	(34)	101	24	33	4,523	457[a]	
1743		60	990	(15)	295	15	38	1,398	15	95
1758	600	84	1,418	(25)	207	800	19	3,128	1,413[a]	225
1773	920	175	1,363	(18)	145	32	18	2,653	12	
1777		229	715	(11)	161		24	1,129	24	
1795	1,600		2,080	(28)		170	12	3,862	28	
1797		251	630	(6)	518	200	24	1,623	113	
1804	88	746	2,660	(21)	680	550	13	4,737	25	
1813 a	5,200	129	1,860	(18)	228	86	36	7,539	50	386
1813 b	363	182	2,090	(21)	449	40	21	3,145	1,654[a]	1,056
1824	1,045		1,163	(15)	120	40	5	2,373	32	

[a]Includes value of a sugar crop. Other personal property includes furniture, silver, cash, etc. *Sources:* APB, inventários: 1713 (S. Francisco 7744/5), 1714 (S. Francisco 7745/1). 1722 (S. Francisco 7743/2), 1733 (S. Francisco 7753), 1743 (S. Francisco 7749/2), 1758 (Cidade 636), 1773 (S. Francisco 7742/4), 1777 (S. Francisco 535/17), 1795 (Cidade 656/2), 1797 (S. Francisco 536/16), 1804 (CWP, pacote ii), 1813 a (Cidade 689/1), 1813 b (Cidade 688/5), 1824 (Cidade 741/3).

and Dutch linens and the ability to afford them, there were ten or twelve millowners who simply struggled to make ends meet.

This pattern is even more apparent for a group of estate evaluations of lavradores de cana for the period 1713 to 1824, shown in Table 8-3. Their investment in consumer goods was minimal, rarely reaching 10 percent of their wealth. In a few places in the table where large sums are noted under personal wealth, these amounts represent the cash value of sugar not yet sold at the time of the inventory. Although the absence of cash or luxury goods usually indicates that, with few exceptions, the lavrador class did not live extravagantly, the relatively small debts of most also argue against their own constant claim of crippling indebtedness. There were a few cases in which debts equaled a quarter or a third of total wealth, but these were matched by others in which no debts were outstanding. As with the engenho owners, the situation and living standard of the cane growers reflected the general health of the industry, but both seem to have managed their finances with caution and good sense.

Many lavradores were renters and did not own land or residences. But when realty did form part of their property, its proportion to the total was well below that found on engenhos. In the fourteen lavrador estates analyzed in Table 8-3, the combined value of land and cane was

30 percent of capital. Slaves were far more important, making up 56 percent of the total. We can take here the example of Felipe Dias Amaral, a lavrador in São Francisco parish who in 1804 owned twenty-one slaves, thirty-five oxen, and a small piece of land. His slave force composed almost two-thirds the value of all his assets. Upward shifts in the price of slaves were felt by the whole industry, but they had an especially hard impact on the cane farmers like Dias Amaral since so much of their operating capital was invested in them.

Costs and returns

Having reviewed the sources and peculiarities of capital and credit and the relative distribution of assets, we can now turn to the problem of operating costs. The question of expenses and, ultimately, of profits is a highly complex matter that in the context of North American and Caribbean plantation economies has generated a heated, if informative debate. The views of the accountant, the economist, and the planter are not the same on these issues, and the discrepancies among them have led to widely varying interpretations. A planter believed, for example, that the value of an asset was its current market price, what he could get for it at sale. An accountant's evaluation would be the original cost less depreciation. The economist would probably agree that the current price did not represent the true value but would probably insist that further calculations of productivity were needed to arrive at an appropriate figure. Modern historians often find that the kind of information needed to make these calculations of profitability are lacking. This is nothing new. Planters themselves were faced with uncertainty and incalculability produced by the vagaries of nature, changes in markets and prices, and government policies over which they had little control. Risk and uncertainty were part of plantership, and cost accounting was no easy matter.[56]

Most Brazilian planters, like most North American ones, "were content with the simplest records and figured profits and losses on the basis of cash income and expenditure."[57] They were primarily interested in what was spent out of pocket in relation to what was sold. "Paper" gains or losses caused by changes in the value of capital stock usually went unrecorded. Their accounts continually mixed current expenses for items such as food, lumber, and tallow with capital outlays for new slaves or equipment. A single entry in the accounts often combined disbursements for labor and materials, so separation into components is impossible.

Beyond the general problem of farm accounts are those characteristic of Brazil. The documentary record is thin, as a result of poor accounting, subsequent disinterest, a humid climate, and voracious insects. There are only two general estimates of profits and expenses: Father

Estevão Pereira's analysis of Engenho Sergipe of 1635 and an estimate of 1751 submitted by a group of protesting planters. Both are examples of special pleading and both must be treated with caution. For the privately owned properties, hundreds of engenhos and thousands of fazendas de canas, hardly any ledgers survive from the colonial era. The only consistent accounts that remain are those of Jesuit and Benedictine mills.[58] These properties are not typical, but if we discount their somewhat larger expenses for charitable contributions and religious observance and their absentee ownership, their expenditures can, along with the general estimates, indicate certain patterns of performance for the Bahian mills.

To simplify analysis, annual expenditures have been divided into a number of broad categories. Labor costs were a major expense item throughout the colonial era. Two types of salaries were paid: *soldadas*, yearly wages that sometimes included room and board, and *salários* or *jornais*, daily or piecework wages paid at a defined rate for a specific task. In addition, the slave force had to be replenished or increased, and although the purchase of new slaves was in reality an addition to capital stock, the planters calculated their purchase as an annual expense. Slaves, moreover, had to be fed, clothed, housed, and maintained. Outlays for these items as well as for medicine, a midwife, a doctor, or a barber-surgeon were normal.[59]

Other major categories of expenses were fuel, transportation, materials, and capital outlay for slaves, livestock, and equipment. Fuel was an essential item, and the supply of firewood to the furnaces was as important as the supply of cane to the mill. Engenhos with their own forest lands were fortunate; those without them incurred considerable expense in the purchase and transport of this item. Transportation costs included payments to shippers and carters, warehousing charges, and various duties and taxes. Material and equipment costs included a wide variety of items, from fence posts and crates to whale oil for candles and copper plates for repairing the kettles. Copper was among the consistently most expensive goods, but an oxcart or a boat purchased or built in a year added considerably to expenses because its unit cost was high. Here, too, planters made no distinction between capital purchases and maintenance that might be considered a current expense. Livestock were also considered a current expense, and they provide a good example of the problems of precise accounting. A planter with his own herd on a ranch in the sertão might enter no expenditure for livestock in a particular year in his engenho account, ignoring the cost of raising the cattle at the ranch and of transporting them to the mill. Moreover, cart oxen were valued at three or four times the price of untrained animals, and the expense of breaking them to the yoke should also have been calculated. None of this was done, and modern attempts to do so are based on so many assumptions and so few consistent data that any attempt at precision is misleading at best.

Finally, the cost of the industry's raw material, sugarcane, was almost never calculated by the millowners. Planters were able to estimate the cost of planting and harvesting a tarefa of cane. In 1751, the câmara of Bahia placed the value of a tarefa of planted cane at 10$ and the total cost of turning it into sugar at 31$600, but since most engenhos depended on cane farmers to supply the majority of the cane, its acquisition was rarely calculated as an expense.[60] In reality, however, the portion surrendered to the lavrador after milling was a cost to the planter, even though they did not identify it as such.

Each engenho was by definition distinct, with its own peculiar advantages and disadvantages that influenced its operations. Engenho Sergipe, for example, was located at the mouth of a river, and it maintained its own boats and boatmen to move sugar and supplies. This increased its expenditures for salaries and equipment but limited its costs for transportation. Conversely, Engenho Sergipe always had its own herds, which supplied fresh oxen each year and thus reduced its livestock expenditures. The sale of lands to lavradores in the early seventeenth century had alienated much of that mill's natural supply of firewood so that its supply was a continually heavy burden at Sergipe. Engenho São Bento dos Lages of the Benedictines, just across the river from Engenho Sergipe, had a similar position, with low costs for livestock and transport but heavy expenditures for firewood. Its sister mill, São Caetano, further inland in the parish of Purificação, had ample supplies of wood and spent nothing for it; but it was faced with the problem of moving goods to and from the coast without water transport. Its livestock costs were always high because it lacked its own herds. These distinctive features contributed to the observed differences in the performances of the producing units.

With these various limitations in mind, let us turn to the surviving records. The first available calculation of operating expenses was made by Father Estevão Pereira in 1635.[61] He had managed Engenho Sergipe, and his report was based on intimate firsthand knowledge as the administrator of a sugar mill. He placed the value of that property at 46,800$, of which the land was worth 24,800$ and the buildings, slaves, and stock composed the remaining 22,000$. The engenho annually produced between ten and twelve thousand arrobas, of which about seven thousand of various grades remained as the mill's share. At the prices of the period, the value of sugar, molasses, and rum was 3,874$ to 4,888$. In addition, the engenho collected certain land rents in kind that also constituted an income. Father Pereira's estimate of costs came to 3,465$ annually.[62] Of these, salaries were important, making up a larger proportion than the purchase and maintenance of

Table 8-4. *Engenho Sergipe expenses, 1707–16*

Year	Salaries	Slaves	Food	Medi-cine	Fuel	Equip-ment	Trans-port	Live-stock	Miscella-neous	Total
1707–8	947	254	158	30	958	38	7	166	112	2,670
1708–9	1,023	450	177	30	778	742	535	24	1,018	4,777
1709–10	825	420	213	42	726	400			372	2,998
1710–11	690	342	168	34	781	318	287		345	2,965
1711–12	797	817	373	33	1,068	305	290		92	3,775
1712–13	663	1,953	944	34	727	292	389	13	524	5,539
1713–14	–	–	–	–	–	–	–	–	–	–
1714–15	701	924	812	32	636	192	433		173	3,903
1715–16	647	590	1,168	32	496	262	524	23	298	4,040
Totals	6,293	5,750	4,013	267	6,170	2,549	2,465	226	2,934	30,667
Percent	20.5	18.7	13.1	0.8	20.1	8.3	8.0	0.8	9.6	

slaves. Equipment and material costs were also high, constituting more than 30 percent of the total.

Father Pereira's "theoretical" accounting can be compared against the actual accounts of Engenho Sergipe for forty-eight safras between 1611 and 1754. The records for the period from 1622 to 1654 have been published and have served as the basis for studies by Frédéric Mauro and Mircea Buescu.[63] Those years, however, were difficult ones for Engenho Sergipe and for the Bahian economy as a whole. For that reason, I have taken as a more representative sample the nine consecutive harvests between 1707 and 1716. Annual expenses for these years are presented in Table 8-4.

A word is in order about the categories used in Table 8-4. Medical costs include an annual salary of 30$ for a doctor; this sum could be counted with salaries and thereby increase the proportion devoted to labor. Livestock costs are low because of Engenho Sergipe's access to its own herds. The column for miscellaneous expenses includes legal fees, charitable gifts, and some payment of debt. When taken together, the nine harvest years indicate the pattern of disbursement of a large Recôncavo engenho in the early eighteenth century. Notably, labor-related costs (salaries, food, medicine, slaves) made up more than 50 percent of the annual outlay, whereas equipment expenses were only 8 percent of the total. If the cost of slaves, livestock, and (arbitrarily) half the material are considered together as capital purchases, about 25 percent of the annual outlay went to restocking capital in a given year.

In Table 8-5, Engenho Sergipe's distribution of expenditures for 1707–16 is compared with earlier safras at that mill, as well as with those on other Bahian estates. Sergipe's fuel costs fluctuated very little

Table 8-5. *Percentage distribution of annual expenses of Bahian engenhos, 1611–1822*

Engenho	Years	Sala-ries	Slaves	Food	Medi-cine	Fuel	Equip-ment	Trans-port	Live-stock	Miscella-neous
Sergipe	1611–12	27.0	4.3	16.0	1.3	1.4	30.0	3.0	–	4.7
Sergipe	1634–5	33.0	4.1	6.0	–	26.0	24.0	3.0	–	3.1
Sergipe	1643–52	26.0	8.2	7.9	–	20.0	35.0	1.1	0.2	–
Sergipe	1669–70	14.0	13.5	3.8	–	18.0	17.2	–	–	–
Sergipe	1707–16	20.5	18.7	13.1	0.8	20.1	8.3	8.0	0.8	9.6
Lages	1711–1800	14.4	14.6	30.0	2.5	19.0	13.5	1.0	3.2	1.4
S. Caetano	1726–1800	13.4	12.3	30.5	0.6	–	14.7	10.0	15.4	3.1
Average Mill	1751	20.6	18.9	11.3	3.1	11.8	28.0	–	9.6	1.7
Buranhaem	1796–1801	12.1	10.7	21.4	3.9	8.5	11.6	5.9	18.8	7.2
Passagem et al.	1822	25.5	(13.5)	12.9	1.9	20.0	10.2	(5.5)	(9.3)	1.3

and remained about 20 percent of the total each year. Its livestock purchases were also consistently low. Salary costs at Engenho Sergipe were lower in the eighteenth century than they had been earlier; this change probably reflects a conscious effort to replace free workers with skilled slaves. Transport costs were considerably higher in the period 1707–16, a change that probably represents higher charges for warehousing associated with the fleet system.

Accounts from São Bento dos Lages and São Caetano, two Benedictine engenhos, can be compared to the Sergipe records. The triennial reports of the Benedictines of Bahia contained a financial record of their properties, and from these it is possible to group their operating expenses so as to compare them with those of Engenho Sergipe.[64] At the two Benedictine mills, between 50 and 60 percent of the outlay was consistently spent on labor. Both devoted roughly 30 percent of expenditures to the purchase of food. São Caetano, further from the coast and powered by oxen, also incurred large transportation and livestock costs, but both mills had equivalent expenditures for materials and equipment.

Slave-related expenses on the Benedictine estates are particularly interesting because they seem to indicate a distinct pattern of practices. Especially toward the end of the eighteenth century, the Benedictines developed an ameliorationist policy, and this was reflected in the large share of expenses devoted to food, the relatively low proportion given to salaries because of the use of slave artisans and technicians, and a low rate of slave purchase because of good conditions and natural increase. In fact, the percentage assigned to slave purchases at these two mills in Table 8-5 represents only an estimate of a maximum based on a replacement rate of 6.25 percent at current average prices. This estimate was made because the Benedictines did not include slave purchases in their engenho accounts but recorded them separately as part of general disbursement in each province of the order. Thus the true replacement rate may have been even lower, further reflecting the benefits of a more humane attitude toward their bondsmen. Benedictine accounts, in fact, indicate periods of positive growth among their slaves, but the data do not exist to permit a calculation of the value of this increase in terms of the capital stock.

Unfortunately, there are no complete working accounts from a privately owned secular mill against which the Jesuit and Benedictine records could be compared. There are, however, the controversial accounts of five safras at Engenho Buranhaem (1796–1801) kept during litigation on that property, and there is another set of partial accounts kept by the court-appointed administrator of Engenhos Passagem, Cachoeirinha, and Santa Ines (1822–3) during another legal dispute. Although each of these accounts presents specific problems of consistency, accuracy, and typicality, together they provide a basis for comparison with the more extensive records of ecclesiastical properties.

The Engenho Buranhaem accounts present a remarkably detailed record of the administration of that mill by Felix de Betancourt e Sá on behalf of the other heirs to the property.[65] During a period of boom in the Bahian sugar economy, this engenho ran at a loss, a situation that caused the other heirs to complain, and it is for that reason that the administrator was forced to prepare such a detailed record. Although the record is thus full, it is also highly suspect. Moreover, during his administration, Betancourt e Sá purchased no slaves or livestock and, quite unlike the general practice in Bahia, rented both slaves and animals when needed for field labor while the forty-seven resident slaves were used exclusively in the mill itself. The other heirs complained of this practice and of the exorbitant levels of slave maintenance and salaries. Still, if we assign the costs of slave and livestock rental to the categories of slave and livestock purchase, the Buranhaem accounts can be made comparable to the other records in Table 8-5. Despite discrepancies, the Buranhaem accounts demonstrate uniformities in the proportion of expenditures made for material, transport, and salaries.

These same uniformities can be seen in the records kept by the administrator of the three Bahian engenhos during the period from November 1822 to March 1823. During these months, he made no purchases of slaves, oxen, or firewood, nor did he pay out money for transportation. To estimate the outlay for these items, I have ascribed 20 percent to fuel and then used the average expenditure of the two Benedictine mills for the other missing categories. Once done, 8-5 indicates disbursement for food, salaries, and medicine in the range established from the fuller records of the ecclesiastical estates.[66] The fragmentary evidence from the secular mills thus indicates that they seem closer to the pattern of Engenho Sergipe than to that of the Benedictine mills with their higher food and lower salary costs. The evidence from the secular mills also suggests that whatever the peculiarities of ownership and administration on the ecclesiastical estates, in their sugar-making operations they were much like the other engenhos. Their records, therefore, provide an excellent view of the industry as a whole.

Although the surviving estate accounts are biased or suspect for a variety of reasons, the more general contemporary descriptions are no freer of such biases or problems. The creation of boards of inspection to regulate the quality of colonial products provoked a number of Bahian planters to prepare in 1751 a theoretical balance sheet to underline their difficulties. They sought to demonstrate that although merchants in the slave trade were making large profits, they were losing money even when the price of sugar was high and the crop was good.

The document was clearly a piece of special pleading. It described the operations of a medium-sized mill of only forty-four slaves, made no allowance for gains to scale, and failed to discount capital expenditures from operating expenses. Generally, it underestimated income and overestimated expenses, especially those for slave maintenance and materials. Still, the relative proportions assigned to various categories and the planter's own vision of the nature and purpose of costs is useful when placed in comparison with the extant accounts. Like the Engenho Sergipe books, the planters estimated the cost for labor acquisition and maintenance at over half of annual expenses.

This last point raises two final issues in regard to operating expenses. Frédéric Mauro, in a pioneering study of this topic based on the Sergipe accounts and Father Pereira's calculations, concluded that labor costs comprised only one-third of annual costs. The discrepancy between Mauro's conclusion and the one offered just above lies essentially in the categories of disbursement used in the two studies. Mauro, for example, included under "salaries" only annual soldadas, whereas money spent for day labor and piecework was assigned to the categories of what was worked on. Thus, his columns for "coppers," "boats," and "works" are inflated and mix wages with materials. These accounting decisions led Mauro to believe that material expenses were about two-thirds of all costs, and from this he concluded that in its distribution of outlay a sugar engenho was much like a modern steel mill.

Although Mauro was correct in believing that for its time an engenho represented "heavy industry," the proportion of its costs devoted to labor was much larger than he believed, and thus the analogy with the steel industry is far less compelling. Moreover, unlike modern industry where labor is essentially a variable cost, slavery turned labor – its re-supply, financing, and maintenance – into a fixed cost. This added to the already large proportion of fixed cost and limited planter flexibility. Engenhos thus continued to operate at a loss during some periods, as long as the variable costs and some portion of their fixed costs were met. To do otherwise would have resulted in even greater damage to their fortunes.[67]

Labor – its acquisition, quality, maintenance, control, and cost – remained the central theme of the sugar economy. The interaction of planters with their slaves or dependent free workers set the social relations of production in human terms, the texture of which sometimes comes through the terse account-book entries. The accounts make clear in many ways the inherent strains of paternalism and proprietorship. Money was spent for presents and alms, for sugar to help slaves celebrate a holiday, or for masses and confessions, but also for manacles, stocks, and slave catchers. We learn from the accounts that sick slaves almost invariably received a special supplemental diet of chicken, eggs, or meat and that small gifts were sometimes exchanged between masters and slaves.[68] But such relations were then carefully recorded as part of an accounting of income and expenditure, profit and loss.

The stacatto language of bookkeeping provides not only a vision of slavery as business but also a composite life history of people as property. Within the simple entries are contained the contradictions of slavery, as the following demonstrate:[69]

For a black named Miguel Bamba ambuilla bought from Antônio de Almeida Pinto on 4 November

45$000

For a black, brother of the above named Pedro Bamba ambuilla, bought on the same day

45$000

For 12 *sirios* [a measure] of manioc flour for the blacks

7$200

Three pieces of cotton cloth with 53 varas bought . . . at 110 rs [réis] which I bought because they were at a good price for the uniform of the slaves for the next safra

58$960

On 24 November I gave to a mulata midwife for delivering of two pregnant blacks

1$280

For hens, eggs, and broilers for the sick slaves

25$780

I received for three blacks that . . . were sold to Santos because they were prejudicial to the engenho, after expenses

83$720

For a black who brought me a present

$160

For the slave catcher who apprehended the slave Caetano

8$600

For alms given to the Brotherhood of Our Lady of the Rosary [of the slaves]
$080

For twelve varas of cotton for three shrouds for deceased slaves

1$680

Sugar planting with slaves was a business but a peculiar one constrained by attitudes and practices and by the give and take of social relations. In the closing of accounts, there was always more than the bottom line. But planters were never unaware of the balance between the cost of slave labor and its returns, and they conceived of slaves in economic terms as well as social ones. In 1751, for example, Bahian planters calculated that the food, clothing, medical, and religious care of a slave came to about 8$400 a year, or 8.4 percent of the average value of an adult slave. Since planters themselves estimated that a slave could produce an annual income of 35$500, even with an underestimate of productivity and overestimate of expense, it would take a slave only three and a half years to earn an amount equal to his or her purchase price and yearly upkeep.[70] In another example, the administrator of Engenho Buranhaem claimed in 1804 that he spent 40 réis a day for slave food and 4$ a year to clothe each slave. Other expenses brought the total expenditure per slave to 21$253. This relatively high figure was disputed by other heirs to Engenho Buranhaem, who claimed that the two shirts, two pairs of cotton drawers, and rough cloth for a blanket normally issued to slaves in Bahia came to only 2$ a year.[71] Even so, we can take the stated Buranhaem figures as a maximum and see that annual costs per slave were about 12 percent of the price of a male field hand (about 180$). Each of the forty-seven slaves produced an average of 78$ a year, so that with costs deducted it would still have taken only three years to recoup the original purchase price of the slave. With such ratios, slavery remained unquestioned as a profitable form of labor.[72]

The final question of plantership was profit. But here, as in other aspects of engenho accounting, the record is unclear or fragmentary. Estimates of profitability or return on capital vary so widely that it is difficult to reconcile them. Obviously, levels of return changed over time and varied in relation to changes in the costs of productive factors and the values of products. Desirous of demonstrating the evils and iniquities of a plantation economy, modern researchers, on the basis of little direct evidence, have calculated returns of between 32 and 50 percent a year on investment in a sugar mill in the seventeenth century as a way of damning sugar and slavery for Brazil's social inequalities and lack of subsequent economic growth. As we have seen, however, it is difficult to reconcile these estimates with the existing accounts and contemporary reports, which indicate much lower figures.[73] But those numbers must also be questioned because special pleading led planters to paint their situation with a consistently somber brush.

Common sense points to the conclusion that, although planters were constrained by a high proportion of fixed costs and sometimes operated at a loss to service existing debts and meet other obligations, the Bahian industry as a whole did not operate at a deficit for long periods. In the British Caribbean, profit levels of 5 percent were considered acceptable to sugar planters and 10 percent excellent. I suspect that similar levels were characteristic of Bahia, although in times of boom much better returns were obtained.[74]

In the seventeenth century, an annual return of 2,000$ to 3,000$ on a mill worth 20,000$, a profit of 10 to 15 percent, was thought to be quite good.[75] Such gains were not always achieved even by large mills. Engenho Santana in Ilhéus operated well below this level in the eighteenth century. Between 1730 and 1750, it remitted to the College of Santo Antão in Lisbon a sum of 17,100$522 while it received in provisions goods worth 7,073$537. This left an annual balance of 501$349 for those twenty years.[76] If we estimate Santana's value at 25,000$, then its rate of return is only 2 percent. Even if we double that figure to compensate for local sales, the return on capital is not impressive. Similar levels, however, are suggested in Father Pereira's 1635 figures, which estimate an annual net return of from 565$ to 1,578$, which when divided by the 46,800$ value of Engenho Sergipe yields a return of 1.2 to 3.4 percent on capital. Such returns are very low and do not seem to coincide with the historical record of rapid growth in the early years of the industry or with the image of planter wealth sketched by early observers of the colony.

Much of the sugar economy's early growth may, in fact, be attributed to an increase in wealth in the form of capital assets rather than simply to income flow. The formation of a sugar works was a process of capital creation. Many of the early colonists acquired land for nothing by means of royal concessions (sesmarias), which were awarded as subsidies with the specific intention of stimulating the sugar economy. Once cleared, fenced, and improved, the unclaimed land became a valuable asset. Buildings were raised, machinery constructed, herds begun. Slaves could always be put to clearing another tarefa, building a tank for the water system, or other such tasks, all of which increased the wealth of the planter with no need to limit current consumption. We do not have the data to calculate the ratio of wealth to income of an engenho or group of them in the process of formation, but I suspect that the value of the assets grew more rapidly than did income. This suggests a high rate of savings and a rapid growth in individual wealth.

Contemporaries noted a pattern of accumulation that emphasized capital gains rather than luxury or great disposable riches. In 1618, the author of the *Dialogues of the Greatness of Brazil* counterposed the immigrant to the East Indies who returned to the metropolis with great riches to those who went to Brazil and whose wealth was primarily in realty. When the Dutch seized Bahia in 1624, they complained that there was little booty. The commander of the Portuguese forces that took the city in the following year explained that fact as evidence of investment in slaves and business rather than as a sign of poverty.

The "rags to riches" imagery and ostentatious lives of the planters dwelled on by clerics and chroniclers in the sixteenth century may have been overstated, but there were features at the industry's inception that made the accumulation of wealth possible. In the sixteenth century, land was commonly acquired through sesmarias at essentially no cost to the grantee, and as we have seen in this chapter land was often calculated to be worth half an engenho's value. Indian laborers were plentiful and cheap in the 1560s, and although their replacement by Africans toward the end of the century did raise the cost of labor, this was apparently offset by increases in productivity. With rising demand and high prices, a boom was created that attracted newcomers who began operations with only a small fraction of the capital needed to set up a sugar works. They did so because the land was acquired by grant and because merchants were willing to extend credit for slaves and equipment on the security of the rapidly growing wealth that an engenho in formation represented. Thus calculation of return on capital was probably made not on the basis of return on total asset value but rather on the income generated by money out of pocket.

To use the example of Engenho Sergipe in 1635 once again, the annual gross income balanced against expenditures yielded a net income of 565$ to 1,578$. As I have argued, this is already an underestimate because the expenses include capital expenditures. The total value of the engenho at that time was estimated at 46,800$, but land made up over half that amount. In such a situation, a planter then might calculate his return on the value of his estate excluding land, in this case 22,000$. By such figuring, the return on capital is now no longer between 1.2 and 3.4 percent but between 2.6 and 7.2 percent. If in addition only a fraction of the working capital had been put up by the planter and the rest provided in the form of credit, then, even with interest payments, the seeming benefits to the planter are even greater. Meanwhile, the wealth of the planter was growing as a result not only of market transactions but also of the building of capital through the development of the estate. When Engenho Sergipe was auctioned in 1638, the starting price was the original 48,100$, but the winning bid of Pedro Gonçalves de Mattos was for 61,200$. The mill had increased in value by an average of 3,275$ a year between 1634 and 1638.[77]

By 1600, conditions began to change. Good caneland was no longer freely available, Indian labor was disappearing, and costs were rising. As we saw in the preceding chapter, the rate of engenho construction dropped from 5 to 2 percent a year for Brazil as a whole and to 1 percent for Bahia in the period from 1538 to 1612. Only the introduction of new, more efficient, cheaper technology, the three-roller mill, increased the growth rate from the latter date to about 1630. By that year, Brazil had already undergone the first major decline in sugar prices and was experiencing the difficulties caused by politics and war. Growth after that date came in fits and starts, responding to market and political forces.

The "mystery" of Engenho Sergipe

The only accounts that shed light on the early period of the sugar economy's development are those of Engenho Sergipe. The problem with them is that they show this large engenho running at a deficit, or at best only a modest profit, during a period when by all other indicators large returns to capital should have been characteristic of the industry. I have suggested that part of the discrepancy can be explained by inattention to capital investments and growth and by a confused system of accounting. But the incongruence between the Engenho Sergipe accounts or Father Pereira's statement and the observed history of the industry also calls for an internal criticism of these documents, especially since most modern analyses have been based on them.[78]

The "Dase rezão da fazenda" of Estevão Pereira was not written to record a plantation's operation for posterity or out of scientific curiosity.[79] It was, instead, an act of self-defense designed to exculpate the author from charges of mismanagement or worse leveled against him by his successor. Father Pereira had administered Engenho Sergipe for five years (four safras) from 1629 to 1633. By March 1634 his successor, Father Sebastião Vaz, complained that the mill was in disrepair, the slaves lax and uncontrolled, relations with nearby lavradores hostile, and, worst of all, the engenho encumbered with heavy debts, continual legal disputes, high expenses, and low income.[80]

Vaz's complaints and the poor state of the engenho led the College of Santo Antão to hold an inquest of Pereira's activities as administrator, and in 1634 a deposition was taken from Pereira, who by then was living in Coimbra. In addition, he submitted his annual accounts to a special commission that had been established to investigate the charges against him. The "Dase rezão da fazenda que o collegio de Santo Antão tem no Brazil, e de seus rendimentos," was composed as part of Pereira's self-defense, and it must be treated with caution as an impartial and accurate accounting of an engenho's operations and expenses. In general, we should expect to find that it tends to underestimate earnings while overestimating expenses in an effort to explain why conditions had become so bad. Pereira was specifically charged with the failure to account for a sum of 3,730$818 and about 275 arrobas of sugar. Moreover, the commission complained that more than 700 al-

quieres (a measure of 36.3 kilograms) of manioc flour and 150 hens a year collected as rents were not reported in his accounts, and it rejected his explanation that because these things were used for the engenho slaves they did not enter into his accounts. More serious still was the enormous debt of 4,214$978 that remained on the engenho, even though Pereira himself in 1633 had promised to eliminate all outstanding liens.[81] Despite his assurances, new debts had been incurred, such as that of 485$ with a carpenter for twenty-two months of work at an exorbitant rate of 22$ a month. The "Dase rezão da fazenda" of Father Estevão Pereira must, therefore, be placed in the context of his own personal situation and of the continuing problem of loss faced by Engenho Sergipe in the seventeenth century.[82]

That Father Pereira was guilty of sloppy bookkeeping if not a certain amount of skimming seems beyond question, but it appears unlikely that Engenho Sergipe's continual losses were due only to his particular sins. In fact, the College of Santo Antão's own accounting of Engenho Sergipe's finances demonstrated that, from the time of its acquisition, the mill had continually lost money and that in fact the small gains registered by the engenho during two of the safras administered by Father Pereira were exceptions to a general history of loss from the time the mill had been acquired by the order. This situation led the Jesuits at the time, and historians subsequently, to ask two questions: First, why did this large engenho, "Queen of the Recôncavo," operate at a loss, and was this "typical" of the sugar estates? And second, why, if it ran at a loss, did the Jesuits continue to hold on to it?

In some ways, it is easier to address the first question than the second. Engenho Sergipe operated at a loss, or close to it, over long periods, and this was not simply a matter of poor bookkeeping. Current expenses more often than not exceeded income. Poor management may lie at the root of the problem, at least in part. During the dispute over Engenho Sergipe between the Jesuits of Bahia and those of Lisbon, the charge was made that administrators had been sent out from Portugal with no experience in managing slave-worked agricultural enterprises and that by the time these men had learned something they were replaced by another inexperienced man. The administrators laid the blame elsewhere. Father Vaz claimed that the father provincial and the rectors sometimes satisfied the obligations of the college to the detriment of the engenho. He gave the following example:

One day, the Father Provincial called me to his cubicle and there I found him with a New Christian named Diogo Lopes Ilhoa; and the Father said the following to me: Your Reverence well knows the many obligations that this College has to senhor so-and-so. He asked me that you take a man of his confidence as crater [*caixeiro*] in the city; and from him I have had as little satisfaction as Father Estevão Pereira had from João Domingues.[83]

Such decisions were not made to maximize the efficiency and output of
Engenho Sergipe but to satisfy the other obligations and responsibilities of the Jesuit order. In this sense, Engenho Sergipe must be viewed
as part of a larger structure, similar in some ways to a modern corporation, and as such with a deficit to be balanced against gains made in
other sectors of the corporation's operation.

The question of Engenho Sergipe's poor performance was first recognized and analyzed by Frédéric Mauro, who pointed out that the
engenho operated at a deficit for ten of the thirteen safras between
1622 and 1635.[84] He noted the deficit nature of the engenho's operations and the fact that expenses exceeded receipts by about 16 percent
during this period. As we saw in the preceding chapter, 1622 to 1635
were particularly bad years for the Bahian sugar industry: They included the price crash of 1623, the Dutch invasion of 1624–5, and the
following period of poor prices until 1633. Added to these difficulties
were the peculiar problems of the Engenho Sergipe: the continual litigation and legal costs incurred by the dispute over the estate of Dona
Felipa de Sá, the inter-Jesuit battle, and perhaps the presence of an
excessive number of lavradores de cana who had acquired their holdings when the count of Linhares had sold off large tracts of surrounding land. These facts help to explain why costs were perhaps excessive
and production was reduced. In addition, there is the matter of confused accounting of capital purchases, so that a deficit of 16 percent did
not necessarily represent a long-term decapitalization of the engenho.[85]

The difficulties at Engenho Sergipe continued into the 1640s. By
1650, the Jesuits were trying to set things right. Father Belchior Pires
reported in that year that Engenho Sergipe was making the best sugar
in Bahia and that he hoped to make over 2,000$ after expenses that
year.[86] His hopes were premature, and shortly thereafter Father Agostinho Lousado, the provincial of Brazil, suggested that the Bahian college sell its interest in Engenho Sergipe because of its poor performance and concentrate instead on Engenho Pitanga, which was owned
exclusively by the Bahian college.[87]

By 1660, the major legal battle between the two Jesuit colleges and
the Misericórdia of Bahia had been decided, and the Jesuits of Santo
Antão began to address the main problems confronted by Engenho
Sergipe. Father Francisco Ribeiro undertook a thorough examination.
He claimed that his engenho was "regal" in its size, water, canefields,
and lands but that it had not been administered well. He suggested
that any lands sold should be "obliged" to the engenho so that the
supply of cane and firewood would remain constant. He also felt that
much money could be saved on salaries if the freemen who held the
positions of skilled labor were replaced by mulattoes and crioulos, who
in two years would recompense in their earnings the money spent for

them as slaves. He was also critical of former administrators who had sold or rented lands good for firewood or manioc cultivation nearby and had incurred the extra costs of buying these items. Purchases of firewood had run as high as 3,000 cruzados a year, a sum that could be considerably reduced. But above all, Ribeiro saw the problem as the control of canefields directly by the engenho rather than dependence on lavradores de cana. "The engenho that does not have its own cane has no remedy, and this engenho until now has not had any, although it has a better opportunity to do so than any other." He argued that during the four or five months when the engenho did not grind cane, the slaves could work in the canefields or on manioc plots, neither of which Sergipe had maintained in the past. Until then, the time between safras had been one of relaxation for the slaves and loss to the mill. "Just look, your Reverence, at how this engenho has been governed all these years!"[88]

Ribeiro's suggestions took effect, and in the 1660s a move was made to increase the amount of caneland controlled directly by the mill. As late as 1655, Engenho Sergipe had depended exclusively on cane supplied by lavradores; by 1670, 38 percent of the sugar it produced came from its own cane; by 1700, occasionally more than 80 percent. After 1670, Engenho Sergipe depended for a much smaller proportion of its cane on lavradores de cana, and by eliminating them it gained the double benefit of keeping a larger proportion of the sugar produced and of making the slaves more productive and more fully employed all year round.[89]

By using the unpublished as well as published accounts of Engenho Sergipe, it is possible to derive a much fuller and more revealing accounting of its profitability. The existing accounts analyzed in Table 8-6 can be grouped according to the time before Jesuit ownership (in 1611–21); the period of Jesuit control (1622–54), for which the accounts have been published; the era (1699–1723) during which the Jesuits made specific reforms in estate management; and the 1740s and 1750s. During only two of these epochs was the engenho continually running a deficit. By 1669, after a concerted effort had been made to reduce the number of lavradores de cana and therefore increase the amount of sugar controlled directly by the mill, the engenho produced a healthy return of 1,117$. It took a loss in the crisis year of 1680–1 but by 1699–1700 was again in the black. The records of the safras in Table 8-6 that survive from 1704–26 indicate a period of loss during the early years of the eighteenth century but a series of very good safras in the second decade of the century. A small profit was registered in the safra of 1722–3, but high costs in 1725–6 caused a deficit of almost 1,000$. This probably signaled another stretch of hard times as Engenho Sergipe like the other Bahian mills suffered through the low prices, droughts, and bad harvests of the 1730s. In 1734, Father Luís da Rocha lamented

Table 8-6. *Income and expenses at Engenho Sergipe, 1611–1754*

Year	Income	Expenses	Difference	Year	Income	Expenses	Difference
1611–12	4,478	3,663	+ 815	1650–1	5,040	7,070	−2,030
1612–13	2,937	3,166	− 229	1651–2–3	7,001	7,110	− 109
1619–20	4,069	3,342	+ 727	1669–0	6,998	5,881	+1,117
1621–2	6,584	4,479	+2,105	1680–1	4,791	6,193	−1,402
1622–3	3,616	4,171	− 555	1706–7	4,012	5,283	−1,271
1623–4	2,567	5,831	−3,264	1707–8	5,050	3,912	+1,138
1624–5	Dutch invasion			1708–9	3,368	4,216	− 848
1625–6	3,096	4,981	−1,885	1709–10	4,787	3,818	+ 969
1626–7	4,928	6,491	−1,563	1710–11	3,564	3,112	+ 452
1627–8	4,495	4,647	− 152	1711–12	6,973	3,818	+3,155
1628–9	3,686	5,113	−1,427	1712–13	8,907	6,509	+2,399
1629–30	6,099	7,027	− 928	1713–14	6,538	5,182	+1,356
1630–1	4,565	5,311	− 746	1714–15	5,533	3,875	+1,658
1631–2	2,257	3,402	−1,145	1715–16	4,112	4,008	+ 104
1632–3	4,609	3,920	+ 689	1722–3	3,830	3,207	+ 623
1633–4	–	–	–	1725–6	6,302	7,203	− 901
1634–5	4,968	3,253	+1,715	+1745–6	1,861	2,957	−1,096
1635–6	4,958	4,135	+ 823	1746–8	9,780	11,711	−1,931
1636–7	3,658	3,997	− 339	1748–0	5,641	7,472	−1,831
1643–4	7,339	9,585	−2,246	1750–1	4,069	5,164	−1,095
1644–5	5,427	7,485	−2,058	1751–2	5,472	6,758	−1,286
1645–6	3,061	2,067	+ 994	1752–3	2,929	3,508	− 579
1647–8	3,571	3,249	+ 322	1753–4	10,406	11,729	−1,323

Source: Livros de contas, Engenho Sergipe, all in ANTT unless otherwise noted: 1611–13, maço 14, nos. 4, 19; 1622–53, *Documentos para a história do açúcar*, vol. III; 1669–70, maço 17, n. 24; 1680–1, maço 17, n. 25; 1699–1700, maço 17, n. 27; 1704–6, maço 17, n. 28; 1705–16, maço 17, n. 29; 1722–4, maço 17, n. 30; 1725–6, maço 17, n. 31; 1745–8, maço 54, nos. 30, 31; 1751–4, maço 54, nos. 35, 54, 57.

from Engenho Sergipe that "Brazil had reached such a miserable extreme that not a milréis appeared in the market and crops were generally worth nothing." "No one speaks any longer of sugar," he said. "Gold, if there is any, only passes through to Portugal and from there to foreign kingdoms."[90]

The early problems of Engenho Sergipe, then, seemed to be related to its peculiar history; absentee and ecclesiastical ownership resulting in mismanagement and an excess of lavradores de cana. By the 1730s, it suffered along with the rest of the industry through bad prices and local climatic disasters. It never really recovered. By the mid-1740s, it was still a large engenho with 184 slaves but with a level of production that was falling. Between 1745 and 1754, it once again operated continually at a deficit.[91]

Sergipe do Conde, for all its importance as a source of information, was not a typical Brazilian sugar mill. But many of the problems it

faced were common to other engenhos. The engenho Pitanga, bought
by the Jesuit College of Bahia in 1643 and enlarged over the next seven
years, also experienced hard times in the 1650s, and some in the order
wanted it sold because of its many expenses and high rate of slave
mortality.[92] Belchior Pires came to its defense, pointing out that he had
excellent land and plenty of wood for crates and fuel, so that unlike
Engenho Sergipe, which spent 2,000$ a year for these items, Engenho
Pitanga was free of such costs. Pitanga, said Pires, could yield a net
profit of 2,800$ a year, but "like a galleon under sail, the Superiors had
taken down the mast and set it in dry dock [estaleiro] by their ignorance
and disinterest." Managers had not fulfilled their obligations, and the
engenho was continually undercapitalized because those in charge did
not realize that "what is spent in benefit of farms is not expense but
profit." Lay senhores de engenho, stated Pires, took much better care
of their properties, and even the Benedictines ran their sugar estates
better, "receiving profit from them while all we get from ours is
misery."[93]

Finally, the Pires memorandum expressed concern over the problem
of slave mortality. Although it was true that many slaves died, Pires
argued that these were often recently purchased Africans who were old
or weak on arrival. Others died, he believed, because they were not
adequately supplied with food or their own plots. And then there were
the slaves themselves.[94] Five witch doctors (feticeiros) had been discovered at Pitanga, and they were held responsible for a number of
deaths. Slave mortality and slavery itself troubled the consciences of
some of the Jesuits, and when in 1667 the rector of the Bahian college
proposed to sell Engenho Pitanga, he listed among its problems not only
low profits and the difficulty of finding someone with the experience
and energy to run an engenho but also slavery itself. Operating a sugar
mill was inconvenient because "of the turbulence of its activity and
because it is very difficult to deal with slaves with the piety necessary for
a cleric."[95] Such self-doubt was overcome, however, and the Jesuits
continued to operate engenhos in Bahia as elsewhere in Brazil until their
expulsion in 1757. In 1684, Pitanga produced a return of 1,200$ to the
College of Bahia, and its interest in Engenho Sergipe brought another
600$.[96] During the eighteenth century, income from sugar accounted for
about one-third the revenue of the Bahian college.[97]

Returns and profits

The Jesuits cast justifiably jealous glances at the Benedictine engenhos
in Bahia because Engenho São Bento dos Lages and later São Caetano
almost never ran at a deficit, even during the hard times of the mid–
eighteenth century. Like the Jesuits, the Fathers of Saint Benedict
owned ranches, cane farms, and urban properties as well as sugar

mills.[98] Each establishment of the order in Brazil supported its religious, educational, and charitable activities on the basis of its properties and investments. The Bahian Benedictines had originally grown cane and milled it at Engenho Sergipe, but sometime after 1604 they constructed their own mill. A second engenho, São Caetano, was constructed between 1720 and 1723. During the seventeenth century, receipts for sugar sometimes comprised almost 70 percent of the order's income in Bahia. But after 1670, when the sugar industry began to experience difficulties, the Benedictines diversified their operations so that sugar's share declined to less than one-third. Only with the boom at the close of the eighteenth century did the proportion of income generated by sugar and rum rise to the levels of the early seventeenth century.

Through good times and bad, the Benedictine engenhos in Bahia generally ran at a profit, although at times it was small. Their history is probably more representative of the industry than that of Engenho Sergipe. Table 8-7 presents the figures for income and expenditures of the Benedictine engenhos. Benedictine success appears to have been the result of good management, better treatment of slaves resulting in lower mortality and higher fertility rates, and savings in expenditures. Moreover, unlike Engenho Sergipe, the Benedictine mills also produced quantities of rum and molasses that were sold locally in Bahia. These sales comprised between 10 and 20 percent of gross income during most of the eighteenth century. The Benedictine accounts show a fall in revenues in the late seventeenth century, with some improvement during the recovery of the 1710s and 1720s after the War of the Spanish Succession. The decline in the following two decades was disastrous. Data from the 1750s and 1760s are missing, but by the 1770s there were already signs of improvement. The last two decades of the century were years of boom created by high prices and expanding markets. The variations observed in the Benedictine accounts loosely parallel the trends for the industry as a whole that were traced in the preceding chapter.

By making a number of reasoned assumptions, we can try to calculate a return on capital for the Benedictine mills. If we assume that slaves comprised about one-quarter of the capital assets of a mill, then we can calculate the value of the slave force and from that the value of the engenho as a whole. The annual net income divided by the capital value will give us a rate of return. Engenho São Bento had a spectacular return of 40.3 percent in 1652–6, but in the mid-1660s the rate was 10.3 percent, and it fell to 8.6 percent in 1700–3. São Caetano outperformed Lages in the 1720s and 1730s, but the rate of return was clearly falling. In 1723–6, São Caetano had a rate of return of 4.5 percent; Lages barely broke even.

Moving from specific mills to general patterns, we can turn to two

Table 8-7. *Income and expenses at Benedictine engenhos in Bahia, 1652–1800*

Dates	Engenho	Slaves	Expenses (milréis)	Income	Profit	Annual average
1652–6	Lages	87	13,373	44,239	30,866	7,717
1657–60	Lages	113	5,960	20,020	14,060	4,687
1663–7	Lages	115	5,527	14,076	8,549	2,850
1700–3	Lages	117	3,450	14,356	10,906	3,635
1707–10	Lages	111		9,769		
1711–14	Lages		3,234	15,326	12,092	4,031
1714–23	Lages		5,018	17,346	13,328	4,109
1726–9	Lages	94	4,971	10,848	5,877	1,959
	S. Caet.	50	2,693	13,988	11,295	3,765
1732–6	Lages	79	2,723	3,296	574	143
	S. Caet.	46	1,570	5,293	3,733	1,244
1736–9	Lages		1,715	1,160	555	185
	S. Caet.		997	1,720	723	241
1764–6	Lages		723	915	73	37
	S. Caet.		1,312	3,687	2,375	792
1765–8	Lages		1,388	3,770	2,382	794
	S. Caet.		1,761	9,168	7,407	2,469
1769–72	Lages		1,448	2,106	658	219
	S. Caet.		1,629	7,709	6,080	2,027
1777–80	Lages		2,675	5,066	2,391	797
	S. Caet.		1,626	7,426	5,800	1,933
1780–3	Lages		4,148	6,051	1,903	634
	S. Caet.		2,811	12,118	9,307	3,102
1783–6	Lages		1,684	4,406	2,722	907
	S. Caet.		4,287	11,459	7,172	2,390
1786–9	Lages		2,121	3,859	1,738	579
	S. Caet.		4,936	9,765	4,859	1,619
1789–93	Lages		3,453	11,196	7,743	2,581
	S. Caet.		5,335	23,140	17,805	5,935
1796–1800	Lages		2,674	6,369	3,695	924
	S. Caet.		7,555	31,703	24,148	6,037

Source: Arquivo Distrital de Braga, Congregaçao de São Bento, 136–7.

attempts to establish the profitability of the sugar economy at the end of the colonial era. In 1781, José da Silva Lisboa, later viscount of Cairú, a man with broad interests and liberal ideas, wrote a long, detailed letter to Domingos Vandelli, director of the Royal Botanical Gardens in Lisbon.[99] The letter contained a description of the society and economy of Bahia, including an estimate of the costs and profits of a sugar planter. Lisboa calculated that a tarefa of cane would yield a minimum of sixteen loaves of sugar with three arrobas per load, or forty-eight arrobas in all. At prices then current, this would equal 48$, to which another 9$ for molasses could be added. And if the engenho had its own still for making cachaça, that was worth a further $700. Thus a tarefa of cane produced 57$700 in gross income. A mill with eighty slaves, fifty of whom were fully able, could maintain 100 tarefas of cane. The value of such a mill would be about 24,000$ on the average.

Although Silva Lisboa realized that the 5,770$ in gross income had to be reduced by expenses, he believed that these were fully recaptured by the division of sugar with dependent lavradores and the rent charged them. Thus his final rate of return was calculated on the gross income and amounted to 24 percent. Beyond this rate, however, he also pointed out that many people began operations with only an out-of-pocket cost of 8,000$; the return to them was much higher. Unfortunately, Silva Lisboa's estimate of operating costs is very imprecise, as is his calculation of the income to the mill generated by the lavradores. His figure of 5,770$ as net income is, therefore, highly suspect, especially because the few existing accounts of the period do not indicate such high levels.

The improbable rate of return suggested by Silva Lisboa is underlined by the "Economic Description of the Province and City of Salvador," penned by an unknown author around 1790.[100] Written to suggest ways of stimulating the economy by a person with obvious firsthand experience in Bahia, its rounded numbers suggest estimate and guess rather than access to hard figures. Nevertheless, it does provide a base point for comparison. The anonymous author stated that Bahia had 170 engenhos, of which 150 were operating. The average value of an engenho was 40,000$, so the total capital stock of the engenhos was 6,000,000$. Annual sales of sugar and rum brought a gross income of 974,000$, which after expenses left a net return of 316,000$ or 2,166$ per mill.[101] This was a net return on capital of 5.4 percent, to which another 1.0 percent from local sales could be added. Because the current interest rate on money at loan was 5 percent, the industry was making roughly 20 percent more than that. When in the late 1790s net incomes soared, the rates of return were surely well above 6.4 percent, but a return of between 5 and 10 percent during much of the eighteenth century is suggested by both general descriptions and engenho accounts.[102]

What, then, was the return on capital in the Bahian sugar industry? The answer must be that it varied greatly from time to time and mill to mill. Surely, the low returns suggested by the Engenho Sergipe and Engenho Santana records did not characterize the industry over long periods of time. No matter what the social advantages of plantership, owners would not have remained in business for extended periods under such conditions. Although there were constraints on the flexibility and mobility of capital in the sugar economy that sometimes compelled planters to operate at a loss, matters were usually not as gloomy as they proclaimed. Conversely, although there were periods of high profits that produced growth and fortunes in the industry, the image of luxury and incredible wealth is also a misleading one. The industry was probably never as rich in its good days and never as poor in its bad ones as contemporaries and historians have painted it.

By inflating levels of production in the sixteenth century, modern observers have made the decline of the industry and its detrimental effects on Brazil all the more striking. Estimates of Brazilian sugar production for 1600 of more than 1 million arrobas by Simonsen or more than 2 million by Furtado were far too high and led to a series of miscalculations about productivity, wealth, and economic development.[103] Furtado, for example, believed that in the early seventeenth century net returns of more than 80 percent on capital could be obtained in a good year and that the sugar sector was an enclave with very little connection to the rest of the economy. He believed that only about 3 percent of the income generated by sugar went to pay for salaries and local products and that the planter class that controlled 90 percent of the income was enormously rich. Thus wealth was concentrated in their hands, and they spent this money profligately on luxury items or new slaves whose labor increased their profit without stimulating economic growth or structural change. In his view, steady decline set in from the seventeenth century on as the Brazilian Northeast lost a major share of the world's sugar market, but fixed costs kept planters in the business.[104]

The shadow of gloomy decline cast by such an interpretation owes much to a miscalculation of early profits as well as an overly negative description of later years. Once contraction had begun in the seventeenth century it was not constant. A portion of the Atlantic market remained available to Brazil even in the hard times of the mid–eighteenth century, and there were periods of expansion, such as the 1760s and 1790s, when hopes were always raised anew. Brazilian sugar filled about 8 percent of Europe's demand in the 1770s and then almost doubled to about 15 percent in the 1790s.[105] At no time from 1600 to 1800 did the value of any other commodity, including gold, ever exceed the value of sugar among Brazilian exports. Sugar remained the leading economic activity in Bahia throughout the colonial period.

Concentration on the ups and downs of the sugar trade has directed attention to the external aspects of the Brazilian economy, but the business of plantership was inextricably tied to other areas of the regional economy.[106] Engenhos stimulated primary production; consumed skills, labor, and raw materials; and, in a reduced fashion, supplied sugar and by-products to colonial consumers. Furtado and others have downplayed these internal connections, but they are important for understanding how the industry coped with difficult periods without major structural changes.

As the population grew and the economy diversified, local sales of sugar and its by-products became increasingly important to the industry. At the close of the seventeenth century, 3 to 4 percent of the sugar produced in Bahia was consumed locally. That percentage surely rose as population grew in the following century.[107] Salvador, as Brazil's largest city for most of the colonial period and a large urban center for all of it, provided a concentrated market for local sugar and rum. By 1757, there were thirty-nine distilleries in the city and another thirty-two in the Recôncavo, all producing rum, most of it for local consumption.[108] Molasses became an essential product on Bahian engenhos. Gonçalo Marinho Falção said plainly in 1763 that "everyone knows the necessity of having molasses is notorious."[109] In times when sugar prices were particularly low, planters may have held back white-sugar production and concentrated instead on making molasses or rum for the local market. In a sense, the drinkers of Bahia offered an alternative to the sugar bowls of Europe.

Rum sales were only part of the activities that increasingly placed the Bahian sugar sector at a central place within the region's economy. Unlike the Caribbean sugar islands, where the level of imports and even of foodstuffs always remained high, Brazil with its great size, varied climate and topography, and potential for expansion provided conditions for increasing linkage between the sugar sector and other aspects of the economy. Imports always made up a significant portion of costs in the sugar industry, especially because of the need for manufactured goods and slaves. But the engenho accounts indicate that the myriad of locally produced goods – lumber, bricks, tiles, forms, whale oil, and services in the form of labor – made up at least two-thirds of the annual expenses. Moreover, the proportion of expenditures devoted to the purchase of imported material tended to decline, as Table 8-5 indicates. With the exception of the inflated figures in the 1751 general statement, engenho accounts from the late eighteenth century indicate lower levels of material costs than had existed. Better management and an increasing ability to obtain some products locally rather than depend on imports probably explains this change. Although copper, iron, and steel were never available from local sources, many other items were, and planters came to depend on local skills and materials.

Sugar-plantation areas have been portrayed as classic examples of enclave economies in which monocultural export agriculture has produced only minimal impact on the regional or national economies. In the Bahian case, it is hard to substantiate this position. The flows of income from the engenhos to other sectors of the economy through the purchase of foodstuffs, skilled labor, wood, and other supplies constituted large transfers of resources. The cattle industry of the sertão was an activity early and directly subsidiary to the growing sugar economy. By the eighteenth century, it had developed its own trajectory of growth based on the supply of meat to populated areas and hides for export, as well as replacement stock to the sugar mills. The tobacco industry of Bahia, the most important in Brazil, depended on molasses for the treatment of lower grades to make them appealing to African buyers. The availability of this sugar by-product gave Bahian producers a comparative advantage over other sellers in African ports.

The refusal of many planters to grow food crops on their own lands stimulated the development of whole areas in the southern Recôncavo and farther south, where agriculture was organized by the market available in the Recôncavo engenhos and the city of Salvador. Jaguaripe, Maragogipe, and eventually Nazaré "of the flours" became the centers of small- and medium-scale producers employing one to ten slaves, often alongside family labor. This was not peasant production but, rather, a small-scale market agriculture tightly oriented to the sugar economy. On engenhos where slaves were allowed to maintain their own gardens, some of their produce also found its way into local markets and linked them to a monetary economy as producers as well as consumers.

The linkages between the sugar sector and the rest of the Bahian economy were varied, continual, and profound.[110] Sugar production originally demanded heavy imports of material and skills, and the planter class imported furniture, clothing, and other "consumer" goods, but many items were eventually obtainable in the colony itself. In periods of low prices and hence low returns on capital, planters found ways to substitute for imported goods, whereas in "boom" times, such as the end of the eighteenth century, demand for fine wines and English pianos increased.[111] To use the terminology of development theory, "backward linkages" between the sugar sector and the producers of materials needed by it were strong, and sugar stimulated the growth of other production. By taxing the flow of income generated by sugar, a "fiscal" linkage was made possible, but the revenues were not reinvested in the colony. Instead, they went to pay for debts, wars, and the extravagance of the Portuguese court. The colonial government did not use these revenues to stimulate further economic development. The Bahian sugar industry also failed to create strong "forward" linkages. Refineries never developed in the colony, partly because the engenhos themselves by producing clayed sugars precluded them and partly because of Portugal's own economic dependency on its European trading partners. Planters paid little attention to road building or other improvements in transportation, and not many were willing or able to ship sugar on their own, let alone take on the risks associated with the role of merchant-shipper. Distance, technology, and predilection separated the producers of sugar from involvement with the staple that might have led to further growth.

Given its ups and downs, the sugar industry proved in the main a profitable business for the planters. The failure of the industry to provide for sustained growth lay, it seems, not in the deficiencies or unprofitability of slave labor but in the policies of a state that taxed the industry but did not put the revenue toward ends that sustained economic development. It also lay in the nature of the commercial organization of the staple, which remained oriented toward, and dependent on, the metropolis. Despite these obstacles, the sugar industry did stimulate a wide range of other economic activities in the colony, and it engendered a society that reflected the hierarchies of the engenho. To that society we now turn.

PART III

SUGAR SOCIETY

CHAPTER 9

A COLONIAL SLAVE SOCIETY

In America every white man is a gentleman.
Alexander von Humboldt (1804)

. . . where a person of the most humble birth puts on the airs of a great gentleman.
A royal official (1718)

Up to this point, we have traced the formation of colonial Brazilian society through the sugar economy and the plantation system on which it was based. During this formative experience, actions and decisions by Europeans, Indians, and Africans contributed to the way in which the historical process took place and the results to which it led. Moreover, the technology and techniques of sugar production and its position within an international market also structured relationships within the society and created or reinforced positions held by various groups: planters, merchants, and slaves. Although from the beginning there were always other groups and other activities in Portuguese Brazil, sugar, the engenho, and slavery played central roles in defining and shaping Brazilian society. They did so not only because sugar remained an important economic activity but also because the principles on which sugar society was grounded were widely shared, adaptive to new situations, and sanctioned by both church and state. Colonial Brazil was a slave society not simply in the obvious fact that its labor force was predominantly slave but rather in the juridical distinction between slave and free, in principles of hierarchy based on slavery and race, in the seigneurial attitudes of masters, and in the deference of social inferiors. Through the diffusion of these ideals, slavery created the basic facts of Brazilian life.

It should be clear from my analysis and description of the plantation economy, the nature and social relations of sugar production, and the economics of the sugar industry and of plantership that a peculiar kind of society had developed. This society inherited classical and medieval concepts of organization and hierarchy. But it added to them systems of rank that grew from the differentiation of occupation, race, color,

245

and status–distinctions resulting from the American reality. It was a society of multiple hierarchies of honor and esteem, of multiple categories of labor, of complex divisions of color, and of varied means of mobility and change; but it was also a society with a profound tendency to reduce complexities to dualisms of contrast–master/slave, noble/commoner, Catholic/gentile–and to reconcile the multiple rankings to one another so that rank, class, color, and civil status tended to converge in each individual.

Social ideology and Brazilian reality

A political and social vision of the world derived essentially from Catholic theologians and especially Saint Thomas Aquinas served as the bedrock of Brazilian society in formation. It defined the goals of political life as pursuit of the common good through an arrangement of society into a hierarchical organization that encouraged complementarity and balance while controlling competition and conflict.[1] By the sixteenth century, state and society were inseparable in theoretical terms; the former represented the ordering of the latter and had a definite role in controlling and regulating the relationship of groups to each other. In theory at least, society was divided into the three distinct traditional orders or estates, the position of each being originally defined by function but subsequently determined by privilege, statute, custom, and manner of living. Whereas the king ruled as the head of the body politic, the nobility were the arms that defended it, the clergy the heart that guarded its soul, and the commoners those who gave it the energy and sustenance to survive.[2] The tripartite division had been an obvious simplification even as it became codified in European thought in the eleventh century, and in reality society was far more varied and complex.[3] Gradations and subranks existed among the nobility and within the hierarchy of the clergy, and the existence of professionals, merchants, and artisans among the commoners created important distinctions there as well. The division of society into three estates was an obvious oversimplification, but at the same time it erred by being too complex; in some ways, the most important distinction was between commoners (peões) and persons of quality or nobles (pessoas de mor qualidade).[4] That distinction was reflected in some of the earliest legislation for the Brazilian colony.

The society of orders or estates was in effect a statutory or juridical construct in which the hierarchy of rank, privilege, and honor was legislated into practice.[5] External signs of rank, forms of address, insignia, privilege, and obligation defined an individual's position. Procedure and precedence took on important symbolic meanings on public occasions and buttressed the position and prerogatives of each group. Leaving the clergy aside (it was small in numbers at its upper levels and somewhat an adjunct to the great nobles), the nobility were the most privileged, honored, and respected order. In return for their theoretical obligation to bear arms, they were entitled to tax exemptions, preference before the law, governmental positions of authority and command, and social deference.

The nobility dominated society and determined standards of performance and behavior. Even a university-trained judge or a wealthy merchant, though bourgeois in origin, usually aspired to the status, titles, and privileges of the nobility. The gradations of the Portuguese nobility, from titled counts, dukes, and marquises to the gentlemen fidalgos or those who were made noble in their own lifetime for some service or deed (*fidalgos da casa del rey*) need not detain us here. Nobility was, in a sense, defined by what a person did not do. Working with one's own hands, shopkeeping, artisan crafting, and other "mean" occupations were the domain of the commoners. Nobles were expected to live without recourse to such activities. Nobles sought instead to live from rents or offices and to maintain an aristocratic way of life, which usually meant a large household of retainers, relatives, and servants. Independent means, seigneurial dominion, command over dependents, the maintenance and furtherance of lineage, and the profession of arms or political service constituted the elements of the noble ideal that infused society and served as a goal for others to achieve.

As originally conceived, the peasantry were persons of lesser quality: the vast majority of the population settled in the countryside, engaged in agriculture, herding, or fishing. But this was a wholly unrealistic representation of society in the sixteenth century. Artisans, though surely commoners, had capital in their skills and shops, servants and employees; their own internal structuring of masters and apprentices; and through their representation in municipal councils, a voice in local government. Similar statements could be made about other functional groups like the merchants and the legal profession, also by statutory definition members of the third estate, but with abilities, skills, knowledge, or wealth that distinguished them from the peasantry and made possible their entry into the nobility. These functional groupings were distinct from the estates but blended into them. Artisans and merchants developed corporate guilds and other associations to express collective interests, often using religious confraternities as the basis for voluntary association. Corporate identity, membership in one of the estates, and affiliation with a guild or confraternity provided the theoretical base of society, and this was expressed in government by the *cortes* (parliament) in which the crown presided over the three estates.[6]

Accompanying the division of society into juridical orders and functional groupings were some other principles of organization. The distinction between Old Christians, those whose families had been Catholics before the forced conversion of all Jews in Portugal in 1497, and

New Christians, converted Jews and their descendants, was main-tained until the mid–eighteenth century. Persons of New Christian descent suffered various disabilities, no matter what the orthodoxy of their religious beliefs. Illegitimacy too brought disadvantages in the inheritance of name and property and in the ability to achieve higher status through entry into royal service or office. Illegitimacy and famil-ial religious orthodoxy were related to the concept of purity of blood. Although the origins and exact meaning of that concept are much debated, by the sixteenth century it was used to distinguish those persons who were unstained by racial or religious deviance from the ideal of a white, Old Christian Portuguese, untainted by the infected races, as the expression went, of "moor, mulatto, negro, or Jew." When purity of blood was then combined with *fidalguia* (nobility), all doors could be opened in the society.[7]

Fidalguia, or more generally higher social status, was, in fact, not beyond reach. Although the society of orders had been conceived as fixed and rigid, social mobility was certainly possible. The growth of commerce and the rise of the state in Portugal as elsewhere in Europe had created opportunities for merchants, lawyers, royal officers, and others to gain wealth or status or both. Although noble titles were relatively few, rewards of fidalgo status or its equivalent were not uncommon in the sixteenth and seventeenth centuries. To some ex-tent, Lawrence Stone's "San Gimignano model" of a large population base from which a series of more or less independent economic and status hierarchies – land, church, law, commerce, and government – rose like towers above it, describes Portuguese society in the age of Brazil's formation.[8] But these multiple hierarchies were still juridically and theoretically conceived within the limits and rankings of the soci-ety of orders with its fundamental division between noble and com-moner. A person might rise within one of the towers, but when he reached an appropriate height there was always a strong tendency to reconcile his position within the more general social hierarchy. Both these elements of Portuguese society, openness to mobility and the desire to reconcile and legitimate higher status with the traditional attributes and lifestyle of the nobility, are crucial for understanding the nature of colonial Brazil, a place "where a person of the most modest circumstances and birth puts on the airs of a great nobleman."[9]

The noble ideal infused Brazilian society at its inception and per-sisted throughout the colonial period. It encompassed attitudes, attri-butes, and traditions that both certified and measured noble status. The ideal rested on a concept of social organization that like society itself was hierarchical, unequal by definition, and paternalistic. A noble lived without recourse to manual labor, and thus manual labor was degrading. A nobleman ensured the maintenance and persistence of his lineage and family. This he did by sponsoring chapels and masses for ancestors; by supporting his present "family," understood as immediate relatives, retainers, servants, and slaves; and by devising appropriate marriage and inheritance strategies to ensure the future. The prefered goal was to possess landed property, which was valued not simply because it brought prestige in and of itself but also because it was the most secure way to maintain the noble life. The senior member of the noble house exercised paternalistic control over its members. He owed them protection; they owed him loyalty and deference. Such noble households might include distant relatives of lower social status, adopted children, and the recognized children of illicit unions, whose position fell beneath that of legitimate offspring. Noble status might be buttressed by entails or membership in a military order, but it was also a matter of attitudes and values. The blooded horse, unbounded largesse, literacy, religious devotion, bravery in the face of danger, and the ability to command subordinates were the marks of a nobleman. A patriarchal family organization grounded on a landed estate over which the noblemen exercised paternalistic and authoritarian power was no less part of this ideal.

American realities transformed or modified the organization and ideals of Portuguese society in the Brazilian colony. The traditional structure of estates and corporations existed but became less important in the American context. The essential distinction between gentleman and commoner tended to be leveled because the sea of Indians that surrounded the Portuguese population made each European in effect a potential gentleman. The availability of Indians as slaves or laborers allowed the immigrants to live out their noble fantasies. With a few Indians to hunt and fish, any man could live without recourse to manual labor. With many Indians, a truly noble life could be achieved. Indians became a surrogate peasantry, a new estate, which permitted the traditional categories to be rearranged. The fact, however, that Indians and later Africans were ethnically, religiously, and phenotypically different from Europeans created opportunities for new distinctions and hierarchies based on culture and color. To describe these opportunities as "new," in fact, may be an overstatement. Blacks had been in Portugal since Moorish times, and by the early sixteenth century there were more than 30,000 in Portugal itself.[10] All the institutions of black life and culture and reactions to them existed in Portugal, so it is impossible to ascribe the Brazilian system of racial discrimination and classification entirely to the colonial regime.[11] What made Brazil distinct from Portugal, however, was the eventual preponderance of persons of color compared to their minority status in the metropolis.

As pagans, Indians and Africans were outside the limits of the body politic. But as Christians, they had to be found a place. Religious orthodoxy and acceptance of European culture became measures by which they were judged. Distinctions between *gentios* (gentiles) and *índios aldeados* (village Indians) or between *boçal* (newly arrived) and *ladino* (acculturated) Africans were essentially cultural rankings to mark off those within and those outside or almost outside society. Once part of society, Indians and Africans could simply be placed in the existing hierarchy as new corporations, strata defined by color. But complexities were introduced by Indians and crioulo blacks born within Portuguese society and thus not easily distinguishable by cultural differences, and even more so by people of mixed origin, the results of miscegenation. The problem of placing these people within traditional social order led to the creation of the peculiar social hierarchy based on race that we have come to associate with many New World colonies.

Acculturated Indians, freed slaves, and free persons of mixed descent were defined by color as much as by functional grouping or traditional estate. Color gave them a corporate existence, although distinctions were recognized. Various labels developed in Brazil, changing with time and place. In Bahia, mulatto, *cabra* (black-Indian), *pardo* (lighter mulatto), and *preto* (black) were in common use. Coloreds generally bore two marks of disadvantage. First, their color clearly indicated origins associated with Africa and therefore lower social status, presumably slavery, at some time in the past. Second, there was a suggestion of illegitimacy in the existence of a person of color, the assumption being that a white man did not usually marry women of inferior racial status. Added to these disadvantages were prejudices about the natural moral inclinations of mixed bloods, who were often characterized as clever, pushy, untrustworthy, and undependable. But such attitudes and discriminatory legislation did not prevent the pardo population from growing and becoming a major part of the artisan, wage-labor, and small-farming sectors.

Free persons of color were, in fact, a heterogeneous group, varied in origin, place of birth, skills, extent of acculturation, and color. Little bound them together except their color. Race had created an alternate system of estates – white, pardo, black, Indian – that both fused with European society of orders and transcended it. Had all blacks been slaves and all slaves remained slaves, then the traditional principles of social organization could have accommodated the Brazilian situation with little change. The complexity was caused by the manumission of slaves, who thus became free, and by the birth of persons of mixed racial origin, who were born some free and others slave but who were favored in the manumission process. These people created new social categories that had to be accommodated in the social hierarchy.

A system that combined social definitions and rankings based on estate, function, corporate identity, religion, culture, and color might have proved so confusing and liable to inherent contradiction as to become no system at all. But such was not the case. The tendency was always for the various criteria of rank to become congruent in a single individual. Thus a boçal African was most likely to be pagan, black, unacculturated, unskilled, a field hand, and certainly a slave. A white was assumed to be free and acculturated, to be defined by estate or function, and to tend toward the top of the various social gradients. Between the two extremes, persons of mixed origin proved less easy to place. The plantation regime did not create the rankings, but its internal structure with ownership by Europeans, coerced labor provided by Indians and then African or black slaves, and artisan or managerial roles filled by poorer whites, freed blacks, and persons of color, reinforced the social hierarchy and reaffirmed the gradations in a practical and demonstrable way. The engenho was both mirror and metaphor of Brazilian society.

A slave society

It has become commonplace to speak of colonial Brazil as a slave society, but we should recognize that the colony's original theoretical base was only partially associated with slavery. Although that institution had existed in Iberia prior to the settlement of Brazil, it was relatively marginal to the essential principles of organization of the society of orders, as it developed in Europe. In the New World, the existence of slaves and the creation of a population of mixed origin created new social realities that had to be reconciled with the transferred Portuguese principles of social organization. It was easy enough to do. Brazil in a way demonstrated the resilience of the society of orders and its adaptability to new social categories and situations. Plantation slavery in Brazil transformed and broadened the traditional categories – it turned into persons of quality some who could have never aspired to that label in Portugal and created a new estate of commoners in the slaves. But at the same time it developed new principles of hierarchy based on race, acculturation, and civil status. Brazilian slave society was not a creation of slavery but the result of plantation slavery's integration with preexisting European social principles.

The ultimate social difference upon which Brazilian society rested was its division into slave and free. This essential juridical distinction inherited from Roman law divided society into those with rights to person and property, those who could theoretically exercise rights as "citizens," and those who could not.[12] In its origins, this division was not based on race. Portuguese law codes like the *Ordenações manuelinas* (1514) still spoke of white and Moorish slaves, but by the sixteenth century's close, slavery in the Portuguese world was increasingly associated with Africans and their descendants.[13] Although the distinction between slavery and freedom had important juridical implications, the ancient precedents of Roman and Iberian domestic servitude, the role of the Catholic church in insisting on slaves' humanity, slaves' eligibility for membership in the church and thus entitlement to its rites and privileges, and the existence of other forms of subordination within the society hedged the relationship of master to slave. Even the status of slave was not without variation, for Portuguese custom in Brazil recognized the status of *coartado*, a slave who had been designated in a will or other document as entitled to pay for his or her freedom and who was thus given a certain freedom of movement or ability to gain or own property to accumulate the needed sum. In short, a coartado was a slave in the process of transition to freeman or freewoman. But although such gradations existed, although the tradition or custom of slave *peculium* – slave-owned property – was allowed, and although the church welcomed slaves as members, the distinction between slave and free truly divided the society. Unable to make contracts, dispose of their lives and property, defend themselves or their families from physical abuse by their masters, testify against freemen, choose their labor or their employer, and limited by law and practice in a thousand other ways, slaves remained the most disadvantaged element in society. In a world in which lineage provided a person with a base, slaves usually had no last names, in effect no recognizable family; in a society in which honor reflected status, slavery was assumed to divest a person of any honor at all. Free people of color may have suffered disabilities and indignities, been subjected to legal and illegal coercion, and been held in low regard, but their status was infinitely better than that of slaves. At least the slaves thought so. Only this can explain why so many Brazilian slaves were willing at great sacrifice and effort to scrape together enough money to purchase their own freedom or that of their children. Legally, freedom mattered.[14]

I emphasize here the crucial legal distinction because I wish at the same time to deemphasize the economic one. If there were in Brazil slaves who grew their own food, marketed their surplus, held skilled occupations, could accumulate money to buy their freedom, and in the cities as *negros de ganho* (slaves for hire) lived and worked on their own; if at the same time there were in Brazil free persons who were subject to coercion, suffered discrimination, received little remuneration for their labor, and were fettered by custom and practice; then as descriptions of a labor system, slavery and free labor are not particularly helpful in understanding colonial Brazil.[15] If slaves acted like peasants and peasants were treated like slaves, then the distinctions begin to lose their meaning and their ability to direct and inform analysis. Like proletarians, slaves were separated from the means of production, and the surplus value of their labor was appropriated by those who owned the productive means. But on the plantations of Bahia, as elsewhere, both slaves and wage earners lived under the paternalistic control of a planter who viewed his labor force, slave and free, as something more than labor. From the slaveowner's point of view, slave labor and free labor were not two separate worlds, but, rather, two points along a continuum, each with its advantages and problems.[16] Either might be used given existing political and economic conditions. The shift from slavery to free labor on the Northeast sugar plantations in the 1870s, before the abolition of slavery in Brazil, is a case in point. Slavery predominated during the colonial period in Bahia, but it was usually accompanied by various forms of wage labor as well.

The point I wish to underline here is the relative similarity and compatibility of various labor forms within the context of the plantation and the principles of a multitiered society of estates. At the same time, I do not wish to diminish the importance of slavery as an institution that thrived within that context and contributed to those principles. In a sense, Frank Tannenbaum had seen the crucial distinction, although he and his followers did not immediately grasp its meaning. His book *Slave and Citizen* (1947) recognized in its title that the real difference in a society was the legal one between those two statuses and that the ease by which a person could move from one to the other was an essential measure of a slave regime.[17] The difference between slave labor and free labor was of less importance and did not in itself inform us about the conditions under which people lived.

Having deemphasized the theoretical distinctions between categories of laborers should not, however, diminish our perception of Brazil as a society profoundly influenced by slavery. Here history played a role, for it was not simply slavery that shaped this society but large-scale plantation slavery, based first on Indians and then on Africans, creating hierarchies based on race or color that reflected the internal organization of the engenhos. Slavery and race created new criteria of status that permeated the social and ideological life of the colony. The plantation allowed a re-creation of the noble ideal, a large landed estate in which the owner could exercise patriarchal control over his family and dependents. Its need for a large labor force created a role for these dependents, and the fact that they were slaves and racially distinct from the owner caused no particular problem for the ideal. Seigneurial society showed itself quite adaptable in this regard. Finally, the sugar engenhos' peculiar need for skilled workers, artisans, and managers created opportunities for differentiation among the slaves and for roles that could be filled by wage workers. These niches provided a place in the engenho regime for freemen and persons of mixed origin, the results of miscegenation and manumission. The slave plantation did not create the structure of Brazilian society, but it meshed with it so well that the specific features it introduced were easily accommodated within that structure.

Racial distinctions and slavery permeated the whole society, reaching into the most mundane aspects of life and affecting the actions and perceptions of everyone, slave and free, white, black, red, and brown.

The many instances of freedmen who owned slaves, of slaveholding even by poor farmers, and even occasional references to slaves who acquired slaves indicate the power and pervasiveness of this institution.[18] Although Africans or slaves might have their own values and cultures, they were always constrained by the necessity of operating within the limits of colonial society. No one in colonial Brazil was free from the presence of slavery.

A feudal society?

I must at this point address an issue that has plagued (and I use the word with intention) the historiography of Brazil, and of the plantation Americas – that is, the feudal or capitalist nature of Brazilian society. As Jacob Gorender pointed out in 1978, much of the writing on Brazilian society has knowingly or unconsciously taken up the issue. Thus, the seigneurial-patriarchal emphases of authors of the 1930s such as Gilberto Freyre or Oliveira Viana were essentially feudal interpretations of Brazil's essence, a view subsequently adopted by such Marxist historians as Nelson Werneck Sodré.[19] But a feudalism without fiefs, without serfs, and without the rites of fealty – a feudalism characterized by plantations worked by slaves growing an export commodity for an international market during Europe's transition to capitalism – has been questioned by a host of authors who prefer to use such terms as *mercantilist*, *commercial capital*, and *capitalist* to describe the society of colonial Brazil.[20]

To some extent, there are really two issues in this debate; at times, the exponents of the main lines of argument have been talking about different things under the single rubric of feudalism. The debate in Portuguese and Brazilian historiography went back to the 1920s and was basically juridical in nature, centering on the origins of the colony and especially on the nature of the donatary captaincies. Of primary concern was the relationship between the crown and the lord proprietor; the powers granted by the former and the obligations of the latter.[21] The donatary captains were thus key figures in the debate, and their charters were the crucial documents to be interpreted. But this was no easy matter. For there was an even older debate in Portugal itself over the issue of whether feudalism had ever existed there during the medieval period.[22] Those who questioned its existence in Portugal also argued primarily on juridical grounds that the lack of military service given in return for seigneurial rights meant that feudalism as such did not exist. Although their contention was probably correct in an extremely narrow sense, it overlooked the fact that feudalism had varied greatly from one place to another in Europe and throughout time. But more importantly, the nature of Brazilian society was not clarified by this debate because feudalism was still being used as a description of an economic system, and one that as Jacques Heers has stated was "almost always weighed down with every conceivable implication of evil."[23] He, like other medievalists, warned us that they were unsure of its exact meaning and if in fact it had ever existed.[24]

For Marx and his followers, the juridical debate of the medievalists that concentrated on the relationship of sovereign to lord was misplaced. Marx demonstrated that it was not necessary to have feudalism as a political system to have a feudal mode of production in which a dependent labor force maintains some control over the means of production, meeting its obligations of rent in payment, kind, or labor. His vision of feudalism emphasized the relations between lord and peasant rather than between king and vassal. Such an understanding allows the possibility of feudal social relations existing within a nonfeudal political organization. This is what Eugene Genovese and Elizabeth Fox-Genovese have in mind when they state: "Colonial and plantation economies, based primarily on monoculture, embody features of two different economic structures, and the macrostructure of the sector as a whole may bear only an indirect relation to the microstructure of the individual firms."[25] In fact, they eschew the term "feudalism" and prefer to use "seigneurialism" because it avoids the burden of confusion that weighs so heavily on the word feudalism and because the social relations between master and slave preoccupy them in their analysis.

Seigneurialism, in fact, is a term that merits some close attention in the Brazilian context because the donatarial captaincies of Brazil are perhaps best understood as extensions of the Portuguese concept of *senhorio* or lordship.[26] But as Harold B. Johnson pointed out, when transferred to the Atlantic islands and then Brazil certain changes had taken place. "Unlike the classical fief, the grant was not dependent upon service, military or otherwise, but rather was given in reward for services, past, present or future."[27] By the time of the Brazilian donatary grants in the 1530s, the grants themselves were different from their medieval precedents. The *foral* or constitution traditionally granted by the lord to the inhabitants on his lands was in Brazil given instead by the crown, reflecting a process that had been under way since the fourteenth century in Portugal in which the "new monarchy" had reduced the powers of senhores over their lands and dependents. Although the forms of medieval Portugal were transferred to Brazil, their content reflected new political realities in which the state played a central role. The judicial and appointive powers in the donatarial grants that were reminiscent of earlier senhorios were quickly abrogated in the colony and much diminished after the creation of royal government in Brazil in 1549. Thus, by the time the sugar economy had begun to flourish in the 1560s, the state had diminished many of the seigneurial powers of the donatary captains and had assumed a central role in the formation of society and economy quite unlike its medieval precedents.

The donatary captaincies then were indeed expressions of Portuguese seigneurialism, but that seigneurialism was itself changing and was increasingly controlled by a centralized, absolutist state. By the time Brazil became a plantation colony, even within the traditional juridical definition, there was little left of the feudal past. The state had assumed a direct role in the allocation of resources and thus in the ordering of society. Contemporaries realized that these changes had taken place. In the 1620s and 1630s, the crown attempted to force the holders of donatarial grants in Brazil to personally develop and defend their lands.[28] They objected, and a crown commission after examining the charters found them to be all of *juro e herdade*, without the obligation that they be defended in person. The "feudal" obligations were absent. The crown eventually found a lawyer to argue that the donataries' responsibilities as governors required their service.[29] Thus military and bureaucratic roles rather than lordship had to be used to mobilize the grantees. As one Jesuit wrote around 1600, "The captains of these captaincies of Brazil are not the lords of them in the same way that in Europe a man is over his entail or *casal*."[30]

In Marxist terms, such debates were arid, if not pointless. For feudalism has a specific meaning as a particular mode of production regardless of the legal-juridical framework in which it is placed. Thus there can be feudalism without the existence of the *feudum* (lordly estate) as long as the other criteria of a peasant or serf class subject to extraeconomic coercion that limits its personal liberty and property rights so that neither labor nor its product is fully commercialized are present. In this context, it is the relationship between the property owner (master) and the laborers (slaves) that is the object of primary consideration, not that between lord and sovereign as in the historical-juridical tradition.[31]

Within the framework of either approach, it seems clear that the usual features of feudalism do not characterize colonial Brazil in general or the plantations of Bahia in particular. Whatever seigneurial aspects may have existed in the original donatarial grants were increasingly abrogated after the creation of royal government in 1549. The slave-based economy that developed in the sugar industry satisfied the criteria of a predominantly agrarian system in which the basic productive unit was a large landed estate, but it lacked other features such as a low level of productive forces and commercial exchange.[32] Above all, there were no peasants since production was overwhelmingly slave-based. Small-scale subsistence farming always existed to some extent in the colony, but this class did not grow in size or importance until the eighteenth century. Moreover, the small-scale farmers who most closely approximate the classic European peasantry were often slaveholders themselves.

But the absence of feudalism in the political sphere and the inapplicability of that term as a description of the organization of production should not deflect us from a recognition of an ideology held by the planters, and others in the society, that was essentially hierarchical, founded on dominance and rank, moved by patronage and fealty at least in theory, and wedded to a Catholic concept of the civil and religious spheres. These attitudes, whether we call them premodern, seigneurial, or feudal, were not indigenous but grew from a solid base of Portuguese, and indeed European, tradition. They served well, however, the interests and position of the planters who, as the arbiters of taste and style and the holders of power, dominated social and political institutions within the colony. Such attitudes did not mean that slaveholders in Brazil were kinder in their treatment of bondsmen than were "capitalistic" slaveholders of nineteenth-century Mississippi. As we have seen, profit was a principal concern throughout the history of the sugar industry, and the nature of sugar production, combined with the principal theory of slave management, produced a regime that was at times as cruel and devastating as any other. Still, that exploitation was set in an ideological context in which the metaphors of family, obligation, fealty, and clientage predominated. When in an act of manumission a slaveowner said, as many did, "I am freeing my slave because I raised her like my own child, because of the many years of faithful service she has provided, and for the 200$ that she has paid me," that unity between profit and paternalism was made clear.[33] Although we may find this to be a contradiction, the slaveowners of Brazil did not.

Just as slaves growing their own food were not exactly peasants, so planters driving for profit were not necessarily capitalists. The slave-based plantations of Brazil were undoubtedly tied to a European economic system in a phase of commercial expansion, dominated at this stage by merchant capital that itself was transforming social and political life in the metropolis, but there was nothing that prevented the development of slave-based or coerced labor relations from feeding into this commercial system. Whether one believes, as Wallerstein does, that the development of archaic labor forms on the peripheries of the European world system was inevitable (I do not), there was certainly no inherent contradiction in the existence of the slave plantations within the mercantilist commercial system.

The intense desire to characterize the New World colonies as either feudal or capitalist has led to an extensive if often less than enlightening debate. A recent and reasonable trend is to move away from typological description toward an analysis of the particular features of these colonies and especially of their dominant labor forms. In Brazil, this approach has led to the definition of the Brazilian slave regime as a "colonial slave mode of production," and various scholars have sought to identify and analyze its peculiarities or specific general features. Up to this point, I have tried to follow this path by looking at the formation of the plantation system in Brazil, at its operation and internal organization, and especially at the nature and social relations of labor. In this, I accepted the suggestion of Octavio Ianni that "it is necessary to study the relation, processes, political, economic structures which give it [the social formation] reality and movement." Like Ianni, I believe that we must not simply limit study to the mode of production but must also address the broader questions of the social, political, and intellectual dimensions of the society as a whole.[34] This, I think, is what Marx had in mind when he spoke of the social relations of production as being the "innermost secrets, the hidden basis of the entire social structure."[35] The penetration of slavery into every aspect of life, its ability to order the society and influence the behavior of not only masters and slaves but also bureaucrats and peasants, freed people and free, whites, browns, and blacks – this was the power of the institution. No action could be taken, no decision made, no thought expressed without at least tacit recognition of the dominant labor form and the servile population it had created.

The state and society

It is insufficient to characterize colonial Brazil as a slave society and leave it at that because to do so is to ignore the central role that a particular political form played in the shaping of that society. The development of colonial Brazil during the period of early modern Europe's experience with centralized monarchies, the absolutist states, marked that development in a variety of ways. It is not simply that laws, administrative institutions, and royal officials set the perimeters of society and created the context of the economy, but that the state itself was the level at which the struggle between groups and interests was finally resolved. The Weberian approach to the state employed in most studies of colonial Latin American government has emphasized the bureaucratization of the state and its increasing political power as independent of a particular economic or social basis.[36] By viewing that state as an increasingly powerful and thus independent force, its role as a regulator of various interests within society and ultimately as an expression of power of certain groups or classes is obscured. Thus far, this book has attempted to demonstrate the way in which the planters sought to control the policies of the state and to use the powers of government for their own ends. Subsequently, we shall give particular attention to changes in Portuguese colonial policy in relation to the interests of competing groups within the metropolis and the colony.

Just as any characterization of the colonial economy or social structure as feudal or capitalist is fraught with problems because it oversimplifies, so too is the attempt to typify the early modern state with a single term. Was the absolutist state, as Marx and Engels suggested, a balance between a "feudal nobility and an urban bourgeoisie," and thus somewhat independent, or was Engels closer to the mark when he stated that "the political order remained feudal while society became more and more bourgeois?"[37] Perry Anderson believes that the absolutist state was a "redeployed and recharged apparatus of feudal domination," but I think that here he has confused the continued presence of nobles in positions of authority with the hegemonic position of the nobility.[38] In the Portuguese case, some have seen the creation of a strong centralized monarchy after 1385 as a manifestation of the rise of mercantile or bourgeois elements to political ascendancy. I think this too is unreasonable in that it assigns an overly precocious role to those elements.

Like the period itself, the absolutist states were transitional and demonstrated a lack of correspondence between political superstructure and economic instance. The state's role was to carry out the transition to congruence. The centralized monarchy in Portugal under the Aviz, Hapsburg, and Bragança dynasties, like the absolutist states elsewhere in Western Europe, was designed not to destroy seigneurial society but to some extent to perserve it. It was not in the least revolutionary in its goals and was certainly conservative in regard to productive relationships. But in its inherent power and bureaucratic structure were potentially dangerous elements that might call forth new forms. Under extreme military or economic pressure, certain economic relationships and practices could be considerably altered in ways that were potentially revolutionary or disruptive to established social and political principles. The creation of monopoly trade companies during the War of Restoration (1640–68), Pombal's policies (1757–76), and political alterations during and after the Napoleonic Wars (1807–20) were all periods and cases in point. How and when these elements might lead to a weakening of seigneurial society and the encouragement of different social relations and manners of thought and expression in each of the European states is a matter for empirical analysis.

This leads me to two caveats that I hope have guided my analysis in the remainder of this book. First, in dealing with the Bahian sugar-plantation regime throughout the colonial period, I have become aware that any attempt to characterize the entire period by a single political or social term tends to disguise or ignore historical specificity, nuance, and the dynamic of change. The plantation regime with Indian labor in the sixteenth century was in some ways different from that regime with African slaves in the eighteenth. To miss that point is to miss all that history is about. Marx's admonition that we will never arrive at an understanding of history "by using as one's master key a general historico-philosophical theory, the supreme virtue of which consists in being super historical," must be kept in mind.[39] Human decisions and actions, and specific events in particular places, mattered as they always do.

Second, I have also become painfully aware that the role of the state in a colonial polity presents a peculiar set of problems because the apparatus of the state does not necessarily represent the interests of the dominant group *within the colony* but instead may be reflective of metropolitan situations and conflicts. At the same time, it is also possible that certain groups in the colony may be allowed control over social and economic resources and in fact be dominant, as long as their well-being benefits those in the metropolis. The Bahian planters had pretensions to noble status that were never fully satisfied by the Portuguese crown. But during long periods when mercantile elements in Portugal itself were important in the formulation of state policy, the Brazilian planters were coddled and protected. Here, there appeared to be a unity of interest between a colonial class hoping to turn itself into a feudal estate and a metropolitan class of merchants aiming to break the power of the nobility in Portugal itself. As long as the value of the Brazilian colony was generated primarily by private investment in the agricultural sector, the state was content to give the planters a free reign in the colony. When in the late seventeenth and eighteenth centuries export agriculture experienced difficulties and gold (after 1695) became important in the Brazilian economy, the state took a much greater role in ordering the colony's productive forces. The actions of Pombal that we shall examine in Chapter 15 are unimaginable a hundred years before. Policy changes, new economic approaches, and shifting social alliances all had to contend with inertia, tradition, and entrenched interest, so the story of the three-century colonial era is essentially one of persistence rather than change. But there is no doubt that the social and economic equation of Brazilian life in 1620 differed considerably from that of 1820. Although the ebb and flow of social alignments and changes in state policies are relatively easy to document, alterations in attitudes are more difficult to perceive. In fact, the seigneurial mentality seems to have remained deeply entrenched and widely diffused throughout the society even after the original basis of its formation had been significantly modified.

Plantation societies cannot be reduced to the relations between masters and slaves but must be studied with some attention to the political and social contexts in which they exist at a given historical moment. The relationship between the metropolitan government and colonial social hierarchies alone could serve as the basis for detailed study. That has not been my goal in this book. Before proceeding with my analysis, however, I do wish to raise two issues that bear most directly on the relationship between the state and the productive forces in the colony: the creation and enforcement of law, and the role of the bureaucracy within the colony.

The increasing power of the Portuguese state was closely tied to the triumph of Roman law and the growth of a judicial bureaucracy that both administered that law and served as royal servants in a variety of governmental capacities. The legal system that this bureaucracy both created and enforced provided a needed framework for the control of property and commerce and for the distribution, exchange, and control of labor.[40] The Portuguese legal codes encapsulated and amplified the Roman legal tradition and represented the victory of an anchored concept of nonconditional, absolute ownership rather than conditional ownership or "feudal tenures."[41] Although the judicial bureaucracy administered both public and private law, it was in the realm of *lex*, or public law, which regulated the subjects' relation to the state, that the role of the bureaucracy as a force in ordering the society was most apparent. Despite the noble ideal of seigneurial control over dependents and property, the Portuguese state and its royal bureaucracy increasingly penetrated every aspect of life or at least had the ability to do so.

Yet in the matter of slavery, the state and its officers are notably absent. Portuguese law codes like the *Ordenações filipinas* (1603) contain few references to slavery, and those that there are clearly pertain to the social relations of an earlier age of domestic servitude when Moors and even whites were still enslaved. They are not concerned in the main with plantation slavery based on African labor. Except for a few admonitions, these laws are essentially designed to limit the slave's actions and mobility and to impose a severe control over the labor force.[42] They do not interfere with the master's control over his bondsmen.

In Brazil, the same situation obtained, and the crown rarely intervened in the internal operation of the slave regime in the colony. Rather than law, it was the internal organization and operation of the engenho, the techniques of production, the theory of slave control, and the dynamic relation between master and slave that ordered Brazilian social relations and shaped the nature of slavery. On rare occasions, the crown might intervene. The late 1680s to 1710 saw a number of cases tried in Bahia in which the abuse of slaves by masters reached the civil courts. But judges tended to be lenient; in one case, when the crown tried to force the sale of a slave who was sure to suffer cruelly from her owner, the governor of Bahia refused to enforce the sale because it would disrupt the whole social fabric of the colony.[43] In short, the Portuguese crown or its officers generally proved unable or unwilling to interfere in the operation of the dominant productive mode or in its fundamental social relationship. It was a matter of malign neglect.

Local government, the câmaras, controlled as they were by the planters, were far more active in setting the standards of behavior and control over slaves and free persons of color than was the metropolitan government. In the matter of slavery, the crown essentially did not interfere. Although there were periods of royal intervention such as under Dom Pedro II (1683–1706) or Pombal, these were relatively limited in scope and only rarely or halfheartedly addressed the productive system itself. Far more concern and legislation were devoted to taxation, mercantile organization, and the relationship between merchants and planters or creditors and debtors than were devoted to the relationship between property owners and their slaves or employees.

During the eighteenth century, a tendency toward increasing state control of the planters and a shift toward policies that favored mercantile groups can be seen in both Portugal and Brazil. But such policies were always limited by attitudes and interests shared by the sugar planters and merchants. We have already seen how in the matter of credit arrangements the market limited the range of possible legislation and created the basis for alliance and cooperation despite inherent antagonisms between merchants and planters. As long as export agriculture remained a primary activity in Brazil, a certain unity of interest existed among the planters, the merchants, and the state, which, whatever its class basis, was willing to give the planters relatively free reign in the colony. This was not done because the state was weak. Quite the opposite, because in the colony the absolutist state was relatively unhampered by feudal rights, representative bodies, or ancient liberties, it exercised an "exclusive and unique authority" that was checked only by geography and the market. It was therefore able to favor or protect whomever it chose.[44]

This brings us to the final point: the role of bureaucracy in the society. It has become popular in Brazilian historiography to see an inherent conflict between state and society rather than to seek the way in which the colonial slave mode of production resulted from class alliance or cooperation between groups. The conflict view has been most cogently argued by Raimundo Faoro, who sees the ever growing power of government aligned against colonial or national interest.[45] Faoro tends to view the bureaucracy as an independent and self-aggrandizing stratum that uses the goals of the state for its own purposes. There are both historical and theoretical grounds for finding this vision of the role of the bureaucracy unsatisfactory. State power is not the same as state apparatus.[46] Institutions do not hold power in themselves; rather, social groups hold power through institutions. Faoro's position tends to separate the state and bureaucracy from the economic relations that define the society.

Historically, government officers and royal bureaucrats were not created by plantation society but were shapers of it and, as individual human beings, were potentially liable to be drawn within that society. Faoro underestimates the ability of local social groups to form alliances with the bureaucracy to further local interests, in this case the interests of the sugar sector.[47] Undoubtedly, the bureaucrats, especially the royal magistrates, had a certain tendency toward careerism and the pursuit of professional goals and developed a corporate identity. But like other groups in the society, they too hoped to gain the status, insignia, and rights of the nobility, to participate in the aristocratic way of life. They too shared the seigneurial ideal, and they often saw alliance with the planter class as one way of satisfying their desires. Rather than taking stances in opposition to the local elites, the royal bureaucrats sought by marriage, kinship, business association, and cooperation to force alliances with them. In colonial Brazil, state and society were not antagonistic phenomena. The absolutist state facilitated and maintained the predominant productive system and the society based upon it, and it did so by allowing that society a certain freedom to develop along lines inherent in the predominant economic relationships within the context of traditional social values and principles.

The remainder of this book, then, is an attempt to describe and analyze the social groups created by the plantation regime and to examine their interrelationship within the context of a slave society. Rather than view these groups in some kind of stasis, however, I hope to show that two parallel processes were under way: First, the slave regime was constantly subject to stresses inherent in its own organization and nature, so resistance, manumission, demography, and the international market all tended in various ways to rend the society's fabric. Second, changes in the society as a whole, in the growth of a free population and in the development of new economic policies and political ideas in response to new historical conditions, brought opportunities for alterations in the slave system. The tension between the persistent power of slavery as a social and productive system and the pressures brought upon it by its own internal structure and features and by external commercial and political events forms the historical thread in the remaining chapters of this book.

CHAPTER 10

THE PLANTERS:
MASTERS OF MEN AND CANE

An engenho is hell and all the masters of them are damned.

Andrés de Gouvea (1627)

No group in Brazilian history has more of a patina of legendary grandeur than the senhores de engenho of the Northeast. Despite the fact that by the nineteenth century it was proverbial to say, *senhor de engenho, morto de fome, cheio de empenho* ("sugar planter, dying of hunger, loaded with debt"), the planters remained at the pinnacle of the social hierarchy, projecting an image of nobility, wealth, and power.[1] This image was based on their continued control of land and slaves and on the traditional role of local potentate that many had assumed. The senhores de engenho, however, are not simply a social type easily transposed from one epoch to another but are also a class formed over time, developing historically and manifesting different characteristics at different dates. Moreover, there was considerable variation within their ranks, so that although many aspired to reach the apex of the social pyramid, only a small proportion attained this goal.[2] The planters set the social standards of the colony and came closest to approximating metropolitan models. Thus, by examining their composition and behavior, we can establish the norm against which others in society were measured.

The planter class

Once the shift from dyewood cutting or other temporary extractive activities to agriculture had been made, the planters had no difficulty in reconciling their occupation to the high status traditionally associated with landholding. Classical and medieval authors echoed the sentiments of Cicero's widely read *De officiis*: "Of all the sources of income, the life of the farmer is the best, pleasantest, most profitable, and most befitting a gentleman."[3] Extensive landholding supported by the control of many dependents had characterized the nobility of Por-

264

tugal, and those colonists in Brazil who established sugar estates saw themselves as the colony's nobility. In a sense, they were a social class posing as a medieval order or estate; men of new wealth seeking traditional forms of social legitimacy.

At the close of the sixteenth century when there were between fifty and sixty engenhos in the Recôncavo, the majority of the senhores de engenho, like the colony's white population as a whole, were European born. For the Portuguese immigrants, and a scattering of Spaniards, Florentines, and Flemings, the position of sugar planter offered in this period the joint advantages of a lucrative activity and the attributes of noble status associated with a seigneurial way of life, surrounded by slaves and retainers and living off the produce of one's own land. Most of the immigrants who become senhores de engenho married in Brazil. Of the fifty planters identified by Gabriel Soares de Sousa in the late 1580s, twenty-four had wed Brazilian-born women and only seven were married to women from Portugal. This pattern of young men immigrating from Portugal; by wealth, family, or good fortune acquiring a mill; and then marrying a local woman long continued in Bahia, although it should be noted that sometimes the marriage itself brought the ownership of an engenho.[4]

The social origins of the first generation of Bahia senhores de engenho were far less distinguished than later generations of planters liked to admit. Although there were men of noble family or high office like governor Mem de Sá, owner of Engenho Sergipe, or Antônio de Barros Cardoso, son of the royal treasurer of Bahia and a fidalgo of the royal household, many of the early senhores came from less distinguished origins.[5] Perhaps a third of the Recôncavo engenhos in the 1580s were owned by merchants who had moved easily from commerce to sugar planting; some continued both occupations simultaneously. A representative case is the story of the brothers Pacoal and Dinis Bravo, who came to Bahia from Oporto in the beginning of the seventeenth century.[6] These two young merchants eventually acquired some land belonging to Engenho Sergipe, and they began to grow cane and supply it to that mill as lavradores de cana. Dinis, along with some partners, then purchased land on Cajaíba Island, where he later set up his own engenho. The Bravo brothers later appeared in the Inquisition investigation of 1618 as New Christians.

New Christian origins, in fact, were common among the first Bahian senhores.[7] Of forty-one engenhos whose owners' origins could be determined in the period 1587–92, twelve were held by New Christians. The 1618 Inquisition records mentioned thirty-four engenhos, twenty of which were owned by New Christians. Inquisition records are surely not an unbiased source in this regard, as they would tend to deal with engenhos whose owners' orthodoxy was questionable, but there can be little doubt that many of the early senhores de engenho were immigrants of New Christian background who came to Brazil to make their fortunes and live their lives beyond the watchful eyes of the Holy Office. Some remained in fact crypto-Jews, and the Inquisition discovered a synagogue on a Matoim engenho in the 1590s. These people maintained ties with their families and coreligionists in Portugal, Italy, and Holland, and some, despite their suspect Christian orthodoxy, achieved positions of prominence as well as power in Bahian society. This was surely true of Diogo Lopes de Ulhoa, a merchant and sugar planter who gained political importance as the confidant of a governor in the 1620s and as a trusted agent of the Jesuits'. Denounced repeatedly to the Inquisition and related to others who were burned for judaizing in Portugal, Diogo Lopes remained a wealthy and important figure in Bahian life, so trusted by the governor that his enemies called him the "count-duke of Brazil," in an ironic comparison to Olivares, the minister and confidant of Philip IV of Spain.[8]

Although claims in the early seventeenth century that most of the Brazilian engenhos were owned by New Christians were exaggerated, there is no doubt that New Christians played an active role in forming the sugar economy and were an important social element among the early senhores de engenho. Of 150 New Christians mentioned in Inquisition records from Bahia between 1620 and 1660, 20 percent were millowners or cane farmers, and, as we have seen, a large proportion of the engenhos were in the hands of New Christians.[9] Both crypto-Jews and those who had fully abandoned the faith of their ancestors were discriminated against and despised by other elements of the population in Brazil, as in Portugal. But Brazil did offer a situation of somewhat less vigilance and a social structure more open to upward mobility that made it particularly appealing to the New Christians. The sugar industry played a central role in that appeal. The discrimination against New Christians also did not prevent unions between them and Old Christians of impeccable lineage. Beatriz Antunes, a New Christian, had practiced Jewish rites while married to an Old Christian senhor de engenho in Matoim, that hotbed of sixteenth-century Bahian judaism.[10] Henrique Moniz Barreto, a senhor de engenho who was the son of one of Salvador's founders and a member of one of the first families of Bahia's aristocracy, married a New Christian woman who was eventually prosecuted by the Inquisition.[11] The Bahian planter class's origins, despite its later aristocratic pretentions, were marbled with elements of the commercial bourgeoisie and New Christians, two groups whose status in Portuguese society was decidedly low.

By the seventeenth century, two strata of planter families could already be defined: a first group who had acquired lands shortly after the creation of Salvador and who dated essentially from the 1550s and 1560s, and a second group who had arrived in Bahia in the 1580s when the sugar boom was well under way. The period from the 1620s to the

1660s witnessed the arrival of a third layer of aspirant planters. The temporary crisis of the 1620s caused by short-term downturns in sugar prices and the fighting with the Dutch created hard times for some planters. Some engenhos were destroyed, others went broke or ceased operations and were sold. Young men arriving in various of the military contingents sent to Brazil during the war against the Dutch took up the opportunity created by the availability of sugar properties at relatively low prices. Other planter families originated in Pernambuco, fleeing to Bahia with slaves and capital during the Dutch occupation of northern Brazil. Lineages like the Brandão Coelhos, Ferrão e Argolos, and the Pires de Carvalho originated in this period, and a review of Jaboatão's genealogy reveals other Bahian families whose progenitors arrived in the mid–seventeenth century.[12]

Of eighty senhores de engenho who lived in Bahia between 1680 and 1725 and for whom detailed information can be obtained, fifty-six (70 %) were Brazilian born, and twenty-two were the sons of immigrants. Increasingly Brazilian in origin, over half the planters were still immigrants or the sons of immigrants. The ties to Europe remained strong a century and a half after the world of the engenhos had begun to take form. Families of great distinction – Argolo, Moniz Barreto, Dias d'A-vila – were represented by fourth or fifth generations, but alongside them were recently arrived immigrants who had also become sugar planters. Most of the Brazilian-born senhores came from families already associated with the sugar economy, although about a third of them had fathers who had been lavradores de cana rather than mill-owners – a sign of upward mobility within the industry. The planters whose fathers had been immigrants were also helped into the industry by their parents' actions, for more than two-thirds of the immigrant fathers had become cane farmers or millowners. Those immigrants who acquired sugar properties were drawn primarily from the mercantile and professional occupations, the latter including lawyers and royal judges. It was common for the immigrant senhores de engenho to continue their original occupation along with plantership; but that seems to have been much less the case with Brazilian-born planters.

By the beginning of the eighteenth century, the planter class was well established and intermarried to a large extent. Invariably white, or taken as such, the senhores de engenho laid claim to the status of nobility as well as to local power. Although continual intermarriage tended to reinforce the dominance and centrality of a relatively small group of families, there was always room for new blood, drawn principally from the royal magistrates, other government officials, or Salvador's mercantile community. Lavradores de cana also moved into the ranks of the senhores de engenho, usually by marriage or by amassing enough capital through successful cane farming. As a social group, the planters generally remained open to new additions, although these were drawn from a relatively limited spectrum of occupations and were invariably white.

Two cases flesh out these generalizations about the formation of the planter class. A good example of the immigrant senhor de engenho was João Lopes Fiuza, who had come to Bahia from Viana do Castelo in Portugal to join his brother, an established merchant in Salvador.[13] Arriving in the 1690s, Lopes Fiuza found his way smoothed by his brother's connections to the sugar aristocracy through marriage to the Moniz Barretos. João Lopes Fiuza went into commerce, trading slaves, sugar, and tobacco and establishing a reputation as an important Bahian businessman. In 1709, he married his sister-in-law, the daughter of senhor de engenho Jerônimo Moniz Barreto. Through this marriage, Lopes Fiuza acquired Engenho de Baixo in Paramerim, to which he later added by purchase Engenho São Pedro de Tararipe in what was to become Rio Fundo parish. Although his rise to social prominence was slow, perhaps due to his continuing identification as a merchant, by the time of his death in 1741 he held militia commissions, was a member of the Order of Christ and of the tertiary orders of the Franciscans and Carmelites, and had served as councilman in the câmara of Salvador. His family remained prominent in the Recôncavo into the nineteenth century.

A somewhat different career is seen in the life of Cristóvão de Burgos.[14] He was born in Bahia in the 1610s, the son of a Portuguese bureaucrat who had married in Bahia and become a respected member of local society. Sent to study law at Coimbra, Cristóvão returned to Brazil after entering royal service as a magistrate. He married the daughter of a prominent sugar planter in Bahia, Helena da Silva Pimentel, a widow and stepmother to seven children who bore the name of Telles Meneses, another important planter clan. Cristóvão de Burgos was thus extremely well connected in Bahian society, and when he was promoted to the position of desembargador (royal judge) of the Bahian Court of Appeals, there were those who believed he was too tied to his own and local interests to be an impartial judge. He owned extensive properties on the São Francisco River, three Recôncavo engenhos, and the five largest canefields in Passé parish. A real power in the seventeenth century, Burgos combined bureaucratic office with family ties and planter status. Unlike Lopes Fiuza, however, he left no descendants, and his name disappeared among the planter class.

By the beginning of the eighteenth century, the Bahian elite had become a more heterogeneous group, and although sugar planters still predominated, there were other sectors of the economy and other professions that thrust men forward. The merchants of Salvador achieved economic and social importance in the sixteenth century, but their status and political influence were undeniable by 1700. Although some married into the sugar-planter families or acquired engenhos and

joined the planter ranks, others rose to prominence without ever joining the sugar sector. Then, too, there were the great landholders of the
sertão, who had opened up the interior and received extensive sesmarias of thousands of acres in return for their services. Men like Garcia
d'Avila to the north of Salvador and João Peixoto Viegas along the
margins of the Paraguaçú had created vast estates. By the late seventeenth century, these had been turned into ranching empires, or in the
case of Peixoto Viegas, tobacco fazendas as well. Although over time
the tendency was for these families to merge with the Recôncavo sugar
elite, their origins were in fact distinct. Also joining their ranks were
crown magistrates and professional military officers, people whose occupations were usually accompanied by high prestige and the symbols
of nobility and considered wholly honorable.

As the elite became more diverse, so, too, did the economic activities
of the planters. By the late seventeenth century, it was not uncommon
for them to have at least short-term investments in commercial ventures,
shipowning, mortgages, ranches, and occasionally tobacco growing.
This was a pattern repeated later when the sugar economy experienced
difficulty. The German travelers Spix and Martius reported similar economic diversification among the planters in the 1810s.[15] These activities,
however, remained secondary. When called on to identify himself, a
planter usually chose the title senhor de engenho as the first label because it was always a metaphor for the seigneurial way of life, the
obedience of slaves and dependents, and potential wealth.

The planter class took form through two interrelated tendencies that
worked in opposite directions. First, a considerable degree of turnover,
of false starts, poor management, barren marriages, and accidental
deaths, prevented the establishment of lineages or the achievement of
personal success. Often it was a matter of misplaced ambition. A number of observers complained that rich lavradores de cana sometimes
invested in a mill, became poor senhores de engenho, and then lacked
the resources to operate successfully. Any list of engenhos always included a few that were fogo morto, abandoned or inoperative for one
reason or another. As F. W. O. Morton has put it, the title senhor de
engenho was a passport to prominence, not a guarantee of it.[16] The
failures, however, have generally been overlooked because they have
disappeared from the record. This has tended to create an image of the
planter class as a tightly knit, relatively small group of interconnected
families, successful generation after generation. Although a core of
planter families fit that description, they were never the only ones who
owned engenhos at any one time. The ups and downs of the sugar
economy created constant opportunities and difficulties for others who
aspired to the status of the "traditional" families.

At the end of the eighteenth century, the internal stratification
within the planter class could be seen clearly. By that time, Bahia had

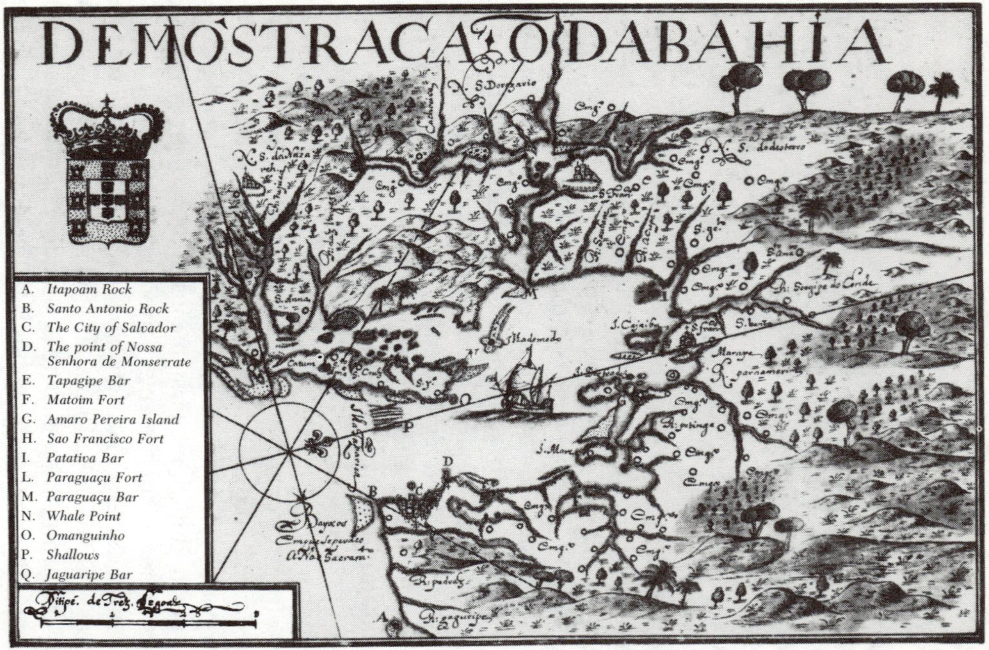
DEMOSTRACAÕ DABAHIA
A. Itapoam Rock
B. Santo Antonio Rock
C. The City of Salvador
D. The point of Nossa Senhora de Monserrate
E. Tapagipe Bar
F. Matoim Fort
G. Amaro Pereira Island
H. Sao Francisco Fort
I. Patativa Bar
L. Paraguaçu Fort
M. Paraguaçu Bar
N. Whale Point
O. Omanguinho
P. Shallows
Q. Jaguaripe Bar

Map 4. "Demonstration of Bahia." An unpublished eighteenth-century map showing the locations of some of the engenhos (emg°). (Courtesy of Dona Lygia Cunha, Biblioteca Nacional de Rio de Janeiro.)

about 220 engenhos owned by 176 individuals and 2 religious orders. By 1820, the number of mills had increased to 340 owned by 250 persons, a sign of the sugar boom of the period and of the industry's ability to attract new participants when conditions were appropriate. Among the senhores de engenho was a group that could be called the traditional sugar aristocracy, identifiable by name and by a series of shared characteristics. All of them owned at least two engenhos and all belonged to families that had been established before the crisis of 1680 and the subsequent years of stagnation after 1730. The engenhos they owned tended to be the largest, oldest, and best situated and were on the Recôncavo coast or at the mouths of the small rivers leading into the Bay of All Saints. These were the traditional sugar parishes of Cotegipe, Matoim, Passé, São Francisco do Conde, and Santo Amaro. The richness of the soil, the lower transportation costs, and the access to seafood for the slaves enabled these engenhos to ride out temporary crises, to survive when others failed. These were the largest mills. In a list of engenhos made in 1757, half the units that produced 3,000 arrobas or more belonged to the traditional families, although their members were less than a third of the owners. By 1818, when there were 316 engenhos in Bahia, 20 interconnected families owned 92 of them. Although the proportion of Bahian engenhos on the coast was less than 50 percent, more than 70 percent of the aristocratic families' properties were on the shore.[17]

The names of these "traditional families" were recognizable to contemporaries, just as they are today in Bahia. Many were related in one way or another to the descendants of Diogo Alvares, Caramurú. The Argolo, Moniz Barretto, Aragão, Bulcão, Rocha Pitta, and Vilas Boas families, to name a few, were woven together in a delicate tracing of endogamic ties, of cousin marriages in multiple generations, and of secondary ritual kinship created at baptisms, confirmations, and weddings. These families were an enduring inner core of the Bahian planter class, the model for others to emulate. By the end of the colonial period, standing in the forefront of these families were the Pires de Carvalho e Albuquerque. The originator of the line, Domingos Pires de Carvalho, had come out from northern Portugal in 1660 and achieved some prominence as a merchant and landowner. His son, José Pires de Carvalho, had married a daughter of the Cavalcanti e Albuquerque family, of long-standing distinction both in Pernambuco and Bahia. Later, the family became linked to the ranching-elite Dias d'Avila clan. By 1805, members of this family owned nine engenhos, thousands of cattle in the sertão, public offices and city mansions, and, despite continual intermarriage, they were also related to most of the other Recôncavo clans.

Although it was difficult to reach the top rank of planter families, there were always some who did. So, over time, new elements were brought in. The Calmons, for example, dated their rise to prominence from the end of the seventeenth century, when they bought properties in Cahipe and made a series of strategic marriages that linked them to the Lopes Franco, Aragão, and Araújo lines. The Costa Pintos, Vieira Tostas, and Bittencourt Berenguers dated from the mid–eighteenth century. They acquired seaside mills or, as in the case of the Bittencourt Berenguers, developed engenhos in the new parishes of Santana de Catú and São Pedro de Rio Fundo that, though further from the bay, still had virgin massapé. By 1807, the Bittencourt Berenguers owned three engenhos in Rio Fundo.[18] But alongside such success stories were always the also-rans, those who bought mills, struggled to succeed and failed, men whose genealogies cannot be traced and who appear in the historical record only as the buyers and sellers of engenhos. The story of Antônio Ribeiro de Migueis – who purchased the former Jesuit engenhos of Sergipe and Petinga, was never able to meet his financial obligations, and despite various appeals for credit extensions eventually lost his properties – is as much a story of the planter class as are those of the Calmons and Bittencourt Berenguers.[19]

Although some men among the original group of planters could lay claim to noble status in Portugal, the majority, as we have seen, came from less distinguished origins. New Christians, merchants, and poorer immigrants were attracted to Brazil because the colony seemed to offer social and economic opportunities not readily available in Portugal. The successful pursuit of wealth in the context of this tropical colony upset Portuguese hierarchies of status, race, and wealth and created a series of negative images that denied the residents of Brazil the social recognition they prized.

Sexual promiscuity and avarice became linked in the minds of those who witnessed the creation of the colony's elites. Magalhães de Gandavo wrote in 1570 that the colonists "shed their humble manners that poverty and necessity had forced them to use in Portugal; and their mestiço sons shed their red skins like snakes and used the most honorific titles in everything."[20] Jesuits such as Father Nóbrega thundered against their inattention to the precepts of the church. The planters, he said, "give consideration to nothing but sugar mills and property although it be with the perdition of all the world's souls."[21] But accompanying these negative assessments of the colonial planters was a recognition of their wealth. Father Cardim's description of the planters of Pernambuco, written in the 1580s, could to a lesser extent be applied to Bahia: the women in damask and silk, a taste for Portuguese wine and blooded horses, wedding banquets that lasted whole days, a highly developed sense of hospitality, and a much less developed sense of religious obligation.[22]

The central point to be made here is that despite a desire for noble status, the planters were essentially an aristocracy of wealth and power who performed and assumed many of the traditional roles of the Portuguese nobility but never became an hereditary estate. Grants of knighthood in the military orders or status as fidalgo de casa de El Rey were occasionally made as reward for military or other service or for payment, but these grants were not inheritable. The Bahian planter class, with its many immigrants, the continual entry of merchants, and the less than distinguished origins of many of its members, remained insecure about its position. This insecurity projected itself in many ways. In the eighteenth century, genealogical histories were produced in various parts of Brazil as a way to provide compensation for social deficiencies. Frei Antônio de Santa Maria Jaboatão's *Catálogo genea-lógico*, produced in 1768, was created to extol the virtues of the main lineages of the Bahian plantocracy, the thirty or so families that constituted the core of the elite.[23] The *Catálogo* created "nobility" for a family by reason of its early arrival in the colony, sought any link with a fidalgo household in Portugal as proof of noble status, and, when all else failed, pointed to the "honorable" origin of a founding father to create a pedigree for the local elite. Like parallel works in other captaincies, Jaboatão's book was the codification of the colonial elite. As such, it was an act of intellectual liberation and self-affirmation.

Their undistinguished European origins and sexual liaisons with the Indian population in Brazil made the planters sensitive to any deprecation of their social position and desirous of the traditional insignia and accoutrements of nobility and gentle birth. A royal investigator who visited Pernambuco in 1591 wrote that the Brazilians were wealthy but lacked honors and that the crown could use these to mobilize the colonists for military ventures.[24]

Nobility, in fact, was a matter of the way one lived and what one did as much as a legal charter. Lacking the titles, the planters demonstrated their noble status by living a seigneurial life with a landed estate, many slaves and retainers, and a responsibility to provide for the region's defense. The early grants of sesmaria in Bahia that required the engenhos to provide arms and defense as conditions of the grant can be viewed as a recognition of the military function of the early planters. It was to them a symbol of their position in Bahian society analogous to that of the nobility in Portugal. Liberality toward equals and dependents, dominion over family and servants, hospitality, and a sense of personal and familial honor allowed the planters to act like a nobility and thus to be one. A life so extravagant that "they seem like some counts" was the sixteenth-century image of the planter class. Antonil put it best in a famous statement: "To be a senhor de engenho is a title which many aspire to because it means to be served, obeyed, and respected by many. . . . To be a senhor de engenho in Brazil is considered like having a title among the nobles of Portugal."[25] The title senhor, in fact, implied the jurisdictional powers that had accompanied senhorio or lordship in Portugal. It was a title in keeping with the pretensions of the planters and was never replaced with the title *fazendeiro,* which would have referred only to property (fazenda). The sugar planters were seeking something more.

In reality, however, the Portuguese crown was stingy in granting to the planter class, or to anyone else in the colony for that matter, the status or rank of nobility. Unlike Spanish America, where the Spanish crown eventually created a titled nobility, in Brazil such titles were never given. There were a few Portuguese titled nobles like the duke of Monsanto or the count of Linhares who owned engenhos in Brazil, but they were absentee owners. No Brazilian titles were created. Some of the early planters could claim the rank of fidalgo. Egas Moniz Barretto, who came from the Azores in the Tomé de Sousa expedition of 1549, Paulo Dias Adorno, the minor Genoese noble who fled to Bahia to escape prosecution for a homicide, and Gaspar de Barros Magalhães, a Portuguese fidalgo exiled to Bahia, all fell into this category. All, however, were of the lesser nobility; none had titles. Those who did not have fidalgo status on arrival found it extremely difficult to obtain it in Brazil. Grants of fidalguia, memberships in the military orders as knights, and entails of property were continually sought by the planters as symbols and perquisites of their status. The incongruity between their perceived station and formal recognition of it intensified their desire for these symbols all the more. As late as the 1790s, when the traditional concepts of nobility were under attack in Portugal itself, observers in Brazil still ridiculed the colonials for their lust for titles, honors, and other signs of noble status.[26]

We must keep in mind that the legitimation of noble status implied disassociation from the stains of religious heterodoxy, mechanic origins, or links to the "infected races" of Moors, Jews, or mulattoes (as the proscription ran). Some of the Bahian planter families, in fact, were not free of such association, begun as they were by New Christians, merchants, and occasionally even artisans. By the early eighteenth century, many of the interrelated core families included descendants of the original settler of Bahia, Diogo Alvares, Caramurú, especially through his Indian wife, Catarina Paraguaçu. Although having such a distinguished Indian "princess" as an ancestor might bring no embarrassment in local circles, it made the planters particularly sensitive to the nuances of the color and status hierarchies that operated in the Portuguese colonial world.

By drawing the line as sharply as possible between themselves and the rest of the population, the senhores de engenho sought also to emphasize their racial and religious purity. Noble status, theoretically dependent on such purity, was one means of doing this. Families tried to ensure that no member would reverse the process. Governor Mem de Sá included in his will a provision preventing inheritance if his descendants married anyone but a white Old Christian. Jerônimo de Burgos did the same in 1664. João Mattos de Aguiar's dowry fund with the Misericórdia limited applicants to white Old Christians. Such attempts were not always successful.[27] New Christian connections were relatively common, and even marriages to blacks occurred. The scandal caused when Manoel Dias Lima, a senhor de engenho in Inhambupe, married Josefa, a former slave from Angola, in the late eighteenth century must have been profound.[28] Surely people less prominent than Dias Lima must have been scandalized by the thought of such unions. In 1803, Isidoro Gomes de Sá, a white man who lived on Ilha de Maré in the Recôncavo, came to blows with his son because of a slave woman whom the boy wanted to marry.[29]

In the hierarchy of Brazilian society, such a marriage was a derogation of status to be avoided at any costs. For the planters with aspirations to be the Brazilian nobility, it was a move in the wrong direction. What they sought were ways to separate themselves from any such taint and to affirm the position to which they believed they were entitled. But in the eyes of metropolitan Portuguese, the Brazilians, of whatever social status, were always somewhat suspect. In the seventeenth century, Brazilians were considered poor material for vocations in the Jesuit order by some who argued that birth in a debilitating climate, low social origins, the prejudice against hard work generated in a slave society, and the lax upbringing of children made the colonials unfit. Although these remarks were aimed primarily against persons of mixed origins, it was felt that even the whites imbibed their first milk from the breasts of slave women, so the defects of race were transmitted to them as well.[30] Such attitudes made the planters ever more anxious to establish their claims to nobility.

Finally, the pressures of insecurity that drove the planters to seek noble status neatly fitted with a variety of economic gains also derived from that position. The privileged exemption from taxes is one example. Members of the military orders were exempted from the tithe, and this was a great attraction for planters. It was also a reason for the crown's reluctance to grant this honor to many in the colony.

The planters in society

Since institutionalized recognition of their position was difficult to obtain, the planters sought by functions, actions, and a way of life to affirm their place in society as a colonial nobility. Medieval concepts of nobility centered on the responsibility to bear arms. The *bellatores* (warriors) were guardians of divinely sanctioned social order, and as the concept developed, the knights or *milites* became an essential and honored estate.[31] By the sixteenth century, the Portuguese military orders, Christ, Aviz, and Santiago, were open to men whose service was not only military but also bureaucratic or financial, and awards of fidalguia were made on such bases as well.[32] Still, the profession of arms was considered an ennobling activity, and the planters made pretensions in that direction. The wars against the Indians in the sixteenth century and against the Dutch in the seventeenth provided some opportunity for military service and subsequent justification for reward. But it is fair to say that the level of royal response to requests for fidalguia or knighthoods never satisfied the demand.[33]

Planters in Bahia found a suitable alternative to the traditional nobility's use of arms in the local militias. Some sort of local defense force had existed in Bahia from the 1550s, and by 1612 the Recôncavo could field twelve companies of militia.[34] The first-line troops, organized after 1626 along the lines of the Spanish *tercios* (regiments of about 2,500 men), were generally officered by professional soldiers. The militia units and the third line of local units called *ordenanças* were not; instead they were usually commanded by locally important individuals – in effect, the senhores de engenho. Recôncavo militia forces were organized geographically, and unlike the city of Salvador's, they included soldiers of different colors commanded mostly by white officers.[35] By 1800, the Recôncavo could field six militia regiments, all of whose senior officers were senhores de engenho; some senhores and lavradores de cana were in junior-officer positions. Landowners held more than 70 percent (23 of 32) of the officer positions in the Recôncavo regiments. A few of the leading planter families sent younger sons into the professional military as career officers, but as a rule the planters preferred the militia units where local prestige and wealth counted in promotion and duties were performed close to home. Otherwise, problems could result like those of João Felix Machado Soares, who owned two engenhos in Santo Amaro and found that his post as captain of an infantry regiment detracted from his responsibilities as a planter. In 1744, he petitioned for a six-month leave each year to manage his affairs.[36] Militia forces were better suited to the planters, and these units tended to reproduce Recôncavo society with planters in command and those dependent on them in the rank and file.[37]

A militia patent, signed by the king, provided the senhores de engenho with not only a stage on which to act out their claim to nobility but also a back door to legitimate noble status. Although unpaid, militia officers were allowed to wear swords and ride horses, the traditional attributes of nobility. They enjoyed the *foro militar* or distinct legal privileges and exemptions, and their sons were entitled to become cadets or officers in training, a rank reserved for the sons of the nobility.[38] Although the Brazilian military system did not reserve officerships exclusively for the nobility and some promotions from the noncommissioned officer ranks were made, the tendency was always to favor the nobility and tie it as closely as possible to the interests of the crown. By the close of the colonial era, virtually all the colonelcies and many of the captaincies in the Recôncavo regiments were held by sugar planters. Their military rank was simply a logical extension and legal affirmation of their social position; they were, in effect, born to it. When in 1786 Antônio de Bittencourt Berenguer Cezar sought a post as colonel, he pointed to twenty-six years of military experience and his ownership of "three first-class engenhos" as evidence of his suitability.[39]

Planters viewed political activity, like the profession of arms, as both a duty and a privilege. As permanent residents of Bahia and as *homens bons*, honorable men of property, the senhores de engenho were entitled to serve in the câmara, the municipal council, principal organ of local government.[40] The multiple functions of the câmaras included many areas of direct interest to the sugar sector: road building, slave control, price fixing, tax collecting, and the like. The câmaras also served as advocates for local interests, petitioning governors or the crown directly on matters of immediate concern. The câmara of Salvador was the sole municipal council in Bahia until 1698, when Jaguaripe, São Francisco, and Cachoeira were elevated to municipal status. Meanwhile, all the câmaras were affected by reforms beginning in 1696 that placed the presidency of the councils in the hands of a royally appointed magistrate and empowered the governor to appoint councillors from the lists of eligible citizens. These changes reduced the independence of the câmaras and made service in them somewhat less attractive. But they still continued to be the principal organs of local government.[41]

Although it is at present impossible to determine the social composition of the Recôncavo câmaras in any detail, existing lists allow us to establish the makeup of the Salvador town council. From its earliest days, the câmara of Salvador was dominated by local landed interests, especially the sugar sector; this pattern clearly persisted throughout the colonial period, as Table 10-1 demonstrates. Merchant representation was always present but, as Table 10-1 also shows, it tended to increase during the eighteenth century. This change reflected the alterations in the governance and selection of councillors made in the 1690s and also the desire of planters in the eighteenth century to serve on the Recôncavo câmaras rather than on the Salvador municipal council. The câmaras of São Francisco do Conde, Santo Amaro, and Cachoeira, closer to the location of their engenhos, came to be seen by the sugar sector as effective substitutes for their political activity. A man like senhor de engenho José Pires de Carvalho served first on the Salvador council and then on the Cachoeira body, and there were others like him.[42] This ruralization of political life did not mean that planter interests were lessened but, rather, that the structure of representation was broadened. On an issue of common cause such as opposition to the creation of agricultural boards of inspection in 1751, the câmaras of Salvador, Santo

Table 10-1. *Occupations of the city councillors of Salvador, 1680–1729, 1780–1821*

	1680–1729		1780–1821	
Occupation	N	%	N	%
Senhores de engenho	132	50.8	32	26.5
Lavradores de cana	33	12.7	–	–
Landed merchants	35	13.5	6	4.9
Landed professionals	8	3.1	11	9.1
[Sugar sector]		(79.1)		(40.5)
Merchants	12	4.6	24	19.8
Professionals	7	2.7	16	13.2
Cattlemen and tobacco growers	9	3.4	–	–
Unidentified	24	9.2	32	26.5

Sources: For 1680–1729: Flory, "Bahian Society," 138–147. For 1780–1821: F. W. O. Morton, "The Conservative Revolution of Independence: Economy, Society and Politics in Bahia, 1790–1840" (Ph.D. thesis, Oxford University, 1974), 65. Their data were not collected according to similar definitions of categories and are thus not exactly comparable. To some extent, Morton's large percentage of unidentified councillors seems related to his exclusion of the lavradores de cana category. Thus, the subtotal for the sugar sector in 1780–1821 can represent only a minimum.

Amaro, and São Francisco united to make joint or simultaneous representation to the crown.[43] The câmara of Salvador continued to be the most prestigious of them and was favored by the aristocratic Recôncavo families, although members of the Calmon and Pires de Albuquerque clans do appear in the lists of the Reconcavo governing bodies. Merchants and professional lawyers or military men made some gains in representation in the late colonial era in the Salvador city council, but they always remained secondary to the sugar sector.

Enjoying status and wealth, or at least the image of it, control of local institutions, and extensive kinship networks, the planters were unquestionably the most powerful segment of Bahian society. It would be wrong, however, to view them as feudal lords virtually unrestrained by any authority at all times and on all issues. After the early-frontier stage of the sixteenth century, the presence of royal magistrates and the Bahian high court of appeals placed some limits on the power of the planters. The crown's officers rarely interfered in matters of slave control, and in that sphere the planters often had a free hand; but their actions were constrained by the royal government when they conflicted with civil government or the administration of justice. The crown's ability to control the world of the engenhos was limited, nevertheless, by distance, difficulty, and the webs of kinship and influence that often incorporated the justices themselves.

In the sixteenth century, when the Recôncavo engenhos were effectively frontier institutions, senhores could and did operate with little fear of government interference. Inquisition investigations of 1591–3 and 1618 uncovered men like André Fernandes Margalho and Fernão Cabral de Atayde, who had murdered their slaves, and Pedro Garcia, owner of four engenhos, who had sodomized servants and slaves on his properties.[44] Although they had been able to commit these crimes, the fact that they were later denounced to the Inquisition indicates that such matters were not beyond the knowledge and control of civil and ecclesiastical authorities. As the population grew and the Recôncavo was settled, effective control improved. Sugar planters were undoubtedly powerful and could sometimes protect wanted men, but they do not seem to have exercised the kind of unbridled independent authority more characteristic of the cattle barons of the far interior. Still, the senhores viewed the protection of relatives and retainers to some extent as a matter of duty. Government displeasure with such activities was sharply expressed. The Engenho da Matta was condemned as a criminal hideout by the viceroy in 1724, and three years later the government moved against an engenho owner in Maragogipe who gave refuge to criminals.[45] As the judicial structure developed in the Recôncavo towns, the central authorities in Salvador were better able to organize and execute police functions. In 1798, Father Gonçalo Manoel de São Boaventura fled to the engenho of his brother in Iguape after committing a crime. The governor in Salvador instructed the district magistrate in Cachoeira to apprehend him.[46] The world of the engenhos was not entirely beyond the reach of the law, nor was the word of only the senhores writ in the canefields.[47]

The extent to which the civil authorities were willing to exercise control and contest the power of engenho owners was made clear in an extraordinary event, revealing of the social dynamics of Recôncavo society. On Sunday, 14 November 1717, a slave of Engenho Sergipe was in the town of Santo Amaro when he was accosted by João Dornellas, a mulatto slave catcher who was drunk at the time.[48] Words passed, among them the insult that the Jesuit master of the Sergipe slave was deficient in his manhood. The slave responded and was stabbed and beaten. Dornellas then arrested him as a fugitive and placed him in a boat to take him to Salvador. On learning of the incident, Father Luís Vellozo, administrator of Engenho Sergipe, sent some armed slaves in canoes to intercept the slave catcher. They did so, fighting took place, and Dornellas was mortally wounded, dying on the dock of Engenho Sergipe. The incident was reported to Salvador, and the governor sent a troop of infantry to arrest the guilty slaves. The soldiers broke into the engenho and stole sugar, and Father Vellozo was placed under house arrest. But the guilty slaves fled, as did all the free employees. The whole Recôncavo was mobilized to search for them. Engenho Sergipe was occupied and under a state of siege for almost three weeks.[49]

Father Vellozo could not understand why so much force had been used in an incident involving a drunken mulatto, who himself had been a slave (an attitude revealing of Vellozo's own frame of reference). This was not, Vellozo said, a matter of conspiracy or *lèse majesté*. The marquis of Angeja, governor of Bahia, put the action into context when he reported to the crown that Vellozo had acted in a high-handed manner and that he was powerful enough to control the Recôncavo and suppress the truth. The senhores de engenho had to be taught an object lesson. Angeja was not too far from the mark. Vellozo had produced a testimonial attesting to his good qualities signed by 230 individuals, including the most prestigious sugar planters in the Recôncavo.[50] The authority of the crown was at stake.

Such direct confrontations with the government were rare in comparison to interpersonal disputes over property, which tended to override all other considerations among the planters, to the dismay of royal judges and ecclesiastical observers. Wills were commonly contested by relatives, disputes even between children and parents were not unknown, and violence against neighbors over land and water was common. The senhores de engenho were, in the words of Antonil, like Cain and Abel, "linked by blood but little united in charity, needing only a missing piece of wood or a stray ox in a canefield to provoke hidden hatred, and to cause legal actions or mortal retribution."[51] Incidents of violence between senhores de engenho can be found from the beginning of the sugar economy to the end of the colonial era and beyond. The Inquisition investigations of 1591 noted the burning of canefields in Passé during a dispute, and similar actions were a fact of life in the Recôncavo.[52]

To some extent, these disputes were endemic and systemic, given the patchwork nature of landholding in the Recôncavo, the relatively few good roads, the competition for water power, and the need to pasture oxen in and around the mills. Unmarked boundaries, the wandering of cattle, the building of a new water course to power a mill usually caused a conflict with some other property owner and led to a civil suit or violence. Clemente Luís Moreira, senhor of Engenho Restinga in Passé, could not keep his oxen out of his neighbors' crops because the lands were "so mixed together." The cattle were killed, and Moreira turned to the courts for help, asking that he be allowed to buy his neighbors out at a just price set by the archbishop.[53] Others found that they had to defend their property with sword or pistol in hand. Tomé Pereira de Araújo of Engenho da Cruz was attacked three times by the overseers and slaves of his neighbor, Dona Maria Ana Rita de Meneses, when he tried to construct a levada for the waterwheel of his engenho. As he put it, armed force was needed to counter the "African aggression" of his neighbor's slaves.[54] Ecclesiastical ownership was no protection in these disputes. The Jesuits at Engenho Pitanga tried to stop their neighbors from cutting firewood on their property. An incident occurred in which one of the Fathers was badly beaten by two men in the employ of the brothers Antônio da Rocha and Manoel Barbosa, both senhores de engenho who lived nearby.[55] Fifty years later in 1740 at Engenho Sergipe, Father Luís da Rocha was involved in a similar incident over a contested property line. His opponents were members of the Caramurú clan, one of the "principal houses of Brazil," and although the matter went to the courts, battles in the fields had also taken place.[56]

Examples of these conflicts could be easily multiplied, but three recurrent aspects of them are particularly revealing of Bahian society. First, although legal actions were common and the planters proved to be a litigious group as a whole, they often found the courts less desirable than direct action. Civil suits were expensive, and they "bled rivers of money" from the hands of the planters into the pockets of the lawyers, solicitors, and scribes (to say nothing of the judges), so that even if a suit was successful, it was often won at excessive cost to purse and soul.[57] Second, justice in the captaincy moved slowly in the hands of self-interested judges who were themselves senhores de engenho or lavradores de cana or often were connected to powerful planter families whose interests they protected.[58] Others were simply venal. It was reported in 1799 that the planter João Pedro sent some small crates of sugar every year to all the judges as "in all times has been done and is done by many others in this city [of Salvador]."[59] Although planters who had greased the proper palms or made the appropriate links found the responsiveness of the judges a most positive aspect of justice, those who lacked these ties found no justice at all and little chance of getting any.

A few cases will suffice to establish the nature of the problem and the elements involved. Antônio Luís Pereira, senhor of Engenho Santo Antônio da Boa Vista in Santo Amaro, tried to get the courts to settle his boundaries.[60] His powerful neighbors suborned the judge sent to do the survey, and the judges of the appeal court (relação) were also partial in the case. Although the Overseas Council in Lisbon felt that judicial misconduct should be severely punished, it also noted that these arguments were common in Brazil and that Pereira had not proven any misdeed. Proof in such matters was always difficult to establish, and thus what usually remains in the historical record are the charges. In 1732, Coronel Bernabé Cardoso Ribeiro, senhor of Engenho Citio da Grama in São Francisco, complained that his mill had been placed at auction to satisfy debts but without proper notice given to him. The court-appointed executor awarded the property to his own nephew, Miguel Moniz Barreto. When Cardoso Ribeiro resisted the sale and refused to vacate, the engenho was stormed, fields burned, and slaves terrorized by Moniz Barreto and his slaves. No witnesses would testify against Moniz Barreto because he was "powerful and well related [aparentado]."[61]

Finally, the linkage between planter families and judges could lead to a tangle of politics and factionalism that simply paralyzed the operation of the judicial structure. In the late 1670s, Captain Tomé Pereira Falcão was involved in a boundary dispute with the heirs of Belchior Brandão Coelho, who owned the neighboring engenho in Iguape parish.[62] Pereira Falcão had asked the courts to appoint a surveyor, but he then complained that the appointed judge was linked to Antônio de Aragão and Pedro Garcia Pimentel, his opponents in the case. He tried to get the judge removed from the case, but was prevented by the chancellor of the high court, another friend of the Aragão faction. Meanwhile, when one of the Aragão group, Manoel Garcia de Mello, was murdered in his engenho, Pereira Falcão was accused of the crime. A judge was appointed to investigate, but he too, was suspect because of his family connections. The Overseas Council bemoaned the fact that there were not enough judges in Bahia to handle the cases since all of them were partial to one side or the other in this dispute. Pereira Falcão, whose petitions leveled charges of family ties and personal relations between high court judges and his opponents, was no innocent. He was himself a former member of the câmara of Salvador, a relative by marriage to the great Dias d'Avila family, probably Bahia's most powerful, and a man noted for his own ties to judges on the high court.[63] Here was a case of two important planter families mobilizing influence and violence to settle a dispute and of the institutions of control being so subordinated to family ties or alliance that they were unable to act.

Litigation, then, provided a mechanism to resolve disputes but was not the only or the always preferred means.[64] Force or the threat of force lay always just beneath the surface, especially in the relations between senhores de engenho and their dependents or inferiors but also in the relations between planters. Despite the sense of nobility and honor involved in the patriarchal ethic, the ritualized duel between equals was virtually unknown. Slaves or dependents invariably carried out force in a subinfeudation of violence. Responsibility for criminal acts was hence more difficult to assign, and it was just so much easier to have one's slaves take the physical and legal risks. In the scale of possible actions to protect or acquire property, influence and intimidation were preferred to violence; but when that was necessary, slaves and dependents carried it out.

Masters of men and cane, the senhores de engenho tried to fulfill a seigneurial ideal in which authority and dominance was widely exercised over dependents without the external interference of the state. Given a relatively unrestrained hand in regard to their families and dependents, royal government and justice could and did intervene in planter life when royal authority was at stake. The planters, however, found that friendship, kinship, and favor could often accomplish the desired end so that royal judges and other officials became responsive to individual planter interests and tended to mediate between the law and the local situation. The result was an accommodation in which the crown gave the planters a relatively free hand in their control of the organization of production and in their sway over slaves but played a more active role in disputes that occurred between different economic sectors or that impinged on royal authority.[65]

The planter way of life

Given the availability of documentary materials and the present state of research, it is impossible to trace the development of the planter way of life in the colonial Northeast. The best approximation of it was made by Gilberto Freyre in his classic *The Masters and the Slaves* (1933), but he was able to do this only by transposing the observations of nineteenth-century travelers backward to earlier times and by adding perceptions of engenho life based on his own childhood experiences.[66] Although his book was filled with insights, its method precluded tracing development over time and was thus flawed as a historical analysis. Still, *The Masters and the Slaves* captured an image that revealed a wide range of attitudes and activities within the rural domestic sphere of the planters, and although that image may be questioned for earlier periods or other social classes, it is the way Brazilians have come to think of their rural past. There is no need here to restate its central themes of interracial contact and cultural fusion within the *casa grande* (great house), but a few aspects of planter life not treated in detail in Freyre's work must be understood to understand the senhores de engenho as a social category and in their relations with one another.

First, the senhores de engenho were a resident planter class. Therefore, with few exceptions, the owners of Bahian engenhos lived in Brazil rather than in Europe. Colonial residence, however, did not mean that Bahian planters stayed in constant personal control of their mills. Until the later seventeenth century, planters seem to have spent a good deal of time in Salvador. Some of the wealthier ones maintained residences in the city, and others came in to transact business, see friends, and take part in civic affairs on a regular basis. This participation of the rural oligarchy in the life of Salvador was made possible by the proximity of many engenhos to the margins of the bay. A trip by sailboat from Salvador to Santo Amaro took only two hours. The participation of planters on the câmara or in the Misericórdia indicates the close ties between city and Recôncavo.

With the expansion of the sugar zone in the eighteenth century, such contacts became more difficult, time consuming, and bothersome. (Even today, a trip from Salvador to Rio Fundo is made over difficult roads.) As such parishes as Rio Fundo and Santana de Catú turned to sugar, the planters there became less tied to the city. Senhores de engenho sought excuses from military or civic responsibilities by arguing that their duties in the countryside called for their personal attention. But the ruralization of the planters did not in all cases mean that each engenho had a resident senhor. Multiple holdings were relatively common among the sugar elite, so some mills were administered by overseers or agents. Moreover, the elite families tended to have the larger and older mills in the seaside parishes and were thus less affected by ruralization. Curiously, then, the very families who owned the large engenhos and great slave forces and most approximated the ideal of the patriarchal domain were those least likely to be full-time residents on their estates watchfully guiding the everyday affairs of dependents, family, and slaves.

Still, given their residence in the captaincy, the Bahian senhores remained in touch with their estates and with the surrounding society. As F. W. O. Morton points out, the distribution of the engenhos meant that a senhor and his family lived in relatively close proximity to his neighbors. This was, of course, the cause of many disputes, but it also meant that there was considerable peer pressure on comportment. Senhores de engenho did not live in isolation, and there were certain limits on their dealings with others and in their personal lives beyond which they could not stray. The *vox publica*, or public opinion, in fact played an important role in Brazilian society, determining relative honor and shame, and public affirmation of status through civic or religious ritual helped create a social map. Isolation, then, was not only difficult to achieve but also undesirable. Municipal service, militia drills, and religious ceremony all gave the planters an opportunity to publicly affirm their status, to gain honor; but doing so also made them susceptible to public censure.[67]

How, then, was a senhor de engenho expected to act? Antonil's famous volume describes the sugar industry in a series of chapters that are essentially models of ideal behavior; how the planter should behave toward his family, his slaves, his dependents. A shorter description of expected behavior was provided by Father Luís Vellozo when, in defense of himself before the law, he produced a statement signed by over two hundred residents of the townships of Santo Amaro and São Francisco do Conde attesting to his character. If allowance is made for Vellozo's clerical vocation as Jesuit administrator of Engenho Sergipe, the following testimonial tells us what was considered proper for a senhor de engenho:

> . . . he keeps the slaves of the said engenho well controlled and instructed, so that they do not bother anyone, he sees to the confessions and the last rites of neighbors . . . he makes a good division with lavradores who give their cane to the said engenho and he helps them cut and transport the cane and gives accounting of the sugar with great care and good processing; he pays and treats the employees of the mill with punctuality as with all those others who supply the engenho.[68]

These were matters of *"boa vizinhança"* (good neighborliness), in the words of Antonil, who in a similar fashion exhorted the senhores to be affable and friendly but who also made it plain that the senhor de engenho was the central strand in the web of rural social and economic relations. We shall examine these relations in detail in the chapters that follow. But it is to the planters themselves that we must now turn in conclusion.

If the few remaining bodies of planter correspondence give us an accurate picture, the problems of this year's harvest and preparations for next year's filled planter life on the engenho. In 1625, Antônio de Sá Doria wrote that he could not leave his engenho on Itaparica Island to visit his father because his brother needed help and since on an engenho "no one person can see to everything."[69] The correspondence of the Pinto da Franças from Engenho Aramaré (1821–4) and of Felisberto Caldeira Brant Pontes from Engenho da Ponta (1819–21) point to the constant occupations of rural life on an engenho. Their letters are filled with the slaves, neighbors, agents, overseers, prices, oxen, weather, sugar, and family that comprised a daily round of the senhores de engenho, occasionally punctuated by weddings, baptisms, funerals, and the feasts of the Catholic calendar.[70]

Catholicism, in fact, provided the spiritual, moral, and social base of rural life.[71] The universal concepts of the Roman church as expressed in the teachings of the Jesuits and the code of behavior set down by the archdiocese of Bahia were recognized, but these were fused with a varied set of folk practices and beliefs. The cult of the saints was particularly important – Saint Gonçalo for finding a husband, Saint Barbara for protection against storms, Saint Anthony for lost items – each had his or her particular powers. People feared the evil eye and magic, especially when practiced by slaves. Local custom was often allowed even when the constitutions of the archdiocese prohibited it. When for a Rio Fundo baptism in 1788 two godfathers but no godmother appeared, the priest noted that this was "against the Council of Trent," but he administered the sacrament anyway.

The engenhos were erected under the invocation of the saints, and many engenhos had chapels attached to them. In 1830, for example, there were ten engenhos with chapels in the parish of Nossa Senhora do Monte and four more in neighboring São Gonçalo.[72] But the presence of churches was not necessarily a measure of the impact of religion. None of the above-mentioned chapels had a resident curate. Priests who lived in the sugar areas were often the younger sons of planters or were themselves lavradores and senhores de engenho as concerned with harvesting cane as saving souls. Those who were not depended on direct support from the planters because the secular church in Bahia was usually without endowment. Precepts of the church that conflicted with the efficient operation of a sugar estate were often honored in the breach. Mills operated on Sundays, slaves were denied the sacraments and sometimes prohibited access to the Mass, and in this local clerics sometimes complained and often complied.[73] There was enough concubinage, sexual deviance, and violation of church doctrine to keep ecclesiastical investigators busy and cause the French consul Guinebaud to write that "the aristocrats of this province are timid, without talent, and contemptible in their profound immorality." But in fact the planters were probably better able than most in this society to fulfill the obligations of the church.[74]

Attentive to business, jealous of honor and rank, serious in their duties to society and religion, especially when these coincided with their own interests, the planters as a group were not much given to intellectual pursuits. Good conversationalists – perhaps a necessary grace given the obligations of hospitality – the Bahian elite were known in the nineteenth century as great orators. But in the colonial era they were not often friends of the pen.[75] There were reasons for this. The lack of a printing press or a university in the colony provided a disincentive to the exchange of ideas. The policy had its intended effects by forcing anyone who wished to publish to do so under the vigilance of crown and church in the metropolis and by requiring those seeking university degrees to attend the University of Coimbra in Portugal. This policy constantly reinforced the intellectual and social ties between the colonial elite and the metropolis.[76] Beyond this was the reality of a planter's life, spent for the most part in the countryside concerned with the day-to-day aspects of sugar growing. To raise children on an engenho was to "raise them rustics [tabareos] so that they know how to talk of dog, horse, and ox and nothing else," said Antonil. The alternative, sending children to Salvador, exposed them to vice and licentiousness, and so Antonil counseled that they be placed in the house of a serious and responsible relative who would keep them attentive to study and closely controlled.[77]

Education for the children of the senhores de engenho was for the most part limited to the fundamentals of reading, writing, and arithmetic. Early lessons were given at home, where the resident cleric or a relative first taught letters. Education for girls often ended with this. Boys continued on at the Jesuit College of Salvador with theology, Latin, and the other courses of the Baroque curriculum.[78] Those who wished to pursue higher studies, usually in preparation for careers in the church or in the royal magistracy, had to do so at the University of Coimbra. There were not many of the planter class who followed this course. Whereas Bahia sent 230 men to Coimbra between 1772 and 1822, more than any other Brazilian captaincy, only 20 or so came from planter families or became senhores de engenho.[79] Although a Rocha Pitta or a Borges de Barros could be found among the published authors of Bahia, in the main the planter class did not concern themselves with such activity. The ephemeral eighteenth-century academies of Salvador were composed almost exclusively of clerics, lawyers, and government officials.

If wills and inventories are any measure, the planters spent little time with books. The occasional volume of prayer or devotional reading appears. The New Christian senhores de engenho in the sixteenth century seem to have had access to some Jewish devotional literature too, but in general libraries were uncommon. There were exceptions. João Lopes Fiuza, senhor of Engenho de Baixo in São Francisco do Conde, left a collection of over fifty volumes in Latin, Spanish, and Portuguese when he died in 1741.[80] Portuguese by birth and a merchant as well as a planter, Lopes Fiuza was not a product of Bahian education. He had a taste for such classical authors as Virgil and Cicero, and he owned the usual moral and pious works, but his main interests seem to have been history and literature. His library included Lope de Vega, Cervantes, Sá de Miranda, and Francisco Manuel de Mello. Lopes Fiuza was an exception among his peers.

Lack of interest did not mean lack of capacity. In the eighteenth century, the Bahian educational system changed considerably, especially after educational reform in 1759. Public education was instituted, and by 1800 primary classes were available in many of the smaller towns of the captaincy. Chairs in Latin, Greek, philosophy, and rhetoric were established in Salvador, and regius professorships supported by a sales tax on meat and cachaça provided advanced studies.[81] When the ferment of the late eighteenth century moved men to take up the pen to advocate political or economic reform, members of the Bahian planter class were well represented in the persons of Manoel Ferreira da Câmara, Felisberto Caldeira Brant Pontes, and Manoel Jacinto de Sampaio e Mello.[82]

Family and property

For most of the colonial era, then, the senhores de engenho concerned themselves not with philosophical abstractions, literature, or civil or divine law but with the practical matters of family rank, property, and power. The cornerstone of the seigneurial way of life was the family, but "family" understood in the broader sense of "house" of "lineage." The precedents for this attitude could be found in the Church Fathers, particularly Saint Augustine, and in that most popular tract of classical philosophy, Cicero's *De officiis*. As Cicero put it, "In the family the broad expanse of human society is compressed into a compact, tightly-knit unit."[83] Moralists continually used the metaphor of the family in efforts to improve the relationships between fathers and children, husbands and wives, masters and slaves, king and people, Christ and his church. It was a metaphor that resonated in this society because the patriarchal ideal was widely diffused and deeply engrained. Like paternalism, family signaled authority and hierarchy, in which the father required the unquestioned respect and obedience of his children, wife, servants, slaves, and dependents, in return for which he was expected to provide sustenance, direction, and protection. Symbolically, both children and slaves were supposed to ask for a blessing (*benção*) on seeing the senhor, and he was expected to give it.

The clearest exposition of the responsibilities of the father of the family in Bahia was made in the work of Nuno Marques Pereira, a Bahian who published in 1728 *The Narrative Compendium of the American Pilgrim*.[84] The book described a journey through the interior of Bahia, during which the author was moved to make moral and philosophical observations on the nature of society. The paterfamilias must be, said Marques Pereira, "like a clean mirror for the family to see itself reflected without stain." The responsibilities of the house were mutual, for whereas the family must honor its parents, the father must provide for the discipline, material welfare, and spiritual life of the family. Like precious jewels, the family must be guarded because the sin of any member tarnished the honor of the house. But Marques Pereira complained that many failed to live up to the ideal. Children or slaves who committed crimes remained in the house because they were too loved or too valuable, clerics failed to perform their function within the family, and moral instruction was often lax. Bahians sinned especially by worshiping their children and failing to punish them for wrongdoing. Discipline was the duty of the head of the household, and he owed this obligation to his dependents and slaves.

This was the hortatory tone of the moralist writers and clerics who admonished the planters on the proper behavior of a father. But we catch a better glimpse of the texture of life inside the big house in a paragraph of Antonil's book intended to deal not with domestic relations but with the danger of leaving account books unattended. Antonil warned planters not to leave papers on a table or in their wives' chests,

... so that later it will not be necessary to order masses to Saint Anthony to find some important paper that has disappeared when it is needed. Because it will happen that a maid or servant will take two or three pages from the wife's chest to wrap something she likes, or the youngest child will take some from the table to draw carts or make paper boats for flies or crickets to sail, or finally the wind will make them fly, without feathers, away from the house.[85]

Wives and their servants, children at play, the familiarity of a popular saint – family life for the planters was more than discipline, obedience, and honor.

Whatever the nature of domestic relations inside the planter family, it was the formation and perpetuation of that family that remained a central concern of the sugar planters' throughout the colonial era. Success in this process ensured continuity; failure spelled obscurity. Marriage was the major act in the process. The standing regulations of the church as expressed in the constitutions of the archdiocese of Bahia (1707) did not differ in essentials from general Catholic practice. Men were to be at least fourteen years old; women, at least twelve. The act was to be permanent and dedicated to reciprocal loyalty and fidelity and to reproduction. Various impediments of blood and other relationships prohibited certain unions.[86] As we have seen, however, the selection of partners and the patterns of choice were made according to a wide range of social and economic decisions. Brothers in one family marrying sisters in another was relatively common as a strategy to limit the dispersal of property. Cousin marriages were a rule rather than an exception, and the church often secured dispensations for these unions.[87] Unwanted marriages were prevented by placing daughters in convents, but a counterpoint to this was elopement and later reconciliation.

There is no adequate demographic study of the planter families in Bahia, so it is difficult to assess size and composition. Nineteenth-century observers commented on wide age differences between husbands and wives, but in eight planter couples in Santo Amaro in 1788 the average difference was only twelve years.[88] The elite families included in Jaboatão's geneaology had an average of six children that survived infancy, but we have no idea of the pattern among the lesser planters and lavradores.

Women were clearly the key in family strategies. The selection of the right wife could initiate success; the proper arrangements for daughters could ensure continuity. The women of the senhores de engenho shared the status and prestige of their husbands but were also constrained by their roles in the paternalistic society of colonial Brazil. The wives of the planters saw themselves as "moons among the stars" in their relations with the other women who inhabited the world of engenhos.[89] They often had the material goods that others could not afford, and they exercised control of the domestic life within the big house. The honor of the house was tied to the honor of the women; daughters were to remain chaste and the wife free of any compromising situation or rumor. Travelers to Bahia commented on the seclusion of women and the jealousy of Portuguese men. The law permitted a husband to kill a wife who cuckolded him, and those who did not wish to take such extreme action could find other means of control. Luiza Francisca do Nascimento was forced into the Lapa convent by her husband because of her behavior, and when in 1800 she appealed for release, the governor showed no sympathy.[90]

The maintenance of family honor was also tied to the perpetuation of the lineage and property. The daughters of the planters were married to partners chosen by the head of the family, or they were placed in convents. In the sixteenth century, this meant sending daughters back to Portugal. But after 1677, when a convent of Poor Clares was established in Bahia, there were local institutions to take on this function. Convents allowed the planter class to isolate daughters and avoid unwanted alliances. Also, in the payment of the dowry required of the entrant, the family could satisfy the daughter's rights to a share in the inheritable property and thus maintain landed property intact. Parental pressure and coercion reinforced religious motives to bring young women of the Bahian elite into the conventual life and thereby separate them from the active world and strategies of the engenhos.[91]

For those who married, time eventually became an ally, albeit often an unwanted one. Women outlived their older husbands and despite attitudes to the contrary, women often became owners of engenhos and fazendas de canas. This was especially common among the traditional elite families, unwilling to contract alliances with any but the most suitable partners or to see property alienated from the children of the first marriage to a second husband and the possible progeny of the new union. By the late eighteenth and early nineteenth centuries, some of the wealthiest slaveowners of the Recôncavo were women, especially in the older areas of Santo Amaro and São Francisco do Conde, where by 1817 10 percent of the cane farms and over 15 percent of the engenhos were held by women.[92]

Female ownership of sugar properties conflicted with prevailing attitudes and created a situation that always seemed inherently unstable and tenuous. Luís Pereira, who fought in the 1790s to keep his engenho, complained that in his absence powerful men had taken advantage of his wife's administration of the property because, "being a woman and by nature timid and unable to deal with such business and surrounded with dear children, she lacked protection and the means to combat the incursions of those evil-doers."[93] This was a clear expression of a commonly held attitude that a woman could manipulate for her own purposes. In 1748, Dona Theresa Borges de Abreu, a widow who lived on her engenho with a daughter, petitioned to have her son released from military service to manage the engenho because as a woman she was not able to do so.[94] Although the patriarchal ideal eliminated women from an active role in estate management and family strategy, the reality appears to have been more complex.

If women were the key to family formation, property was the basis of its survival. Property and family were intimately entwined in the planters' minds. Their concern for honor, lineage, and familial continuity depended on the acquisition and maintenance of fortune, especially landed property. They viewed these assets not as an end in themselves but as a means of securing the continuity of the family. João Pedro Fiuza Barreto, bearer of a distinguished name and owner of two engenhos, described himself in 1798 as "obligated to the guarding of his properties or to their conservation and increase in order to leave them to his children."[95] This was a widely shared sentiment.

In the agrarian society of Brazil, the medieval concepts of land and property were maintained. Like marriage, the acquisition of landed property was encased in a complex covering of legal and symbolic acts. Notarial registration was required for all transfers, and even the act of alienating property (as in the manumission of a slave or bequest to a religious institution) was duly registered to prevent future action by heirs. Roman and medieval precedents were followed in the ceremonies of property acquisition. At the public auction of land, the public crier was required to call three times for other bids and then place a green branch in the hand of the last bidder and say "May it profit you" (bem proveito) to him. On taking possession of an engenho or other property, the new owners had to walk the boundaries symbolically in the presence of a notary and open and close the doors in the buildings, all in the presence of three witnesses. These acts symbolized possession and underscored the social and public nature of property.[96]

The planters' central concern in regard to property was its maintenance in the face of partible inheritance.[97] Portuguese law did not provide for primogeniture except in extraordinary cases. Instead, all recognized children were entitled to share equally in the division of property. In the marriage by dote and arras, the husband and wife brought property into the union that was maintained separately.[98] At the death of one spouse, the survivor retained his or her property when the other portion was divided. Marriage by this arrangement was relatively rare in Brazil. Far more common was a marriage that created community property. In this case, the surviving spouse retained one-half the property. The other half was then divided according to a fixed formula in which two-thirds went in equal portions to the "forced heirs," usually the children, but in their absence then progressively to lineal ascendants, collateral relatives, the surviving spouse, or finally the state. The remaining third (terça) could be assigned by testament to anyone. It was from this portion that charitable bequests, the manumission of slaves, and the favoring of a child or godchild were made. This system did not allow for a great deal of testamentary flexibility, and the necessity to divide the estate equally among the heirs always placed the integrity of the landed property in danger.

To avoid the division of a family's landed property and especially the piecemeal division of the slaves, cattle, equipment, and land that constituted an engenho, the planters sought to entail portions of their property. Various forms of entail (*vinculos*) had existed in Portuguese law from the thirteenth century, but the first consistent legislation on them dated from the Manueline Law Code of 1514.[99] The two forms most common in Brazil were the *morgado* (entail) for secular purposes and the *capella* (lien) for ecclesiastical ends. Such entails were in Portugal usually associated with the nobility, and as in other things, the crown was in general reluctant to extend the emblems and privileges of nobility to Brazil. Establishment of a morgado required royal permission, and although requests were frequent, there is little evidence that such grants were made in large numbers.[100] Morgados tended to be left to the eldest son, and opposition to them came from younger siblings. A law of 1770 severely restricted their use, but in Brazil the period 1820–5 saw a notable increase in petitions for them. Having been under attack for some time in Portugal and Brazil on both moral and economic grounds, they were abolished in Brazil in 1835.[101]

At present, we do not know how many of the engenhos were entailed. By the eighteenth century, clans such as the Garcia d'Avila, Pires de Carvalho, Calmon, and Rocha Pitta had established morgados on their estates, but the number of these entails appears to have been relatively small. Henry Koster, who lived in Pernambuco, claimed that morgados were more frequent and larger in Bahia. But he had little firsthand knowledge of Bahia, and one suspects that he was misled into believing this because of their relative scarcity in Pernambuco.[102] In general, morgados appear to have been infrequent in Bahia and were primarily held by the wealthiest of the traditional aristocratic families. But this was not as bad as it might have been for the planters. The royal policies granting senhores de engenho freedom from foreclosure for debt and from attachments of the parts of an engenho for money owed served effectively like an entail by protecting the unity of the landed properties. This did not ensure the engenhos against division through inheritance, but it did give some safeguard against the breakup of properties during the owner's life.

Another, and perhaps more common, form of entail (although this too is a matter of conjecture) was the capella placed on a property for ecclesiastical purposes. Usually designated for the saying of masses or the erection of a chapel, the income from a defined piece of land was assigned to an administrator, often the principal heir.[103] Since the chapels erected were often on the engenho itself, such liens created no additional financial burden and did provide protection of the attached property, as it could not be divided. An example of the form and purpose of these entails can be seen in those created in 1722 by Desembargador Dionísio de Azevedo Arevalos. He and his wife first created an entail (*patrimonio*) on a canefield in Passé to establish a trust with an income of 25$ a year for João Barbosa de Góis, a cleric. Then, Azevedo Arevalos established in his mother-in-law's name a capella valued at 100$ on her Engenho Jacarancanga to generate 6$250 a year to build and maintain a chapel on that property.[104] Such entails made the sale or mortgaging of properties complicated and, when small amounts were involved, annoying as well. In 1769, abolition of capellas under 200$ was permitted, and by 1796 their elimination was required by law. F. W. O. Morton has pointed out that in practice capella restrictions were often ignored when the heirs to an estate so desired. But through much of the colonial period, the capella and the morgado provided ephemeral solutions to the problem of maintaining sugar properties intact.

Entail and restrictions on the dissolution of landed property, though a desired goal of families hoping to maintain their position and wealth, remained the exception. Most real estate was considered freely disposable property (*bens livres*) and thus subject to the laws of partible inheritance. This system often resulted in joint ownership of an engenho or a cane farm by siblings, but such arrangements led to conflicts. To avoid these disputes, one heir could buy out the interests of the others; or the property could simply be sold and the proceeds divided among the heirs. This system made the entrance of new people into the industry relatively easy and encouraged the circulation of properties, but it also made capital accumulation difficult. It was rare for the child to begin where the father left off.

Family, then, was the text in which property was presented. And conflicts that arose between relatives over property, though common enough, were disruptive to rural society and a matter that caused the most intense feelings. In such disputes, the idiom of society, family, was placed in direct confrontation with the material basis of life. One case, revealing of attitudes and practices, can be used here in conclusion to illustrate this point and the nature of interactions in the sugar zone.

In 1800, Manoel do O Freire and his sister Dona Ana Joaquina Freire brought suit against their own mother, who upon the death of their father had been appointed guardian and administrator of his Engenho Boca do Rio in Paripe parish.[105] They argued that owing to their father's senility, their mother had taken over the administration of the engenho and adjacent cane farms before his death and had dissipated their value because of her intimate relationship with Luís Pereira Lopes, a neighboring lavrador de canas. They claimed that the illicit relationship had allowed Pereira Lopes to rise from poverty to wealth and that to the detriment of the engenho his cane had been the first milled, engenho slaves had been lent to him, and he had been favored in other ways. Francisco Sabino Alvares Costa Pinto, the judge assigned to this case, took up the matter with reluctance, realizing that in such "private and domestic matters proof was almost impossible." Moreover, "public decency and the modesty of a family that has always enjoyed consideration might weigh against making public such matters and the spite with which the plantiffs are moved to make these charges against their own mother."

More than twenty witnesses testified. Their statements tended to refute the charges, but in doing so also revealed commonly held attitudes and practices. Witnesses stated that the deceased father had been of sound mind until his death and that the mother had administered the property not only at the end "but throughout the marriage." Although some agreed that the estate was in decadence because "management by a woman, even an active and efficient one is, as a rule, not the best practice" – thus repeating the expected prejudice against women – others felt that the problem was poor land, too few slaves, and other such problems. As to the charges that Pereira Lopes had used engenho slaves on his own fields, three witnesses testified that the reciprocal use of slaves between engenhos and lavradores was a common practice. The children claimed their mother had sold pieces of the estate and had allowed her lover to take valuable items, but the judge found no evidence that this was true and pointed out that the deceased father had sold some of the property in 1796–7 to satisfy debts.

The judge was scandalized by the case. He believed that the only fruit of his investigation was to learn "to what point someone could be carried by passion and hate." He was not shocked, however, by an intrafamilial suit over property; those were common enough. It was the nature of the charges and the fact that in this case the dispute was intergenerational between parent and children that made this particular suit so potentially disruptive of the social order. The charges had thrown into bleak contrast family authority and property rights, two concepts the planters strove to harmonize. Finally, the fact that a neighboring subordinate, a lavrador de cana, was involved in the suit forces us to recognize that the planters lived in continual contact with other social groups within the context of the engenhos. The nature and composition of those groups and their relations to the planters created the texture of social relations, and it is to these other social categories that we now turn.

CHAPTER 11

THE CANE FARMERS

O life of the farmer
If only well they knew
their disadvantages are but few
and with their sainted efforts
themselves and this world support.
Sá de Miranda

Here, no one is interested in dealing with me about anything except having his cane milled first.
Francisco de Negreiros (1588)

From its earliest days, Brazil differed from other New World sugar
economies in that a large proportion of the necessary raw material –
sugarcane – and the labor force of slaves were controlled not by the
producing mills but by cane farmers. This structure had existed on the
Atlantic islands of both Spain and Portugal and appears to have been
transferred to the Spanish Caribbean islands Cuba and Puerto Rico in
the sixteenth century as well. But until the nineteenth century, only in
Brazil did cane farmers form an essential part of the sugar economy.
Perhaps in the Caribbean there were too many other economic activities, or the attractions of Mexico and Peru were eventually too strong
to make cane farming appeal to poorer colonists. Brazil in its early
years presented fewer distractions. Early royal efforts to stimulate the
sugar economy had been designed to provide aid for colonists who
lacked the capital or credit necessary to establish an engenho but who
wished to participate in the export economy. The earliest engenhos in
various parts of Brazil depended on these cane farmers, and the instructions to Tomé de Sousa on the establishment of royal control in
Bahia contained specific references to them. Lavradores de cana remained throughout the colonial period an essential and integral element in the Bahian sugar economy, providing by their existence certain
peculiarities in social and economic organization that influenced the
lives of both slave and free in the captaincy.[1]

The term "lavrador de cana" calls for explanation and clarification.

295

"Lavrador" in Portuguese simply referred to anyone engaged in agriculture and could be used generically for the meanest dirt farmer or a great senhor de engenho. In practice, however, the term "lavrador" was usually modified by a description of the crop produced; and that in turn, at least in Bahia, also indicated something of social standing. The lavradores de cana, or cane farmers, were a kind of farmer elite, often ranked just below the senhores de engenho but also including among them people of far humbler backgrounds and resources. Although association with the dominant export economy, the political interests of the sugar sector, and slavery gave the lavradores de cana a relatively high social position throughout the colonial period, there were some changes over time that we will have to address. *Lavradores de fumo*, or tobacco farmers, included some people of great wealth with large holdings, but they were, as a group, not as wealthy or prestigious as the cane farmers. Food-crop farmers, *lavradores de roça*, included both subsistence growers and some who raised manioc and other foods for local sale, using slave labor on a small scale. As a group, food-crop farmers enjoyed less status or wealth than those associated with the export crops. In addition, the rural world of Bahia witnessed in the eighteenth century the development of categories defined by their relationship to a landowner rather than by the crop produced. These were the agregados and moradores, which will figure prominently in our later discussion of social change. Although all the agrarian classes shared some characteristics and attitudes, the lavradores de cana stood somewhat apart. Despite antagonism and conflict born in their relationship to the senhores de engenho, the cane farmers took pride in their title and in their association with sugar. Petitions to local or royal councils that emanated from the sugar sector usually included the signatures of both millowners and cane farmers. The lavradores de cana viewed themselves as proto-planters, as indeed they were. They were an essential part of the world of the engenhos (see Figure 11-1).

Tenure and obligations

Land stood at the core of the cane farmers' existence, determining their relation to the engenho and their position in society. The types of tenure used in Brazil had firm roots in Portugal's agrarian traditions, following medieval precedents in form if not necessarily in proportion or frequency of use. By far the most advantaged growers were those who possessed full and clear title acquired by grant or purchase of the lands they worked. Independent ownership gave them considerable flexibility in bargaining with millowners over the pressing of the cane. Although the division of sugar produced from this "free cane" – that is, cane grown by an independent grower – was customarily 50 percent to the grower and 50 percent to the senhor de engenho, the independent

Figure 11-1. An engenho complex: mill, big house, chapel, canefields, corral, pastures, and perhaps a lavrador residence in the distance. Despite many illustrations of sugar-mill machinery, this seventeenth-century view is one of the few that also picture canefields. Note their proximity to the river and the cart road between them.

lavrador de cana could negotiate other advantages such as the loan of slaves or oxen, the mill's supply of firewood, and preferential treatment in the milling schedule. A large independent grower who could bring thirty or forty tarefas of cane to an engenho was in an excellent bargaining position since cane supply was essential for success. When the milling schedules were being prepared, these were the lavradores de cana who the senhores treated with "great pampering." Independent cane farmers with their own land, slaves, and oxen shared the risks of the industry with the engenho owners.

Many persons lacked the capital or credit needed for independent cane farming and turned instead to some form of lease or rental of engenho lands. Planters probably preferred to rent at a fixed rate so that all risk would fall on the lavrador no matter what the production in a given year, but far more common seems to have been the *partido de cana* (canefield) in which the lavrador leased land from the mill with restrictions on its use and on the disposal of cane produced. Engenho owners favored the *partido de terço* (third) or the *partido de quarto* (fourth), in which the lavrador agreed to pay a land rent of one-third or one-fourth of his or her half of the sugar produced from the cane of the partido. In effect, this meant that the lavrador de cana retained between 16.5 and 37.5 percent of the sugar produced.

The contract at a third placed a heavy burden on the lavradores de

cana, for in each safra only a small fraction of the sugar produced from
their cane would be returned to them. But engenho owners usually
rented their best lands in rather large parcels at the "third" rate. At
Engenho Sergipe, lands beside the bay or along rivers where the soil
was good and transportation easy went at a third, whereas lands without such advantages were rented at a fourth. Manoel de Couto reported to the countess of Linhares in 1617 that one cane farm was so
far from the engenho that it could not be leased at the terço because
the lands of twenty other growers would have to be crossed to bring in
the cane. He suggested it simply be sold.[2] But Couto forcefully objected to the sale of lands along the river that could be leased at rents
favorable to the engenho. The countess of Linhares in 1601 had in fact
specifically ordered her agent at Engenho Sergipe to lease lands at the
third, but local lavradores who had been paying minimal fixed rates
were reluctant to change their contracts.[3]

Because of the heavy obligations, only farmers of some substance
accepted a large partido de terço. The millowners encouraged this situation because they wished to place prime lands in the hands of those
who could cultivate them to best advantage. At Engenho Sergipe,
Manoel de Couto refused to lease good lands at the terço to poorer
lavradores de cana because, despite their willingness, he felt that their
offers were "only words since they have not the capital, ability or
slaves necessary for those who must supply cane at the third."[4] The
best cane fazendas, then, went to persons who already possessed some
wealth and could afford to meet the rigors of the third contract. Such
assets did not preclude great effort or hard work. The industry of a
lavrador a terço was proverbial. Bernardo Ribeiro noted in 1612 that
one poor farmer at Engenho Sergipe was "felling trees, hoeing and
planting the land at great cost to his pocket as if he would have to
provide the terço."[5]

Contracts varied from place to place and over time, dependent not
only on the quality and location of the land and resources of the lavrador but also on the state of the economy. In the boom days of the late
sixteenth and early seventeenth centuries, engenho owners found
many people willing to take on contracts at the one-third or one-fourth
rate. By the late seventeenth century, conditions had changed, and in
the 1690s the contract in Pernambuco was commonly one-fifth and in
Bahia one-fifteenth or one-twentieth.[6] Changes in the rent were one
means of attracting lavradores or stimulating their efforts. In 1694, Luís
Ferreira de Araújo leased a partido to Domingos Alvares Mendes at
one-fifth on cane already planted but promised to charge only one-
tenth on any newly planted cane.[7]

Lease (arrendamento) of a partido varied in length of tenure and reciprocal obligations. The papers of Engenho Sergipe are particularly infor-

mative in this regard because that engenho depended on a large number of lavradores, and at certain points in time attempts to renegotiate contracts generated much correspondence. Although Antonil reported that contracts in the 1680s were normally for nine or eighteen years, in the 1640s Engenho Sergipe preferred a six-year contract.[8] There were exceptions, however. Custódio Lobo, who had managed Engenho Sergipe, was replaced in 1617, but he was allowed to become a lavrador a terço.[9] His contract is revealing of the general pattern of these arrangements. Lobo received a fifty-year lease. He agreed to plant new fields and after the first three cuttings to bring his cane to Engenho Sergipe where it would be divided, two-thirds to the mill and one-third to Lobo. If the engenho's administrator did not need the cane in a particular year, Lobo was free to mill it elsewhere, but Engenho Sergipe was still entitled to one-third of the sugar produced. The partido could not be sublet without the agreement of Engenho Sergipe, and then only under the original limitations and conditions. Unlike the situation of most of the lavradores at Engenho Sergipe, however, Lobo was not required to provide firewood to the mill.[10]

Most striking in the Custódio Lobo contract was a clause requiring Lobo or his heirs to surrender the partido and any improvements (*bemfeitorias*) to the owners of Engenho Sergipe upon termination of the lease. Such clauses kept the best sugar land in large parcels under control of the engenhos and also contributed to the impermanence of the lavradores. The inability to acquire permanent title to good land hampered the lavradores in their attempts to establish firm economic bases. A high rate of turnover seems to have been characteristic of the lavradores de cana as a group. Over a period of eighteen safras (1622–52), 128 individuals appeared as cane growers at Engenho Sergipe; but of these, 53 appeared in only one harvest and only 24 supplied cane in more than five safras.[11] Although such instability was probably characteristic of the smaller growers with only a few tarefas, the precarious position of the lavradores de cana is made clear by the pattern. When Pero Bras Rey pleaded in 1609 that the count of Linhares sell him the piece of land he had worked for twenty-five years so that he could leave it to his sons, we can sense the predicament of the cane growers.[12]

Pero Bras Rey's appeal indicates the strong attachments that lavradores de cana could develop for their partidos. Manoel de Couto discovered the strength of these feelings when he tried to expel some cane growers whose long occupancy caused them to "act like masters of their lands."[13] These attitudes led to litigation and violence. Manoel Maciel Aranha used his slaves and followers to drive off the feitor of Engenho Sergipe when he tried to retake possession of a fazenda.[14] The case was still in the courts when Aranha and his family arrived home to find someone else occupying the building. They threw the goods of the new occupant out into the pasture and a fight ensued when other men came to clear the canefieds. Maciel and his family had worked the partido for eighteen years, and there is little wonder that he was willing to fight for it.

Both social and economic reasons impelled senhores de engenho to maintain control of land. Status and recognition of rank derived from landholding to some degree, but there were also strong practical considerations. Once title passed permanently into the hands of others, control was lost and competition could ensue. Enterprising lavradores de cana hoped to create their own mills, and the proliferation of producing units provoked competition for cane, firewood, pasturage, and lavradores de cana. In 1615, the count of Linhares sought to restrain some lavradores on lands they had purchased from him from building their own engenhos. These men were taking advantage of the new technology of the three-cylinder mill to set up small mills. Jorge Lopes da Costa, the count's lawyer, informed him, however, that since the lands had been sold outright, nothing could be done.[15] As we shall see, this tendency toward fission was a continuing problem.

As a compromise solution, millowners turned to *emphyteusis*, lease in perpetuity but with restrictions. Lands were commonly sold with continuing "obligations" of various sorts: most commonly, restrictions on the disposal of cane, timber, or firewood or on the construction of a new mill. Martim Lopes, a resident in Salvador, bought 400 braças of land near Engenho Sergipe in 1613 with an agreement that he could not build a mill without written permission from Sergipe's owners.[16] More common was a purchase like that made by Francisco Machado Passanha in 1701.[17] He bought a fazenda de canas in Cahipe with an obligation to provide all his sugarcane to Engenho Caboto in Matoim, which was the property of the vendor, Antônio da Rocha Pitta. The engenho owner agreed to mill this cane according to a set schedule, but the cane farmer was required to pay stiff penalties if any cane was diverted to another mill. Domingo de Araújo, a lavrador in Iguape, bought lands in Patatiba with the obligation to provide as part of the payment eighty tarefas of firewood a year at a price of 2$ each until the agreed-on price of 500$ was settled. Araújo also agreed to supply timber and cane, if he had it, to the former owner of the property.[18] Araújo and others who acquired lands from Engenho Sergipe also paid a symbolic rent or foro that indicated a continuing attachment to the original owner. These rents were commonly paid with a few chickens or measures of flour. By these arrangements, individuals could acquire caneland, but at the same time their crop became captive to the vendor.[19]

The following examples illustrate the crucial difference between free and captive cane. In a sale made to Simão Borges in 1602, the vendor renounced

. . . all rights, actions, pretentions, control, and usufruct and all present and future power that he or his heirs might have on the said land . . . and it is totally given, ceded, and transferred to the buyer and his heirs to hold, dispose of, and use as their own property as it now becomes by means of this instrument.

Compare this contract with that made between lavrador de cana Diogo de Leão and Engenho Sergipe in 1670, in which the above clause was repeated but with an additional "condition and obligation that all cane planted on the said land is perpetually obligated to be milled at Sergipe do Conde as is already the case with the buyer's [other] farms."[20]

Lavradores de cana did occasionally buy freedom for their captive cane by paying a sum to the engenho, but many illegally disposed of their cane. Engenho owners viewed the alienation of captive cane as a serious offense, and they used both force and the courts to prevent it. Many examples of these disputes can be cited, but the difficult years of the late seventeenth century seem to be particularly rich in violations of lavrador obligations.[21] In 1699, for example, João Francisco Villas Boas brought a suit against Dinis de Merello for selling cane obligated to Vilas Boas's mill to other engenhos.[22] In another instance, Manoel Alvares Melam owned a fazenda supposedly obligated to Engenho Sergipe. In the safra of 1679, Melam had taken his cane to the engenho of Miguel Pereira da Costa, and the Jesuit owners of Engenho Sergipe sued for damages.[23] Complexities could arise. Engenho Sergipe had sold a fazenda with obligation to Father Gaspar Dias in 1602. He then built his own engenho on the land and later sold it to Francisco Gonçalves, who sold it to Pedro de Andrade in 1618. Andrade moved the engenho downriver and then sold it to Duarte Lopes Soeiro. Francisco Gonçalves had retained part of the land in his original purchase, and his heirs had continued to grow cane on it. When the Gonçalves mill ceased operation, they had taken their cane to other mills as they chose. They claimed that if they had brought it to Engenho Sergipe, it was due to "friendship" rather than obligation and that their cane was not captive.[24] Antonil states that illegal disposal of captive cane increased in a poor safra when cane growers tried to help their relatives meet contractual obligations.[25]

The lavradores de cana, therefore, were subdivided into a number of categories according to their relationship to the land they worked. Those who owned land outright, free of obligations, constituted a privileged group. Those with captive cane were further separated into sharecroppers (lavradores de partido), tenants, and those who owned land with obligations. These categories played an important role in determining the relations of lavradores de cana to other groups in the society.

The holdings of the lavradores de cana varied considerably in size and value. Although we lack the precise information to calculate an average-size cane farm within each of the lavrador subdivisions, there are some clues. One observer stated in the 1640s that a cane farmer needed twice as much land as the amount he or she cultivated each year. Keeping this in mind, we can then make some estimates based on production figures. The twenty-five lavradores who supplied cane to Engenho Sergipe in 1626–7 averaged 3.07 hectares of caneland, or twice that amount for total holdings (6.14 ha.).[26] But the distribution was quite unequal, with seventeen of them holding fewer than three hectares and only four with more than eight. Those four controlled more than 52 percent of the land cultivated by these cane farmers.

By modern standards, these holdings seem quite small, and indeed many of the lavradores de cana were marginal producers with only a few slaves and a little land. But the figures may be misleading. Samples of land sales indicate the purchase of land by lavradores de cana in the range of roughly thirty to two hundred thirty hectares. The discrepancy can be explained by the inclusion of large tracts of nonarable land, fallowing, or the existence of contracts with more than one engenho, so that the records of any one mill do not reflect a lavrador's total output. Another manner of calculating the size of lavrador de cana operations is to use slaves as a measure. Most observers used as a rule of thumb a ratio of one slave per tarefa. In 1817, in a partial census of Recôncavo slaveowners, there were 478 lavradores de cana listed with an average of ten to eleven slaves. The range ran from as few as one to as many as forty slaves.[27] This would yield holdings of five to ten hectares on the average. Whatever the average size of lavrador de cana parcels, it was surely greater than the plots of fifty to sixty braças described as the size of holdings in a subsistence-farming area. The disparity between the two indicates the difference in economic status between a lavrador de roça and a lavrador de cana.

In addition to slaves, lavrador de cana concerns centered on oxen, firewood, and lumber, the items necessary to produce sugar. Oxen were indispensable since transportation of cane to the mill remained essentially the growers' responsibility. The number needed varied according to location, but Van der Dussen estimated that a lavrador with forty tarefas of cane needed four to eight carts and six oxen for every two carts. Foraging cattle were a constant problem and the cause of continual disputes. A law of 1700 finally gave lavradores the right to kill such loose cattle in their fields, but the reissue of the law in 1709 and 1740 and subsequent litigation indicates that the problem did not disappear.[28] Firewood was a continuing problem, especially by the mid–seventeenth century, by which considerable deforestation of the Recôncavo had taken place. Wood could always be obtained from the great timber reserves of Jaguaripe and the south coast, but transport made it expensive. Arrangements on the supply of firewood varied. Cristóvão Barroso claimed that the grower was responsible for supplying the fuel to process his cane and that this was the "custom of the land," but others disagreed with him. A contract of 1648 provided that if the grower produced "firewood, boards, crates or foodstuffs, he will sell them, things being equal, to the engenho."[29] By the eighteenth century, engenhos commonly supplied the fuel. This seems to be one of the areas that was negotiable and probably changed according to the state of the sugar economy and the difficulty of securing lavradores de cana. The sale of firewood, crates, and foodstuffs probably provided some of the cane farmers with extra income. As we saw in the preceding chapter, testimony given in 1800 indicated that the reciprocal use of slaves, oxen, and carts was commonly practiced.[30]

Social composition and relations

In social terms, the lavradores de cana are best understood as proto-planters, drawn essentially from the same social origins and sharing similar aspirations as the senhores de engenho. Obviously, a wide gap existed between a grower with one or two tarefas and a lavrador with forty or fifty and a like number of slaves. Among its lavradores de cana, Bahia counted Catholic priests, New Christian merchants, wealthy widows, and threadbare gentlemen. Many among them were officers in the militia units, served in the câmara, or were on the Misericórdia board of directors. Cosme de Sá Peixoto, who held municipal office and whose name figures prominently on petitions from the sugar sector, and Desembargador Cristóvão de Burgos, Bahia's most prominent judge in the 1670s, were both lavradores de cana. They had little in common with someone like Pedro de Lima, who in the safra of 1654–5 produced twenty arrobas of sugar. Still, all these men grew cane and most likely perceived some community of interest between themselves and with the sugar sector in general.

A petition sent by senhores de engenho and lavradores de cana to the crown in 1662 revealed cane growers like Dom Pedro Daça de Mello, "knight of the Order of Christ"; Luís Gomes de Bulhões, "lieutenant general of artillery and knight of the Order of São Bento de Aviz"; Luís Alvares Montarroio, "Provedor da Fazenda e Alfândega"; and Francisco Negreiros Sueiro, "Knight of Aviz, civil judge, many times municipal councillor, and cane grower for over forty years."[31] Such men surely figured among the principal residents of the captaincy and formed a select stratum among the cane growers. These wealthier and more distinguished cane farmers were always present in the industry: men like Felipe Dias Amaral, who died in 1804 leaving twenty-seven slaves, thirty-five oxen, other livestock, a substantial house, twenty-five tarefas of improved pasture, and forty-two tarefas of caneland connected to Engenho Pandalunga and Engenho Fazenda do Meio. Conversely, most lavradores de cana operated at far more modest levels.[32] In 1817, about 57 percent of the Recôncavo lavradores had fewer than ten slaves and about 25 percent owned fewer than five. Although the spectrum of lavradores de cana was broad, socially they remained an adjunct to the planter class, people of the same background but lacking the capital to achieve fully their goal of plantership.[33]

The two groups, in fact, were not only socially homogeneous but were often related by blood. Senhor de engenho Afonso da França's brothers were lavradores de cana, as were the sons and brother-in-law of Manoel Mendes Monforte. Numerous examples throughout the colonial period could be cited. Historian Rae Flory provides a remarkable late-seventeenth-century case centered on Engenho da Ponte and the Araújo de Aragão family. Pedro Camello Pereira de Aragão, owner of Engenho da Ponte, had eleven children, ten of whom become mill-owners or cane farmers. By the early eighteenth century, the engenho controlled six nearby fazendas with obligations; three of these were owned by relatives. Moreover, five more nearby farms were managed by sons, nephews, or sons-in-law of the da Ponte owners.[34] These bonds of blood reinforced those of interest and mitigated the inherent conflicts that also existed in the relationship between millowners and cane growers.

As among the millowners, religious institutions, individual clerics, and women could also be counted among the ranks of the lavradores de cana. As early as 1611, the Benedictines supplied cane to Engenho Sergipe, and in 1670 they acquired more canefields under obligation to the Jesuit mill. Eventually, they developed their own mill, São Bento dos Lages, across the river from Engenho Sergipe. The Carmelites and Franciscans also appear among cane suppliers of Engenho Sergipe, as did the Jesuit College of Salvador in the late seventeenth century and the eighteenth. Individual clerics were among Engenho Sergipe's relatively small producers in the seventeenth century, but priests sometimes became large-scale cane growers as well. Van der Dussen's account of Pernambuco in 1639 notes one priest with sixty tarefas of cane.[35] In Bahia, Father José Carlos Marinho Falcão Pereira, who died in 1789 leaving more than fifty slaves, or Canon Anselmo Dias da Rocha, who in 1833 had 300 tarefas of massapé, were examples of clerical lavradores with extensive holdings.[36] There were also a few clerics who administered engenhos, and a report of 1779 mentioned some Capuchins who were millowners.[37]

Despite the prejudices and stereotypes, women also owned and sometimes managed cane farms. At Engenho Sergipe, hardly a safra passed in which there were not two or three women growers. Often women took over the property and obligations of their husbands. Beatris Delgada, for example, was a major supplier to Engenho Sergipe in the 1620s. The pressures on these women to remarry were great, given the demands of agriculture and the value of their property.

Like the planters, the cane growers included in their ranks merchants, persons of mechanic origins, and New Christians, and until the eighteenth century they were almost invariably white. Although free blacks and mulattoes filled a variety of artisan occupations and practiced other kinds of agriculture, the role of lavrador de cana appears to have been almost exclusively for whites. At Engenho Sergipe, none of the registered lavradores de cana is mentioned as preto or pardo, the usual color designations often noted when speaking of artisans or other workers in that estate's accounts. Rae Flory found that among 400 persons who could be identified as cane growers in the period 1680–1725, only one was a pardo.[38] The demands of cane farming and the financial requirements seem to have been beyond the reach of the free-colored population. Toward the end of the eighteenth century, however, this situation began to change. A partial census of Nossa Senhora da Purificação parish in Santo Amaro revealed in 1788 that although the eight engenho owners or administrators were white, six of the thirty-four cane growers were persons of color.[39] The inclusion of nonwhites among the lavradores de cana seems to indicate a slippage in the social position of this category toward the end of the colonial era.

How many lavradores de cana existed at any one time in Bahia? The question is a difficult one to answer with any precision. The ratio of growers to engenhos changed over time and reflected the state of the industry. Moreover, as an area was opened up to sugar cultivation and then stabilized, the ratio of lavradores to mills also appears to have altered. Evidence from Pernambuco and Paraíba from the early seventeenth century indicates a relatively high ratio of between six and seventeen cane farmers per mill.[40] The accounts of Engenho Sergipe also list a large number of lavradores, especially in the mid–seventeenth century, when the yearly figure was between fifteen and thirty. In this regard, however, I now believe that Engenho Sergipe was atypical and tended through most of its history to have far more lavradores de cana than was the rule in Bahia. In the period 1680–1725, Flory found no engenho with more than eight cane suppliers.[41] In 1817, the average number of lavradores de cana per engenho in the Recôncavo was three per mill, although there were parishes such as Passé and Rio Fundo in which that figure rose to four.

Rio Fundo, in fact, offers an excellent view into the complex structure of the Bahian engenhos. Table 11-1 shows clearly that some engenhos had no lavradores de cana whereas others had as many as eleven, the average being four per mill. Cane farmers controlled an average of 10 slaves each, or about one-third of the parish's slave force employed in sugar; other employees and engenho dependents owned another 9 percent. Thus although the average number of slaves held by a senhor de engenho in Rio Fundo was 62, each mill depended on an average of 112 slaves because of the labor force provided by the lavra-

Table 11-1 *Structure of the engenhos of São Pedro do Rio Fundo, 1788*

Engenho	Slaves	Lavra-dores	Slaves	Free dependents	Slaves	Others	Slaves	Total Slaves
Rio Fundo	40	9	69	8	15			124
Buraco	22	2	8			9	24	54
Pandalunga	64	3	34			11	101	199
Rossado	61	2	14					75
Paramerim	30	4	46					76
Pernagua	30	3	12					42
Papagaio	60	4	34			3	12	106
Felipe	114	3	20					134
Merces	46	2	11					57
Camboata	70	4	34			2	2	106
Jacú	100	9	67			12	19	186
Canabrava	97	11	159	13	26	1	1	283
Quitanga	138	5	38	2	4			180
Outero	51	1	12					63
Coite do Baixo	60	7	67	2	3			130
Coite de Cima	37	5	74	2	3			114
Orobó	33	6	64	1	1	1	1	99
Gamaleira	58	3	26					84
Europa	60	5	24					84
Brejo de André	30	4	50	1	2	1	18	100
Brejinho	28	4	12	3	5			45
Bomjardim	97	7	91					188
Cravatá	80							80
Camorogi	185	2	25	23	56			266
Pajuca	37	5	64	3	5			106
Alumiar	60	5	36					96
Serra Novado	110	4	95					205
Stos Apostolos	32	1	18					50
Peripery	30	3	10					40
Jacuipe do Desterro	70	6	71	2	4			145
Jacuipe	75	9	70	10	51			196
Carapia	60	1	8	1	4			72
Picado	36			1	4			40
Taraquary	7			1	7			14
Inhata	45	4	85			5	8	138
Totals for 35 engenhos	2,153	143	1,448	73	190	45	186	3,977

dores de cana. This complex arrangement gave the Bahian sugar estates a form of organization that distinguished them from other New World sugarworks but not from other Brazilian engenhos.[42]

Together, the senhores de engenho and lavradores de cana formed the sugar sector, united by interest and dependence on the international market. They were the "nerves of the body politic," wrote Wenceslão Pereira da Silva in 1738.[43] Common interests, however, should not obscure conflicts born of their relationship. Millowners looked upon lavradores de cana as retainers who owed not only sugar-cane but also respect and allegiance. The wives of planters followed suit, treating the wives of cane growers like servants. Through pres-sure, payment, or calling on the bonds of kinship and association, senhores de engenho prevailed on cane growers to give false witness or carry out illegal acts.

Antonil admonished senhores to treat their lavradores well, for the success of the mill depended on that of the cane growers. Honest and helpful planters were sought out by the lavradores. The least-powerful planters often proved to be the fairest, lending slaves and oxen and sharing panela, which by right belonged entirely to the mill. Santos Vilhena suggested in 1798 that the more powerful the planter, the more tyrannical his or her dominion over dependent lavradores.

More important than the personality or wealth of the senhor de engenho in determining relations between the lavradores de cana and a mill was the formal contractual status of the grower. Senhores courted those lavradores with free cane, especially at the time of the safra. Lavradores without obligations could bargain with the engenho owners on a more or less even footing. Lavradores de cana were also jealous of their position in society and could prove to be sensitive. One administrator at Engenho Sergipe wrote in 1623 that to succeed with the lavradores one had to be "pleasant and benevolent because in this land everything is respect and courtesies [respeitos e fidalguias], and if you do not treat them in this way, nothing can be done with them nor can fortune be made because much depends on them."[44] Sharecrop-pers and tenants were in a far weaker position, being subject to caprice and "servile oppression," as many observers noted.

The possible abuses were many. The senhor might fail to divide the sugar evenly and give fair measure, or he might keep the best for himself and give the grower only that of inferior quality. In another common abuse, the senhor mixed the sugar of two lavradores to even out the quality, thus depriving one of a premium for good sugar while rewarding another whose product was inferior. Delay in cutting cane caused great damage, but most harmful of all was failure to mill cane immediately after it had been cut. Disruption of the milling schedule could ruin a whole crop. "The poor lavrador," said Santos Vilhena, "can see in less than a week the loss of a year's labor."[45] Personal antagonism and the desire to dominate subordinates lay behind such behavior, but of course the senhor did not want to cause his own loss at the same time. Politics, too, entered the relationship. In 1821, Fran-cisco Manoel da Rocha, a lavrador de cana for Engenho Coite de Baixo, complained that its owner, Antônio Alvares da Silva Pereira, refused to grind his cane at the right time and even burned his fields because of the "spite in his gut against all Brazilians, going so far as to expel from the lands of the engenho all the lavradores and tenants who were not Europeans like himself."[46]

Most lavradores de cana could ill afford to bring these abuses to the attention of the courts, but some did. One such instance occurred in 1677, when a grower argued that, in return for furnishing cane to the engenho, it was obliged "to grind the cane at a fixed time, so many tarefas per week with the condition that the party who fails in his obligation must pay the other for all loss and damage."[47] Other contracts also indicate that cane obligations involved explicit or implicit obligations on the part of the engenho. But in truth the courts did little to temper the relation between senhores de engenho and their dependent cane farmers.[48] By withholding cane or fuel, however, lavradores could exert pressure on an engenho. A seventeenth-century observer noted that the lavradores' unreliability in this regard created the most serious problems for the senhores, who lived "dependent on the will of the cane growers."[49] But the balance in the relationship was unequal and weighted on the side of the engenho owners.

Individual animosities and the tensions that resulted from the relationship between subordinates and inferiors remained, in the final analysis, less important than a perception of common interest between senhores de engenho and lavradores de cana. Often drawn from the same social origins, sometimes sharing ties of kinship, the senhores needed the lavradores to supply cane and help share the risks of plantership, and the lavradores practiced their husbandry to get ahead, many hoping to establish their own engenho someday. The lavradores de cana were proto-planters, owning slaves, oxen, sometimes land, and other assets, and sharing with the senhores a constellation of attitudes and interests. As we saw in Chapter 7, planter petitions for debt moratoriums, protection from foreclosures, lower interest rates, and elimination of merchant abuses were supported by lavradores de cana as well. The law of 1663 protecting engenhos from piecemeal attachment of their assets for debts was extended to cover lavradores de cana, and when in 1720 a test case came before the High Court of Bahia, both planters and cane growers exerted considerable pressure on the court. They argued, "It is all the same agriculture and the same sugar making, for engenhos could make little or no sugar if there were no lavradores to bring the cane of their fields to be ground."[50] The cane growers lived in the shadow of the senhores, but they also enjoyed its protecting shade.

Mobility and conflict

At no time did the symbiotic relationship between senhor and lavrador become more apparent than in the 1660s. During a period when mercantilist restrictions had caused a loss of traditional markets to Brazilian sugar, planters in the colony found themselves faced with falling or stagnating prices and apparent shortages of firewood and other supplies. Planters did succeed in obtaining the law of 1663 limiting foreclosures for debt, but in addition another measure was suggested that caused an uproar in Bahia and brought sharply into focus the relation between growers and engenho owners, revealing at the same time the motives of the cane growers.[51]

In an extraordinary letter, the juiz do povo and the artisan representatives on the Salvador municipal council petitioned the Overseas Council in Lisbon for a royal injunction to halt the creation of new engenhos near the coast. They suggested that only toward the sertão could new mills be set up without damaging the operations of those already in existence. The letter observed that men "gave up being rich cane growers to become poor millowners, as is almost always the case." A lavrador with one hundred tarefas of cane found, on establishing an engenho, that half his land had to be devoted to pasturage and other activities so that, along with new capital expenses, his production was cut in half. Thus, although the number of mills increased, the production of sugar did not keep pace.

The man behind this petition seems to have been Bernardino Vieira Ravasco, a senhor de engenho and the secretary of state of Brazil.[52] In his own letter, he argued that the proliferation of mills caused shortages of cane and fuel and drove up prices. This resulted in a loss of production, so an engenho real that had formerly produced 6,000 to 7,000 arrobas was reduced to an output of 4,000 to 5,000 and the output of an animal-powered mill was reduced from 4,000 to 2,000 arrobas. Within his complaint, however, was another theme: the shifting balance between lavradores and senhores. Vieira Ravasco suggested that the creation of too many engenhos had altered the relationship with the lavradores and those who supplied the engenhos or offered their skills. Thus wages were rising, wood suppliers were "inconstant," and the senhores lived subject to their "whim." Today, said Vieira Ravasco, the owners go "begging at the doors of the lavradores."[53] Rather than profiting from this situation by demanding more favorable terms, the lavradores sought the title of senhor de engenho, driven by vanity or greed ("vaidade de nome ou enganho de cobiça").[54] With few exceptions, the general result was a large number of formerly successful lavradores de cana heavily indebted as millowners.

Vieira Ravasco's position caused a general uproar in the câmara and fiery rebuttal. It was claimed that the juiz do povo was an illiterate who had persuaded the other popular representatives to sign the petition without revealing its contents to them.[55] Moreover, Vieira Ravasco was self-interested in this matter, having mismanaged his own engenhos, and he was seeking to eliminate competition and lower his costs. The crown gathered informed opinions on the matter. Lourenço de Brito Correa argued that if engenhos had gone out of production, it was due to the divisions of legacies made upon the death of senhores rather than the result of competition.[56] Everyone wanted success, he argued, and thus no one would build a mill where there was insufficient cane or firewood, nor would merchants extend credit to someone who had no chance of gain. His statement was supported by others, the most telling of which was a petition signed by 108 senhores and lavradores de cana arguing for no limitation. Engenhos had to be built to increase production and thus generate more revenue for the state. Moreover, engenhos stimulated the economy, generating trade, promoting importation of slaves and manufactured goods, creating work for artisans, and helping to populate the countryside. They put it simply: "Sugar is the head of this mystic body of the state of Brazil."[57]

But if Vieira Ravasco had noted an economic consideration with social implications – namely, the relationship of lavradores to senhores de engenho – his critics also responded directly to this problem. Their proposal, allowing for the unlimited increase of competition, seems to make sense only if the social dimension is accounted for. Cane farming had been a traditional path of social mobility and a route generally available to people already privileged by color or wealth. The move from cane farming to senhor de engenho happened often enough to make the path attractive, and the hope of acquiring a mill is what led people to assume the obligations of a lavrador. As the petitioners put it, "It is unjust to deprive the lavrador or other person who has the capital for it from seeking his best interest in the establishment of a new mill since it is the greater glory of the state to have many rich subjects."[58] Without the hope of eventual millownership, it would be difficult to induce men to become lavradores de cana. The door had to be left open, at least in theory, if the industry was to survive.

If the juiz do povo was correct in his analysis that rich lavradores always became poor millowners, then the lavradores' economic miscalculation can only be explained by the compensating social benefits associated with plantation ownership. For them, the prestige of title, the hope of profit, and the social attributes outweighed the current economic difficulties. The desire of the lavradores de cana to become senhores de engenho led them to perceive a congruence of interests between themselves and those who already owned mills. Those cane growers possessing the capital and skills most likely to lead them to millownership were also those best able to provide leadership among the cane growers and the other free elements in the rural population. The men most qualified to offer a challenge to the political dominance of the planters probably became the first to join their ranks. Social goals offset possible conflict, and real or apparent mobility was fostered by the planters to maintain the structure of the sugar industry and the social relations within it. Lavradores de cana, able to serve in municipal posts, join prestigious brotherhoods, own slaves, amass capital, and hope to become engenho owners in their own right, had a stake in the existing political and social order. The achievement of their dreams depended on the continued vigor and stability of the sugar economy. They were not a group from which demands for broad social change would spring easily.

The problems that had generated this dispute did not disappear. The 1660s witnessed activity on many fronts, all of which related to the internal structure of the industry and the position of the planters and lavradores within it. The 1663 law limiting foreclosure, the attempt to introduce new technology like the Urrey mill, and the limitation of engenho construction must all be seen as part of a general response to Brazil's changing role within the Atlantic sugar economy. The debate continued throughout the 1660s, and by 1667 when the Recôncavo had 130 engenhos, a first step toward the limitation of construction was finally taken, resulting in the law of 1681 that limited the building of new mills to a distance of 1,500 braças from existing engenhos. Other legislation sought to exclude tobacco growing and cattle raising from possible sugar-growing areas. The law of 1681, modified by a second provision of 1684, remained the operating legislation.[59] These had the effect of opening up new areas for sugar in parishes like Inhambupe, Rio Fundo, and Catú. But over time, the law was often ignored. This became apparent in 1797, when Manoel Alvares de São Boaventura tried to stop José de Araújo Barcelar from building a new mill near São Boaventura's own Engenho de Conceição in Cachoeira. Planters in Santo Amaro and Iguape testified that the 1681 law had fallen into disuse and that in Iguape alone 15 engenhos could be found within the space of a league (3,000 braças).[60] In 1801, the law was reissued placing the 1,500 braças limit on engenhos near the coast, but not doing so on those in the sertão. A provision of 1802 required perspective builders of new engenhos to acquire a government license.[61]

It is difficult to estimate the effects of the restrictions and the changes in the sugar economy on the lavradores de cana as a group. Engenho Sergipe in the 1660s moved to sharply reduce the number of lavradores that supplied cane to it, and other engenhos may have followed the same pattern. Certainly by the end of the eighteenth century, the average number of growers per mill had declined from the boom days of the early seventeenth century. The problem may have been one of supply. Persons who before might have taken on the obligations of a contract at the terço or the quarto were, by the eighteenth century, drawn to tobacco farming or to the mines of the interior. The stagnation of the sugar economy made cane farming less attractive and the limitation laws of the 1680s, though protecting existing senhores, did nothing to bring in new ones. The door to plantership was not shut,

but the crack had been made thinner. The contracts in which lavradores de cana paid 7, or 10, percent as a land rent were one way in
which the planters sought to secure cane farmers, but these easier
contracts can be misleading.[62] Dona Francisca Maria de Vasconcelos,
lavradora at Engenho Macaco, produced the cane for eighty-eight
loaves of sugar in the safra of 1821. These produced about 250 arrobas,
which were divided equally between her and the engenho. She then
paid a land rent of 7 percent, but in addition she had to pay crating
costs and transportation and to repay a loan. She cleared less than 30
percent of the sugar produced.[63]

At the end of the colonial era, there were still well-to-do cane farmers
holding large numbers of slaves and working many tarefas of cane,
people who were related by blood and interest to the planters and who
could realistically hope to gain that title themselves. But they were the
exception. Late colonial observers like Santos Vilhena (1798) in Bahia
and Tollenare (1819) in Pernambuco describe the lavradores de cana as
a class in decline.[64] With the exception of the independent growers, the
lavradores de cana appear in these descriptions as subservient dependents, subject to the whim or caprice of the senhores and easily
cheated or dispossessed of their holdings. Planters often violated the
oral contracts commonly used, and a lavrador after improving a canefield would often find himself evicted and paid only a pittance for his
improvements. Given the instability of tenure, lavradores de cana
tended to invest in such moveables as slaves and oxen and limit their
capital expenditures on fences, houses, or land. Many worked themselves, alongside their sons and their slaves.[65]

At best, they were a class hanging on. Racially, they remained predominantly white, although by the end of the colonial period they
were almost exclusively Brazilian born. Increasingly, persons of color
became cane farmers; a sign of their upward mobility, but also an
indicator of the group's social decline. There is something sad in Tollenare's description of the cane farmers of Pernambuco, laboring with
hoe in hand but dressing in city clothes and mounting a fine horse to
ride to mass on Sunday, their silver spurs jingling on their heels as
they left their ramshackle homes.[66] Better off than the majority of the
free rural population and placed in a somewhat higher social niche, the
lavradores de cana remained an essential element of rural society, participants in the plantation economy, slaveowners, themselves subordinate. "This class is truly worthy of interest," said Tollenare, "because
they possess some capital and they work."[67]

CHAPTER 12

WAGE WORKERS IN A SLAVE ECONOMY

He who makes sugar, with reason they call master because his work demands intelligence, attention, and experience, not just any kind, but local experience.

André João Antonil (1711)

Sugar making is given over to ignorance, and generally to stupid blacks who sing but have no measure, no rule, and no proportion.

Sampaio e Mello (1834)

In the world of engenhos, mobility from field hand to proprietor, from slave to freedman, from those who labored to those who owned, or simply from black to white, was most apparent in the categories of wage earners that were always present in the sugar-making process. Although chattel labor characterized the sugar economy in Brazil from its inception until the end of the nineteenth century and slaves were always the predominant laborers, the nature of sugar production and its specific demands created a need for a body of wage earners at the core of the process. Field hands were almost always slaves, usually black, and predominantly Africans; senhores de engenho were invariably free and white; but in the intermediate positions of management, technical skill, and artisian craft were found freemen, freedmen, and slaves; whites, browns, and blacks. Here in the heart of the sugar economy was a sector of workers that by its very existence validated the system of slavery on which the industry was based by providing examples of mobility and advantage to those enslaved.

The skills and services of these workers were essential to the production of sugar, and the existence of this segment of the labor force served as example and goal for at least some of the enslaved workers. Even when millowners replaced free workers in these positions with skilled slaves, a social differentiation of labor remained characteristic of the engenho work force.

In the previous chapters, we examined the importance of sugar-making skills in the transition from Indian to African workers, the specific labor requirements and tasks of sugar making, and some as-

313

pects of the cost of wage labor in plantation operations. In this chapter, we shall be concerned primarily with the characteristics of the skilled workers as a social category and with the manner in which color and juridical status influenced their position in sugar society.

Categories of salaried employees

Four types of salaried employees appear in engenho accounts; it is useful to note the distinctions between these categories because they represented different positions within the society. The first category was composed of salaried professionals or service personnel who provided skills, expertise, or services to the plantations on a recurring basis. Attorneys on retainer are a good example of these. Lawyers were considered a necessary evil, an unavoidable complement to business, and engenhos turned to them with regularity. They often resided in Salvador or Santo Amaro and were paid an annual retainer by an engenho, although they sometimes served more than one planter in the course of a year. Another kind of city resident employed by the engenhos was the city crater (*caixeiro da cidade*). These registered the engenhos' sugar crates at the local warehouse, handled problems of transportation and duties, and also secured supplies to be sent to the mill. They served, in effect, as urban agents for the planters. Chaplains and doctors, two other professionals employed by engenhos, were more likely to be found in the countryside. Many engenhos, however, had neither a permanent chaplain nor a priest, their presence being reserved to the larger mills. Chaplains in the eighteenth century were often related to the senhores de engenho, and Antonil informs us that they sometimes served as tutors for the planters' children as well as the moral and spiritual guardians of the estates' residents.[1] Like other professionals who resided in the countryside, chaplains often engaged in cane farming along with their other activities.[2] Those employed to care for sick slaves and to tend the needs of the planters and their families included a variety of what today are called health-care specialists. University-trained physicians were in short supply, but engenhos also called on the services of nurses, midwives, barber-surgeons, and herbalists. Usually, when a trained physician was employed, he, like other professionals, was hired by contract on an annual basis.

The principal salaried employees engaged on an annual basis were the sugar-making specialists and the field managers or overseers (feitores). The sugar master, his night-shift assistant (banqueiro), the crater at the mill, the purger, kettlemen, overseers in field and factory, and a variety of other workers (like helmsmen on the boats that transported cane, firewood, and sugar chests) were generally hired by contract on a yearly basis. Their annual salary (soldada) was calculated in currency, and adjustments were made if lodging or food was also provided. The monetary salary was known as *soldada seca*. In the seventeenth century, the value of food and lodging was about 110–150 réis per day, and workers who received it earned that much less than those who did not. At the beginning of the nineteenth century, planters claimed that "it took an ox a week to feed chaplains, administrators, craters, sugar masters, and carpenters, masons, blacksmiths, and the sick that are always on such properties."[3]

Accounts were not necessarily paid each year, and advances were sometimes made on a monthly basis.[4] Father Luís da Rocha wrote in 1745 from Engenho Sergipe that accounts with salaried employees "are not customarily settled each year, but only with those who are dismissed or who move to another engenho . . . and as is practiced on all the engenhos, those who remained are clothed and fed so that the soldadas are adjusted only every two or three years."[5] Such a system made sense in an economy chronically short of specie. Soldada employees apparently needed permission to work elsewhere during the safra, but occasional references indicate this practice was not unknown. Salvador Mirandes, a master carpenter at Engenho Sergipe, received permission in the 1570s to work at another mill. Francisco de Abreu died in 1663 owing money for the services of the feitor of another mill.[6] Father da Rocha observed in 1745 that a blacksmith, carpenter, barber, and surgeon could serve two, three, or even four engenhos.[7]

The workers on soldada appear to have been a privileged segment of the labor force because of the dependability of their employment in the short term and because of their special relationship to the planters. Their position, especially that of the sugar-making specialists, was roughly equivalent to that of traditional artisan craftsmen, and the term *master* was applied to those with recognized skill and long experience. In a sense, these occupations constituted what J. R. Hicks called the "regular" trades – those in which workers did not frequently change employers and in which regularity provided some economy.[8] Clearly, there were advantages in this relationship both for the planters who wanted skilled and experienced workers and for those employed on a secure basis who could depend on employment each year. The latter expectation was perhaps exaggerated, for (as we shall see) high rates of turnover in personnel can be observed in some occupations; but the regularity of these positions did have some stabilizing effect on wage rates over long periods of time. Planters could not replace these people without inconvenience, and workers could not respond to higher wages elsewhere without costs and trouble. As long as oscillations in the sugar economy were viewed as transitory, the long-term effect on the employment and compensation of skilled labor on the engenhos was negligible.

The last two categories of paid employees both worked on a daily or piecework basis, but there was a considerable difference between their earning power and relative social position. Artisans such as blacksmiths, carpenters, masons, shipwrights, boat caulkers, and coppersmiths provided services on a constant and recurring basis. No harvest passed when their skills were unnecessary, and in years of major repairs or expansion the annual incomes of these artisans might well exceed those of the soldada employees. In fact, blacksmiths (*ferreiros*) and coppersmiths (*caldereiros*) were sometimes employed on soldada, but they probably preferred piecework. In any case, on the engenhos blacksmiths and coppersmiths sometimes maintained their own workshops, buying raw materials and employing workers or owning slaves. Some capital was needed for such activities, and blacksmiths were among the wealthiest of the rural artisans.

As a group, the engenho artisans also composed a segment of the rural labor elite. Many worked with assistants, journeymen, or slaves. As late as 1626, the câmara of Salvador sought to regulate sugar masters; but such attempts were a dead letter, and engenho workers worked essentially without municipal oversight.[9] The rudiments of a stratified labor hierarchy existed, and the terms *mestre* (master), *oficial* (journeyman), and *aprendiz* (apprentice) appear in surviving documents. But these designations were not as rigidly controlled as in urban areas, which it should be noted, were themselves already weaker than their Portuguese precedents.

In fact, the artisan traditions of regulated ranks, guilds, and associations formed relatively late in Portugal itself and were regularized only after 1572.[10] In Brazil, as I have already noted, the artisan community was small, slow to form, and relatively weak. In the largest city of the colony, Salvador, artisan representation on the municipal council, a commonplace in Portugal, was intermittent and short lived; even from 1641 to 1713, when artisans did sit with that body, they were given little voice in important decisions other than the regulations of the trades.[11] The *bandeiras*, or artisan associations, with civic and religious goals that were characteristic of Portugal, did not exist in Salvador, and the role of artisan confraternities appears to have been limited; their regulations and bylaws dated mostly from the eighteenth century, indicating late development. What role slavery and slave artisans had on lowering artisan status and depressing wages in Brazil remains to be studied.[12]

Rural artisans in Brazil were even less organized and privileged than their urban counterparts. There is no evidence of an extensive organization of brotherhoods or of the regulation of skill and wages in the countryside. Collective action by rural artisans seems virtually nonexistent. An unsuccessful attempt was made in Rio de Janeiro in 1739 to exempt sugar specialists, artisans, and overseers from military service because, as they argued, their skills were essential to the economy; but such action was unknown in Bahia.[13]

The final category of paid workers provided unskilled labor on a short-term or occasional basis – for digging a trench, felling trees, carrying a message, capturing a runaway, or working part time in the field. These tasks were unsuitable or too dangerous for slaves or were performed alongside field slaves. The laborers doing the tasks received the lowest pay and, along with subsistence farmers, constituted the rural poor. This element of the work force, however, seems to have been present from the inception of the sugar industry, providing a pool of occasional labor to the engenhos. The distribution of work to the free rural poor gave the senhores an opportunity to tie workers to the personal control of the planters. By the eighteenth century, numerous individuals were listed without occupation as residents on or around the engenhos. Often they were persons of color – freedmen, freedwomen, or their descendants, the results of miscegenation and manumission.

Although the number of salaried employees and wage workers was small in comparison to the number of slaves, this element of the work force had an importance beyond its numbers. In proportions varying over time, both free and slave workers performed many of the skilled tasks and crafts needed by the engenhos, often laboring side by side. Slaves acquired skills and experience that might serve them or their children well after manumission, and the benefits of acquiring skills and trust were made obvious to them. The existence of this segment of the work force, by serving as example and goal, justified slavery by making that condition appear to be transitory and preparatory. If slaves believed that the passage from slave to citizen, or from slave to employee, was in fact a possibility within their grasp, then their desperation was reduced. Even for those slaves who did not obtain their freedom, the conditions of an artisan's life were in general better than those of a field hand's. But although the existence of free labor at the core of a profoundly slave-based plantation economy seemed to offer hope for a transition from slavery to freedom, that segment of free and remunerated labor was also marked by its existence within a slave-based, multiracial regime.

Workers and wages at Engenho Sergipe

Once again, the only set of extant records that allows us to observe in detail the internal operations of an engenho, in this case the role and scale of engenho wage labor over time, is the Engenho Sergipe account books. Although long gaps in these accounts and variations in recording procedures make them difficult to use for some periods, they provide us with a basic guide to the types of workers employed, the differential levels of payment, the hierarchy of skills, and the influence of race and status on remuneration.[14] Moreover, when used with care, a wage series can be constructed from them that indicates basic levels of worker remuneration over time.

The records of Engenho Sergipe confirm the impresison that the highest-paid workers were the few whose positions can best be described as managerial. These were the men who directed and supervised sugar making at various points along the stream of activity from grinding to purging and crating. As we might expect, the sugar master, valued for his "intelligence, attention, and experience" and responsible for the process from beginning to end, was the most highly paid employee, receiving a salary that was usually over 120$ a year, a sum about 60 percent higher than the salary of the next-best-paid employee.[15] Next in terms of salary were the purger (purgador) and the banqueiro or night-shirt sugar master. They both earned roughly equivalent salaries, which at Engenho Sergipe varied between 50$ and 60$ during the seventeenth century. Although Antonil reported that the various types of kettlemen earned equivalent salaries, the Engenho Sergipe records demonstrate considerable variation among the caldereiros (de melar, de escumas). As a group, however, their average was only slightly less than that of the banqueiro. The crater (caixeiro) also earned a salary roughly equivalent to that of the banqueiro at Engenho Sergipe.

Occasionally, other salaried workers were employed in the milling and clarification process. Those who transported cane and firewood to the engenho or carried sugar crates to the port were another group of paid employees. At Sergipe, this job was done by boatmen of various descriptions whose salaries averaged slightly less than those of the kettlemen.

In the fields and at the mill, the feitores or overseers were essential to a plantation's operations. As Antonil put it, if each feitor exercised independent control, the result would be like Cerebus, the three-headed dog of ancient mythology; but at the same time, overseers had to have some authority to command respect and work efficiently.[16] During the seventeenth century, Engenho Sergipe employed a general overseer (feitor-mór) whose responsibilities included the division of the work force, the regulation and timing of activities, and other management functions. His salary was second only to that of the sugar master. By the 1640s, this position was eliminated, and these functions were taken over by an administrator and perhaps by the sugar master as well. The feitor da moenda controlled the milling process, regulating the labor shifts, the flow of cane to the mill, and the power source, water or oxen. Over two centuries, the Engenho Sergipe accounts list many other feitores assigned to other tasks. In the sixteenth and seventeenth centuries, feitores of "the corral," "the free folk," and the "boats" appeared. In the eighteenth century, each of the separate cane farms had its own feitor to manage its operations. These field managers received annual salaries that averaged about 50$, which made their incomes roughly equivalent to those of the skilled workers at the mill (with the exception of the sugar master).

I must put the Engenho Sergipe accounts into perspective. Although on that estate the feitores were, for the most part, free men, on other estates the role of foreman or driver was filled by both slave and free, by black, mulatto, and white. By the late sixteenth century, it was apparent that both recent immigrants, who found this position a first step on the social ladder, and Brazilian-born mulattoes and mestiços, who saw it as a position of trust and authority, were employed as foremen and drivers. The pattern for whites was later described by the governor of Bahia, who complained in 1775 that there were few sailors because so many who arrived became tavern keepers or slave drivers.[17] Those who were talented and zealous usually married well and were on their way up. For a young immigrant arriving without kin or prospects, the role of foreman seemed a natural calling, since by virtue of their color and origin they possessed inherent characteristics that called for deference in Bahian society. Many learned, however, that driving slaves was no easy business – as planters were quick to point out. By the eighteenth century, many mills had turned to mulattoes as drivers and overseers.

Good overseers and drivers, slave or free, were always at a premium, and senhores de engenho lamented the lack of men with the requisite skills and disposition. Caldeira Brant, senhor of Engenho da Ponta in Cachoeira, wrote that a relative had discovered a mulatto slave who was so good as a feitor that if "half of what was said was true, the man could be canonized." The slave, valued at 600$, after a trial period of a few months, proved unsuitable for the task.[18] The position was also dangerous. In 1822, when the feitor of a Recôncavo engenho was killed by the slaves, an observer noted that this was no novelty.[19]

The driver's position of authority and continual contact with the slaves gave him power and sexual advantage, but his relatively low status also reduced social distance. Two legal actions involving paternity reveal much about the social position of the driver and his role in the sexual life of the plantation world. The first case involved a girl born to a parda slave at Engenho Mombaça. The father of the girl was the overseer of a cane farm owned by Colonel José Pires de Carvalho, the brother-in-law of Mombaça's owner. The overseer had often eaten at the big house at Mombaça where the slave woman served, and he had established a relationship with her. The overseer paid the woman's owner for the freedom of their child on learning that his mistress was pregnant, and the child was born free. But when the owner moved to another engenho, he took the slave woman and her free child with him. The overseer, meanwhile, married another woman. His illegitimate daughter later brought a suit over inheritance, in which she complained that her father "was an ordinary man who served an overseer and had no impediment to marry his mistress [a slave] if he had wished."[20]

Similar sentiments were expressed in the case of José Gonçalves Portela, a feitor in São Francisco parish who had "dishonored" a slave woman who then bore an illegitimate child. Years later, the child sued for paternal recognition, claiming that Portela had arrived in Brazil without shoes or socks (*descalço de pé e perna*) and had lived on his salary as a poor man. The child stated that there was nothing that kept Portela from marrying the woman if he had so desired, for at the time they were both single and "many others much better than Portela had married women of less esteem."[21] The outcome of the two cases need not concern us, but the fact that legal unions between slaves and free feitores could be imagined demonstrates the lack of social distance between the two. Despite the relatively high salaries indicated in the Engenho Sergipe accounts, the status of the feitor was low.

The Engenho Sergipe accounts are filled with references to specific payments to a wide range of artisans and craft workers. Often mentioned by name with reference to the length of service, task performed, and daily or piecework rate, the Sergipe accounts provide something of the human dimension in the relationship of craft workers to the mill. Accounts from the seventeenth century are particularly informative: "to João Fernandes stonemason for forty days he worked at the engenho at 400 réis" (1636); "to Amador Gonçalves mason for installing the kettles and other jobs at 640 réis" (1680); "to the caulker Françisco Pires for repairing the boats in the middle of the safra, 7$500" (1612). Sometimes the terse entries reveal small stories: "to João Fernandes, master smith for the sixteen months he served at the smithy in order to instruct the black master of it in some works he did not know how to do, and because the said black died, Fernandes remained the said sixteen months . . . at a rate of 40$ a year" (1669).

Recording practices are not consistent enough at Sergipe to document with security the turnover or circulation of the artisan labor force, but a close reading leaves some general impressions. Artisans appear and disappear with considerable frequency, indicating considerable movement among them. Moreover, since many payments are to artisans for relatively short periods of time, one suspects that they offered their services to a number of mills during a year. At times Engenho Sergipe employed carpenters, caulkers, and blacksmiths on a soldada basis and thus secured presumably exclusive service, but I suspect that an artisan willing to take the risk could earn more by dealing with a number of mills. The advantage of the soldada was security for the worker and probably an averaging out of costs for the mill.

In the payments made to artisans at Engenho Sergipe, the elements of a hierarchy of labor and a premium for skill and experience were clearly present. A carpenter earned less than a shipbuilder, who earned less than a boat caulker (*calafate*). The going rates for these trades in 1655 were 400 réis for the carpenter, 700 for the shipbuilder, and 740 for the calafate. These wage differentials remained relatively constant in the seventeenth and eighteenth centuries and indicated a ranking and valuation of particular labor skills. In addition, the rank definitions within trades also determined the level of compensation. In 1650, for example, a master shipbuilder (*carpinteiro da ribeira*) received 700 réis per day, an oficial half that amount, and an apprentice 200 réis; but ability and experience also played a role within the designations. In 1655, an apprentice in this craft received exactly one-half the daily wage of an experienced worker.

Although the artisans who worked at the engenhos were free or freed persons, they were also often themselves employers and slave-owners. Engenho Sergipe entries indicate that for many tasks labor was provided by an artisan, his helper, his apprentice, or his slave, and that the rate of payment differed accordingly. In the safra of 1645, for example, two calafates and a slave worked for nine days on the boats, "the men at 700 réis, the black at 320 per day." In 1680, Amador Gonçalves, a mason, had mounted some kettles, working for twelve days at 640 réis while his free workman (*obreiro*) had remained on the job for twenty-eight days at 500 réis. A young slave (*muleque*) who also worked received 100 réis for each of the ten days he labored. The engenho, theoretically at least, paid the artisan for the service of his slave. We do not know what portion, if any, the slave retained. But given the practice of allowing slaves to keep some part of their earnings, which was so common in the urban context in Brazil, one suspects that this also occurred among the artisan slaves.

These artisan salaries can be put in perspective by comparing them to the wages paid for unskilled field labor. In 1669, a free woman was paid 80 réis per day to work in the fields at Engenho Sergipe; compensation for a man was 100 réis at that time.[22] In 1714, the daily wage continued to be 100 réis per day, but in 1751 the câmara of Santo Amaro calculated the journal, or daily, rate for a slave at 6 *vintens* or 120 réis.[23] By 1802, freedmen were paid 160 réis a day for field labor at Engenho Buranhaem.[24] Thus a shipwright who earned 640 réis a day in the eighteenth century earned about five times the wage of a field hand. This ratio appears to have remained relatively constant throughout the colonial period.[25]

In addition to a wage scale that varied according to the type of labor performed, the skill or experience of the individual, and their legal status (slave or free), the Engenho Sergipe accounts, especially those of the seventeenth century, underline the existence of a racial and color hierarchy that also influenced the level and method of payment for labor. Terse bookkeeping entries sometimes note the racial designation of nonwhite employees as a justification of the rate paid for the work performed. In the labor market for artisans, these references to ascriptive characteristics are especially important in distinguishing the levels of compensation. In its original conception in the early sixteenth century, a labor force structured by race had been plausible. The Portuguese had envisioned a separation of tasks by race: whites in positions of skill and management, blacks as slave workers in the fields replacing Indians who became auxiliaries assigned to menial and intermittent tasks. Due to miscegenation and to the acquisition of skills by blacks, Indians, mulattoes, and mestiços, this theoretical order never became a reality. Occupational status provided nonwhites a means of social mobility and incomes considerably above those they might have expected as simple laborers, but the gradient of race and color and the prejudices associated with it were not totally ignored.[26]

We have already examined in Chapter 3 the role of Indians within the sugar economy and the transition from Indian to African labor in skilled as well as unskilled positions. By the seventeenth century, Indians most commonly appear in the Sergipe accounts as woodcutters, slave catchers, boatmen, and in other such jobs. Often they were paid in goods as well as money, usually cloth or manioc, and often on a monthly or task basis rather than by the day as were other workers. All this indicates attitudes about Indians as workers that placed them in a position distinct from European norms.

Whether these attitudes reflected the reality of Indian productivity and work habits, or simply European perceptions of them, is unclear. Nevertheless, in general, Indians' wages were only about 20 percent of other workers' for similar tasks. This differential existed for unskilled labor, but it was also maintained between Indian artisans and their non-Indian co-workers. Indian carpenters in 1628 earned between 40 and 75 réis a day, whereas other carpenters received between 320 and 500 réis for similar work. This devaluation of labor, like the general practice of not recording the names of Indian workers and of simply using the designation "indio," suggests that Indians were not judged to be equivalent to other members of society and remained in an inferior and subordinate position despite their acquisition of skills.

In the seventeenth century, the color of other nonwhite workers was also noted with some regularity at Engenho Sergipe. Entries such as "to Damião mulatto for the time he worked at the kettles" (1623); "to the crioulo calafate who worked nineteen days at the boats" (1636); and "to Alvaro mulatto kettleman" (1625) indicate that color was used to identify and classify workers. But as the mixed-blood and freed population grew, such designations disappeared within the accounting records. Moreover, the attainment of skills and experience that made a worker valuable to the engenho tended to suppress ascriptive and pejorative descriptions. The case of Alvaro the mulatto kettleman (caldereiro de melar) is instructive. In 1625, he was simply described as a mulatto and paid 24$ for the safra of that year. The following year, his salary rose to 25$, but he was still simply Alvaro mulatto. By 1627, he had become Alvaro Fernandes and while still paid 25$ was on his way up.[27] From this point on, the designation "mulatto" disappeared from the accounts, and he was simply called Alvaro Fernandes, receiving 30$ in 1629, 35$ in 1633, and 42$ in 1644. He worked only part of the safra of 1645 and apparently died or retired that year.

During the same period, Engenho Sergipe employed Pedro Alvares, a black carpenter. A man of apparent skill and energy, Alvares earned over 117$ in 1636 as a skilled craftsman, and in the following year he also earned an additional 57$ by selling firewood to the mill. Although the designation "black" always appeared next to his name, Alvares was among the top wage earners at Engenho Sergipe in these years.

Such success stories, tales of upward mobility, should not disguise the fact that they were set in a matrix of continuing discrimination on the basis of color. In the very years that Alvaro mulatto had become Alvaro Fernandes, Engenho Sergipe continued to pay a crioulo calafate 320 réis per day and white calafates 700, a difference of over 50 percent. In theory, Indians received less than blacks and they less than whites for the same service, but in practice this hierarchy was sometimes overcome by supply, demand, and skill.

By 1669, racial designations were no longer used in the Engenho Sergipe accounts in either descriptions of the permanent employees on soldada or of the artisan workers. We can probably assume that by that date, if not before, free people of color had become an integral part of the skilled work force so that the necessity of designating them by color no longer served its purpose. They constituted a very large proportion of the free population in the countryside and of the artisan class by the end of the eighteenth century. By that time, engenhos depended primarily on slave artisans and specialists and on large numbers of free and freed people of color to perform the specialized tasks of sugar production.

But the creation of social space for the colored artisans and skilled workers did not signify a disappearance of the hierarchy of color, nor did it alter the fact that social relations still took color into account. The Engenho Sergipe accounts are filled with entries for the payment of unskilled and occasional workers that are recorded solely by color or racial designation: "to the Indians who worked on the water course" (1633); "to a criuolo who worked five days on the boats" (1636); "for the money I gave to a mulatto" (1625). These payments were made in small amounts and in some cases are more in the nature of presents or gratuities than wages. Money paid to some Indians for capturing a runaway black (1629) and for a suit of clothes (1634), to a black to help him buy his freedom (1669), to pay for a mass for a dead slave (1654), and other such disbursements represented a way for the engenho both to acquire necessary services and work and to create paternalistic ties with slaves, dependents, and poorer neighbors. These small payments stimulated cooperation and rewarded it with such disbursements as 100 réis to a black who brought a present, money to blacks who loaded crates onto a ship or brought lumber to the engenho, and 320 réis to a slave who informed on the escape of another (1644). Out of such relations, converted into the language of accountancy, the fabric of sugar society was woven.

Although Engenho Sergipe's ecclesiastical ownership provokes questions about its typicality in the patterns of racial designation, occasional remarks in secular correspondence and in the few surviving accounts of lay properties confirm the trends noted at Sergipe. Engenhos Buranhaem and Cachoerinha are a case in point. Accounts made for those estates (1796–1800) did not note the racial designation of the artisans and specialists on soldada but did often comment on the color or legal status of occasional employees. All those who cut firewood for Buranhaem in 1769, for example, were paid 160 réis per day, but in the record distinctions were made between Mathias Pinto (presumably a white), "a forro," and a "preto forro."[28] By the end of the eighteenth century, planters saw themselves surrounded by a sea of "coloreds," the *criuolada*.[29] That perception intensified racial antagonisms and fears.

Wage levels

In an economy profoundly influenced by slavery, with a complex interweaving of free and slave aspects in its labor market creating a set of special circumstances, it is difficult to determine the exact meaning and level of wages. It seems clear that medieval concepts of moral theology influenced salaries through the concept of a just wage and that this, along with broad customary practices, tended to keep wages stable over long periods of time.[30] Adam Smith's observation that "in many places the money price of labor remains uniformly the same, sometimes for half a century together," seems borne out by the Engenho Sergipe data.[31] We must also remember that in Bahia, even today, wage earners often have many jobs, so a salary recorded in one place does not necessarily represent the worker's earning power.

Soldadas at Engenho Sergipe display a consistency over long periods of time. Nominal wages rose between 1574–78 and 1611 and then crested in 1622, surely an abnormal year, after which wages fell back to their 1611 levels. Table 12-1 gives the nominal wage levels of the Bahian sugar master, purgador, caixeiro, and others over roughly a century and a half. These salaries are "sticky," with long periods of un-

Table 12-1. *Wages paid or estimated for soldada employees on Bahian engenhos, 1611–1798 (in milréis)*

Occupation	Engenho Sergipe, 1611	Estevão Pereira, 1635	1688	Antonil	Engenho Sergipe, 1704–15	Salva-dor's Câmara, 1752	Engenho Buran-haem 1796–8
General overseer	110	100[a]	80	60			
Sugar master	140	140	100	100–20	115	100	100
Banqueiro	12	50	50	30–40	46	50	
Crater	40	40	50	30–50	50	50	50
Purger		40		50			50
Kettleman	30	100				35	25
Mill overseer			40	30–45	48	32	30
Field overseer	60	50		40–45	47[b]		
Doctor	30	30					
Skimmer	80						

[a] In addition, he received a barrel of wine (20$) and a meat ration valued at 16$ for a total of at least 136$.
[b] This is the average salary for all the field overseers.
[c] The document refers to this man as a forro; the wage thus may be depressed.
Sources: Engenho Sergipe, 1611: ANTT, CSJ, maço 14, n. 4. Estevão Pereira, 1635: *Anais do Musea Paulista* 4 (1931): 773–94. Antonil: André João Antonil, *Cultura e opulência do Brasil,* ed. Andrée Mansuy, (Paris, 1965), appendix III, 513–28. Salvador's câmara, 1688: Câmara to crown (12 Aug. 1688), *Cartas do Senado,* III, 62–73. Engenho Sergipe, 1704–15: ANTT, CSJ, maço 17, n. 28. Salvador's câmara, 1752: AHU, Bahia pap. avul., caixa 62. Engenho Buranhaem, 1796–8: ANRJ, caixa 406.

changing levels. There appears to have been a rise at the end of the sixteenth century and another in the mid–eighteenth century, but some of the variation in the Sergipe accounts, shown in Table 12-2, are due to changes in personnel.

Salaries seem to have been standardized for sugar specialists according to customary usage, and wages do not appear to have varied widely according to the availability of labor or the cost of living. This is not to say that market forces were without influence. Adjustments in productivity expectations, nonmonetary rewards, and other terms of contract may have changed in relation to changing economic situations; but such alterations cannot be traced. Instead, we can observe long periods during which soldadas remained unchanged. Moreover, the Engenho Sergipe soldadas appear to be at levels standard for other Recôncavo engenhos. Compare, for example, in Table 12-1 the various estimates with the actual disbursements made by Engenho Sergipe in the period 1704–14.[32] With allowances made for variations in size, the soldadas appear to be standardized from one mill to another as well as remaining stable for long periods of time.

From the detailed and continuous accounts of Engenho Sergipe for

Table 12-2. *Wages of sugar specialists and overseers at Engenho Sergipe, 1704–15 (in milréis)*[a]

	1704	1705	1706	1707	1708	1709	1710	1711	1712	1713	1714
Sugar master											
Manoel de Abreu	110										
Manoel Gomes		120	120								
Domingos Pinto				110							
João Rodrigues					120	120	120				
João Fernandes								111			
Manoel Carneiro									120	130	(73)-
Banqueiro											
José Pinheiro	45										
Pedro Gomes		48									
Bernardo Gomes			45								
unidentified				46				42			
Tomé Pereira					45						
Manoel Pereira						50					
Francisco de Brito							40				
José Lopes										45	45-
Mill overseer											
Gregorio Pires	50	50	50								
João de Castro				40							
Santos Pereira					48	inc					
Crater											
Rafael da Costa	50	50	50	50	50	50	50	50	50	50	50
Overseer of Fazenda grande											
Manoel Gonçalves	50	50									
Manoel Duarte			50	50	50	50					
Overseer of fazenda nova											
Lourenço Machado	46	46	46								
Manoel Gonçalves				40	45	45	45	45	45	50	50
Overseer of fazenda preguiça											
Antônio Nunes	43	43	43	43	43	43					
Manoel Luís							40	40	40	40	40-

[a] In this table, I have tried to indicate the wages paid to individuals in a number of occupations over the course of a decade. The table is designed to demonstrate the considerable turnover in some occupations. The wages for each individual only appear in the years that each served. A line of dashes indicates the absence of a man from the accounts.

1704–15, it is possible to examine the changing pattern of wages for specific individuals. Table 12-2 analyzes the personnel histories of a number of soldada occupations during this period. First, it is obvious that there was considerable turnover in certain positions and much stability in others. The same crater served the mill throughout the whole period, his wage never changing. Overseers in the fields changed every four or five years on the average, but the more important sugar specialists changed more often. During these eleven years,

Table 12-3. *Purchasing power of a carpenter's daily wage as measured in alqueires of manioc, 1622–99*

Year	Daily wage (réis)	6 days' wages	Manioc flour (réis/alqueire)	Number of alqueires equal to week's wages
1622	320	1,920	165	11.6
1644	400	2,400	336	7.1
1650	480	2,880	360	8.0
1680	500	3,000	–	–
1699	640	3,840	480	8.0

Source: Livros de contas, Engenho Sergipe.

Engenho Sergipe employed three different mill overseers at least, seven banqueiros, and six sugar masters. These last two offices were well paid; but heavy responsibility lay on those who accepted these positions, and a poor safra might mean dismissal. Conversely, there is little evidence that engenhos competed for able and skillful specialists by offering higher wages.[33] Second, fluctuations in the salary level assigned to different positions appear more frequently immediately after a change in personnel, indicating either a lower wage offered because of the lack of experience of a new man at the job or higher wages sometimes offered as premiums. Thus the soldada wages may be even more constant than the record shows.

Although soldadas remained little changed for long periods of time, journais or daily wages, though also sticky, changed with more frequency and showed an upward trend. The daily wage for unskilled labor for a man rose from 100 réis in 1670 to 120 in the 1750s and 160 by 1802.[34] Wages for carpenters, shipwrights, and other craft workers also demonstrated a strong upward tendency in the seventeenth and eighteenth centuries, but few gains were made in real income because of an even stronger rise in the general level of prices. In fact, despite a doubling of wages between 1622 and 1700, the actual purchasing power in terms of food was cut by a third. Table 12-3 shows the changes in the daily wage of a carpenter measured against the price of manioc flour, the dietary staple. The decline in buying power is clear. Recording practices from Engenho Sergipe do not allow similar calculations for the first half of the eighteenth century, but Mattoso's study of Salvador from 1750 to 1800 indicates that by the close of the century wage workers were once again suffering a loss in real income.[35]

Using the Engenho Sergipe accounts, Brazilian economic historian Mircea Buescu has calculated a nonweighted price index in an attempt to establish a general rate of inflation for the second half of the seventeenth century.[36] He determined that prices rose over 160 percent between 1650 and 1703, based on the Engenho Sergipe accounts for the first date and on Antonil's observations for the latter. By comparing the salaries of wage earners in the two years, he also estimated a general loss in buying power of between 20 and 35 percent during this period, a finding that parallels the data presented in Table 12-3. This evidence suggests that in a time of falling sugar prices and of difficulties for the sugar economy, planters transferred part of their decline in profits to their workers.

A loss in real income may, in fact, be one of the explanations of why during this period there were an increasing number of persons of color in artisan and specialist occupations at the engenhos. White immigrants, perhaps perceiving a loss in status and reward in these occupations, sought other opportunities. Freedmen in turn moved into the ranks of the salaried plantation employees, a process that, given the traditional discounting of their labor, probably contributed to a further suppression of wages.

Parallel to the loss of earning power, during the seventeenth century at Engenho Sergipe, two other processes or changes in the structure of the paid labor force took place that may be representative of changes in the industry as a whole. First, there was a tendency over time to reduce the number of employees paid on a yearly basis. In the early seventeenth century, sometimes as many as twenty-five people recieved soldadas. But by the early eighteenth century, that figure had been cut in half. Positions such as boatman, cowhand, water manager (*levadeiro*), kettle skimmer (*escumeiro*), and others were eliminated, their places presumably being taken by skilled slaves (see Figure 12-1). Even extremely important positions disappeared. Engenho Sergipe employed no purger after 1670, his functions being performed by skilled slaves or assumed as the duties of other employees. As late as 1654, Sergipe employed three different types of kettlemen – de melar, de meio, and de escumas – but by the end of the century, these positions had disappeared from its rolls. In part, the impetus for these changes originated in the effort of engenho administrators to reduce annual costs. At the same time, however, certain craft workers like the blacksmiths and specialized carpenters probably preferred to leave the soldada rolls and work on a piecework or daily basis; their services were always in demand, and better contract terms could be obtained on the open labor market.

The second process, one I have already noted, was the increasing presence of free blacks and mulattoes or of slaves as artisans, managers, and specialists at the engenhos. In the 1580s, an observer at Engenho Sergipe had stated that there (as at any similar engenho) about twenty whites were necessary for the mill's operation.[37] But the situation had changed by the seventeenth century. At Engenho Santana in distant Ilhéus, Father Felipe Franco complained in 1671, "These

Figure 12-1. Continuities: a kettleman photographed in the 1930s.

lands are not those of Madeira or even of Bahia, and to this exile of
Ilhéus comes no good sugar master and he, good or bad, is the only
white. All the other sugar workers are our blacks, worse than galley
slaves."[38] Engenho Santana was an extreme case, but Father Franco
had probably overstated the difference with Bahia. There, too, slaves
increasingly served in the specialist occupations alongside an ever-
growing number of free persons of color. In 1706, when the crown
tried to have six Bahian sugar masters sent to Maranhão, the governor
complained that sugar masters were already in short supply; for that
reason, many senhores de engenho used slaves in this position.[39] By
the eighteenth century, about 20 percent of the engenho slave forces
were artisan or fabrica slaves (see Table 6-2). They increasingly lived
and worked alongside a growing population of freedmen, freedwomen, and their descendants.

To summarize, the number and diversity of soldada employees declined over time, and with that reduction also came a decline in the real wages of salaried employees. The social composition and legal status of the engenho labor forces also changed as free whites who had usually filled the specialist and management roles in the sixteenth century were gradually replaced by either freedmen or slaves. In this process, the planters found that operating costs could be reduced, although the long-term effects on productivity and quality could not be calculated. Moreover, the opportunities presented to slaves and freedmen to become skilled engenho workers served as a means of labor control and incentive. Eventually, the planters would complain that the reason for their comparative disadvantage in the world sugar market was the ignorance and "rudeness" of the skilled slaves and colored freedmen who performed the specialized tasks of sugar making. Or, put in another way, the very classes the planters had created or promoted to economize in the short run had come to be a detriment to the industry's progress in Brazil.

Freedmen and freedwomen

Mulattoes and, to a lesser extent, crioulos were favored as house slaves, artisans, and sugar specialists. The favoritism showed to them was based on a complex intertwining of racial perceptions, personal attachments, and cultural bias. Mixed-bloods (pardos) were perceived as quicker to learn and better able to master the skills and artisan crafts of the sugar mill. When they were loyal, they could be very loyal. Antonil noted how often the banqueiro had as an assistant a trusted slave whose work was rewarded by a small salary that made him willing to serve.[40] Africans, on the other hand, were strangers, pagans, or at best recent converts, thought to be untrustworthy or dangerous, although there were certainly exceptions. Still, Table 6-2 indicates that color and place of birth influenced the assignment of tasks within the engenho slave force, favoring the Brazilian born and the lighter in color.

Of course, there were always those who found pardos' cultural proximity, ability to operate successfully in the white world, and upward mobility to be threatening. Father Luís da Rocha wrote from Engenho Sergipe in 1745, "In mulattoes one can have no confidence for in themselves they are more unfaithful than the very blacks."[41] Almost a century before, another administrator of that engenho had refused to buy some mulattoes, claiming that they would do more to disrupt the slave force than their work was worth.[42] Such opinions were not limited to the Jesuits. In 1711, the câmara of Salvador had opposed plans to use mulattoes and crioulo freedmen to fight against the French or guard the interior roads because, as the aldermen argued, in "these people . . . there is united inconstancy and interest."[43] In times of political unrest, such opinions reached levels bordering on paranoia. Luís dos Santos Vilhena, writing in the first decade of the nineteenth century, found mulattoes and crioulos to be "vagrant, insolent, uppity, and ungrateful," ruined by coddling and often the most likely to turn on their masters.[44] But despite such opinions and many other examples that can be shown of racial prejudice and discrimination, pardos and secondarily crioulos were favored in a variety of ways.

The chief advantage given to Brazilian-born slaves was favoritism in the granting of freedom. Manumission (*alforria*) was practiced throughout the history of Brazilian slavery, and although there was, in fact, no civil or canon legislation requiring or advocating manumission, except in extraordinary circumstances, custom and economics led masters to free slaves. Favored slaves were often designated in wills to be freed upon the owner's death, and many others received freedom as a bequest of the owner's in reward for loyal service or because of personal affection. These were the normal workings of a paternalistic system, the just reward for compliance and cooperation. Other slaves, however, were released from service when too old or infirm to continue work or were simply allowed to pay for their liberation.

Quantitative studies of manumission have now been done of a number of regions in Brazil, and at least three have centered on Bahia.[45] Certain patterns emerge from these studies that are useful to note here. First, twice as many women as men received their freedom. A large percentage of the manumissions involved children, and among them the sex distribution was more nearly equal; but after roughly age thirteen, women were favored. A large proportion of the manumissions were purchased, usually by the slave him- or herself, and this proportion varied over time, reflecting perhaps the utility of manumission as a stimulus to productivity. In Bahia, the percentage of paid manumissions rose from 35 to almost 50 in the period 1680– 1750. This was an era of difficulty for the sugar industry and the Bahian economy in general, and the increase of paid manumissions may indicate an effort by slaveowners to stimulate productivity during hard times by offering increased opportunities for freedom.[46] As in training for skilled occupations, mulattoes and crioulos were usually favored in the manumission process, receiving a disproportionate number of the grants. In the period 1684–1745, mulattoes received over 45 percent of the Bahian manumissions but constituted less than 10 percent of the slave population.[47]

Once freed, the former slaves found their opportunities limited by a variety of cultural and legal constraints and barriers, not the least of which was the fragility of the manumission grant itself. All manumissions were in essence revocable and dependent on the appropriate behavior of the former slaves. In 1812 Victoriano, a pardo freed by the planter Antônio Bittencourt Berenguer Cezar on his death, refused to pay respect to his former master's son, who then threatened to reenslave him "as was his right." Victoriano fled.[48] In disputes over property, ex-slaves became matters of contention. The pardo Pedro Gomes de Albuquerque, a freed slave, was seized on the death of his former master and taken to the engenho of a man who had claims on his master's estate.[49] Thus, although the gaining of freedom was desired and to that end slaves were willing to sweat and toil for years, once gained, freedom was often conditional and subject to a variety of limitations. This is what the Angolan Domingos Lopes da Silva discovered after obtaining his freedom. He went to work as a sugar specialist for a planter at 35$ a year, but when he demanded his salary, he was chained and branded. There was little he could do because the planter was "rich and powerful."[50]

The number of manumissions in a single year, the rate or probability of a slave obtaining freedom, has never been calculated for Bahia, but an estimate of about 1 percent per annum seems plausible given existing evidence. The chances for women, mulattoes, and skilled slaves were considerably better than one in a hundred, however. By the time of independence, in 1822, Bahia had a population of about 500,000, of which about a third were slaves and a half free people of color, freed persons, and their descendants. This element was growing rapidly in the late colonial period.[51]

Social positions

Although in the limited world of the engenhos, the small segment of skilled free employees constituted a labor elite, we must use that term with caution. Both in terms of social prestige and income, artisans and sugar specialists were far beneath the planters, whereas in status they were often perceived as not far above the slaves, especially if these free workers were persons of color. Artisans on the engenhos were far better off than the other workers and unskilled slaves, but even in comparison to their urban counterparts they were ranked relatively low. We know this from petitions of Brazilians seeking the title of familiar of the Inquisition, a position of considerable prestige because it certified orthodoxy and purity of blood and exempted the holder from certain fines and obligations. In Brazil, where opportunities for certified privilege were slight, such distinctions were in great demand. In the eighteenth century, only 95 persons, or about 4 percent of the 2,153 who sought the title of familiar in Brazil, were artisans. But with the exception of 4 coppersmiths and possibly some of the 8 carpenters, engenho artisans were not involved in these petitions.[52]

Using evidence from seventeenth-century Pernambuco, we can in fact establish some idea of the relative levels of income distribution

Table 12-4. *Average payment for selected occupations: special assessment for the dowry of Catherine of Bragança and the Peace of Holland, 1664–6 (Pernambuco)*

Occupation	Payment (réis)
Senhores de engenho	36,500
Cane farmer	5,160
General overseer	2,750
Sugar master	2,200
Banqueiro	2,250
Purger	1,220
Sugar journeyman	600
Overseer	525
Goldsmith	1,330
Blacksmith	710
Carpenter	685
Shoemaker	620
Potter	580
Mason	550
Tailor	490
Subsistence farmer	525
Fisherman	438

Source: "A finta para o casamento da Rainha da Grã-Bretanha e Paz da Holanda (1664–1666)," *RIAHGP* 54 (1981): 9–62. The document was edited and published by José Antônio Gonçalves de Mello.

among the various occupations in sugar-plantation society. Tax assessments made in relation to the dowry of Catherine of Bragança and the settlement with Holland (1664–6) allow us to see a hierarchy of income if we assume that these assessments were made according to real or expected income. In Table 12-4, we can see this distribution. Senhores de engenho paid seven times more than lavradores de cana, and they in turn paid almost twice as much as the general overseers, the top category of the salaried employees. Among the artisans, blacksmiths were the most taxed and presumably the wealthiest of the engenho craft workers. Small-scale subsistence farmers and fishermen were near the bottom of the income scale.

The social position of the salaried employees varied according to their occupation but also changed over time. The general overseers and administrators were employees of relatively high social position and were sometimes direct representatives of Portuguese nobles or of local aristocrats. Throughout the colonial period, their social standing remained relatively high. The sugar-making specialists had a different history. The first generation in the sixteenth century had been composed of men with experience in the Atlantic islands of Portugal; men like Baltesar Martins Florença, a sugar master born on Madeira who settled down in Cotegipe, or Gaspar Rodrigues, a sugar master who settled in Ilhéus. Sons followed fathers in these careers, and these positions represented opportunities for the kind of mobility we can see in the life of Gaspar Nunes Barreto, a blacksmith who became a planter on the Paraguaçu in the sixteenth century.[53]

By the mid–seventeenth century, such mobility appears to have been closed to a large extent. Moreover, by that period sugar specialists and artisans on the engenhos were increasingly Brazilian born and increasingly persons of color. This was a pattern quite distinct from that of the urban artisans, among whom the Portuguese born continued to predominate, comprising almost two-thirds of the total in Salvador around the beginning of the eighteenth century.[54] We do not know for sure the situation in the Recôncavo, but I suspect that even at this date the percentage of European-born artisans and overseers had already begun to decline.

A partial census of six rural parishes of Bahia made in 1788 reveals that free people of color constituted about 57 percent of the free population in the countryside and predominated as artisans and managers. Table 12-5 records the reported occupational structure by color for the parishes of Purificação and Rio Fundo.[55] Whites continued to control the sugar economy, composing all the engenho owners and more than 70 percent of the cane farmers. Pardos had penetrated into the lavrador class but were associated more with subsistence farming and fishing, as were the blacks. In the sugar-specialist and managerial roles, pardos held the most positions. In the office of administrator and general overseer, whites still had considerable advantage since these positions probably called for an ability to read and write. The presence of whites in the role of crater probably also rested on literacy because of the need to record the division of sugar between senhor and lavrador and to audit the shipments made to the port.[56] But in the other engenho positions, pardos and blacks held sway.

The predominance of people of color, especially pardos, was even more marked among the craft workers. More than 80 percent of the artisans recorded in these parishes were pardos or blacks. If such partial figures can be taken as indicative of the sugar-growing parishes in general, then whites continued to be important in only a few of the trades, composing about a third of the shoemakers and about 40 percent of the blacksmiths. The fact that smiths needed more capital to purchase raw materials for their shops probably kept the poorer pardos and blacks from entering this trade and thus left some room for continued white activity. The results of the census of 1788 indicate that by the end of the eighteenth century the classical tripartite color division

Table 12-5. *Distribution of occupations by color in Purificação and Rio Fundo parishes, 1788*

Occupation	White	Pardo	Black
Property owners or self-employed			
Senhor de engenho	19	0	0
Cane farmer	26	9	1
Subsistence farmer	7	5	6
Fisherman	0	6	1
Sugar-mill positions			
Mill administrator	1	1	0
General overseer	7	0	0
Overseer	0	6	0
Sugar master	0	8	3
Banqueiro	0	1	0
Kettleman	0	1	0
Crater	4	4	0
Artisans			
Blacksmith	5	6	1
Carpenter	2	22	4
Mason	0	2	0
Shoemaker	4	11	2
Tailor	1	11	0
Potter	0	1	0
Sawyer	0	2	0

of the sugar mills had come into being; white owners and administrators, mostly black slaves in the field, and an intermediate sector of skilled workers and tradesmen composed mainly of pardos.

The free colored artisans and workers had grown as an important segment of the plantation work force during the eighteenth century and had filled a number of economic and social niches of great importance in the plantation world. The skills they acquired were learned as an art, by experience and training, and they were greatly valued for these skills, if depreciated for their color. When at the close of the eighteenth century new technologies were introduced among Brazil's competitors in the Caribbean, Brazilian planters looked upon the "art" of their sugar specialists as a detriment and as a reason for Brazil's inability to compete on the world market. The thermometer, the principles of chemistry, and eventually the steam engine were scientific innovations for which the uneducated engenho artisans, and the specialists who depended on sight, taste, and smell, were unprepared. In Brazil, reformers appeared who advocated the introduction of scientific methods and innovations, all of which they felt were far beyond the capacity of the pardos and blacks in the skilled positions on the engenhos.

The sugar masters bore the brunt of this criticism. Luís dos Santos Vilhena lamented the total ignorance of sugar masters, "mulattoes and blacks so stupid that I never knew one who could read or write his own name, and even the whites in this profession differed not at all in education."[57] What improvements could be hoped for from such people? The Bahian sugar industry and slavery had created and trained an essential class of workers, and now that training and those workers were found lacking. Overseers and sugar masters who depended on experience and traditional practices were accused of ignorance and routinism.[58] Ignorance was linked to social condition. One observer complained in 1798 that sugar masters and purgers were unskilled and that anyone could call himself by these titles. Those who did so were usually of the lowest social strata, and the planters were at their mercy.[59]

The lack of regulation and control of the sugar specialists was a theme taken up by the strongest critic of the Bahian workers, Manoel Jacinto de Sampaio e Mello. Owner of the Engenho Filosofia in the Recôncavo and a leading exponent of the scientific reform of the sugar industry, Sampaio e Mello began in 1809 to publish a series of articles in the *Gazeta da Bahia* that eventually appeared in 1816 as the *Novo methodo de fazer o açúcar*.[60] He, like Santos Vilhena, also complained that though tailors and shoemakers had to pass an exam to be called masters, sugar masters were simply unconscious and lazy men who were masters only because they called themselves such. The sugar masters, he said, "like only their beloved kettles, and the bigger the better so they can have more time to sleep or to cut a swath in the senzalas." Making sugar was a science that demanded knowledge and care, it needed intelligent men, but instead it was in the hands of "ignorance, usually stupid blacks who sing but who lack measurement, rule, or proportion."[61] The sugar economy had created the class of colored sugar workers drawn from the ranks of slaves and freedmen, and now it held them responsible for Brazil's inability to compete. Ignorance and color were two sides of the same coin for the reformers and observers.

Reformers believed they had identified the problem, but planters found that solutions were not quickly found. Felisberto Caldeira Brant also believed that ignorance in the boiling and purging underlay the poor quality of Bahian sugar. In 1820, he made arrangements to bring in sugar masters from the Caribbean to teach the techniques used in Jamaica and Cuba.[62] Two arrived – one was a fake and the other, a drunk, died in three months. Caldeira Brant suggested that perhaps paying the sugar masters on a percentage basis would solve the problem, but he did not abandon the search for a foreign specialist. This led in 1821 to the hiring of John Gyles, who was brought to Engenho Tijuca to institute the Jamaica system.[63] Convinced of Gyles's ability and intelligence, Caldeira Brant gave him free reign. Gyles made various reforms, sent for an English mason, and asked for three youths from Portugal to be trained in planting cane, making sugar, and operating the still because the present workers (Brazilians) were worthless. All these steps met with Caldeira Brant's approval. But when the safra began, Gyles wanted to work for other engenhos, Caldeira Brant refused to pay him, and valuable harvest time was lost. The experience disillusioned Caldeira Brant about the use of foreigners as a way of reforming the engenhos. Brazil would have to seek its own solutions. The Bahian sugar economy continued to be a producer and a captive of the social relations that lay at its core.

CHAPTER 13

THE BAHIAN SLAVE POPULATION

This Bahia is a Land of Hottentots.

The count of Arcos (1765)

The slave class was always little prolific, the number of births being comparatively small.

Opusculo Agricola-politico (Bahia, 1874)

Slaves constituted the broad base of Bahian society, the bedrock on which it rested. By the beginning of the nineteenth century, about one-third of the captaincy's 500,000 inhabitants were enslaved; but in sugar-plantation zones, that proportion sometimes reached as high as 70 percent. We have already examined the nature of slave work, the characteristics of the plantation organization, and some aspects of master–slave relations. In this chapter, we will discuss the demographic features of the Bahian slaves in order to understand their life experiences and the range of opportunities and chances open to them. The use of a demographic approach is necessary because of the personal anonymity imposed on the majority of slaves by the documentary record. What remains is fragmentary, but it still contains enough information to suggest the conditions that Brazilian slaves endured. In the aggregated figures, we can perhaps recover some idea of personal experience.

From the gradual disappearance of Indian slavery in Bahia in the second and third decades of the seventeenth century until the end of the slave trade in 1850, the central fact of Bahian, and indeed Brazilian, slavery was the African origin of the majority of those in bondage. The unhealthy demographic regime characterized by a negative growth rate meant that to maintain, or in some periods to expand, the slave population, constant importation from Africa was required. Bahia became and remained a major terminus of the Atlantic slave trade, developing a local slave-merchant class and products, such as tobacco and cachaça, to trade on the African coast. The existence of an open slave trade, generally easy access to new slaves, and the constant arrival of Africans influenced the perceptions and actions of slaveholders and shaped the culture and attitudes of slaves. Despite the fine work of many scholars, the history of the Bahian slave trade is still to be written, and it suffers from a lack of documentation, especially for the period before 1700. It is a topic somewhat beyond the scope of this book; but because of its centrality in shaping the population of Bahia, we must briefly review its major outlines.

The slave trade

The slaves transported from Africa to Brazil in the sixteenth century came primarily from the area of the Senegambia, what the Portuguese called Guiné. A variety of peoples were caught up in the slavers' trade – Manjacas, Balantas, Bijagos, Mandingas, and Jaloffs, among others. The trade concentrated along the coast at a few spots, although transshipment through the Portuguese outposts at São Tomé and Cape Verde was common. The volume of the trade in this period is unknown, but Mauro's calculation of about 100,000 slaves exported for the whole of the sixteenth century for an average of 1,000 a year seems reasonable if we remember that very few came before 1550 and that the numbers between 1580 and 1600 probably exceeded 2,000 a year.[1] In part, this trade also included slaves shipped from the Congolese port of Mpinda and the area in contact with the kingdom of the Congo, with which the Portuguese also had a long-standing relationship. Increasingly, the Portuguese began to take slaves from the area south of the Dande River in the area that became known as Angola. By the 1620s, the Dutch estimated that Pernambuco alone took 4,000 slaves a year.[2] Bahia, with fewer engenhos, surely had a lower level of importation at that time, so an annual estimate of 2,500 to 3,000 is probably fair for its share.

By the time the Portuguese crown decided to colonize Angola in 1575, a slave trade was already flourishing in the area, and with the foundation of Luanda in that year, the Portuguese slave trade increased in this region. By the last decades of the sixteenth century, between 10,000 and 15,000 slaves from Guiné, the Congo, and Angola disembarked annually in Brazil. Luanda, Benguela, and Cabinda all developed into slaving ports during the seventeenth century as the center of activity shifted to the Angola region.[3] The famous phrase of Padre Antônio Vieira to the effect that "whoever says sugar says Brazil and whoever says Brazil says Angola" was actually a common expression. The connection between sugar and slavery, Brazil and Angola was obvious.

The period of the Iberian union (1580–1640) provided opportunities that led to intensified Portuguese slaving on the African coast, but it also created supply problems for the planters in Brazil. The connection with Spain not only provided access to iron and other trade goods that allowed the Portuguese to monopolize the slave trade in such areas as the upper Guinea coast; it also led to formalized contracts (*asientos*) to supply African slaves to Spanish-American ports.[4] The first of these was awarded to a Portuguese merchant in 1587, and between 1595 and 1640 at least 147,779 slaves were carried to Spanish America on vessels registered in Seville.[5] The demand for slave cargoes in Spanish America, where silver was paid for them, caused problems for Brazilian planters who could only offer sugar or other crops in exchange. Slave prices rose in Brazil, and there was a short-lived resuscitation of Indian enslavement in the period.[6]

More serious was the disruption of the slave trade caused by European rivals. The Dutch had attacked São Tomé in 1598–9, but the end of a twelve-year Spanish–Dutch truce in 1621 led to a series of attacks on Portuguese positions in Africa. El Mina fell in 1637, Luanda and Benguela in 1641, and although the latter ports were recaptured within the decade, Portuguese predominance on the African coast had been lost, especially north of the equator, where the Dutch allowed the Portuguese to trade on the Dahomey coast under license and regulations that favored Brazilian traders carrying tobacco from Bahia while limiting the importation of European goods carried by ships from Portugal.[7]

The warfare and political changes of the mid–seventeenth century had disrupted the patterns of the slave trade, but the ultimate outcome was a situation that favored the Bahian traders and promoted a relatively constant flow of slaves to the captaincy. Although the Portuguese crown insisted on trade with Guiné, Angola, or Mozambique, the Bahian merchants continued to trade with the Mina coast, paying the tax to the Dutch at El Mina and buying slaves with tobacco or the contraband gold that was coming from the Brazilian interior by the first decade of the eighteenth century. In the period 1701–10, 216 ships from Bahia called at the Mina coast.[8] Throughout the 1720s and 1740s, Lisbon and Bahia merchants jockeyed for advantage in the slave trade to Brazil. The Portuguese had created their own fort at São João Baptista de Ajuda (Whydah) in 1721, which despite an unstable relationship with the king of Dahomey, remained the central trading post on the African coast until about 1770. Around that date, a shift toward Porto Novo and Lagos in the Bight of Benin area of the West African coast began to bring out increasing numbers of Yoruba slaves, a result of the demand and of the internal wars in Yorubaland. This pattern continued into the opening decades of the nineteenth century until the English–Portuguese treaties of 1810 and 1826, which made the slave trade illegal north of the equator after 1815 and south of it in 1831.[9]

Both merchants and planters accepted the union between the slave trade and agriculture as a constant of colonial life. Tensions between these two groups intensified in the intermittent periods of shortage and high prices caused by foreign wars, competition from the West Indies or other regions of Brazil, and the usual conflicts of debtors and creditors, but most persons in Bahia realized the symbiotic relationship that tied the planters to the slave merchants. Few free persons in the captaincy would have disagreed with the special pleading of the Bahian merchants who wrote in the 1790s:

The happiness of these colonies consists in the growth of their agriculture which is always the result of the number of workers they possess. The arms of slaves – due to the lack of others – are those that cultivate the vast fields of Brazil; without them there would perhaps not be those things as important as sugar, tobacco, cotton, and the rest which are transported to the Motherland, and which enrich and augment national commerce and the royal treasury of Your Majesty. Any objections to the slave trade are attacks on the population, the commerce, and the income of Your Majesty.[10]

Later opponents of the slave trade like João Maciel da Costa or José Bonifacio were generally European-trained bureaucrats whose criticism began to appear only in the nineteenth century.[11] They met with little enthusiasm on the party of many Brazilians, so many of whom directly participated in the institution of slavery and by extension in the slave trade.

Leaving aside the history of the trade itself, its organization, its horrors, and its changes over time, there still remain two aspects that demand some attention in the context of Bahian slavery's internal development. First, the continuous history of the slave trade to Bahia and its geographical shifts in Africa meant that a constant stream of Africans arrived at the docks of Salvador and that, according to the historical moment, the majority came from different areas of the African coast. This meant, in effect, that in the sixteenth century peoples from the Senegambia predominated, in the seventeenth Angolans and Congolese, and in the eighteenth slaves from the Mina coast and the Bight of Benin. But despite the shifting areas of concentration, the Bahian slave population was always composed of a mixture of peoples. Even at the height of the Bight of Benin trade, from about 1780 to 1820, when Geges (Ewes), Nagôs (Yorubas), Tapas (Nupes), Ussás (Hausas), and other "Sudanese" peoples predominated among the Bahian slaves, about a third of the African-born slaves were Bantu peoples from Angola and central Africa. The twenty-six slave ships landing in Salvador in 1803 carried 6,992 slaves, of whom 555 (7.9%) died in passage.[12] Of those that arrived alive, approximately two-thirds originated on the Mina coast and the remaining third in Angola. This pattern seems to have been fairly typical for the eighteenth and early nineteenth centuries, with Angolans comprising a quarter to a third of the imports.

Planters had their prejudices and preferences in regard to various African peoples, but these varied over time and reflected fashion and availability. Angolans were preferred in the seventeenth century as

hard workers but were depreciated in the eighteenth as "natural enemies to work."[13] The planter Caldeira Brant could complain in 1819
that "the blacks from Mozambique are the Devil," but that did not
prevent him from buying two at that moment.[14] In general, planters
bought what was available, and although they held their prejudices,
when need demanded they seemed to purchase what slaves were
available in the market. Age, health, and sex were certainly more important determinants of a slave's purchase price and desirability than
his or her ethnic origins. Moreover, except for the preference shown to
mulatto and crioulo slaves in manumission and training for skilled
jobs, it is difficult to discern a pattern of preference shown to African-
born slaves on the basis of their origins.

From the slaves' perspective, the constant dependence on the African slave trade meant that cultural forms and traditions were continually reinforced by new arrivals. We cannot know if this process slowed
the pace of acculturation to European norms, but undoubtedly African
practices and traditions persisted in the colony. The present-day African culture in Bahia, which is heavily Yoruba in origin, dates from the
late eighteenth century. Before that, other African traditions existed, of
which only a few hints remain in the surviving documentation. Nuno
Marques Pereira's work of 1728 mentioned *calundus* or rites of divina-
tion and *quinguilla* or taboos, both of which are Angolan in origin. He
complained that such "gentile rites" were condoned by Brazilian
planters in order to get along with their slaves.[15] When in the late
seventeenth century a large escaped slave community was formed at
Palmares, its inhabitants called it *Angola janga* or little Angola. The
image of Africa was still vivid for many slaves, and that fact was not
lost on the masters. As we shall see, a strong debate developed between two schools of slaveowners and royal officials: those who
thought that permitting slaves to maintain their African cultures was a
positive way of stimulating differences among them and thus an effective social control, and those who thought that such cultural persistence stimulated rebellion.[16]

A second aspect of the slave trade that has some importance for our
subsequent discussion is its volume. Figures for the sixteenth and seventeenth centuries are at best only estimates. Mauricio Goulart's calculations of about 2,000 slaves a year to Bahia in the first half of the
seventeenth century for a total of 100,000 in that period, although like
all his estimates on the low side, seem in keeping with the size of the
sugar industry. But the growth of the tobacco and subsistence-crop
sectors later in the century makes calculations based only on the sugar
industry's needs difficult.[17] The problem becomes impossible with the
opening of the interior gold fields after 1695. One estimate for the last
decade of the seventeenth century places the annual figure at about
6,000 slaves from the Mina coast alone. This would suggest a total of

Table 13-1. *Estimates of the Bahian slave trade, 1681–1830*

Year	1. Alden estimate	2. Goulart estimate	3. Verger estimate	4. Eltis estimate
1681–90			17,200	
1691–1700			60,800	
1701–10		83,700	86,400	
1711–20		83,700	67,200	
1721–30		79,200	63,400	
1731–40		56,800	49,000	
1741–50		55,000	39,200	
1751–60	63,500	45,900	34,400	
1761–70	29,500	38,700	36,000	
1771–80	31,500	29,800	30,000	
1781–90	24,000	24,200	32,700	
1791–1800	39,000	53,600	53,100	70,500
1801–10		54,900	72,900	75,400
1811–20			59,000	41,400
1821–30			51,800	50,200

Sources and explanation: Column 1 is from Dauril Alden, "Late Colonial Brazil, 1750–1807," *CHLA*, II, 610–12; he bases his estimates on a variety of sources. I have taken Alden's quinquennial yearly figures and multiplied them to provide decennial totals. Columns 2 and 3 are taken from Patrick Manning, "The Slave Trade in the Bight of Benin, 1640–1890," in Henry A. Gemery and Jan S. Hogendorn, eds., *The Uncommon Market. Essays in the Economic History of the Atlantic Slave Trade* (New York, 1979), 107–41. Column 4 is based on David Eltis, "Imports of Slaves into the Americas, 1781–1867" (unpublished paper). For the period after 1810, I have accepted his estimate, which includes ships known to have disembarked unknown numbers of slaves but for which he has made a calculation based on average ship tonnage.

8,000–9,000 annually if Angolan imports are included. These levels reflect the tentative recovery of the sugar economy after 1689, the growth of other agricultures, and the opening of the mines.

Although figures for the first two centuries of the Brazilian slave trade are only rough estimates and guesses, eighteenth-century records, despite gaps and discrepancies, are more complete. Patrick Manning's estimates of exports from the Mina coast to Bahia in Table 13-1 reflect the decline of the sugar economy between 1730 and 1790.[18] Slave imports in these years fell to levels of 3,000 to 4,000 a year. There was probably some recovery by the 1780s and certainly after 1790, when the rebellion in Haiti and its destruction as a sugar island created new opportunities for Brazilian sugar producers along with a new demand for laborers. Another set of estimates for the period 1780–1830 is available in the work of David Eltis. His figures show a rise in Bahian slave imports from 20,300 for the period 1786–90 to 34,300 for 1791–5 and 36,000 for 1801–5. These levels were generally maintained until 1821–5, when disruption caused by Brazilian independence and British abolitionist pressure caused a decline of the trade. But between

Table 13-2. *The transatlantic slave trade to Bahia as recorded in contemporary sources, 1731–1810*

		Mina			Angola	
Year	Ships	Total slaves	Annual average	Ships	Total slaves	Annual average
1731–33[a]	19	5,953	5,103	9	3,169	2,716
1733[b]		2,749	2,998		1,850	2,018
1741–44[c]		13,425	4,475			
1742–43					2,616	
1745–6[d]		4,872				
1746–8[e]					3,820	2,084
1750–1[f]	15	7,660	4,145			
1750[g]	8	3,488				
1751	15	4,028				
1752	8	3,649				
1753	12	4,288				
1754	5	1,843				
1755	10	3,853				
1759[h]		4,209				
1760		3,319				
1761		4,071				
1762		4,021				
1763		3,427				
1764		2,651				
1765		2,863				
1785–7[i]		12,233	4,077			
1792		2,934			3,327	
1793		3,055			3,615	
1794		4,558			3,498	
1795		4,170			2,910	
1796						
1797		4,600			2,850	
1798		4,903			2,151	
1799		8,200			300?	
1800[j]		6,098			2,085	
1801[k]		5,250			1,450	
1802						
1803		5,486			3,250	
1804		4,214			652	
1805		4,615			1,747	
1806		6,322			2,717	
1807		6,361			2,140	
1808		5,443				
1809		7,348			95	
1810		7,225			893	

Sources and explanation: Data for the different years, noted in table with superscripts *a* through *k*, from AHU, Bahia pap. avul., unless otherwise noted: (*a*) 4 Dec. 1731 to 22 Jan. 1733, caixa 48; (*b*) Jan. to Nov. 1733, caixa 44; (*c*) 1741–4, 22 Nov. 1742 to 29 Sept. 1743,

1826 and 1830, Bahia's slave trade reached new heights, with close to 10,000 slaves a year arriving.[19]

Modern estimates such as these sometimes differ considerably from the contemporary historical record, as Table 13-2 demonstrates. These records usually suggest lower figures than modern estimates. For example, the tax records of Bahia's customshouse recorded the entrance of 40,757 slaves from the Mina coast in the period 1725–44, whereas the estimates of Goulart and Manning are considerably higher.[20] This pattern is common. In any case, we should observe the secular trend of the trade rather than the specific numbers, which remain incomplete and questionable. Here the general pattern of stagnation from the 1750s to the 1770s followed by periods of growth after 1785 seems clear. Imports, even during the height of the Mina and Bight of Benin trades, always included some slaves from the Angolan ports.

Finally, it must be remembered that not all slaves arriving at Salvador remained in Bahia, especially during the mining boom from 1700 to 1760. A report of 1763 estimated that one-third of the slaves landed were sent to the mines. In the 1780s, persons moving slaves to other captaincies were forced to post a bond guaranteeing that the slaves would not be taken to foreign colonies. In 1798, long after the mining boom had subsided, 168 slaves were sent from Salvador to the mines of Minas Gerais, Goias, and southern Bahia. Interestingly, Angolas were favored for reexport. Between 1778 and 1798, 2,844 slaves were sent from Salvador to the sertão: 634 Minas; 47 Nagôs and Geges; and 2,163 Angolas, Benguelas, and Congos.[21] Such reexports made calculations of Bahian productivity or slave mortality based on slave-trade figures highly problematical.[22]

In short, throughout the colonial era, the trade remained relatively open and responded to planter need despite the vicissitudes of war and politics in the Atlantic. The planters could thus generally depend on adequate replacements from Africa at affordable prices, although there were sometimes periods of very sharp price increases. Drawing on a variety of ports from the Senegambia to Angola and occasionally from Mozambique, the slave trade to Bahia introduced a variety of peoples so that although the slave population of the captaincy was always predominantly African, a wide variety of cultures were present.

Sources and explanation for Table 13-2 (*cont.*)

caixa 49; (*d*) caixa 59; (*e*) 15 Oct. 1746 to 1 July 1748, caixa 55; (*f*) 18 March 1750 to 30 Dec. 1751, caixa 30, 2d. ser. uncat.; (*g*) 1750–5, ABP, Ord. reg. 54, 400–5; (*h*) 1759–65, certificate of 26 Nov. 1765, cited in Luís Vianna Filho, "O trabalho do engenho e a reacção do índio-Estabelecimento da escravatura africana," in *Congresso do Mundo Português*, 19 vols. (Lisbon, 1940), X, 11–29; (*i*) 1785–99, documents 15.151 and 16.157 in BNRJ, *Exposição*, as cited in Vianna Filho, "O trabalho;" (*j*) 1800, APB, Cartas do governo 141; (*k*) 1801–10, AMS, Livro de visitas de embarcações 182.1, as cited in Vianna Filho, "O trabalho," 127.

Sex, age, and origins

Bahia's dependence on the African slave trade throughout the colonial period created two characteristics of the slave population that had broad social and demographic effects on the history of slavery in the Recôncavo. First, from the initiation of the trade to Bahia and Brazil in general, males were imported in larger numbers than females. We do not have adequate data from the seventeenth century to determine the degree of this imbalance in those years, but studies of eighteenth-century slaving indicate that in all the transatlantic slave trades there was imbalance in favor of men. To some extent, the predominance of men may have been due to planter preference and to the fact that, in Brazil at least, little emphasis was placed on a woman's childbearing capacity, as we shall see. There is also some evidence, however, that African suppliers were less willing to make women and children available to the Europeans.[23] Second, in any case, children under thirteen probably constituted no more than 2 to 6 percent of the slaves carried in the trade to Bahia and women probably about 30 to 40 percent. It should be emphasized that these estimates are based on patterns found in the slave trade to Brazilian ports other than Salvador, particularly Rio de Janeiro, Pernambuco, and São Luiz, for which the documentary record is much better. Nevertheless, given the patterns of age and sex distribution that can be observed on the Bahian plantations, there is no reason to believe that Bahia differed in this respect from the other Brazilian terminals of the slave trade, although the imbalance was probably worse on sugar plantations than elsewhere.

The sex ratio on Bahian engenhos (expressed as the number of males divided by the number of females times 100) seems to have been consistently high throughout the colonial period. Materials from the late sixteenth and seventeenth centuries are few, but Table 13-3 presents the age and sex structures of a number of early Bahian plantations. Three lists are presented from Engenho Sergipe. In 1591, it was owned by the count of Linhares and still was worked predominantly by Indian slaves. In 1626, it was a Jesuit property and had just suffered from the Dutch attack on Bahia in the previous year. In 1638, it was again in secular hands, having been sold to Pedro Gonçalves de Mattos. The engenho of Antônio de Sá Dória located on the island of Itaparica was a secularly owned estate, as was the cane farm of João Mattos de Aguiar, whereas those of São Bento and do Matto were both property of the Benedictines of Salvador. All these estates, both secularly and religiously owned, demonstrated a strong imbalance between the sexes in favor of males.

This same pattern appears again in plantation lists from the eighteenth century. In a government report after the sequestering in 1739 of nine plantations belonging to the Rocha Pitta family, a list of resi-

Table 13-3. *Engenho and fazenda de canas slave forces*

Region	Source	Type of property		Children		Adults		Elderly		Total	Sex ratio	% children (0–13)
				M	F	M	F	M	F			
Santo Amaro	A	Engenho Sergipe	1591		43	64	39	–	–	146	141	29
	B	Engenho Sergipe	1626	5	3	28	18	23	12	89	167	9
	C	Engenho Sergipe	1638	5	6	41	25	2	3	82	141	6
Itaparica	D	Engenho Sá Doria	1662	5	2	23	10	–	–	40	233	18
S. Francisco	E	Engenho S. Bento	1666	15	11	48	41	–	–	115	121	23
Itapororocas	F	Engenho do Matto	1666	13	9	21	–	–	–	71	137	30
Patatiba	G	Fazenda Mattos de Aguiar	1685	–	–	37	11	1	–	48	336	–
Jaguaripe	H	Fazenda Querado	1631	2	2	7	3	1	2	17	143	24

Sources: A, ANTT, CSJ, maço 13, n. 4; B, ANTT, CSJ, maço 14, n. 52; C, ANTT, CSJ, maço 30, f. 1040; D, ASCMB, Liv. I do Tombo, fs. 147–85; E and F, ADB/CSB 136, fs. 47–70; G, ASCMB, Liv. I do Yombo, fs. 491v.–502v.; H, ASCMB, Liv. I do Tombo, f. 118.

Table 13-4. *Creole and African slaves at nine Bahian engenhos, 1739*

Engenho	Creoles[a] M	F	Angola[b] M	F	Mina[c] M	F	% African	Total M	F
São Bras	12	7	12	5	9	17	69.4	33	29
Pitanganha	14	6	8	1	42	40	81.3	65	47
Acotinga	16	7	7	3	7	18	60.3	30	28
Matoim	21	12	5	2	24	24	65.9	50	38
Pindobas	9	3	9	2	24	48	87.4	42	53
Sapocaya	3	5	2	2	14	17	81.4	19	24
Caboto	6	9	3	1	15	23	73.7	24	33
Pojuca	4	1	14	7	27	14	92.5	45	22
Cornubuçu	1	0	0	0	12	11	97.1	13	11
Total	86	50	60	23	174	212	77.4	321	285
(percent male)	(53.2)		(72.3)		(45.1)			(52.9)	

[a]Includes crioulos, mulattoes, mestiços. [b]Includes Angolas, São Tomés, Benguelas, Congos, Gagos. [c]Includes Minas, Geges, Calabars, Ardas.
Source: AHU, Bahia pap. avul., caixa 90.

Table 13-5. *Sex ratios at engenhos and cane farms in Bahia, 1710–1827*

Property type	African M	F	Sex ratio	Brazilian M	F	Sex ratio	Overall sex ratio
Engenhos	660	257	256	262	196	134	199
Cane farms	146	115	126	146	115	126	126

Source: APB, sec. jud. (Data Set A).

dent slaves was made. The results are presented in Table 13-4. Once again, an imbalance can be noted, although it was only 112 despite the fact that over three-quarters of the slaves were African born. By the beginning of the nineteenth century, it would seem that the imbalance had become even more extreme. Six Bahian engenhos examined in 1816 demonstrated a sex ratio of 275 males for every 100 females and an age structure in which only 14 percent of the slaves were children under the age of eight. This pattern for the end of the colonial era is also confirmed by a study based on fifty-three inventories and wills drawn from the periods 1805–6 and 1810–11 in the city of Salvador.[24] The combined sex ratio during these two periods was 193. A survey of 1,913 slaves listed in engenho and cane-farm inventories contained a similar overall sex ratio of 185, varying from a low of 123 in the period 1710–50 to a high of 233 during the expansion of the sugar industry after 1793.[25] Table 13-5 demonstrates that in the eighteenth century the sex ratio was higher on the large plantations than on the cane farms. Engenhos, with their constant demand for field labor as well as a need for skilled and semiskilled workers, had twice as many men as women, whereas the fazendas de canas had between 20 and 30 percent more men than women. Naturally, the more African the population, the higher the sexual imbalance. Only in the period 1751–89, characterized by depression and a decline in the African slave trade, were the sex ratios of African and Brazilian-born slaves about the same. During this period, the percentage of Africans on Recôncavo properties was at its lowest. The more African the population, the less the dependence on natural growth, the higher the sex ratio.

The proportion of mulattoes and other racial mixtures among the slaves is in some ways an index of the degree to which the slave population is native born. Slaves of mixed ancestry, usually grouped under the designation of pardos, in Bahia were always a small minority of the captaincy's slave force. Our sample of Bahian rural slaves contained only 8.4 percent of mixed ancestry, and even admitting a higher rate of manumission for such slaves, pardos were probably never more than 10 percent of Bahia's slave force in the colonial period.[26] In captaincies less directly dependent on the slave trade, that figure was considerably higher. Throughout the period 1600–1820, Brazilian-born blacks (crioulos) and Brazilian-born pardos never seem to have made up more than one-third of the Bahian slave force.

The predominance of Africans and of males was accompanied by an age structure characterized by few children. Information on slave ages is often difficult to obtain. Aside from the usual problem of age "heaping" (rounding ages off to the nearest five or ten), ages ascribed to slaves, especially those born in Africa, were at best simply a planter's guess or estimate based on appearance. Ages for children under ten were often recorded with care, but after that age, far less attention was given to age until a slave became "old," a term used sometime around fifty years of age, depending on physical condition. For the historian, it is often possible to identify the very young and the very old on slave lists. But those in between remain a problem. In colonial Brazil, various systems of descriptive age categories were used by slave traders and planters to overcome the problem of affixing a numerical age to slaves.[27] In Bahia, a *cria de peito* was a nursing child one year old or younger, and a *cria de pé* was a nursing child able to walk. *Menino* and *menina* were used for young children up to eight or so. *Muleque (mulequa)* was applied to children up to thirteen or fourteen in general, although definitions varied. The Jesuits of Engenho Santana in 1753, for example, listed muleques up to sixteen and muleques grandes up to twenty.[28] The term *rapaz* or *rapariga* (boy or girl) was often used for adolescents, but it too was subject to a variety of uses. In my analyses here and elsewhere, discussions of age will be imprecise because of these problems; but in general, despite the "fuzziness" at the edges of the age categories, it will be possible to discuss the slave population in terms of children up to eight or thirteen, adults fourteen to fifty, and the elderly fifty and above.

All the information available thus far confirms the impression that the percentage of children on the plantations of Bahia was very low. In a population of high mortality that was maintaining itself by natural growth, we would expect to find about one-third the population below the age of fifteen.[29] At none of the engenhos or fazendas listed in Tables 13-3 and 13-4 is such an age distribution apparent. In fact, the highest percentages of children are achieved at Engenho Sergipe in 1591, an estate still worked predominantly by Indians, or at the two Benedictine engenhos in the 1660s, which were noted for their attempts to sponsor a self-generating slave force.[30] Six Bahian engenhos in 1816 had only 14 percent of their slaves under eight, and even if the age boundary is extended to fourteen years of age, that figure probably would not rise to 20 percent. In our survey of rural slaves, only 13 percent fell into the categories of children under fourteen years of age.[31]

The ratios of age and sex that I have just described for Bahia seem to have characterized other sugar-growing regions of Brazil as well. A survey of fifty-one engenhos in the parish of Serinhaem, Pernambuco, made in 1788 revealed that of the 3,829 slaves, only 18 percent (696) were below the age of eight. The sex ratio among these children was 109; but among the adults it was 221, reflecting the patterns in the slave trade and the labor requirements of sugar plantations. These ratios closely parallel those observed in Bahia.[32]

In summary, taking a long view of the period from the late sixteenth to the early nineteenth century, the general patterns of the Bahian slave population seem clear and, although the information we have is spotty, it is in no way contradictory. The Bahian slave population was always heavily foreign in origin, probably averaging about 70 percent African from 1600 to the end of the colonial era. It was also heavily male, with sex ratios of about 130 or 150 for the captaincy as a whole and much higher ratios of 200 or even 300 on engenhos and cane farms. Dependence on the Atlantic slave trade, in which few children were shipped; the shortage of women on the plantations; and, as we shall see, low fertility, high infant mortality, or both – all created a population in which there were few children relative to the rest of the slave population.

When we examine the eighteenth century not as a whole but in chronological periods according to the situation of the Bahian economy, some variations in the patterns of the slave population can be seen that shed light on the basic outlines of Bahian slave demography. The period 1710–50 was marked by some recovery after the disruption caused by the gold rush to Minas Gerais and the agricultural crisis of the 1680s. An active slave trade between Salvador and the Mina coast was established by the 1720s, and a fleet system from Lisbon to Bahia and back regularized the export of sugar and tobacco to Europe. By 1750, however, a period of depression or stagnation began to set in, despite the efforts of the royal government to overcome these problems. Both the agricultural output of the captaincy and the volume of the slave trade decreased in this period. There was some recuperation by the 1770s and 1780s, but it was really after the great slave rebellion on the French sugar island of Saint Domingue (Haiti) in 1792 that the economy of rural Bahia began to expand again.[33] With a new demand for sugar created by the elimination of Saint Domingue from the marketplace, a feverish expansion of production took place in Bahia, where it was accomplished by a great increase in the volume of the slave trade. Between 1798 and 1807, about sixty thousand African slaves arrived at the docks of Salvador.[34]

This new wave of African arrivals exacerbated the patterns that had long existed in the Bahian slave population and cut short any possibility that this population might begin to approach an age and sex configuration that would encourage demographic stability or growth. The sex ratio in the period prior to 1790 was 207, an imbalance due to the importation of Africans, who continued to make up about two-thirds of the Bahian slave population. The importation of African adults, the imbalanced sex ratio, and perhaps a low fertility rate were all contributors to the relative lack of children. There was less than one child under fifteen to every adult slave. After 1750, the proportion of Africans in the population had declined about 10 percent as the trade had slowed. If this pattern had continued, the sex ratio in favor of males would have gradually fallen as the proportion of Brazilian-born slaves had grown. This never really took place in Bahia, which as a principal terminus of the transatlantic slave trade and a major zone of export agriculture was always tightly tied to the African supply lines.

After 1793, with the suddenly available new opportunities for planters, all the old patterns were reinforced or exacerbated. As Table 13-6 demonstrates, the ratio of Africans in the population rose to new heights as the wave of slaves inundated the captaincy. The heavy importation of Africans, most of them young adult males, caused an increase in the sex ratio and a fall in the percentage of children in the slave population. From a demographic standpoint, all of these features were negative. The information contained in Table 13-5 leads us to suspect that the sex and age ratios in this period were worse on the engenhos than in the captaincy as a whole.

We can test our conclusions about the structure of the Bahian slave population by examining that of the neighboring captaincy of Sergipe de El-Rey. In areas less closely tied to the export economy or having less access to the Atlantic slave trade, we would expect to find lower

Table 13-6. *Sex, origin, and age of the Bahian slave population, 1710–1827*

	Male	Female	Sex ratio	African ratio	Child ratio (children/ adults)
1710–89					
African	440	212	207	171	.47
Brazilian	170	144	118		
Totals	610	356			
1790–1827					
African	469	164	226	216	.32
Brazilian	173	119	145		
Totals	642	283			

sex ratios, fewer Africans, more crioulos and pardos, and more women and children than in Bahia. These conditions are in fact what seems to have existed in Sergipe de El-Rey just north of Bahia. A census made in 1785 of plantations in the sugar-growing district of Ribeira de Vazabarris at the mouth of the Cotinguiba River revealed that that area, a sugar-plantation zone but somewhat off the major axis of the Atlantic slave trade, had a sex ratio of 119, well below that of the Recôncavo.[35] To a large extent, that lower sex ratio was due to the high proportion of Brazilian-born slaves in the population. Africans made up only one-third of the Ribeira slave force, whereas in Bahia they comprised about 60 percent of the total, even in this period of depression. While the African-born slaves in Sergipe de El-Rey had a sex ratio of 143, that of the native born was only 107. In comparative terms, there was an excess of 185 males for every 1,000 females in Ribeira de Vasabarris, whereas in the Recôncavo sugar areas there was an excess of 1,070 males for every 1,000 females. (See Table 13-7.)

The situation I am describing for this one district of Sergipe de El-Rey in 1785 seems to have characterized the captaincy as a whole and does not appear to have altered in the period after 1790. Census records for the period 1825–30 also reveal a sex ratio of 110 among the slaves.[36] Moreover, as on the Ribeira de Vazabarris list, the 1825–30 census shows that about a quarter of the slave population was pardo. This is a much higher proportion of slaves of mixed ancestry than existed in Bahia and is an indication of the dominance of native born among the Sergipe de El-Rey slaves. These census returns do not provide good information on the age structure of the slave population, but we suspect that it was considerably younger than that of Bahia. By 1834, pardos were fully one-third of the Sergipe de El-Rey slaves.[37]

Thus far, we have discussed a series of demographic features that set the parameters of Bahian slavery and provided the contours within which decisions made by both slaves and slaveowners were cast.

Table 13-7. *Sex and ethnic origins of the slave force, Ribeira de Vazabarris, Sergipe de El-Rey, 1785*

Origin	Male		Female		Sex ratio	African ratio
Brazilian born (66.4%)						
Crioulo	166		152			
Mulatto	69		70			
Mestiço	19		13			
Cabra	10		10			
Totals	264	(51.8%)	245	(48.2%)	107	
African born (33.6%)						
Mina	41		26			
Angola	106		77			
Gege	1		0			
Congo	2		0			
Benguela	2		3			
Totals	152	(58.9%)	106	(41.1%)	143	.507
	(54.2%)		(45.8%)			

Source: APB, Cartas ao Governo 188.

Although these features of the Bahian slave population provided a context, they were themselves not necessarily givens but, rather, the result of social and cultural choices made by masters and slaves – influenced, to be sure, by the conditions of labor, climate, and morbidity under which both lived. Given the nature of the documentary record, it is extremely difficult to separate or place relative weights on the various demographic, economic, social, and cultural forces that created the structure of slavery in Bahia. At this point in our discussion, it is important to bring the topics of birth and death into consideration, for these were "vital" considerations for both masters and slaves – as well as for slavery as an economic system and slavery as an institution that determined the lives of so many Bahians. Fertility and mortality are the classical subjects of demographic analysis, but our treatment of them will be placed in a social and cultural context that, though complicating the discussion, may also clarify it by bringing us closer to the reality of the complex interaction of masters and slaves.

Fertility and marriage

In 1623, a Father Matias reported with pride from Engenho Sergipe that he had expelled some whites who had congregated at the plantation and had thrown the slave quarters into turmoil.[38] At night, these men had by force or seduction slept with a number of slave women and caused general unrest among the slaves. Some believed that this situation explained why there were so few births at the engenho. It was said that the slave women feared the anger of the slave men and thus refused to bear mulatto children. Instead, they took "some things" that caused them to abort.

Father Matias's brief statement underlined, unknowingly to be sure, three problems that have concerned historians of the slave experience. First, the fact that there were so few births at the engenho was a central problem of Brazilian slavery and was not limited to Engenho Sergipe. Historians and demographers have suggested that the imbalanced sex ratio introduced by the slave trade, exacerbated by a preference for manumitting females, and extremely high levels of infant mortality were the major factors in the negative natural growth rate of the Brazilian slave population. Father Matias, however, touched on another aspect of the problem, a lack of births itself caused in this case by intentional abortion practiced by slaves but that other historians have seen as a result of late age of marriage, unstable unions, and other social and demographic causes. Third, his reference to the anger of the slave men raises the question of the position of the slave as father and husband or brother within the context of slave family life. I shall defer a discussion of this last question to the following chapter, but it is necessary to point out here in the context of fertility that formal church-sanctioned marriages were rare among the slaves and that rates of illegitimacy were very high among them.

Planters in nineteenth-century Brazil sometimes discussed the benefits of allowing consensual unions among the slaves as long as they did not disrupt plantation routine. Some manuals of the period even pointed out that unstable unions led to a lower reproductive rate, to the detriment of the planters.[39] In the colonial period, such discussions of planter attitudes toward slave marriage are extremely rare.

Once again, correspondence from engenhos Sergipe and Santana is revealing of both existing conditions and of attitudes toward them. In 1634, Father Sebastião Vaz complained that the majority of Engenho Sergipe's slaves were single and that this resulted in continual moral sins and general unrest.[40] A century later at Engenho Sergipe, the situation remained the same. Father Jerônimo da Gama wrote from the engenho in 1733 that most of the slaves remained unmarried. Recognizing the relationship between unstable unions and the low rate of reproduction, he asked, "Is it not better that there be more children and fewer illicit affairs [*mancebias*]?"[41] In fact, his rhetorical question had been in a way answered from Engenho Sergipe in 1731: "Many little crioulos have been born but many have also died, and it costs a great deal to raise them."[42] Even the Jesuits could see that, given the high mortality rates and the relatively secure supply of new slaves from the Atlantic trade, the costs and risks of pregnancy and child rearing did not make the fostering of stable unions within the church an economic as well as a moral imperative.

That a divergence of opinion existed among the Jesuit plantation administrators – and we can assume among the other slaveowners – is made clear by a particularly revealing letter from Engenho Santana written in 1733. Two years before, Father Pedro Teixeira had taken charge of the mill and its 178 slaves. He complained that in the preceding twenty-seven years when Father Manoel de Figueiredo had managed the estate there had only been thirty-four marriages and that most of these were between old slaves who had long cohabited. Figueiredo had been of the opinion that slaves should not marry, and he had defended his position "to the fingernails." Teixeira, quick to point out the failings of his predecessor, complained that the slaves still lived in sin and that this situation reduced the rate of reproduction. He also hinted that infanticide was sometimes practiced. His final statement on the matter speaks with unintended eloquence about his own attitude toward the slaves, the slave's attitude toward Catholic marriage, and the demographic realities at Santana:

I made various preachings, examples, and public demonstrations to them, exhorting them in particular to give up their evil state and marry. I spoke to them of marriage, I spoke to them of the Devil, and some who had accepted the Devil seemed to break away. From July 1730 to July 1731 single women bore three children, married women bore another three [and of all these] two died and four are being raised.[43]

The policy of more balanced sex ratios, marriages, and conditions that favored reproduction advocated by some of the Jesuits was apparently followed consistently by the Benedictine Fathers in Brazil. The congregation of São Bento owned various rural properties in colonial Brazil, including large cattle ranches and engenhos in Bahia, Pernambuco, and Rio de Janeiro. In Bahia, their holdings included canefields, a manioc farm, cattle ranches, and eventually two engenhos: São Bento dos Lages in the township of São Francisco and São Caetano in the region of Itapororocas. Unlike most of the slaveowners of colonial Brazil, the Benedictines seem to have encouraged the formation of family units. They became known, in fact, as excellent plantation administrators. In 1662, Father Belchior Pires, a Jesuit, wrote that the Benedictine engenhos were much better and more cheaply run than those of the Society of Jesus.[44] The ability of the congregation of São Bento to depend on crioulos born on their estates for additions and replacements to the slave force, supposedly as a result of sponsoring slave marriages, drew the attention of contemporaries. Data from Bahia suggest that there is some truth in this belief. A review of Benedictine properties between 1652 and 1710 revealed relatively high numbers of children, running between 20 and 24 percent on individual properties.[45]

That the Benedictine congregations may have been particularly concerned with the formation of slave families is also suggested by notations in their records from São Paulo, Pernambuco, and Rio de Janeiro. Between 1783 and 1787, thirty-three women and three men were added to the slaves at Engenho de Vargem in Rio de Janeiro. The triennial report noted by 1787 that "some were already married," indicating that the unusually large number of female additions was made specifically to balance the sex ratio and provide partners for men residing at the mill.[46] This had been exactly the purpose when seven women had been added to the slave force at Engenho da Ilha in 1747–8, "in order that they marry with the slaves of the said estate."[47] A general meeting of the Benedictines in São Paulo in 1752 required that single slaves marry, and by 1783 Benedictines of São Paulo released from all hard work any slave woman with six living children.[48]

The Benedictine Fathers undoubtedly saw in the policy of balanced sex ratios and "stable" families a means of promoting fewer sins and a more moral life among the slaves, but the fact that married slaves might be less restive or likely to run off was probably not lost on them either. The triennial reports or estados that the Benedictine congregation of Brazil submitted to the mother house in Tibães provide some proof of concern with balanced sex ratios and with the ability of plantations to partially meet their labor needs with crioulos born on the estates. The records of the congregation of Olinda are particularly good in this regard. In 1715, the two engenhos of Musurepe and São Bernardo both displayed balanced sex ratios and large numbers of children. Musurepe had twelve married couples, twenty-one single men, twenty single women, and twenty-four children. São Bernardo was smaller, with ten couples, six unmarried males, six unmarried females, and eighteen children. Later estados paid attention to the number of slaves born on the estates who "entered service in comparison to those who were bought."[49]

The intentions or policies carried out by the Benedictines and at least some of the Jesuits in regard to slave-family formation and stability or the fostering of the natural increase among slaves probably do not represent the common reality of the Bahian slave experience. The situation on secularly owned plantations seems to be one in which little concern was given to sponsoring slave marriage or reproduction. In fact, it is difficult to make this assertion since records that provide information on slave families in colonial Brazil are rare.

Historians and demographers concerned with questions of slave demography have usually turned to inventories or property records made at an owner's death, which list slaves by family units. In the United States, Jamaica, Trinidad, and Peru such records have been used to discuss the residence and family patterns of slave populations. In Bahia (and for most of colonial Brazil), the materials needed for this type of analysis are slim. Estate inventories exist in considerable numbers, but although these usually include a careful accounting of the qualities and values of the slaves, they rarely record their marital or family and residence situation. The most common way of listing slaves in an inventory is first the men, then the women, and finally the children and infirm. On other occasions, groupings are made by occupation. The lack of attention given to family units is in itself revealing of the unimportance such matters had for the owners and their heirs. Inventories made at the end of the colonial era in the early nineteenth century pay no more regard to the slave family units than did those of the seventeenth century.

A few scattered inventories and lists from non-church-owned Recôncavo engenhos indicate a pattern of lack of church-sponsored marriage and a low birthrate. Engenho Sergipe in 1591 was a secular plantation still owned by the count of Linhares. At that time, only nine of the twenty-three adult Africans were married, three of them to Indian women. The tendency to import men in the African slave trade surely created problems of finding a mate, but the problem of lack of marriages seems to go beyond the demographic limitations.[50] Evidence from the eighteenth century makes the patterns clearer. An example can be seen in the inventory of the slave force at Engenho Cinco Rios made in 1779. In that year, the engenho had eighty-six slaves, of whom forty-nine (57%) were Africans. Of the eighty adults, only nine couples were listed as married and all the rest either as *solteiros* (single or without any marital designation). The sexual ratio was badly imbalanced, with sixty adult males and only twenty-one females. There were only six identifiable children.[51] The situation in Cinco Rios, though extreme, appears to have been a relatively common pattern on the Bahian plantations.

The inventory made of the estate of João Lopes Fiuza in 1741 included three separate properties, two engenhos and a large cane farm of 50 hectares. The slave force on each of these properties was inventoried separately and reference was made to married couples and to age, the latter usually in descriptive terms. At Lopes Fiuza's Engenho de Baixo in São Francisco, there were 138 slaves, of whom only 20 were identifiable children. Of the 118 adults, only 30 (15 couples) were listed as married. At the smaller, probably newer, Engenho São Pedro de Tararipe in Rio Fundo, Lopes Fiuza had 63 slaves, of whom 54 were adults. Here, only two married couples were listed. The situation was considerably better on his cane farm of Our Lady of Monte, where there were twelve married couples of the 44 adults and more than 35 percent of the resident slaves were listed as children.[52]

As we have seen in Table 13-5, the sex ratio was considerably lower on the cane farms than the engenhos. Cane farms, lacking the need for slave technicians and artisans associated with sugar making rather than sugar agricultures, did not have so imbalanced a sex ratio. Nor was the slave force on cane farms as stratified in terms of occupation. Still,

despite these realities, the life opportunities for slaves were not necessarily better on cane farms than at engenhos. First, many inventories of
cane farms indicate extreme sexual imbalance and low fertility, even
though in general the situation was better than on the engenhos. José
Rodrigues Pereira's fazenda de canas, for example, had twenty males
and only seven females when it was inventoried in 1733. Only one
couple was listed as married, and there were no children.[53] The cane
farm of Felipe Dias Amaral in São Francisco had only two crioulos
among its twenty-one slaves. Of the sixteen males and five females,
only one slave was a child.[54] Such cases demonstrate that the demographic conditions on these smaller properties could also be quite
negative, despite the somewhat better situation of cane farms in general. Conversely, because the general pattern in Bahia was to keep
slaves from marrying or forming relationships beyond the boundaries
of their master's holdings, life opportunities could be more restricted
on cane farms than on engenhos. Although the sex ratio may have
been more balanced on smaller plantations, the limited number of
available partners and the fact that some of those resident on the same
unit may have been kin limited a slave's marital opportunities.

Examples of other engenhos and cane farms that demonstrate similar
patterns of imbalanced sex ratios, lack of formalized marriage, low
rates of reproduction, and high indices of illegitimacy can be produced
for various points in time, but our ability to generalize from them is
limited at best. Instead, let us turn to a different type of source. In
1788, a census was made in the captaincy of Bahia. Its purpose was
apparently military recruiting or tax assessment. The returns from six
parishes have survived, and of these only three record the slave population. Unfortunately, the reports from main Recôncavo parishes such
as Rio Fundo and Santo Amaro de Purificação do not contain information on the slave population, but three districts – Aguafria, Inhambupe,
and Taperagoa, all with sizable slave populations – do. Both Aguafria
and Inhambupe were parishes neighboring the Recôncavo and contained sugar properties, although these districts were somewhat more
diversified than the main sugar parishes. An analysis of these three
parishes' slaves can provide some general idea of the structure of the
Bahian rural slave population, although we should expect that because
of both a more diversified economy and the 1788 date, prior to the
reintensification of the slave trade, in the aftermath of the Haitian
revolt, the demographic indices should be "healthier" than in the
sugar-plantation zones during much of the colonial period.

The structure of the slave populations of the three parishes reveals
the adult sex ratios and, in the percentile distribution of ages, suggests
once again the severe sexual imbalance and indicates high rates of
infant mortality and low rates of fertility. That these features were
more pronounced among the slave population than other segments of

Table 13-8. *Dependency ratios in Bahian parishes, 1788*

(age)	A (0–14 years)	B (45 years +)	C (15–44) years	Ratio (A+B/C times 100)
Free[a]				
Whites	474	316	554	143
Pardos	667	285	761	125
Blacks	107	156	152	173
All free colored	774	441	913	133
All free	1,248	757	1,467	137
Slaves[b]				
Pardos	60	11	84	85
Blacks	309	203	764	67
All slaves	369	214	848	69
All colored (free and slave)	1,143	655	1,761	102

[a]Includes six parishes: Purificação, Saubara, Rio Fundo, Taperagoa, Inhambupe, and Aguafria.
[b]Information available for only Taperagoa, Inhambupe, and Aquafria parishes.

Table 13-9. *Demographic ratios of the population of three Bahian rural parishes, 1788*

Parish	Adult sex ratio			Dependency ratio			Child/woman ratio[d]			Adjusted child/woman ratio[e]		
	W[a]	FC[b]	S[c]	W	FC	S	W	FC	S	W	FC	S
Taperagoa	102	78	135	137	142	57	165	122	72	161	156	53
Aguafria	79	95	134	132	93	69	93	74	49	117	78	37
Inhambupe	92	101	176	109	98	49	59	86	58	64	85	33

[a](W)hites. [b](F)ree (C)olored. [c](S)laves. [d]Calculated by dividing the total population ages 0–9 by the number of women ages 15–45. [e]Adjusted child/woman ratio is the product of the child/woman ratio times 100 divided by the adult sex ratio.

society, white or free or colored, is made clear in Table 13-8. The imbalance in favor of men among slaves was far in excess of that among whites or free people of color, reaching a level of almost three men for every two women. The impact of the slave trade is obviously at work here, because the imbalance is most pronounced in the most productive adult years. The low child–woman ratios presented in Table 13-9 also indicate a low rate of reproduction. Whatever the causes, these data underline the general impression that the Bahian slave population did not reproduce itself and was maintained by the continual forced immigration of Africans.

Two measures, the dependency ratio and the general-fertility ratio (or, as it is sometimes called, the child–woman ratio), help to clarify the inability of the Bahian slave population to reproduce itself. The dependency ratio is calculated by dividing the number of productive adults (age 15–44) into those younger or older, who are assumed to be less productive. The lower the ratio, the greater the likelihood of high infant and child mortality and/or a shortened life expectancy for adults.

Table 13-8 demonstrates that slaves had by far the lowest dependency ratios of any group in the population, at a level less than half that of the whites. To some extent, this comparison is complicated by the introduction of young adults into the slave population through the Atlantic trade, thereby in effect lowering the dependency ratio. But the great disparity between slaves and all segments of the free population indicates that high levels of mortality and low fertility must also be at work. The dependency ratio of pardo slaves, which we can assume was unaffected by importation, was still considerably lower than that of the free population.

The general fertility ratios of the slave and free populations confirm the low rate of slave reproduction. The slave population, with low ratios of 58 to 72, was incapable of self-reproduction. Slave women were simply not bearing enough children for this population to grow or even remain stable without considerable additions from the trade. Finally, it should be noted that the excess of males in the slave population tended to inflate the general fertility ratio among the slaves while deflating it among the free colored, who had an excess of women. Thus, Table 13-9 also presents an adjusted child–woman ratio that compensates for the sex ratios of each group, whites, free coloreds, and slaves, and demonstrates even more clearly the depressed fertility of the slave population.

To place the structure of this slave population in a comparative context, I have indexed it and the total free population against the standard of the white age distribution in the three parishes, as shown in Table 13-10. Because of obvious age heaping, the slave age categories have been converted into ten-year groupings. The results demonstrate that up to age ten the male slave population was almost 40 percent less than that of the whites. Between ages ten to forty, however, the male slave population counted high excesses over whites, an obvious result of the trade's importation of young adults. After age fifty, the earlier imbalance reappears, with slaves at these ages only 50 to 60 percent of the proportion of whites. Slave women demonstrate a similar, but less extreme, pattern in comparison with white women.

From the 1788 census, it is possible to take an even closer look at the fertility levels of the various segments of the population and from them to make some tentative assumptions about the structure and characteristics of the slave population. In Table 13-11, I present some of the

Table 13-10. *Index of Bahian free and slave populations compared with Bahian whites, 1788*

Ages	Whites		All free		Slaves		Slaves by 10-year cohort	
	%M	%F	%M	%F	%M	%F	%M	%F
0–4	13.7	15.8	89.8	90.5	41.6	59.5		
							60.2	69.3
5–9	10.9	11.6	112.8	110.3	83.5	82.8		
10–14	9.2	11.4	118.5	102.6	107.6	89.5		
							130.7	111.4
15–19	7.1	10.5	129.6	111.4	160.6	135.3		
20–4	6.5	7.0	115.4	93.3	169.2	140.0		
							157.4	123.5
25–9	7.5	9.7	102.6	90.7	146.6	108.2		
30–4	5.7	5.5	91.2	94.5	240.4	141.8		
							149.2	122.3
35–9	6.9	5.7	91.3	103.5	73.9	103.5		
40–4	6.2	4.0	82.3	107.5	109.7	167.5		
							99.2	100.0
45–9	6.0	6.5	128.3	92.3	85.0	88.5		
50–4	5.6	3.0	87.5	93.3	83.9	106.6		
							57.9	98.2
55–9	5.8	2.5	75.9	120.0	32.8	88.0		
60–4	3.4	2.1	64.7	85.7	70.6	90.5		
							49.5	95.7
65+	5.7	2.6	77.2	123.1	36.8	80.8		

traditional ratios of age groups within the population and of children to women within population groups. All these demonstrate that slaves, and especially black slaves, had the lowest ratios of children to women in the population. Free and slave pardos had considerably higher ratios than did blacks in similar categories of free or slave status, but their ratios are complicated by the fact that black as well as pardo women could bear pardo children. Thus it probably makes more sense to consider all free colored and all blacks in each category together. These traditional measures of fertility confirm the impression that slaves had lower ratios than other segments of the population.

The traditional measures, however, are unsatisfactory because of the nature of the evidence and the peculiarities of a slave population. The census of 1788, like most colonial Brazilian censuses, consistently underenumerated young children. The problem was probably worst among the free colored and slave populations where infant mortality was high and neither parents nor owners had much assurance of a child's survival. This underenumeration probably inflates the ratio of chidren for whites and deflates it for slaves and free coloreds. On the

Table 13-11. *Indices of fertility of the Bahian rural population compared with model tables*

Population	1 (F,15–44)[a]	2 (P,0–14)[b]	3 (2/1)	4 (F,0–14/ F,15–44)	5 (P,0–4/ F,15–44)	6 (P,0–14/ P,15–45)	7 (P,5–9/ F,20–49)
Model							
West-1 (R = 1)	445	858	1.93	.964	.399	.889	.352
West-1 (R = −.5)	469	656	1.40	.700	.271	.420	.4802
West-1 (R = −1)	470	590	1.26	.628	.237	.387	.427
Bahia							
Whites	321	432	1.320	.872	.505	.749	.593
Free pardos	331	661	1.997	.967	.312	.812	.935
Free blacks	70	98	1.400	.571	.586	.512	.379
All free colored	451	749	1.661	.785	.441	.726	.703
Slave pardos	34	60	1.765	.853	.412	.674	1.43
Slave blacks	313	309	.987	.447	.278	.375	.383
All slaves	404	377	1.102	.426	.213	.404	.436

[a]F means females. [b]P means population.

Sources: Model population estimates are based on Ansley J. Coale and Paul Demeny, *Regional Model Life Tables and Stable Populations* (Princeton, 1966), 26. Data from Bahia are based on the Bahian census of 1788, APB, secção historica, recenseamentos. Columns 1 and 2 are based on a total population of 1,000.

other hand, the tendency to import young adults in the slave trade resulted in a disproportionate number of young women in the slave population and their presence had a tendency to elevate its apparent level of fertility.

To emphasize how negative the slave fertility situation really was, Table 13-11 also includes ratios computed from model life tables compiled by Coale and Demeny. Although these tables were developed for stable populations quite unlike the Bahian slaves, they are useful for comparative purposes because they provide parameters of fertility. I have placed in Table 13-11 figures drawn from a regime of very high mortality (West-1) at three rates of natural growth or decrease (+1% per year; −5%; −1%). These examples demonstrate that, even with an annual rate of loss of 1 percent, the model ratios were usually higher than those experienced by the slave population.

Once again, however, the traditional fertility measures are not entirely satisfactory because of peculiarities in the slave population and because of the nature of the evidence. To compensate for these problems, I have computed the ratio of children 5–9 years old to women 20–49 years of age. This ratio is really a stark measure of the reproductive power of the population. Here the contrast between slaves and free persons is readily apparent. Whereas the ratio for black slaves was only .383, the ratios for whites and free persons of color were .593 and .703 respectively. Also noticeable are the high ratios achieved by the pardos, both slave and free; but it is difficult to evaluate these since pardo chidlren were also produced by white and black parents. If, however, we simply compare all slaves to all free persons of color, the lower ratio for slaves is still clear.

All these various measures corroborate the general impression that slave fertility was depressed and whatever the regime of infant and child mortality among the population as a whole, for Bahian slaves it was worse. The Bahian slave population was simply not reproducing itself, and it does not appear to have done so at any time in the colonial era. The question remains: Why did the Brazilian slave population and, for most of the eighteenth century, that of the West Indies exhibit low rates of fertility? A wide variety of causes have been suggested, including among others delayed mating; poor nutrition, which delays the age of menarche; exhausting labor; sexual imbalance; unstable unions; and promiscuity.[55]

One of the most interesting explanations of depressed fertility among plantation slaves is the "African" custom of protracted lactation. Extended breast feeding has a contraceptive effect and would prolong the period between conceptions.[56] Given the heavily African origin of Bahian slaves, the maintenance of these practices would not be surprising. There is, in fact, evidence that this pattern was followed in Brazil. João Imbert in his guide to farm management complained that slave women prolonged breast feeding "two years or more" and that this and other "African errors" retarded the growth of the slave population.[57]

Extended lactation, however, may be only half the story. Modern studies of the Yoruba have noted a pattern of postpartum sexual abstinence that is widespread in sub-Saharan Africa. This abstinence extends beyond lactation from six to twelve months so that the principal cause of reduced fertility is not postpartum amenorrhoea itself but, rather, the long period without sexual intercourse. The reason for this taboo is a strong belief that the health of the child will be endangered by a new pregnancy, and thus there follows an attempt to delay the time when the child is weaned and hence more vulnerable because of poor nutrition or the absence of the antibodies contained in the mother's milk. Although the length of the abstinence period varies, it has been noted among the Akans and Ewes as well as the Yorubas, or to put it in Bahian terms, among the Minas, Geges, and Nagôs.[58] The studies of modern Yorubas indicate that long periods of culturally accepted abstinence reduce a woman's experience of sexual intercourse to less than half of her fecund years; but, of course, high infant mortality rates would counterbalance this to some extent. The result of this sexual pattern is to "insure a minimum inter-pregnancy period of four years." The low fertility we observe among Bahian slaves may then have resulted from the pattern of extended lactation accompanied by sexual abstinence. It would be paradoxical if, despite the many observations about slave promiscuity, in fact it was an intentional avoidance of sexual relations that underlay the lower fertility.

Death in the tropics

It is generally agreed that slavery was bad for the health. The life expectancy of slaves seems invariably to have been lower than that of free persons living in the same environment, and the conditions of sugar plantations throughout the Americas seem to have been worse than on other kinds of slave properties. Although there is no agreement on the rate of mortality, virtually all observers of slavery in colonial Bahia concur in their belief that its slave population suffered an annual rate of decline; a situation in which the number of births was constantly exceeded by the number of deaths so that maintenance of the population was possible only by continually importing new slaves from Africa.[59]

Observations of the high mortality among slaves begin in the seventeenth century. Bernardo Ribeiro, agent for the countess of Linhares, wrote in 1601, "The properties of engenhos in this state are very laborious and costly because they depend on slaves with whom little can be done; the work is great and many die."[60] In the same decade, Governor Diogo de Meneses wrote of the cost to planters of the many slaves bought on advances from merchants who died leaving the planters with great debts.[61]

By the early nineteenth century, observers began to offer estimates of the rate of decline of the slave population. One author in 1832 placed the rate of decline at 5 percent per year, meaning that the slave force would be reduced to half its size in seven years if no additions were made.[62] Another observer, writing in the mid–nineteenth century, placed the decline at 8 percent a year, with an additional loss of 2.75 percent due to interprovincial sales southward.[63] Although there was a divergence of opinion on the actual rate of decrease, there seems to have been no doubt about the situation of demographic decline. Charles Pennell, the British consul in Salvador and a supporter of the 5 percent a year loss figure, wrote in 1827:

The annual mortality on many sugar plantations is so great that unless their numbers are augmented from abroad the whole slave population would become extinct in the course of about twenty years; the proprietors act on the calculation that it is cheaper to buy male slaves than to raise Negro children.[64]

Plantation-level data are difficult to obtain and are complicated by the fact that ages were often recorded in descriptive categories rather than in years. Once again, engenhos Sergipe and Santana offer some evidence. Engenho Sergipe in the 1630s had about eighty-five slaves. Father Sebastião Vaz reported that between 1633 and 1636 fourteen slaves (in this case, Africans), most of them elderly, and four or five crioulos had died. This would constitute an annual crude mortality rate of 75 per 1,000 and it obviously does not take infant mortality into account. At such a rate, the whole slave force would have to be replaced in under ten years. Vaz went on to report that fifteen new slaves had been purchased, of whom one had died and the rest lived, "thanks to God, and will become good slaves – May God preserve them."[65]

That the extremely high rate of mortality implied by Father Vaz's figure may be atypical is suggested by plantation lists from the other Jesuit engenho in Bahia, Santana. On that estate between July 1730 and July 1731, single women bore 3 children and married women another 3. Of these 6 babies, 2 died; an infant mortality rate of 333 per 1,000. In addition, there were 5 other deaths distributed as follows: Andreza, 90; Gregório, 75; Mariana, 24; Rosalia, 22; and Maria, 30, a recently arrived African. In total then there were 7 deaths among the 178 slaves for a crude mortality rate of 39 per 1,000. From a Santana inventory made twenty years later, in 1752, we learn that in the fifty-seven months between 3 March 1748 and 13 November 1752, 24 children were born and 23 slaves died, of whom 7 were children, 10 were elderly and 6 were adults "of full service." For the engenho's population of about 180 slaves, these figures produce a crude birthrate of 28 and a crude

Table 13-12. *Crude birth and death rates in various slave-based societies in the Americas, 1633–1861*

Place	Date	Population	Crude birthrate	Crude death rate
Brazil				
1. Salvador				
S. Antonio parish	1775	All		35.1
Penha parish	1775	All		33.9
Passo parish	1798	All		34.5
2. São Paulo	1765	Males	64.2	59.2
		Females	56.6	51.5
3. São Paulo	1798	All free		54.4
4. Pernambuco	1775	All	41.4	32.8
5. Maranhão	1798	Whites	16.3	27.9
		Pardo slaves	38	26.7
		Black slaves	24	26.7
		All slaves	26.5	26.7
6. Minas Gerais	1815	Whites	36.6	27.4
		Free colored	41.7	34.3
		Slaves	33.4	32.9
7. Minas Gerais	1821	Whites	40	28
		Free colored	41.5	39.6
		Pardo slave	38	60
		Black slave	29	65
		All slaves	33.7	62.8
8. Espirito Santo	1817	All	44.2	33.5
9. Brazil	1873	All slaves	30	
10. Jamaica	1817–32	All slaves	23	26
11. Jamaica	1844–61	All	40	32
12. Surinam	1826–48	All slaves	27.5	50
13. Surinam (Caterina-Sophia plantation)	1852–61	All slaves	26.8	43.4
14. U.S. South	1850	Whites	46–50	
15. U.S. South	1820–60	Slaves	60	
16. Cuba	1791–2	All blacks	52.5	34.0
	1816–17	All blacks	50	34.2
17. Danish West Indies	1840s	All slaves	40	50
18. Bahia				
S. Amaro Parish	1817	Slaves		47
Engenho Sergipe	1633–6	Slaves		75
Engenho Santana	1730–1	Slaves		39
Engenho Santana	1748–52	Slaves	28	27
Engenho Petinga	1744–5	Slaves		115 (plague)
Fazenda Saubara	1750–60	Slaves	17–26	
		Adult male slaves		115
		Adult female slaves		81

Sources: 1. Johildo Ataide, "Mortalidade na Cidade do Salvador," (unpublished paper, 1972). 2. Elizabeth Kuznesof, "Household Composition and Economy in an Urbanizing

death rate of 27, but to what extent 1730–1 or 1748–52 were typical years at Santana or to what extent Santana was a typical engenho cannot be determined. Jesuit-owned Santana probably represented a situation of somewhat better conditions than those found in most Bahian engenhos. Certainly, parish-level data suggest mortality levels that were higher than those found on this estate.

Despite the fact that crude rates are not a particularly good comparative measure, there is some utility in presenting here crude birth and death rates for segments of the population in a number of slave-based societies to establish a comparative context for the Bahian rates. Before the introduction of birth-control devices, crude birthrates in most populations varied between 35 and 55 per 1,000, whereas crude death rates fell between 30 and 40. In epidemic years, death rates exceeding 100 have been recorded for European populations in the historical past, but such levels are the result of the bad times of plague or famine. Table 13-12 presents a summary of these rates. The range of these figures is very great and to some extent represents problems of underregistration rather than real differences. Still, it is clear when compared with other slave regimes, especially those also dependent on the slave trade and therefore probably somewhat similar in terms of sex distribution and age structure, the rural Bahian figures tend to fall in the low range of birthrates and the high range of death rates. The crude death rate from Purificação parish in 1817 is based on a count of death registrations in relation to the total number of slaves in the parish in that year. If we assume a crude birthrate for slaves in that parish of about 34, similar to that listed for Minas Gerais at about the same time, then

Sources for Table 13-12 (*cont.*)

Community: São Paulo, 1765–1836," (Ph.D. thesis, University of California, Berkeley, 1976), 292–6. 3. Maria Luiza Marcilio, *A cidade de São Paulo* (São Paulo, 1974), 161–2. 4. *ABNR* 43 (1923): 20–111. 5. BNL, Fundo geral. 6. Nathaniel Leff and Herbert S. Klein, "O crescimento da população não européia antes do início do desenvolvimento: O Brasil no século xix," *AH* 6 (1974): 51–70. 7. W. L. von Eschwege, *Pluto brasiliensis* (1821), 2 vols. (Belo Horizonte, 1979), II, appendix. 8. IHGB, lata 17.2. 9. Robert Slenes, "The Demography and Economics of Brazilian Slavery" (Ph.D. thesis, Stanford University, 1976), 341–411. 10 and 11. Herbert S. Klein and Stanley L. Engerman, "The Demographic Study of the American Slave Population," (unpublished paper, 1976). 12 and 13. Humphrey Lamur, "The Demography of Surinam Plantation Slaves in the Last Decade Before Emancipation," *CPSNWS*, 161–73. 14 and 15. Klein and Engerman, "Demographic Study," various sources. 16. Jack Eblen, "On the Natural Increase of Slave Populations: The Example of the Cuban Black Population, 1775–1900," in *Race and Slavery in the Western Hemisphere. Quantitative Studies*, Stanley L. Engerman and Eugene D. Genovese, eds. (Princeton, 1975), 211–48. 17. Hans Christian Johansen, "Slave Demography in the Danish West Indian Islands," *Scandanavian Economic History Review* 29, no. 1 (1981): 1–20. 18. ACMS, Livro de Óbitos, 1817; ANTT, CSJ, maço 69, n. 76; maço 15, n. 24; maço 54, n. 42; maço 54, n. 31; ASCMB, B/3ª/213.

the rate of growth of the slave population would be negative, with a loss of more than 1.3 percent a year, not taking into consideration manumission and escape. Underregistration of infant deaths has probably lowered this figure, and I suspect that a rate of loss of 2.5 to 3.5 percent per year is probably more accurate. Such a rate would approximate the uncompounded estimates of 5 percent a year made by various observers.

A number of problems complicate any attempt to establish rates of mortality among the Bahian population. Mortality rates are particularly susceptible to the age structure of a population. An older population (one with more people in the older age brackets) will have a higher rate of mortality than a younger population. This fact will tell us very little about the conditions of health endured by the two populations. The lack of adequate age-specific data on the Bahian population, therefore, makes the calculation of rates very difficult, a problem even further complicated by the traditional underreporting of children, stillbirths, and infant mortalities. The model life tables are also of limited value because they are designed for stable populations, something that the Bahian slave population, constantly resupplied from Africa, never was.[66]

As with fertility, a number of factors influenced the life expectancy of slaves in Bahia, but inadequate census, registration, and shipping data make it difficult to evaluate the impact of each of the factors that contributed to mortality. As we have seen, the Bahian slave population was heavily African in origin. African-born slaves suffered high rates of morbidity and mortality in the New World with their entry into a new disease environment. Not only did Africans lack the immunities that would naturally be acquired by the native born in childhood, but the passage from Africa probably left them in a weakened physical and psychological state on arrival and more susceptible to sickness.[67] The period of "seasoning" was crucial. During the first year after arrival, African slaves not only acquired a knowledge of the expectations of their masters and the rudiments of the Portuguese language but also passed through a period of high mortality risk. Thus, the listing of a slave as ladino or acculturated was not only a comment on his or her skills but also on his or her potential longevity. The price differential between ladino Africans and the recently arrived boçal was about 15 percent throughout the eighteenth century.[68] The high proportion of Africans in the Bahian slave population also had the effect of pushing up its median age because of the tendency to import young adults, and this in turn would have contributed to a higher crude death rate.

Scholars have long attempted to use mortality figures as a direct measure of "treatment," the physical conditions under which slaves labored. It was common to estimate in Brazil that a slave's life expectancy was seven to fifteen years, but such an estimate is particularly misleading.[69] To be of much value, calculations of life expectancy must be based on age-specific death rates. In Brazil, for example, an adjustment for deaths during seasoning and for infant or child mortality, factors that contributed heavily to the crude death rate, would considerably lower the death rate and would only partially be tied to labor conditions, although infant and child mortality was to some extent linked to the morbidity and nutrition of the mothers. Still, if a large proportion of deaths were suffered in childhood or upon arrival from Africa, crude mortality rates would tell us little about the work regime.

In fact, evidence suggests that infant and child mortality was extremely high among Bahian slaves and probably higher among them than among any other group in the Bahian population. Without knowledge of the age structure, it is difficult to establish meaningful mortality rates or ratios, but some evidence from the parish of Santo Amaro da Purificação is suggestive. Given what we have already established about the low proportion of children in the slave population, the mortality figures from Purificação are striking. Of 226 slaves who died between 1816 and 1819 and whose age was recorded, more than half were children below the age of five years, and another third were elderly people over the age of sixty.[70] The proportion of deaths among the free population was reversed, with children under five making up under 30 percent of the fatalities and those over fifty-five accounting for half the deaths. Although it is impossible to estimate the rate of mortality without figures for the age cohorts, it is probably safe to assume that the percentage of children under the age of fourteen was smaller among slaves than among the free colored or white population.[71]

What did these figures mean in terms of a slave's life expectancy? Using semistable population techniques, a number of authors have attempted to calculate age-specific life expectancy in Brazil. Assuming a severe mortality regime somewhere between the Coale and Demeny model tables of West-1 and West-4, Robert Slenes has estimated life expectancy at birth (e_o) of between nineteen and twenty-seven years for Brazilian slaves in the late nineteenth century, a figure only slightly under the 27.08 years that has been calculated for the Brazilian population as a whole in 1879.[72] Still, he characterized this situation as one of extremely high mortality, considerably above that of slaves in the U.S. South in the mid–nineteenth century. Using a somewhat different technique, Pedro Carvalho de Mello reached similar conclusions, placing a male slave's life expectancy at birth at 18.3 years, compared to 27.4 for the population as a whole in 1872. The male slave's life expectancy at birth in Brazil was thus 30 percent less than that of the whole population, and it was only half that of a male slave in the United States about 1850 ($e_0 = 35.5$), which in turn was only 12 percent less than that of the entire U.S. population.[73]

Using the semistable population method, Stephen Burmeister estimated Bahian slave life expectancy on the basis of the 1788 census. He calculated for male slaves at birth a life expectancy of twenty-three years and for females twenty-five years, but these figures are probably inflated because of underreporting of infant mortality.[74] Even so, they represent non-sugar-growing regions and thus should be taken as reflecting optimum conditions for Bahian slaves. The majority of slaves who labored at engenhos and in the canefields probably had an even lower life expectancy.

The disease environment, poor nutrition, and lack of medical care affected a large segment of the free population as well as the slaves in Bahia, but there is little doubt that the slave condition created certain peculiar conditions of mortality. The apparently very high rates of slave neonatal and child mortality may have been due to poor nutrition and the labor demands made on mothers as well as planter calculations that raising a child until the age of labor was a risky business given its chances of dying first. This attitude and the demands made on pregnant slave women may have also resulted in a higher proportion of stillbirths among slaves than among the rest of the population. Data from Maranhão in 1798 reveal a ratio of stillbirths to total births among slaves of 10.3, compared with 5.7 among whites and 6.5 among free pardos.[75]

Although infant mortality seems to have been a major factor in the pathology of Brazilian slave demography, the work regime, especially that demanded of those in sugar agriculture, also had its costs. Past the age of fifty, slaves suffered higher mortality rates than free persons. At least this is suggested by age distributions in Table 13-10. About 6 percent of the slaves listed as sick in inventories of sugar properties suffered from *cansaço* or exhaustion.[76] Some authors believe that cansaço is a particular disease, but I have never seen a document in which a free person is listed with this ailment in the eighteenth century. I believe that cansaço refers to a condition of slavery, of being worn out or exhausted to the point of incapacity. During the safra, when the work demands were highest, there was little time for rest, especially in the sugar mill itself. Fatigue could have deadly results, as it probably did for Francisco, a slave from Mina, who in 1816 died at an engenho in São Francisco after falling into a kettle of boiling sugar syrup.[77]

Finally, there is the difficult-to-measure but very real psychological effect of slavery on its victims. Plantation accounts hint at infanticide and abortion. Despair in the face of enslavement led to suicides on slave ships and on plantations. Ship captain Felipe Nery reported from Pernambuco in 1812 that he had lost three of his human cargo when on entering the River Zaire three men who had suffered a flogging had "despairingly thrown themselves into the sea."[78] Antonil, who visited the Recôncavo in the late seventeenth century, and Benci, who lived in

Bahia at the same time, both admonished slaveowners to treat slaves with decency because poor care and mistreatment often led the slaves to take their own lives, a matter with serious implications for these churchmen.[79]

Life and death at Fazenda Saubara

The simple statistics of births and deaths do not convey a full image of the past, of the lives and sorrows of the people who underwent the tragedy of Bahian slavery, of those who listened for the cries of life or stood solemnly at the graves. Plantation lists by their "snapshot" nature can only provide a single dimension, frozen in time. One Recôncavo estate, however, provides some evidence of a different nature. Fazenda Saubara was a large property owned by the Misericórdia of Salvador. Located in the manioc zone of the Recôncavo, just south of Santo Amaro in the parish of Saubara, Fazenda Saubara was devoted to producing cattle and manioc for sale and to supplying the needs of the Misericórdia's hospital and other services in Bahia. In addition, the fazenda contained extensive woodlands. Over the years, various pieces of land had been leased or rented to poor farmers, but the Misericórdia had maintained direct control over most of the property and had worked it with about twenty to thirty slaves. Periodically (probably annually), lists of the slaves were made, including their names and sometimes other information about their origins, marital status, working capacity, or other characteristics. For 1750 to 1760, five lists still exist, and by tracing the presence of individuals through these lists it is possible to reconstruct some idea of the confrontation of these people with death in the Recôncavo.

Despite the fact that Fazenda Saubara was owned by a charitable religious institution, its administration often left much to be desired. In 1655, the man hired to reside at the fazenda and manage its operations was dismissed for stealing and branding the slaves with a cattle brand.[80] His replacement, Antônio Alvares de Abreu, was provided with a set of instructions that ordered him to keep the hospital of the Misericórdia supplied with manioc flour and firewood, to prohibit others from cutting brush or timber on the property, and to care for the cattle in the four corrals on the property. As for the slaves, Alvares de Abreu was charged to make sure they served well, were instructed in the faith, and were punished when necessary. Slaves were to be permitted to grow tobacco and sell it so that they could clothe themselves.[81] He proved no better than the man he replaced and lasted only a year. The problems continued. In 1664, João Antunes was dismissed as manager (feitor) for neglect of his duties and because his wife had badly mistreated the household slaves.[82] By the end of the century, mismanagement had taken its toll. The number of slave deaths and the apparent lack of slave births had placed the fazenda in jeopardy, and new slaves had to be purchased. A royal investigator reported in 1755 that poor administration had ruined this property and that better management would lead to more sales of cattle and the birth of more slaves.[83] The problem of low slave fertility seems to have been here as elsewhere in the Recôncavo. In the 1750s, only five children were born to the fifteen women still in their reproductive years.

But despite the low birthrate, conditions at Fazenda Saubara were probably better than those on most Bahian plantations. The instructions set down to guide the estate's managers required that the slaves be allowed to plant their own plots and orchards in scrub brush (*capoeira*) along the coast. Any slave who became ill was to receive all necessary care at the Misericórdia's expense and, should the illness be prolonged, the slave was to be sent to its hospital in Salvador.[84] These measures, which should have ameliorated conditions for the slaves at Fazenda Saubara, were not effective. As Table 13-13 demonstrates, the fifty-six slaves who appeared on the Fazenda Saubara lists between 1750 and 1760 suffered twenty-two deaths, or about two out of every five slaves died in the period. Of the fifteen males on the roll in 1750, only four survived until 1760; of the eight women on the first list, only three remained a decade later. Nor do the 1750s seem exceptional for deaths at Fazenda Saubara. Surviving lists from 1727 and 1735 permit us to trace the survival of individuals between those two dates. Of eleven boys and men listed in 1727 with names and characteristics that allow us to identify them without doubt, only one survived in 1735. Of the women and girls, three and possibly four of the six identifiable in 1727 remained in 1735.[85]

We can, in fact, calculate approximate general fertility and mortality rates for this slave population. For a general fertility rate, we must assume that the recorded births are a minimum since there is no way to know how many infants were born and died between the list dates. In addition, we must assume that, unless designated as young or old, all women are in their childbearing years during the decade under consideration, except, of course, those whose ages are clearly above or below the fertile years. The fifteen women who were capable of bearing children and who appear in the lists bore five children we can account for during the decade under study. These fifteen women, given their ages and mortality history, lived sixty-two and a half years at risk of bearing a child. Thus, their minimum general fertility rate is 80 per 1,000. If this figure is inflated by 50 percent to compensate for intercensal infant deaths, the rate rises to 120 per 1,000.

For comparative purposes, the fertility situation can be expressed in another way. Fazenda Saubara experienced five births during the decade, or 0.5 a year. The average population on the estate during the period was just over twenty-nine slaves. These figures produce a crude birth rate of 17 per 1,000, which, if increased by 50 percent to compensate for unrecorded births, yields a rate of 26 per 1,000 as a maximum. These figures are comparable to the 23 per 1,000 reported for Worthy Park plantation in Jamaica between 1783 and 1834 and for all Jamaican plantations (1817–29), which recorded about 27 per 1,000.[86] The Saubara maximum figures then reach the levels recorded in another slave regime characterized by high proportions of Africans, an unbalanced sex ratio, and tropical agriculture. The minimum figures from Saubara are low but are in keeping with the other information we have gathered from parish registers and census returns. Five children to fifteen women assumed to be in their childbearing years is a general-fertility ratio of 333 per 1,000, which is exactly the average of the slave general-fertility ratio calculated from the three Bahian parishes in 1788. Thus, although the information from Saubara indicates a low level of fertility, it is consistent with other information I have presented concerning slave fertility in Bahia.

Mortality calculations present other problems. Here we are really speaking of an attrition rate from death, sale, or manumission, but I will assume that the disappearance of slaves from the lists is due exclusively to deaths and not to sales. This seems a relatively safe assumption, since the Misericórdia spent a considerable amount of money, according to the lists, to replenish its slave force and seems to have been a purchaser rather than a seller of slaves. No slave was designated on the lists as a chronic troublemaker or runaway, the usual reasons for sale of resident slaves. Since there is no way to recover the history of those children who were born and died between listings, I shall limit my calculation to a general mortality rate for adult men and adult women.[87] Of the thirty males above the age of eight in 1750 or who were probably older than that when they first appear on the lists, thirteen died during the decade. The thirty men lived a total of 113.5 years at risk, for a general mortality rate of 115 per 1,000. The mortality rate for women was considerably lower. The nineteen women of the appropriate ages lived 98.5 years at risk and suffered eight deaths for a rate of 81 per 1,000. This differential in male and female mortality rates has been noted in other slave societies and is usually ascribed to the heavier and more dangerous work performed by the men.

These rates of adult mortality and general fertility are staggering. They are far worse than those recorded in other slave regimes. Jamaica, for example, is thought in the early nineteenth century to have had a crude birthrate of about 23 per 1,000 and a mortality rate of 26 per 1,000. Calculations for slaves in the United States place the crude birthrate at 50 and the death rate at 20–30. The Fazenda Saubara adult mortality rate of 115 for men and 81 for women reaches epidemic levels, although there is no indication that epidemic disease was a problem in the 1750s.[88] Why the rates are so high is unclear. The

Table 13-13. *Slave mortality, Fazenda Saubara, 1750–60*

	Age	1750	1753	1757	1758	1760
Males, 1750						
Alexandre	50	Angola ---- incapacitated --------- †[a]				
Ambrosio	50	Angola ------------------------ †				
Antônio	8	Crioulo -- †
Diogo	20	Angola ---
Francisco	20	Angola ---
João Teixeira	50	Crioulo --
João	45	Angola ---- married ----------- †				
João	4	Crioulo --
José	20	Angola ---- cowboy --- †
José Grande	45	---------- †				
Luís dos Santos	45	----- married, old --------- †				
Manoel	12	Crioulo --- †
Simão	75	---------- †				
Simão da Cunha		married -- incapacitated ----- †				
Vicente	3 mos.	Crioulo (baby) --- †
Males added by 1753						
Ignacio "a boy"			Crioulo ---
Eusebio			Pardo, cowboy --------- †			
Males added by 1757						
Antonio				Angola --- †[b]
Antonio				Mina (new) -------------- (new) -------------------------
Candido				Mulato (young) ---

Domingos Marques,

Francisco	Mina	(new)	
João	Mina novo	(new)	
José	Mina novo	(new)	
Luis	Angola		
Simao	Gege		
Tomas	Angola		
	Mina novo	(new)	

Males added by 1758

Caetano	Mina new	
José	new	†

Males added by 1760

Bernardo	Mina
Pedro	Mina
Ambrosio	Angola
Severino	baby
Bastião	

Females, 1750

Ana	80	married	incapacitated	†
Andreza	50	Crioula	"old"	†
Isabel	30	Crioula	single	
Jacinta	27	Crioula	"baker"	†
Joana	70	Crioula	married	
Luiza	24	Crioula	? (crioulinha)	
Maria	18	Crioula	married	
Micaela	80	Crioula	incapacitated	†

Table 13-13 (*cont.*)

Age	1750	1753	1757	1758	1760
Females added by 1753					
	Joana	Gege	(old)		†
	Esperança	Crioula	(lame)		
	Maria de Mattos	Angola	†		
		Females added by 1757			
		Antônia	Gege (new)	(new)	
		Elena	Gege (new)	(new)	
		Josepha	Gege (new)	(new)	
		Joana	Gege		
		Narciza	Crioula (baby)		
		Rita	Gege nova	(new)	
			Females added by 1758		
			Anita	Gege	†
			Isabel	Angola (new)	
			Tomazia	Crioula (baby)	
				Females added by 1760	
				Ana	Crioula (baby)
				Andreza	Gege

[a]The symbol "†" indicates death.
[b]"New" means recently arrived from Africa.

Misericórdia did care for sick and infirm slaves in its hospitals in Salvador. Were some of those added already ill? It would appear not, since many of those added after 1753 were listed as *nova*, meaning a recently arrived African. High mortality rates during the seasoning period also do not appear to be a major factor. Only one death (José, added 1758) and possibly two others (Antônio, 1757; Anita, 1758) appear to be fatalities during the seasoning of newly arrived Africans. Sixteen of the twenty-two deaths were suffered by slaves who were at Saubara in 1750. Of these, ten or eleven were the deaths of adults over the age of forty-four. The extremely high mortality, then, seems to be a result of the age structure to some extent, although consideration of a slave as "old" at forty-eight (e.g., Luís dos Santos) is in itself a comment on the conditions of slave life. What is still troubling are the large percentage of adult deaths not due to the adjustment of seasoning.[89]

We must not lose sight of the fact that we are dealing here with people, not numbers. Although the materials we have provide only the most cursory and one-dimensional insight into their history, their appearance on the lists is poignant enough. Let us take the case of Ambrósio, born in Angola about the beginning of the eighteenth century. He arrived at Saubara sometime after 1727, at which time he received the name Ambrósio, apparently to replace another Ambrósio, an "old Black" who had recently died. The custom at Fazenda Saubara seems to have been to assign the same names to new slaves as those of former slaves who had died. Thus, we have the instances of a Maria de Mattos, an Arda from Dahomey who appears on the list of 1727, and of another Maria de Mattos, an Angolan purchased sometime before 1753. An elderly Simão died before 1753 and between that date and 1757 was replaced by an Angolan who was given the same name.

In 1750, Ambrósio was listed as fifty years old, and by 1757 he was dead. We do not know his actual age at death, since the age of fity listed in 1750 is clearly, like the other ages on that list, an approximation, at least for Africans. Over fifty years old, however, was considered an advanced age for slaves. This is made clear in the case of Andreza, a Mina who had been at Saubara at least since 1727, at which time she was probably in her twenties. By 1750, she was married and listed as fifty years of age. In 1753, she was listed as "old," and by 1757 she was dead. A similar case of early "aging" is that of Luís dos Santos, recorded as forty-five in 1750, called "old" three years later, and dead by 1757. With only one exception, any slave listed as "old" or incapacitated during the ten years under study did not survive until 1760.

Although "aging" came early, so did the end of adolescence or at least consideration of the slave as an adult. Two crioulo boys, Manoel (twelve) and Antônio (eight), were listed in 1750. By 1753, both were referred to as "already men" (*rapaz alias homen já feito*). Neither survived the decade. The question of adult status also becomes important in considerations of childbearing. We do not have good data for most of the women, but we can assume that most of the Africans purchased were young adults. Nevertheless, of the five babies whom we can identify on the lists, four were definitely born to crioulo women. African women did not seem to be bearing children.

The high levels of mortality called for replacement by the fazenda's owners. The original group of fifteen males and eight females had to be supplemented. By 1753, two new slaves were added to replace two who had died. In that year, three women were brought to Saubara to compensate for one who had died and two others who were incapacitated. By 1757, another ten slaves had died, and a major effort at replacement or expansion of the slave force was made. Ten men, mostly Minas and Angolas, were acquired, as were five women, all Ewes (Geges). In addition, Narciza was born to Maria, the married crioula. Throughout the decade, Fazenda Saubara maintained between fifteen and twenty males and eight and fifteen females. The estate averaged twenty-nine slaves during the decade. The sex ratio was always imbalanced in favor of males.

What the skeleton of lists at Fazenda Saubara cannot convey is the kind of world and perception of it that such high mortality rates must have created. Here we are dealing with pure speculation, but undoubtedly slaves perceived the transitory nature of their existence and the danger of death in which they lived. Those few who survived the whole decade at Saubara would have seen almost half their friends, acquaintances, and companions die in that short time. Was their reaction despair, resignation, or resentment? We cannot know, but one suspects that the very low birthrate may reflect attitudes and decisions on the part of the slaves as much as the influence of sex and age ratios.

CHAPTER 14

THE SLAVE FAMILY AND
THE LIMITATIONS OF SLAVERY

You, so-and-so, in your time you will marry what's her name.

André João Antonil (1710)

. . . they are married before the Church, solemnly by words, André Gege with Eugenia Gege, Antonio Nagô with Rita Nagô, all slaves of Captain Antônio de Araújo Gomes, residents in this parish of Our Lady of Purification, and they then received the blessings according to the rites and ceremonies of Holy Mother Church.

Purificação parish register (1785)

In the face of the deadly demography of Bahian slavery and the limitations imposed by the institution on the life choices and opportunities of those who lived within it, slaves sought to create social and cultural forms that provided solace and support in a hostile world. This chapter will look beyond the demographic structures to examine the cultural boundaries that defined opportunities and then examine the social responses of slaves constantly confronted by the power of the slaveholders. The formation of the family, especially through the sacrament of marriage, and the spiritual birth of the individual through the sacrament of baptism were two moments of extreme importance for anyone living in colonial Brazil, and much of my discussion will center on these acts. We must realize at the outset, however, that the formation of a conjugal unit and ultimately of a family did not depend on church-sponsored marriage for either slaves or free persons. To say that a couple were unmarried and that their children were illegitimate did not mean that they did not form a family unit, despite certain legal disabilities that they might suffer. We can also grant that the impact and meaning of marriage and baptism may have been considerably different for Africans and Portuguese and their respective descendants in the colony. Still, given the difficulty of penetrating the inner world of the slaves, marriage and baptism are two points of entry that promise some return.

The importance of the family – those people related by blood or marriage who recognize these ties – and of kinship in general has long been a subject of intense interest in Brazil, and although a great deal of weight has been given to the impact of these relations on political and social life, there are, in fact, few studies of the organization of the Brazilian family and household in the past.[1] Although this is true of the Brazilian family in general, it is even more so of the slave family, which has been assumed to have been virtually nonexistent or so deformed by slavery that it is believed to be the principal cause of later social ills. Even Gilberto Freyre's classic *Casa grande e senzala*, which studied the relations between masters and slaves in the context of family, was primarily concerned with the patriarchal family of the big house and not with the familial life of the slaves themselves.[2]

The historiographical revolution that has characterized studies of the slave family in the United States and the Caribbean has not been paralleled in Brazil. There, most scholars agree with the approach that in the North American context characterized the work of E. Franklin Frazier or the Moynihan Report of 1965. Slavery is viewed as a destructive force that impeded or deranged the family life of slaves and contributed to a series of postslavery social disorders.[3] We can take here as a leading proponent of this position the distinguished Paulista sociologist Florestan Fernandes, who wrote:

. . . the family failed to set itself up and did not have a sociopsychological and sociocultural effect on the development of the basic personality, the control of egocentric and antisocial behavior, and the development of bonds of solidarity. This can be historically confirmed by a simple reference to the main policy of the seignorial and slaveholding society of Brazil which always sought to hinder the organized life of the family among slaves.[4]

This is basically a view of the slave family in terms of social pathology that ties slave behavior directly to the power of the masters and leaves no room for slaves as actors. It is a view with deep historical roots.

Certainly, by the nineteenth century, abolitionists and ameliorationists in Brazil had joined eighteenth-century ecclesiastical writers in their condemnation of interference in the family lives of the slaves. How can a wife obey her husband and her master, or slave parents protect their children, or these honor their parents, asked one abolitionist, posing the inherent contradictions between slavery and normal family relations.[5] Others, such as João Imbert, as he wrote in his manual on farm management, believed that fostering a strong family among the slaves was good business because "of all ties it is the bonds of family that most closely link a man to his obligations." He advocated giving slaves presents when they married and promises of freedom for their children, but his hortatory comments were by implication a criticism of the attitudes of most planters.[6] But the disregard of planters and the lack of marriages in the church are not in any way a measure of slave reality and of the ability of the slaves to create and maintain bonds of affection, association, and blood that had a real and persistent meaning in their lives. Henry Koster, the English traveler who managed an engenho in Pernambuco in the 1810s, doubted as a man of the Romantic Age that true love could exist in a people that had not reached a certain stage of "civilization," but he personally observed many cases in which "punishments and other dangers have been braved to visit a chosen one; in which journeys by night have been made after a day of fatigue; in which great constancy has been shown, and a determination that the feelings of the heart shall not be controlled."[7] It was, in fact, exactly in the relations with families and friends that the essential humanity of the slaves was made most apparent to Koster and others like him. He observed,

The Negroes show much attachment to their wives and children, to their other relations if they should chance to have any, and to their *malungos* or fellow passengers from Africa. The respect which is paid to old age is extremely pleasing to witness. Superannuated Africans upon the estates are never suffered to want any comforts which is in the power of their fellow slaves to supply them.[8]

The limitations of the slave system were real and often destructive as well, but to believe, as Fernandes does, that the force inherent in the masters' power and the operation of the institution of slavery alone set the parameters of slave life is to miss the essential role of the slaves in creating their own culture. For us, the interpretive problem is one of balance: How do we weigh the problem of the master against the actions of the slaves? Although there is no doubt that the desires of the slaves entered into the selection of marriage partners, family arrangements, childbearing decisions, choices of baptismal sponsors, and other aspects of family life, we can never ignore the overreaching constraints of slavery and those of Catholic law and custom on both masters and slaves.

Here, then, we are dealing with a curious counterpoint, a sort of duel in a dark room in which we see the sparks struck by the wills of the combatants but cannot tell who is striking the blows. It is precisely in the everyday matters of life under slavery, in the most common and mundane aspects of home, family, labor, and recreation, that the documents usually fall silent. Should we have had the opportunity to stop any slave in a canefield in Passé or Rio Fundo, such as those we see in Figure 14-1, and ask him or her about these matters, we would have received an answer filled with insight and understanding that present-day scholars can barely discern after years of study. Moreover, our hypothetical respondent would think us particularly dull to be asking such questions, which surely he or she and all his or her companions could answer as a matter of common knowledge. It is precisely the commonness of this

Figure 14-1. Rural slaves in Bahia in the early nineteenth century. This man and woman seem better dressed than most descriptions of rural slaves would lead us to expect.

knowledge that caused it to go unrecorded. What we have left are certain observable patterns that we can document but whose meaning and function within the slave system remain conjectural.

Constraints on the slave family

Let us first identify the constraints imposed on slave actions, choices, and decisions by slavery and the master–slave relationship. There was, for example, a largely unwritten but generally enforced policy that the social universe of the slave was to be circumscribed – limited when possible to the boundaries of the plantation, cane farm, or slaveholding unit. This policy severely limited familial opportunities for slaves, especially on smaller estates where there were few available partners or where fellow slaves might be blood relatives. In hundreds of registrations of baptisms, marriages, and deaths, I found no slave listed as married to the slave of a different master.[9] It is not difficult to imagine the complications that might arise when such an arrangement existed: divided residence, enforced separation, conflicts of humane treatment and property rights. Such marriages presented real problems for slaves as well as masters, but given the imbalanced sex ratios on many Recôncavo estates, slaves wishing to find mates would undoubtedly have accepted the problems lacking other alternatives. The choice, however, was rarely if ever allowed them.

The clearest exposition of this policy comes to us in the form of the operating instructions in 1692 to Father Bernabé Soares when he was on his way to manage Engenho Sergipe do Conde.[10] The engenho's slaves were not to be permitted to join brotherhoods off the engenho, serve as godparents elsewhere, or take part in religious plays or celebrations off the estate. Similarly, slaves and free persons not attached to Engenho Sergipe could not take part in these activities on that estate. The limitation on marriage off the estate, then, was simply an extension of this general policy designed to circumscribe the slave's world and limit his or her contacts: to isolate an estate's slaves from the possible infection of rebellion or cooperation with others in bondage on other estates and to make them more directly responsive to the commands and desires of their owner.

In the long run, the policy of circumscription or isolation failed. The engenhos were too close to each other. During the safra, men and women going to and from the fields often encountered other slaves of neighboring estates. Contact with Salvador was continual, and boatmen and carters constantly moved between the city and the mills. As the slave revolts of the early nineteenth century later demonstrated, the information and association networks of slaves did expand beyond the boundaries of the rural slaveholdings. Still, the slaveowners' attempts to isolate their bondsmen had some effects. Strong identifications developed among the slaves of a particular institution.[11] Planter rivalries sometimes turned into constant hostility between the slaves of different estates.[12] Strong local attachments developed. Conversely, restriction to the estates' boundaries limited the life opportunities available to slaves in many ways.

The policy of circumscription, enforced in the context of the majority of engenhos' severe sexual imbalances, created another type of constraint on the slaves. There were simply not enough women for the number of men on most estates. This was a result of planter choice in the creation of their slave forces and of the heavy dependence on Africa for new laborers. The effect of this pattern, however, was to preclude the possibility of family formation for many men. Ameliorationists complained bitterly against this "deplorable blindness," since women were necessary to support the men, educate the children, and care for the elderly and sick. The planters, they said, instead of creating "a large and beautiful creole population by fostering propagation among their slaves not only do not do so, but even prevent it."[13] These demographic arguments were accompanied by moral ones as well. Many observers believed that the promiscuity of the slaves was more the fault of the planters than the slaves. Koster is most informative in this regard. He believed that if an adequate number of women were on an estate, that slaves would behave sexually no worse than anyone else. "That many men and women will be licentious has been and still is the lot of human nature, and not the particular fault of the much injured race of which I speak."[14] Once again, his personal experience provides poignant evidence that slaves perceived the problem too. A slave at a Pernambucan engenho, learning of his wife's infidelity, complained to the master. She was ordered to be whipped. But when the punishment began, the husband took pity and pleaded for her release, saying, "If there are so many men and so few women upon the estate, how is it to be expected that the latter are to be faithful? Why does Master have so many men and so few women?"[15]

Imbalanced sex ratios and a policy of restriction limited the social horizons of slaves, who also confronted the direct intrusion of the master in their family life. The power of the slaveowner could be expressed by preventing unions, determining partners, dictating the timing of marriage, and ultimately by breaking up families. In addition, as Freyre and many others make clear, the sexual exploitation of slaves by the planter and his children became a constant aspect of rural life whose effects on the slave family itself were surely negative.

The opportunity for slaves to form permanent unions with some hope that their mates and children would not be separated from them capriciously would seem to be a key to the slave family. Like all aspects of slave life, the problem is complex because we must deal with the forms, strategies, and opportunities used by the slaves and with those provided by the masters within the context of a profound Catholic tradition, sometimes at odds with an even profounder desire for profit. Marriage and the family were not necessarily connected in the sense that officially sanctioned union, marriage as a sacrament of the church, was a prerequisite for either slaves or free people to form families. The problem, then, has four sides: the legal and canonical norms of marriage, the reality within the society, the attitudes and actions of the masters, and the perceptions and performance of the slaves. All are interrelated, and each necessitates the use of different sorts of evidence.

Despite the official ideology that marriage as a sacrament of the church was encouraged among all believers, evidence of various kinds points to a situation in which slaves were regularly denied or discouraged from unions in the church. Observers, most of them clerics, registered their dismay at the failure of planters to encourage or allow slaves to marry. Condemnations of planter attitudes were made as early as the 1580s, and similar criticisms were restated during the next two centuries.[16] The situation in the Recôncavo was outlined in some detail in 1619, when two Jesuit Fathers conducted a mission to the farms and plantations of the region. They reported marrying 308 slave couples who were cohabiting in sin, many of whom had been prevented from marrying by their masters, who "for some reasons and excuses invented by the Devil's art" had impeded them.[17] The Jesuits insisted these couples be allowed to marry and informed the masters that their responsibilities were like those of "fathers of families." Although this paternal image was often used to describe the master–slave relationship, it had little practical meaning in the lives of most slaves.

The church in Bahia gave the matter direct consideration when in 1707 a synod was held to draw up the ecclesiastical regulations for the newly created Archdiocese of Bahia. The resulting code, the *Constituições primeiras* published in Lisbon in 1719, made a number of statements concerning marriage among slaves.[18] On the one hand, it reinforced the slave system by decreeing that the sacrament of marriage did not free a slave from bondage, and it also eased the way for slaves who had been married in Africa before enslavement to marry in Brazil. At the same time, the synod spoke out directly against the common practices of the planters. Canon 303 commanded owners to allow slaves to marry without hindrance or threat, and it exhorted masters not to impede the marriage by separating or selling one of the partners.[19]

That these regulations had little effect on planter actions is made apparent by three works published during the course of the eighteenth century. The Jesuits Andreoni and Benci and the secular priest Ribeiro Rocha all condemned the continuing abuses of slavery, including the restrictions on slave marriages.[20] In the works of the two Jesuits, we catch a glimpse of the abuse and the planter's defense. Slaveowners argued that when slaves were required to marry within the church that the bond then became permanent, and thus when they tired of a spouse they resorted to poison since divorce was impossible.[21] Then, too, planters held that slaves also carried on illicit relations after being married, which was an affront to the church. Planters accepted consensual unions as the normal course of events and tended to leave slaves alone in this regard or to arrange unions without the benefit of clergy. The clerics, of course, found such behavior irresponsible and reprehensible. Benci in his *Economia cristã* (1705) argued with intended irony that if the fact that slaves left their wives to have illicit relations was a reason to discourage them from marrying in the first place, then the many planters who deserted their virtuous and honorable wives for the arms of their own slave women should be an argument aganst whites marrying.[22] Slaves, he felt, should have the full opportunity to marry. The works of these ecclesiastical authors were not widely read, and although they and other clerics had the use of the pulpit to further their ideas, it would seem that the planters continued as before. As late as the 1820s, the Recôncavo slaveowners had a reputation for harsh treatment and not allowing their slaves to marry.[23]

For the slave who did marry according to Catholic practice, the choice of a partner was often not freely made. Antonil tells us plainly that among some masters it was simply the custom to command: "You Fulano, in your time you will marry Fulana," and that was that.[24] Marriage registers that record three or four slave couples belonging to the same master all marrying in the same ceremony seem to indicate direct intervention of the master in the selection and timing of unions. Certainly the paternal model operated here, since in Portuguese society fathers often had the predominant role in the choice of a marriage partner. Clerics often admonished slaveowners to treat their bondsmen like their own families, and in this respect they did so. But given Antonil's tone and the fact that many planters consistently refused to allow their slaves to marry, whatever the ideological justification of equating the management of slaves and families, the treatment of slaves was actually quite a different matter.

Before African slaves could receive the sacrament of matrimony, they had to be accepted within the body of the church through baptism. But here again the planters were negligent of their responsibilities, in the opinion of the clergy. Planters argued that the newly arrived Africans were too uncivilized and ignorant to learn the ten commandments and other basic aspects of Christianity, but Antonil chided them that long after the boçais had learned how to plead with their masters or knew how much cane was in a daily quota, they were still not receiving the instruction necessary for baptism.[25]

The slow pace of Christianization among the slaves became a matter of royal concern toward the end of the seventeenth century. In 1697, the crown ordered that, when possible, baptism take place at the ports of embarkation and that a priest or a pious layman be placed on each slave ship to instruct the slaves in the faith.[26] The Overseas Council in Lisbon proposed that acculturated black catechizers be paid to do this service, but a religious commission in Bahia objected because it feared that if instruction took place in the African languages the black instructors would have too much liberty and power. Instead, the commission suggested that instruction be done in Brazil with the help of ladino slaves and that planters who failed in this regard be punished.[27] In 1718, however, the crown wrote the archbishop of Bahia lamenting the fact that the slaves remained unbaptized.[28]

That the general situation had changed little by the beginning of the eighteenth century was made clear in a report sent to the junta of missions in Lisbon by two Jesuits, Father José Bernardo and Father Francisco de Lima, who visited the Recôncavo in 1701. They baptized 178 Angola slaves who had lived without baptism or had simply had water placed on their head without any instruction before leaving Africa. They also reported that many sugar planters, lavradores, and tobacco farmers kept their slaves from attending mass on Sundays and holy days. To their own satisfaction, and supposedly that of the Lisbon junta, they noted that slaves had ignored threats and punishment to come to the visiting Jesuits.[29]

The failure of planters to indoctrinate their slaves stemmed from a variety of reasons, but their reluctance to allow slaves to marry was probably based more on considerations of the slaves as property than on a desire to guard the honor of the marital state. As long as slaves remained unbaptized and unmarried, the churchmen might complain about the failure of the masters to carry out their moral obligations. But after marriage in the church, there were definite constraints in canon law that argued for the free use of the matrimony. Separation of the partners by sale or for some other reason was condemned as an offense to both charity and natural law. As long as slaves did not have church-sanctioned unions, these restrictions did not apply with any force.

We must, of course, always keep in mind that we are dealing with a slave regime in which the interests of the masters came before the rights of the slaves. Despite occasional interventions from both church and crown intended to ameliorate the conditions of slavery, the normal situation was one in which slaves had little recourse to authority beyond their own masters. As human beings and as Christians, slaves were recognized in civil and canon law as possessing certain rights. This had been true under traditional Portuguese law, and by the mid-eighteenth century some of the more liberal precepts of the Enlightenment had begun to extend these attitudes even farther.[30] The problem remained one of access to the legal system. Most Bahian slaves lived in a situation where their masters were the arbiters of right and wrong, justice and injustice.

One case on the right of a slave to marriage came before the courts in 1770, and it is particularly revealing of the legal attitude toward slave marriage within the context of the slave as property. In that year, Luiza Fernandes attempted to sell away her black slave João. The slave had been able to complain to the civil courts against this. The owner

claimed that João's wife, also a black, had borne a mulatto child, proof
of infidelity, and that the infuriated husband had tried to kill both his
wife and his owner. The case is interesting from a number of view-
points, including the attitude of slave men toward infidelity. But in the
context of the slave's right to marriage, the judgment of the court is
particularly important. The court's opinion was:

> Even though the master should not sell his married slave away so that the use
> of the matrimony is impeded, this can be restricted when because of ill will,
> the master cannot remain without danger to himself or his possession, because
> the right that the married slave has to his matrimony cannot be guarded when
> the crimes of the slave and the need of the master require that he be sold from
> the place where the other partner lives. This separation is more the fault of the
> slave than the master.[31]

We see in this case the basic elements of the problem: The right of
slaves to enjoy their matrimony, that is to remain together, is recognized, but the right of the master to protect his or her property is also
noted. One suspects that in the Brazilian slave regime the latter usually
won out over the former.

There is, of course, another side to this question: the desire or
willingness of slaves to accept Catholic marriages as their own preferred form of bond. Planter complaints that slaves used poison to end
an undesired union were surely excuses, but at the same time we must
admit the possibility that Africans, coming from societies in which
infertility, sorcery, or other causes were grounds for divorce, found the
constraints of indissoluble Catholic marriage undesirable. African reluctance to enter Catholic unions and planter desires to avoid external
interference in the management of their slaves may have been mutually reinforcing attitudes. The fact that so large a percentage of the
slave population of Bahia was African throughout the colonial era undoubtedly contributed to what was a chronic situation. Owners were
reluctant to instruct slaves, baptize them, or allow them to marry in the
church. Slaves may have been less than anxious to accept Catholic
norms.

Whatever the combination of planter and slave reluctance toward
matrimony in the church, the evidence is clear that the vast majority of
slaves did not wed according to Catholic custom. Recorded levels of
illegitimacy are not necessarily a surrogate measure for the lack of
marriage, since couples who eventually wed may have children out of
wedlock, but in the aggregate when used with other materials they do
indicate a general pattern of marital frequency.

First, we must place the levels of illegitimacy in the general context
of Brazilian society. A number of studies have all demonstrated that
although the general rate of illegitimacy in Brazil was high, among
slaves it was always higher. Marcilio's study of São Paulo between 1745

Table 14-1. *Legitimacy of free and slave children baptized in Recôncavo parishes, 1723–1816*

Parish	Years	Status	Legitimate	Illegitimate[a]	Percent illegitimate
Saubara	1723–4	Free	24	10	(29.4)
		Slave	3	28	(90.3)[b]
Rio Fundo	1780–1 and 1788	Free	49	19	(27.9)
		Slave	19	38	(66.6)[c]
Monte	1788–9	Free	52	22	(29.7)
		Slave	15	42	(73.7)[d]
São Francisco	1816	Free	34	13	(27.7)
		Slave	0	21	(100)[e]

[a]Rates for illegitimate slave births may have been slightly higher because in each parish a few *expostos* or abandoned children were accepted and baptized as free. Since their color was often black or mulatto, it is possible that they were children of slave mothers. [b]In addition, 10 adult slaves were baptized. [c]Six adult slaves. [d]Four adult slaves. [e]Twenty-two adult slaves.
Source: ACMS, livros de bautismo for the parishes and years indicated.

and 1845 reveals that 39 percent of the free population was born outside church unions. In Vila Rica in 1804, 52 percent of the free population and more than 98 percent of the slaves were illegitimate.[32] Other evidence suggests the same patterns. Klein showed that in São Paulo in 1800 a higher proportion of adult slaves were unmarried than either whites or free persons of color.[33] Slenes's analysis of the Brazilian slave population in 1872 revealed that although 27.3 percent of the free women were formally married, only 9 percent of the slave women were wed within the church.[34] This scattered evidence all points in the same direction: Although consensual unions outside the church were, and still are, common in Latin America, especially among poorer economic groups, the levels of bastardy that such unions created were considerably higher for slaves than for free persons. Although it can be argued that free persons found it difficult to meet the requirements and do the paperwork necessary to prove their lack of impediments as a prerequisite to posting banns, especially if they had been born in Portugal or in some other part of Brazil, we have seen that the *Constituições primeiras* specifically eased these requirements for slaves.[35] The lack of slave marriages must be attributed to other causes.

The situation in colonial Bahia seems similar to that described in other areas of Brazil. Baptismal registers were sampled in four Recôncavo parishes to determine ratios of illegitimacy. Table 14-1 indicates that although levels of illegitimacy were high for the Bahian population as a whole, the levels for the slave population were two or three times higher than those for the free. The great majority of rural slaves in Bahia were not born to parents who were married in the rite of the Catholic church. Formal marriage in the church was simply not common among slaves, but this did not mean that slaves had no families or that kinship was unimportant in their lives.

Finally, I must reemphasize that while slaveowners held ultimate power in determining the life chances and familial arrangements of slaves, the latter were not without some ability to influence decisions that affected their lives. Within the master–slave relationship there was room for maneuver. Although a slave could not marry in the church without the master's permission, because the priest would not post the banns without it, slaves had ways of making their desires known. Slaves cajoled, bargained, or simply refused to cooperate, often in the face of severe punishment. Masters at times found it easier or more expedient to accede to slave wishes than to ignore them.

What then often appeared as a dictate of the slaveowner was in reality a compromise with the strategies and desires of the slaves. In 1745, for example, a slave woman at Engenho Petinga was sold to a lavrador de cana nearby.[36] Her male companion ran off to join her, and the matter was not settled until the lavrador sent back another slave of equal value in exchange. The slaves had determined that they would not be separated. Henry Koster reported another such "negotiation."[37] A slave woman sought to be purchased by a certain planter with the permission of her present owner. This was done, and on the following day she pleaded with her new master to buy a fellow slave, obviously a kinsman or a lover. The new master sought to do this, but the former owner did not wish to sell the man in question. After three days, however, the sale was arranged because the slave had refused to work and had threatened to take his own life, so that the owner, fearing such a loss with no compensation, agreed to the sale. Slaves did have ways of making their desires known to masters.

To some extent, the larger the estate and the more distant and less intimate the relation with the master, the more freedom the slaves enjoyed in making their own arrangements and decisions. Thus, field slaves would be less subject to interference than house slaves, and those on large units better off in this regard than urban slaves or those who were owned by lavradores and small farmers. Maria Graham, who visited Bahia in 1821, reported that the "out of doors" slaves of the great engenhos were advantaged because, as one was supposed to have said, "The more the master is removed from us in place and rank, the greater the liberty we enjoy."[38] Unfortunately, the great majority of Bahian slaves lived in small- to medium-sized units, so few enjoyed the anonymity that the great plantations with more than one hundred fifty slaves provided.

Family formation

In 1811, the widower Alexandre Francisco, a crioulo forro, was in love. At Engenho Jacuipe do Brito in Rio Fundo, where he resided, there also lived the object of his affection, Joaquina Maria do Sacramento, a crioula who lived at home with her mother, Ana, a Yoruba (Nagô) woman.[39] Alexandre had sought the mother's permission to marry, and his proposal had been accepted. He was welcome in the house, and his prospective wife and mother-in-law cooked for him and washed his clothes. Everything seemed well arranged. Alexandre Francisco was shocked to find when he sought to have the banns posted that his prospective mother-in-law had raised an objection claiming that he was, in fact, not a forro but a slave and was already married. These charges were false, and Alexandre Francisco produced documents to prove them so. The mother, however, was adamant, and Joaquina Maria was so upset at her mother's interference that she left home and sought refuge in the house of the owner of the engenho to avoid the attentions of another suitor her mother had arranged. Why had the mother changed her mind and caused such a furor? According to Alexandre Francisco, it was because the mother was a Nagô, and being of that people, "she allowed herself to be persuaded by those of her nation that her daughter should marry a Nagô black."

The case of Alexandre Francisco suggests that beneath the surface of plantation life and Catholic ritual, African cultural and ethnic affinities continued to play a role in the formation of families among the slaves. In ways usually left unrecorded in the surviving documents, these influenced the decisions and choices of both slaves and free persons of color. Plantation inventories because of their inattention to the marital state of slaves do not usually provide much evidence on this question, but a few lists do survive with the appropriate structure. On the three engenhos and cane farm of João Lopes Fiuza inventoried in the 1750s, twenty-three marriages can be identified in which the origins of the partners are known.[40] Ethnic preference among certain African groups seems strong. Of eleven marriages involving Calabars, for example, ten were between men and women of that group. Although there was a tendency among peoples from the Bight of Benin area to marry endogamously, this plantation list and various parish registers suggest that Yoruba, Ewe, and Akan slaves did intermarry regularly and that for most purposes might be considered a general group sharing certain attributes and serving as a pool of marriage partners.[41]

Some of these patterns become clearer in parish registers. In Purificação parish, the heart of the sugar-growing region of the Recôncavo, sixty-two marriages involving slaves were recorded between 1774 and 1788.[42] A tabulation of these unions indicates patterns of endogamy. Table 14-2 demonstrates that there was a strong tendency for people

Table 14-2. *Origins of slave marriage partners, Purificação parish, 1774–88*

Brides	Grooms			
	Guiné	Bight of Benin	Angola	Brazil
Guiné	2	–	1	1
Bight of Benin	–	19	3	4
Angola	–	3	3	3
Brazil	–	1	2	9

Source: ACMS, livro de casamentos, Purificação, 1774–88.

from West Africa (Guiné) and the Bight of Benin to marry endogamously, or at least to marry partners from their own region of Africa if not from the same ethnic group. Angolan slaves were far less selective and married other Africans or crioulos with apparently less concern for endogamy. In fact, West Africans were about five times as likely to marry endogamously as slaves from central Africa. But whatever the patterns of preference that separated various African peoples, the barriers between Africans and crioulos were even greater. The chances were about eleven to one that Brazilian-born slaves would marry Brazilians and that Africans would marry Africans. This pattern is also borne out in a study of Inhambupe parish, where between 1750 and 1800 more than 80 percent of the marriages were between persons of the same origin or ethnic group.[43] In general, then, common origins, language, and traditions remained important considerations for African-born slaves in their choice of mates. Naturally, those from those groups most prevalent in the captaincy's population had the best chance of finding a partner of their own kind.[44]

The patterns among the Brazilian-born crioulos and pardos deserve separate attention. Brazilian-born slaves preferred partners who were also native born, although they did marry Africans as well. Color and sex seem to have influenced their patterns of selection in ways not apparent among the Africans. Crioula women married native-born blacks and sometimes pardos, but light-skinned women did not marry black men as a rule and preferred pardo men. In this pattern, we see the operation of a hierarchy of color in which women seem to marry "up." The racial hierarchy imposed by the masters became an element in choice, as Fanon's axiom that the oppressed often adopt the ideology of the oppressors became a reality.

One other aspect of crioulo marriage patterns deserves comment. Although slaves of different masters hardly ever married, it was not uncommon to find slaves married to free persons. In Purificação parish, 21 percent of the marriages involving slaves (13 of 63) included a forro as a partner. The predominant pattern was between slave hus-

Table 14-3. *Marriages between slaves and forros,*
Purificação parish, 1774–88[a]

	Slave husband		
Forra wife	Crioulo	Pardo	African
Crioula	5	2	–
Parda	–	–	–
African	3	–	1

[a]In addition, there were two unions between free men
and slave women. In both cases, the husbands were crioulos. In one, the wife was African; in the other, she was
crioula.
Source: Same as Table 14-2.

bands and forro women, and in the majority of cases the partners were
creoles. There were occasional cases of free husbands marrying slave
women, but these were relatively uncommon (see Table 14-3). Although the sample is admittedly small, the patterns are the same as
those discovered in a study of Vila Rica in 1804, when 25 percent of
marriages involving slaves (50 of 200) involved a forro partner, with the
dominant tie (19 percent) again being between slave men and forro
women. Koster, too, noted in Pernambuco that slave–free marriages
were not uncommon.[45]

The marriage links between slaves and forros obviously violated to
some extent the circumscription of slave life aimed at by many masters
but may have served other purposes for both masters and slaves. In
Purificação, this arrangement seems to have been fostered by some
masters and not others. Five of the thirteen cases involved the slaves of
José Pires de Carvalho e Albuquerque, senhor of Engenho Cazumba.
Perhaps he was allowing his slaves to overcome a severely imbalanced
sex ratio by seeking female partners from among the former slaves and
their descendants who lived around the margins of the estate. In this
way he provided mates for his slaves and also secured female laborers
who would become attached to his property. From the slave's point of
view, marriage with a forro would ensure the legal freedom of any
children born, since the status of the children depended on that of the
mother. For a slave woman who married a forro man, the possibility
that he might be able to accumulate enough money to liberate her and
their children may have been a consideration.[46]

Because so few slaves married within the church, the observable patterns of slave unions provide at best a very fragmentary and limited
record of the formation of slave families and the choices or options
available to the slaves. There is, however, evidence of different codes of
behavior and belief operating in the slave community. There appears to

have been an inherent tension between the ethnic preferences of Africa – the desire to maintain cultural ties or links to ancestors through endogamy – and the demands of the hierarchies of slave and free status and of color imposed by the dominant slave-based society. Within the constraints of a master's power and the demographic realities of the sex ratio and age structure, Afro-Brazilians stood at a crossroad between an African past and an American present in their choice of partners and in the formation of family ties. Their decision weighed the comfort and security of a shared past against the manipulation of the colonial slave system for one's personal or family advantage. In a place like Bahia, African affinities weighed heavily; and it is also not surprising that Brazilian-born and African slaves developed different strategies.

Family structure: the example of Engenho Santana

Historians of the family have developed a variety of techniques that allow them to analyze census registers and other lists organized by family or household units in order to examine the structures of residence and familial life. In general, for slaves in colonial Brazil the materials needed for such analyses are lacking. Census schedules infrequently listed slaves, and when they did so usually did not note their family attachments. Plantation lists and inventories rarely noted the social relations of the slaves. Structural analysis of family and household in colonial Brazil has thus concerned itself primarily with the free members of society.[47] The few exceptions are truly exceptions because the lists that permit this kind of analysis for slaves are almost always of properties owned by religious orders or by the state and do not represent the conditions under which the majority of the slaves lived. For example, Richard Graham's pioneering study of the slaves of the former Jesuit fazenda Santa Cruz in Rio de Janeiro deals with a state-owned property with an enormous slave force of 1,347 people, over four times larger than the biggest Bahian engenho.[48] Still, Graham's study and the articles of Craton, Higman, and Laslett on Caribbean and U.S. slave families provide models of analysis that can be used in a limited way in the Bahian context.[49]

We have available two listings of the slave population at the Jesuit-owned Engenho Santana in Ilhéus made twenty-one years apart, the first in 1731 and the second in 1752.[50] These lists are organized by family unit, and although they lack some information such as the slave's place of birth or ethnic origin, they nevertheless offer a rare opportunity to examine slave household structure on a sugar plantation.

Engenho Santana, of course, was in this period a Jesuit estate, and as such its organization immediately raises questions of typicality in regard to the family organization of the slave force and the attention paid to this matter by the owners. Here, however, we may be fortunate.

From 1704 to 1731, Santana had been managed by Father Manoel de Figueiredo, who, as we have seen, had been of the opinion that slaves should not marry.[51] During the period of his control, an average of only one or two marriages a year had been performed. His successor had moved to rectify what he considered a scandalous situation. By 1752, Engenho Santana had passed through the hands of other managers. In that year, a complete inventory of the property was made by Father João Cortes prior to surrendering administration of the plantation to Father Jerónimo da Gama. The two lists, separated by about twenty years, can be taken to represent two models of household structure. The list of 1731 comes after an extended period in which slave marriage has not been encouraged, whereas the list of 1752 represents the result of conscious efforts by the administrators to have slaves form "stable" family units based upon marriage.

Father Pedro Teixeira, who took charge of Engenho Santana in 1731, was shocked by the conditions he found and by the slaves he was to manage. He received 178 slaves, which was the "same as so many devils, thieves, and enemies" – hardly a patriarchal attitude. There were 26 married couples, 66 single males, 4 widowers, 45 single women, and 11 widows. Of the 111 single slaves, about 40 were under the age of twelve or thirteen. In Teixeira's listing of the slave force, he distinguished 57 residential groups or households, giving the age, marital status, and relationship of each individual to the head of the household or to the senior women in the unit. Occasionally, other information as to place of birth, color, or usefulness was also included.

The first aspect of slave-household composition that deserves notice is that, despite a policy of discouraging marriage that had existed at Santana for the two previous decades, most of the slaves lived in units that included a man and a woman stated to be sexual partners or of ages that make that relationship probable; this is shown in Table 14-4. Almost half the households and more than 60 percent of the slaves lived in groupings that were double headed, that is, with both an adult male and female resident. A unit composed of a man, a woman, and children (Type D) was by far the mode, and variations that included the nuclear family as well as other kin were known. We can take, for example, the case of Cosme and his wife, who lived with their two-year-old son. Also residing with them were Cosme's five brothers and sisters, ranging in age from ten to twenty years old. Another example is the household of Policarpo, a man of thirty, who lived with his wife, Maria; their ten-year-old daughter; and his two brothers in their twenties. It is quite clear, at least at Santana, that the two-parent household presented the most common form of family life experience shared by the slaves. High rates of illegitimacy did not necessarily mean that males were absent from the slave child's formative years.

While female-headed households were not uncommon, they were by

Table 14-4. *Slave households, Engenho Santana, 1731 and 1752*

Group	Type		1731 Units	1731 Persons	1752 Units	1752 Persons[a]
I.	A.	Male and female	8	16	13	26
	B.	Male, female, and unrelated others			2	6
	C.	Male, female, and kin	1	3	2	10
	D.	Male, female, and children	15	63	16	61
	E.	Male, female, children, and grandchildren	1	11	2	10
	F.	Male, female, children, and kin	2	13	1	5
	G.	Male, female, children, and others			5	24
	Totals		27 (46.5%)	106 (61.0%)	41 (72.4%)	142 (79.8%)
II.	H.	Female and children	5	16	1	3
	I.	Female, children, and grandchildren	1	3		
	J.	Female, children, and kin	1	6	1	7
	K.	Female and others	4	13	1	3
	Totals		11 (17.2%)	38 (20.4%)	3 (5.2%)	13 (17.3%)
III.	L.	Male and children	3	9	1	4
	M.	Male, children, and grandchildren				
	N.	Male, children, and kin	1	7	1	7
	Totals		4 (8.6%)	16 (10.2%)	2 (3.4%)	11 (6.2%)
IV.	O.	Siblings	1	2		
V.	P.	Solitaries, male	10	10	8	8
	Q.	Solitaries, female	5	5	4	4
	Totals		15 (25.0%)	15 (8.5%)	12 (20.7%)	12 (6.7%)

[a]Deleted from the 1752 list are six slaves. Three – a man, woman, and their child – were on loan from Engenho Petinga. Three others, whose relationship to each other was not given, were reported to be living in Saoguipe, off the engenho.

no means the dominant form of family organization. Of the ten household units headed by women, six can definitely be identified as headed by widows rather than unmarried, or at least unattached, women. Households of men with their children or kin were fewer, as we might expect. Four of the five units of males with children were headed by widowers.

The Santana 1731 list raises a number of issues. One is certainly the lack of evidence pointing to a matrifocal or female-headed family as a predominant form. In terms neither of units nor of persons were such households characteristic of this plantations' slave force. The dominant household types were in Group I, which included subtypes all having

a resident man and woman as co-heads of the family. Despite a reported policy of discouraging marriage, over 75 percent of the households at Santana contained people who were related by blood or marriage. Households included nieces and nephews, grandparents and
grandchildren, siblings of the household heads, and even godchildren.
Kinship in its various forms had an obvious meaning for Santana's
slaves, whatever their attitudes toward, and access to, church-sponsored marriage.

But slavery did have its effects at Santana. One pattern that seems
related to the slave experience is that of synthetic households composed of an elderly woman or women and young unmarried men.
Such was the case of Archangela, a widow of fifty, and Andreza, her
ninety-year-old companion, who lived with four young men in their
late teens. In another household Maria Ganguela, "who had been a
good black," lived with a one-armed woman of twenty-eight and a
thirty-year-old, recently bought bachelor. Such units seem to contain
arrangements in which elderly, less-productive women were assigned
housekeeping and cooking duties for newly arrived unmarried men.
There were also solitaries at Santana. Ten men and five women lived
alone. The men were middle aged. Their mean age was forty-six, and
there is nothing to indicate that they were recent arrivals. The women
were younger, with an average age of thirty-two if the one eighty-year-
old widow is not counted. At Santana, solitaries constituted 25 percent
of the households. This is a high figure when compared to the standard sample developed by the Cambridge group of demographers, in
which the solitaries were about 9 percent of the total of English
villagers; it is also higher than the percentages found in small samples
from the West Indies and the antebellum U.S. South.[52] But of course
the high percentage of solitary units is matched by a low percentage of
slaves who lived alone. Thus only 8.5 percent of the slaves at Santana
lived by themselves.

The Santana lists also permit us to examine in microcosm the patterns of fertility we discussed in the previous chapter. From these lists,
it is impossible to determine the age at which women began to bear
children. What we can do instead is examine the age at which a
woman bore her oldest surviving resident child. Such a measure does
not take stillbirths and infant mortality into consideration, nor can we
determine those who no longer resided with their parents. But when
we make this measure age-specific, it is possible to derive a figure that
permits a suitable estimate of age at first giving birth and thus some
indication of fertility. In 1731, the average age of slave women at the
birth of their oldest surviving resident child was 25.9 years. When we
examine only those six women under the age of thirty, that figure
drops to 20.5 years. This second figure is probably more accurate, since
women in this age group were unlikely to have borne children who

Table 14-5. *The children of slave women at different ages at Engenho Santana, 1731 and 1752*

	1731			1752		
Age group	N women	N children	$\bar{X}^a$	N women	N children	$\bar{X}$
15–19	0	0	0.0	0	2	1.0
20–4	2	2	1.0	3	5	1.7
25–9	3	6	2.0	2	5	2.5
30–4	2	3	1.5	6	10	1.7
35–9	0	0	0.0	2	8	4.0
40–4	5	19	3.8	2	8	4.0
45–9	5	19	3.8	2	3	1.5
50+	7	15	2.1	3	3	1.0
Unknown	–	–	–	5	17	3.4
Totals	24	64	(2.6)	25	61	(2.3)

^{a}Mean number of children per woman.

were no longer living with their parents. In 1731, the mothers at Santana had borne sixty-four children who were still resident with their parents (see Table 14-5). This was an average of 2.6 children per mother, but the figure is somewhat misleading since one woman, Polonia, "who makes children and nothing else," had borne eight and Graça, the wife of Joseph Passube, "honor of the married men," had seven resident offspring. We should note that these observations about the high fecundity of particular women may in themselves be unintended comments on low fertility. Seven or eight children is far from a healthy woman's childbearing capacity. The five women listed between the ages of fifteen and thirty-four averaged 1.3 children each.

By 1752, the conscious efforts to sponsor marriage had changed the patterns of age at birth and fertility. The age at first giving birth was altered considerably, being lowered from 25.9 in 1731 to 19.1; if only women under thirty are considered, that figure had dropped to 18.6. More than twice as many women in 1752 as in 1731 had borne their eldest resident child before the age of twenty, and the 1752 list even included a mother of age thirteen. The earlier age at first birth implied by these figures appears to represent an increased fertility at the younger ages. The five women aged 20–9 on the 1752 list averaged 2.05 children, compared to 1.5 for those of similar age on the 1731 list. Obviously, with such small numbers it is difficult to generalize. But as we might expect, it would seem that a policy of earlier marriage did have some effect on fertility. Nevertheless, when all women with children are considered, it does not seem that the policy change towards marriage overcame the previous low fertility. In fact, the average number of children per woman dropped slightly between 1731 and 1752. Although this ratio is dependent to some extent on the age structure, still the evidence from Santana supports the argument presented in the preceding chapter that fertility among Brazilian slaves was low.

The change in marital patterns at Santana does not appear to have had much effect on the spacing of children. The mean interval between surviving resident children in 1731 was four years (median four years), and the figure in 1752 was only a slightly lower 3.6 years (median 3.5 years). With ages reported only in full years and no way to calculate stillbirths or infant death, these figures on child spacing can at best be only suggestive. But what they suggest is a relatively long interval of about four years between births and thus low fertility among the Santana slaves, as among the Bahian slaves in general.

Whatever the causes, the administrators of Santana were aware of the low fertility of the slaves. Padre Jerónimo da Gama believed that more stable unions might result in more children, but the main thrust of his efforts to have slaves marry at Santana seems to have been the desire to avoid moral laxity and sins. There was of course a long Catholic tradition advocating early marriage as a way of stamping out impure acts and thoughts. For the Jesuits and other European observers, however, Brazil seemed to be a place where the passions ran wild, especially among the slaves. Attached to the 1731 list was a description of the slaves that called them the "worst indoctrinated, thieves, and shameless persons (especially the women) that I have dealt with, lacking in their fear of God and in the service they owe to those who govern them." Instructions for the operation of Jesuit plantations required that the slaves be locked in their houses at night, but at Santana locks and keys had not been the custom. Young boys who worked in the casa grande simply slipped out the windows at night and returned by morning, said the shocked Father. Since the houses in Brazil were all "windows and verandas," it was difficult to stop these forays. He tried. "I gave them all a beautiful beating of lashes [çurra de açoutes], let's see what effect it has."[53]

The transfer of Santana to a new administrator in 1730 created a situation of accusation and counteraccusation. Although the priests and brothers involved disagreed about the gifts and faults of each other, they seemed unanimous in their feeling about the slaves and their lack of morality. Father Pedro Teixeira, who took control of the engenho from Father Manoel de Figueiredo, who had governed it for twenty-three years, saw the slaves as thieves and liars, living in sin, partly as a result of the policies of his predecessors – Father Manoel de Figueiredo and before him Father Luís Vellozo. Teixeira also disliked and distrusted his aides. He accused Brother Antônio de Figueiredo of stealing from the pantry and giving food to a mulatto purgadeira, with whom he carried on in the purging house and with whom he was seen at night in the slave quarters, telling her "little secrets." Figueiredo, in turn, accused the other resident assistant, Brother Mateus de Sousa, of having relations with the slave, Martinha, and fathering a mulatto child.[54] Both Figuereido and Sousa accused Father Teixeira of being too lax in the control of the plantation and letting the slaves run wild. This was due in part to Father Teixeira's gout, and he admitted that he was often bedridden and unable to tend to the slave quarters. "To govern these slave fazendas," he said, "a head is not enough, feet are necessary; it is not enough to command, it is necessary to move."

Although the Jesuits argued about each other's failings, they seemed to agree generally about the moral failings and sexual laxity of the slaves, especially the women. Such attitudes were as common in Brazil as in other slave regimes, and they stemmed from both a racist perception of black behavior and a historiographical tradition that emphasized the unbridled power of the slaveowners. Even those who spoke out against the abuses of the slave system, as Nuno Marques Pereira did, condemned the masters who forced such behavior but did not doubt the promiscuity of the slaves.[55]

"Promiscuity," of course, is a term defined by culture and values. It is, as Sidney Mintz once described it, "someone else's sexual habits." The evidence from Engenho Santana, however, although it does not deal directly with sexual mores among the slaves, has some important implications. Despite the lack of marriages before 1730, living arrangements were far from haphazard. Children lived with one or both of their parents, and in fact the most common type of household unit was the male, female, and children. Women apparently bore their first children in their late teens or even early twenties, and despite the appearance of an occasional thirteen- or fifteen-year-old mother, especially in the 1752 list, the majority of slave women seemed to fit a pattern of delayed motherhood. Although these figures do not speak directly to premarital or early sexual activity, they tend to indicate that either such activity was not extensive or that contraception or birth control was practiced from an early age. The spacing of children in both lists also indicates that unions were relatively stable and long term.

Table 14-4 demonstrates that by 1752 a different attitude toward slave marriage had altered the structure of the household types. By that date, almost 80 percent of the slaves lived in doubled-headed units with resident male and female. These units were of various subtypes in which kin, unrelated others, and children lived. By far the two dominant types were the simple man and woman and the man, woman, and children units. There were only three female-headed households (5.2 percent), a considerable reduction from the ten that had existed at Santana in 1731. The number and percentage of households headed by either a single man or woman and containing children, other kin, or unspecified others were both reduced between 1731 and 1752. The number and percentage of solitaries were only slightly reduced. All the solitary women, however, were widows. In short, it would seem that the change in policy toward marriage had resulted in increased double-headed households, with a concentration of simple family arrange-ments in which kin and sometimes undefined others were added.

Since it appears that a change in attitude on the part of the Jesuit owners or administrators altered the structure of the Santana slave households, it is fair to ask if these units of residence were households at all or whether they were simply units of convenience created by the plantation managers. Examination of two aspects of the lists appears to support my contention that these were in fact functioning household units in the traditional sense of that term. First, the age differential of the spouses seems to conform to a typical European pattern with the men usually older than their mates. Of the twenty-four married couples for whom age data existed from 1731, twenty included older men; of these, two-thirds were ten years older or less. The average age differential was +7.17 years for the men.[56] For 1752, age information is available for twenty couples. In fifteen cases, the males were older than their wives, with an average age differential of +4.1 years. The major difference between the two lists in this regard is the lack in the 1752 account of very great age spreads. In 1731, one man was twenty years older than his spouse; another, thirty years older. One woman was seventeen years older than her mate. By 1752, no man was more than eighteen years older than his wife, and no woman was more than five years older than her husband. Although the policy change toward earlier marriage may have reduced the number of "unequal" or "May–December" marriages between 1731 and 1752, in neither year do the patterns seem to indicate the capricious intervention of the masters in mate selection.

The second aspect of the slave households that argues against these units representing artificial families is that the children resident in them appear in every case to be the biological offspring of one or both of the resident adults listed as husband and wife, or of one of their offspring. Children in each household were listed from oldest to youngest. Since there were no repetitions of ages within the same household, we can assume that children were not simply placed together for convenience and care in these households. More important, the Santana lists state explicitly to which parent the resident children are related.

One of the most striking differences between the Santana lists of 1731 and 1752 is the acquisition of family names by the slaves in the latter list. Except for a Francisco das Minas, all the slaves in 1731 were listed only with their Christian name. This was the usual Brazilian practice. A slave was generally known by his first name only and then further identified by his color or place of origin. A plantation with three slaves named João might have a João Angola, a João Cabinda, and a João Grande because physical characteristics were also used to identify slaves. Official documents usually listed a slave simply by his or her given name, "slave of so and so." A Christian name was acquired at the time of baptism. One estate evaluator noted at the end of a plantation list, "In addition, there are five newly arrived Africans who are not listed here by name, not being baptized."[57] The names chosen were the same for slaves as for the free population, and I shall refer to the patterns of choice in relation to baptism shortly. It is notable that in the lists from Santana there were no cases in which children seemed to be named for parents or grandparents.

When and how slaves acquired family names in Brazil is unclear. Certainly, the acquisition of freedom or manumission was an event that led to the assumption of a family name. In a sense, the family name symbolized free status – but not entirely. Some slaves, especially crioulos and pardos, also had family names. For both slaves and libertos (freed slaves), the pattern was to assume the name of the owner or former owner. Felix Maciel the freedman was the former slave of Belchior Maciel; Josefa Pires was the crioula slave of José Pires de Carvalho of Engenho Cazumba; the Ewe slaves Tomás Marinho and Luiza Marinho who married in Santo Amaro were both owned by Father Pedro Marinho.[58] Some masters found slave adoption of the family name a flattering gratification of their pride and sense of paternalism, whereas others may have been less pleased by the association. In any case, the tendency to choose the master's name was strong.

In 1752, all slaves are listed with family names. Here again, we seem to see the results of the profamilial policy that had characterized that engenho for two decades. In an attempt to regularize family life, the Jesuit administrators had assigned family names or asked the slaves to select them. When and how the names were acquired is unclear, but by that date virtually all the slaves had them. There were about twenty-seven family names in use at Engenho Santana, but of the 108 slaves for whom the family name could be clearly established, more than 70 percent shared the names Figueiredo, Vellozo, Teixeira, and Fernandes. These were the names of administrators of the estate. Father Manoel de Figueiredo had run the plantation from about 1704 to 1730 and had been succeeded by Father Pedro Teixeira in 1731. Father Luís Vellozo had administered Santana in the 1690s, and Antônio Fernandes was there from 1736 to at least 1746.[59] Slaves were apparently assigned the name of the administrator who ran the estate when they were purchased; these then became family names carried forward by their children. Whether slaves recognized any "kinship" with those who bore the same family name but who were not direct blood relatives is a moot point.

Engenho Santana was, of course, not a simple community made up of a collection of households. It was a plantation whose form was determined by the nature of its productive forces and purpose. This was reflected in the composition of its population. The sex and age structure of the population at Santana, with its predominance of males, low percentage of children, and excessive number of young adults, was standard for the engenhos of Bahia. The ratio of those too old or too young to be fully useful to those considered to be productive workers was low, despite Jesuit ownership. The dependency ratio (population 0–14 plus population 50 and above divided by population 15–49) was .41 in 1731 and .33 in 1752. These figures are fully in keeping with the dependency ratios established for Bahian parishes in 1788 discussed in the preceding chapter.[60]

The low dependency ratios reflected the purchase of young adults as well as high infant- and child-mortality rates. In fact, a low dependency ratio, exactly what owners wished to have, reflected the bitter difficulties of slave life. What planters most wished to avoid was a higher dependency ratio caused by temporary illness. At Santana in 1752, it was reported that of the 182 slaves, only 120 were effective workers, and even this number included some old and young slaves who were not fully productive. Of those able to work, however, only 60 or 70 were available for field labor because some of the 120 were artisans and others were sick or feigning to be so. The administrator of Santana complained that no week passed "when six or seven or more fail to come with their complaints, and only with great effort can they be thrown from the house. The patience of Job is inadequate to suffer them in their sickness, which usually amounts to little more than nothing and with which they torment and consume those who govern them."[61]

That slaves sought to avoid work should be no surprise. How much of their complaining was malingering and how much the result of unhealthy conditions cannot be determined. In tropical Bahia, a high-morbidity regime existed for the whole population, and slaves were particularly susceptible to certain illnesses because of the exhausting nature of their labor. From the slaveowners' point of view, a rise in the ratio of nonproductive workers to productive ones was bad business. If we assume that the average sixty-two incapacitated slaves at Santana were productive adults, that engenho's work force will rise from a ratio of 1.9 healthy workers for each dependent to 2.9 workers for each nonproductive slave. No wonder planters avoided whenever possible slaves who were chronically ill or seemed prone to sickness, and no wonder that the inventory value of sick and infirm slaves averaged consistently 20 percent below that of healthy individuals in the same age group.

The structural analysis of a plantation slave list provides only a skele-

ton of family life and sorely needs the flesh and blood of human interaction, custom, and sentiment. The family encompassed roles and attitudes, normative behavior, that the simple lists rarely recapture. In the
case of Santana, however, passing remarks by administrators and observers allow us a glimpse inside the senzala (slave quarters) of the
customs and concerns that regulated relations among the men, wom-
en, and children at this engenho.

The Santana slave quarters were located on a steep hill, "like that of
the Lisbon castle." They were arranged in three rows or streets and
were out of sight of the administrator's residence, a situation that allowed the slaves too much freedom, in his eyes at least. The administrator in 1753 complained against the purchase of slaves from other
owners because good ones were never sold, and he noted that new
slaves were costly because, "having no family, when they fall ill all
responsibility for their care falls on the engenho."[62] Although Engenho
Santana maintained an infirmary, slaves preferred to stay at home.
This observation underlines the role that slave families played in aiding
their members. Given the constant high proportion of Africans in the
Bahian slave population, the problems of forming families and establishing familial ties must have been central for them.

At Santana, slaves had found physical or psychological problems one
of the most effective ways of avoiding the regimentation of plantation
life. Menstruating slave women not only did not work in water, in
accordance with general custom, but also did not work or attend mass
and sometimes stayed in bed for two or three weeks. Women who had
recently given birth, slaves who had had teeth pulled, and those re-
covering from illness all refused to attend mass, claiming that the
"smell of the dead" was harmful to them.[63]

Birth was a matter of the senzala at Santana, as on most plantations.
We have no direct description of delivery at Santana, but it was probably little different from that described by Imbert: The mother, once
labor had begun, was surrounded by midwives, who not only moved
her limbs into different positions and exhorted her at the proper moment to "pucha, pucha" but also offered her relics to kiss, placed
rosaries on her body, and obliged her to pray to the saint of her
name.[64] After the birth, the head of the child was often massaged to
give it better form, and the umbilical cord was cut far from the body
and then smeared with oil and pepper, a custom that perhaps contributed to tetanus infection and the deadly seven-day illness (*mal de sete
dias*), responsible for so many infant deaths in Brazil.

With the birth of the infant, the roles of the parents came into play.
Fathers sought chickens, wine, onions, and other preferred foods for
the babies with such insistence that the overseer was often at his wit's
end trying to put them off.[65] When he refused to provide slaves with
adequate food, they complained bitterly and threated to run off to the

woods. The slave fathers obviously took their paternal roles seriously at Santana and within the constraints of slavery did what they could for their families.

Shortly after the list of 1731 was drawn up, a violent incident took place at Santana that laid bare life in the senzala, the roles of men and women, and the attitudes of the Jesuit administrators. One day on returning at noon from work, a young crioulo caulker discovered his wife, Francisca, in the house of a male friend. Overcome with jealousy, he began to argue with her. This soon led to a beating, which only the intervention of other slaves brought to a halt. The couple returned to their own house, but the argument continued, and shortly thereafter the young woman took up a knife and stabbed her husband fatally in the chest.[66] Padre Teixeira, the administrator, placed the young woman, not yet eighteen years of age, in the stocks; he also placed there her mother, Christina, a forty-two-year-old widow, and her aunt, Marcelina, a twenty-nine-year-old moedeira who had lost an arm because of her occupation.[67] Teixeira, committed to stimulating marriage among the slaves, apparently decided to make an example of the case. The three women and the suspected "friend" were kept in the stocks for three weeks. All the engenho's slaves were then called to hear the charges and witness the punishment. The suspected lover, who had been periodically starved during confinement, was tied to a post. Each of the married men of the estate was required to give him two lashes for his "affront to their [married] state." The house of the couple was razed and a cross planted on the ground to serve as a memorial. The young woman who had killed her husband was kept in the stocks and whipped on nine different occasions, each time receiving forty lashes.

The fate of the mother and the aunt is curious because their involvement in the incident was disputed at the time.[68] Padre Teixeira admitted he did not know if they were directly involved in the killing, since, as he said, "dead men do not talk," but he suspected the two women of selling their bodies and encouraging young Francisca to do the same. Teixeira's opinion was based on information supplied him by the brother of the murdered husband, who was himself married to Francisca's older sister and who had tried unsuccessfully to avenge his brother's death. Teixeira, who had a low opinion of slave women to begin with, was inclined to believe the charges even though his assistant, Brother Mateus de Sousa, doubted them. In any case, Teixeira chose as a punishment to exile these women by sending them to Engenho Sergipe. He selected this punishment because it would serve as an example and because it was something that the women would sorely feel since "almost everyone in the senzala was their relative." Moreover, he had to satisfy the family of the murdered husband, who also had many relatives at the engenho. Such exemplary punishment, said Teixeira, would "make the slaves more humble and docile, and it is better to have a few good ones than many bad ones, and here we have many of the latter, especially the women."

Aside from the misogyny and personal animosities of Father Teixeira, the incident reveals the depths of feeling and the importance of family ties among the slaves of Santana. The jealousy of the husband at the possibility of adultery, the anger of his brother at learning of the murder and his own attempt to avenge the death, the desire of the administrator to satisfy the dead man's relatives, and the use of banishment from the engenho and from their kin as the ultimate punishment for the wife, her mother, and aunt – all underline the importance of family and kinship in the lives of the Santana slaves. Whether the slaves shared Father Teixeira's attachment to the sacrament of marriage is not the question, but their families and kin were central to their lives in a way that the bare structure of household lists can only faintly suggest.

The greater family: ritual kinship

The household structures that we find listed for Santana, or for any other engenho for that matter, present us with only a skeleton of what constituted the slave family, in the sense of those individuals who recognized mutual ties of blood or kinship. Certainly, the "family" extended well beyond the boundaries of any individual household. Recapturing such ties is always extremely difficult. But in the ritual act of baptism and in the religiously sanctioned kinship of *compadrio* (godparentage) that accompanied it, we have an opportunity to see the broader definition of kinship in the context of this Catholic slaveowning society and to witness the strategies of both the slaves and the masters within the cultural boundaries set by this spiritual relationship.[69]

Ritual godparenthood has long been a subject of concern among social scientists. Explanations of it have either been functionalist analyses of what godparenthood does and to what purposes it can be put or more concerned with the meaning of the institution to its participants. Within the context of slavery, however, few studies of either type exist.[70] Drawing data from four Recôncavo parishes, especially from Monte and Rio Fundo in the 1780s, let us examine the patterns of godparentage among the slave population.[71]

Ritual godparentage created a set of bonds, of spiritual kinship, between the godchild (afilhado) and his or her godfather (padrinho) and godmother (padrinha), and between the natural parents and the godparents, who then referred to each other as *compadres* or *comadres* or joint parents of the baptized children in recognition of the union of the spiritual and material essence of the child. The bonds were formed in the church but extended beyond it into secular life. Henry Koster caught the core of the matter when he wrote, "This relationship is accounted very sacred in Brazil, and I believe in all Roman Catholic countries. It is a bond of brotherhood which permits the poor man to speak to his superior with a kind of endearing familiarity, and unites them in links of union, of which the non-observance would be sacrilegious."[72] The idiom of compadrio could only rest uneasily with that of slavery, for the two institutions embodied relationships that appeared to be antithetical. The disjuncture of the two had a profound impact upon who the slaves (and the masters) chose as sponsors for slave children and how slaves used and understood the bonds created by spiritual kinship.

The first pattern that emerges clearly from the Recôncavo baptisms is that masters did not serve as the godparents for their slaves. Despite some authors who have argued that godparentage was used to reinforce paternalism and to bind slave to master by spiritual ties added to the economic ones inherent in slavery, there was no evidence of this either in the Recôncavo or in the city of Salvador. Patron–client relations may in other contexts be covered with ritual ones, but in Bahian slavery this was not the case. Slaves might have a free person as a spiritual sponsor, but they did not have their owner. Whether this was a matter of slaves' avoiding such a choice, masters' refusing to serve, or slaves' realizing that masters would not serve and thus not choosing them is an unanswerable question; but the pattern is clear. Henry Koster noted, "I have never heard of the master in Brazil being likewise the godfather; nor do I think that this ever happens; for such is the connection between two persons that this is supposed to produce, that the master would never think of ordering the slave chastized."[73] His remark is fully borne out by the parish registers of the Recôncavo.

We have seen that in the matter of marriage, as in that of conversion, the church made its reconciliation with slavery. The nonselection of masters as baptismal sponsors for slaves, however, was a direct outcome of a conflict between two different institutions and idioms, the church and slavery, which, when forced to meet in the singular event of baptism, could only turn away in silence. Whatever the social functions that godparentage served, its essence was spiritual. How could the master discipline, sell, or endlessly work his living property while assuming the obligations of godparentage? Baptism represents membership in the church and equality as a Christian. The baptized has been saved from perdition, has gained a new and legitimate family in the church, and has new parents and fraternal relations. For slaves, this meant an ability to establish links beyond those of the immediate family. Baptism, by representing equality, humanity, and freedom from sin, stood for qualities incompatible with slave status and posed a potential contradiction that was resolved not by abolishing either slav-

ery or baptism but by keeping the conflicting elements apart. The re-
birth of slaves through baptism was not to their own masters. Others,
slave, free, or someone else's master, served as godparents for slaves.

The lack of master–slave pairings in the act of baptism did not mean
that at least indirect expressions of paternalism were lacking. For instance, in 1781 the son of the senhor of Engenho Jacuipe sponsored the
child of a slave couple owned by his father, and in 1788 a free pardo
carpenter who was the afilhado of lavrador de cana Clemente Nogueira
sponsored one of Nogueira's slaves. But even these indirect forms
were rare. Frequently, slave women sought "persons of consideration
to become the sponsors to their children in the hopes that the pride of
these will be too great to allow of their god-children remaining in
slavery"; but such hopes were not usually satisfied.[74] In a study of
Bahian manumission between 1684 and 1745, less than 1 percent of all
manumissions and less than 2 percent of all those obtained by purchase resulted from godparents' freeing their godchildren. Whatever
the hopes and designs of the slaves, such cases were few.[75]

To understand the pattern of slave baptisms, it is necessary to view
them in relation to those that occurred among the free population as
well. Free persons sponsored both free and slave children, but slaves
only sponsored other slaves. They did not serve as sponsors for free
persons. The church itself has not concerned itself with the issue of
what social status a godparent should hold, but implicit in many of its
laws is the idea that spiritual paternity is a higher bond than carnal
generation. Godparents are almost invariably of a status at least equal
to that of their godchildren. If godparentage were a relationship con-
fined to the church, social status would be of little relevance. But precisely because these bonds extend into the secular world, consideration
of social position takes on special meaning. With few exceptions, slaves
did not sponsor free children, no matter what their color. The free or
slave status of the child in relation to that of the godparent became an
overriding consideration. Slavery imposed itself on these spiritual acts.
When slave children were baptized, free persons served as sponsors in
about 70 percent of cases, former slaves (libertos) in 10, and other
slaves in 20 (see Table 14-6).

Why did these patterns exist? Slaves did use godparentage instru-
mentally. As Koster suggested, selection of a free person to sponsor a
child in the hopes that they would purchase the child's freedom was
sometimes done. In plantation zones, it was the custom for runaway
slaves to seek the intercession of a "sponsor" who would either ask
that no punishment be given the slave on his or her return or seek to
have the conditions that precipitated the flight changed. Overseers at
Engenho Sergipe were specifically ordered to forgo punishment if such
an approach was made, and in Pernambuco the custom was common
enough so that when a fugitive returned without such a sponsor it was

Table 14-6. *Godparent status of free and slave children, Monte and Rio Fundo parishes, 1780–9*

		Godfathers				
Children	Godmothers	Free	Slave	Liberto	None	Total
Free	Free	88^a	0	0	1	89
	Slave	1	0	0	0	1
	Liberto	0	0	0	0	0
	None	47^b	0	0	1^c	48
	Total	136	0	0	2	138
Slave	Free	48^d	0	0	3	51
	Slave	2	13	4	0	19
	Liberto	0	2	5	0	7
	None	29^e	4	1^f	1	35^g
	Total	79	19	10	4	112

^{a}Includes 3 *expostos* (foundlings). ^{b}Includes 2 *expostos*. ^{c}Includes 1 *exposto*. ^{d}Includes 3 *libertos* (freed at birth. ^{e}Includes 2 *libertos*. ^{f}Includes 1 liberto. ^{g}Includes 1 *liberto*.

cause for suspicion. Thus for slaves to have a free godparent or compadre close by had advantages that might outweigh the close associations or desire for wider family ties that would have led to the selection of other slaves.

The free persons who served as sponsors for baptized slaves were not a homogeneous group. Distinctions of occupations and color operated in the selection pattern here as well. In no cases in the sample of baptisms from Rio Fundo and Monte were the free godparents of slaves of a social status equal or superior to that of the slaves' master. Slaves held by senhores de engenho had other slaves or lavradores as sponsors; slaves of lavradores had carpenters. This pattern recognized the class distinctions among the free and the social distances perceived by both masters and slaves. Here, the hierarchy of color in this slave society also had its effects. Of thirty-two free pardos who served as godparents, almost 70 percent sponsored black children. Free pardo children were more likely to have whites than pardos as sponsors, and they hardly ever had blacks. Color, then, was a further feature used along with free or slave status in the choice of godparents. The preferences were upward in the somatic scale from black to white. In a sample of thirty baptisms of pardo children, whites served in almost 90 percent of the sixty sponsorship roles. Black slaves tended to find sponsors of lighter color, but they also had a high proportion of black sponsors. As Koster noted, "Fellow slaves or free persons of color, are usually the sponsors in Brazil. But it is better, I think, that fellow slaves, that is belonging to the same master, should be sponsors, for they take a considerable interest in their god-children."[76] This was a recognition that slaves understood the meaning of compadrio and made it part of their kinship network.

Added to considerations of color and legal status in the selection of godparents was the matter of gender, which operated at two levels, the sex of the child and the sex of the godparent, in determining certain patterns. Despite ecclesiastical regulations calling for the presence of both a godfather and a godmother at the baptism, children in Bahia were often baptized without one or the other. For both free and slave children, the chances were about fourteen to one that it would be the godmother rather than the godfather who was absent from the font. The presence of the male sponsor was considered to be more important than that of the woman. Status before the law also influenced the pattern. Among slaves, when the godfather was missing, the godmother was free; but when it was the godmother who was absent, there were a few instances when the godfather was a slave or a liberto. When both sponsors were present, their legal status was almost always symmetrical. This pattern in the eighteenth century was different from that in the sixteenth century, discussed in Chapter 3, when a free godfather was sometimes joined by a slave godmother at the baptism.[77]

In a sense, the gender asymmetry reflected in the compadrio records simply underlines that of the society as a whole. Males dominated by controlling to a large extent the means of production and holding a virtual monopoly on political power. The principal means of production was the labor of slave men. The dominance of free males over slave males was the relationship on which the society was founded. Thus, for all persons, the free male was the most sought-after sponsor; and it was slave boys who were most in need of their protection. Greater latitude was shown in the selection of godparents for slave girls. This intense identification of slavery with males evident in the baptismal records is borne out elsewhere in the slave society of Bahia. Manumission, for example, favored females and produced twice as many freed women as men. This suggests that if paternalism operated, it was a far more common attitude toward slave women. A close connection between male slave and master was not fostered, because it was an inherent threat to the society's foundation.

The baptism of adults, recently arrived slaves from Africa, raises another set of issues. First of all, we may ask whether slaves might simply refuse baptism as a rejection of the master's religion and culture. Although this may have been an individual possibility, in general there were too many pressures on both slaves and masters to permit slaves to remain "heathens" or, at least, to reject formal entrance into the church despite whatever other beliefs they might preserve. We have already seen that in the seventeenth century the church campaigned against masters who did not baptize their slaves or instruct them so that baptism was made possible. By the end of the eighteenth century, slaves arriving from Angola usually had been baptized en masse before coming to Brazil, whereas those from Mina had not. Masters were given a year before having to present these slaves for baptism at the parish church. "Pagan" was among the worst epithets that one slave could apply to another, and the newly arrived African soon learned that, in effect, he or she was considered a brute, "nameless" inferior by the master and fellow slaves as long as at least nominal adherence to the Catholic faith was denied.[78]

The difference in the patterns of godparent selection between slave children and slave adults is striking. Whereas slaves were godparents to slave children in only 20 percent of the baptisms examined, slaves served in 70 percent of the baptisms of adults and libertos in another 10 percent. In other words, slaves sponsored adults more than three times more frequently than they sponsored children. This situation can be interpreted in at least two ways. Masters may have been appointing more acculturated slaves or libertos to serve as sponsors in order to smooth the newly arrived African's entry into the labor force. It may also have been the master's recognition that the boçal lacked any kin and that such ties were ultimately essential to his or her well-being as a member of the labor force. This same reason may have been behind slave desires to sponsor their newly arrived fellows. Godparentage might have been seen by them as a way of providing a fictive kinship for people who were sorely in need of some kind of family.

Finally, this discussion of compadrio leads us back to the matter of circumscription and the limitations of kinship within the constraints of slavery. Since canon law prohibited marriage or carnal relations between those who served as godparents and the natural parents of a child, selection of a fellow slave from the same holding, especially on cane farms or smaller units, would limit future marriage possibilities. But as we have also seen, masters tried to circumscribe the contacts of slaves to the holding by impeding conjugal units that crossed ownership boundaries and, in some cases, by trying to limit participation in brotherhoods or in baptisms off the estate. The large plantations may have had some success in this, but the nature of Bahian slaveholding, with many small units interspersed among the larger, frustrated attempts to isolate slaves. The parish registers reveal that about as many slaves who were owned by different masters than that of the baptized served as sponsors as those who were owned by the same owner. Although "broad" marriages off the estate were rare, slaves were able to expand their kinship links beyond the holding through compadrio. It was more often the godfather rather than the godmother who lived in a place different from that of the baptized. In any case, the catchment area was limited for both free and slave. Even when the sponsor was not resident in the same place, he or she usually came from a neighboring estate or village or rarely from the next parish. Although among the planter elite great distances might be traversed by the god-parents (or even proxies used when this was impossible), for slaves this was not done. The estates' boundaries could be transcended, but the distance beyond remained limited.

The rural slaves of Bahia thus lived in a world in which the institution of slavery conspired against their ability to form stable and permanent families and to enjoy the protection and succor that family and kin could provide. At the same time, cultural imperatives inherent in Catholicism urged masters toward recognizing that their slaves as human beings must be provided or allowed to develop "normal" relations of family and kin. The struggles between the ideologies of church and slavery and between the imperatives of masters and the desires of slaves lasted for centuries, but from the conflict a series of compromises resulted that allowed the slaves to have their own lives, to create families and networks of kin. Although always threatened by the very nature of the institution under which the slaves lived, these creations had real meaning in their lives.

PART IV

REORIENTATION AND PERSISTENCE, 1750–1835

CHAPTER 15

RESURGENCE

If abundance has been the cause of our indolence, it must become the reason for our industry.

Sampaio e Mello (1812)

In the Luso-Brazilian world, the second half of the eighteenth century was a period of sweeping reorientations – of new leaders, new ideas of political economy, and a changing international context that forced Portuguese on both sides of the Atlantic to reconsider the traditional relationship between the metropolis and its principal colony, Brazil. Changes in political organization and eventually in political expectations, reforms in fiscal and economic life, and a growing colonial population all contributed to modifications of the colonial relationship, and these in turn altered the positions and interests of groups, classes, and factions in Brazil. But although reorientation and changes were undeniable, to some extent they tended to reinforce and intensify essential features of Brazil's society and economy. Despite innovation, growth, and increasing political maturity, by 1808 Brazil remained a supplier of tropical crops (although some of them were new to the colony) produced by the sweat of slaves. That basic fact was reflected at every level of society, and it set the boundaries of expectation and the horizons of hope.

Tracing the reorientations of this era would amount to writing a broad history of Portugal and Brazil from 1750 to 1830, a task beyond the scope of this volume. For the last two decades, however, others have actively assumed this obligation, and although there remains much to be done, their work allows me to sketch briefly the political and economic trends that bear most directly on the sugar plantations of Bahia and, by extension, on a slaveowning society on the eve and morrow of political independence.[1]

The years between 1750 and 1830 can be usefully divided into two periods. The first roughly coincides with the rule of Sebastião José Carvalho e Melo (after 1770, marquis of Pombal), who dominated Portuguese politics from 1750 until 1777 (purely in economic terms, the

415

mid-1780s make a better point of division). This epoch was marked by a flurry of reforms in the midst of a difficult economic period, during which the demand and price for Brazilian exports were low. The result was a great deal of activity with little apparent improvement in Brazil's commerce or Portugal's revenues. The second period, beginning in the 1780s but intensifying after 1790, saw quickening political life and expanding Brazilian exports; the fruition of the seeds planted by the Pombaline reforms and the result of new opportunities in Atlantic markets. This trend continued until the second decade of the nineteenth century, but by those years political events had pushed the fluctuations of the export sector to the background. In 1808 the Portuguese court, fleeing Napoleon's army, sought refuge in Brazil under British protection, the price of which was the opening of Brazil's ports to foreign shipping and a series of commercial and political agreements between Portugal and England. For a short period, Brazil became the center of the Portuguese empire. When in 1820 the monarch, Dom João VI, was forced to return to Portugal, he left his son Pedro as prince regent. Pressure from the Portuguese parliament (cortes) to reduce Brazil to its former colonial status and to eliminate the equal status it had gained during the crown's exile led to intensification of separatist desires and in 1822 caused a permanent break. Pedro proclaimed Brazil's independence and assumed the title Pedro I, emperor of Brazil. He remained on the throne until his abdication in 1831.

The Pombaline reforms

The marquis of Pombal, architect of the reform and reorganization of the Portuguese empire in the eighteenth century, came to power in 1750 after diplomatic service in Vienna and London and a fortunate marriage. Appointed secretary of foreign affairs by Dom José I, Portugal's then newly crowned monarch, Pombal quickly assumed almost dictatorial powers, which he held until his dismissal in 1777. Autocratic and shrewd, Pombal turned his considerable talents toward centralizing power and redefining Portugal's relationship with England. Hoping to redress the imbalance in Anglo-Portuguese trade and to loosen the ties of economic dependency that had bound Portugal to England since the Methuen Treaty of 1703, if not before, Pombal tried to copy a page from England's own text. With an eye on English commercial, financial, and diplomatic models, Pombal took an activist and interventionist approach to Portugal's affairs of state. His "great new dispositions" were often disguised behind "ancient names and ancient clothing," as historian Kenneth Maxwell has pointed out, but his goal of lessening Portugal's dependency remained clear.[2]

As Portugal's largest colony, Brazil figured prominently in Pombal's designs. The period of his rule witnessed sweeping changes in the colony. In 1751, the judicial structure was altered when a separate high court of appeal was established in Rio de Janeiro, thereby lessening the authority of the appeals court in Bahia. In recognition of the growing population of southern Brazil, the importance of the mining zone of Minas Gerais and the military threat to Brazil's southern frontier, Rio de Janeiro became the colonial capital in 1763. Colonial fiscal administration and accounting procedures were improved in an effort to improve tax collection and thus increase royal revenues. Special efforts were made to impose a more efficient system of taxation in the gold-mining zones and to control the considerable leakage of gold in the contraband trade. The old fleet system was abandoned in 1765 in an attempt to stimulate commerce. To this same end, Pombal created a series of monopoly companies to foment the development and commerce of certain Brazilian regions. He first created in 1755 the Company of Grão Pará and Maranhão, aimed at the economic development of northern Brazil. He then used the same tactic to resuscitate the flagging economy of the Northeast by creating in 1759 the Company of Pernambuco and Paraíba, designed to stimulate the sugar and tobacco trades of that region. With monopoly control over slave imports and certain other commodities, the company was allowed to set prices, and it was expected to provide for safe transport of goods to and from Pernambuco.[3]

Even today, it is difficult to evaluate the effectiveness of the Pombaline companies. Portuguese nationals had been specially encouraged to invest, although shares could be held by foreigners as well. Few Brazilians invested. But the overall result of the investment policy in the companies was to return some portion of control to Portuguese hands and to diminish English control over Portuguese commerce. Both companies eventually promoted new crops or stimulated the expansion of previously undeveloped ones. Cacao production in Pará and cotton in Maranhão became the staples of the northern company's trade. In Pernambuco, sugar and tobacco exports were now joined by a considerable export of cotton and hides. The companies' efforts were paralleled by those of activist Pombaline governors in Rio de Janeiro and São Paulo, who also promoted a diversification of Brazilian agriculture. By 1800, indigo, rice, coffee, cotton, and cacao shared space with sugar, tobacco, hides, and wood as outward-bound cargoes. Still, the companies also created obstacles to growth. In eighteen years before the establishment of the Pernambuco company, that captaincy had received 54,891 slaves, whereas in the seventeen years of the company's existence, only 38,157 slaves entered the port, and this in a period of agricultural expansion.[4]

Whatever the long-term effects of the companies, it is clear that they, like many Pombaline measures, directly conflicted with established interests and upset existing patterns of trade, politics, and convenience.

To express opposition, however, was dangerous. Pombal mercilessly crushed his opponents. The nobility's resistance to royal absolutism met with show trials and executions; merchant resistance to the monopoly companies suffered such swift retaliation as the dismemberment of the Lisbon merchant guild. The Jesuit order with its extensive missionary and economic interests in northern Brazil particularly disliked the northern monopoly and also opposed Pombaline policies in diplomacy, education, and government. The order's wealth, ultramontanism, and political activity made it a primary target and caused, in 1759, its expulsion from Brazil and the confiscation of its extensive properties.[5]

It was not the Jesuits but English commerce, however, that formed the central target of Pombaline policy. Pombal had learned his lessons well in England, where he had observed firsthand the manner in which English commerce and naval power had combined to enable that nation to dominate the Atlantic world. English trade tripled between 1702 and 1772, and Pombal realized that England had emerged from the Seven Years War virtually uncontested. Portugal remained an English client to some extent in diplomatic and military matters, but Pombal was determined to reduce the flow of contraband and gold smuggling passing through the hands of English factors in Portugal or in the thinly disguised illegal trade directly with Brazil. British merchants voiced their complaints. Pombal seemed to accede to their interests in 1765. He abolished the fleet system and abandoned plans for monopoly companies for Bahia and Rio de Janeiro where English interests were strong. But given the lack of capital in Portugal, Pombal may have taken steps to appear malleable when in reality he lacked the resources to do otherwise. What he sought was not to eliminate ties with England but to balance commerce and reestablish Portuguese control over colonial revenues.

Despite imagination, energy, and ruthlessness, Pombal could do little to resolve the underlying economic problems of the empire. Despite all the programs and efforts, the value of Brazilian exports in 1777 was only half what it had been in 1760. Gold production reached its crest in 1750–60 and then steadily declined. Export agriculture experienced a series of ups and downs, but the trend in both price and production was downward. The fluctuations are themselves interesting because they demonstrate how Portugal's position as a witness rather than participant in the major European confrontations determined the type and volume of its colonial exports. Peace in Europe caused prices and production of Brazilian exports to fall in the early 1750s, a situation that made planters sensitive to new government controls typified by the boards of inspection that Pombal created in the major Brazilian ports. With the outbreak of European hostilities in 1756, the Brazilian situation improved, and major gains in sugar prices and production were made until the Peace of Paris in 1763. When England and France were at war and shipping to the Caribbean was disrupted, Brazil made gains; when peace returned, Brazil suffered.[6]

The reestablishment of peace in 1763, although temporary, ushered in a particularly difficult period for Brazilian exports. Caribbean colonies supplied the needs of their metropoles, and Brazil's share of the Atlantic sugar market was reduced to less than 10 percent. Many measures were tried to turn the tide. Pombal's abolition of the fleet system in 1765 was an attempt to increase the volume of trade. A royal order of the following year noted that "agriculture and commerce are the two bases of a people's wealth, and the latter having been made free and open . . . it now remains to stimulate the former."[7] Various reforms were attempted. Old taxes were eliminated or reduced, and in 1766 freight rates were set at lower levels in an attempt to lower planter costs and stimulate commerce.

But despite good intentions, the following decade was disastrous on most fronts. Revenues from mining slumped badly in the 1760s, and the return of Caribbean competitors drove down the demand and price for Brazilian sugar. Unfortunately, fighting with Spain broke out in 1762. The conflict turned into a long-smoldering war on Brazil's southern frontier, lasting until 1777.[8] The defense of this border and campaigns in the Rio de la Plata consumed resources in a period of declining revenues.

Bahia and the Pombaline reforms

Depending on the force with which they were imposed and the interests they upset, the Pombaline reforms met with a variety of reactions in Bahia, the most negative of which extended to remonstrance and nothing more. The transfer of the capital from Salvador to Rio de Janeiro provoked resentment, but nothing could be done.[9] The local merchant community, however, in conjunction with British merchants, was powerful enough to forestall the creation of a Bahian monopoly company on the model of Pernambuco's or Maranhão's. The end of the fleet system was generally welcomed as an opportunity for more open and therefore increased trade. The expulsion of the Jesuits was probably deeply felt in a place like Salvador, but the response was muted as it was politically unwise to raise public objections.

The Jesuit properties seized by the state in Bahia were eventually auctioned or sold to local residents. Although these estates were no longer the best in the captaincy, they were still valuable assets. At the time of the expulsion, the Jesuits owned five engenhos with 698 slaves in the captaincy of Bahia.[10] Engenho Sergipe do Conde was still a large mill, but it was no longer "Queen of the Recôncavo." It had been running an annual loss of about 1,000$ in the hard 1750s, and its production in 1754–5 had been listed at only 3,000 arrobas; but these figures may be misleading.[11] When it was sold in 1760, its annual profit was estimated at 900$. Engenho Santana, its sister mill, had also fallen on hard times. It operated at a deficit, and its managers complained of unruly slaves, exhausted canefields, and isolation. The managers had turned to food-crop production to supplement falling sugar revenues. Still, its annual profit was estimated, perhaps wishfully, at 500$ by state evaluators. The Lisbon College of Santo Antão owned not only these two mills but also Engenho Petinga, an ox-powered engenho neighboring Engenho Sergipe, having acquired it in 1745. Royal evaluators had probably overestimated the value of these properties. Antônio Ribeiro de Migueis, who bought both Sergipe and Petinga for 54,000$ and 25,600$ respectively, found that he was unable to meet his obligations or sell these properties for their supposed value on the open market.[12] Finally, the Jesuit College of Salvador also owned two mills, Engenhos Petinguinha and Santo Antônio de Cotegipe, the second having been acquired by bequest in the 1750s and estimated to produce an annual profit of 800$.[13]

For the sugar industry as a whole, the Jesuit expulsion and confiscation was a relatively minor matter when compared to the implications of Pombal's policies toward agricultural and commercial reform. The Bahian planters felt the impact of these measures first and most directly when in January 1751 boards of inspection (*mesas da inspeção*) were created in the major Brazilian ports of Recife, Rio de Janeiro, São Luiz, and Salvador.[14] Designed to restore confidence in the quality of Brazilian products by eliminating abuses in grading, shipping, and financing, the boards were faced with a difficult and unpopular task. The elimination of false grading and dishonest crating procedures caused some grumbling, but the fixing of sugar prices and eventually the increasing of warehouse and freight rates were far more disliked. Planters complained that, although merchants operated freely in a commercial system that imposed no controls on their activities, the producers were not allowed to charge the highest price possible in the marketplace.[15]

The idea of fixing the price of Brazilian sugar was certainly not new. Since 1688, a form of price fixing set by negotiation between planter and merchant representatives in the câmara of Bahia had been in place. In 1737, the Lisbon Board of Trade suggested a more rigid system of price control, but European wars in the 1740s had created enough demand for Brazilian sugar to keep prices and sales at acceptable levels. The system instituted in 1751 simply realized a long-discussed plan, but that made it no more palatable to the planters.[16]

Sugar planters throughout Brazil registered their complaints. Planters in Pernambuco and Rio de Janeiro wrote directly to the throne. Those in Sergipe de El-Rey complained that the costs of registering their crates in Bahia further impoverished them.[17] All the Recôncavo towns petitioned the crown directly and sought to cooperate with each other in making joint representation. The câmara of Santo Amaro chose to ask the rector of the Jesuit College of Lisbon to represent its interests, feeling that the Jesuit sugar estates in Bahia gave that order interests parallel to its own.[18] The câmara of Salvador as well as groups of planters and cane farmers bombarded the Overseas Council and the governor with petitions and complaints. In Lisbon, the royal councillors remained unconvinced by these pleadings. To them, it was simply a matter of differing approaches, two tactics to achieve the same goal. Everyone wanted to increase the sale of Brazilian agricultural products. The planters understandably wanted to obtain the highest price for their sugar and tobacco, but in the long run, the councillors argued, high prices would only allow foreign competitors to undersell Brazil and injure trade. The planters' short-term gains had to be sacrificed for the good of the economy.

The outpouring of planter complaints against the boards of inspection, though filled with self-pleading and perhaps self-indulgence, nevertheless reveal something about the state of the sugar economy and planter perceptions of it. In 1752, one inspector of the board noted that twenty-five or thirty years before, more than 200 engenhos had existed in Bahia, but now fewer than 120 operated in the captaincy.[19] The key problem was the supply of slaves and their exorbitant costs. The planters complained that the price of sugar was being fixed too low, since the average price of slaves had risen from 25$ to 150$; and this was an unavoidable expense because of the many slaves who "died or became incapacitated with the work." Slaves were, they said, "the most precious and the riskiest property in Brazil."[20] But while the planters labored under this disadvantage, 40 to 50 people controlled the twenty-four registered ships in the Mina trade using the risk capital of about another 150 investors. With a similar 20 owners in Pernambuco, only 70 or so individuals had brought the economy to its knees through their monopoly control of the Mina trade. The "misery of Brazil" merited royal concern and especially that of the senhores de engenho and lavradores de cana who, as they argued, were "no less Portuguese than those who lived in Portugal and who at the cost of their own blood and fortune or that of their ancestors had conquered Brazil for the crown."[21] The planters saw themselves as stepchildren of a distant monarch, and they viewed the boards of inspection as not a remedy but an evil.

The planters lamented in vain. The Bahian Board of Inspection was not abolished; in fact, its powers and scope increased over time. Its first director, Wenceslão Pereira da Silva, the intendant of gold, became more powerful than the viceroy himself, and he tended to favor metropolitan interests. The membership of the board was eventually expanded to include tobacco planters, who like their sugar-planter colleagues, were elected by an assembly of merchants and planters to serve as inspectors at the warehouses.[22] Planter complaints about the merchants' freedom of operation were soon answered by regulation in that sphere, but it brought little relief to the planters. The Bahian slave trade to the Mina coast had been in the hands of Bahian merchants since the beginning of the eighteenth century. Despite various Portugese plans to limit that direct trade, the Bahian merchants had held out; in 1743, a system of controlled sailings had been instituted by the crown, permitting only twenty-four vessels from Bahia to engage in the Mina coast trade. Under the boards of inspection, a new law of 1756 ended the regulated system of direct trade and opened it to all Portuguese ships. The Bahian merchants especially disliked this attack on their position, but the planters also gained very little from it. Rather than lowering the price of slaves in Bahia by increasing the supply, trade at Whydah, the main slave port, was thrown into disarray by the new arrangements.[23] In short, neither planters nor merchants perceived much advantage in the measures imposed by Lisbon.

Sugar's recovery

Throughout the eighteenth century, despite the value of gold production and the increasing importance of tobacco, hides, rice, cotton, and other commodities, sugar remained the single most valuable item in Brazilian trade. At no time in the century did any other product, including gold, exceed its value (at least in legal trade). Brazil by 1780 was no longer simply a sugar colony, but the sugar economy still dominated the colony's trade. This was true of Brazil as a whole, especially of Bahia. But, although sugar remained predominant, Brazil's share of the Atlantic sugar market fell precipitously during the first three-quarters of the century – a result of declining production in Brazil and the rise of foreign competitors. Accurate statistics are lacking, but the trend seems clear. A nineteenth-century estimate placed Brazil's sugar production in 1730 at about 2.5 million arrobas, a figure equivalent to one-third of the sugar produced in the Americas. By 1776, production had fallen to 1.4 million arrobas while the output of competitors had increased, so Brazil at that date supplied less than 10 percent of the market.[24] An English estimate placed Brazil's share as low as 7 percent by 1787. Although scholars vary on the depth and timing of this decline, there is little question about the secular trend. Sugar still predominated in the colony, and planters still held regional power. But by 1790, Brazil was a secondary sugar producer in international terms.

The sugar economy's central problem in the second half of the century was not so much production as it was price, although the two were certainly related. Yearly harvest variations of some size were common, and governors kept a close watch on climatic conditions, which in the 1750s and 1760s they reported with care. Production in these years fluctuated between 1.5 and 2.5 million arrobas for the colony as a whole; Bahia's output averaged about four hundred thousand arrobas. The value of this product, however, varied greatly. The 1720s were years of poor sugar prices, and although these recovered somewhat in the 1740s, they fell badly in 1750. The Seven Years' War (1756–63) disrupted trade in the Caribbean and thus raised European sugar prices to the pleasure and benefit of the Brazilian planters. But a sharp downward turn followed the return of peace.

Low sugar prices characterized the next decade. This period of difficulty lasted long enough to dampen the usual sanguinity of the planters, and the industry appears to have contracted during these years. But beginning in 1776, a new surge in prices again raised expectations. The outbreak of hostilities in North America, leading to a more generalized conflict in the Caribbean and Atlantic, once again worked to the advantage of Brazilian producers. In Bahia, sugar prices rose steadily to 1782, suffered a sharp decline to 1785 (although levels remained high), and then rose again. Then, with the outbreak of the Haitian revolution in 1792 and the eventual elimination of that island as a sugar producer, the price of sugar rose dramatically on European markets and remained high until about 1800, slipped until 1803, and then recovered until 1809.[25]

One event, more than any other, stimulated the recovery and expansion of the Bahian sugar industry and created the conditions for the growth of sugar and coffee production in other parts of Brazil (and in such places as Cuba, Puerto Rico, and Louisiana that had been relatively minor producers). That event was the great slave uprising in the French Caribbean colony of Saint Domingue in 1791.[26] This revolt eventually turned into a movement for independence, and during a decade of warfare, Saint Domingue, the largest producer of sugar and coffee in the 1780s, was virtually eliminated as an exporter of these commodities. A vast new demand for sugar waited to be filled by traditional producing areas or by new ones. Although the Bahian economy had shown some signs of recovery in the 1780s, the Haitian revolt sparked a headlong expansion of the sugar industry and with it an intensification and expansion of the slave trade and of social tension and fears that resulted from a growth of the slave population and an increase of the proportion of Africans in it.

The expansion of the Bahian sugar economy can be documented in a number of ways. In 1759, the captaincy counted 166 engenhos, of which 122 were located in Bahia proper and 44 in Sergipe. By 1798, the total may have reached 400 mills, 260 of which were in Bahia. By 1820, the number hovered around 500 producing units. Some of the new engenhos must have been small because the output per mill remained

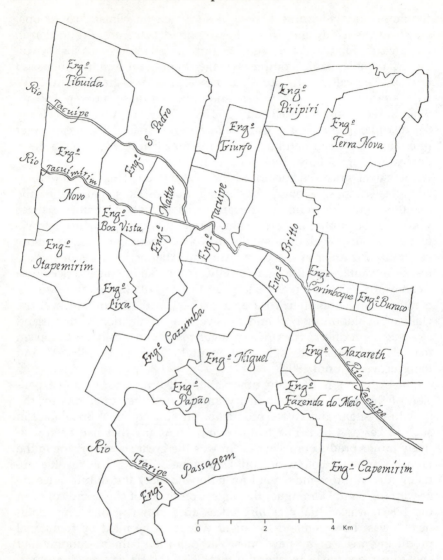

Map 5. Plantation boundaries along the Jacuipe River. (Note the lack of small holdings between the engenhos. Based on an 1864 map in the Monastery of São Bento in Salvador.)

relatively low. Between 1796 and 1811, Bahia's sugar export averaged 652,121 arrobas annually. If we use a figure of about 450 mills as the average number of this period, then output per mill averaged fewer than 1,500 arrobas, a figure well below Antonil's over 3,000 arrobas per mill at the close of the seventeenth century.[27]

New areas were opened up away from the Recôncavo at the same time that older sugar-growing parishes near the bay intensified production. A register of engenhos begun in 1807 documents one of the reasons why. Not only did the new demand raise prices, thus offsetting increased transportation costs, but to compensate for these costs the government also provided a cash subsidy on a sliding scale in relation to the distance of the mill from the port. Planters located beside the bay received only 4$400 per crate as a subsidy, but those in such inland parishes as newly developing Inhambupe and Itapororocas received up to 1$ for every league from the port that their crates had to travel. This allowance obviously served as an incentive to expand the sugar industry. Far from the coastal massapé, small engenhos sprang up, taking advantage of the good prices and government subsidy. But expansion in the core sugar parishes also took place. Traditional mills expanded operations, and new mills were formed on former cane farms, with a resultant competition for firewood, cane, and workers.

Evidence of the expansion can be seen in many ways. Numerous petitions were registered with the câmara of Salvador by those seeking permission to purchase oxen in the sertão without compensation to the municipal monopoly. Most of these petitions dated from the period after 1803 and were similar to that of Antônio José de Queiroz, who asked for permission to buy thirty oxen for the "reform of his engenho Santo Antônio da Ribeira" in the inland district of Ipitanga.[28] When in 1805 Captain José Ferreira da Costa sought to buy 300 head for his three engenhos in Cotegipe, the câmara permitted the purchase but only in small lots, "in order to avoid any shortage for consumption in the city."[29] The câmara had recognized a growing competition between the expanding plantation sector and the urban population of Salvador, now numbering about fifty thousand inhabitants. The government attempted to increase the food supply of the city, but this competition for food led to rising prices.

Other evidence of the expansion of the sugar economy and the construction of new mills is provided by numerous petitions for chapel construction. A law of 11 October 1785 required those who wished to erect a new chapel to secure both royal permission and a license from the local bishop. Beginning in 1797, petitions became numerous. Dona Brites Francisca Cavalcanti e Albuquerque sought to raise a new chapel on her engenho Nossa Senhora de Piedade to provide the sacraments to the eighty slaves who lived there as well as to the surrounding population. Others sought the same privilege as the Bahian sugar industry responded to new opportunities in the 1790s and 1800s.[30]

By 1798, Governor Fernando José de Portugal could report to the Minister Rodrigo de Sousa Coutinho in Lisbon that sugar and tobacco exports had risen markedly "because of the infinite number of engenhos that have been newly constructed during my government and which continue being built." The governor was able to report the existence of 138 mills, 90 stills, and other farms.[31] The expansion continued for another decade, and export levels remained high until 1808. These were boom times for the planters. New people were attracted to the industry: both the relatively humble, who scraped together enough capital to begin, and families like the Ferreira da Câmara, who had made their fortunes in Minas Gerais and now sought solid agricultural investments as the returns from mining declined. Engenhos long in operation also benefited. Many of the still-standing plantation houses, like those of Pouca Ponta and Vitória in Iguape, were rebuilt in the first decades of the nineteenth century.[32] A patina of success gradually covered the past history of struggle and difficulty, creating as it spread a myth of seemingly continuous wealth extending back to the sixteenth century.

The industry in Bahia and Sergipe de El-Rey continued to expand until 1840. Despite a disruption of exports in the period 1808–11 due to European events and local conditions, engenho construction picked up again after 1817. Between that date and 1828, 110 new mills were erected, and in the following decade another 220 began production. A law of 13 November 1827 ended the limitation on new mill construction and made it possible for anyone with the necessary credit or capital to begin operations. Between 1827 and 1834, new engenhos were raised at the rate of 23 a year. Although estimates of production and counts of engenhos varied, the trend of expansion is clear in all cases. An estimate of 1818 listed the number at 325 mills for Bahia and 156 in Sergipe de El-Rey for a total of 511 engenhos. A report of 1834 placed the total figure for both regions at 603.[33]

Export statistics for Bahia seen in Figure 15-1, though deficient for the period after 1808 and especially bad for the years after 1822, indicate the same trend. In the 1770s, Bahia's annual production was estimated at 10,000 crates. That figure rose somewhat in the 1780s, but between 1796 and 1811 Bahia averaged more than 16,300 crates of 40 arrobas each a year (even if we include the extraordinarily bad years 1808 and 1810–11). In 1817, the captaincy exported almost 30,000 crates of sugar.[34] Although numerous suggestions for technological improvements and experiments with new cane types and other reforms were made in this period, essentially the growth of the sugar economy was made by expanding the number of producing units and intensifying the existing system of slavery. Bahia experienced resurgence, not transformation. And Bahia was not alone.

Other regions of Brazil either initiated sugar production or expanded existing industries. A Pombaline monopoly company had already stimulated Pernambucan sugar output. When the company had been formed in the mid-1750s, the price of sugar had been good. At that time, the captaincy had about 268 functioning mills and an annual production of perhaps 6,000 crates or 3,500 tons. By 1762, the company was carrying all the legal sugar exports of the Northeast captaincies,

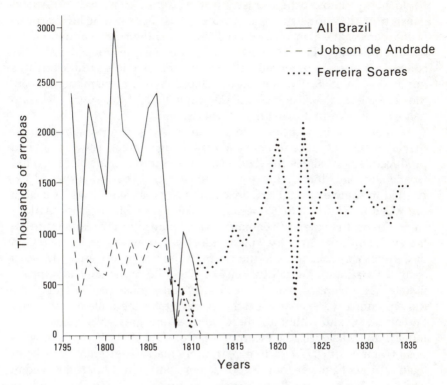

Figure 15-1. Bahian sugar exports, 1796–1836.

which over the course of the next fifteen years averaged about 9,200 crates a year. Although the Bahian figures are not available for these years, it appears that Pernambuco and its associated captaincies outstripped Bahia in these years. Under the control of the company, prices remained relatively stable with slight upward adjustments in 1765, 1770, and 1777, but production after 1762 was about one-third higher than before 1750.[35] In the post-Haitian expansion, the level of sugar exports increased again. Between 1796 and 1811, Pernambuco averaged about 11,000 crates a year. Levels fell back between 1811 and 1815 to 9,000 crates, but exports rose rapidly over the next fifteen years. Between 1826 and 1830, Pernambuco averaged an annual export of over 28,000 crates.[36]

During the middle decades of the eighteenth century, other areas had joined Bahia and Pernambuco as sugar exporters of some importance. Belem at the mouth of the Amazon shipped some sugar to Europe, but despite various attempts to stimulate sugar in the North, high costs and labor problems stifled production.[37] At the other extreme, in the Brazilian South, an activist Pombaline governor of São

Paulo had promoted the industry in that captaincy after 1765. An expansion of the industry began in the 1770s, but once again the post-Haitian era of the 1790s was crucial.[38] By the nineteenth century, sugar became a leading Paulista export, opening the way for its successor, coffee. But even so, in comparative terms, São Paulo's production was minuscule. In 1808, Bahia exported 20,000 crates, Pernambuco 14,000, Rio de Janeiro 9,000, and São Paulo only 1,000. Still, sugar made up half the value of that captaincy's exports.[39]

As these figures indicate, Rio de Janeiro was firmly established by the late eighteenth century as a major sugar area. The region had produced sugar since the late sixteenth century, especially around Guanabara Bay, but in the eighteenth century the industry had expanded to some extent in response to the Angolan slave trade. Cachaça produced in Rio de Janeiro became a major trade item on the African coast, filling the role that Bahian tobacco played in the Mina trade. In the eighteenth century, the sugar industry had expanded in the region of Campos de Goitacazes to the north of the city of Rio and southward around Parati and Angra dos Reis. In 1799, the captaincy had approximately 324 engenhos, and by 1819 400.[40] Like those of São Paulo, the Rio engenhos were smaller on the average than the mills of Bahia and Pernambuco, and although there were a few great plantations with more than 200 slaves, the mean number of slaves was 36 on the engenhos of Campos in 1778. In that year, more than 60 percent of the slaves lived in units of fewer than 50 bondsmen, and only 12 percent lived in groups of 100 or more. This pattern was repeated in São Paulo, where until 1822 that captaincy's mills never averaged production of more than 1,700 arrobas each.[41]

It is important to recognize that sugar's resurgence was not due only to the Haitian rebellion and the opportunities it created, important as that event was. Nor was the sugar industry singular in its expansion and development. The policies of economic improvement and agricultural diversification begun by Pombal had met only limited success because of poor market conditions and political difficulties. But in many cases, the seeds of the future had almost literally been sowed by the Pombaline administrators. Educational reforms and the founding of the Lisbon Academy of Sciences in 1779 presaged changes in attitude and expectation among the Portuguese intelligentsia and bureaucracy. An abortive conspiracy for independence in Minas Gerais in 1788 and growing Brazilian agitation for free trade and a more equitable relationship with Portugal led royal administrators in the 1790s to seek ways of improving the economy and the colonial relationship. Influenced by physiocratic doctrines, much of their effort went to improve agriculture. Surveys were made in the colonies, and the royal bureaucrats sought ways to modernize production and increase output. Much of this was done with a growing awareness of the techniques and advances made in other areas of the world, especially in those that competed directly with Portugal's colonies.[42]

Between 1780 and 1830, such traditional exports as tobacco and hides also registered major increases along with sugar, and they were joined by a series of relatively new products. Cotton, a crop of the drier interior (agreste) became a major export of Maranhão, Pernambuco, and to a lesser extent Bahia. Spurred by high prices after 1770, cultivation of cotton expanded dramatically. Most of what Portugal imported from Brazil it reexported to England and France, so by the 1790s 30 percent of British cotton imports were Brazilian in origin. Only competition from the United States in the 1830s brought an end to the boom. Rice had a similar history. New varieties were introduced from the Carolinas in the 1760s and production – centered principally in Maranhão, Pará, and Rio de Janeiro – began to rise in the following decade. Brazil by the 1820s met its own requirements and those of Portugal, which reexported large amounts of this grain. Added to these successes were cacao, coffee, and wheat. This last crop, grown in Rio Grande do Sul in the far South, by the 1790s was being sold in various Brazilian ports along with dried beef and hides, the other major products of that region.

The result of this agricultural renaissance was an alteration of the existing relationships between Brazil and Portugal and between Portugal and its European trading partners. Whereas Portugal had long been a deficit trader with Europe, after 1796 it developed a positive balance of trade, based primarily on the reexport of Brazilian products. By 1806, more than 60 percent of its exports were Brazilian in origin. Simultaneously, Portugal became a deficit partner in its trade with its own colony Brazil. Specie flowed from England to Portugal and then from Portugal to Brazil. Little wonder that Brazilians began to question the bases of the colonial relationship.[43]

The resurgence of the export economy in the 1790s brought on by the crisis of Saint Domingue was to some extent promoted and intensified by a remarkable group of Portuguese administrators and colonial intellectuals who, sometimes in concert and sometimes in conflict, sought to strengthen the Brazilian economy.[44] To some extent, they were the intellectual godchildren of the Pombaline reforms, and in fact the central figure, Dom Rodrigo de Sousa Countinho, who became prime minister of Portugal in 1790, was literally Pombal's godson. He and his immediate predecessor were men of wide reading and firsthand experience in Brazil or Europe. They sent scientific missions to the capitals of Europe to study improvements in agriculture and mining, they sought reports and studies of commercial, industrial, and agricultural innovations, and they provided in general an atmosphere favorable to practical experimentation. Bahia received a series of able and activist administrators in this period. Men like Dom Fernando José de Portugal (1788–

1801), João de Saldanha da Gama, count of Ponte (1805–10), and Dom Marcos de Noronha e Brito, count of Arcos (1810–18), were forceful representatives of royal government who as governors of Bahia sought to promote economic development while controlling political dissatisfaction and social unrest.

These activist governors provided a climate for institutional change. The first insurance company in the captaincy was created in 1808, and by 1821 there were three in operation. The first bank, the Caixa do desconto, was created by the count of Arcos in 1816 to provide funds for further agricultural development; he was also responsible for creating a commercial exchange the following year.[45] Colonials closely tied to plantation agriculture and export commerce responded to the stimulus provided by the government and the marketplace. These were men like Bishop Azeredo Coutinho, a former administrator of an engenho who penned a memorial against the regulation of sugar prices and later wrote in defense of the slave trade. Although other Brazilian intellectuals tended to be less adamant on the latter issue, most shared his attitudes on the freedom of commerce. Manoel Ferreira da Câmara, who was European educated, had family ties to the elite of Minas Gerais and Bahia, and from 1801 to 1807 administered his family's Engenho da Ponte, advocated practical reforms in mining, agriculture, and sugar making. João Rodrigues de Brito, a high-court judge in Bahia, wrote against any restrictions on the freedom of commerce or on planters' choices. The learned José da Silva Lisboa (later viscount of Cairú) expressed similar sentiments and played an important role in promoting the royal order of 1808 that opened the ports of Brazil to foreign commerce.

If such men were the godchildren of Pombal, they were also the stepchildren of Adam Smith. Their goal was to loosen restrictions on production and commerce in order to benefit from favorable conditions in the marketplace. But if these colonial intellectuals and activist administrators sought reform, they did so always within the context of the colonial system. Some, like Ferreira da Câmara, might attack the boards of inspection or the public granary, but what they envisioned was unimpeded opportunities to profit from a favorable economic situation, not a redefinition of the colonial relationship with Portugal.[46] When in 1808, however, events pushed the Portuguese crown to open the ports of Brazil to foreign commerce, colonial merchants and planters immediately recognized the advantages of the change. Not only would the measure bring new opportunities for trade; it might also dampen the fires of Jacobinism by eliminating one of the complaints of the more radical exponents of reform.[47]

The economy of Bahia had surged ahead in the 1790s, stabilized between 1800 and 1807, and regained a forward momentum after 1808 that it maintained for another decade. During these years, the Bahian elite looked optimistically at the future. It hoped to consolidate the gains already made and to ensure the continued prosperity of the captaincy's economy. Within the general movement of agricultural growth and diversification, sugar continued to remain Bahia's principal export.

Prosperity fueled experimentation and a fevered search for improvements among the Bahian sugar planters. To some extent the movement was government sponsored, but in large part it was generated by the more enlightened and progressive planters, who hoped to find cheaper and more efficient ways to bring their sugar to market. This search for improvements was made in many areas.

One can point first to the raw material, sugarcane. Since the sixteenth century, Brazilian sugar had been produced from one variety of cane, the so-called *cana crioula* that had been brought from Madeira. Around 1790, a new type of cane from the Pacific, called *otahiti*, was introduced into Brazil by way of French Guiana, or Caienne, whence its Brazilian name, *cana caiena*.[48] First planted in Bahia in 1810 at Manoel Pereira de Lima's Engenho da Praia, the new cane variety seemed to offer certain advantages.[49] It was strong and tall with a fibrous stalk resistant to wind damage. The woody nature of the cane also made it preferable for use as fuel in the mill's furnaces.[50] Until its introduction, Brazilian planters had made no use of bagasse or pressed canes as a fuel source. The new cane type now seemed to make this possible. Enlightened planters experimented. In 1820, Caldeira Brant thanked an English correspondent for sending him samples, noting that an experimental field had been planted in it to make comparisons.[51] It is unclear, however, if the new cane type was rapidly adopted. Problems with it arose. Although the fibrous stalk was better for bagasse, it also made grinding with wooden rollers more difficult. Planters in the southern Recôncavo reported that the quality of the new seed cane deteriorated so that diseases damaged the cane and thus each year's safra was smaller than the last.[52] Despite enthusiasm, adoption of caienne cane appears to have been slow. Other varieties such as Batavia, crystalline, and purple that began to make inroads in the Caribbean after 1820 were known in Brazil but were not widely adopted until the late nineteenth century.[53]

A similar pattern of discussion or experimentation followed by reluctant adaptation or rejection could be noted in other aspects of sugar production: milling, furnace construction, planting, the use of bagasse, and changes in the nature or treatment of the labor force. As we have seen, suggestions for technical improvements in the Bahian sugar industry had never been lacking, but the period after 1790 was especially active. Luís dos Santos Vilhena proposed a new type of mill in 1804, and he was but one of many reformers of the period. Something of the tenor of the times was expressed by articles in the *Idade do Ouro*, Bahia's first periodical, published after 1813. Articles and editorials

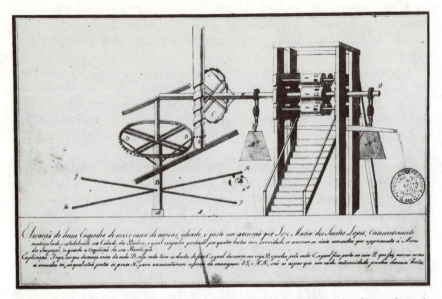

Figure 15-2. The search for reform and improvement: José Maria dos Santos Lopes's plans for a new type of engenho, submitted to the Overseas Council in 1803.

stressed the need for improvements and for the application of science to the sugar industry. "Science," said Manoel Jacinto de Sampaio e Mello, "is not studied to argue in classrooms or to conserve in assemblies, but to discover truths interesting to the common good."[54] He and other Bahian reformers and enlightened planters wished to introduce modern techniques but believed that such innovations had to be tempered by experience.[55] The problem remained that the combination of sugar-making experience and science was rarely found in the same individuals. Still, there were Bahian planters willing to experiment, men like Felisberto Caldeira Brant Pontes, Ferreira da Câmara, and others for whom the principles of the enlightenment were essentially practical.

All sorts of innovations and improvements were suggested or tried. The merchant José Maria dos Santos Lopes submitted plans for a new five-roller mill in 1803 (see Figure 15-2). Ferreira da Câmara proposed a new design for the furnaces at the mill so that less wood could be used.[56] Others suggested the use of the "Jamaica Train," a system of flues that allowed a single furnace to heat a number of kettles and thus reduce the amount of wood needed. The use of bagasse as a fuel and of the steam engine as a power source were also popular proposals.

This last innovation, the use of the steam engine to power the mill, presents a good opportunity to examine the level of planter interest in technical change and to confront the centuries-old claim that Brazilian planters were atavistic and little concerned with improvements. As early as 1618, Ambrósio Fernandes Brandão accused his fellow colonists of having "no desire to add anything new" and of being "stepfathers to Brazil while to them she [was] a very kind mother."[57] The exact sentiment was expressed two hundred years later in the *Idade de Ouro*, which claimed that Bahian planters were so attached to the ways of their fathers that they "looked with exclusive indifference on any innovation."[58] In fact, Caldeira Brant and another planter had contacted an English firm in 1810 to obtain a steam engine. By 1815, a steam-powered mill was operating on Itaparica Island. Planters expressed considerable interest, but the machine broke down easily and planters felt that the "inattention of the slaves" made its use unprofitable. By claiming this, they placed the responsibility for the steam engine's slow adoption on the workers. This, of course, was the argument that other slaveowners made and one that led Marx to see an incompatability between technological progress and slave labor. Historians who accept this contention have not explained why uneducated coolies or ex-slaves were any better adapted to a mechanized sugar industry than were slaves, many of whom had filled the most responsible and skilled positions at the mills.[59]

The early nineteenth century was a period of considerable innovation in the sugar economies of the New World, and the Bahian planters were not unaware of the need to make those adaptations vital to their survival in competition with places like Cuba, Jamaica, and Louisiana. Although much criticized by later historians for their lack of progressive attitudes, in truth there were some every much as interested in modernization as their Cuban and Jamaican counterparts. The technological progress of those islands, in fact, was not really noticeable until the 1840s, and until then Brazil kept apace. Still, it is true that local conditions and practices directed the nature of planter response and limited their willingness to experiment. With heavy massapé soil characteristic in the seaside parishes, the wealthy planters who were also the principal innovators were not much interested in the plow. With local cane and seemingly endless supplies of firewood in the southern Recôncavo, Bahian planters had not been interested in bagasse or the Jamaica train system of furnaces. When conditions began to change, many were slow to change with them. But these people were no fools, and the wealthier and more educated among them were willing to make adjustments. In 1812, Engenho da Filosofia was established in the Recôncavo as an experimental plantation, a place where new techniques and materials could be tried. It symbolized the curiosity of the Bahian planter class but itself remained a curiosity. The traditional engenho and slavery had made Bahia a sugar colony, and they would now be the chief factors in sugar's resurgence.

The revitalizaton of the sugar economy before 1840 took place essentially by intensification and expansion of the existing industry, with little alteration in the mix of productive factors or in the social organization of production. By increasing the number of mills and greatly raising the levels of slave importation, Bahia responded to the opportunities presented in the Atlantic sugar trade at the turn of the century. But this policy was not without costs, especially in a period of political turmoil, demographic growth, and potential social unrest. It is to these costs and to the strains that the resurgence of the sugar economy engendered that we now turn.

Economic growth and social stress

The Bahian population grew considerably during the second half of the eighteenth century. Salvador remained the largest center, with a population of more than 50,000 by 1808, but a considerable expansion of settled territory into the sertão of the São Francisco River and into the southern area of the captaincy toward the mines of Jacobina and Minas Gerais had been matched by an increase in population in these areas. The Recôncavo also experienced a rise in population, and although census counts of the early nineteenth century are unreliable and inconsistent, it seems clear that Bahia had at least a population of 500,000 by the 1830s.[60] Roughly one-third of the population were enslaved, but the slave percentage was considerably higher in the sugar-growing parishes of the Recôncavo. Not only had the Bahian population grown considerably in the second half of the century, but new elements were now present or at least were so numerous that they now merited attention whereas previously they had been ignored. A census of 1788 listed large numbers of *agregados* (dependents) among the free population. These were "attached" persons who resided in the household of others. They might be servants, boarders, relatives, or other dependents, and they now constituted a relatively large segment of the free rural population. In addition, the category morador began to appear with frequency. This was perhaps truer of Pernambuco than of Bahia, but moradores were also found in the latter captaincy. These were free persons dependent on a large landholding such as an engenho. They might own a slave or two, but in general they constituted a poor rural working class that lived in the shadow of the engenhos, providing labor in subsidiary activities. Others were small farmers producing subsistence crops or living by their wits. To a great extent, this population was pardo, the result of two hundred years of manumission and miscegenation.[61] Agregados, moradores, and unattached subsistence farmers were elements of a Brazilian peasantry that had grown in the second half of the eighteenth century. Free, and in the main colored, this portion of the population presented a new factor in political and social calculations.

The fear of slave unrest or rebellion was endemic in Bahian society, but in the late eighteenth century the apprehensions of planters and merchants began to include as well the growing free population of color, much of which comprised the rural peasantry. Control of the *mulatada* (mulatto crowd) became a matter of growing concern among the propertied classes. Complaints were registered against gypsies and vagabonds, and conscription was often used as a way of handling the social problem.[62] Santos Vilhena spoke directly against the presumptions and the degeneracy of the mulattoes in almost classic terms of racial intolerance, but at the same time he was intelligent enough to realize that the issue was not simply race. He wrote in words that previewed Marx:

Political society is divided into proprietors and those who own no property; the former are infinitely fewer than the latter, as is well known. The proprietor tries to buy as cheaply as possible the only possession of the propertyless or wage-earner, his labor. The latter in turn tries to sell it as dearly as possible. In this struggle the weaker contestant although greater in numbers usually succumbs to the stronger.[63]

In late colonial Bahia, the specter of a barefoot mob of pardo peasants or urban workers who might join with the slave population created a frightening image and placed severe restrictions on the plans and programs of liberal reformers who sought increasing liberty from commercial restrictions and metropolitan policies. Together, slaves and free persons of color probably constituted two-thirds of the captaincy's population by the 1820s. Their numbers weighed heavily in political calculations.

Moreover, this population was hungry and poor. The expansion of export agriculture and the profits to be made planting sugarcane or cotton exacerbated another of Bahia's endemic problems: shortages of food. Ensuring an adequate supply of manioc flour to feed the urban population of Salvador and the slaves of the sugar estates had been a problem from the beginning of the seventeenth century, and various measures had been undertaken to eliminate the shortages that occasionally threatened the captaincy. Royal legislation in 1688 and 1701 required sugar producers to plant enough manioc to feed their slaves and to produce a surplus that could be sold in local markets. Similar measures were taken in the eighteenth century, forcing merchants in the slave trade to plant manioc sufficient for the ships' crews and cargoes. Merchants and planters strongly objected to these requirements, and the law was often disregarded. As we have seen, a certain regional specialization took place in which areas of the southern Recôncavo like Maragogipe and Jaguaripe, towns to the south like Cairú and Boipeba, and regions like the Rio Real and the interior of Sergipe de El-Rey to the north of Salvador specialized in food production. This left the planters of the Recôncavo relatively free to plant only the export crop.[64] Royal officials, in fact, prohibited farmers in these regions to grow anything except manioc in an effort to assure adequate supplies of flour to the captaincy.[65] These measures, and government price fixing to prevent speculation, kept the situation under control until the 1770s; but that decade brought new strains. Growers unhappy about the controlled prices and attracted by the improved market for tobacco and sugar either left for areas where those crops were permitted or began to grow them illegally. The crown judge of Ilhéus complained in 1780 that the poverty of his area was due to the "most damnable indolence of the farmers, who forgetting royal orders and moved by greed had planted cane" instead of manioc.[66]

This issue preoccupied government in the 1780s because of the increasing cultivation of sugar, tobacco, and cotton, even by the humblest farmers. A series of censuses were drawn up of all manioc producers in some regions, the number of *covas* (holes; manioc plantings) each planted, and the number of slaves each employed, in an effort to establish the basis of the captaincy's food production.[67] In addition, in 1785 a public granary (*celeiro público*) was established in Salvador. These were stopgap measures, and with the boom of the 1790s poorer farmers increasingly deserted food production for the profits of sugar. The senhores de engenho, of course, had long resisted planting manioc on any land that would support sugarcane. As Manoel Ferreira da Câmara put it in 1807, he cultivated not one plant of manioc to avoid the absurdity of "renouncing the best agriculture of the country for the worst."[68]

The abandonment of manioc and food-crop agriculture and the increasing concentration on exports in the face of a growing population caused a rise in the price of basic commodities and, most likely, a worsening in the material conditions of the enslaved laborers. The price of manioc rose from 1770 to 1800, fell somewhat in the 1810s, and then peaked about 1825. Its trajectory was accompanied by rising meat prices brought on by droughts in the sertão in 1774, 1791–3, and 1819–21 and by sugar planters' increased demand for livestock.[69] A worsening of material conditions led to a growing sense of class division.

The specter of class conflict clouded the horizon of the principal planters and merchants as well as royal bureaucrats. Santos Vilhena had said, "With the exception of a few merchants and well-heeled lavradores such as the senhores de engenho, the rest of the people are a congregation of the poor."[70] This situation he ascribed to slavery's negative influence. But others saw in slavery a barrier to social strains, for the distinction between slave and free united, in some minds at least, rich and poor in an alliance against the servile population. After independence, observers could speculate on the unity created by nationality and free status, although to do so they had to disregard the profound distinctions of color. As the *Correio oficial* editorialized in 1834:

. . . the class of masters concentrates all political power in Brazil . . . if the proletariat as a class has little importance they are [at least] free men, and have no grounds for complaint because they possess all the constitutional rights and privileges without bias whatever of caste, color or custom. . . . Two great interests tend to reunite and join all members of an association so constituted . . . the sentiment of nationality and the necessity of conserving dominion over the slaves.[71]

The sense of nationality was not purely rhetorical. Distinctions had long been made between crioulo or mulatto slaves and those born in Africa, but the period of resurgence intensified the distinctions and reinforced the perceptions of slaves as foreign and dangerous. During the mid–eighteenth century, slave imports had averaged 4,000 to 5,000 annually, but imports to Bahia doubled with the resurgence. Between 1812 and 1830, legal slave imports averaged more than 7,000 a year, even though imports in 1822 and 1823 were, because of political problems, much lower.[72] The slaves were deposited like alluvium atop the existing strata of the plantation world. They arrived in large numbers, many from a rather restricted area of the Bight of Benin. This was a period of major arrivals of Nagôs (Yorubas), Geges (Ewes), and some Muslim Hausas.[73] These groups constituted perhaps one-third of the captaincy's slave population in the early nineteenth century. At the very moment when Brazilians speculated on the nature of their distinctiveness and nationality in relationship to Portugal, a flood of foreign-born Africans, boçais, distinctive in their language and religion, arrived together in large numbers. This situation permitted the slaves to maintain strong cultural and religious associations but also increased the fears and apprehensions of the slaveowners, who viewed this rising tide of Africans as a servile and foreign danger.

Increased importation of African slaves to meet the needs of the expanding sugar economy produced many effects. As we have seen, the slow movement toward demographic balance begun in the mid–eighteenth century was irrevocably reversed as the sexual imbalance and predominance of Africans were reinforced.[74] The presence of large numbers of newly arrived Africans raised well-founded apprehensions, as the series of Bahian slave rebellions beginning in 1807 underlined clearly. The resurgence of the Bahian economy made the role of slavery clear, and it made free Bahians, like other Brazilians, sensitive to British pressures to abolish the slave trade. Treaty arrangements between Portugal and Britain in 1810, 1815, and 1817 increasingly limited the trade and added to Bahian fears that Portugal was no longer able to defend the colonial interest.[75] Moreover, they drove up the price of slaves. The average value of a slave in Bahia tripled between 1780 and 1830. Only the great demand for sugar lessened the impact of that rise.[76]

Despite British pressure, the trade to Bahia continued. But even those who refused to abandon the institution feared its potential consequences. The treaty of 1810 had spoken of the disadvantages of "continually renewing a foreign and factious population," and this theme was eventually adopted by those few Brazilians who advocated abolition of the slave trade.[77] "France in the greatest enthusiasm and delirium of its republican equality refused to admit the propagation of Africans in its midst, while we work in these delicious regions . . . to establish a Congo kingdom," wrote Maciel da Costa in 1821.[78] But although many shared his fears, few were willing to accept the remedy. Slavery held too fast a grip, its roots were too deep, and its role was too central to the economic life of Brazil. If commitment to slavery had been limited to a few planters and merchants, it would have been relatively easy to dismiss its persistence as a political imposition by the ruling class. But instead a wide spectrum of the population participated in the slave regime. Slavery was a pernicious institution that pervaded every level of society. It was a way of life that touched all.

CHAPTER 16

THE STRUCTURE OF
BAHIAN SLAVEHOLDING

It is proof of extreme poverty to not own a slave; they may have
every domestic inconvenience, but a slave at any cost.
                                        Domingos Vandelli (Bahia, 1781)

The resurgence of the sugar economy in the last decades of the eighteenth century and the first decades of the nineteenth accompanied an
intensification of the traditional patterns of Bahian slave society among
both masters and slaves. Increased demand for laborers called for high
levels of slave imports, exacerbating the demographic structure of slavery while intensifying the African cultural presence among the slaves.
This presence and a general increase in slave resistance generated fears
and insecurity among the slaveholders, but they were also distracted to
some extent by their own growing sense of identity as Brazilians and
the preoccupations of colonial politics. Still, the threat and danger
created by slave revolts moved colonial administrators to take extraordinary measures: In September 1816, the count of Arcos, governor of
Bahia, ordered a census of all slaveowners in the Recôncavo to determine the size and location of the servile population.[1] This action did
little to stem the tide of rebellion, as we shall see in Chapter 17, but it
does present us with an opportunity to examine the structure and
significance of slaveholding in the Recôncavo at the close of the colonial era. Once done, we can compare this structure with that of other
American slave regimes and then suggest how slavery and property in
slaves determined the way Bahia faced its future as part of an independent nation.

The lists themselves were collected between September 1816 and
January 1817. Notaries were required to testify that all slaveowners had
reported fully and accurately. Lists were probably submitted from all
the Recôncavo parishes; but those of the suburban parishes of Paripe,
Cotegipe, Pirajá, and Matoim have apparently not survived.[2] A more
serious gap is created by the disappearance of the returns from the
township of Cachoeira and its parishes. Center of the tobacco economy

of the Recôncavo, Cachoeira in 1819 had a regional population of almost 69,000 and 34 engenhos.[3] Its absence from the lists and the failure
of the lists from Maragogipe and Jaguaripe in the southern Recôncavo
to record the slaveholder's occupation are deficiencies that complicate
my analysis. The extant lists do, however, include twelve of the
Recôncavo's seventeen parishes within four of the six principal townships. Both urban and rural settings are represented because slaveowners in the towns of Santo Amaro, Jaguaripe, and Maragogipe are
separately recorded and, most importantly, all the lists from the core of
the sugar zone, the townships of Santo Amaro and São Francisco,
survive. The surviving returns record more than 4,000 owners of 33,750
slaves in parishes representing all the major physiographic and economic subareas of the Recôncavo. In 1819, Bahia's total slave population was about 147,000, or approximately 31 percent of the captaincy's
500,000 souls.[4] About one-half of Salvador's population of 50,000 were
slaves, and perhaps another 30,000 slaves lived in the Cachoeira region
for which no returns have survived. Other slaves lived in the sertão, in
the forests of Ilhéus, and in the transitional agreste (which now produced some cotton for export). Thus, the surviving lists contain about
23 percent of the captaincy's slaves and perhaps one-half of those who
lived in the Recôncavo. In addition, the senhores and slaves of 165
engenhos, or more than two-thirds of the Recôncavo's 240 mills and
almost one-half of the captaincy's 340 mills, are recorded in the surviving lists.[5] The engenhos of Santo Amaro and São Francisco were the
biggest and best in the captaincy and should represent the upper limits
of slaveholding in Bahia.[6] And if any slaveholding structure in Brazil
was comparable to that on the Caribbean islands, slaveownership in
these two townships should have been.

Patterns of slaveholding

The distribution of slaveownership in Bahia was related to the land-
usage patterns of the region. As might be expected, the districts of the
southern Recôncavo devoted primarily to subsistence farming or manioc production for local markets were characterized by small holdings,
which is reflected in the mean number of slaves per holding and by the
ratio of the proportion of slaveholders recorded to the proportion of
slaves listed[7] (see Table 16-1). The unit size of holding was notably
smaller in Jaguaripe and Maragogipe than in the sugar-growing parishes of Santo Amaro and São Francisco and, although the southern
townships contained more than one-half of the owners listed (54 percent), these men and women held only slightly more than one-third of
the slaves reported (34.1 percent). Jaguaripe provides an extreme example of a lack of concentration in slave property and a wide distribution of ownership.[8] Almost three-quarters of the slaveowners in this

Table 16-1. *Slaveholding in the Bahian Recôncavo, 1816–17*

Parish	Number of owners	Percent of total owners	Number of slaves	Percent of total slaves	Mean number of slaves per owner	Median number of slaves per owner
Jaguaripe	1,167	25	5,071	15	4.5	2.6
Maragogipe	1,347	29	6,450	19	4.8	3.9
Santo Amaro	(1,363)	29	(12,168)	36	(8.9)	(3.3)
Purificação	481		4,807		10.0	3.1
Oliveira	252		1,303		5.2	2.6
Rio Fundo	491		5,178		10.5	4.2
Saubara	139		880		6.3	2.5
São Francisco	(776)	17	(10,061)	30	(12.9)	(4.3)
São Gonçalo	271		2,823		10.4	3.6
Socorro	72		854		11.9	2.6
Monte	125		2,448		19.5	5.1
Catú	152		1,420		9.3	4.4
Passé	156		2,516		16.1	5.6
Totals	4,653	100	33,750	100	7.2	

region held fewer than five slaves, and only twenty-five owners possessed more than twenty slaves. The largest units of ownership were those of the few engenhos of the region; but these were rather small, and only three slaveowners held more than fifty slaves.

Maragogipe, a district of transition from the forests and manioc farms of Jaguaripe to the tobacco and sugar zones of Cachoeira, possessed a mixed economy including some six sugar plantations, but it depended largely on manioc and to a lesser extent on tobacco agriculture. Because the Maragogipe lists do not include owners' professions or occupations, it is difficult to evaluate the effect of tobacco planters on the structure of slaveholding. But the somewhat higher mean and median figures for Maragogipe in comparison with Jaguaripe must reflect the presence of tobacco planters. In addition, the Maragogipe district included two medium-sized sugar plantations, Engenho Sinunga of José Alexandre de Quierós with eightly slaves and Engenho Capanema of Jerónomio da Costa Almeida with seventy-three slaves, and four small mills, all of which probably drew on cane supplied by tenant or sharecropping lavradores de cana. These larger units associated with sugar production increase the average number of slaves per holding and disguise somewhat the degree to which Maragogipe was a region of small slaveholding – two-thirds of the owners held fewer than 5 slaves, although only 29 percent of the slaves lived on units of that size. More than 11,500 slaves lived in Maragogipe and Jaguaripe, demonstrating clearly that subsistence-crop agriculture was not exclusively a free peasant activity in colonial Brazil–slave labor was consistently applied to this agriculture.

The parishes of Santo Amaro and São Francisco do Conde townships, the core of the Recôncavo's sugar economy, contained the largest engenhos and the most slaves. Not all the parishes were alike in size or other characteristics. Saubara, for example, lay to the south of the Subaé and Sergi rivers, along which most of the Santo Amaro engenhos were located. Although Saubara had a few sugar plantations, it also produced large quantities of manioc and other food crops. The parishes of São Gonçalo and Rio Fundo, somewhat inland from the Bay of All Saints, had developed as sugar-growing areas in the mid–eighteenth century. These parishes were, therefore, sugar districts still in formation and tended to exhibit a less concentrated ownership of slaves and a more diversified economy than the older seaside parishes of Nossa Senhora do Monte and Nossa Senhora da Purificação. In these traditional sugar parishes, the average-size holding was high, reaching almost 20 slaves per unit in Monte, a parish that contained twenty engenhos, three of which held more than 150 slaves. The parishes within Santo Amaro and São Francisco do Conde townships contained fewer than one-half of the recorded slaveowners (46 percent), yet these masters controlled almost two-thirds of the slaves listed (65.9 percent). The strong association of sugar and slavery is certainly borne out in these figures.

In this rural world of sugar, manioc, and tobacco, small villages and towns were scattered, usually on the banks or at the mouths of important rivers. Towns such as Jaguaripe, Maragogipe, and the larger Santo Amaro were closely integrated into the countryside that surrounded them. They were places of commerce and administration rather than centers of production; and, except for a few stills that produced cachaça, the local rum, and a small number of artisan establishments, these towns lived off the activity of the surrounding agriculture. Slaveholding in this urban context differed considerably in scale and purpose from that in the countryside. Slaves in rural towns were employed as porters, dockmen, servants, and cooks, as well as in other domestic and artisan occupations. The mean size of the urban slaveholdings was small, and the distribution of slaves among the owners was more equal than it was in rural areas.

To discuss the structure of Bahian slaveholding in a comparative framework, I have computed two statistical measures that reveal the pattern of distribution. The Gini coefficient is a measure of relative inequality or of dispersion–in this case, wealth in slaves–from a hypothetical situation of absolute equality. The Gini coefficient is expressed over a range from 0.0, or perfect equality, to 1.0, or absolute concentration. The higher the Gini coefficient, the more concentrated the slaveholding or the less equal the distribution between slaves and owners.[9]

Table 16-2. *Distribution of slaveholding in Bahia*

Location (economic setting)	Gini coefficient of inequality	Size share held by top 10 percent (SSTT) of owners	Mean number of slaves per owner
Recôncavo (urban)			4.0
Maragogipe	.23	–	
Jaguaripe	.34	–	
Santo Amaro	.36	–	
Recôncavo (manioc)			4.5
Jaguaripe	.38	–	
Maragogipe	.45	–	
Sertão (cattle, manioc), 1788[a]			5.2
Inhambupe			
Agua Fria	.48	–	
Taperagoa			
Recôncavo (mixed sugar and manioc)			6.6
Oliveira	.52	47%	
Catú	.55	43%	
Saubara	.59	56%	
Recôncavo (sugar)			11.7
Rio Fundo	.62	53%	
São Gonçalo	.64	54%	
Passé	.65	63%	
Purificação	.67	54%	
Socorro	.70	58%	
Monte	.77	78%	

[a]Slaves in the 1788 census were listed by the household to which they belonged rather than by owner. The Gini coefficient is calculated on households and the mean number of slaves is per household head. When slaves of all persons are included, the mean number rises to 5.7.

As a statistical measure, the Gini index shows the distribution of wealth in slaves at a particular time and provides a measure for comparing distributions across time and place. In addition to the Gini coefficient, I have computed the size share in slaves held by the top 10 percent (abbreviated SSTT) of owners. This simple measure, expressed as a percentage, is particularly sensitive to changes in the sizes of the larger slaveholdings.

The impact of specific economic activities on the distribution of slaves is apparent from these two measures and from the arithmetic mean size of the slaveholding units in the Recôncavo (see Table 16-2). Organization of the data according to location and type of economic activity, in ascending order of slave concentrations, clearly reveals the degree to which all the lowest measures are associated with urban slavery. In rural areas, the lowest indices are found in the zones of subsistence-crop (manioc) agriculture in Jaguaripe and Maragogipe; the slightly higher measures for Maragogipe reflect the presence of some tobacco and sugar agriculture. The concentration of wealth in slaves and the mean size of holding increases from the manioc region to the areas of mixed manioc and sugar agriculture and finally reaches the highest levels in those parishes most thoroughly devoted to export sugar production. Within the traditional parishes, all but one of the newer plantation parishes like Rio Fundo and São Gonçalo – further from the coast and on the outer edge of the Recôncavo – had a lower concentration of slave wealth than did the seashore parishes like Socorro and Monte. Table 16-2 includes data from three parishes in the Bahian interior taken from the census of 1788.[10] These parishes were primarily devoted to cattle ranching and subsistence-crop agriculture, and they represent an intermediate stage in the association of levels of concentration and size with specific kinds of economic activity.

Certainly the most striking aspects of Tables 16-1 and 16-2 are the relatively smooth distribution of slaveowning in the Bahian Recôncavo and the concomitant small size of an average holding. The Recôncavo was, despite its diversity, a major sugar-plantation region, the leading Brazilian exporter of that crop in the early nineteenth century. As such, it should present the upper limits of inequality of wealth and resources traditionally associated with plantation zones. The relatively low concentrations of slave wealth in all areas except the seashore sugar parishes, the rather moderate concentrations even in the majority of these locations, and the quite low concentrations for the Recôncavo as a whole all suggest that our general conception of the structure of slaveownership in late colonial Brazil needs to be considerably modified.

Sugar production had become an important activity elsewhere in the colony, but the plantations and mills in other regions were generally smaller than those in Bahia. A census of the plantations of Rio de Janeiro in 1778 lists 109 estates with an average of only 36 slaves and a median of 30 slaves per estate (for a Gini coefficient of 0.35). The engenhos of São Paulo were of comparable size.[11] Thus the Bahian sugar plantations were among the largest units and had the highest concentrations of slaves in the colony. Yet the majority of slaveowners were not active in sugar production but were instead involved in other economic activities or in urban settings, which had much lower concentrations of wealth in slaves. Slavery as an institution, an economic system, and a form of wealth was widely distributed among the Brazilian population. By the end of the colonial era, neither Brazil as a whole nor its Bahian Recôncavo was simply a sugar plantation writ large.

The slaveowners were as varied as the types of settings in which slaves were held. Men, women, and religious institutions all held property in slaves. Men and women held slaves in proportionate ratios – that is, 80 percent of the owners were men, and men held 80 percent of the slaves. Subtracting the less than 1 percent of the slaves held by religious institutions, women as a group held a proportionate 20 percent share; but there was considerable variation among the female owners. The lists carefully record women who used the title *dona*, an honorific term of prestige usually associated with wealth, respect, and, presumably, white skin. The average size of a holding for women without this title was four slaves; for women with the dona, twenty-three. These figures reflect the fact that women with the title owned twenty-seven of the sugar-parish engenhos, which included some of the largest plantations in Bahia.

Feminine ownership of property reached its apex in Purificação, one of the oldest and most traditional of the sugar parishes. There, thirteen of the district's thirty-seven engenhos were owned by women, who in a number of cases held more than one plantation. Dona Maria Joaquina Pereira de Andrade, for example, owned the two former Jesuit estates of Pitinga (with 164 slaves) and Sergipe do Conde (with 237 slaves), which was the largest single slaveholding in the Recôncavo. In addition, she owned two other engenhos in the parish – Botelho (with 66 slaves) and Santa Catherina (with 87 slaves). To feed her bondsmen, Dona Maria Joaquina owned three fazendas in neighboring Saubara, which were worked by another 34 slaves. Holding a total of 588 slaves in two parishes, Dona Maria Joaquina was the largest single slave-owner in the Recôncavo. Her case is extraordinary, but she was by no means unique. Her neighbor Dona Ana Joaquina de São José Aragão owned two mills, Engenho São Miguel (with 64 slaves) and Engenho Rosario (with 62 slaves). Other instances of large-scale feminine ownership of slaves can be cited. In the townships of Santo Amaro and São Francisco, women owned about 16 percent of all the engenhos and 10 percent of the cane farms.

The active participation of elite women in the control of land and slaves belies some of the common generalizations often made about the incongruity between the reality of these women's lives and the roles expected of them.[12] Whatever the reality of economic activity among elite women, societal attitudes toward such roles remained negative.

Although elite women who controlled large engenhos are colorful examples of feminine power and activity, women made up only 20 percent of the property owners and as a group tended to own smaller slaveholdings than did men. Three-quarters of the women who owned slaves held fewer than five, whereas only one-half of the men fall into that category. Small-scale and probably domestic slaveowning by women was especially noticeable in urban areas like the town of Santo Amaro, where 30 percent of the slaves were held by women.

Both individual clerics and religious institutions were also counted among the Recôncavo's slaveholders. By 1817, the former Jesuit estates were in secular hands, but the Benedictines and the Carmelites still owned engenhos and canelands. The individual clerics who owned slaves were very much a part of the society in which they lived, and

Table 16-3. *Ranking of occupations according to wealth in slaves*

Occupational activity	Mean number of slaves per owner	Number of owners	Percent of total owners
Primary activities			
Senhor de engenho[a]	65.5	165	7.7
Tobacco farmer	19.3	4	0.2
Fazenda or sitio owner	13.4	63	2.9
Lavrador de cana	10.5	478	22.2
Manioc farmer	6.2	128	5.9
Lavrador de cal[b]	5.9	42	2.0
Fazenda renter	5.2	125	5.8
Agregado	2.8	85	3.9
Morador	2.4	25	1.2
Fisherman	1.7	3	0.1
Secondary activities			
Distillery owner	12.1	23	1.1
Artisan	2.4	18	0.8
Tertiary activities			
Warehouse owner	6.0	2	0.1
Priest	4.5	19	0.9
Homeowner	4.2	41	1.9
Bureaucrat or professional	2.2	11	0.5
Small businessman	2.4	64	3.0
Suas agencias[c]	1.9	30	1.4
Overseer	1.5	2	0.1
No occupation listed	3.4	824	38.3
Totals		2,152	100.0

[a]The senhor de engenho figures represent single units of ownership (engenhos). There were in 1816–17 four cases of multiple ownership encompassing thirteen units. [b]Lime worker. [c]Translates as "their activities."

little distinguished them from the secular slaveowners. In the towns, priests held small numbers of slaves as butlers, cooks, and other servants; but in the countryside clerics employed slave labor in agricultural pursuits.[13] As sons of the rural elite, some priests acquired or inherited engenhos and cane farms. Six priests were listed as senhores de engenho and another thirty as lavradores de cana. In a number of cases, arrangements existed that permitted priests to perform their clerical functions while participating in the sugar economy. Such was the situation of Father Rafael de Sousa Gomes, who served as chaplain at Engenho Retiro and employed nine slaves to grow cane for that mill.

The lists for Santo Amaro and São Francisco townships record considerable occupational information for the 2,152 slaveowners and permit the ranking of these slaveholders according to their productive or economic sector[14] (see Table 16-3). Such a ranking contains few surprises, although what is missing is as interesting as what is present.[15] In the primary sector of agriculture, the ownership or control of property most closely linked to the export economy was the crucial element determining the size of the slave force. This may, however, be a somewhat circular argument, since certain kinds of agriculture demanded specific levels of labor input. The senhores de engenho held the largest slave forces and stood at the top in terms of wealth in slaves, just as they did in social prestige. Among their number were seven men who rented rather than owned plantations and whose holdings in slaves were considerably smaller than those of the plantation owners as a whole. No renter owned more than fifty-eight slaves, and the mean size of a holding for the renters was only thirty-seven slaves, compared with sixty-six for the senhores de engenho as a whole. Operation of a mill was not, in and of itself, an explanation of the level of wealth in slaves, and the ownership of land seems to have been an important factor in wealth accumulation.

Given the importance of the sugar economy in Bahia and the traditional position of the lavradores de cana as proto-planters, cane farmers might be expected to fall just below the senhores de engenho. But instead they follow the tobacco farmers and other farm owners. This anomaly is probably the result of the lack of extant lists from Cachoeira, center of the tobacco economy, and the growing prominence of other farm owners, some of whom produced some sugarcane. Of the four tobacco growers listed for Santo Amaro and São Francisco townships, three owned fewer than nine slaves, but one held sixty bondsmen, which pushes the mean size of holding to unexpectedly high levels. In general, a large tobacco farm in the early nineteenth century might have had twenty-five slaves, and many had only two or three. Using notarial contracts for a century earlier, Flory has found that at that time, tobacco farms were, on the average, one-third the value of cane farms.[16]

The other types of agricultural property commonly found in the Recôncavo were the fazenda and the sítio,[17] both of which roughly translate into English as "farm." The distinctions between them are difficult to ascertain. Fazendas could be devoted to a variety of activities ranging from cattle to food crops and occasionally sugar cane. Sítio was the term preferred for tobacco farms but was not exclusively used in this way. Size, crop type, tradition, and probably personal preference all influenced the designation of a property as a fazenda or a sítio. For convenience, I have combined the fifty-one owners of fazendas and the twelve proprietors of sítios. Together the mean size of the holdings is just over thirteen slaves. Those who rented fazendas or pieces of them were poorer than both fazenda owners and lavradores de cana and held only about one-third to one-half the number of slaves. Thus, ranking the owners and tenants of agricultural properties by the size of their slaveholdings tends to confirm the impression created by travelers to Pernambuco, who described the decline of the lavrador de cana class in wealth and prestige,[18] for a similar process seems to have been taking place in the Bahian Recôncavo. The lavradores de cana were still a substantial class of rural slaveholders; but those who owned or controlled land in fazendas and sítios apparently were, as a group, wealthier. Moreover, evidence from the census of 1788 suggests that lavradores de cana increasingly included people of color among their ranks, a situation that in Brazil was a sure sign of a decline in social prestige.[19]

On a different scale of wealth were those slaveowners who were not directly connected to the major export crop or whose limited access to land and capital kept their operations small. The manioc farmers who owned their own plots averaged slightly more than five slaves a unit, as did the renters of fazenda land. In the parish of Boqueirão, a number of individuals made a living by preparing cal (lime), a material essential for building construction. At the bottom of the agricultural slaveholders were the dependents of the engenhos and fazendas.[20] Contemporary observers in the early nineteenth century always described these people as the poorest of the free rural population, so those listed here as slaveowners must surely have been somewhat wealthier than the majority of their class. This group falls into two categories – agregados and moradores. In 1817, moradores probably constituted about 20 percent of the rural population of Pernambuco. If a similar situation existed in Bahia, then the presence of only twenty-five moradores among the slaveholders is an indication of their poverty, not their numbers.

The secondary economic sector includes those activities associated with manufacturing or with artisan crafts. In the Recôncavo lists, the number of individuals with these occupations is very small. There are several possible explanations for this situation, some structural and some accidental. Some notaries may have listed only "properties" in the sense of land or possessions and not bothered to include occupation. There were 824 slaveowners listed without occupational designation, and included among them may have been some artisans. A second possible explanation is that artisans did not in general own slaves, but this is, as we have seen, unlikely. Perhaps most plausible is an explanation that emphasizes the impact of slavery itself on the artisan trades. In the Recôncavo, many of the traditional artisan skills were in this period practiced by the slaves. The only manufacturing done in Santo Amaro and São Francisco townships was the distilling of cachaça, the local rum. The alambiques (stills) varied in size from household enterprises with four to five slaves up to factories with twenty to forty enslaved workers.

The tertiary sector, that of "service" occupations, actually includes a wide range of professions and activites, many of which were associated with the towns and villages of the Recôncavo. The two trapiche (warehouse) owners obviously provided a necessary service for the sugar planters. But the tertiary sector here also encompasses those who were listed simply as homeowners in the towns and for whom slaveowning was primarily a form of domestic employment. The same can probably be said of the priests who served the Recôncavo. Included in the bureaucrats-and-professionals category are lawyers, notaries, a doctor, tax collectors, teachers, and minor officials. Perhaps of most interest in the tertiary sector are those involved in small-scale commerce: shopkeepers, *mascates* (traveling peddlers) and individuals who simply lived *de negocios* (by business). All those lists were from the parishes of São Francisco township, which suggests that the officials responsible for recording the parishes of Santo Amaro simply did not bother to note this form of occupation. Some individuals who were listed as living by *suas agencias* (their activities) probably rented out their slaves or put them to work in the towns as market women or porters and lived off their earnings. Later in the century, Thomas Ewbank noted that, in Brazil, "hundreds and hundreds of families have one or two slaves on whose earnings alone they live."[21]

It was not the slaveowners with one or two slaves who set the patterns of the society and economy in the Recôncavo but the senhores de engenho, who for two and a half centuries had dominated Bahian life. The 1816–17 lists offer an excellent opportunity to examine the slaveholding of that class in a quantitative way and to analyze the organization of the plantation economy. By 1817, the effects of the sugar industry's expansion in the wake of the Haitian Revolution and the Napoleonic Wars could be seen in the increased number of mills. By that date, Bahia had about 316 engenhos, an increase of about 100 plantations since 1790.[22] About twenty interconnected traditional families – such as the Calmon, Fiuza Barreto, Costa Pinto, and Pires de Carvalho – controlled about one-third of the engenhos. These "aristocratic" families were especially dominant in the coastal parishes and on lands fewer than ten miles from the shore. In this group, there often were instances of ownership of more than one plantation. They were particularly well represented in the lists from Santo Amaro and São Francisco do Conde.[23] Since the largest mills were concentrated in these townships, the 165 engenhos are an excellent and large sample of the Bahian plantations – a sample that, if it has any particular bias, probably tends to exaggerate the average size of an engenho slave force.

Two features of the Recôncavo engenhos immediately stand out. First, there was a relatively smooth distribution in the size of the slave force among the engenhos – that is, there were few very small or very large units (see Table 16-4). The most common size was between 60 and 100 slaves, but a considerable number of plantations operated with

Table 16-4. *Distribution of slaveownership among engenhos in Recôncavo parishes, 1816–17*

Size of holding in slaves	Number of owners[a]	Percent of total owners	Number of slaves	Percent of total slaves	Gini coefficient of inequality
São Francisco township (São Gonçalo, Catú, Passé, Socorro, Monte)					
5–9	0	0.0	0	0.0	
10–19	0	0.0	0	0.0	
20–39	14	17.5	408	7.4	
40–59	18	22.5	862	15.5	
60–99	34	42.5	2,759	49.6	
100–49	14	17.5	1,531	27.5	
150 or more	0	0.0	0	0.0	
Totals	80	100.0	5,560	100.0	.21
Santo Amaro township (Rio Fundo, Purificação, Saubara, Oliveira)					
5–9	2	2.4	14	0.2	
10–19	3	3.5	49	0.9	
20–39	24	28.2	745	14.2	
40–59	14	16.5	687	13.1	
60–99	31	36.5	2,231	42.5	
100–49	7	8.2	787	15.0	
150 or more	4	4.7	740	14.1	
Totals	85	100.0	5,253	100.0	.30

[a]The total number of owners does not include one whose mill was fogo morto in the parish of Passé in São Franciso township.

20 to 60 workers (and the Gini coefficient of slaveownership among the senhores de engenho is low). Second, the 165 engenhos listed averaged only 65 slaves per engenho, if only those slaves who were owned directly by the mills are counted. Estates with a slave force of this size do not seem to fit the common image of the Brazilian plantation as a great latifundium with hundreds of slaves laboring under the unitary and patriarchal hand of a resident planter-lord. In fact, only Engenho Sergipe do Conde had a slave force of over 200 bondsmen, and only about 15 percent of the mills counted 100 slaves or more.

The crucial point here is that the unit of production, the engenho, drew not only on the labor force of its owner but also on the slaves of the lavradores de cana and sometimes on those of the other tenants and employees. The listed number of slaves for a senhor de engenho does not fully disclose the size of the labor force associated with the mill; when all the slaves are considered,[24] the sizes of the "great" plantations are approached. Because ownership of the labor force was divided, slaves lived in smaller groups than historians have heretofore thought, and this probably had considerable impact on the lives of both masters and slaves.

Although it is possible to speak of an average number of slaves on a Bahian engenho, it is more useful to view plantation scale in terms of optimal sizes. More than 80 percent of the Bahian engenhos had between 20 and 100 slaves. Large mills with direct control over more than 100 slaves were concentrated along the coast. They were few in number and controlled fewer than 30 percent of the plantation slaves. If those engenhos with fewer than 20 slaves – presumably plantations in the process of formation or decay – are discounted, then small mills can be defined as those with 20 to 59 slaves, medium-sized engenhos are those with 60 to 99 hands, and large plantations are those with more than 100, of which mills with 150 or more bondsmen are a small subcategory. These great engenhos came closest to the romantic image of the colonial sugar plantation; but they were atypical, forming only a small fraction of all engenhos and holding about 17 percent of the plantation slaves. Neither the typical planter nor the typical slave lived on the great plantations of colonial Brazil And these dimensions of slaveownership and plantation size were quite unlike those of other sugar-plantation zones in the Americas. In Jamaica, for example, more than half the slaves on the island in 1832 lived in units of 150 or more.[25]

The sugar-plantation structure in Bahia was a complex arrangement in which the engenhos were the central and crucial units of production, serving as the industry's core but dependent on the contributions of the free rural population that lived within their shadows. This free population entered into a variety of contracts and arrangements with the engenhos, providing them with supplementary slave forces, labor and management, and an enlarged capital credit base for the industry. This nonmillowning population of the lavradores de cana, agregados, moradores, and renters, who often owned property in slaves and rarely in land, characterized the Recôncavo. Labor as a factor of production was not so concentrated in the hands of the great planters as in other regions of the New World; thus the risks of sugar agriculture were more widely shared, which meant that the brunt of a natural disaster or of falling prices was not borne solely by the planters. The existence of these groups of free people who participated in significant numbers in sugar agriculture made the organization of that activity more complex than it was in other regions of the Americas.

The key group within the structure of Bahian sugar agriculture was the lavradores de cana.[26] By 1817, there were between three and four of them for each mill, although some engenhos depended on the cane from ten or more lavradores, and a few had none. These cane farmers owned their own slaves and livestock and also held about one-third of all the slaves directly employed in sugar agriculture. Lavrador slaveholdings varied widely in size but had a relatively low level of concen-

Table 16-5. *Distribution of slaveownership among lavradores de cana in Recôncavo parishes, 1816–17*

Size of holding in slaves	Number of owners	Percent of total owners	Number of slaves	Percent of total slaves	Gini coefficient of inequality
São Francisco township (São Gonçalo, Catú, Passé, Socorro, Monte)					
1–4	69	25.4	211	7.6	
5–9	90	33.2	590	21.3	
10–19	75	27.7	977	35.2	
20–39	36	13.3	944	34.1	
40–59	1	0.4	51	1.8	
Totals	271	100.0	2,773	100.0	.37
Santo Amaro township (Rio Fundo, Purificação, Saubara, Oliveira)[a]					
1–4	48	23.2	152	6.8	
5–9	66	31.9	435	19.4	
10–19	64	30.9	875	39.1	
20–39	27	13.0	695	31.1	
40–59	2	1.0	80	3.6	
Totals	207	100.0	2,237	100.0	.37

[a]In the parish of Oliveira, occupations were not recorded. There were probably twenty-one lavradores de cana who owned 133 slaves (or about 5.6 percent of the slaves held by lavradores in Santo Amaro township), but the table has been calculated without these lavadores and their slaves.

tration of slaves (see Table 16-5). Approximately one-quarter (24.5 percent) of the cane farmers were marginal producers with fewer than five slaves, and almost three-fifths (57.1 percent) held fewer than ten workers.

The disparity between lavradores de cana who held 1 or 2 slaves and those who held 40 reflects the wide range of social and economic variation within this group and suggests reasons why care must be used in treating them as a homogeneous class. Earlier research has provided some idea of the size of lavrador slaveholdings, but the 1816–17 lists offer for the first time an opportunity to examine the distribution of slaveownership within this group in a comprehensive manner.[27] In the townships of Santo Amaro and São Francisco do Conde, there were 478 individuals who can positively be identified as lavradores de cana. They owned 5,010 slaves for a mean size of slaveholding of 10.5. In both Santo Amaro and São Francisco do Conde, just more than 60 percent (61.7) of the lavrador owners held slaves in groups of 5 to 19, and slightly fewer than 60 percent (57.4) of the slaves held by lavradores de cana in the two townships lived in units of this size. This situation made slaveholding patterns in Bahia quite dissimilar to those in other sugar-plantation areas. In Jamaica, for example, where the small and medium-sized slaveholdings had been eliminated in the mid–eighteenth century, only 11 percent of the slaves lived in units of 5 to 20 at the time of registration in 1832. In Louisiana in 1850, fewer than 20 percent of the sugar-plantation slaves lived on estates of 50 or fewer. Even in Trinidad in 1814, with its more diversified economy not so fully committed to sugar, more than 60 percent of the agricultural slaves lived in groups of 60 or more, and only 17 percent of the slaves lived in units of fewer than 20.[28] In contrast, 53 percent of all the Recôncavo's slaves lived in groups of 1 to 20. This slaveholding structure reflects both the agricultural diversity of the region and the role of the cane farmers in the sugar economy.

The existence of the lavradores de cana as slaveowners with medium-sized holdings whose labor forces were committed to the sugar industry explains the curious and distinctive structure of the Bahian (and, by implication, Brazilian) sugar industry. The 165 engenhos of the Recôncavo depended on an average of three lavradores for each mill, and these lavradores owned an average of 10 to 11 slaves each. Thus, about one-third of the slaves directly employed in sugar agriculture were owned not by the engenhos but by the cane farmers.[29] This division of ownership is essential to understanding the scale of plantation operations in Bahia. If the engenho slave forces include not merely the slaves held by the senhores de engenho but also those held by the lavradores de cana (see Table 16-6), then the mean number of slaves per mill rises to 96, a figure much more in line with the 100 slaves estimated by various observers in the seventeenth and eighteenth centuries.[30] Apparently contradictory statements, like that of the town council of Salvador in 1751 placing the average number of slaves at an engenho at 40, now also make sense, because of the implicit assumption that additional labor will be supplied by the lavradores de cana through their slaves.[31]

Finally, it must be pointed out that the arrangements between lavradores de cana and engenhos reveal only a part, albeit a major one, of the complexity of plantation labor structures. Also resident on the lands or at the boundaries of many plantations were other free people who provided labor services themselves or whose slaves could be used by the engenhos at certain times of the year. It is difficult to know to what extent these slaves were employed regularly in sugar agriculture, and I have not included them in my calculations of engenho size up to this point. In some parishes, however, slaveowners were recorded by their residence in relation to engenhos; thus it is possible to see the relationship between plantation owners and other resident slaveowners. In Rio Fundo parish, the thirty-eight engenhos averaged four lavradores each, as well as two agregados and one other resident slaveowner each. This group of "other" slaveowners was made up of moradores, artisans, and managers. Although the mean size of an en-

Table 16-6. *Slaveholding by engenhos and lavradores de cana in Recôncavo parishes, 1816–17*

Parish	Number of engenhos	Number of slaves held by engenhos	Percent of slaves held by engenhos	Number of lavradores	Number of slaves held by lavradores	Percent of slaves held by lavradores	Lavradores per engenho
São Francisco							
São Gonçalo	19	1,298	62.0	62	791	38.0	3.3
Catú	10	182	58.8	41	338	41.2	4.1
Monte	20	1,732	74.7	59	588	25.3	3.0
Socorro	9	562	77.0	13	168	23.0	1.4
Passé	22[a]	1,486	62.7	96	885	37.3	4.4
Subtotals	80	5,260	66.7	271	2,770	33.3	3.4
Santo Amaro							
Purificação	38	2,560	80.5	54	622	19.5	1.4
Rio Fundo	38	2,245	60.4	143	1,474	39.6	3.8
Oliveira[b]	6	239	100.0	0	–	0.0	–
Saubara	3	209	59.7	10	141	40.3	3.3
Subtotals	85	5,253	70.1	207	2,237	29.9	2.4
Totals	165	10,813	68.3	478	5,010	31.7	2.9

[a]Figure does not include one engenho that was fogo morto.
[b]In the parish of Oliveira, occupations were not recorded. There were probably 21 lavradores de cana who owned 133 slaves (or about 35.8 percent of the slaves employed in sugar agriculture), but the table has been calculated without these lavradores and their slaves.

genho's slave force in Rio Fundo was 59 if only those slaves owned directly by the plantation are counted, the figure rises to 112 when the slaves of all associated owners are included.

When "reconstructed" by aggregating the slaves of all the dependents as part of the engenho work force, the scale of the Bahian plantations falls more closely into line with the size of sugar plantations found in the Caribbean and the U.S. South. The complex arrangements of slaveownership and its diffusion within the sugar economy had important implications for both masters and slaves. With small-scale slaveholding a predominant feature in Bahia and medium-sized holdings common in the sugar economy, we need to reexamine our long-held notions about master–slave relationships and the basis of pervasive patriarchal attitudes held by many slaveowners. In the slave communities, marital arrangements must have been difficult when the units of slaveholding were small, unless permission to marry outside the group of slaves held by one master was readily given; if normally granted, then extended family ties must have been tenuous, with various family members under different owners. And, for the planters, a major concern had to be the coordination of the engenho's schedule with the use of the existing labor force, much of which was under the control of others; management skill became crucial to a mill's success. Little wonder, then, that many Bahian planters were reluctant to leave the big house and allow stewards to direct operations. Plantation structure set the context for the social relations of production.

Bahian slaveholding in the Brazilian context

The relatively low levels of concentration of slaves in large units, the predominance of small and medium-sized slaveholdings, and the apparently broad distribution of slaveownership among the free population revealed in the Bahian lists – these facts suggest a number of problems. The first problem is one of "typicality." The Recôncavo was not Bahia, and Bahia was not Brazil. It is fair to ask what the slaveholding structure revealed in the 1816–17 lists represents in terms of the colony as a whole. As a major plantation zone, Bahia should present the upper levels of concentration of wealth and median and mean size of slaveholding in comparison to those of other Brazilian regions characterized by subsistence agriculture, ranching, cotton, or products that were less labor intensive than sugar. Information to support this hypothesis is difficult to obtain; but there is enough evidence, both direct and circumstantial, to suggest its validity.

Comparative quantitative data are available from São Paulo and Minas Gerais. On the basis of local tax records and census for five districts in Minas Gerais between 1718 and 1804, Francisco Vidal Luna has demonstrated that the size of an average slaveholding was small and that ownership of slave property was widely diffused in the population. In Minas Gerais, slaveowners with 1 to 4 slaves predominated, few owners held more than 40, and only one owner held more than 100. During the eighteenth century, the mean size of a slaveholding varied between 3.7 and 6.5 slaves (Gini coefficient 0.40 to 0.57), depending on time and place. Holdings in the mining region, then, were somewhat smaller and less concentrated than in the Recôncavo. Minas Gerais was a slaveowning economy of "small property."[32] A similar situation characterized São Paulo in 1804 where, despite the existence of engenhos in some regions, the mean number of slaves per owner in the captaincy was about 5.0, and 72 percent of the owners owned fewer than 6 slaves. More than 35 percent of the slaves in the captaincy lived in these small units, and if we raise the limit to 10 slaves, the proportion of slaves held in such units rises to almost 60 percent.[33] The hypothesis that Bahia represents the upper levels of size and concentration of slave property is supported by this evidence and, although similar quantitative studies of other regions are lacking, other, nonquantitative evidence confirms this supposition.

Slavery in Brazil was broadly distributed among the free population, providing the economic basis of the society as a whole and an extremely common and accessible form of investment. Travelers often commented on the widespread and profligate use of slave labor and spoke against its deleterious moral effects.[34] For example, an Englishman, the Reverend Robert Walsh, described seeing a black freedwoman in Rio de Janeiro with her slave:

Her young slave was her only property, and she made a good livelihood by hiring her out as a beast of burthen, to whoever wanted her, and for whatever purpose. Many persons black and white, about Rio live in the same manner. They possess a single slave, whom they send out in the morning, and exact at night a *patac* [*pataca:* a coin equivalent to 320 réis]. They themselves do nothing, lying indolently about and living on this income.[35]

Other observers noted the use of slaves in gangs to do the labor that a single horse or pulley could have performed more quickly and efficiently. The acquisition of slaves by people of humble means and the wasteful use of slaves indicate that this form of labor was cheap, relatively abundant, easy to obtain, and, most important, easy to replace. The key here seems to have been the slave trade itself; open throughout the colonial period, operating at levels not merely adequate to compensate for natural losses but, in certain periods, to meet demands created by economic expansion as well. Although planters invariably complained that the price of slaves was too high, evidence suggests that ownership of a slave was a relatively accessible goal that, whether for reasons of prestige or economic gain, promised a reasonable return on the investment.

The moralistic observations of foreign travelers, some of whom had their own abolitionist causes to promote, cannot always be taken at face value concerning the distribution of slavery in Brazil. And although lists like the Bahian rolls of 1816–17 provide excellent information on the distribution of slaves among slaveowners, they cannot resolve another and perhaps more important question: What part of the Brazilian population participated through ownership in the institution of slavery? That question is more complex and difficult than it first appears. Colonial Brazilian census materials are notoriously poor and often contradictory, so simply establishing the size of the population is no easy task. And shifting the question slightly, to calculations of the distribution of wealth, should slaves themselves be counted as part of the population "at risk?"[36] Slaves were human beings, not just property, and they constituted about 30 percent of the total population at the close of the colonial era. Obviously, their inclusion in estimates of wealth distribution will affect the outcome. The lack of sound demographic data complicates this question in other ways. If the acquisition of wealth is in some ways cumulative, and thus linked to age, then the older an individual, the more likely he or she is to own wealth in slaves and the greater would be the number owned. Without age-specific demographic data, analyzing the distribution of slaves in a population becomes more difficult.[37]

Given these problems, a useful way to approach the question of the diffusion of slaveownership is to ascertain the number of households that contained slaves as a function of total households. This rough measure can suggest the pervasiveness of slavery in Brazilian society. The general impression from the Bahian lists of a broad diffusion of slaveownership is supported by scattered evidence from other regions of Brazil. About one-half of the households in the urban centers of São Paulo and Ouro Preto, for example, contained at least one slave. In São Paulo, the percentage decreased between 1778 and 1836, but even at the later date 46 percent of the free households in the town held slaves. In Ouro Preto, capital of the old mining district of Minas Gerais, the figure was 41 percent of the households in 1804.[38] This level of diffusion in urban areas is borne out by a published census for the parish of São Pedro in the city of Salvador in 1775;[39] 47 percent of the households in that central parish contained slaves. The evidence is scattered, to be sure, but it supports the impression given by the foreign travelers that slavery was a ubiquitous institution in the cities and towns of Brazil.

It is more difficult to establish the proportion of slaveholding households in rural areas. In part, the problem is a lack of sources; but in addition, the variety of economic and ecological settings in Brazil makes any attempt to generalize from one region to another risky. Early evidence of a broad diffusion of slavery is provided by a census from Moucha in the cattle-ranching and subsistence-farming captaincy of Piauí. Of the 302 households recorded in the parish in 1762, slaves were present in 209 (or 69.2 percent) of them. On the cattle ranches, more than 90 percent of the households (*fogos*) contained at least one slave.[40] Similar evidence is not available from the Recôncavo, but the 1788 census includes some parishes just beyond the Recôncavo in which the presence or absence of slaves can be calculated. Inhambupe, a district of some sugar production as well as cattle and food-crop husbandry, had 115 free fogos, of which 56 (48.7 percent) contained slaves; and in Agua Fria, only 6 of the 69 fogos (8.7 percent) did not contain at least one slave. In the southern captaincy of São Paulo, a region characterized in the main by a dispersed rural peasantry, about one-quarter of the fogos contained slaves. The proportion declined slightly between 1798 and 1818 as the captaincy moved toward production of export crops and a concentration of wealth began to take place. Small-scale slaveholding was the rule in São Paulo; in its agricultural communities, about 45 percent of the slaveowners held fewer than three slaves, and two-thirds of the slaveowners held fewer than seven.[41]

Finally, yet another demonstration of the ubiquity of slaveholding and the pervasiveness of the institution is the now substantial evidence of slaveholding by former slaves (libertos). Mahommah G. Baquaqua, a West African enslaved in Brazil before reaching the United States, where he eventually published his story, commented that he was almost purchased by a man of color in Rio de Janeiro. "Slaveowning," he stated, "is generated in power, and anyone having the means of buying his fellow creatures with the paltry dross can become a slaveowner no matter his color, his creed, or his country, and . . . the colored man would as soon enslave his fellow man as the white man, had he the power."[42] Although the abolitionist who recorded Baquaqua's story may have been unaware of alternative functions that slaveowning could have had for people of color, the evidence of liberto slaveholding is clear. A study of 259 wills and testaments left by former slaves in nineteenth-century Bahia reveals that 207 (78.3 percent) left at least one slave among their property.[43] In Minas Gerais between 1743 and 1811, libertos made up between 3.3 and 14.6 percent of the slaveholders. In the diamond-mining district of the Serro do Frio in 1738, more than 22 percent of the slaveowners were former slaves.[44] The great majority of liberto owners held only one or two slaves, but their very presence as slaveowners indicates that even the most disadvantaged group of free people could, and did, participate in the institution of slavery. There are even documented cases of slaves who "owned" slaves.[45]

Let us examine a Bahian example, one that reveals slaveholding by former slaves and something of a slave biography as well. In 1752, Gonçalo de Almeida, a black former slave, drew up his will in Pirajá in the Recôncavo.[46] After making the usual statements of piety and the desire to die in the arms of the church, he recounted his life story. Born in the Congo, he had come to Bahia as a slave and been sent to the sertão. But when his master, Antônio de Almeida, had died, Gonçalo had bought his freedom. While still a slave, he had married a slave woman and fathered a number of children; but she and they were all dead by 1752. He had wed a second time, with a woman who for some time had been his slave and whom he had married after granting her freedom. At the time of his death, he owned six slaves, mostly Angolans. One of these was coartada at the time of the will, and was given the right to buy his freedom. Among the others was a child of his wife, born while she was still a slave. Gonçalo de Almeida's will indicates that even among the libertos who owned slaves there was no single pattern; rather, the institution was adapted to familial and economic needs.

This evidence, scattered through time and space, all points in the same direction. There was a wide distribution of slavery throughout the free population, and a large segment of the population directly participated in the system. In the cities, chances were about fifty-fifty that a free individual lived in a house with a slave. In rural areas, the range was wider, depending on the local economy, extending from about 25 percent of the households in São Paulo to more than 90 percent in some Northeast parishes. Furthermore, Gini coefficients calculated on this scattered data indicate that the concentration of wealth in slaves was relatively low. In sum, the existing evidence strongly suggests that slavery as an institution and a form of property pervaded Brazilian society and often touched and drew upon the participation of a broad spectrum of the population, including people of humble circumstances.

The analysis thus far is not intended to support an argument for "economic democracy" in colonial Brazil. Far from it. Whether the levels of concentration of wealth are considered "great" or "small" depends on one's expectations and some sort of comparative perspective. The level of concentration of slaves in the Bahian Recôncavo was a moderate Gini coefficient of 0.59, a figure quite like that found for the U.S. South and quite unlike that found for Jamaica. That figure, however, says little about the distribution of wealth among the whole population. At present, data do not exist that permit an examination of the general distribution of wealth in Bahia. But this analysis of slaveholding demonstrates that its level of concentration was lower than might be expected in an export-oriented, slave-based colonial economy.

Bahian slaveholding and the Americas

Comparisons across time, space, and cultures are problematic, to be sure, but they do offer a context in which a specific case can be used to examine more general patterns–in this case, the owning of slaves. The engenho slaveholdings in the Recôncavo, to recapitulate, were generally smaller than historians have assumed; the majority of the owners held fewer than four slaves, and more than half the slaves lived in units of fewer than twenty–all this in a region traditionally associated with a sugar-plantation economy. Just how surprising these patterns really are becomes clear when we compare them with those for the other slaveholding regions of the Americas. Slaveowning seems to have been somewhat more concentrated in the mid–nineteenth-century U.S. South than in late colonial Brazil, and the relative concentration of land and slaves seems to have differed in the two regions. But these small differences aside, what is striking is the overall similarity of slaveholding patterns in Bahia and the United States, particularly when these patterns are then compared with Caribbean slaveholding regimes.

In the United States, scholars have made an intensive examination of slaveholding patterns between 1790 and 1860. These studies have led to a series of conclusions about the inequality of wealth before the Civil War, the structure of the Southern economy, and the role of slavery within it. Many of these studies have emphasized considerable regional variations in the patterns of slaveholding according to soil and type and economic activity, an approach that underscores the diversity of the Southern economy. But despite such diversity, the findings to date also make clear that before 1850 the institution of slavery was broadly diffused throughout the South and that approximately one-third of all households were associated with it by ownership of slaves. In spite of a long historiographical tradition that concentrated on the plantation and on the political power of the planter class, scholars as diverse as Lewis Gray, Frank Owsley, and Gavin Wright have noted the importance of small-scale slaveowners and free farms.[47] Gray spoke of the "large number of small slaveowners–men who are hardly to be called planters. . . . Their main ambition is to produce cotton and own slaves."[48] Wright, though not wishing to overstate the case for equality of wealth in the South, still found that on many issues there was little difference between the attitudes of the large planters and those of the small slaveowners and that "the minority holding slaves was by no means tiny–roughly half of the cotton South, better than one-fourth of all families in the slave states."[49] On the basis of these figures, Wright has argued convincingly that Southern society's stake in the slave regime was broadly based.

The existence of census schedules from 1790 onward has enabled historians of the U.S. South to establish a firm quantitative basis for analyzing Southern slaveholding. The main thrust of many studies has been to use slaveownership as a measure of wealth and then to compare its concentration with patterns in the North or to trace changes over time; but their findings have revealed the structure of Southern slaveholding.[50] Attention has been focused on this structure in the antebellum period, especially in the years 1850 to 1860. But the work of Lee Soltow, which uses data from 1790 and 1830, is particularly useful for comparison with the late colonial materials presented here. Soltow examined a four-region area – Maryland, North Carolina, South Carolina, and the District of Columbia – for 1790 and found that an average-sized holding comprised eight slaves and that one-third of the families held slaves.[51] The Gini coefficient of concentration was 0.60, a moderate level. All these indices change slightly for 1830, when the average holding size rose to 9.6 slaves and the Gini index barely declined to 0.59. Soltow also calculated these statistics for all fourteen southern states in 1830 and found only minor variations from his four-region sample. His main conclusion was a notable stability in the patterns of slaveholding, at least until 1830; within these general patterns, however, there was considerable regional diversity.[52]

In marked contrast to the United States were the plantation islands of the Caribbean. There, the large plantations dominated, and the ratio of whites to slaves in the population was much lower than in the United States. The history of how sugar turned the Caribbean islands black has been told in other places and need not be repeated here, but the results are significant for comparative purposes. By the end of the eighteenth century, the larger British and French islands were characterized by big agricultural units and overwhelmingly slave populations. Grenada in the 1780s, for example, was over 91 percent slave; Saint Domingue in 1779 was 86 percent slave.[53]

Jamaica, a large island with a variety of landscapes, also fits this pattern. A careful accounting of the slave population made during the period of emancipation allows us to examine the structure of Jamaican slaveholding in 1832. In Jamaica, slaves totaled 86.5 percent of the population, and more than half of them lived on great plantations with more than 150 slaves.[54] The average size of a slaveholding was 25, and the Gini coefficient of inequality was a high 0.83. Jamaica, for all intents and purposes, resembled in its overall demographic configurations the plantation writ large: Slaves on large estates predominated within the population, and very large estates dominated the economy. Slaveowning in Jamaica was on a different scale from that in the United States. On that island, 61.5 percent of all slaves lived on plantations of over 100 slaves. In the United States in 1850, only 8.6 percent of the slaves lived on units of that size; even if only the lower South is considered, that figure rises to but 14.1 percent.[55]

When the analytical data of the Bahian slaveholder lists are compared with the same sort of data for the U.S. South and Jamaica, it becomes clear that the structure of slaveholding in colonial Bahia looks much more similar to that in the antebellum South than it does to that

in preemancipation Jamaica. The proportion of slaves in the total population, the average size of holding, the coefficient of concentration of
ownership, and the percentage of slaves living on large plantations in
the South and the Recôncavo are far more similar to each other than
either is to Jamaica (see Table 16-7). To be sure, Bahia as a sugar-plantation zone had a higher median figure of ownership at 29.0 than the
U.S. South did in 1850 at 20.6. But the lower South provides a better
comparison in terms of its agricultural structure; there, the median was
a remarkably similar 30.9 slaves.[56] In only one regard did Bahia probably stand far apart from both the United States and Jamaica, and in fact
from virtually all other slave-based societies of the Americas: The percentage of the Bahian population composed of free people of color was
almost certainly 40 percent or higher.[57] In the upper South, people of
color were never more than 6 percent of the total free population before 1850, and in the lower South the percentage was about one-half
that figure. Of course, in the United States free people of color had the
alternative of moving to the North, but in 1820 only 3.4 percent of the
total population of the United States was composed of free people of
color. By 1850, that percentage had fallen to 1.8. In Jamaica in 1800,
with its very small white population, free people of color were only 3
percent of the total population but composed one-third of the free
inhabitants.[58] Similar proportions were typical of the other British islands. Only on the Spanish Caribbean islands of Cuba and Puerto Rico
did free people of color constitute proportions of the total population
even approaching that in Brazil.

The sugar economy itself imposed certain patterns and structures on
slavery and slaveholding, so that it is useful to separate Louisiana from
the United States as a whole and from the South as a region in order to
observe patterns in that sugar-growing area. Unfortunately, data for
the early nineteenth century are not readily available; but there are
data for 1850 – thirty years later than the data from the Bahian lists. Not
surprisingly, Louisiana's structure of slaveholding was in some ways
closer to that on the Caribbean sugar islands. More than 20 percent of
the slaves in the state lived in units of more than 100, compared to 8.5
percent for the South as a whole. Although large units were more
characteristic of Louisiana than of any other state, still more than one-
third of Louisiana's slaves resided in units of fewer than 20, and more
than one-half of the slaveowners held fewer than 5 slaves.[59] There are
remarkable similarities between the percentile distribution of slaveholding units in the Bahian sugar parishes and Louisiana. The major
difference lies in the larger percentage of slaves held in Bahia in groups
of 50 to 99, reflecting the smaller size of the plantation slave force
because of the engenho's dependence on the slaves held by the lavradores de cana. Without a class of cane farmers, Louisiana plantations

Table 16-7. *Comparative distribution of slaveholding in Bahia, Jamaica, and the U.S. South, 1790–1832*

Place and time	Mean number of slaves per owner	Median number of slaves per holding	Gini coefficient of inequality	Mean proportion of families holding slaves	Percent of slaves in the total population	Percent of free people of color in the total population
Bahia, 1816–17	7.2	29.0	.590	.25–.50	30.8[a]	40.0 (?)
Jamaica, 1832	25.0	–	.825	–	86.5	3.0 (1800)
U.S. South						
Four-region area, 1790	8.0	–	.602	.34	33.5	–
Four-region area, 1830	9.6	–	.599	.33	–	3.4 (1820)
Entire South, 1830	8.7	20.6[b]	.597	.36	33.5	–

[a]Data for Bahia in 1819 taken from Joaquim Norberto de Sousa e Silva, as presented in Maria Luiza Marcilio, "Crescimento histórico dc população brasileira ate 1872," *Crescimento populacional,* Centro Brasileiro de Análise e Planejamento, no. 16 (São Paulo, 1974), 14.

[b]This is Lewis Gray's estimate for 1850; see his *History of Agriculture in the Southern United States to 1860,* 2 vols. (Washington, 1932), I, 500.

Sources: For the South, Lee Soltow, "Economic Inequality in the United States in the Period from 1790 to 1860," *Journal of Economic History* 31 (1971): 825–8; and Gray, *History of Agriculture,* 482, 529–40. For Jamaica, B. W. Higman, *Slave Population and Economy in Jamaica, 1807–1834.* (Cambridge, 1976). 144–5, 374–5; and Douglas Hall, "Jamaica," in David W. Cohen and Jack P. Greene, eds., *Neither Slave nor Free: The Freedman of African Descent in the Slave Societies of the New World* (Baltimore, 1972), 194. For Bahia, see Thomas Merrick and Douglas H. Graham, *Population and Economic Development in Brazil, 1800 to the Present* (Baltimore, 1979). 66.

Table 16-8. *Comparative distribution of slaves and slaveowners according to size of holding in slaves (in percentages), 1816–50*

Size of holding	Bahia Recôncavo, 1816–17	Bahia Sugar parishes, 1816–17	Jamaica 1832[a]	United States South, 1790[b]	United States South, 1830[b]	United States Louisiana, 1850[b]
Slaves						
1–9	36.3	24.9	8.7	29.9	28.5	20.2
10–19	17.1	15.2	6.3	26.3	27.4	15.0
20–49	17.1	20.6	9.5	28.0	25.3	23.4
50–99	20.2	27.7	14.0	9.3	10.3	20.5
100–99	8.7	10.5	25.6	4.5	6.2	15.5
200 or more	0.7	1.1	35.9	1.9	2.2	5.4
Slaveowners						
1–9	83.6	76.5	69.1	79.3	73.4	73.5
10–19	9.5	11.5	11.2	13.5	17.1	12.7
20–49	4.3	6.9	7.5	6.4	7.7	8.5
50–99	2.1	3.7	4.6	1.3	1.4	3.5
100–99	0.5	1.4	4.4	0.4	0.4	1.3
200 or more	0.0[c]	0.0[c]	3.2	0.0	0.0[c]	0.5

Ratio of owners with 1 Slave to total owners					
.23	.20	.11	.24	.20	.23

[a]Calculations for Jamaica are based on B. W. Higman, *Slave Populations and Economy in Jamaica, 1807–1834* (Cambridge, 1976), 724–5. Higman's size categories are 1–5, 6–10, 11–20, 21–30, 31–40, etc. Such divisions inflate the percentages in the lower size units. The ratio of owners with 1 slave to total owners has been calculated by dividing the 1–5 unit by 5; this surely overestimates the ratio, since the number of owners with 2 slaves exceeds the number with 1 slave in most distributions.
[b]Calculations for the South in 1790 and 1830 are based on Lee Soltow, "Economic Inequality in the United States in the period from 1790 to 1860," *Journal of Economic History* 31 (1971): 825, using a midpoint in each size category to estimate the number of slaves from each class size. Percentages for Louisiana are calculated in the same way from J. D. B. DeBow, *Statistical View of the United States* [seventh census] (Washington, 1854), 95.
[c]In these cases, the percentage was less than 0.1.

were larger, and more than 20 percent of the slaves lived in units of more than 100.

When the distribution of slaveholding according to the size of the unit for the three regions is examined, the similarity between Bahia and the United States and the dissimilarity between the two and Jamaica are plain (see Table 16-8). In both the U.S. South and the Bahian Recôncavo, fewer than 10 percent of the slaves lived in units of more than 100, compared to more than 60 percent in Jamaica. Emphasis is probably more appropriately placed on the similarity of the United States and Bahia at the bottom rather than the top of the scale of holdings – that is, in the number of slaves and owners associated with units of fewer than 5 slaves. In Bahia, this category comprised 64 percent of the masters and 15.4 percent of the slaves. Presumably, the figures for Brazil as a whole would be as high or higher, given its economic diversity. For the United States, it is possible to provide comparable estimates for 1790, 1830, and 1850. The trend across these sixty years was a decline in the ratio of small slaveholders to total slaveowners; but the proportion remained roughly half, decreasing from 54.9 percent in 1790 to 50.2 in 1850. These small owners controlled about 15 percent of the slave force in 1790, 13 percent in 1830, and 10 percent in 1850. In Jamaica, holders of fewer than 5 slaves were 54 percent of the owners, but these owners controlled only 4.4 percent of the island's slaves. And the ratio of those with only 1 slave to all slaveowners was one-half that of the United States or Bahia.

Slaveholding and Bahian slavery

This quantitative analysis of Bahian slaveholding underlines a number of patterns of property and social organization discussed elsewhere in this volume, and it also suggests a series of implications about the actions and perceptions of both the slaves and the free in Bahian society. First, it is clear that no longer can the differences in the size of slaveholdings or their distribution within the population be posited as an element of central importance in explaining variations between the slave systems of the United States and Brazil. Those two areas, in fact, were quite similar in that regard, and both stood in sharp contrast to Jamaica and other plantation islands. Second, the complex arrangements of slaveownership in sugar production, the large numbers of small and medium-sized slave units, and the broad distribution of slaveholding among the free population meant that this was not a society of simply planters and their bondsmen. Rather, hundreds of individuals or families with one or two or five slaves, whose investment in slavery was quantitatively small but whose attachment to the institution was no less real, must also be considered integral to the slave system. They were the majority of the slaveholders, and they held a substantial proportion of the slaves. Any discussion of slave life, acculturation, familial opportunities, and rebellion must take this pattern into consideration. Contrasts between Brazil and the U.S. South become even more striking when the differences in the size and distribution of slaveholding are shown to be minimal. Certain similarities, however, become understandable.

In *The World the Slaveowners Made*, Eugene Genovese pointed out what seemed to him to be an anomaly: Slaveholders in the U.S. South and Brazil closely resembled each other.[60] He argued that, despite the bourgeois origins of the Southern slaveowners and the seigneurial traditions of the Bahian planters, both "most closely approximate the standards of paternalism we associate with the patriarchal plantation." Genovese ascribed this similarity to the plantation regime and the contact between black and white on it, and in this he is probably correct. But what neither he nor anyone else suspected is that the structures of Southern and Brazilian slaveholding were so similar. Genovese emphasized the importance of a resident planter class in the formation of these patriarchal societies, but what may be even more important is that the majority of the planters lived on estates with fewer than one hundred slaves, places large enough to develop all the basic structures of everyday life but of a size that allowed the owner to know his or her slaves well enough to intervene in their lives in a direct and personal way. In contrast, Jamaican plantations were usually much larger, and more than half the slaves on that island lived on these great estates. With three to five hundred slaves, how much difference did it make if the plantation was run by the owner or by an administrator? Neither could know all the slaves in any but the most general way. Despite Genovese's essentially ideological interpretation of the similarity between these two slaveowning classes, the material basis of their existence was in fact closely parallel.

It would seem that the problem in Bahia and the United States was not that patriarchalism faced the constraints of slaveholding units that were too large. Quite the opposite: The majority of the slaveholders and the majority of the slaves lived in residences under working conditions in which the ideals of paternalism were difficult to maintain. The great aristocratic planter families did set the social tenor of the slave societies. But given the prevalence of small-scale slaveholding, the hegemony of aristocratic attitudes and their general diffusion within a population that lacked the material basis to support them symbolize the strength of slavery as an ideology as well as an economic system. Relations of production were typified by the large plantations, but in reality neither the majority of the slaveholders nor the majority of the slaves interacted within that context.

In Brazilian historiography, there has developed an interpretation of the movement toward independence and its relationship to social change that might be called neopopulist. At times clearly stated and at times implicit, this interpretation holds that in the efforts to achieve independence the existing structures of property and society were not seriously questioned, because the primary figures in such movements as the Minas Gerais conspiracy of 1788 and the republican Pernambucan revolt of 1817 were representative of the merchant and planter elites, the very people most firmly tied to the continuance of slavery.[61] For them, the ideas of European liberalism centered on freedom of trade, the abolition of state interference through metropolitan-controlled monopolies, and the sacred rights of property. Except for a few Europeanized and enlightened intellectuals or for those racists who wished to save Brazil by ending the importation of blacks, the leaders seeking independence opposed any change in the social organization of Brazil, which was built on slavery and profoundly influenced by it. In effect, this interpretation shifts the onus of political decision to the planters and merchants, the elite, and thus exculpates the "people" from the sin of perpetuating slavery. Surely the elite determined the trajectory of political independence, but the program they put forward was not extraneous to the context of Brazilian society as it had developed in the colonial period. In fact, a large number of Brazilians participated in, or were otherwise attached to, the institution of slavery and were willing, even anxious, to see its continuance. Had the only supporters of slavery been the planter and commercial elites, the efforts of the slaves might have met with success, as they had in Saint Domingue. But slavery was not the exclusive interest of any one group; in that lay its strength.

Finally, we cannot disregard the influence of slaveholding patterns on slave life and culture. Many Bahian slaves lived not in great masses of fellow bondsmen, relatively isolated from free society, but rather in daily proximity to free people of various colors and degrees. Acculturation throughout much of the colonial period was probably facilitated by this contact. Although few have questioned the rebelliousness of Bahian slaves, we can no longer hold that it was the large size of the slave units and their isolation that stimulated their resistance. In fact, the dispersion of slaves throughout the population, their presence in both urban and rural contexts, and their close proximity to white society may have led directly to a slave consciousness or political awareness that contributed to flight or rebellion. At city fountains, on country roads, in canefields, and while serving at tables, slaves watched and planned. In the tumultuous closing years of the colonial era and the heady but uncertain ones of independence after 1822, slaves perceived opportunities for successful resistance on a scale rarely possible before. They seized the moment, and for a while they shook the foundations of the world that constrained them.

CHAPTER 17

IMPORTANT OCCASIONS:
THE WAR TO END BAHIAN SLAVERY

But it is true old Marx
that history is not enough
Important occasions,
man makes them.
It's a real live man who does it, who masters it who will fight
History by itself does nothing, dear friends.
It does absolutely nothing.

Heberto Padilla (1971)

At the beginning of the nineteenth century, Bahian society had reached a breaking point, a moment when the political and economic contradictions of a headlong export boom constrained by colonial restrictions seemed to sow the social and demographic seeds of its own destruction. Sugar's rapid post-Haitian recovery, the expansion of the world of the engenhos, and the rising wave of African imports combined with the political changes brought about by the transfer of the Portuguese court to Brazil and the subsequent development of nationalist and republican sentiments to create conditions of instability and unrest. Between 1790 and 1837, Bahia experienced turmoil unprecedented in its history, or in the history of Brazil for that matter. Here was a slave society in the midst of disintegration, a social fabric rent by ancient injustices and present animosities. But despite the strains, the conflicting interests, the political shifts, and the violence, this society held together and survived the crisis to reach another period of relative stability. Institutions and forces of social control had been mobilized to protect the existing order, and the hierarchies and divisions that structured social life provided barriers to any sharp change. Under attack, this multiracial slave society had demonstrated its inherent strength and its ability to rise to its own defense.

It was not, however, for lack of will or courage that slavery persisted in Bahia. Slaves and freedmen at different times, and occasionally in concert, rose to challenge slavery's hold. From their attempts and from their failure, we can draw some conclusions about the nature of both Bahian slavery and Bahian society. In effect, I shall, in this concluding chapter, give the final word to the slaves themselves, although they left few records. We must instead seek their voice in the sum of their actions.[1]

This discussion of slave resistance is placed at the end of the book not simply because it is chronologically convenient but also because I wish to emphasize the endemic nature of resistance to slavery in Brazil. Throughout, I have attempted to demonstrate that the system of slavery – which developed from Iberian precedents and the plantation economy and which eventually extended into every aspect of Brazilian life – integrated a wide range of social, cultural, and economic phenomena in a malleable, adaptive, and imaginative system of labor organization and social stratification. Force and incentive, punishment and reward, rejection and favor began in the workplace and extended outward into the society as a whole; there, the distinction between slave and free shaded into hierarchies based on color, occupation, and rank. Although in material conditions there was often little to distinguish slave from freedman or freedwoman, crioulo from African, black from brown, or even brown from poor white, the juridical divisions and perceived distinctions served to divide and thus to cement the base of social action. But by stressing the integrative features of the slave system, I do not wish to fall into a functionalist trap, overemphasizing the features of the slave system that made it work smoothly while disregarding the extensive evidence of continual opposition and resistance that emanated from the slaves themselves.

There were always those men and women heroic or foolhardy enough to brave the considerable force that this slave society could bring to bear in its own defense. In a critical period, slaves sought to create "important occasions" and struggled to make their own history. This question must remain, however: Why, despite their bravery and the preponderance of slaves and free people of color in Bahian society, were they unsuccessful in the long run? In an age of revolution that ignited the hopes of men and women of all colors, the slaves of Bahia carried out a war against slavery. But they fought against military, social, and ideological odds that gave them little hope of victory.

Endemic resistance: the mocambos

Although the slave rebellions of the nineteenth century have captured the attention of scholars and the imagination of political activists, organized insurrection was not characteristic of slave resistance in Bahia until after 1790, when political events, economic conditions, and patterns in the slave trade created a set of conditions that made such movements possible. Instead, slave resistance in the captaincy historically took other forms, varying from individual acts of despair or violence to work slowdowns and recalcitrance, often with the intent of securing better conditions. Among the most common expressions of resistance was flight. The swamps and woods of the Recôncavo, the forests of southern Bahia, the scrub and mountains of the sertão, and the growing free-colored population of Salvador all offered environments friendly to runaways. Fugitives appear regularly in plantation inventories, and although some of this was *petit marronage,* that is, temporary absence to see a friend, to visit a relative, or for another, similar reason, there were others who fled with the definite intention of leaving slavery altogether. Some slaves developed reputations as continual runaways; about 1 percent of inventoried plantation slaves had this designation.[2] Evaluators placed this observation along with remarks on health because repeaters were considered to suffer from "illness." Persistent attempts at flight demonstrated that, whatever the effects of paternalism or the attempts to construct an adaptive slave regime, some slaves were never convinced or terrorized into cooperation. To the planters, these fugitives were ill. Their rejection of paternalism or desire for freedom was a sickness.

Fleeing slaves began to form fugitive communities, called at first *mocambos* and by the eighteenth century *quilombos.*[3] Although under certain conditions (e.g., the Luso–Dutch wars of the mid–seventeenth century) these communities could reach the great size and power of settlements like the quilombo kingdom of Palmares, the majority were much smaller and relatively short lived. In Bahia, they dotted the margins of the engenhos and fazendas, tucked in marshes and woods but relatively close to the plantations and towns, which they raided for supplies, arms, and new recruits.[4] There were references to mocambos in Bahia as early as the 1580s, and some regions like the southern Recôncavo and the area further south of Cairú, Camamú, and Ilhéus were, because of their isolation, particularly vulnerable to the attacks of escaped slaves. Expeditions in 1663, 1692, 1697, and 1723 were sent out to suppress mocambo activities in that region, but their repetition suggests the difficulty of the task. Camamú itself was attacked by fugitive slaves in 1692, and the whole Recôncavo was thrown into panic by the threat and example of these escapees. Some regions were chronically threatened by runaways. Sergipe de El-Rey was one. Its captain-major complained in 1751 that the runaways were innumerable and that the only solution was the use of black and pardo regiments to suppress the fugitives. By 1767, the runaways were bold enough to march armed into the capital city with drums beating and banners flying to demand letters of manumission from the captain-major, who was unable to arrest them because there were no troops available.[5] A litany of known mocambos could be recited across the course of the colonial period in Bahia. They were a constant feature of the plantation slave regime.

Located relatively near population centers and farms, most quilombos lived by a form of social banditry or guerrilla depredation. Although in some fugitive communities aspects of African religion, language, and social organization can be observed, most mocambos seem not to have attempted the re-creation of an independent African world; rather, they followed a strategy of survival on the margins of the Brazilian world. Colonial officers thus considered these activities purely criminal and doubly dangerous because of their immediate effect and because of the threat their example posed to slave society as a whole. The chance meeting with a group of fugitives was common enough to make travel in the interior a hazardous event. A law prohibiting the use of firearms in the 1740s drew complaints from many who had to journey in the countryside. Domingos Nunes Pereira argued in 1745 that the bands of blacks and mulattoes who raided the highways around Santo Amaro made carrying arms necessary, and similar sentiments were expressed in 1752 by residents of Maragogipe and Cachoeira.[6] Such statements were common enough to indicate that the number of fugitives was large and potentially dangerous. When questioned about the existence of quilombos in his district, the governor of Itaparica Island reported no knowledge of them but added that nighttime thefts and the continual disappearance of slaves provided much evidence of fugitive raiding. Despite no evidence of quilombos on the island, he reported that "still terror has spread among the families."[7]

The threat posed by fugitives and the fear they provoked moved colonial society to seek protection and a means of control. From the earliest days of the sugar economy, Indians were used to hunt down runaways. Engenho Sergipe's accounts are dotted with small payments to Indians who returned fugitives. Whole Indian villages were mobilized to serve as anti-quilombo troops, and virtually every major military effort mounted against Bahian mocambos included Indian auxiliaries.[8] These operations were usually directed by a rural constabulary created specifically to control this problem. Beginning in the early seventeenth century, bush captains (capitães do campo [field], do mato [forest], de assalto [assault]) were assigned in rural districts to catch fugitives and destroy quilombos. That these posts were in the service of the slaveowners was made clear by regulations issued in 1676, which stated that their income was to be derived directly from charges paid by the owners of the fugitives rather than by the royal treasury.[9] These offices were often filled by free blacks and mulattoes, who found in such positions some authority and respect. But the bush captains themselves sometimes caused problems, bullying rural residents, arresting slaves without cause, or trying to extort money from planters. Such was the case with a certain pardo, Daniel Dias, who was extorting money to buy a bush captain's position in Sergipe de El-Rey and who was drunk most of the time. He was, said a superior officer, a disgrace to the uniform he wore.[10] Still, despite such problems, colonial society could not dispense with their services. That fact became painfully clear after 1790, when resistance and insurrectionary activity reached new levels of intensity. Bush captain Severino Pereira, petitioning for promotion in 1798, could list among his services capturing planter Bento Simões de Brito's slaves, who had risen up in 1789; destroying a quilombo at the headwaters of the Jacuipe River in 1791; leading a major expedition against three quilombos in the Orobó range in 1796; and capturing a highwayman and his gang – all to "protect the internal security of the people and the dominion of masters over slaves and evildoers who otherwise would all flee or rise up against the very Country."[11]

The cost of control – of militia units, Indian auxiliaries, and bush captains – was a price that slaveowners bore with few complaints as a necessary expense for the maintenance of slavery. Marauding slaves, insecure highways, and nighttime visits to the senzalas were unpleasant but unavoidable features of Bahian slavery. In some ways, the planters were better off having the most troublesome slaves off the estates rather than disrupting operations in fields and at the mill. Still, mocambos caused consternation and sometimes fear, and planters were usually unwilling to seek any compromise with fugitives and fully disposed to eliminate their depredations. But although the problem sometimes reached threatening proportions, it was usually kept at levels acceptable to planters and other slaveholders. It was a nuisance, and sometimes a deadly one, but a certain amount of resistance and flight were simply endemic and accepted as such. What occurred after 1790, however, was a level of slave resistance that no slave society could accept and still survive.

The revolts: contexts and consciousness

The cycle of Bahian slave revolts presents important and difficult theoretical questions about the nature of slave resistance, especially when placed in comparative perspective. Michael Craton in his examination of the British Caribbean and Genovese in a broad comparative study have both stressed (with certain differences between them) an important change in the nature or type of slave resistance before and after the period roughly beginning in 1776–93 when the American, French, and Haitian revolutions changed the substance of political discourse and the expectations of slaves as well as masters.[12] Craton noted an earlier tradition of maroon-style rebellions led by unassimilated Africans, subsequently replaced by movements led by elite creole slaves. Genovese goes even farther and claims that after Haiti, slave rebellions became part of the bourgeois revolution, not simply seeking freedom in a kind of African restorationism but aiming at more revolutionary goals, based on a desire not simply to escape or destroy society but to transform it. Certain elements in this thesis are supported by the Bahian revolts; there is also much (admittedly given the limited present evidence) that does not seem to fit the universal model.[13]

Bahia certainly had a long history of endemic resistance, of maroons, runaways, recalcitrance, and individual violence or despair. It also produced in 1798 what appeared to be a classic case of a movement inspired by the principles of the French Revolution and led by assimilated mulattoes. But, in truth, the great series of slave rebellions of the early nineteenth century seem in the main to be ethnic revolts, organized around African affiliations or religion and combining a rejection of slavery and of white society with deep and persistent motives related not to France or Haiti but to traditional African polities and religious divisions.

It is not that Haiti and France were without their effect in Bahia; but different groups in Bahian society responded differently to the conditions and opportunities presented in this revolutionary period. Those elements of the slave and free-colored population most receptive to the impact of international events and ideas, the crioulos and mulattoes, were noticeably absent from many of the slave rebellions. In fact at times, as in 1835, some were killed by rebels for failing to join the insurrection. By 1808, these groups, surely desirous of change in their status and willing to fight for it on occasion, saw in the political changes that eventually led to Brazilian independence in 1822, and in the period of political organizing that followed, a better opportunity to achieve their goals. Some of the freedmen and freedwomen were themselves slaveowners, and although the whites always feared the collaboration of the free coloreds and the slaves, there was little evidence of it. Colonial slave society had created a set of racial and status divisions that effectively interdicted cooperation. From a North American perspective, one may question the failure of these various exploited sectors of the population to make common cause, but this is a naive application of our scheme of racial classification to Brazilian society. The distinctions between crioulos and Africans and between blacks and mulattoes were not simply census takers' conveniences or descriptive designations. They were important categories that described the multiple and complex divisions of Bahian society and circumscribed political action.

Part of the historiographical confusion about the slave revolts has resulted from treating them without regard to the round of political and social unrest carried out by nonslaves during the same period. At very few junctures did the slave and nonslave movements intersect. Free blacks and mulattoes often figured prominently in the movement for independence, in various barracks revolts, in nationalist anti-Portuguese violence, and in republican agitation. Rarely, however, did they make common cause with slaves. Their agenda for the future lay not in crushing the exploitative regime that held them but in gaining access to the benefits that structure promised, especially during a period of rapid political change. The slave rebellions, then, serve here as a measure not of resistance or oppression but, rather, of consciousness and strategy and of the internal workings of this slave society in a moment of crisis.

Scholars have long tried to identify the causes of slave rebellions and resistance. Interpretations have varied from simplistic models of direct reaction to oppression (the corollary of which would be: the more oppressive the slave regime, the more common and violent the resistance) to other analyses that argue that rebellions were more common in areas of mixed economy or in cities where the physical conditions of slavery were not as harsh as in plantation regions. Certainly, geography, demography, ethnicity, the structures of slaveholdings, the relations of masters and slaves, political realities within the society as a whole, and personality all must enter into the analysis of slave resistance. I have already touched on a number of these issues elsewhere in this volume. Here, by making a somewhat unrealistic separation between the endemic resistance and slave rebellions, I try to identify the factors that contributed directly to the insurrectionary swell after 1800.

The post-Haitian sugar boom, the expanding engenhos and perhaps intensifying demands on workers, food shortages, price rises, and political change and unrest all created the context for increasing slave resistance. These conditions produced patterns within the slave community itself that also influenced the level and nature of resistance. Certainly, the demographic situations of Bahian slaves must be taken into account as a feature that contributed to instability during the post-Haitian boom. As we have seen in Chapter 13, the slave sex ratio in rural areas reached 200, and the excess was composed mostly of young African males. Never good, the possibilities of finding a mate and forming a family were probably worse for Bahian slaves in this period than at any time since the early seventeenth century. The proportion of children in the slave population decreased. The high level of imports also altered the proportion of Africans in the population, increasing it to more than 60 percent (see Tables 13-5, 13-6, and 13-7). This was an unstable population, it did not reproduce itself, it suffered from high levels of importation, and it had few opportunities for social stability. These conditions certainly created a base for unrest, to which were added increasing pressures generated by the demands of the plantation economy and the resultant hardships for slaves.[14]

Not only the volume of the slave trade but also its composition played a role in the patterns of rebellion. Bahia had long received its slaves from both central and West Africa, and even during the great period of importation from the Bight of Benin, slaves from Angola continued to make up more than 40 percent of the African born. Still, after 1790, the numbers of West Africans that arrived at the wharves of Salvador far exceeded earlier import levels.

The Bight of Benin region at the beginning of the nineteenth century was swept by political and religious revolution. To the north, Usuman dan Fodio launched a campaign with the help of Muslim Fulani to take control of the Hausa kingdom in the first decade of the century. Further to the south, among the city-states of Yorubaland, the Oyo empire was in the process of breakup. In the eighteenth century, Oyo had exercised influence over Dahomey and the Ashanti kingdoms, but by the 1790s it was in political decay. As subject provinces wrested their autonomy, especially after 1817, the number of Yoruba slaves flowing to the coast increased. Disintegration was furthered by a separatist revolt of the city of Ilorin, which was also a center of Muslim penetration into the region.[15] These civil and religious conflicts produced large numbers of captives, which could be safely and profitably disposed of in the slave trade. The long-standing Bahian trade with the Bight of Benin area proved especially advantageous to warring polities and factions in Africa. Thus, at a time when Bahian demand for slaves increased, the network of trade was well established and the supply of slaves, a result of the internal conflicts of the area, was great.

This combination of demand and supply resulted in the large numbers of Hausa, Yoruba, Ewe, and (some) Nupe (Tapa) slaves who arrived at Bahia. The chronology of their arrival is important. The Hausaland conflicts took place in the first decade of the nineteenth century, the Yoruba civil wars somewhat later. There were some Nagôs in Bahia listed in the late eighteenth century, but they did not come in preponderant numbers until after 1815. Although there is no way to calculate, many of the slaves who came in this period must have been young men of defeated armies. The Nagôs were disproportionately used in the city of Salvador. Of a sample of more than two thousand slaves in the city, the African born were two-thirds of the total, with Nagôs composing 19 percent, Geges about 11 percent, and Hausas slightly more than 6 percent. In a rural sample, the relative proportions of Geges and Yoruba were reversed.[16] As we shall see, the Bahian rebellions were mostly organized around ethnic affiliations. Not surprisingly, Hausas carried out the early revolts, Nagôs the later ones. But although it is important to recognize the ethnic and cultural affinities of the Bahian slaves and slave rebels, we must also keep in mind that the Portuguese classification "Nagô" might mask deep religious and political divisions among the slaves. The struggles in Yorubaland had, after all, been between warring political units and between the active and aggressive Islamic expansion and the traditional religion of the Orishas. Thus, despite the faulty ethnography of the Portuguese, not all Hausas or Nagôs were alike, to say nothing of the deep-seated animosities between groups like the Geges and Nagôs.

But the matter is complex. A Gege defendant in 1835 might argue, as one did, that he could not have joined the rebels since they were all Nagôs, enemies of his people, but this may have been a self-serving and convenient defense.[17] In some of the revolts, there is clear evidence of cross-ethnic cooperation among the West Africans. There seems to have been far less between West Africans and those Bantu speakers from the Congo and Angola who also made up a considerable proportion of the Bahian slave population. In any case, tradition and association molded the manner in which many African slaves saw themselves and their condition.

The perception of Brazilian-born slaves derived from other bases. The failure of most of the crioulo and mixed-blood (pardo, cabra, mulatto) slaves or freedmen and freedwomen to participate in the slave rebellions is a troubling question. The Brazilian born made up perhaps 35 to 40 percent of the captaincy's slave population, and their absence from rebel ranks severely limited any hopes for success. In fact, not only did they fail to cooperate, but often it was loyal black or mulatto militia forces that were used against fugitive communities or slave rebellions. The relative absence of Brazilian-born slaves from many of the rebellions undercuts any analysis of these movements as simple uprisings of the "servile class," and the fact that the Brazilian-born free-colored population of the captaincy refused in most cases to join these movements implies that its perception of realities and possibilities was distinct from those of the Africans.

That perception was due to harsh experience. Mulatto freedmen and a few Brazilian-born slaves had in fact initiated political activity in the late eighteenth century, when in 1798 a number of them had become involved in an insurrectionary plot, generally called the Tailors' Revolt.[18] News from France of a more or less revolutionary nature had seeped into Bahia in the 1790s despite the government's attempts to suppress it. Revolutionary republicanism found some adherents in the colony, and on 12 August 1798, the citizens of Salvador awoke to find posters in the city calling for independence, freedom of trade, an end to racial discrimination, and higher pay for troops, among other things. Eventually, forty-six individuals from Salvador and the Recôncavo were arrested for this seditious activity; four were executed; others were exiled, flogged, or imprisoned. Most of the plotters were lower-class artisans and soldiers; twelve of them were slaves; and many were pardô tailors, craftsmen, or soldiers. Although only three free blacks were involved, and only one of them an African, there were thirty mulattoes. The slaves were urban house servants or artisans, and almost all were crioulos. In addition, five whites of the educated elite were implicated and arrested.[19] If they adhered at all to the principles of racial equality, it seems to have been only peripherally. "My friend, caution with the African rabble," was a phrase found in a letter of

Cipriano José Barata de Almeida, one of the conspirators.[20] In the judicial investigations, the white prisoners, some of whom were slave-owners, showed little interest in the slavery and racial-discrimination issues but considerably more ardor for free trade.

The division of goals between the whites and the colored conspirators, slave and free, made any hope of success sadly utopian. The white conspirators received relatively light sentences; the mulattoes and blacks were treated far more harshly. The mulatto João de Deus had hoped for a rising of the engenho's slaves, but that was probably wishful thinking. Had this happened, in any case, Recôncavo planters and other slaveowners whatever their political proclivities would have withdrawn support. Investigations after the arrests did reveal that some of the conspirators had sought the end of slavery and the establishment of equality without regard to race. But such ideas would have been difficult to advocate openly, and probably for that reason abolitionist goals did not appear in the public posters. As Portuguese administrators pointed out, there was little danger of a general movement for independence as long as the people of property and substance could not accept slave rebellion or social upheaval.[21]

In the Tailors' Revolt, free mulattoes and crioulos had been willing to cast their lot with whites and slaves. But when the hammer of justice fell, the free coloreds and slaves had borne its force. After 1798, free mulattoes and blacks found alliance with slaves, and especially with the large numbers of African slaves, to be a tactic with few chances of success and deadly risks. At various moments, free blacks and mulattoes and occasionally crioulo slaves would seek to better their condition or to bring about political change; but they often did so with no attempt to forge an alliance with the slave population, and sometimes by distancing themselves from that population as much as possible.

The conspiracy of 1798 was a solitary event, after which the movements of slaves and free people of color followed essentially separate trajectories. This was made clear by an event at the end of the period under study here. In the Sabinada, the great and bloody federalist revolt of 1837–8 in which rebels took and held Salvador and drove the imperial government from the city, attempts made to integrate slaves into rebel military units met with opposition not only from slaveowners but also from free people of color who objected to being placed on the same level with the enslaved. When separate slave units were formed, only crioulos were allowed to join.[22] Even in the midst of revolution, the divisions of slave society could not be overcome.

Although slaveowners had long preferred to think of their slaves as ignorant workers whose intellectual horizons were limited to the satisfaction of immediate goals or needs, there are indications of a consciousness among slaves more developed than owners liked to admit. As early as 1710, a group of slaves apparently petitioned the crown for freedom, so municipal concillors of Salvador were forced to argue that slavery was essential to the colony and that both the law of nations and the laws of God upheld its existence.[23] Slaves were certainly not unaware of the nuances of law and custom within the system that bound them. Pombal's abolition of slavery in Portugal itself (19 Sept. 1761) provoked some unrest among Brazilian slaves.[24] Although Pombal had taken this step to ensure adequate supplies of slaves to the colonies, Brazilian slaves recognized the contradiction inherent in abolition in Portugal and continued enslavement in Brazil. Occasionally, those slaves traveling in ships to the metropolis sought to secure their liberty.[25] A further Pombaline statement in 1773 led in Paraíba to a movement among slaves and free pardos in which they sought extension of abolition to Brazil. A hastily formed junta quickly disabused them of this "erroneous opinion," but it was clear that the implications of Portuguese reforms and European events were not lost on slaves and freedmen.[26] They had seen clearly the logical connection between their situation and the changes taking place in Europe. Slaveowners and colonial administrators were no less perceptive, realizing the implications and "dire consequences" implied by the diffusion of the news.

Thus, although slaveowners spoke of slaves as brutes, they feared that the most subtle of them, the mulattoes and crioulos, might take advantage of changes in law or politics. This fear was great, but it sometimes exceeded reality. As late as 1822, in the midst of the agitation for independence, the French consul in Bahia could write, "The ideas of liberty continue to germinate among the crioulo and mulatto slaves. There have been some revolts in the larger plantations. The blacks have not demanded their freedom, but they have committed acts of independence . . . refusing to obey this or that overseer or master."[27] The same year, the mistress of Engenho Aramaré mixed bravado with her fear. She noted that the "crioulada" of Cachoeira had sought their freedom. "They are crazy, but the whip will deal with them." Even so, she warned her correspondent in Lisbon that there were those who might carry the pleas of the slaves to the Portuguese parliament (cortes) and that all her correspondence should be destroyed because of the possible effect if such news reached Aramaré.[28]

A conservative faced with the political turmoil of independence, Aramaré's mistress was nervous, but she was certainly not alone in her sentiments and fears. White apprehensions had greatly intensified during the late eighteenth century with the growth of the free-colored population in Brazil and with news of the Haitian revolution. The image of a plantation-based colony turned upside down by slave insurrection provoked the worst fears of slaveowners in Brazil, as throughout the Americas. Many Brazilian and foreign commentators in the early nineteenth century wrote of the dangers of replicating Haiti and of the anarchy that might result from political divisions if slaves took advantage of them.[29] But despite such fears, the mass of the slave population seems to have been little affected by the Haitian revolution. Instead, it was the free-colored population who saw in Haiti a parallel to their own situation. In 1804, crioulo and mulatto militiamen in Rio de Janeiro wore portraits of Dessalines, the Haitian leader, suspended from their necks, to the dismay of local officials. In Sergipe de El-Rey, the free-colored elite toasted the equality of the races and the great revolution of Saint Domingue at a banquet in 1824.[30] During the period of the Regency (1831–40), the term "Haitianism" was used as an epithet against newspapers that supposedly represented the interests of the free-colored population and harped on the racial issue.[31] Evidence of insurrection spurred by news or the example of Haiti appears in none of the judicial inquiries during the repression of the Bahian slave rebellions. The Bahian slaves found the sources for their movements in their own traditions and condition.

— *The war against Bahian slavery*

Divided by color and place of birth, by juridical status and hope of improvement, slaves and free people of color did not for the most part make common cause. The war against slavery in Bahia was a war carried out or led after 1798 almost exclusively by African slaves and by those freed persons of African birth for whom ethnicity was more vital than juridical status.

It is impossible to make a sharp break between the current of endemic resistance and the outbreak of insurrections around the turn of the century. The uprising and flight of the slaves of Engenho Santana in 1789 was perhaps an early manifestation of the new cycle of resistance, although in that case the leadership was crioulo or cabra and there were clear signs of competition with Africans.[32] By 1795, royal officials and rural residents were concerned about an increase in fugitive activities. Two quilombo settlements in the region of Cachoeira moved the government to action. Plantations had been burned, property stolen, and other slaves induced to run off. The governor dispatched Severino Pereira, captain-major of assaults of Itapororocas, and 200 men to attack the well-fortified mocambo in the Orobó Mountains. Two encampments, Orobó and Andrah, were destroyed and thirteen slaves taken captive, but a great number escaped to another quilombo, Tupim.[33] The expedition was a traditional response to a recurring problem, but the problem seemed to intensify in the opening years of the nineteenth century. The governor of Bahia, João de Saldanha da Gama, count of Ponte, launched an active campaign against quilombos all over the captaincy. In Rio das Contas, the captain of assaults and a troop of Indians from the Pedra Branca mission were sent to destroy quilombos in the area but failed. Poor farmers accused of harboring fugitives were tried and their property confiscated.[34] Ponte sought to stem the rising tide of resistance because he understood its potential threat to the captaincy's economy and tranquility.

Although 1809 is usually taken as the beginning of the cycle of Bahian slave rebellions, a plot was uncovered in 1807. The Hausas had elected a "governor" who had as his "secretary" a free pardo. The pardo had been dispatched to the Recôncavo to enlist the engenho slaves for a concerted uprising; but when the plot was exposed, the governor threw guards around the city's fountains because of a supposed threat to poison the drinking water.[35] The Hausa leaders were tried for having violated the rights of their masters and for disrupting "the public tranquillity on which the conservation of states depends."[36] A slave and a freedman were sentenced to death, and eleven others were flogged. The plot had been revealed by a slave (presumably not a Hausa), and the arrests brought discovery of two arms caches. The rebels had sought to rise up on 29 May during the Corpus Christi festivities, when security would be lax.

Here at the very outset of the insurrectionary cycle, some features common to many of the Bahian revolts were already apparent. Organization of the movement had apparently been along ethnic lines, in this case Hausa. The plotters had sought to take advantage of the distractions of the colonial religious cycle. Corpus Christi, Holy Week, and Christmas came to be favored by those who sought freedom, and during Christmas slaveowners were particularly on guard. Noticeably, here in the very first instance, the insurgents had planned to coordinate a rising in the city with a rebellion in the Recôncavo. The mass of rural slaves held the key to success – and both slaves and masters realized this. Salvador provided a milieu for conspiracy, a place where interaction and communication between slaves was possible and might pass unnoticed, a locale where freedmen or freedwomen of a particular ethnic group might be enlisted to help. But the key to ultimate success lay in the mass of slaves at the engenhos and farms of the countryside (see Figure 17-1). The slaves' victory over slavery had to be won in the Recôncavo if it was to be won at all.

The abortive insurrection placed the government on guard. The governor of Bahia, the count of Ponte, alarmed by the abortive plot and by natural inclination a man with no sympathy for slaves, intensified his vigorous campaign against fugitives and quilombos. In Rio das Contas, the capitão dos assaltos and a troop of Indians from Pedra Branca were dispatched against quilombos, but the fugitives were forewarned and the expedition failed. Justice fell on a number of poor farmers, who were accused of employing fugitives or harboring them.[37] He had already attacked two quilombos on the outskirts of Salvador, capturing seventy-eight people. By January 1809, Ponte expressed his concern to Lisbon that the rising number of fugitives in the city and the Recôncavo threatened the captaincy and that the repercussions on the

NÈGRES CANGUEIROS.

DIFFERENTES NATIONS NÈGRES.

Figure 17-1. Top: Slave porters moving a cask of wine. Bottom: European visitors to Brazilian cities in the early nineteenth century were impressed by the many slaves in the streets and by the distinctive markings and coiffures of the various African nations.

engenhos could be disastrous. Repression followed. A 9:00 p.m. curfew for slaves was set and *batuques* (gatherings of slaves for music, dance, and probably African religion) were prohibited as the governor sought to bring the problem under control.[38]

The governor's measures could not stem the tide of resistance. The first blow was struck at Christmastime in 1808. Slaves in the southern Recôncavo near the towns of Nazaré and Jaguaripe rose up, burning canefields and marching on Nazaré. A pitched battle was fought as a few hundred slaves tried to take the town, but the rebels were unsuccessful and were forced to retreat with heavy losses. On 4 January 1809, either as a result of prior arrangement or stimulated by news of the Recôncavo rising, about four hundred Hausas, Nagôs, and Geges fled Salvador and headed in the direction of the Recôncavo rebels, burning and killing along the way. The rebels were surprised by government troops on 6 January and quickly defeated. Ninety-five prisoners were taken, but many others escaped into the woods.

The count of Ponte was particularly concerned that word of the rebel defeat and capture should precede news of the revolt when it reached the engenhos, but the whole captaincy was thrown into a state of uneasiness. The municipal judge of Maragogipe reported that groups of four and five rebel slaves had drifted into that town and that their effect on local slaves would lead to "funeral results." He passed an ordinance, in view of the "slaves principally of the Hausa nation who with total disregard and resistance to the laws of slavery have become revolutionaries and disloyal" and who might stimulate further revolt. The ordinance imposed curfews, prohibition of batuques and other gatherings, limits on slave movement and residence, and a shoot-to-kill provision against resisters.[39] By February, the câmara of São Cristóvão, Sergipe de El-Rey, discussed the threat of fugitives and the special danger caused by the arrival in the area of some who had taken part in the Bahian rising.[40] In April, the captain-major of Sergipe arrested a number of Geges who were thought to be involved in insurrectionary activities.[41] Salvador, in February 1810, witnessed another unsuccessful uprising.

In 1810, the count of Ponte was replaced by Dom Marcos de Noronha, count of Arcos, an experienced administrator who launched a number of reforms in Bahia, including the construction of a commercial-association building, a public theater, improved highways, and a number of projects of agricultural reform. But despite certain progressive attitudes, Arcos was a conservative on political issues and a loyal subject of the Portuguese crown, as his suppression of the republican movement of 1817 in Pernambuco was to demonstrate. Arcos's presence seems to have had no effect on the level of slave resistance, and between 1814 and 1816 he was faced with a continuing series of uprisings in Bahia, Sergipe de El-Rey, and Alagoas. The slave war continued.

The first outbreak occurred north of Salvador in the fishing and whaling stations of Itapoam. On 18 February, the slaves rebelled and killed a number of whites, burned the buildings, and then marched toward Itapoam. They set two engenhos ablaze and killed some people enroute, and they seized arms and horses. Arcos dispatched cavalry and infantry contingents, which intercepted the rebels and left more than fifty dead on the field. Many were arrested. A subsequent trial led to stiff penalties of 400 to 500 lashes and penal exile for some and the firing squad for four. The punishment was to be exemplary, but even here the slaves disrupted the proceedings. One of the defendants, on being led to the whipping post, began to mutter that his friends in the crowd would begin to kill the whites. Execution of sentence was suspended, and the crowd dispersed.[42]

Now it was the turn of the Recôncavo. A plot involving Hausa slave dockworkers in Cachoeira was uncovered in 1813. The câmara of Cachoeira petitioned Arcos for arms and supplies in preparation for a suspected Hausa-led revolt. Arcos thought this simply planter paranoia, the imagination of those who treated slaves cruelly and therefore had much to fear. Although this may have been true, the slaveowners of Cachoeira did not simply suffer from guilty consciences. On 20 March 1814, the royal magistrate of Maragogipe received word that the slaves in the Iguape district had risen up and were gathering at Engenho da Ponta, property of Felisbeto Caldeira Brant Pontes. The militia was mobilized and Iguape brought under control, but the uprising and Arcos's slow reaction to planter pleas now made him the target of both the Salvador and the Recôncavo slaveowners. In December 1815, a threatened slave uprising in the town of Alagoas was discovered; and earlier that year, troops had had to be dispatched against a large quilombo near that town.

In the heart of the sugar region of Santo Amaro and São Francisco do Conde, slaves at the engenhos Caruassu, Guaiba, and others, returning from Sunday festivities, rose up apparently spontaneously. They attacked Engenho Casarangongo, burned part of the property, and then moved against Engenho Quibaca. There the owner quickly mustered a defense by local residents and loyal slaves. The rebels took to the woods near Engenho Cabaxi and from there raided the town of Santo Amaro, causing some deaths. Residents fled, and although word reached Salvador, Arcos made no public announcement, fearing general panic or an uprising in the city.[43] Only prompt military action led by Colonel Jerônimo Muniz Fiuza Barreto, an important senhor de engenho of the region, saved the day. He received the title "Saviour of the Recôncavo" in recognition of his actions.

This round of slave insurrections from 1813 to 1816 brought the Bahian slaveowners and the count of Arcos into direct conflict over the best method of slave control. Arcos was no particular friend of the slaves', but he felt that Bahians were unreasonably fearful of their bondsmen and unnecessarily cruel. The slaveowners viewed him as overconcerned with the sons of Africa and as a stepfather to his Bahian subjects. Eventually, in somewhat more refined words, they called him a "nigger lover."

His first confrontation with the slaveowners had come over the issue of slave cultural independence, specifically the batuques. African religion and culture had long posed a problem for colonial authorities and slaveowners in Brazil. The debate was always the same. Some wished to allow slaves freedom to keep their African traditions as a way of giving them a respite from slavery and as a means of maintaining ethnic distinctions. Others saw slave gatherings as socially disruptive and potentially threatening, occasions when plots and rebellions could be hatched. In 1790, the count of Povolide, governor of Pernambuco, had refused to suppress the batuques of the slaves. But he did note that those done in secret by the Minas with black female leaders, altars of idols, and blessings with cock's blood were dangerous. Clearly, he was describing the *maes-de-santo* (female cult leaders) and practice of the *candomblé* (ceremonial site) religion of the Orishas.[44] Povolide had sought the advice of Lisbon, and although the Inquisition felt that these practices should be slowly eliminated, it counseled toleration of this "lesser evil in order to avoid greater ones."[45] In 1796, an attempt was made to stop batuques at the engenhos in Goiana, Pernambuco, but once again the governor intervened, arguing that "this was the greatest pleasure that they [the slaves] have in all the days of their slavery."[46]

Thus the debate in Bahia had its precedents. But the rising level of slave resistance now made the issue a matter of serious concern and violent opinion. The count of Ponte had followed a hard line on the issue, and especially after 1807 he had strongly opposed the gatherings and batuques of the slaves. his successor, the count of Arcos, had taken a much more lenient position on the batuques, and this had led, after the revolt of 1814, to a direct confrontation with the planters and slaveowners of the captaincy. The merchants of Salvador complained directly to the king that the batuques allowed at Graça and Barbalho in the city had made the city like the "backlands of the Mina coast," and they denounced the profane disregard of Catholicism that these dances implied. But above all, they feared that in these meetings, where foreign tongues and secret signs were used, plans for the next revolt were being laid. Whereas Arcos's permit had spoken of the batuques as a release from the "sad state" of captivity, the slaveowners fretted that the slaves used them to plan insurrection and to spread word of the "fatal events of Saint Domingue."[47] The imperial government in Rio de Janeiro supported Arcos but asked that he move to abolish these activities gradually.[48] Arcos's policy was not so much humanitarian as practical. The mutual distrust among the slaves was "the strongest guarantee for the cities of Brazil." To prohibit the one act that promoted slave disunity would be the same as fostering their union, an act of "disastrous consequences."[49] Arcos had realized the ethnic orientation of most of the revolts, and he hoped to limit the scale of these movements by promoting ethnic divisions. Apparently, the Itapoam rebels had marched along with shouts of "death to the whites and mulattoes," and other manifestations of such division could be noted. The critics of Arcos's policies, however, pointed out that in 1814 slaves of a number of nations had joined together, a dangerous precedent and a proof that the policies were not producing the hoped-for divisions.

Arcos had in fact taken firm steps against further rebellions. Patrols (*rondas*) were established in a number of Recôncavo districts. In Sergipe de El-Rey, ordinances established curfews, passes for slaves, and arbitrary arrests of freedmen or slaves suspected of criminal actions.[50] As we saw in the preceding chapter, Arcos also ordered a detailed listing of all the Recôncavo slaveowners and the number of slaves held by each in an attempt to control the slave population.

For the slaveowners, all this was not enough. In São Francisco do Conde, the principal senhores met under the direction of Caldeira Brant to discuss their predicament, share their apprehensions, and call for the governor's removal. They wished to have the right to deport any suspected rebel and to hang any caught in rebellion. They sought to impose subjugation. Given the governor's attitude, there was nothing remarkable, they felt, in the "daring of the blacks and the fright and confusion of the whites."[51] But although the planters realized that their control over the servile population had to be tightened, they were already willing, at least in theory, to voice a desire for an end to slavery. Racial fears, British pressure to abolish the slave trade, and progressive attitudes led to a call for the abolition of the slave trade and the importation of European immigrants.[52]

The residents of the city clamored no less strongly for the governor's dismissal. In an 1814 letter to the king, they outlined their own perception of the situation. The frightened citizens wrote that they were surrounded by a sea of blacks, more than 40,000 in the Recôncavo, a ratio of almost twenty to one in comparison with the number of whites and mulattoes. And these blacks were a barbarous people, used to hardship and used to killing at whim. They understood only force, and the governor's leniency had only stimulated greater misdeeds. Slaves, they said, responded only to rigor and punishment, not to kindness.[53]

After the uprising of 1816 and the repression that followed, a time of uneasy quiet set in among the slave population. Slaveowners were nervous, to be sure, and on the lookout for any manifestation or rumor of rebellion. In 1818, for example, the senhor of Engenho Maçape in Sergipe de El-Rey reported that during the celebrations in honor of Saint Benedict, it was customary among the slaves and freedmen to take crowns as "kings." Given the rumors of planned rebellion, he asked the governor whether it was wise to permit the festival that year.[54]

In truth, however, Bahians were distracted from the servile threat by the rapid political changes between 1818 and 1824. The return of the court to Portugal, the Oporto revolt of 1820, the actions of the Lisbon cortes, and finally the declaration of independence in September 1822 all produced political repercussions and sometimes fighting in the captaincy. The strong Portuguese garrison in Salvador resisted independence, and royalist sympathizers seized the capital. Proindependence forces organized in the Recôncavo towns under the direction of the major planters, who were also the principal militia officers. Troops arrived from Rio de Janeiro, and Bahia was the scene of military operations for over a year, until July 1823, when the city finally fell to Brazilian forces.

Curiously, during this period when colonial society was split into royalist and Brazilian factions, the slaves remained relatively quiet. There were three minor incidents in 1822, the last of which, instigated by the Portuguese, brought harsh retribution and the summary execution of fifty slaves. But despite these rumblings, the slaves did not mount a major effort during the war for independence. Historian João Reis has aptly pointed out that although the divisions within slave society presented what appeared to be an excellent opportunity for the slaves, a moment to be seized, at no time was Bahian society more mobilized and armed than from 1821 to 1823. Although rebellion may have been politically appropriate, it was tactically hopeless.[55]

By 1824, matters had returned to normal in what was now the province of Bahia in the empire of Brazil. "Normal" meaning in this case a return to the festering and sporadic war against slavery carried out by the slaves. The 1820s witnessed ten uprisings in Bahia and another five in Sergipe de El-Rey. The Recôncavo was aflame. A "king" of the blacks in Cachoeira led an insurrection in August 1826. In December, a pitched battle was fought against a quilombo at Cabula, on the outskirts of Salvador. The quilombo had served as a candomblé for the Yoruba religious activities of the cult of the Orishas. The Nagôs were now taking a lead in resistance. Arrests revealed that the quilombo's depredations were intended to draw troops away from the city to set the stage for a general uprising. More arrests of slaves, freedmen, and even some mulattoes in Salvador disrupted the plan. Runaways terrorized Abrantes in 1827, and in March of that year the slaves of Engenho Vitoria and two other engenhos near Cachoeira, all owned by Pedro Rodrigues Bandeira, rose in rebellion. Troops were dispatched, and the rebellion was quelled with thirty slaves arrested. The fires continued to smolder and ignite, in Cachoeira again on 17 and 22 April 1828, and then at engenhos in Santo Amaro in December. In Pirajá in March, Nagôs attacked a number of engenhos and then marched on the fisheries at Itapoam, already a target in 1814. Government forces intercepted the insurgents and killed twenty. The following year saw more of the same. The slaves of three engenhos owned by José Maria de Pina e

Mello rebelled, killed three people, and burned an engenho before they could be subdued. Planters drew up plans in 1828 to improve military preparedness in the face of servile insurrection, and the government supported them. But it was clear that little could be done to stop the outbreaks and that the only hope was to prevent their spreading into a general rebellion.

In fact, the outbreaks in the Recôncavo and Salvador may have stimulated the slaves in other parts of the captaincy to seize their own destinies. At least this is what planters and slaveowners believed. The sugar plantations of the Cotinguiba district of Sergipe de El-Rey were alive with insurrection in the same period. In 1824, insurrectionary broadsheets in Laranjeiras read, "Long live blacks and mulattoes, death to the Portuguese and whites."[56] Some of this agitation appears to have been republican and racial, uniting free blacks and mulattoes against whites; but more limited slave revolts were not lacking. In September 1827, a great uprising occurred. Slaves of at least ten engenhos, mostly Nagôs, killed masters and those slaves who would not join them. The revolt began to spread. A battle with government forces left fifteen to eighteen slaves dead, but many fled into the woods, and two weeks later militia forces were still seeking their capture. News of the battle at Cabula, near Salvador, had apparently sparked the Sergipe rising. Rebellions and rumors of rebellions continued in Sergipe until at least 1837, and hardly a Christmas season passed when local authorities did not report some slave agitation or threat of revolt.

In 1830, the Nagôs rose up again in Salvador. Stevedores seized arms in city shops and proceeded to the slave markets, where about one hundred newly arrived slaves joined in the revolt. An attack on a police station failed, and the garrison turned out to meet the rebels. A number were killed outright, forty-one were captured, and some were lynched by the terrified city residents. Restrictions on slave movements and a 9:00 p.m. curfew were imposed after the rising, but the captaincy remained nervous. During the abdication turmoil of 1831, the câmara of Cachoeira reported that the slaves of Pedro Rodrigues Bandeira, who had risen up in 1827, were again plotting, this time instigated by the pro-Portuguese faction.[57]

In any political dispute or public disturbance, the underlying possibility of a slave uprising cast a shadow over all other events. The early 1830s were filled with garrison revolts, urban disturbances, nativist riots, and political struggles, but the specter of slave insurrection was never far off. The final slave revolt took place in January 1835, when Muslim Africans in Salvador, mostly Nagôs but including some Hausas, Geges, and Tapas, attacked police and military installations and for two days waged a war in the city. The revolt was planned to take place during the festival of Our Lady of Guidance, held at the church of Bomfim on the northern edge of the city, a time when civil authorities would be distracted. Once again, the plot was betrayed by a slave; but when the police moved to apprehend the plotters, the insurrection began. For two days, the city was thrown into turmoil. The rebels were met and defeated at Agua de Meninos, on the road to the Recôncavo. Once again, the rebels realized that the key to success lay in raising up the plantations. Perhaps three hundred rebels had been involved. Fifty were killed in battle, and the trial of those captured led to five executions, "dozens" of public floggings of up to 600 lashes, deportations of the free Africans who had participated, and a general turning of the screws on the slave and especially African population.

The extent of this rebellion and its Islamic aspects have generated curiosity and interest in this "great insurrection."[58] For our purposes, however, it was simply the last in a long chain of revolts marking the passage of Bahian slave society into the nineteenth century. The war against Bahian slavery had failed; each August, the slaves trod to the canefields anew, and the mills began to turn again. The odds had been too great, the forces that defended slavery were too strong, and the society was so permeated by slavery's ethic and convinced of its value that it could not be destroyed by heroic action. But the revolts had made the dangers and costs of slavery clearer than they had ever been. Brazilians increasingly sought and considered other alternatives for the nation's labor requirements and social composition. The war, perhaps, had not been in vain.

THE PROBLEM OF
ENGENHO SERGIPE DO CONDE

Each engenho had a separate history, each served as a microcosm where the relations between master and slave, white and black, capital and labor were worked out. Yet, curiously, it is nearly impossible to reconstruct the operational history of any single mill. At the end of the colonial era, Bahia had more than three hundred engenhos, but the internal records of almost none of them have survived. And planters did keep accounts. They recorded the division of sugar with lavradores, kept a record of production for the tithe, and as wills indicate, knew precisely their active and passive debts. But such records have not survived for secular estates. Deeds and land titles were carefully guarded; annual accounts were not. Historian Wanderley Pinho was able to make his wonderful reconstruction of the history of Engenho Freguesia of the Rocha Pittas by weaving a few documents together around a general discussion of the Recôncavo. But he concentrated on the family's relation to the property rather than on the mill's structure and operations. For some engenhos, it is possible from wills and notarial records to trace changes of ownership, and we have occasional glimpses of internal operations from inventories made at the time of transfer. But these are momentary visions, snapshots in time, lacking continuity.

Only for the mills of the religious orders does a documentary record exist that allows us to trace a mill's operations and production over time. The periodical reports of the Bahian religious houses to superiors in Portugal have in the cases of the Jesuits and Benedictines survived in European archives. Whatever the peculiarities of these corporately owned estates, their records provide an invaluable documentary record of the social and economic history of Brazil.

The record is fullest for Engenho Sergipe do Conde; founded by Mem de Sá, owned by the count of Linhares, eventually administered by the Jesuits of Lisbon, and in the seventeenth century considered the "Queen of the Recôncavo." Although its peculiar history and size made this engenho atypical, its role as a point of dispute between the Jesuit colleges of Lisbon and Bahia generated a vast collection of correspondence, memorandums, legal briefs and decisions, and annual accounts that have made it the best-documented engenho in colonial Brazil. A small portion of the annual accounts covering 1622–53 was published by the Institute of Sugar and Alcohol of Rio de Janeiro in 1956 as part of the *Documentos para a história do açúcar;* since no other such accounts have been available in published form, these records have been the subject of intensive analysis, most notably by Mauro, Buescu, and Amaral Ferlini.[1] The published accounts are only a small part of the existing documentation on Engenho Sergipe and the related mills of Santana and Petinga, most of which is currently housed in the Arquivo Nacional da Torre do Tombo, Lisbon, and the Archivum Romanum Societatis Iesu, Rome. Historian Andrée Mansuy made extensive use of the unpublished materials in Lisbon in her excellent edition of Antonil's *Cultura e opulência do Brasil*.[2] In this study, I have sought to make full use of these records.

Although Father Serafim Leite briefly traced the history of the intra-Jesuit dispute over Engenho Sergipe in his *História da Companhia de Jesus no Brasil*, that story has never been outlined in any detail. Given the importance of the records produced by that dispute for all analyses of the colonial sugar economy in general and this book in particular, I believe it is useful to unravel the tangled legal history to set this fundamental body of information in its proper historical context.

The history of Engenho Sergipe begins in the middle decades of the sixteenth century with the arrival of the third governor-general, Mem de Sá. This active and intelligent soldier and statesman is remembered as the one who drove the French from Rio de Janeiro, cleared the Bahian Recôncavo of Indians, and set the legal and administrative structure of Brazil on a firm basis during his rule from 1557 to 1572. Like most royal officers of his age, Mem de Sá had a patrimonial attitude toward his office and was not above providing for himself and his family by using his extensive powers in the colony. This attitude appears to be the origin of a grant in 1559 of a large sesmaria to his friend Fernão Rodrigues de Castelobranco, *almotácel-mor* (court provisioner). This grant of two leagues along the coast by four leagues toward the interior was to include "the lands and waters of Ceregippe," and it was given for the express purpose of constructing a sugar mill. The following year, Rodrigues de Castelobranco renounced all his rights to this property in favor of Francisco de Sá, the only son of Mem de Sá. Obviously an understanding had been worked out enabling the governor to acquire this prime land for himself and his son by means of a rather transparent legal detour. The original grant was enlarged by subsequent sesmarias of 1561 and 1564, and the transfer to Francisco de Sá was later reconfirmed by the crown in 1571.[3]

The problem with this whole arrangement was that both the original grant and the subsequent transfer were illegal under the code governing the distribution of sesmarias. Fernão Rodrigues de Castelobranco never resided in Brazil, as was required of all those receiving sesmarias in the colony. Moreover, the charter for sesmarias required that they not be transferred or alienated for three years after the original grant. Rodrigues de Castelobranco's renunciation within a year violated this restriction, as did the fact that Francisco de Sá also lived in Portugal and was not a resident of Brazil. Finally, governors were forbidden to grant entails (morgados) to themselves or their children. Thus on at least three counts the land grant in Sergipe rested on illegal bases, and this illegitimacy of its birth was to complicate the subsequent history of what was to become in the seventeenth century the greatest engenho in Bahia, and perhaps in all Brazil.

Despite the fact that title to the lands of Sergipe was held by Mem de Sá's son Francisco, the governor treated them like his own property, adding them to lands that he had acquired in Ilhéus and Camamú before ever coming to Brazil. Mem de Sá claimed to have spent 20,000 cruzados in constructing an engenho at Sergipe, and in his will he passed the engenho and the lands to his heir along with his other possessions.[4] Later, a question would arise over Mem de Sá's ability to will the lands to anyone. Although his right to cede the improvements on the land made at his own cost was not questioned, his ability to dispose of the land itself would become a matter of contention. Did Mem de Sá own the lands of Sergipe at the time of his death, or were they owned by his son? And was the claim of either legitimate under the law of sesmarias?

At his death, on 2 March 1572, Mem de Sá was survived by only two children. His wife had died in 1542. He had lost one son in Ceuta in battle against the Moors and another in Brazil fighting Indians. A twelve-year-old daughter had died as well, leaving him only a son, Francisco, and a daughter, Felipa. Francisco was already launched on a career in the church when his father's death made him the principal heir. He left the religious life to take charge of his family's estate, but he died only eight months after his father and had little time to enjoy the fortune or to further the family line. With no heirs, Francisco left all his property to his sister, Dona Felipa de Sá. This property included the engenho of Sergipe in Brazil, which Mem de Sá had taken as his terça, or the portion of his estate that he could freely will. Francisco had received the engenho and lands of Sergipe as an entail (*vinculada em morgado*), but with the provision that should Francisco and Felipa die without heirs then the estate was to be divided. The properties in Brazil were to be sold off and the money divided into thirds between the charitable brotherhood of the Misericórdia of Salvador, the Jesuit college of that city, and the poor and orphans of Salvador. Possessions in Portugal were to be ceded to the Misericórdia of Lisbon.

At the time of her inheritance of the Engenho Sergipe, Dona Felipa de Sá was living a religious life in the Dominican convent of Santa Catherina de Sena in Evora. She had entered the convent in 1560 at the age of twelve, but with the death of her brother and her inheritance of the family properties she now became a desirable bride responsible for continuing the family line. In 1573, her marriage was contracted with Dom Fernando de Noronha, heir to the title of count of Linhares.[5] The marriage was arranged according to a contract of *dote e arras e metade dos adequiridos*. By this arrangement, both husband and wife declared the portions and properties that they were bringing into the marriage and could limit the access or control of their spouse over certain properties.[6] Dona Felipa declared in the marriage contract that among her properties were the Engenho "that is called Sergipe," with 282 slaves and another at Ilhéus with 130 slaves. These, like the other properties inherited from her father and brother, were to be considered part of the entail and thus subject to the conditions and restrictions stipulated in their wills.[7] Realizing the shaky legal ground on which her family's claim to these properties rested, Dona Felipa, through her husband, petitioned for and received in 1576 royal confirmation of the grant made originally by Mem de Sá and the transfer made by Francisco Rodrigues de Castelobranco to Francisco de Sá.[8]

Between 1576 and 1618, Engenhos Sergipe and Santana were owned by the absentee count and countess of Linhares and managed by resident administrators sent from Portugal. During this period, the mill in Sergipe came to be known as the Engenho Sergipe do Conde (of the count), or, after his death, sometimes as the Engenho da Condessa (of the countess). Dom Fernando de Noronha, count of Linhares, had accompanied the king, Dom Sebastião, on the ill-fated crusade that met disaster in Morocco in 1578. Captured, Dom Fernando was forced to ransom himself. He returned to Portugal, where he exercised the important office of inspector of the treasury (*veedor da fazenda*). He took an active interest in his wife's properties in Brazil, along with his own estates in Portugal and his business interests in Spain. From 1586 to 1607, the count of Linhares was represented in Bahia by his retainer, Francisco de Negreiros, who had been captured and ransomed along with his lord in Morocco.[9]

These were difficult years for the engenhos. Both Santana and Sergipe suffered from Indian attacks. Santana was besieged in the 1590s, and during a general uprising of the Aimoré in 1601 it suffered the loss of slaves and supplies.[10] Engenho Sergipe was burned sometime in the 1580s and then rebuilt at considerable cost.[11] In addition, Francisco de Negreiros on his own initiative or under orders from the count of Linhares sold off large amounts of the original land grant. There were at least eighty-one separate sales, totaling 49$770.[12] Although these sales were usually made with the purchasers' agreement to supply sugarcane to Engenho Sergipe, later observers believed that the alienation of these lands caused severe problems in the supply of firewood and foodstuffs to the engenho. Moreover, a question later arose about the legality of these sales if the lands of Engenho Sergipe were indeed an entail as stipulated in the will of Mem de Sá.

The count of Linhares died in 1617, and Dona Felipa at that point retired to her estate at Telheiras where, under the influence of her confessor, the Prior of Lumiar, she decided to endow a church for the newly created Jesuit College of Santo Antão in Lisbon.[13] The church was begun in 1613. By 1618, Dona Felipa was in ill health. On 20 July, she drew up her first will, and she revised it in a second one, composed on 31 August. In this testament, she left all her possessions in both Brazil and Portugal to the Jesuit College of Santo Antao. She died on 1 September 1618.[14]

It was at this point that the legal complexities concerning the two engenhos began to multiply. The already shady origins in the grant of Mem de Sá to a nonresident friend at the Portuguese court and its quick transfer to Mem de Sá's own son, who then allowed his father to use and benefit from these lands during his life, opened the property and its owners to the threat of suit or legal nullification of property rights. The count of Linhares's sale of lands theoretically held in morgado created another set of legal uncertainties. But the central problem was created by Dona Felipa's decision to leave all her property to the Jesuit College of Lisbon. Mem de Sá's testament had stipulated that should his children die without heirs that his properties in Brazil should be sold and the proceeds divided equally between the Misericórdia of Bahia, the Jesuit College of Bahia, and the poor of the city of Salvador. His goods in Portugal were to be left to the Misericórdia of Lisbon. Dona Felipa, by leaving all her possessions to the Jesuits of Santo Antão, thus ignored her father's desire and created a situation in which the engenhos in Brazil were willed to different parties – by Mem de Sá to the Misericórdia, poor folk, and Jesuit College of Bahia, and by Dona Felipa, countess of Linhares, his daughter, to the Jesuit College of Lisbon.

Dona Felipa, in fact, had foreseen the problem and had stated specifically in her will that Engenho Sergipe had been inherited directly from her brother as his property and was not affected by the limitations set on her father's legacy. Francisco de Sá did have legal title to the engenho and its land through the sesmaria transferred to him by Fernão Rodrigues de Castelobranco, although it is clear that since his father maintained control over the "use and fruits" of this property that Francisco's possession was only "on paper" as long as his father was alive. Whatever the agreement that had existed between father and son, it was, by the time of Dona Felipa's death, forgotten. The legal question now was, Did Francisco own the engenho outright or did he inherit it, and the restrictions on it, from his father? The answer to this question determined the right of Dona Felipa to dispose of the Engenho Sergipe and its land only as she saw fit without concern for the provisions of her father's will.[15]

The battle for the engenhos of Mem de Sá began almost immediately upon the death of the countess of Linhares.[16] On 6 September, the College of Santo Antão sent a legal representative to take possession of Engenho Sergipe, but the Jesuit College of Bahia was already in possession when he arrived. The Lisbon college and the Misericórdia of Bahia, the other interested parties, could do nothing. Legal action was initiated by the Misericórdia on 22 July 1621, when the provedor, or senior officer, of that body brought suit against the Father Provincial of the Jesuits in Bahia. The provedor claimed that Mem de Sá's will provided that his property be sold and the proceeds divided among the three named testators. The Bahian Jesuits had not done this, nor had they shared the annual profit of the engenhos. The following day, Father Manoel do Couto, representing the Lisbon college, asked for the right to enter the suit as a third party. On 24 July, the Bahian Jesuits submitted their defense. The probate judge (*juiz dos difuntos e ausentes*) delivered his decision in September 1622, finding in favor of the Jesuit College of Lisbon. Now the appeals began. The Misericórdia appealed to the Relação of Bahia. Failing there, it carried the case to the High Court of Appeals in Lisbon (Casa da Suplicação) in 1623,[17] which heard the case in 1627 and in January 1629 issued a decision. The Casa da Suplicação found that although the Misericórdia had not been aggrieved by the Bahian Jesuits' forced possession, it was justified in demanding that the engenho be sold and the proceeds divided.

The College of Santo Antão had been in possession of Engenho Sergipe since 1622 and was so when the Dutch destroyed much of the mill in 1625 and stopped production. Now it was Santo Antão's turn to appeal. Three times appeals were made, all of them unsuccessful. During this period, an inventory of Engenho Sergipe was drawn up in preparation for the ordered sale and division of property. The "final decision" (the first of many) was handed down in 1627. At this point, the Jesuits of Santo Antão raised another problem. If a division of Mem de Sá's property was to be made, then it should be the property as Mem de Sá left it. In other words, improvements made by the College of Santo Antão had to be separated from the division. This position generated a whole new round of claims and counterclaims concerning the improvements and their value. The crown magistrate (*ouvidor geral*) of Bahia wanted to include everything in the division. The Jesuits of Santo Antão complained to the Casa da Suplicação, which agreed with their position and ordered that they be left in possession of Engenho Sergipe until an appropriate partition of the property could be made. This decision reached Bahia in January 1639. The Misericórdia registered a complaint, and the ouvidor geral refused to enforce the decision. Appeals against the decision went back to the Casa da Suplicação twice, each time being rejected with a new order to execute. Finally, in January 1642, the College of Santo Antão sought and received a royal order requiring the ouvidor geral to execute the sentence of the Casa da Suplicação without delay and to return the Engenho Sergipe to the College of Santo Antão.

Although the Jesuits of Santo Antão were carrying their appeals to the Lisbon high court after 1637, the ouvidor geral in Bahia, apparently no friend of the Lisbon Jesuits, was forcing the issue in Brazil.[18] He "violently" removed them from possession of the engenho and ordered it sold at public auction in March 1638. The death of the ouvidor geral soon after this event was taken by the Lisbon Jesuits as proof of God's punishment for the injustice he had done. With their appeal still before the Lisbon tribunal and the Misericórdia in possession of the engenho, it was sold to Pedro Gonçalves de Mattos in Salvador on 30 March 1638.[19] He remained in possession until the harvest of 1643.

Meanwhile, the Casa da Suplicação had ruled that the College of Santo Antão was entitled to credit for the improvements they had made at Sergipe and that possession should be returned to them until a fair evaluation of these could be made. The new ouvidor geral balked, and the Misericórdia appealed to Portugal without success. The ouvidor geral then accepted an evaluation of the improvements at 8,000 to 10,000 cruzados but refused to honor other aspects of the Casa da Suplicação's ruling. Once again the College of Santo Antão appealed, the Lisbon tribunal ruled in their favor, and the ouvidor geral was forced to comply – not, of course, without another appeal by the Misericórdia, which proved unsuccessful. By 1643, possession of Engenho Sergipe was returned to the College of Santo Antão, but with it now came a new legal action initiated by Pedro Gonçalves de Mattos, who had been dispossessed from the engenho he had owned for five years. Father Simão de Vasconcelos, representing the Bahian Jesuits, could write in October 1643 that only the litigation with Pedro Gonçalves de Mattos remained unresolved. But the Jesuits both of Lisbon and of Bahia agreed that no settlement could be made with him or the Misericórdia until an understanding was reached between the two Jesuit colleges.[20]

At this point, the dispute between the two Jesuit colleges, which had been pushed to the background during the other litigation, reemerged. The Jesuits realized that this legal battle between two houses in the same order was not to the best interests of either or of the company of Jesus in general. In fact, in the early stages, Fernão Cardim as Jesuit provincial in Brazil had prohibited the representative of Santo Antão in Brazil from pursuing his suit without express license from the father general of the order.[21] In 1643, however, the Jesuit College of Bahia brought suit against the College of Santo Antão and appealed the previous decisions in its favor. The ouvidor geral forwarded this appeal to Lisbon, but even so the Jesuit provincial in Bahia considered him an interested party and sought his removal. This was done, and his successor then overturned previous decisions favorable to Santo Antão. Santo Antão appealed this action to the Casa da Suplicação, which found in its favor and reversed the judge's action. The Jesuit provincial of Bahia appealed this action, but to no avail. The litigation involving Engenho Segipe had by 1645 been in the courts for almost twenty-five years with little progress made toward resolution of the knotty legal problems, claims, and counterclaims. Rather than resolving the issues, the quarter of a century had brought further complications and new litigants.

By 1648, the battle had entered a new stage. To some extent, the claims of the Jesuits of Lisbon and Bahia and of the Misericórdia had all been recognized, and now the questions became: What was the value of the property when Mem de Sá died? What improvements had been made while Engenho Sergipe was in the hands of the College of Santo Antão? What value did they add to the property and to the annual production?[22] Santo Antão argued that Engenho Sergipe was not worth 20,000 cruzados when Mem de Sá died, but only later when improvements had been made, and that from this amount deductions had to be made for depreciation, debts, slave deaths and runaways, and upkeep. Moreover, by 1648 none of the buildings on the plantation dated from the time of Mem de Sá – all had been rebuilt by the Jesuits of Santo Antão at considerable cost. In short, Santo Antão was trying to reduce as far as possible the portion of the estate to be included in the court-ordered division. Of course, the College of Bahia and the Misericórdia had their own arguments on these matters. When, for example, the College of Santo Antão argued that only 125 tarefas of cane existed at Engenho Sergipe in the time of Mem de Sá and that cane in excess of that amount was a result of subsequent improvements made by lavradores during its administration, the Misericórdia pointed out that improvements made by lavradores on leased land always became property of the owner of the land, "as was the usual custom in Brazil." The Misericórdia also complained that Santo Antão had, during its management of the plantation, sent people of little intelligence or ability to run it, with the result that Engenho Sergipe was less profitable than less advantaged but better managed estates.[23]

Some resolution of the legal battle took place in the 1650s. A decision of the Casa da Suplicação in May 1654 recognized the improvements made by the College of Santo Antão at Engenho Sergipe, but it also required its payment of a large sum of money to the other parties of the suit as their portion of the harvests while Santo Antão had been in possession. The decision also ordered that the engenho be sold and its value divided.[24] This writ probably made the Jesuits of Lisbon more disposed to settle the matter out of court. Moreover, the Jesuit order, despite its recognition of the independent financial arrangements made by each of its colleges, felt that a civil suit between two houses of the order was unbecoming and divisive.[25] Pressure from the father general in Rome as well as the continuing costs and uncertainties of the suit led, on 20 April 1655, to a friendly settlement out of court between the Lisbon and Bahian colleges. They agreed to equal ownership of the engenho, with the Bahian college appointing an administrator experienced in sugar making and the Lisbon college appointing his assistant. The Misericórdia's claim would be settled by payment from annual profits or by selling parcels of land.[26] In recognition of the advantage the Bahian college had won in the suit (*melhoria*), Santo Antão agreed to pay it 10,000 milréis in sugar. Any new engenho built on the land of Sergipe or any new canefields planted had to be on a half-and-half basis. No land could be sold and no obligation on a lavrador's cane could be ended without the agreement of both houses.[27]

With the issue now seemingly settled between the two Jesuit colleges, the other parties in the suit could be satisfied. In September 1659, the provedor of the Misericórdia was approached by no less a figure than Salvador Correa de Sá, the distinguished soldier and administrator whose family dominated affairs in Rio de Janeiro. Recently appointed captain-general of the South, he was en route from Lisbon to Rio de Janeiro when he stopped in Bahia. Salvador Correa's relations with the Jesuits had always been particularly close, and it is not surprising that he had been asked to serve as their intermediary with the Santa Casa. On 22 September 1659, a general meeting of the Misericórdia was called, and a majority of the brothers voted "according to their conscience" to accept an agreement with the Jesuits. They were moved to this decision because the suit had lasted forty years, and "could continue another forty," and "because it was against powerful people in this State and in Portugal," and finally because the ultimate outcome was uncertain in any case.[28]

The vote of the Misericórdia now permitted matters to progress. On 13 October 1659, the Jesuit provincial of Brazil, Father Baltesar de Siqueira, the rector of the Bahian College, Father Sebastião Vaz, and a representative of the College of Santo Antão, Father Agostinho Lousada, met with the officials of the Misericórdia and with Father Eusebio de Mattos, a Jesuit who represented his relatives, the heirs of Pedro Gonçalves de Mattos. An agreement was reached in which the Misericórdia's claim would be settled for the sum of 7,000 milréis, from which 600 milréis would be subtracted to satisfy the heirs of the Gonçalves de Mattos estate.[29] On 27 June 1660, the outstanding balance was paid to the Misericórdia, and their claim to the Engenho Sergipe and its lands was eliminated.[30]

It is unclear if the original intention of the two Jesuit colleges in 1655 had been to sell the engenho and its lands and divide the sale price, but by 1663 such a sale was no longer contemplated. In that year, the next step was taken. The Engenho Sergipe was divided into two parts: The buildings and two large canefields deemed necessary for its operation were evaluated at 24,000 milréis; the other lands were valued at 16,000 milréis.[31] The College of Santo Antão was offered the choice of the two parts with the understanding that it would pay the difference if it selected the first. The College of Santo Antão took the engenho, and the College of Bahia took the lands with an obligation on the engenho to grind their cane. Both sides took care to state that this agreement would not prejudice any outstanding claims they had still in litigation. Both sides agreed that together they would satisfy the claims of the last remaining party in the original suit, the poor of Salvador, as soon as possible. The poor were, in fact, represented by a Jesuit father in the College of Bahia who bore the title procurator of the poor.[32]

Father Serafim Leite, the most prominent historian of the Jesuits in Brazil, wrote that by 1669 the matter was settled. This was not exactly true. The College of Santo Antão did not take full possession of the Engenho Sergipe until 15 March 1676, and as late as 1680 money matters betweeen the two colleges were still not completely settled.[33] After that date, Engenho Sergipe produced sugar for the College of Santo Antão and for the College of Bahia, which owned extensive canefields formerly part of the engenho. The sugar for each college was shipped and accounted for separately. Engenho Sergipe remained in the hands of the College of Santo Antão, administered by Jesuit priests sent out periodically from Portugal, until the expulsion of the order from Brazil in 1759.

With the departure of the Jesuits, Sergipe and the neighboring Engenho Petinga, which the Jesuits had acquired in 1745, were auctioned by the state. Sergipe was first acquired by a priest, Father Luiz de Sousa Oliveira, and Petinga by Dr. Antônio Ribeiro de Migueis (Guimarães), and Migueis subsequently took possession of Engenho Sergipe as well. By 1770, he was in arrears in the payments on both properties. The mills were sold again and passed through the hands of a number of owners. In the 1790s, they were held by the brothers of Gaspar Alvares de Sá. By 1812, they, along with three other mills, belonged to Simão Alvares da Silva, and in 1817 they were listed as the property of Dona Maria Joaquina Pereira de Andrade, one of the wealthiest slave-owners in the Recôncavo. The record of Engenho Santana is less full. It was owned at the end of the eighteenth and beginning of the nineteenth centuries by Manoel da Silva Ferreira and passed in 1810 into the hands of Felisberto Caldeira Brant, the future marquis of Barbacena, a major figure of the independence period. Conde and Petinga, by the mid–nineteenth century, had become the property of the baron of Pirajá.[34] The engenhos of a count had become the engenhos of a marquis and a baron.

The long, complex, and sometimes bitter lawsuit over Engenho Sergipe produced a mountain of paper. Briefs, transcripts, certified copies, deeds, decisions, appeals, reports, inventories, and position papers were produced in Portuguese, Italian, and Latin throughout the dispute. These materials, scattered in Brazil, Portugal, and Italy, provide an incredible record of one engenho's history. More important, because of the contested ownership of the property and testamentary obligations on it, extremely careful annual accounting records were kept over long periods of time. These livros de safra, as they were called, were probably kept by other engenhos as well, but they have not survived. Only those of Engenho Sergipe and its associated sister mills of Santana and Petinga have been uncovered for the colonial period. Together with the other documentary evidence, these series of accounts are an indispensable source for understanding the operations and dynamics of the Bahian engenhos.

Sergipe and Santana were by no means typical engenhos. Because they were not, great care must be taken in positing generalizations based solely on their records. Founded by a governor, owned by a count, and later held by the Jesuits of Lisbon, their pattern of ownership was unlike that of most mills. Absentee ownership was not characteristic of Bahian engenhos for the most part, but Sergipe and Santana were almost always owned by absentees or administered by religious institutions. In Brazil, as in Mexico and Peru, Jesuit ownership seems to have provided considerable stability. And Jesuit management practices emphasized safe policies, with perhaps lower returns but fewer risks than for lay owners.[35] The role of the administrator, clerical constraints on sexual contacts, the observance of religious precepts and obligations, and perhaps in some periods a different concept of slave control all may have set these Jesuit mills apart. But in the last analysis, supporting evidence indicates that, in markets, agricultural techniques, and management practices, the similarities were greater than the differences.

THE ESTIMATED PRICE OF WHITE SUGAR AT THE MILL IN BAHIA

This table has been constructed by combining a number of price series and adjusting them in an attempt to create a consistent series of Bahian at-the-mill prices for white sugar. The observed prices are the actual figures reported. After 1675, these are based primarily on the series created by Dauril Alden and are indicated in the table by parentheses. In all other cases wherever possible, the average annual price at Engenho Sergipe has been used. Two adjustments have been made to the observed prices. For the period before the devaluation of Portuguese currency in 1688, an upward adjustment of 20 percent has been made. In addition, after 1675 a downward adjustment of 10 percent has been made to the Alden series since those prices were based on purchases by the Misericórdia hospital and should be discounted somewhat to represent what the millowner could hope to receive. When observed prices existed from both Engenho Sergipe and the Misericórdia, the former were usually 10 to 20 percent below the latter; I have used the lower figure for my calculations. All figures are in réis per arroba. The sources for the table are : (a) Wanderley Pinho, *História de um engenho do Recôncavo* (Rio de Janeiro, 1946), 247 (various sources); (b) *DHA*, III, 406ff.; (c) Miguel Dias de Santiago Papers, PRO, State Papers 1/104; (d) Engenho Sergipe Accounts, ANTT, CSJ, various maços; and (e) Dauril Alden, "Commodity Price Movements in Brazil" (unpublished paper, 1983).

Year	Observed price	Adjusted price	Source
1550	400	480	a
1552	400	480	
1572	450	540	
1576	630	756	b
1578	880	1,056	b
1584	800	960	a
1592	800	960	a
1596	865	1,038	c
1597	910	1,092	
1598	950	1,140	
1600			

Year	Observed price	Adjusted price	Source
1607	1,100	1,320	d
1608	1,083	1,299	
1611	1,287	1,544	
1613	1,147	1,376	
1614	1,000	1,200	
1620	955	1,146	
1622	850	1,020	
1623	580	696	
1625	675	810	
1626	617	740	
1627	730	876	
1628	896	1,075	
1629	810	972	d
1630	673	807	
1631	619	743	
1632	780	936	
1633	852	1,022	
1634	1,042	1,250	
1636	1,378	1,654	
1637	1,420	1,764	
1643	1,218	1,462	
1644	1,035	1,242	
1645	1,128	1,354	
1646	1,157	1,388	
1650	1,147	1,376	
1651	1,350	1,620	
1654	1,200	1,440	
1655	1,206	1,447	
1660	1,090	1,308	
1665	1,200	1,440	
1669	1,177	1,412	
1675	(1,356)	1,220	e
1676	(1,112)	1,001	
1677	(1,206)	1,085	
1678	(1,200)	1,080	
1679	(1,200)	1,080	
1680	(1,392)	1,109S	
1683	(1,392)	1,109	
1688	(1,020)	918	
1689	(864)	778	
1691	(1,200)	1,080	
1692	(1,200)	1,080	
1695	(1,600)	1,440	
1696	(1,500)	1,350	
1697	(1,500)	1,350	
1698	(1,264)	1,138	
1699	(2,200)	1,980	
1701	(1,800)	1,620	
1702	(1,600)	1,440	
1704	(1,350)	1,215	
1705	1,600		d
1706	1,295		

Year	Observed price	Adjusted price	Source
1707	1,343		
1708	1,335		
1709	1,341		
1710	1,600		
1711	1,600		
1712	1,602		
1713	1,760		
1714	2,020		
1715	1,815		
1716	(2,000)	1,620	
1717	(2,100)	1,890	
1718	(1,920)	1,728	
1719	(1,920)	1,728	
1720	(1,920)	1,728	
1721	(1,350)	1,215	
1722	(1,550)	1,395	
1723	(1,550)	1,395	
1724	(1,500)	1,350	
1725	1,692		d
1728	(1,663)	1,491	
1729	(1,575)	1,418	
1730	(1,475)	1,327	
1731	(1,530)	1,377	
1732	(1,240)	1,116	
1733	(1,280)	1,152	
1735	(1,265)	1,138	
1736	(1,974)	1,777	
1738	(1,066)	959	
1739	(914)	823	
1740	(1,010)	909	
1741	(1,266)	1,139	
1742	(1,189)	1,070	
1743	(1,600)	1,440	
1744	(1,333)	1,200	
1745	1,800		d
1746	1,800		
1747	1,800		
1748	1,273		
1749	1,273		
1750	1,273		
1751	1,255		
1752	1,273		
1753	1,400		
1754	1,400		
1755	(1,320)	1,188	
1756	(1,400)	1,260	
1757	(1,472)	1,325	
1758	(1,598)	1,439	
1759	(1,870)	1,429	
1760	(1,575)	1,420	
1761	(1,417)	1,276	
1762	(1,440)	1,296	

Year	Observed price	Adjusted price	Source
1763	(1,360)	1,224	
1764	(1,486)	1,337	
1765	(1,413)	1,272	
1766	(1,327)	1,194	
1767	(1,360)	1,224	
1768	(1,294)	1,165	

THE VALUE OF BAHIAN SUGAR EXPORTS, 1698–1766

Like Appendix B, this table is based on the export records of the Junta do Tabaco. Here, I have taken the total number of crates exported – including *feixos* (small boxes) at a ratio of 3:1 – and then assumed that on the average two-thirds of Bahia's sugar exports were white sugar and one-third was muscavado. I have then multiplied these amounts by the estimated price of those sugar types in that year in Bahia to produce an estimate of the value of the sugar exports in a particular year. Because of the irregularity of the fleets, there are considerable variations in these figures, especially when after a year in which no fleet sailed, the following fleet carried two years' harvest. Figure 7-5 attempts to compensate for this situation by presenting five-year averages. The reader, however, may wish to have the annual figures, and for that reason they are presented here. The total value has been rounded to the nearest milréis. Numbers in brackets are contemporary estimates.

Year	Total caixas	Caixas, white	Caixas, muscavado	Price, white	Price, muscavado	Total value
1698	9,444	6,296	3,148	1,138	683	326,023
1699	11,223	7,482	3,741	1,980	1,188	674,053
1700	10,606	7,071	3,535	2,035	1,221	654,700
1701	4,143	2,762	1,381	1,620	972	203,587
1702	14,397	9,598	4,799	1,440	864	628,861
1703	5,844	3,895	1,948	1,362	817	241,378
1704	22,000	14,667	7,333	1,350	810	900,906
1705				1,600	1,100	
1706	24,141	16,094	8,047	1,295	785	950,552
1707				1,343	640	
1708	29,096	19,397	9,699	1,335	657	1,129,353
1709				1,341	651	
1710	20,000	13,333	6,667	1,600	800	933,324
1711		8,480		1,600	800	
1712	21,383	14,255	7,128	1,602	900	1,023,810
1713	15,206	10,137	5,069	1,760	961	734,935
1714	10,488	6,992	3,496	2,020	1,248	647,040
1715	10,985	7,323	3,662	1,815	1,282	629,508
1716	11,379	7,586	3,793	1,800	1,080	647,844

Year	Total caixas	Caixas, white	Caixas, muscavado	Price, white	Price, muscavado	Total value
1717	5,105	3,403	1,702	2,080	1,248	322,082
1718	6,377	4,251	2,126	1,928	1,037	334,264
1719	8,113	5,409	2,704	1,928	1,037	425,278
1720				1,928	1,037	
1721	19,849	13,233	6,616	1,215	729	731,541
1722	12,843	8,562	4,281	1,395	837	543,452
1723				1,395	837	
1724	12,350	8,183	4,167	1,350	810	504,781
1725	25,225	16,817	8,408	1,539	923	1,630,365
1726	13,000	8,667	4,333	1,428	857	453,145
1727						
1728	9,223	6,149	3,074	1,497	898	418,793
1729	10,222	7,175	3,074	1,418	851	446,850
1730	5,839	3,893	1,946	1,327	796	235,025
1731	12,927	8,628	4,309	1,377	826	540,400
1732	13,100			1,116	670	
1733	17,404	11,603	5,801	1,152	691	608,130
1734						
1735	12,732	8,488	4,244	1,138	683	439,530
1736				1,777	1,066	
1737	873	582	291	[1,000]	[500]	25,462
1738	9,123	6,082	3,041	959	575	265,342
1739	10,905	7,270	3,635	720	432	238,165
1740	11,000	7,333	3,667	1,000	600	333,662
1741	14,661	9,774	4,887	1,139	683	506,464
1742				1,000	600	
1743	12,529	8,353	4,176	1,440	864	547,273
1744				1,200	720	
1745	13,441	8,961	4,480	1,800	1;080	733,887
1746	8,258	5,505	2,753	1,800	1,080	450,878
1747	8,891	5,927	2,964	1,800	1,080	485,440
1748	20,087	13,392	6,696	1,364	818	831,041
1749				1,365	819	
1750	11,398	7,599	3,799	1,255	753	433,909
1751	10,998	7,329	3,664	1,273	764	424,519
1752	12,000	8,000	4,000	1,400	840	509,600
1753	11,198	7,465	3,733	1,400	840	475,535
1754	3,853	2,575	1,278	1,325	795	154,976
1755	6,486	4,324	2,162	1,188	713	233,745
1756	10,234	6,823	3,411	1,260	756	391,149
1757	10,685	7,111	3,555			
1758	11,557	7,705	3,852	1,439	863	504,412
1759	12,000	8,000	4,000	1,429	858	520,240
1760				1,420	850	
1761	15,000	10,000	5,000	1,276	765	580,475
1762	17,000	11,333	5,667	1,296	778	668,377
1763	23,000	15,334	7,666	1,224	734	853,848
1764	7,000	4,667	2,333	1,337	802	283,890
1765						
1766	13,959	9,306	4,653	1,194	716	505,502

NOTES

Chapter 1. The sugar plantation: from the Old World to the New

1 Noel Deerr, *The History of Sugar*, 2 vols. (London, 1950), and Edmund von Lippmann, *História do açúcar*, 2 vols. (Rio de Janeiro, 1942), are the standard histories of sugar. An excellent history of sugar in the Portuguese empire is still found in João Lucio de Azevedo, *Épocas de Portugal económico*, 2d ed. (Lisbon, 1947), 223–98.

2 Charles Verlinden, "The Transfer of Colonial Techniques from the Mediterranean to the Atlantic," in *Beginnings of Modern Colonization* (Ithaca, N.Y., 1970), 18–21. A useful summary is presented by J. H. Galloway, "The Mediterranean Sugar Industry," *Geographical Review* 67, no. 2 (April 1977): 177–94. Particularly useful because of the Venetian documentation it incorporates in E. Ashtor, "Levantine Sugar Industry in the Late Middle Ages: A Case of Technological Decline," in A. L. Udovitch, ed., *The Islamic Middle East, 700–1900: Studies in Economic and Social History* (Princeton, 1981), 91–133.

3 There is some possibility that sugar was known in North Africa before Arab conquests, but it was most surely there under the Almoravides in the ninth century. Moroccan sugar grown on irrigated estates was occasionally marketed in England and France during the sixteenth century. Eventually war, political unrest, and competition from Madeira and Brazil drove the Moroccan product from international markets in the 1570s. See Paul Berthier, *Les anciennes sucreries du Maroc et leurs resaux hydrauliques*, 2 vols. (Rabat, 1966), 273–4.

4 Moacyr Soares Pereira, *A origem dos cilindros na moagem da cana* (Rio de Janeiro, 1955), casts some serious doubts on the assertion of Lippmann and Deerr that the *trapetto* of Sicily was, in fact, the cylindrical press. The matter remains open to question, but Soares Pereira's claim that the cylindrical rollers are a Brazilian innovation cannot be accepted in the face of the documentary evidence from the Canaries, which indicates that it was already in use there by the sixteenth century. On Sicily, see Carmelo Trasselli, "Produzione e commercio delle zucchero in Sicilia dal XII al XIX sécolo," *Economia e Storia* 2 (1955): 325–43. The Sicilian sugar industry fell on hard times in the early sixteenth century but lasted until the general crisis of the 1680s. See Carmelo Trasselli, "Sumário duma história do açúcar siciliano," *Do Tempo e da História* 2 (1968): 49–78, and especially Giovanni Rebora, *Un' impresa zuccheriera del cinquecento* (Naples, 1968), which contains accounts from the 1580s.

5 The best discussion of this problem is Antônio Barros de Castro, "Brasil, 1610: Mundanças técnicas e conflitos sociais," *Pesquisa e planejamento econômico* 10, no. 3 (1980): 679–712.

6 Verlinden, "Transfer of Colonial Techniques," 21; Immanuel Wallerstein, *The Modern World System*, 2 vols. to date (New York, 1974–78), I, 43; Virginia Rau and Jorge de Macedo, eds., *O açúcar de Madeira nos fins do século xv* (Funchal, 1962), 11.

504

See also Ruth Pike, *Enterprise and Adventure* (Ithaca, N.Y., 1966). On Valencia, see Jose Perez Vidal, *La cultura de la caña de azúcar en el Levante español* (Madrid, 1973).

7 Lippmann, *História do açúcar*, II, 190–238.

8 Charles Verlinden, *L'esclavage dans l'Europe médiéval*, 2 vols. (Bruges, 1955). He has summarized his major points in the context of Iberian expansion in "Medieval Slavery in Europe and Colonial Slavery in America," *Beginnings of Modern Colonization*, 33–51. See also Marc Bloch, "How and Why Ancient Slavery Came to an End," *Slavery and Serfdom in the Middle Ages* (Berkeley, 1975), 1–32. A useful summary is also provided by David B. Davis, *The Problem of Slavery in Western Culture* (Ithaca, N.Y., 1966).

9 John L. Vogt, "The Lisbon Slave House and African Trade 1486–1521," paper presented to the Society of Spanish and Portuguese Historians (1971), gives somewhat lower estimates of 300–700 a year, including both those arriving in Lisbon and Lagos.

10 Manuel Correia Lopes, *A escravatura: subsídios para a sua história* (Lisbon, 1944), 15–18; Verlinden, *L'esclavage*, I, 626–7. On slavery in the Algarve, see Joaquim Antero Romero Magalhães, *Para o estudo do Algarve económico no século xvi* (Lisbon, 1970), 32 passim. The most complete account of Portuguese slavery is A. C. de C. M. Saunders, *A Social History of Black Slaves and Freedmen in Portugal 1441–1551* (Cambridge, 1982).

11 Rau and Macedo, *O açúcar da Madeira*, 14; Fernando Jasmins Pereira (Rodrigues) *Alguns elementos para o estudo da história económica da Madeira* (Coimbra, 1959); Frèdèric Mauro, *Le Portugal et l'Atlantique au xvii siècle* (Paris, 1960), 184–8. Also of general interest is Carlos Montenegro Miguel, "Um ciclo económico – o açúcar," *Das Artes e da História da Madeira* 5, no. 19 (1955): 13–15.

12 See T. Bentley Duncan, *Atlantic Islands* (Chicago, 1972), 7–53, for a good discussion of the early history of the Azores and Madeira.

13 Joel Serrão, "Sobre o 'trigo das ilhas' no século xv e xvi," *Das Artes e da História da Madeira* 1, no. 2 (1950): 2–6. This problem is also discussed in Sidney Greenfield, "Madeira and the Beginnings of New World Sugar Cane Cultivation and Plantation Slavery: A Study in Institution Building," *CPSNWS*, 538–52. Greenfield also summarizes much information in "Plantations, Sugar Cane and Slavery," in *HR/RH* 6, no. 1 (1979): 85–119.

14 Joel Serão, "O Infante D. Fernando e a Madeira (1461–1470)," *Das Artes e da História da Madeira* 1, no. 4 (1950): 10–12.

15 Duncan, *Atlantic Islands*, 30–1.

16 Rau and Macedo, *O açúcar da Madeira*, 12; Carlos Montenegro Miguel, "O açúcar e a sua importância na economia insular," *Das Artes e da História da Madeira* 3, no. 15 (1953): 33–5.

17 The arroba of sugar on Madeira equaled 28 *arratéis* until 1504 when the weight was standardized at 32 arratéis. All figures given here are in the "peso novo" of 32 arratéis per arroba. The *aratel* is the equivalent of the pound (lb.).

18 A good short summary of Madeiran production is found in Vitorino Magalhães Godinho, *Os descobrimentos e a economia mundial*, 2 vols. (Lisbon, 1963–8), II, 419–56. The decline is documented in Joel Serrão, "Rendimento das alfandêgas do arquipélago da Madeira (1581–1587)," *Das Artes e da História da Madeira* 1, no. 5 (1951): 2–5; 1, no. 6 (1951): 14–18. These findings are summarized in Mauro, *Portugal et l'Atlantique*, pp. 186–7. Indispensable for the sixteenth century is Fernando Jasmins Pereira, *O açúcar madeirense de 1500 a 1537: Produção e preços* (Lisbon, 1969), which revises downward the production estimates of Magalhães Godinho.

19 Consulta, Con. da Fazenda (31 July 1613), AGS, sec. prov. 1472, fs. 284–5. A similar request was made again in the 1620s. Duncan, *Atlantic Islands*, 33–5, points out that the Twelve Year Truce (1609–24) reopened the Brazilian sugar trade and spelled disaster for Madeira.

20 Rau and Macedo, *O açúcar de Madeira*, 13.

21 Damião Peres, ed., *Libro 2° das Saudades da Terra do Doctor Gaspar Fructuoso*, 2d ed. (Oporto, 1926), 114. Fructuoso is not a reliable source in this matter. His volume on Madeira was written in the Azores, and he is sometimes less than exact on specific matters. Rau, Mauro, and others have cast doubts on his figures. He claims that the Esmeraldo engenho had a yearly capacity of 20,000 arrobas, almost twice that of the largest Brazilian mills. Such a production would also mean that each slave produced over 3 tons of sugar, 3 times the normal Caribbean and Brazilian calculations.

22 Horacio Bento de Gouveia, "A escravatura na Ilha da Madeira do fim do século xv até meados do xvi," *Das Artes e da História da Madeira* 1 (1950–1): 9–10. On the trade in Canarian slaves, see also Leopoldo Piles Ros, *Apuntes para la historia economica social de Valencia durante el siglo xv* (Valencia, 1969).

23 Rau and Macedo, *O açúcar da Madeira*, 25–6. Complaints against Jewish and foreign merchants in the sugar trade were made throughout the 1470s and 1480s.

24 Ibid., 35. The *lavrador* system was also practiced in the Azores. See Maria Olimpia da Rocha Gil, "O porto de Ponta Delgada e o comércio açoriano no século xvii," *Do Tempo e da História*, 3 (1970): 75.

25 "Capitulaciones que presenta al Rey la isla de Tenerife" (1513), cited in Elias Serra Rafols and Leopoldo de la Rosa, eds., "Acuerdos del Cabildo de Tenerife (1508–1513)," in *Fontes rerum canarium* (La Laguna, 1952), 277.

26 "Canary" sugar was preferred over that of São Tomé and other sources on the Brussels market in the 1540s. Brussels served as a major sugar entrepôt in this period, receiving shipments from the Atlantic islands and Brazil and then exporting it to Germany and the Baltic region. Relative sugar prices can be learned from the 100th penny export tax in Archives Generaux du Royaume, Cambre des Comptes, nos. 23357–61,63 (Feb. 1543–Sept. 1545). I owe this information to my colleague James Tracy.

27 Guillermo Camacho y Pérez Galdos, "El cultivo de la caña de azúcar y la industria azucarera en Gran Canaria (1510–1535)," *Anuario de Estudios Atlanticos* 7 (1961): 15. See also Maria Luisa Fabrellas, "La producción de azúcar en Tenerife," *Revista de Historia* (Tenerife) 18 (1952): 455–87.

28 Camacho y Perez Galdos estimates a *tarea* or daily work load of 5,000 kilograms of cane with a yield of 6 percent sugar to cane. In a working month of 24 days, an ingenio would produce during the 6-month harvest season a total of 4,320 arrobas (of 25 lb.) or 49 tons. See "El cultivo," 45.

29 Serra Rafols, "Acuerdos," ix–x; Camacho y Pérez Galdos, "El cultivo," 58; Charles Verlinden, "Italians in the Economy of the Canary Islands at the Beginning of Spanish Colonization," *The Beginning of Modern Colonization* (Ithaca, N.Y., 1970), 132–57.

30 Camacho y Perez Galdos, "El cultivo," 15–16.

31 Ibid. The Spanish not only enslaved the Guanches on their native islands but sent them to Spain as well. See Vincente Cortés, "La trata de esclavos durante los primeros descubrimientos (1489–1516)," *Anuario de Estudios Atlanticos* 9 (1963): 23–50.

32 "Capitulaciones," 282–3.

33 "Cuadernos de las Ordenanzas del Melgarejo," cited in Camacho y Pérez Galdos, "El cultivo," 26. See also Felipe Fernández-Armesto, *The Canary Islands after the Conquest* (Oxford, 1982), 84–5.

34 Serra Rafols, "Acuerdos," 2.

35 Duncan, *Atlantic Islands*, 21.

36 Francisco Tenreiro, *A Ilha de São Tomé* (Lisbon, 1961), 62–3; António de Oliveira Marques, *History of Portugal*, 2 vols. (New York, 1972–4), I, 374–6; Virginia Rau, *O açúcar de São Tomé no segundo quartel do século xvi* (Lisbon, 1971).

37 Tenreiro, *A Ilha*, 68–9. See also Robert Garfield, "A History of São Tomé Island, 1470–1655" (Ph.D. thesis, Northwestern University, 1971).

38 The history of sugar production in São Tomé is a subject of total disagreement among

historians. There is no accurate series of consecutive production figures, and thus authors have put forward fragmentary estimates based often on contemporaneous commentators. Oliveira Marques (*History of Portugal*, I, 375) follows Mauro (*Portugal et l'Atlantique*, 190–1), stating production as follows: 1570s, 20,000 arrobas; 1602, 40,000; 1610, 23,000. Edmundo Correia Lopes (*A escravatura* [Lisbon, 1944] presents figures of a wholly different magnitude: 1529, 5,000; 1554, 150,000; 1610, 100,000; 1630, 60,000. Francisco Tenreiro (*A Ilha*, 70–3) is more in line with Correia Lopes, claiming a production of 300,000 in the 1590s and only 60,000 by 1610.

39 Fernando Castelo-Branco, "O comércio externo de S. Tomé no século xvii," *Studia* 24 (Aug. 1968): 73–98, is a revisionist account that demonstrates that though the sugar economy declined it did not become moribund, as Tenreiro and others had argued.

40 Correia Lopes, *A escravatura*, 29; on pp. 38–44, he also publishes the "Regimento do negoceo e trato que foy para a Ilha de Sam Tome sobre os escravos (8 Feb. 1519)." See also Marian Malowist, "Les debuts du systeme des plantations dans la période des grandes découvertes," *Africana Bulletin* 10 (1969): 9–30.

41 Valentim Fernandes, "Navegacão de Lisboa à ilha de São Tomé," published in *Collecção de noticias para a história das grandes nações ultramarinas* 2 (Lisbon, 1821), is the most commonly used source for the sixteenth century. Tenreiro, *A Ilha*, 66–7, describes the free population at this date as white, but this was surely not the case.

42 A. F. C. Ryder, *Benin and the Europeans, 1485–1897* (London, 1969).

43 This description is based on Tenreiro, *A Ilha*. He argues that the system instituted on São Tomé was more akin to serfdom than slavery. Francisco Tenreiro was, however, an ardent exponent of the Portuguese miscegenation mystique, and I do not believe that his conclusions are entirely trustworthy on this question. Moreover, the serfdom-vs.-slavery issue persisted on São Tomé into the twentieth century, when it became a matter of contention between Great Britain and Portugal. It is possible that this more recent debate influenced Tenreiro's historical judgments. See Tenreiro, *A Ilha*, 70. Ryder, *Benin and the Europeans*, 55, demonstrates that the crown used slaves in transit on the local plantations. He claims that the fear of slaves running off to join the fugitive rebels led the crown to urge a constant turnover on the plantations.

44 A. F. C. Ryder, "An Early Portuguese Trading Voyage to the Forcados River," *Journal of the Historical Society of Nigeria* 1, no. 4 (1959).

45 Tenreiro, *A Ilha*, 66–7.

46 Carta régia (20 Oct. 1620), *Col. chron.*, III, 31.

47 Oliveira Marques, *History of Portugal*, I, 375–6. An important contemporaneous history that documents this situation is published in Antónia Ambrosio, "Manuel Rosario Pinto. A sua vida e a sua História de S. Tomé," *Studia* 30–1 (1970): 205–330.

48 Correia Lopes, *A escravatura*, 66–8; Tenreiro, *A Ilha*, 73; Fernando Castelo-Branco, "Subsídios para o estudo dos 'angolares' de S. Tomé," *Studia* 33 (1971): 149–59.

49 Carl O. Sauer, *The Early Spanish Main* (Berkeley, 1966), 210–11.

50 Mervyn Ratekin, "The Early Sugar Industry in Española," *HAHR* 34, no. 1 (Feb. 1954): 1–19. On Columbus's career in Madeira, see Samuel Eliot Morison, *Admiral of the Ocean Sea*, 2 vols. (Boston, 1942), I, 48–53.

51 On Cuba, see Julio Le Riverend, *Historia economica de Cuba* (Barcelona, 1972), 92–8; Levi Marrero, *Cuba: Economía y Sociedad*, 7 vols. (Río Piedras, Puerto Rico, and Madrid, 1972–8), II, 305–21.

52 Relevant sources are cited and an adequate survey is presented in Deerr, *History of Sugar*, I, 117–33.

53 Surveys of the beginnings of the Brazilian sugar industry are found in Lippmann, *História do açúcar*, II, 99–112; Varnhagen, *HGB*, I, 164–91. Also see Basilio Magalhães, *O açúcar nos primordios do Brasil colonial* (Rio de Janeiro, 1953).

54 Magalhães, *O açúcar*, 17–20; David Denslow, "The First Brazilian Sugar Cycle, Growth and Maturity" (unpublished paper, Yale University, 1970). The evidence

from Antwerp is mentioned in Eddy Stols, "Os mercadores flamengos em Portugal e no Brasil antes das conquistas holandesas," *AH* 5 (1953): 21.

55 The sugar specialist was Pedro Lopes Silveira. Among the foreigners were João Veniste and the Genoese João Adorno. See Magalhães, *O açúcar,* 26.

56 A somewhat outdated but still useful survey of the donatarial system especially valuable for the many published documents it contains are the chapters contained in *HCPB,* III, 167–271. The debate on the feudal vs. capitalistic elements of the captaincies has been considerably clarified by Harold B. Johnson, "The Donatary Captaincy in Perspective: Portuguese Backgrounds to the Settlement of Brazil," *HAHR* 52, no. 2 (May 1972): 203–14.

57 Alexander Marchant, *From Barter to Slavery: The Economic Relations of Portuguese and Indians in the Settlement of Brazil, 1500–1580,* Johns Hopkins University Studies in Historical and Political Science, ser. LX, no. 1 (Baltimore, 1942 [reprinted Gloucester, Mass., 1966]), 62.

58 W. F. Harrison, "A Struggle for Land in Colonial Brazil: The Private Captaincy of Paraíba do Sul, 1533–1753" (Ph.D. thesis, University of New Mexico, 1970), 19–21.

59 Ambrósio de Meira to Crown (Espirito Santo, 26 Sept. 1545), *ABNR* 62 (1940): 12.

60 Gabriel Soares de Sousa, *Tratado descritivo do Brasil em 1587* (São Paulo, 1971), 92. This is a reprint of the edition of 1851 published in Madrid by Francisco Adolfo de Varnhagen. Because of its accessibility, I have made all references to it, although the reader should be aware that the edition published by Pirajá da Silva contains important annotations. See *Notícia do Brasil,* 2 vols. (São Paulo, 1940).

61 The first three engenhos were built by the Adorno brothers and by the brothers Pero and Luís de Góes. Pero de Góes later became the donatary of São Tomé (Paraíba do Sul). See Alberto Lamego, "Onde foi iniciada no Brasil a lavoura canavieira?" *Brasil Açúcareiro* 5, no. 32 (July–Aug. 1948): 165–8.

62 On the Engenho São Jorge dos Erasmos, see Carl Laga, "O engenho dos Erasmos em São Vicente; resultado de pesquizas em arquivos belgas," *Estudos Históricos* 1 (1963): 14–43; Eddy Stols, "Um dos primeiros documentos sobre o engenho dos Schetz em São Vicente," *RH* 76 (1968): 407–20; Stols, "Os mercadores flamengos," 9–54.

63 See Maria Schorer Petrone, *A lavoura canavieira em São Paulo* (São Paulo, 1968).

64 Suely Robles Reis Queiroz, "Algumas notas sobre a lavoura do açúcar em São Paulo no período colonial," *AMP,* 21 (1967): 109–277, especially 109–28.

65 Serafim Leite, ed., *MB,* II, 292.

66 The Schetz ownership continued until the beginning of the seventeenth century but was quite secondary to their other interests. Eventually, the social status of the Schetzes changed when they assumed the title of Lord of Grobbendonk and Hoboken, a change in rank accompanied by a diminished interest in commerce. This, along with the difficulty of contact with Santos, led them to sell the engenho. See Hermann Kellenbenz, "Relações económicas entre Antuerpia e o Brasil no século xvii," *RH* 5, no. 37 (1968): 293–314.

67 A. Pereira da Costa, "Origens historicas da industria assucareira em Pernambuco," *Arquivos* (Recife, 1945–51), 257–329; Costa Porto, "Os primeiros cinco engenhos pernambucanos," *Revista do Museu do Açúcar* 2 (1969): 7–14; Magalhães, *O açúcar,* 60–5.

68 José António Gonçalves de Mello and Cleonir Xavier de Albuquerque, eds., *Cartas de Duarte Coelho a El Rei* (Recife, 1967), 29–33.

69 Ibid., 104, n. 2; Costa Porto, "Os primeiros," 7–14.

70 Gonçalves de Mello and Albuquerque, *Cartas de Duarte Coelho,* 114.

71 Mauro, *Portugal et l'Atlantique,* 193.

72 Duarte Coelho to Crown (Olinda, 15 April 1549), Gonçalves de Mello and Albuquerque, *Cartas de Duarte Coelho,* 71.

73 Flávio Guerra, *Evolução histórica de Pernambuco* (Recife, 1970), I, 148–9 (1 vol. to date). On the Lins family, see Carlos Xavier Paes Barreto, "A estirpe dos Lins," in *RIAHGP*

46 (1967): 209–16; and Henrique Oscar Wiedrspahn, "Dos Lins de Ulm e Augsburgo aos Lins de Pernambuco," *RIAHGP* 46 (1967): 7–98.

74 Engel Sluiter, "Os holandeses no Brasil antes de 1621," *RIAHGP* 46 (1967): 188–207.

75 Mauro, *Portugal et l'Atlantique*, pp. 192–6, discusses the figures and their sources.

76 Good summaries of the early history of Bahia can be found in Thales de Azevedo, *Povoamento da Cidade do Salvador*, 2d ed. (Bahia, 1969), 31–159; J. F. de Almeida Prado, *A Bahia e as capitanias do centro do Brasil* (1530–1626), 3 vols. (Rio de Janeiro, 1945–8), I, passim.

77 T. de Azevedo, *Povoamento*, 119–26.

78 Edward Haskins, "An Economic Geography of the Bahian Recôncavo" (Ph.D. thesis, University of Minnesota, 1956).

79 Pedro de Azevedo, "A instituição do Governo Geral," *HCPB*, III, 327–83; Varnhagen, *HGB*, I, 232–74. On the struggle of the crown against the donataries of Pernambuco, see Francis A. Dutra, "Centralization vs. Donatarial Privilege: Pernambuco, 1602–1630," in Dauril Alden, ed., *Colonial Roots of Modern Brazil* (Berkeley, 1973), 19–60.

80 The regimento has been printed in various places. See, e.g., *DHA*, I, 45–62. An easily accessible collection of regimentos is found in Marcos Carneiro de Mendonça, ed., *Raízes da formação administrativa do Brasil*, 2 vols. (Rio de Janeiro, 1972).

81 That these instructions were carried out is clear in the *sesmarias* (land grants) granted to Fernão Rodrigues de Castelobranco (n.d.), ANTT, CSJ, maço 14, doc. 59, and that given to D. Antônio de Athaide, count of Castanheira, to build an engenho on Itaparica island (27 April 1552). See APB, Sesmarias, 599.

82 Alvará of 20 July 1551 and an extension of 23 July 1554, granting five-year exemptions from the tithe to those who go to Brazil to rebuild or set up new engenhos. *DHA*, I, 111–13.

83 Regimento do Provedor mor da Fazenda (17 Dec. 1548), *DHA*, I, 63–72.

84 Alvará (5 Oct. 1555), *DHA*, I, 121–3. Gabriel Soares de Sousa reported that this mill was in operation in 1587, at which time the leasee paid 650 arrobas of white sugar a year for the rent. *Tratado*, 156. See also [José] Wanderley [Araújo] Pinho, *História de um engenho do Recôncavo* (Rio de Janeiro, 1946), 30–2.

85 Herbert Ewaldo Wetzel, *Mem de Sá: Terceiro Governador Geral* (Rio de Janeiro, 1972), 179–224. See also the classic accounts in Varnhagen, *HGB*, I, 299–348; Frei Vicente do Salvador, *Historia do Brasil*, 5th ed., with notes by Capistrano de Abreu, Rodolfo Garcia, and Frei Venâncio Willeke (São Paulo, 1965), 171–204.

86 Wanderley Pinho, *História*, 25–31, describes in some detail the conquests and land grants of Mem de Sá.

87 Mauro, *Portugal et l'Atlantique*, 193–5.

88 Pero de Góes to Martim Ferreira (18 Aug. 1545), *HCPB*, III, 262–3.

89 Stols, "Um documento," 418–20.

90 Ward J. Barrett and Stuart B. Schwartz, "Comparación entre dos economías azucareras coloniales: Morelos, México y Bahía, Brasil," in Enrique Florescano, ed., *Haciendas, latifundios, y plantaciones en América Latina* (Mexico City, 1975), 532–72. For a contemporaneous estimate of engenho production from the early seventeenth century, see Ambrósio Fernandes Brandão, *Diálogos das grandezas do Brasil*, José Antônio Gonçalves de Mello, ed., 2d complete ed. (Recife, 1966), 88. I have assumed throughout, in agreement with Gonçalves de Mello, that the author of this work is Ambrósio Fernandes Brandão.

91 Marchant, *From Barter to Slavery*, 61–5.

92 Costa Porto, "Os primeiros cinco engenhos," 7–14; Gonçalves de Mello and Albuquerque, *Cartas de Duarte Coelho*, 114, n. 56.

93 Gonçalves de Mello and Albuquerque, *Cartas de Duarte Coelho*, 104, n. 2.

94 *HCJB*, III, 262.

95 Stols, "Um dos primeiros," 418–20.

96 It appears that in the sixteenth century the term morador was sometimes used interchangeably with lavrador. Morador was also used to mean simply a resident. In the eighteenth-century lexicon of the rural Northeast, a morador was a part-time free laborer who lived on a fazenda or engenho and was quite distinct from the lavrador who grew cane.

97 Gonçalves de Mello and Albuquerque, *Cartas de Duarte Coelho*, 112, n. 42; *Arquivo Histórico da Madeira* 12 (1960–1): 93–5.

98 Antônio Pires to Brothers of the Company (Pernambuco, 2 Aug. 1551), Afranio Peixoto, ed., *Cartas Jesuítas. Cartas avulsas 1550–1568* (Rio de Janeiro, 1931), 83–4. (Further references to this collection are cited as *Cartas avulsas.*) See also Serafim Leite, ed., *Cartas dos primeiros Jesuítas do Brasil*, 3 vols. (Rome, 1956–8).

99 T. de Azevedo, *Povoamento*, 133–52; Marchant, *From Barter to Slavery*, 92.

100 Leite, *HCJB*, V, 110.

101 *DHA*, I, 111–13; Wanderley Pinho, *História*, 173–4.

102 ANTT, CSJ, maço 13, doc. 15.

103 Pero de Góes to Martim Ferreira (Vila da Rainha, 18 Aug. 1545), *HCPB*, III, 262–3.

104 References to Madeira appear with some frequency in this connection. Ambrósio de Meira wrote in 1545 that the sugar specialists had not yet learned the peculiarities of the land but that good sugar from Espirito Santo was, in their opinion, as good as that of Madeira. Individuals like Baltesar Martins Florença, a sugar master born in Madeira, also appear in the Inquisition records. See *ABNR* 57 (1939): 11–13; *PVCB*, 25–7.

105 Stols, "Um dos primeiros," 418; cf. Fernão Cardim, *Tratados de terra e gente do Brasil* (1583) (Rio de Janeiro, 1925), 283. There is a more recent edition of 1978.

106 Cardim, *Tratados de terra e gente*, 283.

107 Letter of 15 April 1549, Gonçalves de Mello and Albuquerque, *Cartas de Duarte Coelho*, 71.

Chapter 2. A wasted generation: commercial agriculture and Indian laborers

1 Large sections of this chapter and the one that follows appeared as "Indian Labor and New World Plantations: European Demands and Indian Responses in Northeastern Brazil," *AHR* 83, no. 3 (June 1978): 43–79.

2 Immanuel Wallerstein, *The Modern World System*, 2 vols. to date (New York, 1974), I, 86–90. His bibliography provides an excellent introduction to the historical and theoretical literature. Wallerstein has anticipated my criticism and similar observations made by Domenico Sella by stating that "the alternatives available to each unit are constrained by the framework of the whole even while each actor opting for a given alternative in fact alters the framework of the whole." Thus, the difference in our positions may be one of emphasis, although it is clear that, for him, the alternatives are still determined by the system and not by the actors. See his essay "The Three Stages of African Involvement in the World Economy," in Peter C. W. Gutkind and Immanuel Wallerstein, eds., *The Political Economy of Contemporary Africa* (London, 1976), 30. Also see Domenico Sella, "The World System and Its Dangers," *Peasant Studies* 6 (London, 1976): 29–32. For an important set of essays on these problems, see Carlos Sempat Assadourian et al., eds., *Modos de producción en América Latina*, vol. 40 of Cuadernos de Pasado y Presente (Buenos Aires, 1973).

3 See the survey presented in Estevão Pinto, *Os indígenas do Nordeste*, 2 vols. (São Paulo, 1935–8), I, 168–246; Carlos Ott, *Pre-história da Bahia* (Salvador, 1958), 11–33; Alfred Metraux, "The Tupinambá," in Julian Steward, ed., *Handbook of South American Indians*, 6 vols. (Washington, 1948), III, 95–135; Julio Cezar Melatti, *Indios do Brasil* (Brasilia, 1960). The best single sixteenth-century source on the indigenous peoples of Bahia is Soares de Sousa, *Tratado*, 299–341.

4 Florestan Fernandes, *Organização social dos Tupinambá*, 2d ed. (São Paulo, 1963), 149–308; Metraux, "Tupinambá," 119–26.

5 Florestan Fernandes, *A função social da guerra na sociedade Tupinambá*, 2d ed. (São Paulo, 1970).

6 Alfred Metraux, *La religion des Tupinambas* (Paris, 1928), 170–1. Metraux calls the Tupinambá an "agricultural people," but it is clear from his own work and that of Fernandes that agriculture was not a major ceremonial force in Tupinambá society. Cf. Fernandes, *Organização*, 82–98; Arthur Ramos, *Introdução à antropologia brasileira*, 2 vols. (Rio de Janeiro, 1943), I, 110–37.

7 Fernandes, *Organização*, 84–5. Trade was not entirely lacking. For an important theoretical essay, see Claude Levi-Strauss, "Guerra e comércio entre os índios de América do Sul," *Revista do Arquivo Municipal* (São Paulo) 87 (Dec. 1942): 131–46.

8 Manoel da Nóbrega, "Informação das terras do Brasil," *MB* (Bahia, 1549), I, 153.

9 These comments are based on Marshal Sahlins, *Stone Age Economics* (Chicago, 1972), 1–41. Although his analysis deals with stone-age peoples in general, it is directly applicable to the economics under discussion here, as will be clear from the contemporaneous observations.

10 Martim da Rocha (Sept. 1576) as quoted in *HCJB*, II, 90; Nóbrega, "Informação," 153; *MB*, II, 249 (1555). Observations like these are probably not entirely correct. Most Indian peoples recognized individual ownership of goods of production (bows, axes, etc.) but made collective use of goods of consumptions. See Melatti, *Indios do Brasil*, 68–9.

11 *DH*, 37–8, passim; Marchant, *From Barter to Slavery*, 87–95.

12 Diogo de Meneses to crown (1 Sept. 1610), ANTT, Fragmentos, caixa 1, n. 6.

13 "They are great friends of leisure (*folgar*)," Os Capitulos de Gabriel Soares de Sousa, *ABNR* 62 (1940): 373. This work, edited by Serâfim Leite, also appeared in *Ethnos* 2 (1941): 5–36.

14 Ott, *Pre-história*, 11–33.

15 Soares de Sousa, *Tratado*, 78–80.

16 Ott, *Pre-história*, 16. It is highly probable that Aimoré became like Tapuya a generalized term used to describe any hostile people in the central coastal region. The Gerens, the Cutacho, and others were all identified as Aimoré at various times.

17 Pero de Magalhães de Gandavo, *Histories of Brazil* (New York, 1922), 139–40; Gonçalo Soares da França, "Dissertações da historia eclesiastica," SGL (1724), ms. Reservados 1-C-147, 33–5, is an excellent example of eighteenth-century Portuguese attitudes toward the Aimoré.

18 The law of 1570 exempted "aquelles que custumam saltear os Portugueses ou a outros gentios para os comerem assim como são os que se chamâm Aymores e outros semelhantes" (those who are accustomed to attacking the Portuguese or other gentiles in order to eat them such as those called Aimoré and others like them), *DHA*, I, 225–6.

19 Alfred Metraux, "The Revolution of the Ax," *Diogenes* 25 (1959): 28–40.

20 Karl Polanyi, *Primitive, Archaic, and Modern Economies*, ed. George Dalton (New York, 1968), 3–37, provides a brief introduction to the vast literature on primitive economics. Also see George Dalton, ed., *Tribal and Peasant Economies* (New York, 1967). I have quite consciously taken a "substantivist" position in the continuing controversy over the nature of primitive economies because I feel the weight of evidence on precontact Indian cultures in Brazil does not indicate that social forms were produced out of or by the means or modes of production. When faced with a situation such as contact with Europeans, Indian societies were forced to adapt certain institutions to new economic purposes and were sometimes transformed in the process, but the divergence between Indian and European economic concepts remained great. Thus, even if the arguments of the formalists (who see all societies organized around general

economic principles) or of the neo-Marxists (who see the forms of social organization in primitive societies as responses to economic needs) have some validity, the continuing disparity between Indian and European economic concepts and forms still served as a major barrier to the integration of Indians into the colonial economy. For an interesting review of the literature on this controversy, see B. Marie Perinbaum, "Homo Africanus: Antiquus or Oeconomicus? Some Interpretations of African Economic History," *Comparative Studies in Society and History* 19 (1977): 156–78.

21 Sahlins, *Stone Age Economics*, 76.
22 Nóbrega, "Informação," *MB*, I, 153.
23 Gandavo, *Histories of Brazil*, 153.
24 I have reviewed this struggle in some detail in *Sovereignty and Society in Colonial Brazil* (Berkeley, 1973), especially ch. 4, "Judges, Jesuits, and Indians," 122–39. See also Dauril Alden, "Black Robes versus White Settlers: The Struggle for 'Freedom of the Indians' in Colonial Brazil," in Howard Peckham and Charles Gibson, eds., *Attitudes of Colonial Powers Toward the American Indian* (Salt Lake City, 1969), 19–46. The best study of Portuguese Indian policy is Georg Thomas, *Die portugiesische Indianerpolitik in Brasilien, 1500–1640* (Berlin, 1968).
25 Marchant, *From Barter to Slavery*, 63, 72.
26 Gandavo, *Histories of Brazil*, 132–3.
27 Marchant, *From Barter to Slavery*, 131, based on a number of contemporary sources.
28 Almeida Prado, *A Bahia*, II, 7–123, contains a survey of these actions. The expedition commanded by Mem de Sá, the War of the Paraguaçu, was caused to some extent by the fact that Indians in that region refused to return runaway slaves to the Portuguese. Cf. Letter of Padre Nóbrega (Bahia, 5 July 1559), in Serafim Leite, ed., *Cartas do Brasil e mais escritos do P. Manoel da Nóbrega* (Coimbra, 1955), 343. (Cited hereafter as *Cartas Nóbrega*.) Also cf. Wetzel, *Mem de Sá*, 59–68.
29 Leite, *HCJB*, II, 96, 194.
30 Serafim Leite, "Emformação dalgumas cousas do Brasil por Belchior Cordeiro, 1577," *Anais da Academia Portuguesa de História*, 2d series, 15 (1965): 187.
31 Ibid.
32 Leite, *Cartas Nóbrega* (Bahia, 5 July 1559), 346.
33 Leite, "Emformação," 187–8.
34 *PVCB*, 144–5.
35 Father Ruy Pereira to Brothers of the Company in Portugal (Bahia, 6 April 1561), *Cartas avulsas*, 283–4, recounts the hospitality with which he was received on engenhos in Ilhéus. Cf. Cardim, *Tratados da terra e gente*, 192–4. Jesuits were disliked on the fazendas because they asked whether the workers were free or slave. *HCJB*, II, 231.
36 Father Manoel da Nóbrega to D. João III (Olinda, 14 Sept. 1551), *Cartas Nóbrega*, 101.
37 *DHA*, II, 64, 350.
38 Edmundo Zenha, *Mamelucos* (São Paulo, 1970), 130–4; Alcântara Machado, *Vida e morte de um bandeirante*, 2d ed. (São Paulo, 1965), 163–81.
39 Leite, "Resoluções da Junta da Bahia sôbre as aldeas dos padres e os Indios," *MB*, IV, 354–7.
40 Marchant, *From Barter to Slavery*, 132–3.
41 Francisco Soares, *Coisas notáveis do Brasil* (Rio de Janeiro, 1966), 71.
42 Thales de Azevedo, "Catequese e aculturação," in *Ensaios de antropologia social* (Bahia, 1957?), 33–62. E.g., the following statement: "Como esta gente era rude y sin ninguna policia humana" (Since this people was simple and without any human order), in "Historia dos Collegios do Brasil," *ABNR* 19 (1897): 75–144.
43 Cardim, *Tratados da Terra e gente*, 280; cf. Letter of Father Antônio Pires (Pernambuco, 5 June 1552), *Cartas avulsas*, 124.
44 Letter of Inácio de Azevedo (Bahia, 19 Nov. 1566), Serafim Leite, *MB*, IV, 369–70.

45 Plans of some Jesuit aldeias are preserved in the AHU, secção de iconografia. The plan of the Vila de Abrantes in Bahia is reproduced in Nestor Goulart Reis Filho, *Evolução urbana do Brasil (1550–1720)* (São Paulo, 1968), fig. 23.

46 Claude Lévi-Strauss, *Tristes Tropiques* (New York, 1961), 203–5. His discussion deals with the intentional modification of a Bororo village by Silesian Fathers.

47 Nóbrega (Bahia, 8 May 1558), Leite, *Cartas Nóbrega*, 292.

48 Regimento of Tomé de Sousa, *DHA*, I, 53. See also the discussion in Marchant, *From Barter to Slavery*, 90–1. See the interesting theoretical discussion in Juan Carlos Garavaglia, "Un modo de producción subisdiário: la organización economica de las comunidades guaranizadas durante los siglos xvii–xviii en la formación regional altoperuanarioplatense," in *Modos de producción en América Latina* (Cordoba, 1973), 161–92.

49 Leite, *MB*, III, 530–1. On Mem de Sá's support of the Jesuits, see Wetzel, *Mem de Sá*, pp. 205, 215–17.

50 Alvará (21 Aug. 1587), *DHA*, I, 321–2.

51 Shepard Forman and Joyce Riegelhaupt, "Bodo was Never Brazilian: Economic Integration and Rural Development Among a Contemporary Peasantry," *Comparative Studies in Society and History* 12 (1970): 188–212.

52 Soares, *Coisas notáveis*, 77. The wages paid to a boatman in 1574 at Engenho Sergipe were 16$500, or an average of 1$365 per month. See Mircea Buescu, *300 anos da inflação* (Rio de Janeiro, 1973), 60–1.

53 Moradores of Bahia asked in 1561 that the probate judge "desse a soldada os moços e moças orfans e outros pedião os casados" (give them at wages young orphan boys and girls, and others asked for married couples). Padre Luís de Grã to Padre Miguel de Torres (Bahia, 22 Sept. 1561), in Leite, *MB*, III, 431. On Indian workers at Engenho Sergipe, see Paul Silberstein, "Wage Earners in a Slave Economy: The Laborers of a Sugar Mill in Colonial Brazil" (unpublished paper, 1970).

54 *DHA*, I, 404–5.

55 Ibid.

56 Marvin Harris, *Patterns of Race in the Americas* (New York, 1964), 20–1. Harris follows the argument of John Phelan that Amerindians "took to earning a living European fashion when adequately compensated." It should be remembered, however, that Phelan is referring to highland peoples already integrated into larger state structures before the arrival of the Europeans.

57 A brief but accurate account of the plague is found in Fernandes, *Organização*, 40–1.

58 *Cartas avulsas*, 207–8.

59 Leonardo do Valle to Brothers of the Company (Bahia, 23 Sept. 1561), *Cartas avulsas*, 334.

60 Leonardo do Valle to Gonçalo Vaz (Bahia, 12 May 1563), *Cartas avulsas*, 378–93.

61 Fernandes, *Organização*, 40; "Historia dos Collegios do Brasil," *ABNR* 19 (1897): 84, places the plague in 1563–4.

62 Cited in Fernandes, *Organização*, 40.

63 Gandavo, *Histories of Brazil*, 229. A similar situation occurred in Pernambuco in 1583–4, when a famine in the sertão drove 3,000–4,000 Amerindians onto the coastal plantations.

64 The susceptibility of Indians to European disease continued. In 1565, so many died in the Jesuit aldeia of São João in Espirito Santo that the site had to be abandoned (*MB*, IV, 267–8). In 1616–17, Indian and African slaves were decimated by smallpox. See Brandão, *Diálogos das Grandezas do Brasil*, 64. The impact of disease on Indians in the aldeias was not lost on the colonists. In 1610, the câmara of Paraíba argued against the aldeias for exactly this reason. ANTT, Corp. cron., part 1, maço 115, n. 108.

65 Leite, *HCJB*, II, 182–3; T. de Azevedo, *Povoamento*, 81.

66 Vicente do Salvador, *História do Brasil* (Saõ Paulo, 1965), liv. iv, cap. 35, 333. See also the account in Robert Southey, *History of Brasil*, 2 vols. (London, 1810), I, 404–5.

67 Ibid. Some Potiguares under the chieftainship of Zorobabé eventually returned to Pernambuco, where they were used against escaped African slaves.

68 Câmara of São Jorge to count of Linhares (30 July 1601), ANTT, *CSJ*, maço 8, n. 108. Also, BA, 51-VIII-48, f. 139–139v.

69 Letter of 16 March 1603, ANTT, CSJ, maço, n. 125.

70 Letter (Bahia, 28 Aug. 1585), ANTT, CSJ, maço 8, n. 9.

71 Provisão to count of Linhares (1586), ANTT, CSJ, maço 16. The duke of Aveiro, donatary of Porto Seguro, received a similar grant to "descer índios para duas veces somente" (to bring in Indians on only two occasions). AGS, sec. prov., 1487 (Vallado-lid, 7 Oct. 1603), f. 33–33v.

72 *DHA*, I, 321–2.

73 For Diogo de Meneses's very strong support of the colonists, see his correspondence in *ABNR* 57 (1939): 37–40. He even turned some aldeias over to the planters. The crown ordered his successor, Gaspar de Sousa, to prohibit such actions under any circumstances. See BI, Correspondência Gaspar de Sousa, king to Gaspar de Sousa (Lisbon, 28 March 1613), f. 207.

74 "Historia dos collegios do Brazil," *ABNR* 19 (1897): 89.

75 Pedro Correia to Brothers in Africa (São Vicente, 1551), in *Cartas avulsas*, 97–8. Cf. Alfred Metraux, *Religions et magies indiennes d'Amerique du sud* (Paris, 1967), 12–23.

76 This paragraph is based on two letters by Nóbrega and that of Pedro Correia cited above. See *Cartas avulsas*, 97–8; Leite, *Cartas Nóbrega*, 70–71, 297–8. Also used were Southey, *History of Brazil*, I, 371–3; F. A. Pereira da Costa, *Anais pernambucanos*, 7 vols. (Recife 1951), I, 572.

77 The letters of Nóbrega give the details. The letter of Father Leonardo do Valle, the great Jesuit linguist, to Father Gonçalo Vaz (Bahia, 12 May 1563) also contains inter-esting details of the Indian sorcerer who claimed to be a "prophet from the sky." *Cartas avulsas*, 378–93.

78 The confession of Fernão Cabral de Atayde is most revealing since he was an eye-witness to the rites of santidade. He had brought this group of santidade followers to his estate probably in an attempt to secure occasional laborers. See *PVCB*, 28–9.

79 *Cartas avulsas*, 378–93. Leite, *MB*, IV, 9.

80 José Calasans, *A santidade de Jaguaripe* (Bahia, 1952), is the most complete study to date. It does not include the seventeenth-century materials presented here.

81 Pereira da Costa, *Anais pernambucanos*, I, 572. This is about the same date that Fernão Cabral de Atayde turned over the santidade leaders on his fazenda to the authorities. Perhaps these are two variant accounts of the same event.

82 Regimento of Francisco Giraldes, *DHA*, I, 360. Giraldes never served in Brazil. His ship was turned back by rough weather, and he never returned.

83 Diogo de Meneses to crown (Bahia, 1 Sept. 1610), ANTT, Fragmentos, caixa 1, n. 6.

84 King to Gaspar de Sousa (Lisbon, 19 Jan. 1613), BI, Correspondência de Gaspar de Sousa, 185–185v.

85 Ibid. (Lisbon, 24 May 1613), 218–218v.

86 Provisão de Diogo Luís de Oliveira, ACS, Provisões e portarias 1624–42, Livro 155, fs. 24v–26.

Chapter 3. First slavery: from Indian to African

1 Historians of sixteenth-century Brazil depended to a large extent on Jesuit letters and reports and on governmental correspondence and legislation. The account books of engenhos Sergipe do Conde and Santana from 1572–4, 1591, and 1638, along with other supporting documentation, are, for that reason, particularly valuable. These materials reveal a great deal about the labor force in that period. Moreover, the chapel of Engenho Sergipe served as the parish church, and its fragmentary register that

survives for the period 1595–1626 is another valuable source on various social relationships. These materials, limited as they admittedly are, at least provide a glimpse of life on the Bahian engenhos in their early, formative period. Engenhos Sergipe and Santana were originally built by Governor Mem de Sá and later became the property of the Jesuits. See Appendix A for a history of these two estates.

2 The term negro de terra seems to have persisted in São Paulo well into the seventeenth century. In Bahia, although it was occasionally employed in the period after 1600, it was gradually replaced. Cf. Zenha, *Mamelucos*, 52–72 passim.

3 The inventories of engenhos Sergipe and Santana made between 1572 and 1574 are printed, along with the will and testament of Mem de Sá and other relevant materials, in *DHA*, III; Inventário Engenho Sergipe (1572), *DHA*, III, 65; Livro de contas do procurador (1574), *DHA*, III, 406.

4 ANTT, CSJ, maço 15, doc. 9.

5 Ibid.

6 *Feitor* (overseer) of Engenho Santana to count of Linhares (15 Aug. 1599), ANTT, CSJ, maço 8, doc. 105. The feitor called them "gentio do sertão tapuyas do catingua" (gentiles of the backlands, savages of the forest).

7 Domingos Fernandes da Cunha to count of Linhares (Ilhéus, 16 March 1603), ANTT, CSJ, maço 8, doc. 125. Fernandes da Cunha was sent by the count of Linhares to rebuild Engenho Santana sometime in 1601. It was he who in concert with Alvaro de Carvalho brought in the Potiguares, and at one point he went to the Recôncavo to bring settled Indians back to Ilhéus. See ANTT, CSJ, maço 8, doc. 108.

8 Biblioteca Nazionale di Roma, Fondo Gesuitico 1367, "O que pareceo ao Padre Visitador Cristóvão de Gouvea ordernar na visita deste Collegio da Bahia (1 Jan. 1589).

9 Bahia (1 March 1589), ANTT, CSJ, maço 8, doc. 136.

10 *PVCB*, 1591–2, J. Capistrano de Abreu, ed. (Rio de Janeiro, 1935). Although Indians did not come in to make depositions, except in one instance, many who appeared before the inquisitors spoke of their relations with Indians, of the aldeias, of *entradas* (expeditions) to the sertão to bring more Indians down to the coast, and of considerable interaction. A number of mestiços also admitted to practicing Indian customs and speaking Indian languages. See, e.g., 34, 36–7, 64–5, 93–5, 96–7, 104–5, 123–4, 164–5, 167–72.

11 Sebastião Vaz to Diogo Cardim, provincial of the College of Santo Antão (Bahia, 5 June 1629), ANTT, CSJ, maço 69, doc. 74. This letter is most revealing of the history of the Indians in the village near Sergipe do Conde. They had been brought in at great expense by the count of Linhares, but by the time his wife and heir had died there were few left. When the Jesuits had assumed control of the engenho, these Indians were incorporated with those of the Jesuit aldeia called São Sebastião located nearby. When, however, the village was moved elsewhere, the engenho Indians went along. This situation moved Vaz to petition for their return.

12 Safra 1611–12, ANTT, CSJ, maço 14, doc. 4, 24. The *dizimos* (tithe) for the aldeia was 10$400 for 2 years.

13 *DHA*, III, 406, 102.

14 *DHA*, III, 298, 311.

15 *DHA*, III, 92.

16 *DHA*, III, 392–4.

17 *PVCB*, 1591–2, 87, 104–5, 167–72. See also the petition of Luís de Aguiar, AGS, *Guerra antigua*, legajo 906.

18 Carijó was the name sometimes given to the Guaraní of Paraguay and southern Brazil. The Tamoio inhabited the area near Rio de Janeiro, whereas the Cayté had lived near the mouth of the São Francisco River. A war of extermination and enslavement had been declared against them for killing the first bishop of Brazil and eating him. The presence of Carijó and Tamoio at Engenhos Sergipe and Santana may have

been atypical. Mem de Sá's expeditions in the south probably gave him access to the Indians of that area that other planters in Bahia did not have. Moreover, his son, Estácio de Sá, had left a group of slaves on these estates that were the result of his exploits in the Rio de Janeiro area.

19 The chapel register of Engenho Sergipe was mistakenly bound together with materials from another parish. It is presently located in the ACMS, Conceição da Praia, Baptismos 1649–76. It will be cited hereafter as chapel register 1595–1628.

20 Alfredo Ellis Júnior, "O bandeirismo na economia do século xvii," in *Curso de bandeirologia* (São Paulo, 1956), 55–76. For the opposite opinion, see Zenha, *Mamelucos*, 193–6.

21 *DHA*, III, 58.

22 Fernandes, *Organização*, 64–74.

23 Stols, "Um dos primeiros," 407–20.

24 *DHA*, III, 348–9.

25 These figures are my calculations based on the census of Pernambuco (1774) in *ABNR*, 40 (1918), 21–111. Undoubtedly, they reflect underreporting of infant mortality. For the nineteenth century, see Peter Eisenberg, *The Sugar Industry of Pernambuco* (Berkeley, 1974), 148–51; Brainbridge Cowell, "Cityward Migration in the Nineteenth Century: The Case of Recife, Brazil," *Journal of Interamerican Studies and World Affairs* 17, no. 1 (Feb. 1975): 43–63.

26 BNL, Fundo geral, Codice 6936.

27 Michael Craton, *Sinews of Empire* (New York, 1974), 194–5.

28 *DHA*, III, 348–9.

29 Ibid., 93.

30 Inventory of 1591, ANTT, CSJ, maço 13, n. 4.

31 The chapel register is presently located in the Arquivo da Curia Metropolitana of Salvador. It is bound and erroneously titled Book I of Conceição da Praia. I consulted it in 1968 and realized that it was mislabeled, but not until David Smith called it to my attention again in 1973 did I realize what it was. The chapel, dedicated to Nossa Senhora da Purificação, served as the parish church for the region until a new parish church was erected in Santo Amaro in 1722. The register contains information, therefore, about the population of the whole surrounding parish and not solely Engenho Sergipe. Unfortunately, there are also drawbacks that limit the utility of the register for historical analysis. First, its present physical state is poor. Many entries are illegible because pieces of the pages are missing, and, in fact, most of the pages covering the sixteenth century have been lost, as have most of the marriage entries. There are also problems created by imprecision in registry. The term negro was used to describe both Indians and Afro-Brazilians; thus it is impossible to distinguish between them on this basis alone. Whites were never identified as such in the chapel register, and thus when an individual has both Christian name and family name and no other ethnic or color designation, I have assumed him or her to be white. This method probably results in a slight inflation of the white category at the expense of mulattoes and mestiços, but since my major concern here is with Indians and Africans this is not a serious distortion. Also, many individuals are simply described as *escravo* (slave) with no more specific identification as to color or origin. These problems complicate any analysis, and therefore the results presented here are tentative at best.

32 Slave marriages at Engenho Sergipe, 1601–26, were as follows: Indian–Indian, 6; same nation–African, 7; mixed nation–African, 6; crioulo–crioulo, 1; unidentified origins, 9.

33 Inventory, Engenho Sergipe, 1591.

34 This pattern continued throughout the colonial period in Bahia. In the parish of Inhambupe between 1750 and 1800, 80 percent of the 1,294 registered marriages were between couples of the same racial category. See Consuelo Pondé de Sena, "Relações

interétnicas através de casamentos realizados na freguesia do Inhambupe, na segunda metade do século xviii" (unpublished paper, Salvador, 1974).

35 Cristóvão de Bulhões, who appeared before the Inquisition in 1591, called himelf a mameluco despite the fact that this father was not a Portuguese but a mulatto. See *PVCB*, 104–5.

36 Chapel register, Engenho Sergipe, 1595–1628, f. 75v.

37 Inventory, Engenho Sergipe, 1572–4, *DHA*, III, 65; see the discussion in Stuart B. Schwartz, "The Mocambo: Slave Resistance in Colonial Bahia," *Journal of Social History* 3, no. 4 (summer 1970): 318–19.

38 Cf. Sergio Buarque de Holanda, *Caminhos e fronteiras* (Rio de Janeiro, 1957), 15–180.

39 Confessions of Rodrigo Martins, Paulo Adorno, Cristóvão de Bulhões, *PVCB*, 94–5, 104–5, 164–5.

40 Ibid., 96–8. The confession of João Gonçalves, a tailor from Ilhéus, is interesting because it reveals a number of mameluco artisans like himself who also went in search of Indians.

41 Ibid., 79–87.

42 Ibid., 64–5.

43 Ibid., 167–72. The deposition of Tomacauna, described in the next paragraph, on the santidade cult is the most complete eyewitness account that remains in the historical record. He and other mamelucos with him all claimed that they practiced the rites to deceive the Indians and that Christ never left their hearts. The fact that these statements were made during the proceedings of the Inquisition makes their claims somewhat suspect.

44 Mauro, *Portugal et l'Atlantique*, 192–4. The Jesuits of Bahia asked for two dozen Africans in 1558, "and these can come together with those the King may send to the [Royal] engenho because often he sends ships here loaded with them." Leite, *Cartas Nóbrega* (Bahia, 8 May 1558), 288.

45 Pereira da Costa, *Anais pernambucanos*, I, 455.

46 Inventário de Mem de Sá in *DHA*, III, 1–22, 73–6. Engenho Santana had the same distribution, with 7 Africans in a slave force of 107, or 6.5 percent; ANTT, CSJ, maço 13, n. 4; "Treslado do inventário do Engenho Sergipe," ANTT, CSJ, maço 30, f. 1040.

47 Stols, "Um dos primeiros," 418–20.

48 The Portuguese slave trade in the sixteenth century was concentrated in the Senegambia. On the cultural and agricultural traditions of the peoples in that region, see Phillip D. Curtin, *Economic Change in Precolonial Africa: Senegambia in the Era of the Slave Trade*, 2 vols. (Madison, Wis., 1975), I, 3–58; and Walter Rodney, *A History of the Upper Guinea Coast, 1545–1800* (Oxford, 1970), 1–38.

49 Paul Silberstein, "Wage Earners in a Slave Economy," BNM, Codice 2436, fs. 105–9.

50 See Antonio Garcia, "Regimenes indigenas de salariado: El salariado natural y el salariado capitalista en la historia de América," *América Indigena* 8 (1948): 250–87.

51 Silberstein, "Wage Earners," based on *DHA*, II, passim; and Leite, *HCJB*, II, 63. Also see Adrien van der Dussen, *Relatório sobre as capitanias conquistados no Brasil pelos holandeses*, ed. José Antônio Gonçalves de Mello (Rio de Janeiro, 1947), 88–9.

52 Almon Wheeler Lauber, *Indian Slavery in Colonial Times within the Present Limits of the United States*, Columbia University Studies in History (New York, 1913), 298–300, presents scattered references to relative prices from New England, New York, and the Carolinas. Verner Crane, *The Southern Frontier, 1670–1732*, (Ann Arbor, Mich., 1929), 113–15, provides data showing that Indians were valued at one-half to one-third the price of black slaves. Peter H. Wood, *Black Majority* (New York, 1974), 38–40, reviews the literature on Indian slavery in Carolina but is silent on this point. Instead see John Donald Duncan, "Servitude and Slavery in Colonial South Carolina, 1670–1776," 2 vols. (Ph.D. thesis, Emory University, 1972). On French Canada, see Marcel Trudel, *L'esclavage au Canada Français: Histoire et condition de l'esclavage* (Quebec, 1960); and Guy

Fregault, *La civilisation de la Nouvelle-France* (Montreal, 1944), 83–4. Colin Palmer, *Slaves of the White God: Blacks in Mexico, 1570–1650* (Cambridge, Mass., 1976), 34, provides considerable evidence from the 1520s in Mexico, as does Silvio Zavala, *Los indios esclavos en Nueva España* (Mexico City, 1968). Most important is Gonzalo Aguirre Beltrán, "El trabajo del indio comparado con el del negro en Nueva España," *México Agrario* 4 (1942): 203–7.

53 As quoted in Duncan, "Servitude and Slavery in Colonial South Carolina, 1670–1776," 36. For the traditional racist arguments of the nineteenth century, see Herman Merivale, *Lectures on Colonialism and Colonies* [1861] (London, 1967), 283.

54 Gabriel Soares de Sousa's account of 1587 lists 36 engenhos for Bahia, but he also speaks of 8 *casas de melles* (molasses-producing units). He gives an annual production of 120,000 arrobas for the captaincy, or somewhat less than 4,000 arrobas per mill. Fernão Cardim also speaks of 36 engenhos in Bahia, but José de Anchieta lists 46. I have taken Father Soares's figure of 50 – because it yields the lowest ratio of slaves to engenhos – as a control on my argument that the ratio is extraordinarily high. Using the estimates of Soares de Sousa or Cardim yields over 333 slaves for each mill; see Mauro, *Le Portugal et l'Atlantique*, 193; and Mauricio Goulart, *Escravidão africana no Brasil* (São Paulo, 1950), 100.

55 Soares, *Coisas notáveis*, 11.

56 See Barrett and Schwartz, "Comparación entre dos economías azucareras coloniales," 550–5. Also see Ward Barrett, *The Sugar Hacienda of the Marqueses del Valle* (Minneapolis, 1970), 98–9.

57 Gandavo, *Histories of Brazil*, 153.

58 M. Goulart, *Escravidão africana no Brasil*, 100.

59 Buescu, *300 anos da inflação*, 44–5.

60 Sebastião da Rocha Pitta, *História da America portugueza*, 2d ed. (Lisbon 1880), 196–7.

61 Gaspar da Cunha to the count of Linhares (Bahia, 28 Aug. 1585), ANTT, CSJ, maço 8, no. 9. For a similar opinion, see Martim Leitão's *Parecer*, in which he valued 1 Indian equal to 4 Guiné slaves. BA, 44-XIV-6, fs. 185–93v.

62 These requests reappeared from time to time. It was suggested in 1653 that the Tapuyas of Maranhão could be used to develop sugar engenhos in that captaincy, thereby "advancing [them] by removing them from the misery in which they live and teaching them in this way to get along by agriculture." Duarte Ribeiro de Macedo to a friend (Paris, 20 Jan. 1653), LC/Port. Mss. P-271.

Chapter 4. The Recôncavo

1 Maria Graham, *Journal of a Voyage to Brazil and Residence There* (London, 1824).

2 "Relação dos navios de diferentes qualidades que ha na capitania da Bahia," IHGB, Arq. 1.1.19 (1775).

3 Schwartz, *Sovereignty and Society*, 201–2; José Honório Rodrigues, *Historiografia del Brasil siglo xvi* (Mexico, 1957), 70–4.

4 The best succinct geographical description of the Recôncavo is found in Katia M. Queiros Mattoso, *Bahia: A cidade do Salvador e seu mercado* (São Paulo, 1978), 5–60. See also Edward C. Haskins, "An Agricultural Geography of the Recôncavo of Bahia," (Ph.D. thesis, University of Minnesota, 1956).

5 Diogo de Campos Moreno, *Livro que da razão do estado do Brasil*, facsimile ed. (Rio de Janeiro, 1968), 39.

6 On colonial Salvador, the essential monographs are Mattoso, *Bahia*, and T. de Azevedo, *Povoamento*.

7 Mesa de Inspeção to crown, 8 Oct. 1810, ANRJ, caixa 416.

8 William Dampier, *A Voyage to New Holland, etc., in the Year 1699*, 3 vols., 2d ed. (London, 1709), II, 379.

9 Soares de Sousa, *Tratado*, 132; José Pinheiro da Silva, "A capitania da Bahia," *Revista Portuguesa de História* 8 (1959): 71–2. For the 1724 figures, see Table 5-1.

10 Padre Gonçalo Soares da França, "Dissertações da história ecclesiastica do Brasil," SGL, Res. 43-C-147, fs. 87–123.

11 Soares da Sousa, *Tratado*, 102.

12 AHU, Bahia pap. avul., caixa 41, 1st ser., uncat.

13 AHU, Bahia pap. avul., caixa 70, 1st ser., uncat. (1792). A later document of 1808 estimated that the free population of the captaincy was 156,199 and that it was divided into 66 parishes – 23 in Salvador and its suburbs, 26 in the Recôncavo, and the remainder in the interior. This account did not include the 15 parishes of Sergipe de El-Rey or those of Ilhéus and the southern towns. See "Mappa geral das 4 divisoes eleitoraes," AHU, Bahia pap. avul., caixa 100, 1st ser., uncat.

14 AHU, Bahia pap. avul., caixa 46 (19 Aug. 1732).

15 Soares da França, "Dissertações ecclesiastica."

16 APB, Cartas ao Governo 216 (12 July 1809).

17 APB, Ord. reg. 55, f. 248.

18 Soares de Sousa, *Tratado*, caps. xix–xxxi.

19 Soares de Sousa speaks of 120,000 arrobas plus various *conservas* (sweets). The account actually names or identifies 44 mills; four of these are not in the Recôncavo, but further south along the coast. A map giving approximate locations and listing the owners can be found in Diego Gonzalo Rivero, "Brazil: The Crucial Years 1570–1612" (Ph.D. thesis, University of Georgia, 1981), 181–2.

20 Pedro Tomas Pedreira, "As terras de Acupe, Itapema, e Saubara," *MAN* 7, no. 4 (April 1976): 22–3.

21 On Fernão Cabral de Ataide, see Sonia A. Siqueira, "A elaboração de espiritualidade do Brasil colônia: o problema de sincretismo," *AMP* 36 (1975): 211–28; José Calazans, *A santidade de Jaguaripe* (Bahia, 1952).

22 Southey, *History of Brazil*, I, 339.

23 Schwartz, *Sovereignty and Society*, 158–9, and the sources cited therein. Some ginger was produced thereafter. See José Roberto do Amaral Lapa, "O problema das drogas orientais," *Economia colonial* (São Paulo, 1973), 111–40.

24 Conde de Óbidos to Paulo Mirandes Garro, 24 April 1665, BNRJ, 8, 1, 3, f. 44–44v.

25 APB, Ord. reg. 1, n. 45 (Lisbon, 26 March 1688); n. 91 (Lisbon, 27 Nov. 1690).

26 The best description of the tobacco-growing region of Cachoeira is found in Rae Jean Flory, "Bahian Society in the Mid-Colonial Period: The Sugar Planters, Tobacco Growers, Merchants, and Artisans of Salvador and the Recôncavo, 1680–1725" (Ph.D. thesis, University of Texas, 1978). Also useful is Catherine Lugar, "The Portuguese Tobacco Trade and Tobacco Growers of Bahia in the Late Colonial Period," in Dauril Alden and Warren Dean, eds., *Essays Concerning the Socioeconomic History of Brazil and Portuguese India* (Gainesville, Fla., 1977), 26–70.

27 Report of Belchior da Cunha Brochado (Lisbon, 7 Dec. 1697), ANTT, Junta do Tabaco, maço 96.

28 See Figure 7-3.

29 ANTT, Junta do Tobaco, maço 97A.

30 See Chapter 1, section titled "Brazilian beginnings."

31 "Carta de S. Mg^e em que ordena o avisarem do numero de engenhos que ha no recôncavo desta cidade de Bahia," BNRJ, 7, 3, 53, n. 327; report of Sebastião Sampaio, AHU, Bahia pap. avul., caixa 12.

32 ABNR 31 (1909): 130–1. The best summary of eighteenth-century population lists for Bahia is contained in T. Azevedo, *Povoamento*, 181–201. Portuguese lists submitted in religious censuses made a distinction between those *de confissão* (above the age of 7) and those *de comunhão* (over 9 years of age). I have inflated the reported figure by 12 percent to provide a rough estimate of the total population.

33 Cited in Susan Soeiro, "A Baroque Nunnery: The Economic and Social Role of a Colonial Convent–Santa Clara do Desterro, Salvador, Bahia, 1677–1800" (Ph.D. thesis, New York University, 1974), 58.

34 Letter of archbishop of Bahia (Salvador, 25 Jan. 1733) to Conselho Ultramarino, AHU, Bahia pap. avul., caixa 48, 1st ser., uncat. The letter reported that the original order had been dated 6 Nov. 1726 and that the census was included with this response. It is now lost.

35 Soares da França, "Dissertações ecclesiasticas," fs. 87–123.

36 T. de Azevedo, *Povoamento*, 181–200. Also Mattoso, *Bahia*, 130–5.

37 Azevedo reports that the 1759 census counted 62,833 for the Recôncavo and a total population of 250,142, but in the set of instructions issued by Martinho Mello e Castro to the new governor of Bahia (Queluz, 10 Sep. 1779), the 1759 population of the captaincy was recorded thus:

Salvador	6,782	40,263
Recôncavo	8,315	72,833
South	3,782	24,982
Sertão de Baixo	4,893	38,514
Sertão de Cima	4,870	38,550
Totals	28,612	215,142

See AHU, Bahia pap. avul., caixa 364; Dauril Alden, "The Population of Brazil in the Late Eighteenth Century: A Preliminary Survey," *HAHR* 43, no. 2 (May 1963): 173–205, demonstrates that the population under age 7 averaged 11.75 percent in Brazilian captaincies other than Bahia.

38 The 1757 parish figures are found in ABNR 31 (1909): 178–234. I have adjusted them by 12% when necessary to include children under 7, clerics, and Indians. The figures for 1780 did not include the suburban parishes, and I have adjusted them to do so by using the per annum growth rate of neighboring Santo Amaro and São Francisco and applying it to the figure reported for the suburban parishes in 1774. The 1780 census reported births and deaths in each township. These indicate a natural rate of increase in the Recôncavo of 1.0% a year, but the growth rate indicated by the total figures for 1774 and 1780 is 3.3%. There was surely underrecording of births and deaths, but it is probably safe to assume that at least half the annual growth rate in the period was due to inmigration, primarily of slaves.

39 On the Benedictines, see ADB/CSB 136 Estado 1700–3. On the Jesuit holdings, see ARSI, Brasi 6 (1), f. 62.

40 Capoame is discussed in *AAPB* 26 (1945): 46. See, too, AHU, Bahia pap. avul., caixa 46, 1st ser., uncat. (23 July 1723). Rollie Poppino, "The Cattle Industry in Colonial Brazil," *Mid-America* 31, no. 4 (Oct. 1949): 219–47, presents the best short summary of the topic. See also Rollie Poppino, *Feira de Santana* (Bahia, 1968); Consuelo Ponde de Sena, *Introdução ao estudo de uma comunidade do agreste bahiano* (Salvador, 1979).

41 "Mapa que trouxe a frota da Bahia" (1735), NL/GC, ms. 344.

42 King to governor of Bahia, 24 April 1727, APB, Ord. reg. 21, n. 35.

43 Dauril Alden, "Commodity Price Movements in Brazil Before, During and After the Gold Boom, 1670–1769, the Salvador Market" (unpublished paper), 6–7.

44 T. de Azevedo, *Povoamento*, 318–340; Mattoso, *Bahia*, 256.

45 Cf. Flory, "Bahian Society," 26–7; Richard Dunn, *Sugar and Slaves* (Chapel Hill, N.C., 1972), 203. I have included a table with various production estimates in my essay Schwartz, "Colonial Brazil, c. 1580–c. 1750: Plantations and Peripheries," in *CHLA*, II, 431.

46 Wanderley Pinho, *História*, 13–23.

47 Harry William Hutchinson, *Village and Plantation Life in Northeastern Brazil* (Seattle, 1957), 25–46.

48 "Lista das informações," *ABNR* 31 (1909): 201–5.
49 Stuart B. Schwartz, "Patterns of Slaveholding in the Americas: New Evidence from Brazil," *AHR* 87, no. 1 (Feb. 1982): 74.
50 Varnhagen, *HGB*, II, 29–68.
51 APB, Cartas ao Governo, 188.
52 Luís dos Santos Vilhena, *A Bahia no século xvii*, 3 vols. (Bahia, 1969), II, 569–72. The work was originally entitled "Noticias soteropolitanas e brasilicas."
53 Our knowledge of the population size and configuration in Sergipe de El-Rey are due to the research of Luiz R. B. Mott. See especially "Brancos, Pardos, Pretos e Indios em Sergipe, 1825–1830," *Anais de História* 6 (1974): 139–84; "Pardos e pretos em Sergipe, 1774–1851," *RIEB* 18 (1976): 7–37.
54 This calculation is made by comparing the census of 1757 contained in *ABNR* 31 (1909): 178–234, and the census of slaveowners in the Recôncavo of 1817 contained in APB, Cartas ao Governo, maços 232–4.
55 On Engenho Jacarancanga, consult Soares de Sousa, *Tratado*, cap. xxiii, 149–50; Schwartz, *Sovereignty and Society*, 333–4; Santos Vilhena, *A Bahia*, I, between 44 and 45.
56 Wanderley Pinho, *História*, on Engenho Freguesia.
57 F. W. O. Morton, "The Conservative Revolution of Independence: Economy, Society and Politics in Bahia, 1790–1840" (Ph.D. thesis, Oxford University, 1974), 16.
58 Stuart B. Schwartz, "The Plantations of St. Benedict: The Benedictine Sugar Mills of Colonial Brazil," *The Americas* 39, no. 1 (July 1982): 1–22.
59 Dauril Alden, "Sugar Planters by Necessity, Not Choice: The Role of the Jesuits in the Cane Sugar Industry of Colonial Brazil, 1601–1759," in Jeffrey A. Cole, ed., *The Church and Society in Latin America* (New Orleans, 1984), 139–70.
60 Morton, "Conservative Revolution," 14–16.
61 Ibid.

Chapter 5. Safra: the ways of sugar making

1 The most complete modern description of sugar making in colonial America is contained in Barrett, *Sugar Hacienda of the Marqueses del Valle;* see also his discussion of sources in "Caribbean Sugar-Production Standards in the Seventeenth and Eighteenth Centuries," in John Parker, ed., *Merchants and Scholars* (Minneapolis, 1965), 147–70. See also Ward J. Barrett, *The Efficient Plantation and the Inefficient Hacienda* (James Ford Bell Lecture No. 16; Minneapolis, 1979).
2 André João Antonil, *Cultura e opulência por suas drogas e minas*, ed. Andrée Mansuy (Paris, 1965), liv. 1, cap. 9. There are a number of modern versions, of which this fully annotated one is the best. I have made all references to it but have used citations to book (livro) and chapter (capítulo). See also Henry Koster, *Travels in Brazil*, 2 vols. (Philadelphia, 1817), I, 330–1. Antonil clearly indicates that the ceremony of blessing the mill was commonly practiced in Bahia. Koster, writing about Pernambuco at a later date, provides the details. Gilberto Freyre, *The Masters and the Slaves* (New York, 1956), 436, makes some interesting observations based on a nineteenth-century sermon preached at the blessing of a mill. See Lino do Monte Carmelo Luna, *A benção do Engenho Macauassu* (Recife, 1869).
3 Koster, *Travels*, II, 119. Other travelers made the same observation about the drowsiness of engenho slaves. See the remarks cited by Antônio Barros de Castro, "Escravos e senhores nos engenhos do Brasil," (Ph.d. thesis, State University of Campinas, 1976), 11–14.
4 The description of a mill's working day comes from the memorial of Joseph Israel de Costa, who lived in Bahia and later (ca. 1636) wrote a report for the Dutch West India Company. He provided many interesting insights and details about the Brazilian

sugar industry. The statistical part of his report has been printed by José Antônio Gonçalves de Mello, "Uma relação dos engenhos de Pernambuco em 1623," *Revista do Museu de Açúcar*, 1, 25–37, but for the text of the memorial the reader must consult Algemein Rijksarchief (Hague) Staten Generaal, West Indische Compagnie loketkas 6. Fernão Cardim, in *Tratados da terra e gente*, writing about 1584, stated the workday of the mill began about midnight and continued until 3 or 4 p.m. the following day. Although the timing is different, the length of the day is about the same. At Engenho Santana in 1730, the workday was 20 hours. See ANTT, CSJ, maço 69, n. 207.

5 Both the Jew da Costa and the Jesuit Cardim used the same image of hell to describe the engenho.

6 Estevão Pereira stated in his report of 1635 that the traditional day to begin the safra was 25 July; the day of Santiago, and the day to stop was between 20 and 25 April. The records of Engenho Sergipe themselves, however, indicate somewhat later starting and closing dates. See "Dase rezão da fazenda que o collegio de Santo Antão tem no Brazil e seus rendimentos," ANTT, CSJ, maço, n. 20 (reprinted as an appendix in Antonil, *Cultura*, 513–27).

7 Jacob Gorender, *O escravismo colonial* (São Paulo, 1978), 216, makes a number of arguments on the rigidity of slave labor in the face of seasonal constraints, but he errs in this because the basis of his argument is the Caribbean, and he tends to overlook other "productive" tasks to which slaves could be applied.

8 Throughout the text, I will refer to safras by the year of their inception or use the present method, viz., 1612 or 1612/13.

9 See, for comparison, William A. Christian, Jr., *Local Religion in Sixteenth-Century Spain* (Princeton, 1981), and Stephen Gudeman, "Saints, Symbols and Ceremonies," *American Ethnologist* 3, no. 4 (Nov. 1978): 709–29. I wish to express my sincere thanks to Father Matias Kieman, O.F.M., Father Charles Ronan, S.J., and Professor Manoel Cardozo, friends and colleagues, who shared their knowledge of the church calendar with me.

10 Devotion to St. Francis Xavier began in Salvador during the plague of 1686, and he was then chosen patron of the city. See João da Silva Campos, *Procissões tradicionais da Bahia* (Salvador, 1941), 210–16.

11 Charles Herbermann et al., eds., *The Catholic Encyclopedia*, 15 vols. (New York, 1906), VI, 21–3 ("feasts").

12 See, e.g., Koster, *Travels*, II, 219; Santos Vilhena, *A Bahia*, I, 186.

13 Instructio abius qui officinam sacchaream administrant servanda data a P. Rector Bernaba Soares (1699), ARSI, Bras. 11.

14 Domingos do Loreto Couto, "Desagravos do Brasil e glórias de Pernambuco," *ABNR* 24 (1902): 180–6.

15 Jorge Benci, *Economia cristã dos senhores no governo dos escravos*, 2d ed. (Oporto, 1954), 171–7.

16 Religious observance also had its cost. Thomas Ewbank reported a conversation with a slave in Rio who labored on an estate owned by a devout woman. Her custom of waking the slaves at 2 a.m. for prayers caused the man to complain, "Work, work, work all day, pray, pray, pray all night. No Negro should stand for that." See Thomas Ewbank, *Life in Brazil* (New York, 1856), 75.

17 Johann von Spix and Karl von Martius, *Viagem pelo Brasil*, 3 vols. (São Paulo, 1961), II, 172. The original, published in German, dates from 1823. The two travelers visited a few Recôncavo estates and were hosted by Manoel Ferreira de Câmara at Engenho da Ponta. They refer in the text to Engenho Santa Maria in Ilhéus, but this is surely an error; they are referring to Engenho Santana. Their description of urban slavery is quite negative, but their view of slave conditions on rural estates seems to have been colored by the information supplied them by their hosts.

18 The same discrepancy can be seen in the literature on the Caribbean. See Barrett, "Caribbean Sugar Production," 147–70. In Rio de Janeiro, planting was done from June to Sept., to take advantage of the tops of the harvested cane to be used as seed, or in March, when climatic conditions were more appropriate. See José Caetano Gomes, "Memoria sôbre a agricultura e produtos de cana de açúcar," *Brasil Açucareiro*, March 1965: 34–47.

19 In Pernambuco, uplands were planted from July to Sept. and lowlands from Sept. to Nov. In Paraíba, planting took place from Aug. to Oct. or Nov. Koster, *Travels*, II, 115; Irineu Ferreira Pinto, *Datas e notas para a história da Parahyba*, 2d ed. (João Pessoa, 1977), 191–2.

20 AHU, Bahia pap. avul. (1751); a ratio of 1:20 was made at Fazenda Santa Cruz in Rio de Janeiro in the 1790's, but this was probably unusual. See ANRJ, Codice 618.

21 Assento, 27 March 1700, BGUC 711, f. 123; ANRJ, Codice 540. See the *requerimento* of Captain Cristóvão Marques de Azevedo of Jaguaripe for a typical series of complaints; BNRJ, 2–34, 4, 36.

22 Inventories of engenhos rarely mention fences. On fencing of canefields, see J. A. Gonçalves de Mello, "Um regimento de feitor-mor de engenho, de 1663," *Boletim do Instituto Joaquim Nabuco* 2 (1953): 80–7.

23 Zacharias Wagner, "Thierbuch." The illustrations can be seen in E. van den Boogart, ed., *Johan Maurits van Nassau Siegen 1604–1679* (The Hague, 1979), 262.

24 An acre contains 4,050 sq. m., whereas a tarefa has 4,356 sq. m. A tarefa is thus 7 percent larger.

25 The word jornal has the same double meaning as tarefa, both a daily quota and an areal measurement. In eastern Spain, the origin of the jornal can be established as far back as 934 as the area that oxen could plow in a day. Both the Catalonian-Valencian and Portuguese measures probably originate in the Roman *iugerum*. See S. Llensa de Gelcen, "Breve historia de las medidas superficiales agrarias de la antigüedad y estudio particular de aquellos cuyo uso es tradicional en Cataluña," *Annales*, Escuela Técnica de Peritos Agricolas (Barcelona, 1951), X, 65–128. My thanks to Ward Barrett for his help in directing me to this information.

26 Santos Vilhena, *A Bahia*, I, 178–9.

27 Inventory; Antonil, *Cultura*, liv. 2, cap. 4.

28 Francisco Ribeiro to College of Santo Antão (Bahia, 12 March 1660), ANTT, CSJ, maço 68, n. 268. He said, "O engenho que não tem canas proprias não tira lucro algum" (the mill that has no cane of its own will have no profit).

29 Francisco Negreiros to count of Linhares (2 July 1588), ANTT, CSJ, maço 8, n. 25.

30 Report of Ouvidor geral do Civel Francisco Sabino Alvares da Costa Pinto, APB, Cartas ao Governo (23 Sept. 1800), "Pelo costume practicado geralmente entre os proprietarios dos engenhos e seus lavradores de serem os escravos delles reciprocos no serviço e de o retribuirem nas ocaziões competentes" (by the custom generally practiced between the planters and their cane farmers of having their slaves reciprocal in service and exchanging them on appropriate occasions).

31 Antonil, *Cultura*, liv. 2, cap. 2.

32 The remark was made by Antônio Paes de Sande, governor of Rio de Janeiro. See Stuart B. Schwartz, ed., *A Governor and His Image in Baroque Brazil: The Funeral Eulogy of Afonso Furtado do Castro do Rio de Mendonça by Juan Lopes Sierra*, trans. Ruth E. Jones (Minneapolis, 1979), 162.

33 Antonil, *Cultura*, liv. 1, cap. 5.

34 Koster, *Travels*, II, 113.

35 My comments here are based on the perceptive remarks of Barrett, *Efficient Plantation*.

36 Bryan Edwards, *The History Civil and Commercial of the British Colonies in the West Indies*, 2 vols., 3d ed. (London, 1801), II, 252.

37 ABD/CSB 136, "Estado" of 1652–6 for Engenho São Bento.

38 In a full 24 hours, a mill could process 25 to 30 cartloads of cane. This was called a *tarefa redonda*.

39 The best study of the oxcart in Brazil is Bernardino José de Souza, *Ciclo de carro de bois no Brasil* (São Paulo, 1958).

40 Cardim, *Tratado da terra e gente* (1583), noted that a form of .5 arroba was used in Bahia and of 1 arroba in Pernambuco. Records of Engenho Sergipe confirm the use of small forms. Van der Dussen's *Relatório* noted forms in Pernambuco of 1 arroba. By the eighteenth century, the larger form of 2.5–3.5 arrobas was in general use.

41 José da Silva Lisboa, "Carta . . . para Dr. Domingos Vandelli," in *ABNR*, 32 (1910), 494–507.

42 ANRJ, caixa 406, pacote 1.

43 Barrett, "Caribbean Sugar-Production," 153; *Efficient Plantation*, 22.

44 Koster, *Travels*, II, 132. The carts described by Koster (72 by 30 in., = 2,160 sq. in.) were much smaller than those seen by Antonil (72 by 63 in. = 4,536 sq. in.).

45 Antonil, *Cultura*, liv. 2, cap. 4.

46 Slaves from inventories, Data Set A.

47 João Peixoto Viegas, "Parecer e tratado, feito sobre as excessivas impostos que cahirão sobre as lavouras do Brasil," *ABNR* 20 (1898): 214–16.

48 Letter from the merchants of Salvador (1797), AHU, Bahia pap. avul. 75, 1st series uncat.; APB, Ord. reg., 83, 274–7.

49 The best printed collection of Post's Brazilian landscapes appears in Erik Larsen, *Frans Post, Interprete du Bresil* (Amsterdam, 1962).

50 Loreto Couto, "Desagravos do Brasil," 174; Antonil, *Cultura*, liv. 2, cap. 5.

51 Loreto Couto, "Desagravos," 174, and Antonil, *Cultura*, liv. 2, cap. 6, spoke of the canes being passed two or three times into the rollers, but Santos Vilhena (*A Bahia*, I, 179–80) spoke of the need with a horse-driven mill to put them through 10 or 12 times and with oxen as many as 24! He compares this negatively to the West Indies, where only a few passes were necessary. A report from 1798 on the sugar industry of Paraíba stated that bunches of 12 to 18 canes were placed in the rollers 6 or 8 times to squeeze them sufficiently. See Pinto. *História da Parayba*, 2, 193.

52 Eugenio Andrea Cunha e Freitas, "Documentos para a história do Brasil, III; Notícias da Bahia em 1625," *Anais Academia Portuguesa da História*, 2d series, 21 (1972):479–80.

53 Van der Dussen, *Relatório*, 80, 93–6.

54 The building was sometimes called the *casa dos cobres* or copper house because the kettles were usually made of that metal.

55 Inventories made at sales or other transfers sometimes included a listing of the kettles. Engenho Santa Cruz das Torres was sold in 1691 with two caldeiras, three parões, and seven tachas, along with smaller necessary kettles (APB, notas 3, 47–52A). Engenho Cachoeirinha in Cotegipe was sold in 1757 with one caldeira, one parol, three tachas, and a shallow receiving pan (APB, notas 99, 233–8). Loreto Couto speaks of four caldeiras and eight tachas, but this is for two trains or series in a large engenho. See Loreto Couto, "Desagravos," 174.

56 These were the tachas: (1) *de receber;* (2) *da porta;* (3) *de cozer;* (4) *de bater.*

57 Various suggestions were made in Brazil to improve the design and the operation of the furnaces. One was simply to reduce their height and thus reduce the need for wood to produce the proper amount of flame. For an example of suggested improvements, see Santos Vilhena, *A Bahia*, I, 193. He suggests that the traditional furnaces on an engenho burned 1 cart of wood per hour or about about 20 per working day.

58 José da Silva Lisboa, "Carta muito interessante para o Dr. Domingos Vandelli (1781)," *ABNR* 32 (1910): 494–507; ANTT, CSJ, maço 13, n. 14.

59 Loreto Couto states that each caldeira weighed between 25 and 40 arrobas ("Desagravos," 174). Antonil, *Cultura*, liv. 2, cap. 9, 206–13, gives the weight of copper as

follows: *parol do caldo*, 20 arrobas; *parol da guinda*, 20 arrobas; caldeira do meio and caldeira de melar, 60 arrobas; parol de escuma, 12 arrobas; parol de melado, 15 arrobas; parol de coar, 8 arrobas; in the four tachas, 36 arrobas or 9 in each, and in the bacia, 4 arrobas. Antonil's figures are confirmed by the reported weights of the "coppers" at Engenho Barbado in 1769. See APB, sec. jud. São Francisco 535, no. 16.

60 "Regimento do feitor-mor," 85.

61 Lavradio to Principal Almeida (1 May 1769), Marquês de Lavradio, *Cartas da Bahia, 1768–1769* (Rio de Janeiro, 1972), 158. Planters did not agree on the utility of having an olaria on the engenho. The cost of 6 or 7 slaves assigned to this task in addition to the salary of the master potter and the large amount of firewood it consumed were thought to outweigh the benefit of having brick, tile, and forms produced on the estate. Antonil suggested placing a crioulo slave at an olaria as an apprentice so that his salary would help defray the expenses of buying forms. Engenho Sergipe did not have an olaria, whereas Engenho Santana did. See Antonil, *Cultura*, liv. 3, cap. 4.

62 Antonil, *Cultura*, liv. 3, cap. 12.

63 Dampier, *Voyage to New Holland*, III, 55–6.

64 The molasses drained from macho sugar was called *mel*, that from batidos *remel*. Either could be processed into *aguardente* or used to make batido sugar.

65 Silva Lisboa, "Carta," 500.

66 Antonil, *Cultura*, liv, 1, cap. 8.

67 Anita Novinsky, *Inquisição. Inventários de bens confiscados a cristãos novos* (Lisbon, 1976), 191–8. Lopes Henriques owned Engenho Santa Theresa in Matoim. His inventory contains many references to the *livro de razão* (account book) of his caixeiro Agostinho Calheiros.

68 Diogo Brochado to council of war (24 Oct. 1608), AGS, Guerra antigua 690. He noted caixas of sugar weighing 18 to 20 arrobas. Other sources are cited in Robert Simonsen, *História económica do Brasil (1500–1820)*, 4th ed. (São Paulo, 1962), 110.

69 Records of Miguel Dias de Santiago are housed in PRO, SP 9/104. Those of the Engenho Sergipe are from ANTT, CSJ, maços 11, 14.

70 Patricia Aufderheide, "Ships and Sugar: Quantitative Analysis of Shipping Records, 1595–98, 1608–17" (unpublished paper, 1973).

71 Alvará, 29 Oct. 1695; Alvará, 20 Nov. 1698. See APB, Ord. reg. 5, n. 76A.

72 The weight of the wooden crate had been established at 3.5 arrobas (112 pounds) for purposes of customshouse weighing in 1641. Alfandega de Lisboa, n. 113 (23 May 1641).

73 Lista dos caixas q. se carregarao . . ., ANTT, Junta do Tabaco maço 101. The 382 caixas averaged 38.7 arrobas each. The 8 fechos averaged 18 arrobas.

74 Appelação civil contra os senhores dos trapiches (1792), APB, ord. reg. 77, fs. 173–7.

75 Bando (6 Dec. 1657), ACS 125.4 Provisões; ACS Livro 159, f. 239.

76 *Alvará* (15 Dec. 1687), BNRJ, 2–33, 28, 27. See also Peixoto Viegas, "Parecer e tratado," 214–16.

77 See, e.g., ANTT, Junta do Tabaco, maço 96.

78 King to Lourenço de Almeida (Lisbon, 4 Aug. 1709), Almeida to crown (16 June 1710), APB, Ord. reg. 7, ns. 703, 704.

79 "Termo da resolução sobre os senhores de engenhos nas faltas que ouverem nas caixas de açúcar," ACS 9.29, f. 270–270v.; "Termo de Vereação (11 Aug. 1736), ACS 9.30, f. 120–120v.

80 Ofício de José Diogo de Bastos, BNRJ, 2–33, 19, 27.

81 Mesa da Inspeção (27 May 1805), ANTT, Junta do Tabaco, maço 62.

82 Barros de Castro, "Senhores e Escravos," 3.

83 Richard Ligon, *A True and Exact History of the Island of Barbadoes* (London, 1673), 85; Carl and Roberta Bridenbaugh, *No Peace Beyond the Line: The English in the Caribbean, 1624–1690* (New York, 1972), especially ch. 3.

84 Novinsky, *Inquisição*, 46–9.
85 *Estado* (Rio de Janeiro, 1766–1770), ABD/CSB 135.
86 "Le cane tagliate, le pongono sotto una mola agitata de la acqua . . . ," Giulio Landi, *La descrittione de l'isola de la Madera* (Piacenza, 1574), 26; Barros de Castro, "Brasil, 1610, 679–712.
87 Ibid., 689–90. Barros de Castro presents a long discussion of the error of Deerr and others in believing that the roller mill was used in Sicily in the fifteenth century. Another article on sugar technology in colonial Brazil still of value is Alice P. Canabrava, "A força motriz: Um problema da técnica da industria do açúcar colonial," *Anais do Primeiro Congresso de História de Bahia*, 5 vols. (Salvador, 1950), IV, 337–49.
88 Vicente do Salvador, *História do Brasil*, 365–6.
89 ANTT, CSJ, maço 13, n. 32. In a letter to the count of Linhares, the administrator of Engenho Sergipe reported that one engenho do palitos driven by oxen had been built and another, water-powered, was being constructed. In 1620, Antônio Barrieiros offered to construct one old-style or two new-type (palitos) mills in Maranhão in return for certain royal favors. One of the royal councillors noted that "todos se dispoem a querer fazellos." See AHU, Codice 32, fs. 58–60.
90 Consulta of the conselho da Fazenda (Lisbon, 19 July 1620), AGS, sec. prov. 1473, fs. 38–9v. See also AHU, Codice 34, fs. 24v.–30 (23 Feb. 1622).
91 Barros de Castro, "Brasil, 1610," 700–1.
92 I have written at some length on the mysterious figure Juan Lopes Sierra in Schwartz, ed., *A Governor and His Image*, 27–30.
93 AHU, Bahia pap. avul., caixa 8, 1st ser., uncat. (30 Aug. 1663).
94 ACS, *Provisões* 124.1, fs. 3v.–4; *Provisões* 59, f. 2v.
95 APB, Ord. reg. 5, n. 70; Ord. reg. 2, n. 136. Both are letters of the crown to the governor of Brazil (23 Feb. 1693; 13 Nov. 1698).
96 Consulta, Con. Ultra., AHU, Codice 252 (30 Jan. 1703); ACS, Liv. 24, fs. 250–1 (12 Dec. 1705).
97 APB, Ord. reg. 29, ns. 14A, 14B; AHU, Bahia pap. avul., caixa 48, 1st se., uncat. (2 June 1733).
98 Câmara to crown (24 May 1766), APB, Cartas do Senando, 132.
99 Câmara to crown (12 Nov. 1766), APB, Cartas do Senado 132; Câmara to câmaras of other towns, ACS, Cartas do Senado aos governos das Vilas e Capitães, f. 36.
100 Wallerstein, *World System*, 88. Cf. Gorender, *O escravismo*, 74–7. On Max Weber's view of slavery, especially as expressed in his *Theory of Social and Economic Organization*, see the comments by Orlando Patterson in "Slavery," *Annual Review of Sociology* 3 (1977): 407–49.

Chapter 6. Workers in the cane, workers at the mill

1 Antonil, *Cultura*, liv. 1, cap. 9.
2 Joan Nieuhof, *Memorável viagem marítima e terrestre ao Brasil (1682)* (São Paulo, 1942), 309.
3 A very full, if somewhat unorganized, accounting of slave punishments in Brazil is contained in José Alípio Goulart, *Da palmatória ao patíbulo* (Rio de Janeiro, 1971). On slave conditions, see the historiographical discussion in Gorender, *O escravismo*, 348–58.
4 Joannes de Laet, "História ou anais dos feitos de companhia privilegiada das Indias Ocidentais," *ABNR* 41, no. 2 (1925), cited in J. A. Goulart, *Da palmatória*, 82.
5 Antonil, *Cultura*, liv. 1, cap. 9.
6 Nuno Marques Pereira, *Compendio narrativo da Peregrino da America* (Lisbon, 1765), 160.
7 Benci, *Economia cristã*. This work was originally published in Rome in 1705. It was written in Brazil about 1700 by Benci, a Jesuit attached to the college in Salvador.

8 Ibid., 136.

9 Manoel Ribeiro da Rocha, *Ethiope resgatado, empenhado, sustentado corregido, instruido, e liberto* (Lisbon, 1758). See the discussion in C. R. Boxer, *Some Literary Sources for the History of Brazil in the Eighteenth Century* (Taylorian Lecture) (Oxford, 1967), 12–14.

10 *Alvará de perdão* (21 April 1678), APB, Relação 495, f. 75v.

11 AHU, Bahia pap. avul., caixa 42, 1st ser., uncat.

12 Provisões (20 March 1688, 23 March 1688) in BGUC, Codice 711, f. 173. Some of the relevant documents can be found in *DH* 67 (1948): 174, and *DH* 68 (1949): 160.

13 King to governor of Bahia (11 Jan. 1690), BGUC, Codice 706, f. 25; king to archbishop of Bahia (11 Jan. 1690), APB, Ord. reg. 1, n. 56.

14 King to governor of Bahia (1 March 1700), reprinted in Ignácio Accioli de Cerqueira e Silva, *Memorias historicas e politicas da Provincia da Bahia*, ed. Braz do Amaral, 6 vols. (Bahia, 1925), II, 149. See also J. A. Goulart, *Da palmatória*, 28.

15 Petition of Marcelina Diaz Silvestre, APB, Ord. reg. 6, n. 139A.

16 *DH* 34 (1936): 217.

17 AHU, Bahia pap. avul., caixa 53, 1st ser., uncat. In 1761, two men were remanded from Maranhão to Lisbon for abusing their slaves. See AHU, Codice Con. Ultra. 593, fs. 27v.–28. For a case in which the crown intervened to free a slave who had been mistreated, there is the story of Ignácio Xavier, a *pardo* artisan in AHU, Bahia pap. avul., caixa 48, 1st ser., uncat. (21 June 1733).

18 AHU, Bahia pap. avul., doc. 24, 011 (1802). This case involved a group of slaves who trespassed onto Engenho São José in the Recôncavo and who were then beaten by the millowner.

19 Report of the ouvidor geral do crime (Bahia, 1806), BNRJ, I = 32, 28, 25.

20 E.g., APB, *Livro de perdões* 495, f. 75v.; 503, fs. 27–8.

21 Patricia Aufderheide, "Order and Violence: Social Deviance and Social Control in Brazil" (Ph.D. thesis, University of Minnesota, 1976), ch. 6.

22 "Apontamentos para huma nova lei dos escravos do Brazil," AHU, Bahia pap. avul., caixa 44, 2d ser., uncat. (no date but apparently from the 1790s); Luiz R. B. Mott, "A tortura dos escravos na Casa da Torre" (unpublished paper, 1984), based on ANTT, Inquisição, processo 16,687.

23 Inventory of Engenho Agua Boa of Manoel Antônio Campello (1795), APB, secção judiciaria 656A.

24 Testament and Inventory of João Lopes Fiuza (1741), APB, secção judiciária 623.

25 Santos Vilhena, *A Bahia*, I, 186.

26 Graham, *Journal of a Voyage to Brazil*, 114.

27 "Trabalhar de manha cedo até tarde de noite, nús e expostos às intempéres" (To work from early morning to late at night, naked and exposed to the weather). Dierick Ruiter, "A torcha da navegação," *RIHGB* 269 (1965): 83. See also Marques Pereira, *O peregrino*, 159, who stated that in Brazil many planters forced their slaves to work day and night, "broken, naked and without sustenance."

28 Larsen, *Frans Post*, plates 33–6, 46–7.

29 ANTT, CSJ, maço 54, n. 55 (1753).

30 AHU, Bahia pap. avul., caixa 51 (1751).

31 Santo Vilhena, *A Bahia*, I, 186.

32 Koster, *Travels*, II, 231.

33 Barbara Marie-Charlotte Wanda Lasocki, "A Profile of Bahia As Seen by Jacques Guinebaud, French Consul General," (M.A. thesis, University of California, Los Angeles, 1967), p. 127.

34 João Imbert, *Manual do fazendeiro, ou tratado domestico sobre as enfermidades dos negros* (Rio de Janeiro, 1832), xx.

35 King to Council of India (30 April 1606), BA, 51-VIII-48, fl. 88.

36 Antonil, *Cultura*, liv. 1, cap. 9. Cf. remarks made by Israel da Costa and Ruiters that

slaves spent their few free hours in the workday searching for shellfish and other supplements.

37 King to Dom João de Lencastre (Lisbon, 31 Jan. 1701), APB, Ord. reg. 6, n. 103.
38 Patricia Mulvey, "The Black Lay Brotherhoods of Colonial Brazil: A History" (Ph.D. thesis, City University of New York, 1976), 80.
39 "The Most Reverend Dom Abbott ordered all the Father Administrators of our fazendas to give one day a week to all adult slaves, even in weeks with many holy days because all masters should sustain their slaves," in ADB/CSB 135 (Rio de Janeiro, 1763–6); Marques Pereira, O peregrino, 147–51.
40 Pedro Teixeira to College of Santo Antão (Santana, 11 Nov. 1731), ANTT, CSJ, maço 15, n. 26; ANTT, CSJ, maço 54; n. 51 (1753). From Engenho Sergipe on the same theme is the letter of Padre Fernandes (30 June 1748), ANTT, CSJ, maço 69, n. 140.
41 Koster, Travels, II, 116.
42 AHU, Bahia pap. avul., caixa 61 (1751).
43 ANTT, CSJ, maço 15, n. 26.
44 The argument that slaves were well fed, better fed in fact than their masters, appears in Freyre, Masters and the Slaves, 50–4. The argument seems to be based on the observations of nineteenth-century authors who wished to counterpose the condition of plantation slaves with that of industrial laborers, "captives of the machine." To this, Freyre added his belief that to feed slaves poorly was irrational. See D. F. L. C. Burlamaque, Monographia da canna d'assucar (Rio de Janeiro, 1862), 325.
45 Imbert, Manual do Fazendeiro, 366–8.
46 Federico Leopoldo C. Burlamaqui, Memoria analytica a'cerca do commercio d'escravos e acerca da escravidão domestica (Rio de Janeiro, 1837), 79.
47 Marco Antônio de Sousa, Memoria sobre a capitania de Serzipe (1800), 2d ed. (Aracajú, 1944), 17.
48 Koster, Travels, II, 112–13.
49 Marques Pereira, O peregrino, 68.
50 R. Walsh, Notices of Brazil in 1828 and 1829, 2 vols. (Boston, 1831), II, 18–19.
51 ANTT, CSJ, maço 15., n. 27.
52 Deerr, History of Sugar, II, 57–8.
53 The testimony is cited in ibid., II, 352–3.
54 Antonil, Cultura, liv. 2, caps. 2, 3; Ligon, True and Exact History, 88.
55 "Fouce, a saber hum escravo que corta a cana e outro que o vai amarrando em feixes, e pondo em tulhas no agro para o carro correr ao engenho" (fouce, that is a slave who cuts the cane and another who binds it in bundles and places it in stacks in the field for the cart to carry it to the engenho), ACS, Cartas do Senado 28.5 (Letter of the câmara of Santo Amaro, 3 July 1751). See Antonil, Cultura, liv. 2, cap. 4, as well.
56 Antonil, Cultura, liv. 2, cap. 4. Santos Vilhena, A Bahia, I, 179, indicates the same measure was used a century later.
57 Stuart B. Schwartz, "Resistance and Accommodation in Eighteenth-Century Brazil: The Slaves' View of Slavery," HAHR 57, no. 1 (Feb. 1979): 69–81.
58 E.g., at Engenho Vargem in Rio de Janeiro, the derubada or felling of trees was done by hired Indians before slaves were placed in the field to work it. See ABD/CSB 135 (estado of 1772–7).
59 Deerr, History of Sugar, II, 58.
60 Estimate is from Fazenda Santa Cruz in Rio de Janeiro (1798), ANRJ, Codice 618, fs. 57–61.
61 AHU, Bahia pap. avul., caixa 61. This is probably an intentional overestimate of cost or an error in recording. If slaves could cut 4,200 canes a day, as Antonil states, then only 10 or 11 slaves were needed to cut 44,000–45,000 canes in a tarefa. Since these estimates were prepared to justify planter complaints about high costs, I suspect that the error was intentional.

62 ANTT, CSJ, maço 69, n. 83 (1629).
63 "Memorial of Joseph Israel da Costa." Almost two centuries later, the French traveler Tollenare described a rural scene, "30 negres et négresses courbés ver la terre et excites à travailler par un commandeur armé d'un fouet, qui punit le moindre repos" (30 black men and women bent over the land and urged to work by an overseer armed with a whip who punishes the least repose). See Louis-François de Tollenare, *Notes Dominicales*, ed. Leon Bourdon, 3 vols. (Paris, 1972), II, 363.
64 Cf. Marques Pereira, *O peregrino*, 159; *Economia cristã*, 33–62. Ruiter, "A torcha de navegação," *RIHGB* 269 (1965): 3–84, contains observations on slave treatment in translation from the Dutch classic *Toortse der Zee-Vaert* (1623).
65 The three-roller trapiche mill came in Santo Domingo to be called the "bone breaker" (*quiebra-huesos*) because of its power.
66 Antônio de Encarnação, Administrator of Engenho Musurepe, ADB/CSB 322.
67 Matias de Sousa to Padre Luís Vellozo (23 July 1733), ANTT, CSJ, maço 70, n. 170.
68 Tollenare, *Notes Dominicales*, II, 420–1.
69 Padre Antônio Vieira, Sermon to the slaves of Engenho Sergipe (1633), cited by Barros de Castro, *Escravos e senhores*, iii.
70 Santos Vilhena, *A Bahia*, I, 184.
71 Slaves from Inventories, Data Set A. One of the few listings of an engenho slave force in which the slaves were grouped by occupation was that of Engenho Sergipe when in 1638 it was sold to Pedro Gonçalves de Mattos. At that time, 8 males were listed as metedor de fogo. See ANTT, CSJ, maço 30, f. 104.
72 P. Antônio de Gouvea to Provincial (Bahia, 4 May 1626), ANTT, CSJ, maço 68, n. 395. PVCB, 28–9, reports an even more macabre incident when Fernão Cabral de Atayde placed a slave woman near a furnace to "frighten her" but she fell in and was killed.
73 Task requirements are described in Antonil, *Cultura*, liv. 2, caps. 10, 11.
74 ASCMB, Livro do Tombo I, 147–85. By the eighteenth century, Engenho Sergipe had given this task to slaves.
75 Inventory of Felipe Dias Amaral (1804), CWP.
76 Inventory of Col. José da Rocha Dorea, Engenho Barbado (1769), APB, Sec. judiciária São Francisco 535, n. 16.
77 ANTT, CSJ, maço 15, n. 26 (Santana, 11 Nov. 1731).
78 APB, Livro das Notas 25 (23 March 1715), 208–10.
79 Ribeiro to Collegio de Santo Antão (Bahia, 12 March 1660), ANTT, CSJ, maço 68, n. 268.
80 Cf. Antonil, *Cultura*, especially livs. 1, 2. Santos Vilhena, *A Bahia*, I, 183–4, mentions the various occupations and suggests some numbers but in an inconsistent manner.
81 See Chapter 12.
82 For a discussion of the data on which this section is based, see page 582 of the present volume.
83 Gorender, *O escravismo*, 69–77.
84 AHU, Bahia pap. avul., caixa 90 (Treslado das penhoras . . .).
85 There are rare instances of women in supervisory positions. E.g., the slave Monica was listed as the feitora at the Jesuit fazenda of São Bras in Maranhão in the 1750s. See StL/VFL, roll 161.
86 Câmara to king (6 Sept. 1736), APB, Cartas do Senado 131, 117–25.
87 On the matter of the length of the workday, the observation of travelers in other sugar colonies is instructive. In nineteenth-century Cuba, 4.5 hours of rest out of 24 during the safra was common, and a move to 6 hours of rest at a plantation in Matanzas was considered especially "philanthropical." See the sources cited in Magnus Morner, *European Travelogues as Sources to Latin American History From the Late Eighteenth Century Until 1870* (Stockholm: Institute of Latin American Studies, no. 30, 1981), 40.

88 Barros de Castro, "Escravos e senhores," 7–8.
89 Theo Santiago, "A manufatura e o engenho de açúcar no Brasil," in José Roberto de Amaral Lapa, ed., *Modos de produção e realidade brasileira* (Petropolis, 1980), 195–205.
90 Karl Marx, *Capital*, 3 vols. (New York, 1967), I, pt. iv, ch. 13, 322–4.
91 Antônio Barros de Castro, "A economia política, o capitalismo e a escravidão," in Amaral Lapa, *Modos de produção*, 67–107.
92 These calculations were made by Caetano Gomes, "Memoria sobre a cultura e productos de cana-de-açúcar (1798)," 43.
93 Vicente do Salvador, *História*, 366.
94 Loreto Couto provides this information in his justification of the continual operation of mills on Sundays. See *ABNR* 24 (1902): 183–4.
95 ABD/CSB 135 (Rio de Janeiro, 1766–70).
96 Antonil, *Cultura*, liv. 2, cap. 8; Ruiters, "A Torcha," 83.
97 Gonçalves de Mello, "Um regimento," 80–7.
98 Santos Vilhena, *A Bahia*, I, 184.
99 ANTT, CSJ, maço 70, n. 104.
100 See the discussion of the foremen in Daniel Nelson, *Managers and Workers* (Madison, Wis., 1975), 34–54.
101 Gonçalves de Mello, "Um regimento," 83; Nora Barlow, ed., *Charles Darwin's Diary* (Cambridge, 1934), 55.
102 Ciro F. Cardoso, "A brecha camponesa no sistema escravista," *Agricultura, escravidão e capitalismo* (Petropolis, 1979), 133–54. See also the discussion in Barros de Castro, "Escravos e senhores," 17–19.
103 See my discussion in "Resistance and Accommodation," 69–81. Jacob Gorender, "Questionamentos sobre a teoria econômica do escravismo colonial," *Estudos Econômicos* 13, no. 1 (1983): 7–40, has questioned both the typicality of the Santana document used in "Resistance and Accommodation" and my interpretation of it. It is clear, however, that Santana's system was not the result of Jesuit paternalism, because it had not been a Jesuit estate for 30 years and because the Jesuits themselves had been most unpaternalistic at Santana, as the final quotation of this chapter indicates.
104 Father Matias (?) to Father Estevão da Costa (Bahia, 3 Oct. 1623), ANTT, CSJ, maço 70, n. 89.
105 Robert W. Fogel and Stanley L. Engerman, *Time on the Cross: The Economics of American Negro Slavery*, 2 vols. (Boston, 1974), I, 191–257; Paul David et al., *Reckoning with Slavery* (New York, 1976), 69–80. On slaves in industry, see Ronald L. Lewis, *Coal, Iron and Slaves* (Westport, Conn., 1979).
106 P. Felipe Franco (Santana, 15 March 1671), ANTT, CSJ, maço 70, n. 383; P. Pedro Teixeira to Colégio de Santo Antão (Santana, 11 Nov. 1731), maço 15, n. 26; P. Luís da Rocha (1739), maço 69, n. 207 (10 Oct. 1739), maço 68, n. 413.
107 P. Jerônimo da Gama, "Custumes q. achey e vou emendando . . .," ANTT, CSJ, maço 54, n. 55. I have published this statement previously in Schwartz, "Colonial Brazil," *CHLA*, II, 440–1.
108 My "Resistance and Accommodation" discusses the treaty in detail and reprints it.
109 A number of recent studies have begun to search for the interconnections between labor organization and social forms. See T. Maeyama, "The Masters *versus* the Slaves under the Plantation Systems in Brazil," *Latin American Studies* (University of Tsukuba, Japan) 3 (1981): 115–41; Claudinei Magno Magre Mendes, "No Mundo do Quinguingoo," *AH* 8 (1976): 93–106. For comparison, see Philip D. Morgan, "Work and Culture: The Task System and the Lowcountry Blacks, 1700–1880," *William and Mary Quarterly*, 3d. ser., 39, no. 4 (1982): 563–99.

Chapter 7. The Bahian sugar trade to 1750

1 See the review of existing merchant accounts and other materials in Dauril Alden, "Vicissitudes of Trade in the Portuguese Atlantic Empire During the First Half of the Eighteenth Century: A Review Article," *The Americas* 32, no. 2 (Oct. 1975): 282–91.

2 Mauro, *Portugal et l'Atlantique*, 225–32.

3 Engel Sluiter, "Dutch Maritime Power and the Colonial Status Quo, 1585–1641," *Pacific Historical Review* 11, no. 1 (March 1942): 29–42. On German sugar trade to Brazil, see Hermann Kellenbenz, "Der Brasilienhandel der Hamburger Portugiesen zu Ende des 16 und in der Ersten Haltte des 17 Jahrhunderts," *Actas III Colóquio internacional de estudos Luso-Brasileiros* 2 (1957): 277–96.

4 Alvará (Madrid, 7 June 1629).

5 ANTT, CSJ, maços, 11, n. 5.

6 StL/VFL, roll 162 (16 Jan. 1653).

7 Flory, "Bahian Society," 241–2. On merchant shipping arrangements, also see Anna Amelia Vieira Nascimento, *"Letras de risco" e "Carregações" no comércio colonial da Bahia, 1660–1730* (Bahia: Centro de Estudos Baianos, 1977), note 78.

8 John McCusker, "The Rum Trade and the Balance of Payments of the Thirteen Continental Colonies, 1650–1755" (Ph.D. dissertation, University of Pittsburgh, 1970), 94; see also Deerr, *History of Sugar*, II, 449–59.

9 Richard B. Sheridan, *Sugar and Slavery: An Economic History of the British West Indies 1623–1775* (Baltimore, 1974), 29–30.

10 Cf. Richard Pares, "The London Sugar Market, 1740–1769," *Economic History Review* 9, no. 2 (1956): 254–70.

11 McCusker, "Rum Trade," 94.

12 The prohibition of cachaça, dated from 25 Oct. 1646 in Bahia, was opposed by the sugar producers, and the order was rescinded. See Consulta, Con. Ultra., AHU, Bahia pap. avul., caixa 6 (17 Feb. 1647).

13 On the relation of sugar prices to the general price index, see Buescu, *300 anos de inflação*, 39–68.

14 These sources are listed and discussed in Mauro, *Portugal et l'Atlantique*, 192–211.

15 My estimate here is based on calculations made by Mircea Buescu and on my own reading of the sources. Elsewhere, I have seriously questioned an earlier estimate of production presented by Simonsen, *História econômica do Brasil 1500–1820*, 382–3 which set production in 1600 at 1,200,000 arrobas. This estimate is far too high, as I tried to demonstrate in Barrett and Schwartz, "Comparación entre dos economias azucareras coloniales," 532–72. See also Mircea Buescu, *História econômica do Brasil* (Rio de Janeiro, 1970), 81–90. The 1623 estimate is that of Jan Andries Moerbeck. See *DUP*, II, 214–23.

16 I have presented a fuller discussion of these data in "Society and Economy in Brazil: Plantations and Peripheries, 1580–1750," *CHLA*, II,

17 See Chapter 5.

18 Barros de Castro, "Brasil, 1610," 679–712.

19 Carta régia to Governor Gaspar de Sousa (Lisbon, 24 May 1614), BI, Correspondência de Gaspar de Sousa, f. 315.

20 I have attributed to Pedro Cadena de Vilhasanti, provedor mor (royal treasurer) of Brazil, the anonymous report of 1629 entitled "Descripción de la provincia del Brasil," published by Frédéric Mauro in *Le Bresil au xviiᵉ siècle* (Coimbra, 1963), 167–91. Except for the date, it is the same as the report offered by a Pedro Cudena (sic) to the count-duke of Olivares in 1634. This later memorial is printed by Martin Franzbach in *JGSWGIA* 7 (1970): 164–200.

21 Brandão, *Diálogos*, 87–90.

22 José Antônio Gonçalves de Mello, "Uma relação dos engenhos de Pernambuco em 1623," *Revista do Museu do Açúcar* 1 (1968): 25–36.

23 ABD/CSB, 322.

24 See Appendix B for the price series. The price series has been constructed by using the average sale price of white sugar at Engenho Sergipe and adding to those observations for years in which no prices were available the price for white sugar collected by Dauril Alden. Since his series were based on local purchases, I have deflated them by 10 percent to approximate at-the-mill prices. In addition, to make the series consistent, all prices for the years prior to 1688 have been inflated by 20 percent to adjust for the currency reform of that year. See Alden, "Commodity Price Movements."

25 In 1604, the crown arranged to pay the Jesuits their support in sugar according to the price of 1601. AGS, SP 1473, fs. 493–4; SP 1489, fs. 22v.–3. See also Wanderley Pinho, *História*, 243–7; his quotations of 1601, 1604, and 1621 are obviously not market prices.

26 Buescu, *300 anos da inflação*, 41–3.

27 PRO, SP 9/104.

28 AHU, Bahia pap. avul., caixa 1, 1st ser., uncat. (9 Oct. 1623).

29 Barry E. Supple, *Commercial Crisis and Change in England, 1600–1642* (Cambridge, 1959), 1–22. The words "crisis" and "contraction" are used carefully here because much debate centers on the nature, profundity, and meaning of the depression. See the discussion in Wallerstein, *World System*, II, 13–34.

30 The remark was made in Parliament in 1621, cited in Supple, *Commercial Crisis*, 54; Wallerstein, *World System*, II, 25.

31 Supple, *Commercial Crisis*, 73–81; Jan de Vries, *The Economy of Europe in an Age of Crisis, 1600–1750* (Cambridge, 1976), 21–5. Especially important is Ruggiero Romano, "Tra xvi e xvii século, una crisi economica: 1619–1622," *Rivista storica italiana* 74, no. 3 (1962): 480–531.

32 See Frédéric Mauro, "Espaces maritimes et economie coloniale bresilienne," *Des produits et des hommes* (Paris, 1972), 72–92, in which he discusses the period 1600 to 1621 as a contraction or b-period in the Kondratieff cycle. For sugar, however, prices for the 1610s moved strongly upward.

33 Jan Andries Moerbeeck, *Motivos por que a Companhia des India Ocidentais deve tentar tirar a Rei de Espanha a terra do Brasil* (*Amsterdam*, 1624) (Rio de Janeiro, 1942).

34 Eugenio Andrea Cunha e Freitas, "Documentos para a história do Brasil III: Notícias da Bahia em 1625," *Anais Academia Portuguesa da História*, 2d ser., 21 (Lisbon, 1972): 479–80.

35 Relação do estado em que achey o engenho de Sergipe (July 1625), ANTT, CSJ, maço 14, n. 52.

36 André de Gouvea to College of Santo Antão (Bahia, 18 April 1626), ANTT, CSJ, maço 68, n. 394; ARSI Lusitania 77, fs. 71–7. In 1613–14, the tithe for Bahia was 45,000 *cruzados* out of a total for Brazil of 135,000.

37 Manoel Cardozo, "Tithes in Colonial Minas Gerais," *Catholic Historical Review*, 38, no. 3 (1953): 175–82; Oscar de Oliveira, *Os dízimos eclesiásticos do Brasil*, 2d ed. (Belo Horizonte, 1964).

38 Mauro, *Portugal et l'Atlantique*, 219–22.

39 For an example of miscalculation, see the petition of Manoel Rodrigues Sanches, who farmed the tithe in 1613–14 when Bahia was struck by a drought and he was unable to pay. AHU, Bahia pap. avul., caixa 1, 1st ser., uncat.

40 See Chapter 7, note 114.

41 The contract in 1619 was farmed for a three-year period, a technique that was to reemerge in the twentieth century. See AHU, Bahia pap. avul., caixa 1-A, n. 147.

42 See AHU, Bahia pap. avul., caixa 3 (9 Jan. 1681); AHNM, Estado 81, fs. 262–3. The Jesuits' exemption is discussed in Leite, HCJB, III, 148, 178–9, 240.

43 Joseph Joyce, Jr., "Spanish Influence on Portuguese Administration: A Study of the

Conselho da Fazenda and Hapsburg Brazil, 1580–1640" (Ph.D. dissertation, University of Southern California, 1974), 266–271, covers the period 1608 to 1624. For the subsequent years, see the report of Jorge Seco de Macedo (6 Feb. 1656), AHU, Bahia pap. avul., caixa 6, 1st ser., uncat.

44 Pernambuco's tithe dropped from 81,000 cruzados in 1622–3 to 51,500 in 1623–4, a fall of 36 percent. See Joyce, "Spanish Influence," 268.

45 *Livro primeiro do governo do Brasil, 1607–1633* (Rio de Janeiro, 1958), 314–16.

46 Ibid.

47 The version in *Livro primeiro* says 300 ships were involved in the Brazil trade, but if these averaged 400 crates or 7,200 arrobas, Brazil's production would have been over 2,000,000 arrobas, a figure far above its potential. In 1626, the council of state in Portugal discussed the matter and noted that 120 ships were involved in the Brazil trade. Because crates at the time were estimated at 18 to 20 arrobas, Brazil's annual export would have been between 1,080,000 and 1,200,000 if each ship averaged 500 crates. See Consulta, Conselho do Estado (23 July 1626), Cadaval n. 43.

48 The figure of 3,700 arrobas per mill is confirmed by a petition of 1632, in which the town council of Salvador reported that 16 engenhos had gone out of production with a loss of 6,000 arrobas of tithes. This indicates a production of 60,000 arrobas for the 16 mills, or an average of 3,750 arrobas per mill. See ACS, Livro 155, fs. 88–91.

49 The 3 classic accounts are C. R. Boxer, *The Dutch in Brazil, 1624–1654* (Oxford, 1957); Francisco Adolfo de Varnhagen, *História das lutas com os Hollandezes no Brasil* (Lisbon, 1872); and Herman Wätjen, *O domino colonial hollandez no Brasil* (São Paulo, 1938), which is a translation of the German edition of 1921.

50 The best work on the impact of the Dutch invasion on the sugar economy is Evaldo Cabral de Mello, *Olinda restaurada* (São Paulo, 1975).

51 In the previous year, the senhores de engenho had petitioned the câmara for tax relief because of the low sugar price. ACS, Livro 155, fs. 88–90.

52 Estimate of the marquis of Niza in Cabral de Mello, *Olinda*, 123–5.

53 Ibid., 91, 167, 256–7. For a specific case, see Gilberto Osorio de Andrade, "D. Catarina Barreto e a retirada de 1635," *Ciência e Trópico* 7, no. 1 (Jan.–June 1979).

54 Cabral de Mello, *Olinda*, 155. Under the Dutch, planters also complained of taxes, especially that on molasses, which had been untaxed. Planters also objected to measures forcing them to grow foodstuffs. See José Antônio Gonçalves de Mello, *Tempo dos flamengos* (Rio de Janeiro, 1947), 175, 180–1, 188–9.

55 A useful but sometimes confused account of these events is Carlos Valeriano de Cequeira, "Historico da cultura da cana na Bahia," *Anais do Primeiro Congresso de História da Bahia*, 5 vols. (Bahia, 1950), IV, 263–333.

56 I have followed Boxer, *Dutch in Brazil*, for these events.

57 The complaint against the order signed by some eighty senhores and lavradores is found in BI, Cartas do Conde de Torre, liv. 2, n. 102 (28 Feb. 1639). See also liv. 3, n. 155. See also ANTT, Coleção de São Vicente, liv. 23, f. 140.

58 BI, Cartas do Conde de Torre, liv. 1, n. 166.

59 An accounting of ship losses is found in Joannes de Laet, "História ou Annaes dos Feitos da Companhia Privilegiada das Indias Occidentais," *ABNR* 61–2 (1919–20): 201–15.

60 Kenneth Andrews, *Elizabethan Privateering* (Cambridge, 1964), 133, 201–4.

61 Ibid., 206–7.

62 See Sluiter, "Dutch Maritime Power," 29–41; Mauro, *Portugal et l'Atlantique*, 463.

63 Andrade e Silva, *Col. chron.* 1 (5 Jan. 1605): 104.

64 Consulta, Consejo de Estado (13 Jan. 1607), AGS, Estado Sicilia 1171.

65 Mauro, *Portugal et l'Atlantique*, 465.

66 "Alvará" (15 Jan. 1605), ANRJ, Codice 541, f. 116.

67 Aufderheide, "Ships and Sugar." Aufderheide examined the records of Miguel Dias

de Santiago in PRO, SP 9/104, and the shipping records of Engenho Sergipe 1608–17, ANTT, CSJ, maço 11, n. 5.

68 Engenho Sergipe used a number of caravels captained by men from the Alfama district of Lisbon. Each shipment contained between 4 and 20 crates. ANTT, CSJ, maço 11, n. 5.

69 Vieira's remark and a discussion of the caravel is found in Boxer, *Salvador de Sá*, 209–91.

70 AGS, Guerra Antigua, 690.

71 AGS, Sec. prov. 1527, fs. 181–181v. (Madrid, 6 Oct. 1632).

72 Cabral de Mello, *Olinda*, 49.

73 *CSPS*, (10 Nov. 1586): 651; letter of D. Diego Sarmiento de Acuña discussed in a consulta of the council of state (18 July 1615), AGS, Estado Inglatierra 2514.

74 AGS, Sec. prov. 1520 (Madrid, 11 Sept. 1626), fs. 107–7v.; BNM, 2848, f. 165 (5 Sept. 1626), Memorial (1627), *Livro primeiro*, 314–15. Proposals for the creation of a Spanish-style *casa de contratacción* (board of trade) were made at the same time. See *BNR*, 1, 2, 35, n. 14 (7 May 1627). On a later proposal, see "Papel que dio a SMgd. Nicholas Salvago en que offerece hazer una armada de ocho navios para asegurar los açucares del Brasil (1630)," BNRJ, 1, 2, 35.

75 The standard work on the company is Gustavo de Freitas, *A companhia geral do comércio do Brasil (1649–1720)* (São Paulo, 1951), which studies its structure but not its operations. The best description in English is found in Boxer, *Salvador de Sá*, 290–2. On the New Christians, see Chapter 9.

76 AHU, Codice 14, f. 146v.

77 On the Brazil fleets, see Eulália Maria Lahmeyer Lobo, "As frotas do Brasil," *JGSWGLA* 4 (1967): 465–88. Virgilio Noya Pinto, *O ouro brasileiro e o comércio anglo-português* (São Paulo, 1979), is essentially a study of the fleets based on the reports of French consuls. It should be compared with M. Morineau, "Or bresilien et gazettes hollandaises," *Revue d'Histoire Moderne et Contemporaine* 25 (Jan.–March 1978): 3–59, which is based on Dutch sources.

78 Robert Carlyle Batie, "Why Sugar? Economic Cycles and the Changing of Staples on the English and French Antilles, 1624–54," *Journal of Caribbean History* 8 (Nov. 1976): 1–41. See also Matthew Edel, "The Brazilian Sugar Cycle of the Seventeenth Century and the Rise of West Indian Competition," *Caribbean Studies* 9 (April 1967): 24–44.

79 The Portuguese complained that these barriers were contrary to their trade agreements with England. See Consul Maynard to Lord Arlington (Lisbon, 18 April 1671), PRO, SP 89/11.

80 Sir Josiah Child, *A New Discourse on Trade* (London, 1669), 220, cited in Sheridan, *Sugar and Slaves*, 397.

81 McCusker, "Rum Trade," 128.

82 Sheridan, *Sugar and Slavery*, 45–53.

83 Gaspar de Brito Freire to Crown (Bahia, 13 Aug. 1644), AHU, Bahia pap. avul., caixa 4.

84 AHU, Bahia pap. avul., caixa 10 (3 Nov. 1669). It was reported in 1666 that 16,000 slaves had died in Brazil. PRO, SP 87/7, f. 319.

85 Ibid. (19 Dec. 1667).

86 P. Manuel de Oliveira to P. Manuel Morras (16 June 1668 and 11 Sept. 1668), in ANTT, CSJ, maço 68, n. 107, n. 123; AHU, Bahia pap. avul., caixa 10 (3 Nov. 1669).

87 Alden, "Commodity Price Movements," 4–5.

88 Sheridan, *Sugar and Slavery*, 404.

89 Vitorino Magalhães Godinho, "Portugal, as frotas do açúcar e as frotas do ouro (1670–1770)," *Ensaios*, 3 vols. (Lisbon, 1968–70), II, 295–315.

90 Vitorino Magalhães Godinho, "Portugal and Her Empire," *New Cambridge Modern History*, 14 vols. (Cambridge, 1970), VI, 509–40, especially 508–12.

91 Carl Hanson, *Economy and Society in Baroque Portugal, 1668–1703* (Minneapolis, 1981), 108–42; Wallerstein, *World System*, II, 75–125.
92 See my discussion in *A Governor and His Image*, 5–17.
93 Hanson, *Economy and Society*, 240.
94 Pierre Verger, *Flux et reflux de la traite des negres entre le golfe de Benin et Bahia de Todos os Santos* (Paris, 1968), 97–127.
95 Consulta, Con. Ultra. (24 Aug. 1672), Bahia pap. avul., caixa 1ª, n.c.; in 1662, Bahia's annual contribution was reported at 20,000 cruzados a year. See ACS, 4 (24 April 1662): 136–40.
96 AHU, Codice 252, f. 5.
97 *Cartas do senado. Documentos históricos do Arquivo Municipal*, 3 vols. (Bahia, 195?–3), III, 17–20, III, 212.
98 Albert O. Hirschman, "A Generalized Linkage Approach to Development with Special Reference to Staples," *Economic Development and Cultural Change* 25 (Supplement, 1975): 67–98.
99 I have presented a capsule biography of Peixoto Viegas in *A Governor and His Image*, 165–7.
100 "Parecer e tratado feito sobre os excessivos impostos que cahirao sobre as lavouras do Brazil," *ABNR*, 20 (1898): 213–23.
101 Hanson, *Economy and Society*, 142–59.
102 Boxer, *Portuguese Seaborne Empire*, 152–4.
103 For an analysis of the effect of the lack of specie in Portugal, see "Papeles do Duque de Cadaval," BM, Additional Ms. 15170, fs. 201–8 (4 July 1692).
104 Godinho, "Portugal and Her Empire," 509–12, 523–8.
105 Alden, "Commodity Price Movements," 4–5.
106 Godinho, "Portugal and Her Empire," 533–7; Noya Pinto, *O ouro*, 112–18.
107 A good example of this official support for the agricultural sector is the letter of Governor Dom João de Lencastre (12 Jan. 1701) reprinted in Antonil, *Cultura*, 586–90. See also the letter of Governor Dom Rodrigo da Costa, APB, ord. reg. 7, n. 107 (20 June 1703), and Ord. reg. 6 (28 June 1703), f. 59. Cf. Consulta, Con. Ultra. (26 Sept. 1703), AHU, Codice 252.
108 Law of 17 Nov. 1704 prohibited reexport of goods coming from Portugal to Bahia. In 1706, the governor of Brazil tried to stop export of foodstuffs from Bahia to Rio de Janeiro, APB, Ord. reg. 7, nn. 402, 403.
109 Alvará (Lisbon, 20 Jan. 1701), APB, Ord. reg. 6, n. 83. This law limited the Paulistas to 200 slaves a year from Angola purchased through the port of Rio de Janeiro. Royal attempts to prohibit planters from selling slaves to the mines were opposed by those who argued that some slaves were unsuited to agricultural labor and should be available for sale to the mines. See APB, Ord. reg. 8, n. 66A (Lisbon, 22 Feb. 1711). See also King to count of Vimioso (Lisbon, 5 May 1719), APB, Ord. reg. 14, n. 49.
110 Câmara of Salvador to crown (15 Nov. 1723), APB, Cartas do Senado 131, f. 47–9.
111 P. Luís Vellozo to College of Santo Antão (Engenho Sergipe, 16 July 1727), ANTT, CSJ, maço 70, ns. 1, 2 (8 April 1728), 3 (16 Aug. 1728), 4 (28 Sept. 1728).
112 Buescu, *300 anos da inflação*, 94–121; Mircea Buescu, *Evolução econômica do Brasil* (Rio de Janeiro, 1974), 52, 87, 96–7.
113 Mauro, *Portugal et l'Atlantique*, 213–57; Boxer, *Portuguese Seaborne Empire*, 150–76; Buescu, *300 Anos da inflação*, 39–74; Buescu, *Evolução econômica do Brasil*, 38–57, 96–8; Celso Furtado, *The Economic Growth of Brazil* (Berkeley, 1963), 15–32, 43–50.
114 J. H. Galloway, "Northeast Brazil, 1700–1750: The Agricultural Crisis Reexamined," *Journal of Historical Geography* 1, no. 1 (1975): 21–38, presents a stimulating revisionist argument, but one that I do not find fully convincing. Although he is certainly correct that gold alone did not cause the agricultural crisis of the late seventeenth and early eighteenth centuries, the monographic literature had already rejected that

idea. Galloway's contention that, in fact, the crisis was much exaggerated by self-interested parties is, however, debatable. Although planters and royal bureaucrats certainly sought to influence royal policy on behalf of agriculture, there is a great deal of evidence that indicates their complaints were not unfounded. One need only examine the relative price of sugar and slaves in the early eighteenth century to see that the planters were caught in a price squeeze. Galloway points out that the tithe figures did not fall badly until the 1730s, and he assumes that in Bahia planters were able to absorb the rise in slave prices through the new profits made in the growing tobacco trade. Tithe figures are, as we have seen, difficult to use as a gauge of the sugar economy, especially if we do not know the relative proportion of sugar to other exports. Moreover, the connection between the sugar sector and the tobacco growers remains to be shown. There is little evidence of sugar planters involved in tobacco as well, and the two crops were even geographically separated in the Recôncavo. By 1723, some 24 engenhos in Bahia had ceased operations because of the high costs of operation. Although slaves were still imported to Recife and Salvador, many planters could not afford them. Import figures as used by Galloway do not tell the full story. Even in the 1750s, 60 percent of the slaves that arrived at Recife were reexported to the mines.

115 This discussion is based on ANTT, Junta do Tabaco, maços 96A–106, which reports the caixas deposited and shipped from Bahian warehouses (trapiches) and the discussion of Morineau, "Or bresilien et gazettes hollandaises," 26–30; see also Noya Pinto, *O ouro*, 190–200.

116 Although the anonymous "Discurso preliminar, historico, introductivo com natureza de discrição económica da comarca e cidade do Salvador," published by Pinto de Aguiar, ed., as *Aspectos da economia colonial* (Salvador, 1957), outlines essentially the same story, its figures, cited by many, are not to be fully trusted. The author, whoever he was, wrote in the 1780s, and his knowledge of production and prices 4 or 5 decades earlier was very general.

117 José Jobson de Andrade Arruda, *O Brasil no comércio colonial* (São Paulo, 1980), 605–12.

118 Diogo de Meneses to king (8 May 1610), *ABNR* 57: 67–71; ANTT, Corp. cron., pt. 1, maço 115, n. 105. See also Schwartz, *Sovereignty and Society*, 120–1.

119 "Homens de negocio de Lisboa pedindo para ser revogada a provisão de 1612," AHU, Bahia pap. avul., caixa 1 (28 Nov. 1613).

120 "Requeremento q. fazem os senhores de engenho e lavradores a Câmara desta Cidade (1632)," ACS, livro 155, fs. 88–92.

121 Governor Pedro da Silva to Ouvidor geral (31 Aug. 1636) in Accioli, *Memorias*, II, 93–4. Governor da Silva was acting upon a decision of the Bahian high court.

122 AHU, Bahia pap. avul., caixa 8 (26 Sept. 1663). On Rio de Janeiro, see BNL, Chancelaria D. Pedro II, livro 59, f. 206v (1695); livro 25, f. 361 (1700); *Arquivo do Distrito Federal* 2 (1896): 172–3. The câmara of Rio de Janeiro in 1686 petitioned for a six-year extension of the exemption, citing the precedent of 1673 and 1681. It was authorized. See *DH*, 92 (1951): 274.

123 BNM, 2436, fs. 105–9; Parcer de João Rabello de Lima (1630), BNRJ, 1, 2, 35; Petition of Senhores de engenho and lavradores de cana of Bahia, AHU, Bahia pap. avul., caixa 53, 1st ser., uncat. (30 Oct. 1747).

124 The relevant documentation including many of the written opinions is found in APB, Ord. reg. 15, nn. 149–57. See also BGUC, 706, fs. 42–3v.

125 AHU, Bahia pap. avul., caixa 46, 1st ser., uncat.

126 See Chapter 11, section titled "Social composition and relations." Also see my discussion in Stuart B. Schwartz, "Free Labor in a Slave Economy: The Lavradores of Colonial Bahia," in Dauril Alden, ed., *Colonial Roots of Modern Brazil* (Berkeley, 1973), 147–97.

127 The most important documents are published in Maria Izabel de Albuquerque, "Liberdade e limitação dos engenhos d'açúcar," *Anais do primeiro congresso de história da Bahia* (Salvador, 1950), II, 491–9, and in Frédéric Mauro, *Le Brésil au xviie siecle*, 270–307.

128 Petitions of the senhores de engenho can be seen in ACS, 125.4 (fragmento), Bahia (26 June 1669 and 27 June 1669). The established planters were led in their opposition by Bernardino Vieira Ravasco and Lourenço de Brito Correa, both of whom held important government posts. They argued most strongly that no more engenhos should be built on the coast but that new ones could be built inland as long as they were sufficiently separated and did not prejudice already established mills.

129 The law of 1681 was modified in 1684. See AHU, Codice 252 (7 Oct. 1681), fs. 69–69v.

130 A case involving Engenho da Conceição in Cachoeira generated considerable debate over the earlier provision. Some planters testified that the laws of 1681 and 1684 had not been consistently applied and that in Rio Fundo, Engenhos Santo Antônio, Paciencia, Buraco, Pandalunga, and Paranagua were all built close together with no adverse effects. By 1800, the law was considered to be dead (*não está em vigor*), but the case provoked renewed interest and resulted in a royal provision of 13 May 1802 restating it. See AHU, Bahia pap. avul., caixa 51 (1797, 1798); Governor Rodrigo de Sousa Coutinho to D. Fernando José de Portugal (30 April 1800), APB, Cartas do governo 140, ff. 19–21; *Provisão* (Lisbon, 13 May 1802).

131 Eulalia Maria Lahmeyer Lobo, "As frotas do Brasil," 465–88.

132 AHU, Bahia pap. avul., caixa 2 (27 July 1641). The alvará reserving one-third of cargo space on all ships for planters shipping their own sugar on consignment is registered in ANTT, Chan. Felipe II, liv. 23, f. 121v.

133 ACS, 125.4 Provisões (29 Aug. 1652); Consulta, Con. Ultra., AHU, Codice 252 (5 Feb. 1693). The privilege was granted in 1665, 1681, 1689, and 1693.

134 C. R. Boxer, *Portuguese Society in the Tropics* (Madison, Wis., 1965), 107.

135 AHU, Bahia pap. avul., caixa 6, 1st ser., uncat.

136 Boxer, *Portuguese Society in the Tropics*, 107.

137 King to governor to Brazil (Lisbon, 2 March 1697), APB, Ord. reg. 3, n. 98. It was ordered that 15 days after the arrival of the flagship of the fleet the price should be set by appointed representatives and that after three days if no agreement was reached then the chancellor and two disinterested judges (those without their own sugar holdings) should arbitrate the price. If they could not decide, then the average of the three proposals was to be used.

138 Consulta, Con. Ultra., AHU, Codice 252 (25 Sept. 1673), fs. 31v.–2v.; (16 Oct. 1683), fs. 86v.–87.

139 For some of these arguments, see count of Galveas to crown (21 April 1742), APB, Ord. reg. 36, fs. 30–3.

140 *Vereação* (5 May 1700), ACS, liv. 923, fs. 119–24.

141 *Vereação* (25 June 1718), ACS, 9.29, f. 3v. For examples of a petition from the sugar sector, see BI, Cartas Conde de Torre, n. 102 (28 Feb. 1639); ACS, livro 155.

142 Rae Flory and David G. Smith, "Bahian Merchants and Planters in the Seventeenth and Early Eighteenth Centuries," *HAHR* 58, no. 4 (Nov. 1978): 571–94, fall into the error, I believe, of confusing social fusion with lack of class conflict.

143 A good discussion of this problem is found in McCusker, "Rum Trade," 805–7.

144 E.g., the tax levied in Bahia to maintain the local garrison and that assessed in Lisbon to pay for the convoy system were both charged per crate. See AHU, Codice 252, f. 5.

145 Pares, "London Sugar Market," 254–70.

146 See the figures in Jobson de Andrade, *O Brasil no comércio*, 359–64.

147 Marquês de Lavradio, *Cartas da Bahia 1768–1769* (Rio de Janeiro, 1972).

Chapter 8. A noble business: profits and costs

1 Schwartz, "Free Labor in a Slave Economy," 161–5.
2 Stuart B. Schwartz, "Patterns of Slaveholding in the Americas: New Evidence From Brazil," AHR 87, no. 1 (Feb. 1982): 73–5.
3 Vitorino Magalhães Godinho, "Portugal and Her Empire, 1680–1720," NCEH, VI, 509–40. Mauro, Portugal et l'Atlantique, 425–8. Mauro's chapters on money provide the best summary of the currency supply in the Portuguese empire and its effects on the economy.
4 Magalhães Godinho, "Portugal and Her Empire," 529.
5 Alfredo Carlos Teixeira Leite, Gênese socio-econômica do Brasil (Pôrto Alegre, 1963), 195–211.
6 Cited in Wanderley Pinho, História, 204.
7 Cf. Jacob Price, Capital and Credit in British Overseas Trade: The View From the Chesapeake, 1700–1776 (Cambridge, Mass., 1980).
8 José da Silva Lisboa to Domingos Vandelli (18 Oct. 1781), ABNR 32 (1910): 494–506.
9 Some capital came directly from Portugal. Manuel Teixeira, a New Christian merchant in Lisbon, advanced 1,400$ to a planter in Paraíba to be paid in sugar. See Hermann Kellenbenz, "Das Testament von Manuel Teixeira," Studia Rosenthaliana 3, no. 1 (1969): 53–61. Conversely, there is no evidence in the notarial archives of Amsterdam that Portuguese Jews were financing the Brazilian sugar economy prior to 1640. See the notarial entries published by E. M. Koen, "Notarial Records in Amsterdam Pertaining to the Portuguese Jews in That Town Up to 1639," beginning in Studia Rosenthaliana 1, no. 1 (1967) and published serially in each issue to date. On the Brazilian side, see Flory, "Bahian Society," 69–80; Soeiro, "Baroque Nunnery, 115–54.
10 Flory, "Bahian Society," 69–80.
11 I am referring here to the laws of 1663, renewed many times thereafter. See Chapter 12.
12 Soeiro believes that each borrower was committed to one lender because of the indivisibility of sugar properties, but this is obviously wrong, as wills and testaments make clear. Some engenhos had 10 or 15 liens on them. Cf. Soeiro, "Baroque Nunnery," 152.
13 APB, Livro de Notas 13 (3 July 1698). (All citations to Livros de Notas are from Salvador unless otherwise indicated.)
14 AHU, Bahia pap. avul. (25 July 1694). I consulted a microfilm copy at the Bancroft Library, University of California, Berkeley. The document has been reproduced with commentary by American Pires de Lima in "A Situação da Misericórdia da Baia no fim do século xvii," Brasília 5 (1959): 556–600.
15 Other loans were secured on ranches, sugar warehouses, and farms. Livro de Notas 18 contains many loan contracts in which fazendas de cana were mortgaged to the Misericórdia during 1700–1. The large number of contracts made at approximately the same time probably indicates the difficult period through which the sugar economy was passing at the turn of the century.
16 The Misericórdia continued to face the problem of uncollected and uncollectable debts. See AHU, Con. Ultra., #1265 (1755). The author wishes to thank Dauril Alden for access to this document.
17 APB, Livro de Notas 87, f. 180 (3 Feb. 1749).
18 Cf. Soeiro, "Baroque Nunnery," 115–54; A. J. R. Russell-Wood, Fidalgos and Philanthropists: The Casa Santa da Misericórdia da Bahia, 1550–1755 (Berkeley, 1968), 149–65 passim.
19 Soeiro, "Baroque Nunnery," 146.
20 APB, Livro de Notas 15 (28 May 1699).
21 APB, Livro de Notas 195, fs. 136v.–7 (10 Sept. 1817).

22 Flory and Smith, "Bahian Planters and Merchants," 571–94.

23 Catherine Lugar, "The Merchant Community of Salvador, Bahia, 1780–1830" (Ph.D. thesis, State University of New York, Stony Brook, 1980), 157–62.

24 APB, Livro de Notas 134, fs. 154v.–6 (20 Feb. 1794); Consulta, Con. Ultr., AHU, Codice 252, fs. 31–2.

25 *ABNR*, 32 (1910), 494–506.

26 Lugar, "Merchant Community," 158.

27 Smith, "Mercantile Class of Portugal and Brazil in the Seventeenth Century: A Socio-Economic Study of the Merchants of Lisbon and Bahia, 1620–1690" (Ph.D. thesis, University of Texas, 1975), 367–8.

28 ANRJ, Papers of Manoel Gomes Correa, caixa 411.

29 AHU, Bahia, doc. 25395 (1803); also see ANTT, Junta do Tabaco 51 (5 Dec. 1803), which deals with Engenho Cinco Rios.

30 BNRJ, II-34, 5, 24; *DH*, 34 (1936): 57–60.

31 Assento (2 March 1709), ANRJ, Codice 540, f. 96.

32 Antonil, *Cultura*, liv. 1, cap. 11.

33 Processo de Senhor de engenho Capitão João da Fonseca Villas Boas contra lavrador de cana Alferes Dinis de Merello (São Francisco do Conde, 18 March 1699), MHN/CWP, pacote 10. For a similar case involving a fazenda de canas in Jacarancanga, see AHU, Bahia pap. avul., caixa 17 (26 Jan. 1689).

34 Petition of Francisco de Brito Freyre, AHU, Bahia pap. avul., caixa 13 (28 Nov. 1678). The petition was approved by the Overseas Council.

35 Escritura de debito e obrigação que faz Capitão Antônio de Sousa ao Francisco de Brito Freyre (21 June 1681), APB, Livro de Notas 3, fs. 26–8.

36 Ibid., Livro de Notas 18 (4 Aug. 1701).

37 "A experiência brasileira de Robinson Crusoe," in Buescu, *História econômica do Brasil*, 132–9.

38 "Memoria dos guastos que faz todos os annos," ANTT, CSJ, maço 17, n. 35 (undated).

39 My discussion is based on 25 rental contracts from the period 1793 to 1830, drawn from the APB, Livros de Notas.

40 In the rental of Engenho São João in São Francisco parish (8 June 1824), the renter Antônio Joaquim Abreu Pinto de Almeida agreed to pay 50 crates of sugar a year, 25 with white and 25 with muscovado sugar and each containing 40 arrobas. Half the rent was to be paid directly to the owner and the other half used by the renter to satisfy outstanding debts on property. APB, Livro de Notas 212, fs. 118–19.

41 APB, Livro de Notas 231, fs. 50v.–3 (6 April 1830). In this contract, Manoel Joaquim de Vilas Lobos and his wife rented their engenho but with the understanding that the owners would continue to grow cane on the property and that the renter would have to mill their cane whenever they so desired.

42 ANTT, CSJ, maço 13, n. 20.

43 Mauro, *Portugal et l'Atlantique*, 218.

44 Pinheiro da Silva, "A Capitania da Baía," 1, 183.

45 Letter to the Board of Inspection (1751), AHU, Pernambuco pap. avul., maço 24.

46 Flory, "Bahian Society," 64–8.

47 APB, Ord. reg. 58.

48 Ten engenhos selected for completeness of information from the series of wills and inventories, APB, Judiciaria.

49 Silva Lisboa, *ABNR*, 32 (1910): 494–506; "Discurso preliminar, histórico, introdutivo com natureza de descrição econômica de comarca e cidade do Salvador," which is printed in João Pinto de Aguiar, *Aspectos da economia colonial* (Salvador, 1957), 35–6.

50 Flory, "Bahian Society," 64–5.

51 Schwartz, "Free Labor in a Slave Economy," 176.

52 Estimate is based on José Antônio Caldas, *Notícia geral de toda esta capitania da Bahia* (facsimile of 1759) (Bahia, 1951), 425–45.
53 See Gorender, *O escravismo*, 18–22, for a discussion of the historiography on this topic.
54 Sheridan, *Sugar and Slavery*, 230–1.
55 Phyllis Deane, "The Role of Capital in the Industrial Revolution," *EXEH* 10, no. 4 (1972): 349–64.
56 Douglas Hall, "Incalculability as a Feature of Sugar Production During the Eighteenth Century," *Social and Economic Studies* 10, no. 3 (Sept. 1961): 340–52. On the debate in the British West Indies, see R. B. Sheridan, "The Wealth of Jamaica in the Eighteenth Century," *EHR*, 2d ser., 18 (1965): 292–311; R. P. Thomas, "The Sugar Colonies of the Old Empire: Profit or Loss for Great Britain?," *EHR*, 2d ser., 21 (1968): 30–45; R. B. Sheridan, "The Wealth of Jamaica in the Eighteenth Century: A Rejoinder," *EHR*, 2d ser., 21 (1968): 46–51; J. R. Ward, "The Profitability of Sugar Planting in the British West Indies, 1650–1834," *EHR*, 2d ser., 21, no. 2 (1978): 197–213.
57 My discussion here is based on Thomas P. Govan, "Was Plantation Slavery Profitable?" in Hugh G. J. Aitken, *Did Slavery Pay?* (Boston, 1971), 107–32. See also A. C. Littleton, *Accounting Evolution to 1900* (New York, 1933), in which the role of F. Paciolo's *De computis et scripturis* (1494) is emphasized.
58 I have discussed the nature of the Benedictine accounts in "Plantations of St. Benedict," 1–22. For the Jesuits, I have used the Engenho Sergipe materials. Records for Engenho Petinga exist for the period 1745–8, but this was a time of rebuilding, and the records are therefore of less comparability. See ANTT, CSJ, maço 54, n. 36.
59 Occasional costs for capturing escaped slaves have been assigned to the category of miscellaneous expenses.
60 See Chapter 6.
61 ANTT, CSJ, maço 13, n. 20. It has also been published as an appendix to Mansuy's edition of Antonil, *Cultura*, 513–27.
62 See Table 8-5. I have used as a working figure for expenses 3,464$633. This differs from Pereira's own calculation because he did not include the manioc flour that was paid to the engenho as a land rent and was then consumed by the slaves. About 600 *alquieres* (a measure of 36.3 Kg.) worth 156$ should thus be credited to both income and expenditure.
63 Buescu, *História econômica do Brasil*, 98–131; Buescu, *300 anos da inflação*, 39–68; Frédéric Mauro, "Contabilidade teórica e contabilidade prática na America portuguesa no século XVII," in *Nova história e novo mundo* (São Paulo, 1969), 135–48.
64 São Bento safras 1711–14, 1783–6, 1786–1800; São Caetano 1726–9, 1790–3, 1783–6, 1786–9, 1796–1800 are found in ADB/CSB.
65 ANRJ, caixa 406, pacote (1802). In 1806, engenho Buranhaem was valued at 38,000$. See petition of Francisco Joaquim da Rocha Pitta (27 March 1806), ANTT, Junta do Tabaco, 51.
66 "Conta das despezas que tenho feito . . .," APB, Cartas ao Governo 196.
67 "Comptabilité théorique et comptabilité pratique en Amérique portugaise au xvii siècle," *Etudes économiques sur l'expansion portugaise (1500–1900)* (Paris, 1970), 135–50; Edel, "Brazilian Sugar Cycle," 36–8.
68 Cf. ADB/CSB, 136–8.
69 These representative entries are drawn from Engenho Sergipe accounts for 1643–4, 1669–70, 1699–1700, and 1711–12, and from Engenho Buranhaem for 1796–1801.
70 AHU, Bahia pap. avul., caixa 63 (1751).
71 Engenho Buranhaem, ANRJ, caixa 406, pacote 1.
72 Gorender, *O escravismo*, 188–90, deals with the theoretical problem of capital invested in the purchase of a slave. See also Mircea Buescu, "Notas sobre o custo da mão-de-obra escrava," *Verbum* 31, no. 3 (Sept. 1975), 33–4.

73 See Kit Sims Taylor, "The Economics of Sugar and Slavery in Northeastern Brazil," *Agricultural History* 44 (July 1970): 3.
74 Sheridan, *Sugar and Slavery*, 263–6.
75 ANTT, CSJ, maço 30.
76 "Conta de tudo o q. esta Igreja tem recebido pertencente ao Engenho de Santana dos Ilhéus desde o anno de 1730 ate o fim do anno 1750," ANTT, CSJ, maço 54, n. 22.
77 Rematação do engenho Sergipe (20 March 1638), ANTT, CSJ, maço 52, n. 15; see for comparison Russell R. Menard, Lois Green Carr, and Lorna S. Walsh, "A Small Planter's Profits: The Farm Accounts of the Cole Estate and the Growth of the Early Chesapeake Economy," *WMQ*, 3d ser., 40 (April 1983): 171–96.
78 The document is printed in full as an appendix to Mansuy's edition of Antonil, *Cultura*, 513–27. It had appeared earlier in *Anais do Museu Paulista* 4: 775–94.
79 Authors who have used the Pereira document to good advantage are Alice Canabrava in her edition of Antonil, *Cultura* (São Paulo, 1967); Buescu, *300 anos da inflação*; and especially Mauro, "Contabilidade teórica," 135–48.
80 Sebastião Vaz to rector of Santo Antão (5 March 1634), ANTT, CSJ, maço 68, n. 70.
81 "Reposta q. o P. Estevão Pereira deu," ANTT, CSJ, maço 15, n. 17 (30 September 1635).
82 ANTT, CSJ, maço 68, n. 70.
83 P. Sebastião Vaz to rector of Santo Antão (5 March 1634), ANTT, CSJ, maço 68, n. 70; maço 68, n. 267.
84 Mauro, "Contabilidade teórica," 136–9.
85 Mircea Buescu, *Exercicios de história econômica do Brasil* (Rio de Janeiro, 1968), 32.
86 Belchior Pires to College of Santo Antão (11 Feb. 1650), ARSI Bras. 3(1), 277–7v.
87 Agostinho Lousado, ARSI Bras. 3 (1), 317–17v.
88 Father Francisco Ribeiro to College of Santo Antão (12 March 1660), ANTT, CSJ, maço 68, n. 268.
89 See Schwartz, "Free Labor in a Slave Economy," 194–5.
90 Luís da Rocha (Engenho Sergipe, 11 Feb. 1738), ANTT, CSJ, maço 69, n. 172.
91 Alden, "Sugar Planters by Necessity," 139–70.
92 Ibid.
93 Father Belchior Pires to superiors (Bahia, 26 Feb. 1662), ARSI, Bras. 3 (II).
94 Ibid.
95 Father Joseph de Seixas to Father General (Dec. 1677), StL/VFL, roll 160 (Bras. 2).
96 StL/VFL, roll 160, Bras. 2.
97 Alden, "Sugar Planters by Necessity," 157.
98 Schwartz, "Plantations of St. Benedict," 1–22.
99 *ABNR* 32 (1910): 500–1.
100 "Discurso preliminar," 33–6.
101 If the same ratio of costs to gross income is applied to the Silva Lisboa estimate, then the rate of return is 16 percent.
102 Cf. R. Keith Aufhauser, "Profitability of Slavery in the British Caribbean," *JIH* 5, no. 1 (summer 1974): 45–67.
103 Celso Furtado, *The Economic Growth of Brazil* (Berkeley, 1971), 54–7.
104 Ibid.
105 Seymour Drescher, *Econocide: British Slavery in the Era of Abolition* (Pittsburgh, 1975), 48.
106 See the critique of export-oriented analysis in José Roberto do Amaral Lapa, *O antigo sistema colonial* (São Paulo, 1982), 38–47.
107 John Monteiro, "A Study of Sugar Output in Seventeenth-Century Brazil" (unpublished paper, University of Chicago, 1979). The rum industry grew in Bahia despite the objections of the Portuguese wine interests and the complaints of local authorities about its consumption. See *ACB* 1, nos. 75–6 (1 Sept. 1627; 16 Oct. 1627).

108 José Antônio Caldas, *Noticias geral desta capitania da Bahia desde o seu origen ate o presente anno de 1759* (facsimile edition) (Salvador, 1959), 169, 445.

109 APB, Cachoeira, *inventários* (1763).

110 On the theory of "linkage," see Hirschman, "Generalized Linkage Approach to Development," 67–98.

111 Planter desire for European luxuries came to be seen in the correspondence of Felisberto Caldeira Brant Pontes, Marquis of Barbacena, covering the period 1819–21. See *Economia açucareira do Brasil no século xix* (Rio de Janeiro, 1976).

Chapter 9. A colonial slave society

1 L. N. McAlister, "Social Structure and Social Change in New Spain," *HAHR* 43, no. 3 (Aug. 1963): 349–79, presents an excellent analysis of essentially the same set of problems that this chapter confronts.

2 E.g., John of Salisbury, *Policraticus: The Statesman's Book*, ed. Murray F. Markland (New York, 1979). See also Jacques Le Goff, "A Note on Tripartite Society, Monarchical Ideology, and Economic Renewal in Ninth- to Twelfth-Century Christendom," in *Time, Work, and Culture in the Middle Ages* (Chicago, 1980), 53–7.

3 Le Goff, "Note," argues that the early theorists of medieval society had already begun to make distinctions within the third estate and that *laboratores* had a more specific meaning than is usually believed. See pp. 56–7.

4 Vitorino Magalhães Godinho, *A estrutura na antiga sociedade portuguesa* (Lisbon, 1971), 59–60.

5 Roland Mousnier, *Social Hierarchies* (London, 1969), 49–66. Mousnier has become the leading analyst of the society of orders. For a critique of his ideas as essentially Parsonian in origin, see Armand Arriaza, "Mousnier and Barber: The Theoretical Underpinning of the Society of Orders in Early Modern Europe," *Past and Present* 89 (Nov. 1980): 34–57.

6 On the theory of government and society in the Hispanic world, see Louisa Hoberman, "Hispanic American Political Theory as a Distinct Tradition," *Journal of the History of Ideas* 41, no. 2 (1980): 199–220; Richard M. Morse, "Toward a Theory of Spanish American Government," *Journal of the History of Ideas* 15, no. 1 (1954): 71–93. Particularly helpful on Portugal is Martim de Albuquerque, *O poder político no renascimento português* (Lisbon, 1968).

7 A. J. R. Russell-Wood, "Class, Creed, and Colour in Colonial Bahia: A Study in Prejudice," *Race* 9, no. 2 (1967): 133–57. See also the discussion in James Lockhart and Stuart B. Schwartz, *Early Latin America* (Cambridge, 1983), 225–7.

8 Lawrence Stone, "Social Mobility in England, 1500–1700," *Past and Present* 33 (April 1966): 16–55.

9 *DH* 97 (1928): 190. This remark, made in 1718 by a royal attorney, is reported in Russell-Wood, "Class, Creed, and Colour," 143.

10 Saunders *Social History of Black Slaves*, 59–60. Saunders believes that there were about 35,000 black slaves and freemen in Portugal in about 1531. This would have been a figure representing about 2.5 to 3 percent of the population.

11 Ibid., 89–134, 166–76. Saunders's careful book shows that similar forms of discrimination and racial hierarchy existed in Portugal, where blacks were a very small portion of the population. See also A. J. R. Russell-Wood, "Iberian Expansion and the Issue of Black Slavery: Changing Portuguese Attitudes, 1440–1770," *AHR* 83, no. 3 (June 1978): 16–42.

12 See the long discussion in Orlando Patterson, *Slavery and Social Death* (Cambridge, Mass., 1982), 77–105, 172–208. Still important is the survey presented in David B. Davis, *Problem of Slavery in Western Culture* 62–90.

13 Saunders, *Social History of Black Slaves*, 113–20.

14 Stuart B. Schwartz, "The Manumission of Slaves in Colonial Brazil, Bahia, 1684–1745," *HAHR* 54, no. 4 (Nov. 1974): 603–35.

15 Some suggestive remarks on this perspective are found in Sidney J. Mintz, "Was the Plantation Slave a Proletarian?" (unpublished talk, Fernand Braudel Center, State University of New York, Binghamton, 2 Feb. 1977). See also Barros de Castro, "A economia política, o capitalismo e a escravidão," 67–108.

16 Peter Eisenberg, "O escravo e o proletário," *Anais da semana de estudos de história agraria* (Assis, 1982), 31–62. Eisenberg makes a number of suggestions for comparison in terms of work organization, costs, and results.

17 Frank Tannenbaum, *Slave and Citizen: The Negro in the Americas* (New York, 1947).

18 See Chapter 16.

19 Gorender, *O escravismo*, 15–22.

20 Parts of this discussion have been previously presented in my article "Colonial Brazil: The Role of the State in a Slave Social Formation," in Karen Spaulding, ed., *Essays in the Political, Economic, and Social History of Colonial Latin America* (Newark, Del., 1982), 1–24.

21 Carlos Malheiro Dias, ed., *História da colonização portuguesa do Brasil*, 3 vols. (Oporto, 1924–6); Alexander Marchant, "Feudal and Capitalistic Elements in the Portuguese Settlement of Brazil," *HAHR* 22, no. 3 (1942): 493–512. See also the bibliography in Celia Freire A. Fonseca, *A economia européia e a colonização do Brasil* (Rio de Janeiro, 1978), 216–17.

22 See the discussion in Albert Silbert, "O feudalismo português e a sua abolição," *Do Portugal de antigo regime ao Portugal oitocentista* (Lisbon, 1972), 85–108. See also the discussion by Torquato de Sousa Soares in "Feudalismo em Portugal," *Dicionário de História de Portugal*, 4 vols. (Lisbon, 1963–71), II, 228–30. For a Marxist view of feudalism in Portugal, see Armando Castro, *Portugal na Europa do seu tempo* (Lisbon, 1970).

23 Jacques Heers, "The 'Feudal' Economy and Capitalism: Words, Ideas, and Reality," *Journal of European Economic History* 3, no. 3 (winter 1974): 625.

24 Elizabeth A. R. Brown, "The Tyranny of a Construct: Feudalism and Historians of Medieval Europe," *AHR* 79, no. 4 (Oct. 1974): 1063–88.

25 Elizabeth Fox-Genovese and Eugene D. Genovese, *Fruits of Merchant Capital* (New York, 1983), 93.

26 Charles Verlinden, *The Beginnings of Modern Colonization* (Ithaca, N.Y., 1970), 203–40. The article originally appeared as "Formes féodales e domaniales de la colonisation portugaise dans la zone atlantique aux XIVe et XVe siècles et spécialement sous Henri le Navigateur," *Revista Portuguesa de História* 9 (1960): 1–44.

27 Johnson, "Donatary Captaincy in Perspective," 207.

28 I have developed this argument in some detail in Schwartz, "Colonial Brazil: The Role of the State," 5–8. The crown had been able to mobilize the nobility according to traditional obligations as late as the 1620s, but by the 1630s that was much less the case. When a royal attorney attempted to force knights of the military orders to serve in the colonies in person or pay for substitutes, they vigorously objected. The crown was calling on traditional military-feudal obligations; the knights were rejecting them. BNM, Papeles de Orden de Christo 938, fs. 202–10.

29 BNL, Fundo geral 7626, fs. 41–6.

30 "Informação de las tierras del Camamu," ARSI, Bras. 15 (StL/VFL, roll 159).

31 Marxist views of feudalism vary widely, although there are certain shared assumptions. See the discussion in *Sobre o feudalismo* (Lisbon, 1973), especially the remarks of Charles Parrain. Also, a broad theoretical discussion is provided in Barry Hindess and Paul Q. Hirst, *Pre-capitalist Modes of Production* (London, 1975), 221–60. They emphasize the fact that feudalism, or feudal relations of production, does not suppose serfdom nor landlords' seigneurial rights. For an interesting review essay on some of the recent literature, see Adrian Foster-Carter, "The Modes of Production Controversy," *New Left*

Review 107 (Jan.–Feb. 1978): 47–77. Marcello Carmagnani, *L'America Latina del '500 a oggi* (Milan, 1975), presents an ardent defense of the feudal nature of colonial Latin America based on the existence of a dual market and unequal exchange.

32 Witold Kula, *An Economic Theory of the Feudal System* (London, 1976), 9.

33 Schwartz, "Manumission," 603–35.

34 Octavio Ianni, *Escravidão e racismo* (São Paulo, 1978), 16–17.

35 Marx, *Capital*, v, iii, 791.

36 I have summarized much of the literature on bureaucracy in Spanish America in "State and Society in Colonial Spanish America: An Opportunity for Prosopography," in Richard Graham and Peter H. Smith, *New Approaches to Latin American History* (Austin, Tex., 1974) 1, 3–35. Mark A. Burkholder and D. S. Chandler, *From Impotence to Authority* (Columbia, Mo., 1977), seem unconcerned with the theoretical implications of their data on royal bureaucrats.

37 Perry Anderson, *Lineages of the Absolutist State* (London, 1974), 23, following Friedrich Engels, *Anti-Duhring* (Moscow, 1947), 126.

38 Anderson, *Lineages*, 18–19.

39 Cited in Sholomo Avineri, *Karl Marx on Colonialism and Modernization* (New York, 1969), 467–70.

40 Nicos Poulantzas, *Political Power and Social Classes* (London, 1973), 56.

41 Anderson, *Lineages*, 24–7.

42 See the *Repertório das ordenações e leis do reino de Portugal*, 5 vols. (Coimbra, 1857), II, 146–9.

43 See Chapter 6 for the details of the case. Important in this context is Aufderheide, "Order and Violence," especially pp. 209–18.

44 Sholomo Avineri, *The Social and Political Thought of Karl Marx* (Cambridge, 1968), 48–52.

45 Raimundo Faoro, *Os donos do poder* (Pôrto Alegre, 1958). This work, ignored at first, has been "rediscovered" and is now in its fifth edition.

46 Poulantzas, *Political Power*, 333.

47 My earlier book, *Sovereignty and Society*, deals with this integration of bureaucrats and local society in detail.

Chapter 10. The planters: masters of men and cane

1 Burlamaqui, *Memorial analytica*, 79.

2 I am depending heavily on the studies of Eduardo d'Oliveira França, "Engenhos, colonização, e cristãos-novos na Bahia colonial," *Anais: IV Simpósio Nacional dos Professores Universitarios de História* (São Paulo, 1969), 182–241, for the sixteenth and early seventeenth centuries; on Flory, "Bahian Society," for the late seventeenth and early eighteenth centuries; and on Morton, "Conservative Revolution," for the late eighteenth and early nineteenth centuries.

3 John Higginbotham, ed. and trans., *Cicero on Moral Obligation* (De officiis) (Berkeley, 1967), ch. 42, 93.

4 Oliveira França, "Engenhos," 192–3.

5 A distinction was made between a *fidalgo da casa de El Rey* (noble of the king's household) and a *moço fidalgo* (hereditary nobleman). The former rank was awarded for some service but was not inheritable and thus was less esteemed.

6 The Bravo brothers figure prominently among the lavradores de cana of Engenho Sergipe in the early seventeenth century. See ANTT, CSJ, maço 13, n. 6; also see Schwartz, "Free Farmers," 166–7. Later, Diogo Lopes Ulhoa used his nephew André Lopes Ulhoa as administrator of his engenho at Cajaíba Island. The Lopes Ulhoa family was widespread and prominent in Bahian life in the early seventeenth century, but later genealogists preferred to gloss over them for obvious reasons. See Anita Novinsky, *Cristãos novos na Bahia* (São Paulo, 1972), 76–138 passim.

7 Novinsky, *Cristãos novos*, 57–102; Oliveira França, "Engenhos," 217–28; Arnold Wiznitzer, *Jews in Colonial Brazil* (New York, 1960), 12–32.

8 Anita Novinsky, "A inquisição na Bahia (um relatório de 1632)," *Revista de História* 36, no. 74 (1968): 417–23.

9 Novinsky, *Cristãos novos*, 176.

10 Wiznitzer, *Jews*, 19.

11 Afonso Costa, "Genealogia baiana," *RIHGB* 191 (April–June 1946): 31–2. The wife of Henrique Moniz, Ana Rodrigues, was later burned at the stake in Portugal, and her picture was hung in the portal of the parish church in Matoim as a symbol for ridicule. Too much for the family to endure, the portrait was torn down by them with great scandal. See the discussion in Wanderley Pinho, *História*, 42–5. Among other Recôncavo families with New Christian origins that remained important during the colonial period were the Lopes Francos, Ulhoas, and Paredes.

12 See Afonso Costa, "Genealogia baïana," *RIHGB* 191 (1946): 3–279.

13 I am following the account given in Flory, "Bahian Society," 126–8, and the will of João Lopes Fiuza, APB, Jud. 623, n. 4 (1741).

14 I have given more detail to the story of Christóvão de Burgos in *Sovereignty and Society*, 354–5. Most of the information included here is drawn from notarial sources cited in those pages.

15 Spix and Martius, *Viagem pelo Brasil*, II, 164–6.

16 Morton, "Conservative Revolution," 20.

17 Ibid., 13–18.

18 Ibid., 19–20.

19 Antônio Ribeiro de Migueis acquired Engenho Petinga in 1761 and Sergipe sometime thereafter. He was constantly in debt and by 1779 unable to pay. When the crown placed these properties for auction, no bidders came forward, and Guimarães was arrested for debt. See APB, Religião 610; AHU, Bahia pap. avul., caixa 62 (31 July 1779); caixa 363 (31 July 1779).

20 Gandavo, *Histories of Brazil*, 34.

21 Leite, *Cartas Nóbrega*, 346.

22 Cardim, *Tratados da Terra e gente*, 201–2.

23 *RIHGB* 52 (1889), prints the *Catalogo genealogico* (1768).

24 Domingos Abreu e Brito, *Um inquérito à vida administrativa e econômica de Angola e do Brasil*, ed. Alfredo de Albuquerque Felner (Coimbra, 1931), 9.

25 Antonil, *Cultura*, liv. 1, cap. 1.

26 Santos Vilhena, *A Bahia*, I, 51–2.

27 Russell-Wood, *Fidalgos and Philanthropists*, 181–8.

28 Pondé de Sena, "Relações interétnicas" (unpub., 1974).

29 Petition of Isodoro Gomes de Sá (June 1802), APB, Cartas ao Governor 205. Gomes's son, Manoel Gomes, almost killed him over a woman named Francisca Josefa do Bomfim, a cabra slave whom the son wished to marry against his father's objections.

30 Leite, *HCJB* 6: 233–5.

31 Georges Duby, *The Three Orders: Feudal Society Imagined* (Chicago, 1981), 156.

32 Originally, membership in the Portuguese military orders had depended on noble birth. But in the inflation of honors during the reign of Dom João III (1521–57), the relationship was inverted so that membership in a military order was used as proof of nobility. Dispensations of ignoble origins were granted with some frequency in the seventeenth century. About 40 percent of these dispensations were in return for military service and about 45 percent for the service of others, i.e., as a dowry given to a woman that she could then offer a suitor. See Francis A. Dutra, "Artisans and the Order of Christ: The Search for Status in Portugal, 1668–1727" (unpublished paper, 1972); "Membership in the Order of Christ in the Seventeenth Century," *The Americas* 27, no. 1 (July 1970): 3–25.

33 See Cabral de Mello, *Olinda*, 243–8.

34 Schwartz, *A Governor and His Image*, 173–8.

35 Salvador fielded four regiments by the late eighteenth century: the first of leading merchants, the second of free whites, the third of *Henriques* or free blacks, and the fourth of pardos. Similar units were occasionally suggested for the Recôncavo but were not formed. In 1721, Antônio José Barbosa, captain in the Henriques of Salvador, petitioned to have a similar unit formed in Santo Amaro. AHU, Bahia pap. avul., caixa 70, 1st ser., uncat. (12 Jan. 1721).

36 AHU, Bahia pap. avul., caixa 49, 1st ser., uncat. (5 Dec. 1744).

37 F. W. O. Morton, "The Military and Society in Bahia, 1800–1821," *Journal of Latin American Studies* 7, no. 1 (1975): 249–70. See also John N. Kennedy, "Bahian Elites, 1750–1822," *HAHR* 53, no. 3 (1973): 415–39.

38 Morton, "Military and Society," 252–3. Governors did not always appreciate the exemptions that military service provided to Brazilians or the reluctance of many Brazilians to serve in the first-line regiments. See Governor Manoel da Cunha Menezes to Martinho de Mello e Castro (16 Oct. 1775), *ABNR* 32 (1919): 319.

39 APB, Ord. reg. 86, f. 198.

40 Boxer, *Portuguese Society in the Tropics*, 77–8; Afonso Ruy, *História da câmara municipal da cidade do Salvador* (Salvador, 1949).

41 Boxer, "Portuguese Society in the Tropics," 69–102.

42 Flory, "Bahian Society," 144–6; Morton, "Conservative Revolution," 63–7. At its foundation, the câmara of Cachoeira included Manoel de Araújo de Aragão and Antônio Barbosa Leal, both sugar planters. APMC, Posturas e vereações (1698).

43 See, e.g., letter from câmara of Santo Amaro (3 July 1751), ACS, Cartas ao Senado 28.5.

44 Oliveira França, "Engenhos, colonização," 194; Patricia Aufderheide, "True Confessions: The Inquisition and Social Attitudes in Brazil at the Turn of the XVII Century," *Luso-Brazilian Review* 10, no. 2 (winter 1973): 238–9.

45 Vasco Fernandes Cezar de Meneses to Crown (13 July 1724), APB, Ord. reg. 18, 7A; Ouvidor geral Pedro Gonçalves Cordeiro Pereira (4 July 1727), APB, Ord. reg. 21, n. 39. See also Schwartz, *Sovereignty and Society*, 239–62.

46 APB, Cartas do Governo 130.

47 In a list of cases awaiting investigation prepared in 1829, there were a number that indicated the ability of the civil courts to intervene in engenho life, e.g., the death of the creole slave Claudio at Engenho Subae (7 Aug. 1823) and the murder of a man at Engenho dos Britos (5 Jan. 1828) among others. APB, Presidência da Provincia 1425 (*Rol de devasas*).

48 This was probably João Dornelas de Vasconcelos, a mulatto slave who had been freed by Desembargador Miguel de Siqueira Castelobranco on the eve of his departure for Portugal in 1708. APB, Livro de Notas 22, 67.

49 Velloso's side of the story is reported in his letter to Jesuit procurator Antônio Correa (Engenho do Conde, 26 Nov. 1717), ANTT, CSJ, maço 69, n. 13. See also AHU, Bahia pap. avul., caixa 27, 1st ser., uncat. (Aug. 1722).

50 AHU, Bahia pap. avul., caixa 27, 1st ser., uncat. (16 Dec. 1720).

51 Antonil, *Cultura*, liv. 1, cap. 3.

52 *PVCB* (1591), 34.

53 AHU, Bahia pap. avul., caixa 66, 1st ser., uncat. (1756).

54 APB, Pres. da Prov. Engenhos, 1824–54 (1819).

55 Pinheiro da Silva, "*A Capitania da Baìa*," *Revista Portuguesa de História* 8 (1959): 45–76; 9 (1960): 210–45.

56 ANTT, CSJ, maço 70, n. 247.

57 Antonil, *Cultura*, liv. 1, cap. 2.

58 I have written extensively on this question. See *Sovereignty and Society*, 341–56.

59 Desembargador Francisco Antônio Moura to Governor (20 June 1799), APB, Cartas do Governo 39, 154v.

60 Petition of Antônio Luís Pereira (24 April 1799), AHU, Bahia pap. avul., caixa 75, 1st ser., uncat.

61 Petition of Bernabé Cardoso Pereira (4 March 1732), AHU, Bahia pap. avul., caixa 45, 1st ser., uncat.

62 Consulta Con. Ultra., AHU, Bahia pap. avul., caixa 12, 1st ser., uncat.; Petition of Tomé Pereira Falcão (12 Feb. 1680), caixa 14.

63 See Schwartz, *Sovereignty and Society*, 337–8, 347–8.

64 Aufderheide, "Order and Violence," 255–87.

65 Schwartz, "Colonial Brazil: The Role of the State," 1–24.

66 Freyre, *Masters and the Slaves*.

67 Morton, "Conservative Revolution," 30. On the role of the resident planter, see Eugene D. Genovese, *The World the Slaveowners Made* (New York, 1971), 76–7.

68 AHU, Bahia pap. avul., caixa 17, 1st ser., uncat. (16 Dec. 1720).

69 Cunha e Freitas, "Documentos para a história do Brasil," *Anais Academia Portuguesa de História*, 2d. ser., 21 (1972): 465–89.

70 Antônio de Oliveira Pinto da França, *Cartas baianas, 1821–1824* (São Paulo, 1980); Felisberto Caldeira Brant Pontes, *Economia açucareira do Brasil no século xix* (Rio de Janeiro, 1976).

71 "O catolicismo rústico no Brasil," in Maria Isaura Pereira de Queiroz, *O campesinato brasileiro* (Petropolis, 1973), 72–99.

72 "Rellação das freguesias e capelas filiaes . . . da Vila de São Francisco" (1830), APB, Pres. da Prov. 1433.

73 On the interference of masters in the religious obligations of slaves, see APB, Ord. reg. 2, n. 150 (Lisbon, 17 March 1698).

74 Report of Guinebaud (25 April 1825) printed in Barbara Lasocki, "A Profile of Bahia (1820–1826), as Seen by Jacques Guinebaud, French Consul General" (M.A. thesis, University of California, Los Angeles, 1967). See also Luiz R. B. Mott, *Os pecados da familia na Bahia de Todos os Santos (1813)* (Salvador, 1982).

75 U. B. Philips makes this same point about the planters of the U.S. South. See *American Negro Slavery* (Baton Rouge, 1973), 107.

76 I have discussed this problem at some length in "The Formation of Colonial Identity in Brazil" (unpublished paper, 1982).

77 Antonil, *Cultura*, liv. 1, cap. 10.

78 Some courses were also offered by the Carmelites and Franciscans. See Leite, *HCJB* 5: 69–106, 167–97, for the Jesuits' educational role in Bahia.

79 Morton, "Conservative Revolution," 55.

80 APB, sec. jud., maço 623, n. 4.

81 Santos Vilhena, *A Bahia*, I, 273–87. The *subsídio literário* (literary subsidy) was established in 1772 to support public education.

82 Manoel Ferreira da Câmara Bittencourt e Sá, owner of Engenho da Ponta in Cachoeira, wrote and published on natural history and natural resources; Felisberto Caldeira Brant Pontes, senhor of Engenho Santana in Ilhéus and later Marquis of Barbacena, was a widely read and educated man whose correspondence attests to his accomplishments. He played a major role in the Bahian independence movement. Manoel Jacinto de Sampaio e Mello, senhor of an engenho in Cachoeira, published *Novo methodo de fazer o açúcar* (Bahia, 1816).

83 Higginbotham, *Cicero on Moral Obligation*, ch. 17, 58.

84 Marques Pereira, *Compendio narrativo*, 164–6.

85 Antonil, *Cultura*, liv. 1, cap. 2.

86 Maria Luiza Marcilio, "Mariage et remariage dans le Bresil traditionnel: Lois, intensité, calendrier," in J. Dupaquier, E. Helin, P. Laslett et al., eds., *Marriage and Remarriage in Populations of the Past* (New York, 1981), 363–74.
87 There is a collection of dispensations in the archive of the Curia Metropolitana de Salvador, but they were not open to the public at the time of this writing.
88 APB, Recenseamentos (1788).
89 Antonil, *Cultura,* liv. 1, cap. 3.
90 APB, Cartas do Governor 140 (13 Dec. 1800), f. 222v.–3.
91 Soeiro, "Baroque Nunnery," 38–61, 87–114.
92 Schwartz, "Patterns of Slaveholding in the Americas," 63.
93 APB, Ord. reg. 86, fs. 234–6.
94 AHU, Bahia pap. avul., caixa 55, 1st ser., uncat. (14 Dec. 1748).
95 APB, Ord. reg. 85, fs. 268–9.
96 E.g., see testaments of Antônio de Sá Doria (1662) in ASCMB, Livro do Tombo I, 147–85.
97 Cf. J. P. Cooper, "Patterns of Inheritance and Settlement by Great Landowners from the Fifteenth to the Eighteenth Centuries," in Jack Goody, Joan Thirsk, and E. P. Thompson, eds., *Family and Inheritance* (Cambridge, 1976), 192–327.
98 See Chapter 5.
99 Vera Lucia Vilhena de Morais, "O morgado de Marapicu" (M.A. thesis, University of São Paulo, 1977), 5, 12–14.
100 Morton, "Conservative Revolution," 26–7.
101 Morgados were abolished in Portugal in 1863. The classic attack on them is Tomaz Antonio de Villanova Portugal, "Qual foi a origem e quais os progresos e as variações da jurisprudencia dos morgados de Portugal," *Memoria da Literatura Portugesa. Academia Real das Ciencias,* 3 (Lisbon, 1792).
102 Cited in Morton, "Conservative Revolution," 26. There is no full study of the morgado in Brazil in quantitative or qualitative terms. Vilhena de Morais, "O morgado de Marapicu," claims that morgados in Brazil were innumerable, but she lists only 5 in the Northeast, 5 in Rio, 2 in São Paulo, and 2 in Minas Gerais. There were certainly many more than this, but the documents she cites in the ANRJ are only petitions, not grants. The truth is that innumerable in this case simply means uncounted. See also Cid Teixeira, *O morgado na Bahia* (Salvador, 1953), for a short introduction.
103 Morton, "Conservative Revolution," 25–7.
104 APB, Livro de Notas 37, fs. 91–2v, 220.
105 APB, Cartas ao Governor 209 (23 Sept. 1800).

Chapter 11. The cane farmers

1 The disappearance of the cane growers in the Caribbean has not merited any study, although some authors have noted their early existence. See, e.g., Marrero, *Cuba: Economía y Sociedad,* II, 317. This chapter includes large sections of my earlier article, "Free Labor in a Slave Economy: The Lavradores de Cana of Colonial Bahia," in Dauril Alden, ed., *Colonial Roots of Modern Brazil* (Berkeley, 1973), 147–97. The reader is directed there for a more detailed exposition and a fuller set of citations. I have in the present chapter, however, added new materials drawn from documentary sources and secondary works.
2 Manoel de Couto to countess of Linhares (3 May 1617), ANTT, CSJ, maço 9, n. 241; (20 Aug. 1617), maço 13, n. 7.
3 Apontamentos que levao Cristóvão Barroso que agora mando por feitor da fazenda . . . (Lisbon, 23 March 1601), ANTT, CSJ, maço 13.
4 Couto to countess of Linhares (20 Aug. 1617), ANTT, CSJ, maço 13, n.7.

5 Ribiero to Countess of Linhares (17 March 1612), ANTT, CSJ, maço 8, n. 190.
6 Antonil, *Cultura*, liv. 1, cap. 3. See the discussion of lavrador rents in Gorender, *O escravismo*, 397–408.
7 APB, sec. jud., Livro de Notas 9, fs. 110v.–12 (cited in Flory, "Bahian Society," 34).
8 See Schwartz, "Free Labor," 156, n. 23.
9 "Treslado de escritura," ANTT, CSJ, maço 12, n. 36.
10 "Arrendamento de Custodio Lobo" (8 Aug. 1617), ANTT, CSJ, maço 12, n. 7.
11 Buescu, *História econômica do Brasil*, 110–13.
12 Pero Bras Rey to count of Linhares (20 April 1609), ANTT, CSJ, maço 8, n. 188.
13 "Lembrança para a Senhora Condessa de Linhares (Bahia, 20 Aug. 1617), ANTT, CSJ, maço 13, n. 7.
14 ANTT, CSJ, maço 52, n. 32.
15 Schwartz, "Free Farmers," 158; Barros de Castro, "Brasil, 1610," 703.
16 "Venda e obrigação" (Lisbon, 30 Oct. 1613), ANTT, CSJ, maço 12, n. 31.
17 Escritura de débito e obrigação, APB, Notas 18 (4 Aug. 1701), fs. 217–18v.
18 Treslado de escritura de venda, ANTT, CSJ, maço 12, n. 36.
19 These symbolic rents seem to have been more characteristic of contracts with ecclesiastical institutions or with the nobility. Thus they are found in the transactions between the count and countess of Linhares and lavradores in the early seventeenth century.
20 Cf. *DH* 62 (1943): 234, 240; Schwartz, "Free Labor," 159.
21 E.g., AHU, Bahia, pap. avul., caixa 15 (23 Jan. 1686); caixa 17 (26 Jan. 1689).
22 MHN/CWP, pacote 10 (São Francisco do Conde, 18 March 1699).
23 *DH* 62 (1943): 220–32.
24 Ibid.
25 Antonil, *Cultura*, liv. 1, cap. 3.
26 Schwartz, "Free Labor," 165–7.
27 Schwartz, "Patterns of Slaveholding in the Americas," 74; also see Chapter 16. Since the data are drawn from a list of slaveowners, those with no slaves are unlisted.
28 For details, see notes to Schwartz, "Free Labor," 168.
29 ANTT, CSJ, maço 13, n. 32.
30 Antônio Joaquim Pires de Carvalho e Albuquerque, owner of engenhos, testified that mutual use of slaves was "practica constantemente observada entre todos os proprietarios com os seus lavradores" (a constant practice observed by all the owners with their cane farmers). APB, Cartas ao Governo 209 annexo (14 Aug. 1800).
31 Maria Izabel de Albuquerque, "Liberdade e limitação dos engenhos d'açúcar," *Anais do primeiro congresso de história da Bahia*, 6 vols. (Salvador, 1950), II, 491–9.
32 Inventário, Felipe Dias Amaral (1804) registered in São Francisco do Conde, MHN/CWP, pacote 2.
33 Schwartz, "Patterns of Slaveholding in the Americas," 72–3. See Chapter 16 for a fuller treatment.
34 Flory, "Bahian Society," 44–5, and the sources she cites drawn from the notarial registers of Salvador and Cachoeira.
35 Adriaen van der Dussen, *Relatório, sôbre as capitanias conquistadas no Brasil pelos holandeses (1639)*, ed. José Antônio Gonçalves de Mello (Rio de Janeiro, 1947), 73.
36 Morton, "Conservative Revolution," 21–2.
37 Report on the Captaincy of Bahia (1779), IHGB, 1, 1, 19.
38 Flory, "Bahian Society," 41.
39 Lista dos moradores que comprende a companhia de ordenança nos distritos da Patatiba, . . . 1788, APB, Recenseamentos.
40 For the details, see Schwartz, "Free Labor," 180–1.
41 Flory, "Bahian Society," 40–1. My article "Free Labor" apparently caused Flory some confusion. Although I used 30 lavradores per mill as a maximum in an attempt to

calculate the total number, I did suggest that perhaps one-half or one-third that number was probably closer to the correct figure. Flory used 15 per mill as a basis for calculation and then, finding far fewer than that, she assumed that there must have been a high number of independent growers that were unlisted in the materials she was investigating. I suspect that she was misled and that her figure of 15 lavradores per mill is simply too high.

42 Schwartz, "Patterns of Slaveholding in the Americas," 73. Also see Chapter 17.

43 *ABNR* 31 (1909): 27–31.

44 Mateus (?) to Father Christóvão de Castro (8 June 1623), ANTT, CSJ, maço 70, n. 87.

45 Santos Vilhena, *A Bahia*, I, 80–3; cf. Silva Lisboa (1781) as cited in Wanderley Pinho, *História*, 311–12.

46 APB, Pres. da Prov. Engenhos 1824–54.

47 Cited in Wanderley Pinho, *História*, 312 note.

48 Document of 1660 printed in Mauro, *Le Brésil*, 293.

49 Five lavradores de cana at Jesuit-owned Engenho Santana complained that the engenho was in poor repair and not fulfilling its obligations. Their letter brought a visit from Father Felipe Franco, who discovered that in fact there was a shortage of slaves and kettles. The lavradores had stopped planting cane, and shortages resulted that impeded the next 5 safras. See ANTT, CSJ, maço 56, n. 19 (1660).

50 Report of Joseph de Araújo Pinto (15 July 1722); APB, Ord. reg. 15, 52c.

51 I have presented this argument in "Free Labor," 189–93. A good short summary of the story is Boxer, *Portuguese Society in the Tropics*, 104–6. Also essential is Mauro, *Le Brésil*, 270–307, which prints essential documents, as does Albuquerque, "Liberdade e limitação," engenhos d'açúcar," 2: 491–9.

52 For a short biography of Vieira Ravasco, see Schwartz, "A Governor and His Image," 163–5.

53 AHU, Bahia, pap. avul., caixa 8, 1st ser., uncat. (8 Sept. 1660).

54 Mauro, *Le Brésil*, 279–307.

55 This was admitted by one representative. See Albuquerque, "Liberdade e limitação," 498.

56 Correa to Overseas Council (23 May 1662), AHU, Bahia, pap. avul., caixa 8, 1st ser., uncat.

57 Letter of 8 Jan. 1662, in Albuquerque, "Liberdade e limitação," 491–9.

58 Mauro, *Le Brésil*, 297–307.

59 Pinheiro da Silva, *A capitania da Bahia*, part 1, 187–9; Conde de Óbidos to crown (23 March 1665), APB, Cartas do Governor 134, fs. 178–9; Consulta, Con. Ultra. (7 Oct. 1681), AHU, Codice 252, fs. 69–69v.

60 AHU, Bahia, pap. avul., caixa 51, 1st ser., uncat. (1797); Rodrigo de Sousa Coutinho to Fernando José de Portugal (30 April 1800), APB, Cartas do Governo 140. The planters of Santo Amaro had pointed out that engenhos Santos Apostolos, Rio Fundo, Paciencia, Buraco, Parnagua, and Pandalunga were all close together.

61 NL/GC, Privisão (Lisbon, 3 Nov. 1801); Provisão (Lisbon, 13 May 1802). A petition to erect a new mill was directed to the local *juiz de fora* (district magistrate). See that of Luis Paulinho de Oliveira Pinho and Manoel de Oliveira Mendes in APB, Cartas ao Governo 238 (14 June 1819).

62 Cf. Barros de Castro, "Brasil, 1619," 710.

63 MHN/CWP, pacote 1 (Inventário, 19 Oct. 1825).

64 Santos Vilhena, *A Bahia*, I, 180–2; Louis-François de Tollenaire, *Notas dominicais tomadas durante um a viagem em Portugal e no Brasil em 1816* (Bahia, 1956), 93–5. See also Stuart B. Schwartz, "Elite Politics and the Growth of a Peasantry in Late Colonial Brazil," in *From Colony to Nation* (Baltimore, 1975), ed. A. J. R. Russell-Wood, 133–54.

65 João Maciel da Costa, *Memória sobre a necessidade de abolir a introdução dos escravos*

africanos no Brasil (Coimbra, 1821), 74–5, states: "Muitos destes lavradores não tem outro auxillio senao o de seus braços e de seus filhos" (Many of these lavradores have no other help except that of their own strength and of their children).
66 Tollenaire, *Notes Dominicales*, 95.
67 Ibid., 94.

Chapter 12. Wage workers in a slave economy

1 Antonil, *Cultura*, liv. 1, cap. iv.
2 In 1798, Father José da Fonseca Neves, chaplain on the engenhos of Paulo de Argolo e Teive in Nossa Senhora do Monte, complained against a physician and a musician who lived nearby as lavradores de cana and whose actions were offensive to the dignity of the church. See APB, Ord. reg., 128, f. 259.
3 Livro de Contas, 1669–70. In this safra, a boat caulker received 750 réis a day without food or 640 daily with it. ACS, Livro de requerimentos da partes 1787–1814, fs. 344r.–5.
4 E.g., Antônio de Sá Doria died owing salaries to a former sugar master, a crater, and a kettleman. See ASCMB, Livro I do Tombo, fs. 147–85 (1663). See also Contas Engenhos Passagem, Cachoerinha, Santa Ignes (1822), APB, Cartas ao Governo 196, for monthly payments of soldadas.
5 Luís da Rocha (22 May 1745), ANTT, CSJ, maço 70, n. 124.
6 *DHA*, III, 393; ASCMB, Livro I do Tombo, fs. 199–201.
7 ANTT, CSJ, maço 70, n. 124.
8 J. R. Hicks, *The Theory of Wages* (New York, 1932), 69–71.
9 *ACB*, I, 6.
10 Boxer, *Portuguese Society in the Tropics*, 76–7; see also Antônio de Oliveira, *A vida económica e social de Coimbra de 1537 a 1640*, 2 vols. (Coimbra, 1971), I, 443–556.
11 On Portugal, see Franz-Paul Langhans, *As corporações dos ofícios mecânicos*, 2 vols. (Lisbon, 1943), I, x, xii–lxxxiii.
12 Maria Helena Flexor, *Oficiais mecânicos na cidade do Salvador* (Salvador, 1974), 20–4; Flory, "Bahian Society," 291–300.
13 Harry Bernstein, "The White Workingman in Brazil From Pedro I through the Regency," *RIHGB* 301 (1975): 234–53.
14 Citations to specific examples in this section will be made to the year the safra began. The reader should consult the bibliography for the specific location of each of the safra accounts of Engenho Sergipe.
15 Antonil, *Cultura*, liv. 1, cap. 6. Estevão Pereira reported in 1635 that the sugar master's salary was estimated at 100$ in cash, a barrel of wine worth 20$, and an arroba of meat each week or 16$ for the year. Thus full compensation equaled 136$ annually. See Mansuy's appendix to Antonil, *Cultura*, 513–27.
16 Antonil, *Cultura*, liv. 1, cap. 5.
17 Manoel de Cunha Meneses to the crown (3 March 1775), LC/Port. Mss., P-21.
18 ANRJ, Caldeira Brant Papers, caixa 20A, 188–90 (Bahia, 19 Sept. 1820).
19 Maria Barbara to Luís Paulino (23 May 1822), Antônio d'Oliveira Pinto da França, *Cartas baianas 1821–1824*, 60.
20 MHN/CWP, pacote 1 (Santo Amaro, 1766).
21 Juiz dos orfãos de São Francisco (1760), IHGBa, pasta 27, n. 9.
22 In fact, a crioulo who worked for a while in the blacksmith's shop received 100 réis a day during the 1669–70 safra.
23 Testament of Maria da Silva (1714), APB, sec. jud. 619; ACMS, Cartas ao Senado 28: 5 (3 July 1751).
24 ANRJ, caixa 146.
25 Katia M. de Queiros Mattoso, "Sociedade e conjunctura na Bahia nos anos de luta pela Independência," *Universitas* 15–16 (1973): 5–26.

26 This aspect was examined by Paul Silberstein, "Wage Earners in a Slave Economy: The Laborers of a Sugar Mill in Colonial Brazil" (unpublished seminar paper, University of California, Berkeley, 1970).

27 The printed account has Gonçalves, but this is probably a recording error.

28 Accounts of Engenho Buranhaem, ANRJ, caixa 406.

29 Pinto da França, *Cartas baianas*, 36.

30 On the concept of just wage, see Manuel Rocha, *Les Origines de Quadragesimo Anno; Travail et Salaire a Travers la Scolastique* (Paris, 1933); James Healy, *The Just Wage, 1750–1890* (The Hague, 1933).

31 Cited in E. H. Phelps-Brown and Sheila V. Hopkins, "Seven Centuries of Building Wages," *Economica*, new series 22 (1955): 195–206. See also their companion pieces, "Seven Centuries of the Prices of Consumables, Compared with Builder's Wage-Rates," *Economica*, new series 23 (1956): 296–314; and "Wage-Rates and Prices: Evidence for Population Pressure in the Sixteenth Century," *Economica*, new series 24 (1957): 289–306.

32 Antonil actually gives ranges of wages depending on the nature of the duties and the size of the engenho. Mills that produced 4,000–5,000 sugarloaves a year paid more for purgers, craters, and other employees.

33 In 1706, the câmara of Salvador complained that the soldadas of sugar masters had risen markedly, but the Engenho Sergipe accounts present no evidence of such a rise. See Wanderley Pinho, *História*, 175.

34 Jan de Vries has demonstrated that wages in Holland also rose to a height in the early seventeenth century and then leveled off. Also, during the course of the seventeenth and eighteenth centuries masters' wages in Antwerp were less able to keep pace with inflation than those of unskilled workers. See "An Inquiry into the Behavior of Wages in the Dutch Republic and the Southern Netherlands from 1580 to 1800," in Maurice Aymard, ed., *Dutch Capitalism and World Capitalism* (Cambridge, 1982), 75–92.

35 Queirós Mattoso, "Sociedade e conjuntura," 21–2.

36 Buescu, *300 anos da inflação*, 74–7.

37 ANTT, CSJ, maço 13, n. 15.

38 P. Felipe Franco to Provincial (Santana, 15 March 1671), ANTT, CSJ, maço 70, n. 383.

39 Governor of Bahia to crown (6 Nov. 1706), APB, Ord. reg., 7, nn. 440, 441.

40 Antonil, *Cultura*, liv. 1, cap. 6.

41 Rocha to P. Francisco Guerra (25 Sept. 1745), ANTT, CSJ, maço 70, n. 109.

42 P. Agostinho Lousada to College of Santo Antão (17 March 1660), ANTT, CSJ, maço 68, n. 132.

43 Registro da proposta que fizerão o povo e os homens de negocio (3 Dec. 1711), ACMS, 124: 7, Provisões, fs. 171–3.

44 Santos Vilhena, *A Bahia*, I, 135–7.

45 Schwartz, "Manumission," 603–36; Katia M. de Queiros Mattoso, "A propósito de cartas da alforria na Bahia, 1799–1850," *AH* 4 (1972): 23–52; Arnold Kessler, "Bahian Manumission Practices in the Early Nineteenth Century" (unpublished paper, American Historical Association, 1973). See the notes in Schwartz, "Manumission," for another relevant bibliography.

46 Schwartz, "Manumission," 624. It should be noted that the occupation of the slave rarely appears in the Bahian cartas de alforria. The patterns of age, sex, and color observed were the same for both rural and urban slaves in ibid.

47 Kessler, "Bahian Manumission," found a very high proportion of African manumissions in the early nineteenth century. The reasons for this difference are not clear.

48 Juiz de Fora of Santo Amaro to governor (21 Nov. 1812), APB, Cartas ao Governo, 241.

49 Pedro Gomes to crown (17 Nov. 1747), AHU, Bahia pap. avul., caixa 53, 1st ser., uncat.

50 King to governor of Bahia (Lisbon, 25 Jan. 1695), APB, Ord. reg. 3, n. 59.

51 See Alden, "Late Colonial Brazil, 1750–1807," *CHLA*, II, 602–62.
52 Sonia Aparecida Siqueira, "Artesanato e privilégios. Os artesãos no Santo Oficio no Brasil do século xvii," *III Simpósio dos professores universitários de História (França)* (São Paulo, 1967). See also Neusa Esteves, ed., *Irmãos da Santa Casa de Misericórdia da Bahia – seculo xvii* (Salvador, 1977), in which no person defined as an engenho artisan appears as a brother of the Misericórdia.
53 *PVCB*, 1591, 25–7, 125–6; ANTT, Inquisição de Lisboa processo 11,075. The correspondence of Felipe Dias do Amaral, feitor mor of Engenho do Meio (1799–1803), is revealing of the responsibilities of this position. See IHGBa, pasta 27.
54 Flory, "Bahian Society," 302. Of a sample of 125 artisans resident in Salvador, 64 percent were born in Portugal or the Atlantic islands in the period 1680–1725.
55 APB Recenseamentos. The returns for these parishes are only partial.
56 MHN/CWP, pacote 14, Inventory of José Rodrigues Pereira (1733), notes the register of the crater from the engenho of Francisco da Cunha Barbosa. In a dispute, the crater of Engenho Pitinga offered testimony "in a rustic hand," in 1744 (MHN/CWP, pacote 1). The inventory of Manoel Lopes Henriques (1706), senhor do engenho Santa Teresa in Matoim, made many references to the register maintained by his crater. See Anita Novinsky, "Fontes para a história económica e social do Brasil. Inventários dos bens confiscados pela Inquisição," *Revista de História* 48, no. 98 (1974): 359–92.
57 Santos Vilhena, *A Bahia*, I, 189. See also Wanderley Pinho, *História*, 173–7.
58 João Rodrigues de Brito, *Cartas economico-politicas sobre a agricultura e commercio da Bahia* (Lisbon, 1821); Maria Beatriz Nizza da Silva, "Os senhores de engenho e a cultura científica," *Ciência e cultura* 31, no. 4 (1979): 389–94.
59 Irineu Ferreira Pinto, *Datas e notas para a história da Parahyba*, 2 vols., 2d ed. (João Pessoa, 1977), I. 197.
60 Manoel Jacintho de Sampaio e Mello, *Novo methodo de fazer o açúcar* (Bahia, 1816), 39–42. Deerr, *History of Sugar*, II, 534–95, presents the best discussion of technological change in the industry.
61 Sampaio e Mello, *Novo methodo*, 42.
62 Caldeira Brant to Sr. Branford (19 May 1820), ANRJ, Caldeira Brant papers, caixa 20A. See the selection of letters from this collection published as *Economia açucareira do Brasil no século XIX* (Rio de Janeiro, 1976).
63 Caldeira Brant to John Gyles (24 June 1821), ibid., caixa 20A.

Chapter 13. The Bahian slave population

1 Goulart, *Escravidão africana*, 98–104. For recent estimates based on African ports of origin, see Paul E. Lovejoy, *Transformations in Slavery* (Cambridge, 1983), 44–65.
2 Ibid.; on the later trade with Guiné and the peoples involved, see "Mapa dos costumes . . .," BNL, Codice 6938. See also Mauro, *Portugal et l'Atlantique*, 147–52.
3 Boxer, *Portuguese Seaborne Empire*, 100–4. See also Joseph C. Miller, "The Slave Trade in the Congo and Angola," in Martin Kilson and Robert I. Rotberg, eds., *The African Diaspora: Interpretive Essays* (Cambridge, Mass., 1976), 75–113; Herbert Klein, "The Portuguese Slave Trade from Angola in the Eighteenth Century," *Journal of Economic History* 32, no. 4 (1972): 894–918. Also see Phyllis M. Martin, *The External Trade and the Loango Coast 1576–1870* (Oxford, 1972).
4 Walter Rodney, "Portuguese Attempts at Monopoly on the Upper Guinea Coast," *Journal of African History* 6, no. 1 (1965): 307–22.
5 Boxer, *Portuguese Seaborne Empire*, 104. On the asientos in this period, see Enriqueta Vila Vilar, *Hispano-américa y el comercio de esclavos. Los asientos portugueses* (Seville, 1977), and the still-important extended article of Rozendo Sampaio Garcia, "Contribuição ao estudo do aprovisionamento de escravos negros da América espanhola (1580–1640), *AMP* 16 (1962): 7–196.

6 I have discussed the outlines of this issue in "Colonial Brazil: Plantations and Peripheries, 1580–1750," CHLA, II, 423–99.

7 Boxer, Portuguese Seaborne Empire, 109–16; Albert van Dantzig, Les hollandais sur la côte de Guinée à L'époque de l'essor de l'Ashanti et du Dahomey, 1680–1740 (Paris, 1980).

8 The best short survey of these developments is Pierre Verger, Bahia and the West Coast Trade (1549–1851) (Ibadan, 1964).

9 Ibid., 31.

10 "Homens de negocio da praça da Bahia" to crown (no date), APB, Ord. reg. 83, fs. 135–6.

11 Emilia Viotti da Costa, A Abolição (São Paulo, 1982), 19–21.

12 ACS, Livro 182.1.

13 Imbert, Manual do fazendeiro, 2. See also Gaspar Barleus, Rerum per Octennium in Brasilia (Clèves, 1660).

14 ANRJ, Arquivo particular de Caldeira Brant, caixa 20A (Bahia, 25 Nov. 1819).

15 Marques Pereira, Compendio narrativo, 115–28.

16 See Chapter 17.

17 M. Goulart, Escravidão africana no Brasil, 112–28.

18 Patrick Manning, "The Slave Trade in the Bight of Benin, 1640–1890," in The Uncommon Market. Essays in the Economic History of the Atlantic Slave Trade, ed. Henry A. Gemery and Jan S. Hogendorn (New York, 1979), 107–41.

19 David Eltis, "The Direction and Fluctuation of the Trans-Atlantic Slave Trade, 1821–1843: A Revision of the 1845 Parliamentary Paper," in Gemery and Hogendorn, Uncommon Market, 273–99. Other figures come from Eltis's unpublished manuscript on the slave trade, which he provided to me and for which I thank him. See also Alden, "Late Colonial Brazil," 611–12, which presents different estimates but also shows a recovery in volume in the late eighteenth century.

20 "Relação de todas as parcellas de receita e despeza dos tezoureiros q. servirão na Alfândega desta Cidade de 19 de Junho 1725 até 29 Abril 1744 pelo q. respeita aos direitos de 3500 reis q. pagão por entrada os escravos vindos da costa da Mina em direitura a esta Bahia," AHU, Bahia, pap. avul., caixa 59.

21 APB, Ord. reg. 65 (Feb. 1753); APB, termos de fiança 1765–1824; ANTT, Erario régio livro 91 (1788); APB, passaportes; catalogo de alvarás (1779–98).

22 Herbert Klein, The Middle Passage (Princeton, 1978), 34–5. On a sample of fifteen ships carrying slaves between Guiné and Maranhão and Angola-Pará or Angola-Maranhão between 1758 and 1765, there were 2,314 males and 976 females. Females thus constituted 30%. See Antônio Carreira, As companhias pombalinas de navegação, comercio e trafico de escravos entre a costa africana e o nordeste brasileiro (Bissau, 1969), 161–9. See also José Ribeiro Junior, Colonização e monopólio no nordeste brasileiro (São Paulo, 1976), 130–2.

23 Klein, Middle Passage, 35–7, 49–50.

24 Katia M. de Queirós Mattoso, "Os escravos da Bahia no alvorecer do século XIX," Revista de História 97 (1974): 109–35.

25 These figures are based on a sample of 1,914 slaves listed in inventories attached to wills. All are drawn from sugar engenho and fazenda de canas properties in the Recôncavo between 1710 and 1827. For a fuller discussion of this material, see the discussion Data Set A near the beginning of Sources and Selected Bibliography in this volume.

26 Mattoso, "Os escravos," 119. She found the percentage of pardos to be 7.1 in the period 1805–6 and 6.3 in the sample of 1810–11. Some interesting comparative data from Minas Gerais can be found in Francisco Vidal Luna and Iraci del Nero da Costa, "Algumas caracteristicas do contingente de cativos em Minas Gerais," AMP 29 (1979): 79–98. They demonstrated that the percentage of Africans fell from about 80 in 1718 to 40 in 1804. Pardos never constituted more than 12% of the Brazilian-born slaves in

the captaincy. Although the information on age contained in this article is not presented in a manner helpful to our purposes, it is clear that there was a shortage of children.

27 Luís Lisanti, *Negocios coloniais*, 5 vols. (Brasilia, 1973), I, clviii, presents another schema of descriptive ages based on merchant correspondence. He lists old (*velho*) slaves at age 36 and above. This attribution does not seem applicable to plantation slaves in Bahia. The earliest designation of "old" I found applied to a slave for whom an actual age was known was 48 years old.

28 ANTT, CSJ, maço 54, n. 51.

29 Using the Cole and Demeny life tables at West-7 at a growth rate of .5% a year, 32.42% of the population would be age 15 or younger and 16% 8 years of age or younger. If we assume an even more unhealthy demographic regime and use West-1 at a rate of decline of 1% per annum, still over 18% of the population would be 8 years or younger. See Ansley J. Cole and Paul Demeny, *Regional Model Life Tables and Stable Populations* (Princeton, 1966).

30 Henry Koster, who visited the Carmelite engenho of Camasari in Pernambuco, wrote, "The estates of friars are worked almost exclusively by negroes who have been born upon them. Everything goes easily upon them. If much is made, the better satisfied is the chief for the time being; but if, on the contrary, little is obtained, still the affairs of the community go on." *Travels*, I, 313.

31 Data Set A.

32 IHGAP, Estante A, gaveta 5 (1788).

33 A good discussion of the economic stages in the history of Bahia in the late colonial period is provided in Katia M. de Queiros Mattoso, "Conjuncture et société au Bresil a la fin du xviiiᵉ siècle," *Cahiers des Ameriques Latines* 5 (1970): 3–53.

34 Table 13-1.

35 "Mapa feito pelo Capitão da ordenança Francisco Xavier de Oliveira . . . a respeito das mandiocas q. ha plantadas em a Ribeira de Vasabarris, termo deste cidade de Sergipe de El-Rey (1785), APB, Cartas ao Governo 188.

36 Luiz R. B. Mott, "Brancos, Pardos, Pretos, e Indios em Sergipe, 1825–1830," *AH* 6 (1974): 139–84.

37 Luiz R. B. Mott, "Pardos e pretos em Sergipe, 1774–1851," *Revista do Instituto de Estudos Brasileiros* 18 (1976): 7–37.

38 F. Matias to F. Estevão da Costa (Bahia, 3 Oct. 1623), ANTT, CSJ, maço 70, n. 89.

39 Stanley J. Stein, *Vassouras*, 2d ed. (New York, 1970), 155.

40 Vaz to Collegio de Santo Antão (Bahia, 5 March 1634), ANTT, CSJ, maço 68, n. 7.

41 Gama to Collegio de Santo Antão (Engenho Sergipe, 20 Sept. 1733), ANTT, CSJ, maço 70, n. 428.

42 ANTT, CSJ, maço 70, n. 390 (15 Jan. 1731).

43 Estado do Engenho Santana, ANTT, CSJ, maço 15, n. 23.

44 ARSI, Bras. 3 (II) (Bahia, 26 Feb. 1662). He wrote that the *Bentos* managed their estates better, "e por isso tirão delles muito proveito e nos das nossas tirão muita mizeria" (and because of this they derive much benefit, and from ours we get much misery).

45 ADB, CSB, 136–7.

46 ADB, CSB, 135 (Estado 1783–7).

47 ADB, CSB, 134 (Estado 1747–8).

48 ADB, CSB, 135 (Estado 1763–6); MSSB, Livro 18, visitas e juntas de São Paulo.

49 ADB, CSB, 139 (Estados, 1778–80, 1784–6, 1789–93).

50 ANTT, CSJ, maço 3, n. 4.

51 [José] Wanderley [Araújo] Pinho, "Uma partilha de bens no Recôncavo da Bahia em 1779, com informações de caráter econômico social e industrial." *ACCBTSGB*, I, 315–17.

52 APB, secção jud., Testamento e inventário de João Lopes Fiuza, maço 623, n. 4.

53 MHN/CWP, pacote 14.
54 Ibid., pacote 2.
55 Much of the literature is ably summarized in Robert Fogel and Stanley Engerman, "Recent Findings in the Study of Slave Demography and Family Structure," *Sociology and Social Research* 63 (1978–9): 566–89; Stanley L. Engerman, "The Realities of Slavery: A Review of Recent Evidence," *International Journal of Comparative Sociology* 20, nos. 1–2 (1979): 46–66.
56 Herbert S. Klein and Stanley L. Engerman, "Fertility Differentials between Slaves in the United States and the British West Indies: A Note on Lactation Practices," *William and Mary Quarterly*, 3d. ser., 35, no. 2 (April 1978): 357–74.
57 Imbert, *Manual do fazendeiro*, 254–5.
58 J. C. Caldwell and Pat Caldwell, "The Role of Marital Abstinence in Determining Fertility: A Study of the Yoruba in Nigeria," *Population Studies* 31, no. 2 (July 1977): 193–217. See also Frank Lorimer, *Culture and Human Fertility* (Paris, 1954), a UNESCO study, and John C. Caldwell, ed., *Population Growth and Socioeconomic Change in West Africa* (New York, 1975).
59 There were also losses to the slave population due to manumission and flight.
60 Ribeiro to countess of Linhares (27 Sept. 1601), ANTT, CSJ, maço 8, n. 152.
61 ANTT, Corpo cronológico, part 1, maço 115, n. 113.
62 In an estimate made from Barbados in 1689, the rate of decline there was set at 8–10% a year. Newly arrived slaves were expected to suffer a one-third loss during "seasoning." Accidents were common, as was suicide, "and sometimes comes a mortality amongst them which sweeps a great part of them." See *Groans of the Plantations* (London, 1689), 17–18.
63 The 1832 estimate is in an unsigned manuscript. BNL, F. G. Codice 599. João Monteiro Carson, *Primeiro relatório apresentado a Presidência da Bahia sobre os melhoramentos da cultura da cana e do fábrico do assucar* (Bahia, 1854), 7. Hereafter cited as *Os melhoramentos*. All these statements of rate of loss were made without attention to compound figures. A calculation that the slave force would disappear in 20 years implies an annual compound rate of loss of 3.6%.
64 Cited in Leslie Bethel, *The Abolition of the Brazilian Slave Trade* (Cambridge, 1970), 41–2.
65 Sebastião Vaz (Bahia, 2 Dec. 1636), ANTT, CSJ, maço 69, n. 76.
66 The best discussion of the technical problems involved in mortality estimates for Brazilian slaves is presented by Robert Slenes, "The Demography and Economy of Brazilian Slavery, 1850–1888" (Ph.D. thesis, Stanford University, 1976), 341–411.
67 Philip Curtin, *The Atlantic Slave Trade: A Census* (Madison, Wis., 1969), 19; Philip Curtin, "Epidemiology and the Slave Trade," *Political Science Quarterly* 83 (1968): 190–216; Russell Menard, "The Maryland Slave Population, 1658 to 1730: A Demographic Profile of Blacks in Four Counties," *William and Mary Quarterly*, 3d ser., 32, no. 1 (Jan. 1975): 45.
68 The percentage difference is based on calculations made in Data Set A: Slaves from Inventories.
69 The 7–15 year estimate can be found in various authors. See the discussion in Slenes, "Demography and Economy," 361–2, 400–1.
70 ACMS, Livro de Óbitos, Santo Amaro da Purificação.
71 This assumption is based on my discussion of the 1788 Bahian census and on evidence from other captaincies. E.g., in a census of Sergipe de El-Rey made in 1834, the percentage of children 0–10 for each segment of the population was: whites, 26.2%; free colored, 21.9%; Indians, 24.5%; pardo slaves, 21.9%; black slaves, 16.6%; all slaves, 18.3%. See Mott, "Pardos e pretos em Sergipe," 7–37.
72 Slenes uses mortality regimes of West-1 to West-4 as the parameters of mortality. Given that the slave trade had ended and a larger proportion of the Brazilian slave force was native born, I believe the population he studied in the late nineteenth

century experienced healthier rates of mortality and fertility than those that character-
ized Bahian slaves in the colonial era. His estimate is very close to that of Eduardo E.
Arriaga for Brazil in 1879. See *New Life Tables for Latin American Populations in the
Nineteenth and Twentieth Centuries* (Berkeley, 1968), 29. Cf. Slenes, "Demography and
Economy," 348–53.

73 Pedro Carvalho de Mello's estimates were made in an unpublished paper that has
been used by Thomas W. Merrick and Douglas H. Graham, *Population and Economic
Development in Brazil* (Baltimore, 1979), 56–7, and that has since appeared as "Estimativa da longevidade de escravos no Brasil na segunda metade do século XIX," *Estudos
Econômicos* 13, no. 1 (1983): 151–81.

74 Stephen Burmeister, "The Slave Population in Three Bahian Parishes: A Profile and
Comparisons" (unpublished paper, University of Minnesota, 1980).

75 AHU, Maranhão pap. avul., caixa 37.

76 Data Set A.

77 ACMS, Libro de Óbitos, São Francisco (1816).

78 Cartas de Felipe Nery to Antônio Estes de Costa (Pernambuco, 6 Aug. 1812), BNL,
F.G. caixa 224, nn. 31–3.

79 Antonil, *Cultura*, 128–31. For documentation on slave suicides in the nineteenth century, see José Alípio Goulart, *Da fuga ao suicídio* (Rio de Janeiro, 1972), 123–30.

80 ASCMB, "Assento que se despidisse a Luís de Araújo," Liv. 13.

81 ASCMB, Liv. 13, fs. 51–2, 57–8.

82 ASCMB, Liv. 13, fs., 101–2 (19 Oct. 1664).

83 Report of Desembargador Antônio José de Affonseca Lemos (16 May 1755), APB,
Cartas do Senado 152.

84 "Copia do Regimento que ha de seguir o Feytor de Fazenda de Saubara que adminis-
tra a casa da Santa Misericórdia. . . ," ASCMB, B/3ª/213.

85 ASCMB, B/3ª/213. Lists exist for 1713, 1727, 1735, 1750, 1753, 1757, 1758, and 1760.

86 Michael Craton, *Searching for the Invisible Man* (Cambridge, Mass., 1978), 95.

87 We do not know the date of death for the listed slaves. Thus I have taken the
midpoint year between the last listing and absence from a list year as the period at
which the slave was at risk in both fertility and mortality calculations.

88 Klein and Engerman, "Demographic Study of the American Slave Population," 3.

89 I am assuming here that all slaves purchased after 1750 were prime adults unless
otherwise noted.

Chapter 14. The slave family and the limitations of slavery

1 For a review of the literature, see Maria Salete Zulzke Trujillo, "A Familia brasileira,"
Noticia Bibliografica e Historica 67 (May 1975): 139–46.

2 Gilberto Freyre, *Casa grande e senzala* (Rio de Janeiro, 1933).

3 The main issues in the history of the slave family are discussed by Herbert Gutman,
Barry Higman, and Stanley Engerman in *HR/RH* 6, no. 1 (summer 1979): 183–212. An
interesting study of the slave family in southern Brazil is Robert Slenes, "Slave Marriage and Family Patterns in the Coffee Regions of Brazil, 1850–1888" (unpublished
paper, 1978). For a comparative perspective, see Quintard Taylor, "Slave Family Life
on the Fazenda and Plantation: A Comparison of Brazil and the United States, 1750–
1850" (unpublished paper, 1979); and A. J. R. Russell-Wood, "The Black Family in the
Americas," *JGSWGLA* 16 (1979): 267–309.

4 Florestan Fernandes, *The Negro in Brazilian Society* (New York, 1969), 84.

5 Burlamaqui, *Memoria analytica*, 8.

6 Imbert, *Manual do fazendeiro*, 358–9.

7 Koster, *Travels*, II, 203.

8 Ibid., II, 242.

9 Cf. Slenes, "Slave Marriage," which describes a similar pattern, especially on large estates.

10 Instructio abius qui officinam sacchaream administrant servenda data a P. Rectore Bernaba Soares (27 Dec. 1692), ARSI, Bras. 11(1), 132–4. A supplementary set was issued on 18 Jan. 1693.

11 Koster, Travels, I, 322, gives a number of examples from Pernambuco.

12 Richard Price, "Commentary" on Monica Schuler, "Afro-American Slave Culture," suggests this development in Surinam as well. See HR/RH 6, no. 1 (1979): 144.

13 João Severiano Maciel da Costa, Memória sôbre a necessidade de abolir a introdução dos escravos africanos no Brasil (Coimbra, 1821).

14 Koster, Travels, II, 204.

15 Ibid.

16 See the discussions in Magnus Morner, "Los Jesuitas y la esclavitud de los negros," Revista Chilena de Historia y Geografia 35 (1967): 92–109; David Sweet, "Black Robes and 'Black Destiny': Jesuit Views of African Slavery in Seventeenth-Century Latin America," Revista de Historia de America 86 (July–Dec. 1978): 87–133.

17 Report on Mission to the Recôncavo (1619), StL/VFL, roll 159.

18 Sebastião Monteiro de Vide, Constituições primeiras do Arcebispado da Bahia (Lisbon, 1719). See the discussion in Gentil Avelino Titton, "O sínodo da Bahia (1710) e a escravatura," Trabalho Livre e trabalho escravo, 3 vols. (São Paulo, 1973), I, 285–306; Thales de Azevedo, Igreja e estado em tensão e crise (São Paulo, 1978), 78–80.

19 Titton, "O sínodo," 300.

20 Antonil, Cultura, 120–34, contains liv. 1, cap. 9, on slave treatment; Jorge Benci, Economia cristá dos senhores no governo dos escravos, 2d ed. (Oporto, 1954). This edition is enhanced by Father Serafim Leite's notes and introduction to the original edition of 1705. Manoel Ribeiro Rocha, Ethiope Resgatado, empenhado, sustentado, corregido, instruido, e liberto (Lisbon, 1758).

21 Antonil, Cultura, 124–5.

22 Benci, Economia cristá, 82–5.

23 Marcos Antonio de Sousa, Memoria sobre a capitania de Serzipe . . ., as cited in Mott, "Brancos, pardos, pretos e indios em Sergipe, 174.

24 Antonil, Cultura, 124.

25 Ibid.

26 King to D. João de Lancastre (Lisbon, 5 March 1697), APB, Ord. reg. 4, n. 100.

27 Pinheiro da Silva, "A capitania," pt. 1, 126; AAPB 24 (1943): 89–91.

28 AHU, Con. Ultra. 247, f. 73v.

29 StL/VFL, roll 160 (Bras. 10).

30 Colin M. Maclachlan, "Slavery, Ideology, and Institutional Change: The Impact of the Enlightenment on Slavery in Late Eighteenth-Century Maranhao," Journal of Latin American Studies 11, no. 1 (1979): 1–17.

31 APB, sec. jud., maço 638, n. 6; Maria Luiza Marcilio, A cidade de São Paulo. Povoamento e População (São Paulo, 1974), 157–9, discusses illegitimacy.

32 Iraci del Nero da Costa, Vila Rica: População (1719–1826), 249; Marcilio, A cidade de São Paulo, 157–9.

33 Herbert Klein, "Nineteenth-Century Brazil," in David Cohen and J. P. Greene, eds., Neither Slaves Nor Free (Baltimore, 1973), 321.

34 Robert Slenes, "The Demography and Economics of Brazilian Slavery, 1850–1888" (Ph.D. thesis, Stanford University, 1975), pt. ii, 412–20.

35 Maria Beatriz Nizza da Silva, "Casamentos de escravos na Capitania de São Paulo," Ciência e Cultura 32, no. 7 (July 1980): 816–21, shows that canonical and bureaucratic difficulties arose over slave marriages as well.

36 Luís da Rocha to Padre Francisco da Guerra, ANTT, CSJ, maço 70, n. 124 (22 May 1745).

37 Koster, *Travels*, II, 203.
38 Graham, *Journal of a Voyage to Brazil*, 114.
39 Luiz R. B. Mott, "Revendo a história da escravidão no Brasil," *MAN* 11, no. 7 (1980): 21–5, reprints this document in full.
40 APB, sec. jud., maço 623, n. 4 (1741).
41 The Nagô and Gege "nations" began to arrive in Bahia in some numbers toward the middle decades of the eighteenth century and then in large numbers after 1790. This was especially true of the Nagôs with the breakup of the Oyo state in the 1790s. Yoruba and Ewe are related languages, and there were many other cultural affinities between the two groups. See Abiodun Adetugbo, "The Yoruba Language in Yoruba History," in S. O. Biobaku, ed., *Sources of Yoruba History* (Oxford, 1973), 176–204. On the Geges (Ewes), see A. B. Ellis, *The Ewe-Speaking Peoples of the Slave Coast of West Africa* (Oosterhaut, 1970), which is a reprint of the original edition of 1890.
42 ACMS, Livro de casamentos, Purificação 1774–88.
43 Consuelo Ponde de Sena, "Relações interétnicas através de casamentos realizados na freguesia do Inhambupe, na segunda metade do século xviii" (unpublished paper, 1974). The paper is based on a tabulation of 1,294 marriages. Unfortunately, the author used the general category "African" and did not report her results by "nation."
44 This point is also made by Barry Higman in "African and Creole Slave Family Patterns in Trinidad," in Margaret E. Crahan and Franklin W. Knight, eds., *Africa and the Caribbean* (Baltimore, 1979), 41–65. Higman's article is the only one I know that deals with this problem. His data enable him to show differences in family patterns between Africans and creoles. This is a provocative question with wide implications in the Bahian case but unanswerable with the data presently available.
45 Nero da Costa, *Vila Rica*, 34–6; Koster, *Travels*, II, 202. In Purificação parish between 1774 and 1788, there were 13 recorded slave–free unions. Eleven of these were between slave men and free wives, and 7 involved marriages in which both partners were Brazilian born. In only two cases did free men wed slave women, and in both of these the men were crioulos.
46 These explanations are suggested by John Tutino, "Slavery in a Peasant Society: Indians and Africans in Colonial Mexico" (unpublished paper, St. Olaf College, 1978). Tutino refers to this pattern as "emancipationist marriage" and places great emphasis on it as a reason for the decline of the slave population.
47 Donald Ramos, "City and Country: The Family in Minas Gerais, 1804–1838," *Journal of Family History* 3, no. 4 (winter 1978): 361–75; Kuznesof, "Household Composition and Economy"; Donald Ramos, "Marriage and the Family in Colonial Vila Rica," *HAHR* 55, no. 2 (May 1975): 200–25; Marcilio, *A cidade de São Paulo,*
48 Richard Graham, "Slave Families on a Rural Estate in Colonial Brazil," *Journal of Social History* 9, no. 3 (1976): 382–402.
49 Michael Craton, "Changing Patterns of Slave Families in the British West Indies," *JIH* 10, no. 1 (summer 1979): 1–34; Barry Higman, "Household Structure and Fertility on Jamaican Slave Plantations: A Nineteenth-Century Example," *Population Studies* 27 (1973): 527–50; and his "Slave Family and Household in the British West Indies, 1800–1834," *JIH* 6, no. 2 (1975): 261–87; Peter Laslett, "Household and Family on the Slave Plantations of the U.S.A.," in *Family Life and Illicit Love in Earlier Generations* (Cambridge, 1977), 233–60.
50 "Estado em que achey e faz este entrega do Engenho de S. Anna dos Ilheus o Padre Manoel de Figuereido aos 7 de Agosto de 1731," ANTT, CSJ, maço 15, n. 24; "Informe do estado pasado e presente de Engenho de S. Ana dos Illheus ano 1753," ANTT, CSJ, maço 54, n. 42. There is also a list made slightly later in 1753 and dated 13 June, ANTT, CSJ, maço 54, n. 55.
51 Chapter 13, section titled "Fertility and marriage."
52 Laslett, "Household and Family on the Slave Plantations," 250.

53 ANTT, CSJ, maço 15, n. 23.
54 Letters of P. Pedro Teixeira (11 Nov. 1731; 10 Aug. 1732), ANTT, CSJ, maço 70, nn. 405, 469.
55 Marques Pereira, *Compendio narrativo*, 162.
56 These figures are similar to those reported by Ramos for the population of Vila Rica in 1804. See Ramos, "Marriage and Family," 200–25.
57 APB, sec. jud., São Francisco 535.
58 Examples here are drawn from marriage registers of Nossa Senhora da Purificação de Santo Amaro, 1778–90.
59 Information on the men who staffed Engenho Santana in a given year is from the "Catalogus tertibus triennalis" supposedly drawn up every three years for the Jesuit province of Brazil. See StL/VFL, roll 160, which includes materials from ARSI, Bras. 6A, 6, 11, 8.
60 See Chapter 13, section titled "Fertility and marriage."
61 ANTT, CSJ, maço 54, n. 55.
62 Father Jerônimo da Gama (Santana, 20 Oct. 1753), "Informe do estado pasado e presente do Engenho Santana," ANTT, CSJ, maço 54, n. 51.
63 Jeronimo da Gama, ANTT, CSJ, maço 54, n. 55.
64 Imbert, *Manual do fazendeiro*, 249–50.
65 ANTT, CSJ, maço 54, n. 55.
66 My description of the incident is based on Father Pedro Teixeira to Father Simão Estevens (Santana, 20 Aug. 1733), ANTT, CSJ, maço 70, n. 425, and on an alternative account in the letter of Brother Mateus de Sousa to Father Luís Vellozo (Santana, 23 July 1733), ANTT, CSJ, maço 70, n. 170.
67 Ages and other characteristics have been obtained from the Santana list of 1731. The loss of an arm by the women who fed the cane into the sugar mill was a common accident. See Chapter 6, section titled "Work in field and factory."
68 Brother Mateus de Sousa believed that Padre Teixeira had acted without cause and with excessive rigor. On their continuing feud, see ANTT, CSJ, maço 70, ns. 405, 420.
69 Stephen Gudeman and I have discussed the theoretical aspects of godparentage and slavery in detail in "Baptismal Godparents in Slavery: Cleansing Original Sin in Eighteenth-Century Bahia," in Raymond Smith, ed., *Kinship Ideology and Practice in Latin America* (Chapel Hill, N.C., 1984), 35–58. See also Stephen Gudeman, "The Compradrazgo as a Reflection of the Natural and Spiritual Person," *Proceedings of the Royal Anthropological Institute* (1971): 45–71. Much of the discussion that follows is drawn from Gudeman and Schwartz, "Baptismal Godparents," which includes a more detailed presentation of the data.
70 Donald Ramos, "A Social History of Ouro Preto: Stresses of Dynamic Urbanization in Colonial Brazil" (Ph.D. thesis, University of Florida, 1972), 242–55; David Smith, "Cor, ilegitimidade, e compadrio na Bahia seiscentista: Os livros de batizado de Conceição da Praia" (unpublished paper, Third Congress of Bahian History, 1973); Robert Slenes and Pedro Carvalho de Mello, "Paternalism and Social Control in a Slave Society: The Coffee Regions of Brazil, 1850–1888" (unpublished paper, Ninth World Congress of Sociology, Uppsala, Sweden, 1978); and Robert Slenes, "Coping with Oppression: Slave Accommodation and Resistance in the Coffee Regions of Brazil, 1850–1888" (unpublished paper, Southern Historical Association, 1978). On an earlier period in Bahia, see Schwartz, "Indian Labor and New World Plantations," 43–79.
71 Registers of baptism from ACMS, Saubara, 1723–4 (75 entries); Rio Fundo. 1780–1, 1788–9 (131 entries); Monte, 1788–9 (133 entries); and São Gonçalo, 1816–17 (92 entries) were consulted. All quantitative analyses and percentages are based on 264 cases from Rio Fundo and Monte (Data Set C).
72 Koster, *Travels*, I, 316.
73 Ibid., II, 196.

74 Ibid.
75 Schwartz, "Manumission," 113–18.
76 Koster, *Travels*, II, 196 n.
77 See Chapter 3, section titled "Acculturation and interaction."
78 Koster, *Travels*, II, 199.

Chapter 15. Resurgence

1 The historiography of the period 1750–1822 has experienced a remarkable development since 1960. The best short survey is Alden, "Late colonial Brazil," 601–60. Among the essential monographs and broader studies are Kenneth Maxwell, *Conflicts and Conspiracies: Brazil and Portugal 1750–1808* (Cambridge, 1973); Fernando A. Novais, *Portugal e Brasil na crise do antigo sistema colonial (1777–1808)* (São Paulo, 1979); Jobson de Andrade, *O Brasil no comércio;* Carlos Guilherme Mota, *Nordeste 1817* (São Paulo, 1972); Virgilio Noya Pinto, *O ouro brasileiro e o comércio anglo-português* (São Paulo, 1979); José Ribeiro, Jr., *Colonização e monopólio no nordeste brasileiro* (São Paulo, 1976); and Dauril Alden, *Royal Government in Colonial Brazil* (Berkeley, 1968).
2 Kenneth Maxwell, "Pombal and the Nationalization of the Luso-Brazilian Economy," *HAHR* 48, no. 4 (Nov. 1968): 631.
3 On the monopoly companies, see Ribeiro, *Colonização*, on Pernambuco, and Manuel Nunes Dias, *Fomento e mercantilismo: A Companhia geral do Grão Pará e Maranhão (1755–1778)*, 2 vols. (Belem, 1970).
4 Cf. Antônio Carreira, *As companhias pombalinas* (Lisbon, 1983), 232–4.
5 Dauril Alden, "Economic Aspects of the Expulsion of the Jesuits From Brazil," in Henry H. Keith and S. F. Edwards, eds., *Conflict and Continuity in Brazilian Society* (Columbia, S.C., 1969), 25–65.
6 See Buescu, *Evolução econômica do Brasil*, 96–103.
7 The statement was made by Pombal on 22 July 1766. See Suely Robles Reis de Queiroz, "Algumas notas sôbre a lavoura do açúcar em São Paulo no período colonial," *AMP* 22 (1967): 129.
8 See Alden, *Royal Government*, 83–116, 176–246.
9 Gilberto Ferrez, *As cidades do Salvador e Rio de Janeiro no século xviii* (Rio de Janeiro, 1963).
10 Chancellor Tomas Rubi de Barros to Conselho Ultramarino (5 April 1760), IHGB, Arquivo 1.1.19, f. 124; Sequestros dos bens dos Jesuítas, APB, Religião 610.
11 Alden, "Sugar Planters by Necessity," 152–3. Alden emphasizes the poor state of Engenho Sergipe, but its production of ca. 2,600 arrobas may be atypical in that an investigation of about 1750 stated that the mill produced 160 crates annually, of which only 40 to 50 belonged to lavradores. This would mean the engenho itself retained about 4,800 arrobas on its own account. (See ANTT, CSJ, maço 54, n. 62.) The same report stated: "From the bar of Santo Antonio around the bay it is well known around the Recôncavo that there is no better engenho than [Sergipe do] Conde."
12 AHU, Bahia pap. avul., caixa 62 (31 July 1779).
13 AHU, Bahia pap. avul., n. 5584 (1 Oct. 1761); "Relação dos bens sequestrados da companhia," n. 6120.
14 The relevant legislation was dated 16 and 27 Jan. 1751 and 2 April 1751. See Alden, *Royal Government*, 12.
15 Câmara of Salvador to câmara of Santo Amaro (6 Nov. 1751), ACS, Cartas do senado aos governadores das villas; "Representação dos senhores do engenho" (1751), AHU, Bahia pap. avul., caixa 60; caixa 61 (26 Oct. 1751); IHGB, Arquivo 1.1.17, fs. 40–8. See also José Honório Rodrigues, "Dois documentos sôbre o açúcar no século xviii," *Brasil Açucareiro* 20, no. 2 (1942): 159–69, which presents a good summary of the mesas' operations.

16 Report of Wenceslão Pereira da Silva (26 Oct. 1751), AHU, Bahia pap. avul., caixa 61.
17 Câmara of Sergipe de El Rey to crown (30 April 1753), AHU, Bahia pap. avul., caixa 61; APB, Cartas da Câmara 132 (2 July 1751).
18 Consulta, Con. Ultra. (23 Nov. 1752), IHGB, Arquivo 1.1.17.
19 Parecer of Manuel de Saldanha (1752?), AHU, Bahia pap. avul., caixa 63.
20 Petition of Senhores de engenho (Jan. 1751), AHU, Bahia, pap. avul., caixa 60.
21 Petition of senhores de engenho and lavradores de cana (1753), AHU, Bahia pap. avul., caixa 63.
22 João Lucio de Azevedo, *Novas epanáforas* (Lisbon, 1932), 34–9.
23 Verger, *Bahia and the West Coast Trade*, 18–23, provides a short summary.
24 F. L. C. Burlamaqui, *Monographia da canna d'assucar* (Rio de Janeiro, 1862), 329–31; Henri Raffard, *A industria saccharifera no Brasil* (Rio de Janeiro, 1882); Seymour Drescher, *Econocide: British Slavery in the Era of Abolition* (Pittsburgh, 1977), 15–37, 200.
25 Katia M. de Queirós Mattoso, "Conjoncture et société au Bresil a la fin du xviiie siècle," *Cahiers des Ameriques latines* 5 (1970): 3–53.
26 Drescher, *Econocide*, 65–91; see the classic account by C. L. R. James, *The Black Jacobins*, 2d ed. (New York, 1963).
27 Morton, "Conservative Revolution," 152–84, provides the best summary of the Bahian economy in this period. I have depended on his analysis.
28 ACMS, Livro de requerimentos das partes, 1787–1814, fs. 186–7 (18 June 1804).
29 Ibid., f. 191 (24 April 1805). Cf. Queirós Mattoso, *Bahia: A cidade do Salvador*, 295–302.
30 APB, Ord. reg. 281 (Lisbon, 29 Nov. 1797), Ord. reg. 83, fs. 245–278.
31 APB, cartas ao governo 170, fs. 310–13 (24 May 1798).
32 See Paulo O. D. de Azevedo, coordinator, *Inventário de proteção do acervo cultural da Bahia*, 4 vols. (Salvador, 1978–80), especially vol. 2, 2, and vol. 3, 2, on the Recôncavo.
33 Morton, "Conservative Revolution," 207–8; Francisco Marques de Goes Calmon, *Vida econômico-financeira da Bahia* (Bahia, 1925; facsimile ed., Salvador, 1979).
34 The export figures for Figure 15-1 are taken from two sources. Jobson de Andrade, *O Brasil no comércio*, provides export figures from Bahia and all Brazil drawn from the official trade records submitted to Lisbon. The series provided by Sebastião Ferreira Soares, *Notas estatísticas sobre a produção agrícola e carestia dos gêneros alimentícios no império do Brasil* (2d. ed., Rio de Janeiro, 1977), 228–9, is less trustworthy, having been constructed after the fact (1860), but it is also based on official provincial records. See also Spix and Martius, *Viagem pelo Brasil*, II, 148.
35 Cf. Relação dos engenhos (ca. 1751), ANTT, Mss. do Brasil, n. 43, which lists 275 mills, of which 43 were fogo morto; Ribeiro, *Colonização*, 132–45.
36 These figures have been calculated from Jobson de Andrade, *O Brasil no comércio*, 372–9, and Peter Eisenberg, *The Sugar Industry of Pernambuco* (Berkeley, 1974), 16. For purposes of standardization, crates (caixas) have been calculated at 40 arrobas or 1,280 pounds each.
37 "Relação dos engenhos . . . de Belem," IHGB, lata 44, n. 10, listed 17 mills and 36 *engenhocas* (small, animal-powered mills) for low-grade sugar and cachaça production at the beginning of the nineteenth century.
38 Maria Thereza Schorer Petrone, *A lavoura canavieira em São Paulo* (São Paulo, 1968), is the best account to date, although it does not provide details on production.
39 Simonsen, *História econômica*, 235, cited in Suely Robles Reis Queiroz, "Algumas notas sôbre a lavoura do açúcar em São Paulo no período colonial," 109–67; Petrone, *A lavoura*, 155.
40 Rudolph W. Bauss, "Rio de Janeiro: The Rise of Late Colonial Brazil's Dominant Emporium, 1777–1808" (Ph.D. thesis, Tulane University, 1977), 93–6. For the Campos region, see "Relações parciaes apresentadas ao Marquez de Lavradio (1778)," *RIHGB* 76 (1913): pt. 1, 290–360; "Mappa dos engenhos . . .," ANTT, Mss. do Brasil, n. 4, fl. 291.

41 See Petrone, *A lavoura*, 106–9.
42 See Alden, "Late Colonial Brazil," 627–48; J. H. Galloway, "Agricultural Reform and the Enlightenment in Late Colonial Brazil," *Agricultural History* 55, no. 4 (Oct. 1979): 763–79.
43 Alden, "Late Colonial Brazil," 651–3, provides a good general overview. See also Novais, *Portugal e Brasil*, 287–303.
44 Kenneth R. Maxwell, "The Generation of the 1790s and the Idea of Luso-Brazilian Empire," in Dauril Alden, ed., *Colonial Roots of Modern Brazil* (Berkeley, 1973), 107–44.
45 Pinto de Aguiar, *Bancos no Brasil colonial* (Salvador, 1960).
46 Maxwell, "Generation," 126.
47 Ibid., 128–31; Morton, "Conservative Revolution," 108–12.
48 Gileno de Carli, "Geografia econômica e social de canna de açúcar no Brasil," *Brasil Açucareiro* 10, no. 1 (Sept. 1937): 24–41; Morton, "Conservative Revolution," 199.
49 The Engenho da Praia was located in Iguape. De Carli places the date of introduction at 1810 and Morton at 1816.
50 Cf. Manuel Moreno Fraginals, *The Sugarmill* (New York, 1976), 86; Deerr, *History of Sugar*, I, 19.
51 Caldeira Brant to Robert Graham (7 Aug. 1820), ANRJ, caixa 20A.
52 Planters of Nazaré to president of the province of Bahia (n.d., but probably late 1820s), BNRJ, II-33-38-69.
53 Wanderley Pinho, *História*, 174–5.
54 Maria Beatriz Nizza da Silva, *A primeira gazetta da Bahia: "Idade d'Ouro do Brasil"* (São Paulo, 1978). See also her "Os senhores de engenho e a cultura científica, *Ciência e cultura* 31, no. 4 (1979): 389–94.
55 Manoel Jacinto Sampaio e Mello, *Novo methodo de fazer o açúcar* (Bahia, 1816). See also António Barros de Castro, "Escravos e senhores nos engenhos do Brasil," (Ph.D. thesis, State University of Campinas, 1976), 68–90.
56 AHU, Iconografia 28366; Morton, "Conservative Revolution," 160–5.
57 Brandão, *Dialogos*, IV, 123; Nizza da Silva, "Os senhores," 391.
58 Cited in Nizza da Silva, "Os senhores," 394. On the issue of technological change, see Morton, "Conservative Revolution," 329–35; also see Eul-Soo Pang, "Modernization and Slavocracy in Nineteenth-Century Brazil," *JIH* 9, no. 4 (spring 1979): 667–88.
59 Moreno Fraginals, *Sugarmill*, 40–1; Nizza da Silva, *A primeira gazetta*, 95–8.
60 The population of late colonial Brazil is discussed in Alden, "Late Colonial Brazil," 602–10; counts for the period are untrustworthy, but most authors agree that from one-third to one-half of the captaincy's population was enslaved and about two-thirds to three-quarters were persons of color, free and slave.
61 I have dealt with this issue at some length in "Elite Politics and the Rise of a Peasantry," 133–54. See the notes therein for further references.
62 For examples from the period, see APB, Cartas ao governo 210 (Sergipe de El-Rey, 19 Jan. 1807); 235 (Vila Real, 10 March 1817). During the political unrest of the 1830s, more stringent measures and curfews were enforced. See the order of the juiz do paz of Santo Amaro (20 Sept. 1831), APB, Pres. da Prov., juizes 2580.
63 Santos Vilhena, *A Bahia*, III, 919. On the increasing fears of the Bahian propertied classes, see João José Reis, "A elite baiana face os movimentos sociais: Bahia, 1824–1840," *RH* 108 (1976): 341–84.
64 See my discussion in "Colonial Brazil," 462–5.
65 E.g., APB, Cartas do governo 188, f. 36 (22 Dec. 1786).
66 *Provisão* (1780), APB, Cartas ao governo 180.
67 These censuses have never been fully exploited for the considerable social and economic data they contain. They indicate that despite governmental urgings, many planters grew no manioc for their slaves and that many manioc growers owned slaves, albeit in small numbers. See the lists in APB, Cartas ao governo 188, which

includes returns from Sergipe de El-Rey and also those from Cairú in BNRJ, I, 31, 30, 51.

68 Cited in Barros de Castro, "Escravos e senhores," 62.

69 The situation is discussed in more detail in João José Reis, "Slave Rebellion in Brazil: The African Muslim Uprising in Bahia, 1835" (Ph.D. thesis, University of Minnesota, 1982), 1-57.

70 Santos Vilhena, A Bahia, III, 919.

71 Correio oficial 3 (16 Dec. 1834): 561.

72 Goes Calmon, Vida econômico-financeira, 49-50. See Chapter 13 on the slave trade.

73 Reis, "Slave Rebellion," 197-9, presents a discussion of the ethnic origins of slaves in Salvador drawn from wills, testaments, and other sources. His results should be compared with those of Queirós Mattoso, "Os escravos na Bahia," 109-35.

74 See Chapter 13.

75 The standard account of Britain's role in abolishing the Brazilian slave trade is Leslie Bethell, The Abolition of the Brazilian Slave Trade (Cambridge, 1970). On the Brazilian role in the process, see Luís Henrique Dias Tavares, "O processo das soluções brasileiras no exemplo da extinção do tráfico negreiro," RH 71 (1967): 524-37. On the much debated issue of why Britain pushed for the abolition of slavery and the slave trade in the first place, see Roger Anstey, The Atlantic Slave Trade and British Abolition (London, 1975).

76 Katia de Queirós Mattoso, Ser Escravo no Brasil (São Paulo, 1982), 94-5.

77 Cited in Bethell, Abolition, 8.

78 Maciel da Costa, Memoria, 35.

Chapter 16. The structure of Bahian slaveholding

1 Much of this chapter, including the tables, appeared originally as "Patterns of Slaveholding in the Americas: New Evidence from Brazil" AHR 87, no. 1 (Feb. 1982): 56-86.

2 The lists are found in APB, Cartas ao governo, maços 232, 233, 234.

3 In 1819, the parishes of Cachoeira had 12,523 households with 77,500 people and 48 engenhos, according to the German travelers J. B. von Spix and C. F. P. von Martius. Subtracting the area of Santo Amaro, which was included in their calculation but for which lists survive, the totals for Cachoeira are: 10,723 households, 68,700 inhabitants, and 34 engenhos. See Spix and Martius, Viagem pelo Brasil, II, 49-79.

4 Maria Luiz Marcilio, "Crescimento histórico da população brasileira até 1872," in Crescimento populacional, Cuardernos de Centro Brasileiro de Analise e Planejamento (CEBRAP), no. 16 (São Paulo, 1974): 1-26. Also see Merrick and Graham, Population and Economic Development in Brazil, 49-79.

5 The parishes for which lists have been found are: Vila de São Francisco; Nossa Senhora de Socorro; São Sebastio de Passé; Santa Anna do Catú; Nossa Senhora do Monte; São Gonçalo, Madre de Deus de Boqueirão (São Gonçalo and Boqueirão were listed together and are analyzed jointly in the discussion presented here); Vila de Santo Amaro; Nossa Senhora da Purificação; São Pedro de Rio Fundo; Nossa Senhora de Oliveira; São Domingos de Saubara; Vila de Jaguaripe; and Vila de Maragogipe. The lists from the last two were made by district rather than by parish. For a brief discussion of the Recôncavo towns, see Santos Vilhena, A Bahia, II, 475-86.

6 There are 166 engenhos listed in the townships of Santo Amaro and São Francisco, but Engenho do Campo in Passé parish was inactive and thus has been eliminated from all calculations. In addition, although the lists from Maragogipe township did not identify property type, from the names of slaveowners it is possible to recognize 6 other engenhos so that the total number of engenhos appearing on the surviving lists is at least 172. All further calculations, however, are based on the 165 operating mills in the two major Recôncavo townships of Santo Amaro and São Francisco.

7 I have used slaveholdings as units of slaveownership, just as the lists record them. This makes sense from the slaves' point of view, since these units formed the context in which they lived; but it does not resolve problems of multiple ownership – one individual holding 2 or more separate units. Data were not coded by the owner's names, so I have been unable to aggregate the holdings of persons with 2 or more slaveholdings. For the largest units, the sugar plantations, the problem is not acute, because notaries often listed all units held by a single planter together so that multiple holdings are made clear. In 4 instances, however, this causes the opposite problem because the number of slaves is given in a total and not by unit. In these cases, I have simply taken the average per plantation unit. Holdings in more than 1 parish present more of a problem, but there do not seem to have been many of these. One Bahian slaveowner held 500 slaves and at least 3 held more than 300, but no single unit of ownership was composed of more than 237 slaves.

8 I have eliminated 5 owners from my calculations because the condition of the documents does not permit a reading of the number of slaves they held. The Bahian lists record 4,662 individual units of slaveownership that, because of 4 cases of joint recording, can be reduced to 4,653 "owners." Minus the 5 Jaguaripe owners whose slaves cannot be determined, the total number of owners becomes 4,648, holding 33,750 slaves.

9 For an excellent description of the Gini coefficient, see Charles M. Dollar and Richard J. Jensen, *Historian's Guide to Statistics* (New York, 1971), 121–6. The formula for computing the Gini Index is
$$G = 1 - 2 \sum_{i}^{n} P_i \operatorname{Cum} Y_i + \sum_{i}^{n} P_i Y_i.$$

10 APB, Colônia, Mss. Recenseamentos. The bundle of these census returns was created in the Colonia section after I discovered them scattered throughout the Cartas ao Governo section.

11 I have based the calculations for Rio de Janeiro on "Relações parciães apresentadas ao Marquez de Lavradio (1778)," *RIHGB* 76 (1913): 289–360. For São Paulo, see Robles Reis de Queiroz, "Algumas notas sobre a lavoura do açúcar," 109–277.

12 A. J. R. Russell-Wood has provided, in a different context, a brief discussion of inheritance practices; see Russell-Wood, "Women and Society in Colonial Brazil," *Journal of Latin American Studies* 9 (1977–8): 1–34.

13 Katia M. de Queirós Mattoso, "Parocos e Vigários em Salvador no século xix: As multiplas riquezas clero secular da capital baiana," *Tempo e Sociedade* 1 (1981): 13–47.

14 Colin Clark, *The Conditions of Economic Progress*, 3d ed. (New York, 1960), 490–2. Clark has defined the primary sector of economic activity as that which provides the products of agriculture and the sea and which depends on the direct use of natural resources. The secondary sector produces movable goods on a continuous basis through craft manufacture. The tertiary sector includes transport, communication, commerce, finance, professional services, and domestic employment, among quite a wide range of services. I have followed the application of these definitions to the Brazilian situation as outlined in Marcilio, *A cidade de São Paulo*, 129–35.

15 Instructions for making the lists required that the names and properties of the masters be listed but were not clear about the recording of the masters' professions. In some parishes, such as Maragogipe and Jaguaripe, no attempt was made to record either property or occupation. In Oliveira, the list was organized around rural properties, engenhos, and fazendas, so that by inference the occupations of the owners of these properties can be deduced; but many persons remain without occupational information. Despite such gaps and problems, if we view slave property as a form of wealth, then it is possible to rank occupations according to that wealth and, by doing so, to suggest the relative power of classes and groups in Bahian society.

16 Flory, "Bahian Society," 182.

17 *Sítio* was a term also used simply to mean "place."

18 For a discussion of the decline in prestige of the lavradores de cana, see my "Elite Politics and the Rise of the Peasantry," 133–54.

19 In the parish of Rio Fundo in 1788, there were 13 heads of household listed as lavradores de cana, of whom 4 were people of color. See APB, Colônia, Mss. Recenseamentos.

20 Schwartz, "Elite Politics and the Rise of the Peasantry," 150–2.

21 Ewbank, *Life in Brazil*, 184.

22 "Quadro dos engenhos das visinhanças da Bahia" lists 354 engenhos in Bahia and Sergipe; BNJR I-7, 3, 27. Also see the calculations in Morton, "Conservative Revolution," 13–19.

23 Morton, "Conservative Revolution," 20–9.

24 For calculations on this point, see Table 11-1.

25 Barry W. Higman, *Slave Population and Economy in Jamaica, 1807–1834* (Cambridge, 1976), 274–5.

26 Schwartz, "Free Labor in a Slave Economy," 147–97.

27 Ibid., 173; and Flory, "Bahian Society," 30–45. Both studies offer estimates of land and slaveownership among the lavradores de cana based on notarial documents, and both offer correct estimates for the range of unit size; but, until now, it was impossible to determine the distribution of unit size among the lavradores de cana, so that some calculation of "typicality" and concentration could be made.

28 Higman, *Slave Population and Economy in Jamaica*, 174–5; Frank Wesley Pitman, *The Development of the British West Indies, 1700–1763*, 2d ed., reprinted (New York, 1963), 108–27; and Mark Schmitz, Economic Analysis of Antebellum Sugar Plantations in Louisiana (New York, 1977), 127–8. Information on Trinidad was kindly supplied by Stanley L. Engerman.

29 The 1816–17 lists may reveal a process of concentration within the sugar industry. Flory suggested that each engenho required an average of 15 cane farms for sugar production in the Recôncavo during the period 1680–1725; "Bahian Society," 31–5. This number would include both tenants and those lavradores who owned their own land. If Flory is correct, then the percentage of the total slave force controlled by lavradores was probably higher in the early eighteenth century than at the start of the nineteenth. If she is correct, moreover, then there appears to have been a process of contraction and centralization that diminished the number of lavradores de cana in the Recôncavo, since the average number of lavradores declined from her estimate of 15 per engenho to the one presented here of between 3 and 4.

30 For two such estimates, see "Discurso preliminar descrição económica da Comarca e Cidade do Salvador," in Pinto de Aguiar, ed., *Aspectos da economia colonial* (Salvador, 1957), 36–7; and Ruiters, "A torcha," 82–3.

31 AHU, Bahia pap. avul. (1751), caixa 61.

32 Francisco Vidal Luna, *Minas Gerais: Escravos e senhores – Analise de estrutura populacional e econômico de alguns centros mineratórios* (São Paulo, 1981), 157.

33 Francisco Vidal Luna and Iraci del Nero da Costa, "Posse de escravos em São Paulo no início do século xix," *Estudos Econômicos* 13, no. 1 (1983): 211–22.

34 This sort of observation and argument was characteristic of many of the foreign travelers in Brazil in the nineteenth century. For a guide to this literature, see Manoel Cardozo, "Slavery in Brazil as Described by Americans, 1822–1828," *The Americas* 17 (1961): 241–60.

35 Robert Walsh, *Notices of Brazil in 1828 and 1829*, 2 vols. (Boston, 1831), II. 20.

36 For a discussion of how to count the slaves themselves in calculations for wealth distribution, see Robert E. Gallman, "Trends in the Size Distribution of Wealth in the Nineteenth Century: Some Speculations," in Lee Soltow, ed., *Six Papers on the Size Distribution of Wealth and Income* (New York, 1969), 1–24. And for an interesting approach to the problem, see Richard Lowe and Randolph Campbell, "Slave Property

and the Distribution of Wealth in Texas, 1860," *Journal of Economic History* 63 (1976): 316–24.

37 The question of wealth distribution has generated a large and much-debated literature in the history of the United States. Gloria L. Main has identified some of the major trends and problems contained in this literature; see her "Inequality in Early America: The Evidence from Probate Records of Massachusetts and Maryland," *Journal of Interdisciplinary History* 7 (1976–7): 559–82. Also helpful to me was Jeffrey G. Williamson and Peter Lindert, "Three Centuries of American Inequality," in Paul Uselding, ed., *Research in Economic History* 1 (1976): 69–123.

38 Kuznesof, "Household Composition," 135–40; and Nero da Costa, *Vila Rica*, 164.

39 Avelino Jesus da Costa, "População da Cidade da Baia em 1775," *Actas: V Colóquio Internacional de Estudos Luso-Brasileiros*, 5 vols. (Coimbra, 1965), I, 191–205.

40 Luiz R. B. Mott, "Estrutura demográfica das fazendas de gado do Piauí-colonial: Um caso de povoamento rural centrifigo," *Ciência e Cultura* 30 (1978): 1196–1210.

41 Maria Luiza Marcilio, "Tendências e estruturas dos domicilios na Capitania de São Paulo segundo as listas nominativas de habitantes, 1765–1828," *Estudos Econômicos* 2 (1972): 131–44. Also see Emilio Willems, "Social Differentiation in Colonial Brazil," *Comparative Studies in Society and History* 12 (1969–70): 31–49; and Table 16-2. Fernando Henrique Cardoso has pointed out the lack of concentration of slaves in the hands of powerful agriculturalists in the early years of Rio Grande do Sul's settlement; see his *Capitalismo e escravidão* (São Paulo, 1962), 47.

42 Baquaqua, as noted in Samuel Moore, *A Biography of Mahommah G. Baquaqua, A Native of Zoogoo, in the Interior of Africa* . . . (Detroit, 1854), 48. Baquaqua was employed as a baker's assistant and then as a sailor on coasting voyages from Rio de Janeiro to Santa Catarina and Rio Grande do Sul.

43 Maria Inés Cortes de Oliveira, "O Liberto: O Seu Mundo e os outros" (M.A. thesis, Federal University of Bahia, 1979), 90.

44 Francisco Vidal Luna and Iraci del Nero da Costa, "A presença do elemento fôrro no conjunto de proprietários de escravos," *Ciência e Cultura* 32 (1980): 836–81. The authors emphasized that the majority of the liberto slaveowners were women, but they have not provided a sex ratio of the liberto population, so the significance of this distribution is unclear.

45 For the phenomenon of slaves "owning" slaves, see my "Manumission," 6.

46 APB, sec. jud., maço 2170, n. 1.

47 For a critical review of this literature, see Gavin Wright, " 'Economic Democracy' and the Concentration of Wealth in the Cotton South, 1850–1860," *Agricultural History* 44 (1970): 63–94. Albert W. Niemi, Jr., has, for the whole South, supported Wright's conclusions about the cotton South; see Niemi, "Inequality in the Distribution of Slave Wealth: The Cotton South and Other Southern Agricultural Regions," *Journal of Economic History* 37 (1977): 747–53.

48 Lewis C. Gray, *History of Agriculture in the Southern United States to 1860*, 2 vols. (Washington, 1932), I, 500.

49 Gavin Wright, *The Political Economy of the Cotton South: Households, Markets and Wealth in the Nineteenth Century* (New York, 1978), 142, 144.

50 See, e.g., Main, "Inequality in Early America," 559–82; Lee Soltow, *Men and Wealth in the United States, 1850–1870* (New Haven, 1975); and Williamson and Lindert, "Three Centuries of American Inequality."

51 Lee Soltow, "Economic Inequality in the United States in the Period from 1790 to 1860," *Journal of Economic History* 31 (1971): 822–39.

52 Ibid., 29–31.

53 Eric Williams, *From Columbus to Castro: The History of the Caribbean, 1492–1969* (New York, 1970), 104–7, 282–5; and Higman, *Slave Population and Economy in Jamaica*, 45–61, 274–5.

54 I have based these calculations on the table in Higman, *Slave Population and Economy in Jamaica*, 274–5.
55 Gray, *History of Agriculture in the Southern United States*, 530.
56 Ibid., 530–9.
57 There is no adequate census of Bahia for the period in question that provides figures for the relative proportions of the free and slave populations by color. Data do exist, however, for Minas Gerais in 1821, where the free people of color constituted 40 percent of the population. Travelers' observations and comments lead me to believe that the proportion in Bahia was certainly no smaller (and probably larger) than that in Minas Gerais. See especially Klein, "Nineteenth-Century Brazil," 309–40.
58 Ibid., 335–40.
59 See Schmitz, *Economic Analysis*, 127–8; and J. D. B. DeBow, *Statistical View of the United States* (seventh census) (Washington, 1854), 95.
60 Genovese, *World the Slaveholders Made*, 96. Also see Genovese's vigorous and informative defense of his position in "A Reply to Criticism," *Radical History Review* 19 (1977): 94–100.
61 This position is most clearly stated in Maxwell, "Generation," 107–44. Traces of the position are found in Florestan Fernandes, *A Revolução burguesa no Brasil* (Rio de Janeiro, 1974), 35–74; and Emilia Viotti da Costa, "The Political Emancipation of Brazil," in A. J. R. Russell-Wood, ed., *From Colony to Nation* (Baltimore, 1975), 86. The most detailed account of the revolutionary process and its limitations is Mota, *Nordeste 1817*.

Chapter 17. Important occasions: the war to end Bahian slavery

1 The historiography of the Bahian slave revolts is well developed, despite a lack of documentary evidence on many of the uprisings. Essential outlines are provided by Clovis Moura, *Rebeliões da Senzala*, 3d ed. (São Paulo, 1981); Décio Freitas, *Insurreições escravas* (Pôrto Alegre, 1976); Howard Prince, "Slave Rebellion in Bahia, 1807–1835" (Ph.D. thesis, Columbia University, 1972); and Verger, *Flux et reflux*, 324–54. Shorter pieces, important for their interpretations, are R. K. Kent, "African Revolt in Bahia: 24–25 January 1835," *JSH* 3, no. 4 (1970): 334–56; and João José Reis, "Slave Resistance in Brazil, Bahia, 1807–1835," *LBR* (in press). All these works depend to some extent on such earlier scholars as Nina Rodrigues, Manuel Querino, and E. A. Caldas Brito, who did much of the essential archival spadework but whose interpretations, though often repeated, are not to be trusted. A whole new dimension has been added by the work of Luiz Mott, which shows the extent to which Sergipe de El-Rey was also a scene of major slave insurrection in this period. See especially his "Pardos e pretos em Sergipe: 1774–1851," *RIEB* 18 (1976): 9–37; "Violência e repressão em Sergipe: Notícias sobre revoltas de escravos (século xix)." *MAN* 11, no. 5 (May 1980): 3–21.
2 Of 1,689 rural slaves listed in Bahian inventories from 1710 to 1830, 12 bore the designation of *fujão* or runaway.
3 The etymology of the term quilombo has never received the attention it deserves. The word became common only in the late seventeenth century during the struggle against Palmares. It seems to have originally referred to an Imbangala military adaptation of an Ovimbundu male initiation camp. It had important military and magical functions in Angolan society. I have provided a short discussion in "Le Brésil: le royaume noir des mocambos," *L'Histoire* 41 (Jan. 1981), 38–48, based on Joseph C. Miller, *Kings and Kinsmen* (Oxford, 1976).
4 A fuller discussion of the incidence and nature of Bahian fugitive communities is

provided in my article "The Mocambo: Slave Resistance in Colonial Bahia," *JSH* 3, no. 4 (1970): 313–33.

5 Capitão-Mor of Sergipe to crown (16 Sept. 1751), APB, Ord. reg. 76, fs. 178–81. He pointed out the utility and importance of regiments composed of blacks and mulattoes "in these parts of America" to hunt down such fugitives.

6 Domingos Nunes Pereira to governor of Bahia (24 Jan. 1745), BNRJ, II-34, 6, 32; AHU, Bahia pap. avul., caixa 63 (18 Nov. 1752).

7 Antônio de Sousa Lima to Pres. da Prov. (20 Jan. 1825), BNRJ, II-33, 26, 35.

8 Schwartz, "Mocambo," 322–7. See also Roger Bastide, *Les Amériques noires* (Paris, 1967), 77–94.

9 Governor of Bahia to Martinho de Mello e Castro (30 April 1788), in *ABNR* 34 (1913): 82.

10 Manuel Ignácio de Morais de Mesquita Pimentel to governor of Bahia (16 Nov. 1806), APB, Cartas ao Governo 208.

11 APB, Ord. reg. 86, fs. 242–5.

12 Michael Craton, *Testing the Chains: Resistance to Slavery in the British West Indies* (Ithaca, N.Y., 1982); Eugene D. Genovese, *From Rebellion to Revolution* (Baton Rogue, 1979); and Davis, *Problem of Slavery*. The definition of the period varies from 1770–90 to 1825 or 1830.

13 Reis, "Slave Resistance," addresses a number of these issues directly.

14 An argument for the relation between demography and revolt is found in Michael Craton, "Jamaican Slavery," in Engerman and Genovese, *Race and Slavery*, 249–84.

15 Nina Rodrigues, *Os africanos no Brasil*, 5th ed. (São Paulo, 1977), originally published in 1905, was one of the first works to give some interest to African internal affairs. Reis, "Slave Rebellion," 143–81, integrates more recent scholarship. See also J. D. Fage, *A History of West Africa* (Cambridge, 1969), 102–10; Robin Law, *The Oyo Empire c. 1600–c.1836* (Oxford, 1977). A concise summary of these events and their relation to the slave trade is found in Paul Lovejoy, *Transformations in Slavery* (Cambridge, 1983), 140–41.

16 Queirós Mattoso, "Os escravos na Bahia," João José Reis, "Slave Rebellion in Brazil: The African Muslim Uprising in Bahia, 1835" (Ph.D. thesis, University of Minnesota, 1982), 198. My observation on rural slaves is based on the sample of 1,689 drawn from plantation inventories.

17 Reis, "Slave Rebellion," 325–47. Vivaldo da Costa Lima, "O conceito da 'nação' nos candomblés da Bahia," *Afro-Ásia* 12 (1978): 65–90, provides a useful discussion of ethnic differences in the present African religious groups in Bahia.

18 The key studies of the Tailors' Revolt are Affonso Ruy, *A primeira revolução social brasileira, 1798* (Bahia, 1951); Luís Henrique Dias Tavares, *História da sedição intentada na Bahia em 1798* (São Paulo, 1975); and Katia M. de Queirós Mattoso, *Presença francesa no movimento democrático baiano de 1798* (Bahia, 1969).

19 Morton, "Conservative Revolution," 113–44, presents the best summary and interpretation in English.

20 Cited in ibid., 139. Some question remains about whether this statement represents Barata de Almeida's true feelings or whether it was written to exonerate him from complicity in the plot.

21 Maxwell, "Generation," 122.

22 Morton, "Conservative Revolution," 355–6.

23 Actas, ACS (1710), fs. 79v.–80.

24 Francisco C. Falcon and Fernando A. Novais, "A extinção da escravatura africana em Portugal no quadro da política econômica pombalina," *Anais VI Simpósio Nacional dos Professores Universitários de História* (São Paulo, 1973), 405–25.

25 E.g., APB, Ord. reg. 74, f. 38 (22 Feb. 1776); AHU, Bahia pap. avul., caixa 42 (8 April 1824), 2d ser., uncat.

26 The documentation on Paraíba is presented in Antônio Jorge de Siqueira, Jaconira Silva Rocha, and Noêmia Maria Zaidan, "Dados para a história da resistência escrava" (unpublished paper, Federal University of Pernambuco, 1983).

27 Letter of Jacques Guinebaud (Bahia, 22 May 1822), cited in Lasocki, "Profile of Bahia," appendix.

28 Maria Barbara Garces Pinto de Madureira to Luís Paulino d'Oliveira Pinto da França (Bahia, 13 April 1822), Cartas Baianas, 36.

29 The theme constantly appeared in the writings of many educated Brazilians of the period. See the comments and citations in Luiz R. B. Mott, "A revolução dos negros do Haiti e o Brasil," MAN 13, no. 1 (1982): 3–10.

30 Mott, "A revolução," 8.

31 Thomas Flory, "Race and Social Control in Independent Brazil," Journal of Latin American Studies 9, no. 2 (1977): 199–224.

32 Schwartz, "Resistance and Accommodation," 77–81.

33 APB, Ord. reg. 86, fs. 242–5. This document is an account of Pereira's services from 1786 to 1798.

34 Devassa, 1806, APB, Quilombos 572-2, caixa 287.

35 Bahia 1806–8, ms., IHGB, lata 399, doc. 2.

36 Count of Ponte to Fernando José de Portugal (17 May and 6 Oct. 1808), ANRJ, IJJ 317, fs. 205–8.

37 Devassa, 1806, APB, contains the inventory made of the accused. There were obviously poor manioc farmers.

38 Reis, "Slave Resistance," 6; Freitas, Insurreições, 36–7.

39 Joaquim Ignácio da Costa to count of Ponte (31 Jan. 1809), APB, Cartas ao governo 216.

40 Mott, "Violência e repressão," 3–22.

41 APB, Cartas ao governo 213.

42 Marquis of Aguiar to count of Arcos (Rio de Janeiro, 10 June 1814), BNRJ, II-33, 24, 27.

43 Prince, "Slave Rebellion," 117–20.

44 J. A. Gonçalves de Mello, "Um governador colonial e as seitas africanas," RIAHGP (1948–9): 41–5; Rene Ribeiro, "O negro em Pernambuco – retrospecto de suas prácticas religiosas," Revista do Arquivo Público (Recife) 7–8 (1950–1): 571–88. See also Roger Bastide, The African Religions of Brazil (Baltimore, 1978), 78–96. The term batuque is still used in Belem do Pará for candomblé-type ceremonies.

45 Con. Ultra. to Povolide (no date), AHU, Codice 583.

46 Ribeiro, "O negro," 580.

47 Corpo do Comércio to crown (1814), BNRJ, II-34, 6, 57. See the translated letter in Robert Conrad, Children of God's Fire: A Documentary History of Black Slavery in Brazil (Princeton, 1983), 401–6.

48 Marquis of Aguiar to Arcos (Rio de Janeiro, 6 June 1814), BNRJ, II-33, 24, 29.

49 Ribeiro, "O negro," 580–8; Reis, "Slave Revolts in Bahia," 6–8.

50 APB, Cartas ao governo 229 (7 Jan. 1815).

51 Cited in Freitas, Insurreições, 47.

52 Prince, "Slave Rebellion," 153.

53 Conrad, Children of God's Fire, 404–6.

54 Mott, "Pardos e pretos," 18.

55 Reis, "Slave Resistance," 13.

56 Mott, "Violência e repressao," 6.

57 APB, Documentos da Vila de Cachoeira (25 April 1835).

58 Reis, "Slave Rebellion in Brazil," provides an in-depth study of this revolt and a perceptive discussion of the previous historiography. Reis's analysis of the judicial investigations that followed the revolt is the most complete examination of such records from any of the slave revolts of this period in Bahia.

Appendix A. The problem of Engenho Sergipe do Conde

1 Frédéric Mauro, Le Portugal et l'Atlantique (Paris, 1960), 213–19; "Contabilidade teórica e contabilidade prática na America portuguesa no século xvii," Nova história e novo mundo (São Paulo, 1969), 135–48; Buescu, 300 anos da inflação, 39–121; Vera Lucia Amaral Ferlini, "O engenho Sergipe do Conde (162–1653), Contar, Constar, Questionar," (M.A. thesis, University of São Paulo, 1980).

2 Antonil, Cultura.

3 The legal history of Engenho Sergipe has been outlined in Leite, HCJB, 5, and more extensively in Wetzel, Mem de Sá, 225–54. The most perceptive study is [José] Wanderley [Araújo] Pinho, "Testamento de Mem de Sá. Inventário de seus bens no Brasil," Terceiro Congresso de História Nacional, 10 vols. (Rio de Janeiro, 1939–44), III, 5–161.

4 ANTT, CSJ, maço 68, n. 167, P. Simão de Sottomaior to P. Rector Manoel Fagundes (Bahia, 3 Jan. 1622.

5 Victor Ribeiro, "A fundadora da igreja do Colégio do Santo Antão," História e memorias da Academia das Ciências de Lisboa, new series, 2ª class, 14, no. 1 (1911): 14–21.

6 The contract is found in DHA, III, 313–21. A brief description of the two principal types of Portuguese marriage contracts is found in Alida C. Metcalf, "Household and Family Structure in Late Eighteenth Century Ubatuba, Brazil" (M.A. thesis, University of Texas, 1978), 44–6.

7 DHA, III, 320.

8 The count of Linhares stated in his will that he had rebuilt the engenho and that for his services the crown had confirmed his possession of the lands of Sergipe, which he then ceded to his wife. DH 63 (1944): 19–20, 93–4.

9 SGL, Disertações ecclesiasticas, f. 102.

10 Domingos Fernandes da Cunha to count of Linhares (Santana, 16 March 1603), ANTT, CSJ, maço 8, n. 132.

11 Simão de Sottomaior to Rome (Bahia, 22 May 1655), ARSI, Lusit. 78, fs. 94–6.

12 Report of Father Francisco Riberiro (undated), ANTT, CSJ, maço 90, ns. 99, 100. Ribeiro reported that there were other sales as well but that Dutch invasion in 1624 had destroyed the notary records to that their number and value could not be determined.

13 Ribeiro, "A fundadora," 18.

14 Wetzel, Mem de Sá, 246–7.

15 Leite, HCJB, V, 243–5.

16 The chronology presented here follows the unsigned report of about 1645 drawn up by the College of Santo Antão. See ANTT, CSJ, maço 90, n. 91.

17 ANTT, CSJ, maço 13, n. 21.

18 The high court or relaçao of Bahia was abolished in 1626 and not reestablished until 1652. During the interim, the highest legal authority in the colony was the ouvidor geral.

19 Sale contract (30 March 1638), ANTT, CSJ, maço 12, n. 37. Pedro Gonçalves de Mattos was the grandfather of the famous Bahian poet Gregório de Mattos e Guerra. See Fernando da Rocha Peres, "Documentos para uma biografia de Gregório de Mattos e Guerra," Universitas (Bahia), 2 (Jan.–April 1969), 53–66.

20 ARSI, Bras. 3 (StL/VFL, roll 160). The Jesuit colleges had been seeking an amiable settlement throughout most of the suit. The memorial prepared by Father Francisco Pires on 6 Sept. 1634 demonstrates an attempt to find the basis of settlement. ARSI, Bras. 8 (StL/VFL, roll 159); Gonçalves de Mattos had bought the engenho from the Misericórdia, which now demanded that his claims be settled along with their own. The Misericórdia rejected a settlement of 4,800 milréis in 1644 and held out for 8,000 milréis. See Russell-Wood, Fidalgos and Philantropists, 89–90.

21 Father Simão de Sottomaior to Father Manoel Fagundes (Bahia, 3 Jan. 1622), ANTT, CSJ, maço 68, n. 167.

22 ANTT, CSJ, maço 30, ns. 43. 66.
23 ANTT, CSJ, maço 90, n. 91; *Sentença* (21 May 1654), ANTT, CSJ, maço 90, n. 90.
24 ANTT, CSJ, maço 90, n. 90.
25 Leite, *HCJB*, V, 248.
26 The contract of agreement is found in *DH* 62 (1943): 141–59. See also ANTT, CSJ, maço 53, n. 56.
27 Report of Father Simão de Sottomaior (22 May 1655), ARSI, Lusit. 78, fs. 94–6.
28 ASCMB, assento (12 Oct. 1659), liv. 13. See C. R. Boxer, *Salvador de Sá and the Struggle for Brazil and Angola 1602–1686,* (London, 1952), 303.
29 Escritura de composição, *DH* 62 (1943): 159–87.
30 Ibid., 197. The Misericórdia had decided in 1644 to accept 20,000 cruzados as a settlement with the College of Santo Antão "with the participation and approval of Pedro Gonçalves de Mattos, without whose agreement nothing could be done . . . " ASCMB, assento (5 Nov. 1644), liv. 13, fs. 1–1v.
31 Copia dos concertos . . . (27 Jan. 1663), ARSI, Lusit. 75, f. 64–64v; Bras. 11 (StL/VFL, roll 160).
32 Leite, *HCJB*, V, 250.
33 Rationes quibus fundatur iusta PP Brasiliensum querimonia adversus PP Lusitarum nolentes solvere vigintiquinque millia ducatorim . . . (25 April 1680), ARSI, Fundo Gesuitico 1453 (Lisbon 33).
34 APB Religião 610, "Sequestros dos bens dos Jesuítas"; AHU, Bahia pap. avul., caixas 52, 353. For the 1790s, see "Quadro dos engenhos das visinhanças da Bahia," BNRJ, I-7, 3, 27. Dona Maria Joaquina owned almost 700 slaves on her 7 properties. On Engenho do Conde in 1859, see APB, Pres. da Prov., Viação 4795. On Engenho Santana, see Wanderley Pinho, "Testamento de Mem de Sá," 143–61.
35 On Jesuit estate management in Mexico and Peru, see Herman W. Konrad, *A Jesuit Hacienda in Colonial Mexico: Santa Lucia, 1576–1767* (Stanford, 1980), 301–31; and Nicholas B. Cushner, *Lords of the Land: Sugar, Wine, and Jesuit Estates of Coastal Peru, 1600–1767* (Albany, 1980), 58–80. See also the perceptive review essay by A. J. Bauer, "Jesuit Enterprise in Colonial Latin America: A Review Essay," *Agricultural History* 57, no. 1 (1981): 90–104.

GLOSSARY

afilhado (afilhada)	godson (goddaughter)
agregado	dependent in a household or on a rural property
aguardente	strong alcoholic drink made from sugar; rum
aldeia	village, especially an Indian village under Jesuit control
alfândega	customshouse
alforria	granting freedom to a slave; manumission
almoxarife	customs officer, especially of imports and exports
alvará	royal decree having force for one year, but usually extended
Angolares	escaped slaves on island of São Tomé
aprendiz	apprentice
areias	sandy soils unsuitable for sugarcane
arrendamento	rental contract
arroba	measure of weight; by sixteenth century, it was set at 14.75 kilograms or approximately 32 pounds

avería	Spanish shipping tax applied to Portuguese commerce with Brazil during period 1580–1640
baeta	baize, a woolen cloth
bagaço	bagasse, stalks of the sugarcane after pressing, often used as fodder and in Caribbean as fuel
balcão	platform where sugar was dried and separated for crating
banquero	sugar master's assistant, who often directed operations during the night shift at sugar mill
batido	sugar made from reheated skimmings of cane juice, considered of secondary quality
beixigas	smallpox
bemfeitorias	improvements; on a rural estate, buildings, fences, cleared land
boçal	slave born in Africa; unacculturated slave; in modern times, uncouth person
boubas	buboes, venereal ulcers
braça	measure of length equal to 2.2 meters; corresponds to English fathom
cachaça	skimmings from first kettle often fed to livestock; rum
calafate	ship caulker
calcanha	slave worker who tended lamps in sugar mill
caldereiro	kettleman who tended kettles in sugar mill; more rarely in Brazil, kettlemaker
calumbá	worker who placed water on cogs of sugar

	mill to reduce friction and who tended receptacle for cane juice
cara	face of a sugar form, whitest part
casa de caldeiras	building that housed battery of kettles
casa do engenho	building where mill was located
coartado (coartada)	slave (female slave) designated for freedom and allowed to raise money for self-purchase
decoada	wood ash added to heated cane juice to cleanse it
doação	donation, grant given to donatary or lord proprietor
engenho (ingenio, Span.)	sugar mill; by extension, sugar plantation
engenho real	sugar mill powered by waterwheel
engenhoca	small or crude sugar mill, usually animal powered
escumeiro	skimmer; early term for caldereiro
esterco	manure
farinha	flour; in Brazil, usually manioc flour
fazenda	(1) rural property, a farm or ranch; (2) the Treasury
fazendeiro	owner of a rural property of moderate or large size
fechos	small crates
feitor (-mor)	overseer (general overseer)
fidalgo	nobleman
fino	highest-quality sugar

fogo morto	"dead fire," description of an inoperative *engenho*
fornalha	furnace
foro militar	privileges and exemptions enjoyed by the military
forro	(1) freed slave; (2) Indian legally free but under Portuguese control
fouce	(1) short scythe; (2) a team of two slaves, usually a man and a woman who cut cane and bound it in bundles
freixe	bundle of sugarcanes, the number of canes varying with time and place
gangorra	large screw press for squeezing *bagaço* to extract more juice from sugarcane
garapa	drink of low alcoholic content made from skimmings of heated cane juice; another term for *cachaça*
guinda	hoist used to move cane juice from mill to kettles
guindadeira	slave woman who tended *guinda*
ladino	acculturated slave
lavrador de cana	cane farmer
levada	aqueduct to bring water to the waterwheel of an *engenho*
levadeiro	worker who tended and repaired *levada*
liberto (liberta)	freedman (freedwoman)
louvados	representatives of merchants and planters selected to fix fair price for sugar
macho	sugar made from first process of heating

and claying and considered of higher
quality than *batidos* made from reprocessing
skimmings and molasses from first process

madrinha (padrinho)	godmother (godfather)
maes de balção	slave women who took sugar from pots and prepared it for crating
malungo	shipmate; an African term used to indicate a fictive kinship between slaves who came in same ship
mameluco (mameluca)	person of mixed Indian and European origin, a *mestiço*
mancebia	consensual union, the common form of slave marriage
mangue	swamp or saltwater marsh
maré	tide
massapé	a heavy, dark, clay soil preferred for sugarcane
meios de sola	hides prepared for shoe leather
melado	cane juice (*caldo*) transformed into a syrup by heating
meladura	cane juice after reaching a thicker consistency through clarification in second kettle
melles	molasses that drained from sugar pots; small amounts were exported, the rest used to make *cachaça*
mestre de açúcar	sugar master, who directed operations of an *engenho*
metedor de lenha (fogo)	slave who fed furnaces
mó	millstone

moço	young; usual age description of a young slave
moedeira	woman who fed cane into mill's rollers
moenda	mill rollers
molinete	small sugar mill
moradores	(1) inhabitants; (2) residents in a town; (3) agricultural dependents allowed to live on an estate
morgado	entailed estate
muscavado	brown sugar considered of second quality after white sugar
nao	a large merchant vessel
ofícios mecânicos	artisan crafts, skilled trades
olaria	pottery where sugar pots, roof tiles, and other ceramic items were made
ordenanças	militia regiments
ouvidor geral	superior magistrate
panela	dark, low-grade sugar
pano	cloth, a common item used to pay Indian laborers; *pano da serra:* homespun
partido	the holding of a *lavrador de cana*
povoação	small village or settlement
purgadeira	slave woman assigned to drain sugar forms in purging house (*casa de purgar*)
quingingo	extra tasks assigned to slaves beyond daily quota

regimento	standing order or instructions
resgate	rescue; process of "temporarily" enslaving Indians who had been "liberated" from Indian enemies
resoca	second rattoon; sugar cane that grew after second cutting
safra	harvest
salão (pl.-ões)	reddish soils, less favored for sugarcane than *massapé*, but often highly productive
saltos	raids for Indian captives
santidade	religious cult or movement that focused Indian resistance against Portuguese
senado da câmara	municipal council
senzala	slave quarters
sesmaria	land grant
soca	rattoon; sugarcane that grew after first cutting
soldada	salary
tabuleiro	(1) bluffs; (2) division of canefield; (3) peddler's tray
tacha	teache, small kettle or boiling pan
tacheiro	worker who tended *tacha*
taipa	wattle and daub construction
tamina	ration given to slaves
tarefa	(1) task; (2) daily quota

urca   large merchant ship

vara   measure of length of 1.10 meters;
                                corresponds to English yard

várzea   floodplain of a river

vizinho   resident householder in a community

SOURCES AND SELECTED BIBLIOGRAPHY

In the historiography of Latin America, there has been a tendency in recent years to reject the traditional dependence on official government administrative documentation in favor of more "primary" local sources such as notarial records, wills, parish registers, and the like. Although this study has depended to a large extent on these local materials, I have also made an effort to use the fullest range of documentation possible. In colonial Brazil, state and society cannot be separated, nor can the documentary evidence be associated primarily with one or the other.

Because the history of sugar and the plantation regime are so intimately linked to the general history of Brazil, the documentary evidence for this study is widely scattered in all the major archives and collections that concern colonial Brazilian history. These archives and libraries are listed in the guide to abbreviations found at the front of this volume. In a previous book, *Sovereignty and Society in Colonial Brazil* (Berkeley, 1973), I discussed the nature of the holdings in many of these same archives noting the major guides to research, and the reader is directed there for a more detailed discussion. There are, however, a few archival collections that were used extensively in this volume that relate directly to the history of sugar and Bahian society and thus merit comment here.

In Brazil, the most important archive for this study is the Arquivo Público do Estado of Bahia (APB), Salvador. Its *colônia* section contains a vast collection of official government correspondence on a wide variety of topics. Letters to and from the governors, records of the high court, and the series of royal orders (*ordens régias*) were particularly useful. In the judicial section (*judiciária*), two fundamental sources are located. The first is the large but incomplete collection of notarial registers from Salvador and the Recôncavo towns, which contain bills of sale, records of transfer, letters of manumission, and records of borrowing and lending. These proved particularly important for this study. The second is a large but haphazard series of wills and inventories organized by district. These are often in a precarious physical condition, and only by a reading of each can the nature of the property held be determined. Still, the listing of property and its values contained in these documents made the analysis of engenho values, planter wealth, slaveholding, and other related matters possible. Moreover, from the inventories it was possible to obtain considerable information about the composition of the slave force.

In Portugal, the Arquivo Histórico Ultramarino, Lisbon, remains the single most important repository of materials from the colonial era. I have used its collections extensively, especially the series of loose papers (*papéis avulsos*) organized by captaincy and the discussions (*consultas*) of the Overseas Council (Conselho Ultramarino). For this study, the collection of Jesuit-related documents (Cartório dos Jesuítas) at the Arquivo Nacional da Torre do Tombo was indispensable. This series contains the papers and accounts of Engenho Sergipe do Conde and Engenho Santana, as well as thousands of related documents. A portion of the Engenho Sergipe accounts was published by the Brazilian Institute of Sugar and Alcohol, and many works have depended exclusively on this partial publication. The collection, however, is far richer than the limited published accounts suggest. Supplementary documents on the sugar-planting activities of the Jesuits were consulted at the Archivum Romanum Societatis Iesu, Rome. My work there was greatly facilitated by a prior visit to the excellent microfilm collection at the Vatican Film Library at Saint Louis University, Saint Louis. Finally, the collection of triennial reports sent by the Benedictines of Brazil to their mother house at Tibães and now housed in Braga reveals much about the Brazilian sugar economy and had been previously ignored for the social and economic history of Brazil.

From various archival sources, it was possible to construct a number of data sets that permitted quantitative analysis. The wills and inventories at the APB often listed the slaves with information concerning their age, color, origin, occupation, health, and value. Information on 1,914 slaves listed on engenhos and cane farms between 1710 and 1827 (Data Set A) was used to analyze the composition and characteristics of the slave force in sugar. The notarial registers for Salvador at the APB provided a series 1,015 letters of manumission (Data Set B) for the period 1684–1745 that allowed a quantitative analysis of that practice in Bahia. This examination was carried out as part of a parallel project in which Professor Katia Mattoso of Bahia studied a similar set of materials from the nineteenth century. From the Arquivo da Curia Metropolitana of Bahia in Salvador, a series of parish registers were used to examine a number of social and demographic phenomena. My work concentrated on the parishes of Monte, Rio Fundo, Purificação, São Gonçalo, and Saubara. For an analysis of baptismal sponsorship (Data Set C), I used 264 entries from Rio Fundo and Monte from the periods 1780–1 and 1788–9; for illustrative purposes, I consulted another 167 entries from Saubara and São Gonçalo. These materials were used in conjunction with an unpublished census of 1788 from the APB (Data Set D). That census included portions of six Bahian parishes and listed 5,275 individuals, but unfortunately for the three parishes located in the Recôncavo, the slaves were not included. Still, the census provided considerable information about the social, demographic, and racial structure of rural Bahia, and it has been used in various places in this book. Finally, the listing of slaveowners made in 1817 (Data Set E), which serves as the basis for Chapter 16, was found in the APB.

The best guide to the literature and the history of sugar in Brazil is the excellent and long-ignored series of articles written by José Honório Rodrigues for the pages of *Brasil Açucareiro* between 1942 and 1945. Unfortunately, these articles ran serially in short excerpts, which makes them difficult to use, and they have never been gathered together in a single volume as they deserve. Particularly useful to me were: "A literatura brasileira sôbre açúcar no século xviii," 20:1 (1943), 6–25; "A literatura brasileira sôbre açúcar no século xix," 19:5 (1942), 16–38; "Notas à literatura brasileira sôbre açúcar no século xvii," 25:5 (1945), 420–4; "Agricultura e economia açucareira no século xvii," which appeared throughout volume 26 (1945); and "O açúcar segundo o depoimento de José da Silva Lisboa," 25:3 (1945), 45–52.

Published documents and contemporary works

Abreu e Brito, Domingos. *Um inquérito a vida administrativa e económica de Angola e do Brasil* (1591). Ed. Alfredo de Albuquerque Felner. Coimbra, 1931.

Antonil,André João (João Antônio Andreoni). *Cultura e opulência do Brasil por suas drogas e minas*. Ed. Andrée Mansuy. Paris, 1965.

Cultura e opulência do Brasil por suas drogas e minas. Ed. A. P. Canabrava. São Paulo, 1967.

Barleus, Gaspar. *Rerum per octennium in Brasilia*. Clèves, 1660.

Benci, Jorge. *Economia cristã dos senhores no governo dos escravos*. Ed. Serafim Leite. 2d ed. Oporto, 1954.

Brandão, Ambrósio Fernandes (supposed author). *Diálogos das grandezas do Brasil*. Ed. José Antônio Gonçalves de Mello. 2d complete ed. Recife, 1966.

Brant Pontes, Felesberto Caldeira. *Economia açucareira do Brasil no século xix*. Rio de Janeiro, 1976.

Burlamaque, D. F. L. C. *Monographia da canna d'assucar*. Rio de Janeiro, 1862.

Burlamaqui, Federico Leopoldo C. *Memória analytica acêrca do commercio d'escravos e acêrca da escravidão doméstica*. Rio de Janeiro, 1837.

Caldas, José Antônio. *Notícia geral de toda esta capitania da Bahia*. Facsimile of 1759 ed. Bahia, 1951.

Campos Morenos, Diogo de. *Livro que dá razão do estado do Brasil*. Facsimile ed. Rio de Janeiro, 1968.

Livro que dá razão do estado do Brasil (1612). Edited by Helio Vianna. Recife, 1955.

Capistrano de Abreu, João, ed. *Primeira visitação do Santo Officio ás partes do Brasil. Confissões Bahia, 1591–92*. Rio de Janeiro, 1935.

Cardim,Fernão. *Tratados da terra e gente do Brasil (1583)*. 3d ed. São Paulo, 1978.

Child,Josiah. *A New Discourse on Trade*. London, 1669.

Collecção chronologica da legislação portuguesa. Ed. José Justino de Andrade e Silva. 10 vols. Lisbon, 1854–9.

Conrad, Robert Edgar. *Children of God's Fire: A Documentary History of Black Slavery in Brazil*. Princeton, 1983.

Cunha e Freitas, Eugénio Andrea. "Documentos para a história do Brasil III Notícias do Baía em 1625." *Anais Academia Portuguêsa da História* (Lisbon) 2d series, 21 (1972): 465–89.

Dampier, William. *A Voyage to New Holland, etc., in the Year 1699*. 3 vols. 2d ed. London, 1709.

Dussen, Andrien van der. *Relatório sôbre as capitanias conquistadas no Brasil pelos holandeses*. Ed. José Antônio Gonçalves de Mello. Rio de Janeiro, 1947.

Esteves, Neusa Rodrigues, ed. *Irmãos da Santa Casa de Misericórdia da Bahia–século xvii*. Salvador, 1977.

Gandavo, Pero de Magalhães de. *The Histories of Brazil*. Trans. John B. Stetson. New York, 1922.

Gonçalves de Mello, José Antônio. "Um regimento de feitor môr de engenho de 1663." *Boletim do Instituto Joaquim Nabuco* 2 (1953): 80–7.

Gonçalves de Mello, José Antônio, and Cleonir Xavier de Albuquerque, eds. *Cartas de Duarte Coelho a El Rei (Documentos para a História do Nordeste II)*. Recife, 1967.

Graham, Maria. *Journal of a Voyage to Brazil and Residence There*. London, 1824.

"História dos Collegios do Brasil." *ABNR* 19 (1897): 75–144.

Imbert, João. *Manual do fazendeiro ou tratado doméstico sôbre as enfermidades dos negros*. Rio de Janeiro, 1832.

Instituto do Açúcar e do Álcool. *Documentos para a história do açúcar*. 3 vols. Rio de Janeiro, 1954–63.

Koster, Henry. *Travels in Brazil*. 2 vols. Philadelphia, 1817.

Laet, Joannes de. "História ou Annaes dos Feitos da Companhia Privilegiada das Indias Occidentais." *ABNR* 61–2 (1919–20): 201–15.

Landi, Giulio. *La descrittione de l'isola de la Madera*. Piacenza, 1574.

Lavradio, Marquês do. *Cartas da Bahia 1768–1769*. Arquivo Nacional publication n. 68. Rio de Janeiro, 1972.

Leite, Serafim, ed. *Cartas do Brasil e mais escritos do P. Manuel da Nóbrega (ópera omnia)*. Coimbra, 1955.

Cartas dos primeiros Jesuitas do Brasil. 3 vols. Rome, 1956–8.

"Emformação dalgumas cousas do Brasil 'por Belchior Cordeiro' 1577." *Anais da Academia Portuguêsa da História* 2d series, 15 (1965): 175–202.

Monumenta Brasiliae. 5 vols. Rome, 1956–60.

"Os Capítulos de Gabriel Soares de Sousa." *Ethnos* (Lisbon), 2 (1941): 5–36.

Lisanti, Luís, ed. *Negócios coloniais*. 5 vols. Brasilia, 1973.

Livro primeiro do govêrno do Brasil, 1607–1633. Rio de Janeiro, 1958.

Loreto Couto, Domingos do. "Desagravos do Brasil e glórias de Pernambuco." *ABNR* 24 (1902): 1–611.

Maciel da Costa, João. *Memória sôbre a necessidade de abolir a introdução dos escravos africanos no Brasil*. Coimbra, 1821.

Malheiro Dias, Carlos, ed. *História da colonização portuguesa do Brasil*. 3 vols. Oporto, 1924–6.

Mauro, Frédéric. *Le Bresil au xviiᵉ siécle*. Coimbra, 1963.

Mawe, John. *Travels in the Interior of Brazil*. London, 1812.

Moerbreck, Jan Andries. *Motivos por que a Companhia das Indias Ocidentais deve tentar tirar a Rei da Espanha a terra do Brasil (Amsterdam, 1624)*. Rio de Janeiro, 1942.

Monteiro Carson, João. *Primeiro Relátorio apresentado a presidência da Bahia sobre os melhoramentos da cultura da cana e do fábrico do assucar*. Bahia, 1854.

Monteiro da Vide, Sebastião. *Constituições primeiras do Arcebispado da Bahia*. Lisbon, 1719.

Moore, Samuel, ed. *Biography of Mahommah G. Baquaqua, a Native of Zoogoo in the Interior of Africa*. Detroit, 1854.

Mott, Luiz R. B. *Os pecados da família na Bahia de Todos os Santos (1813)*. Salvador, 1982.

Nieuhof, Joan. *Memorável viagem marítima e terrestre ao Brasil*. São Paulo, 1942.

Novinsky, Anita. *Inquisição. Inventários de bens confiscados a cristãos novos*. Lisbon, 1976.

Oliveira Pinto da França, Antônio. *Cartas baianas, 1821–1824*. São Paulo, 1980.

Peixoto, Afranio, ed. *Cartas Jesuitas*. Vol. 2: *Cartas avulsas, 1550–1568*. Rio de Janeiro, 1931.

Pereira, Nuno Marques. *Compendio narrativo do Peregrino da America (1728)*. Lisbon, 1765.

Rau, Virginia, and Jorge de Macedo, eds. *O açúcar de Madeira nos fins do século xv*. Funebal, 1962.

Ribeiro Rocha, Manoel. *Ethiope resgatado empenhado sustentado corregido instruido e libertado*. Lisbon, 1758.

Rocha Pitta, Sebastião da. *História da America portugueza*. 2d ed. Lisbon, 1880.

Rodrigues de Brito, João. *Cartas Económico-Políticas sôbre a agricultura e commércio da Bahia*. Lisbon, 1821.

Ruiters, Dierick. "A torcha da navegação." *RIHGB* 269 (1965): 3–84.

Salvador, Vicente do (Frei). *História do Brasil*. 5th ed. With notes by Capistrano de Abreu, Rodolfo Garcia, and Frei Venâncio Willeke. São Paulo, 1965.

Sampaio e Mello, Jacinto de. *Novo methodo de fazer o açúcar*. Bahia, 1816.

Santos Vilhena, Luís dos. *A Bahia no século xviii.* 3 vols. Bahia, 1969.

Schwartz, Stuart B., ed. *A Governor and His Image in Baroque Brazil: The Funeral Eulogy of Afonso Furtado de Castro de Rio de Mendonça by Juan Lopes Sierra.* Trans. Ruth Jones. Minneapolis, 1979.

Silva Lisboa, José da. "Carta muito interessante para o Dr. Domingos Vandelli." *ABNR* 32 (1910): 494–507.

Soares, Francisco. *Coisas notáveis do Brasil.* Rio de Janeiro, 1966.

Soares de Sousa, Gabriel. *Notícia do Brasil.* Ed. Pirajá da Silva. 2 vols. São Paulo, 1940.

"Os capítulos de Gabriel Soares de Sousa." *ABNR* 62 (1940): 340–81.

Tratado descritivo do Brasil em 1587. São Paulo, 1971.

Sousa, Marco Antonio. *Memória sôbre a capitania de Serzipe (1800).* 2d ed. Aracajú, 1944.

Spix, Johann von, and Karl von Martius. *Viagem pelo Brasil.* 3 vols. São Paulo, 1961.

Tollenare, Louis-François. *Notes Domincales. Prises pendant un voyage en Portugal et au Bresil.* Ed. Leon Bourdon. 3 vols. Paris, 1971.

Walsh, Robert. *Notices of Brazil in 1828 and 1829.* 2 vols. Boston, 1831.

Wanderley [Araujo] Pinho, [José]. "Testamento de Mem de Sá. Inventário de seus bens no Brasil." *Terceiro Congresso de História Nacional.* 5 vols. Rio de Janeiro, 1941.

Books and articles

Accioli de Cerqueira e Silva, Ignácio. *Memórias Históricas e políticas da Provincia da Bahia.* Ed. Braz do Amaral. 6 vols. Bahia, 1925.

Albuquerque, Maria Izabel de. "Liberdade e limitação dos engenhos de Açúcar." *Anais do Primeiro Congresso da História da Bahia* 2 (1950): 491–9. 5 vols.

Alden, Dauril. "Black Robes Versus White Settlers: The Struggle for 'Freedom of the Indians' in Colonial Brazil." In Howard Peckham and Charles Gibson, eds., *Attitudes of Colonial Powers Toward the American Indian,* 19–46. Salt Lake City, 1969.

"Economic Aspects of the Expulsion of the Jesuits From Brasil." In Henry H. Keith and S. F. Edwards, eds., *Conflict and Continuity in Brazilian Society,* 25–65. Columbia, S.C., 1969.

"Late Colonial Brazil, 1750–1807." In Leslie Bethel, ed., *The Cambridge History of Latin America,* vol. 2, pt. 2. 3 vols to date. Cambridge, 1985.

"The Population of Brazil in the Late Eighteenth Century: A Preliminary Survey." *HAHR* 63, no. 2 (May 1963): 173–205.

Royal Government in Colonial Brazil. Berkeley, 1968.

"Sugar Planters by Necessity, Not Choice: The Role of the Jesuits in the Cane Sugar Industry of Colonial Brazil, 1601–1759." In Jeffrey Cole, ed., *The Church and Society in Latin America,* 139–70. New Orleans, 1984.

"Vicissitudes of Trade in the Portuguese Atlantic Empire During the First Half of the Eighteenth Century: A Review Article." *The Americas* 32, no. 2 (Oct. 1975): 282–91.

Almeida Prado, J. F. *A Bahia e as capitanias do centro do Brasil (1530–1626).* 3 vols. Rio de Janeiro, 1945–8.

Amaral Ferlini, Vera Lucia. *A civilização do açúcar séculos xvi a xviii.* São Paulo, 1984.

Amaral Lapa, José Roberto. *O antigo sistema colonial.* São Paulo, 1982.

Aufderheide, Patricia. "True Confessions: The Inquisition and Social Attitudes in Brazil at the Turn of the Seventeenth Century." *Luso-Brazilian Review* 10, no. 2 (Dec. 1973): 208–40.

Aufhauser, R. Keith. "Profitability of Slavery in the British Caribbean." *Journal of Interdisciplinary History* 5, no. 1 (summer 1974): 45–67.

Azevedo, João Lucio de. *Épocas de Portugal económico.* 2d ed. Lisbon, 1947.

Novas epanáforas. Lisbon, 1932.

Azevedo, Thales de. *Povoamento da cidade do Salvador*. 2d ed. Bahia, 1969.

Barrett, Ward. "Caribbean Sugar-Production Standards in the Seventeenth and Eighteenth Centuries." In *Merchants and Scholars: Essays in the History of Exploration and Trade*, 147–70. Minneapolis, 1966.

The Sugar Hacienda of the Marqueses del Valle. Minneapolis, 1970.

and Stuart B. Schwartz. "Comparación entre dos economias azucareras coloniales: Morelos, México y Bahía, Brasil." In Enrique Florescano, ed., *Haciendas, latifundios y plantaciones en América Latina*, 532–72. Mexico City, 1975.

Barros de Castro, Antônio. "Brasil, 1610: Mudanças técnicas e conflitos sociais." *Pesquiza e planajemento econômico* 10, no. 3 (1980): 679–712.

"A economia política, o capitalismo e a escravidão." In José Roberto Amaral Lapa, ed., *Modos de produção e realidade brasileira*, 67–107. Petropolis, 1980.

Bastide, Roger. *The African Religions of Brazil*. Baltimore, 1978.

Batie, Robert Carlyle. "Why Sugar? Economic Cycles and the Changing of Staples on the English and French Antilles, 1624–1654." *Journal of Caribbean History* 8 (Nov. 1976): 1–41.

Bethel, Leslie. *The Abolition of the Brazilian Slave Trade*. Cambridge, 1970.

Boxer, C. R. *The Dutch in Brazil*. Oxford, 1957.

The Portuguese Seaborne Empire, 1415–1825. London, 1969.

Portuguese Society in the Tropics. Madison, Wis., 1965.

Salvador de Sá and the Struggle for Brazil and Angola, 1602–1686. London, 1952.

Some Literary Sources for the History of Brazil in the Eighteenth Century. The Taylorian Lecture. Oxford, 1967.

Buescu, Mircea. *História econômica do Brasil*. Rio de Janeiro, 1970.

300 Anos da inflação. Rio de Janeiro, 1973.

Cabral de Mello, Evaldo. *Olinda Restaurada. Guerra e açúcar no nordeste, 1630–1654*. São Paulo, 1975.

Canabrava, A. P. "A Força Motriz: Um problema da técnica da industria do açúcar colonial." In *Anais da Primeira Congresso da História da Bahia*, vol. 4, 337–50. 5 vols. Bahia, 1950.

Cardoso, Ciro. "A brecha camponesa no sistema escravista." *Agricultura, escravidão e capitalismo*. Petropolis, 1979.

Cardoso, Fernando Henrique. *Capitalismo e escravidão*. São Paulo, 1962.

Cardozo, Manoel. "Slavery in Brazil as Described by Americans, 1822–1828." *The Americas* 17 (1961): 241–60.

Carli, Gileno de. "Geografia econômica e social da canna de açúcar no Brazil." *Brasil Açucareiro* 10, no. 1 (Sept. 1937): 24–41.

Carneiro de Mendonca, Marcos, ed. *Raizes da formação administrativa do Brasil*. 2 vols. Rio de Janeiro, 1972.

Carvalho de Mello, Pedro. "Estimativa da longevidade de escravos no Brasil na segunda metade do século XIX." *Estudos Econômicos* 13, no. 1 (1983): 151–81.

Cequeira, Carlos Valeriano. "Histórico da cultura da cana na Bahia." In *Anais do Primeiro Congresso de História da Bahia*, vol. 4, 263–333. 5 vols. Bahia, 1950.

Costa, Afonso. "Genealogia baiana." *RIHGB* 191 (April–June 1961): 3–279.

Costa, Avelino Jesus da. "População da Cidade da Baía em 1775." In *Actas: V Colóquio Internacional de Estudos Luso-Brasileiras*, vol. 1, 191–205. 5 vols. Coimbra, 1965.

Costa Lima, Vivaldo. "O concepto da 'nação' nos candomblés da Bahia." *Afro-Ásia* 12 (1978): 65–90.

Craton, Michael. "Changing Patterns of Slave Families in the British West Indies." *Journal of Interdisciplinary History* 10, no. 1 (summer 1979): 1–36.

Searching for the Invisible Man. Slaves and Plantation Life in Jamaica. Cambridge, Mass., 1978.

Curtin, Philip. *The Atlantic Slave Trade: A Census*. Madison, Wis., 1969.

Davis, David B. *The Problem of Slavery in Western Culture.* Ithaca, N.Y., 1966.
DeBow, J. D. B. *Statistical View of the United States* (seventh census). Washington, 1854.
Deerr, Noel. *The History of Sugar.* 2 vols. London, 1950.
Dias Tavares, Luís Henrique. *História da sedição intentada na Bahia em 1798.* São Paulo, 1975.
Drescher, Seymour. *Econocide. British Slavery in the Era of Abolition.* Pittsburgh, 1975.
Dutra, Frances A. "Membership in the Order of Christ in the Seventeenth Century: Its Rights, Privileges and Obligations." *The Americas* 27, no. 1 (July 1970): 3–25.
Edel, Mathew. "The Brazilian Sugar Cycle of the Seventeenth Century and the Rise of West Indian Competition." *Caribbean Studies* 9 (April 1967): 24–44.
Eisenberg, Peter. *The Sugar Industry of Pernambuco.* Berkeley, 1974.
Eltis, David. "The Direction and Fluctuation of the Trans-Atlantic Slave Trade, 1821–1843: A Revision of the 1845 Parliamentary Paper." In Henry A. Gemery and Jan S. Hogendorn, eds., *The Uncommon Market. Essays in the Economic History of of the Atlantic Slave Trade,* 273–99. New York, 1979.
Engerman, Stanley L. "The Realities of Slavery: A Review of Recent Evidence." *International Journal of Comparative Sociology* 20, nos. 1–2 (1979): 46–66.
Faoro, Raimundo. *Os donos do poder.* Porto Alegre, 1958.
Fernandes, Florestan. *Organização social dos Tupinambá.* 2d ed. São Paulo, 1963.
Ferreira Pinto, Irineu. *Datas e notas para a história da Parahyba.* 2 vols. 2d ed. João Pessoa, 1977.
Flexor, Maria Helena. *Ofícios mecânicos na cidade do Salvador.* Salvador, 1977.
Flory, Rae, and David Smith. "Bahian Merchants and Planters in the Seventeenth and Eighteenth Centuries." *HAHR* 58, no. 4 (Nov. 1978): 571–94.
Flory, Thomas. "Race and Social Control in Independent Brazil." *Journal of Latin American Studies* 9, no. 2 (1977): 199–224.
Fogel, Robert W., and Stanley L. Engerman. "Recent Findings in the Study of Slave Demography and Family Structure." *Sociology and Social Research* 63 (1978–9): 566–89.
Time on the Cross: The Economics of American Negro Slavery. 2 vols. Boston, 1974.
Freire A. Fonseca, Celia. *A economia européia e a colonização do Brasil.* Rio de Janeiro, 1978.
Freitas, Decio. *Insurreições escravos.* Pôrto Alegre, 1976.
Galloway, J. H. "Agricultural Reform and the Enlightenment in Late Colonial Brazil." *Agricultural History* 53, no. 4 (Oct. 1979): 763–79.
"The Mediterranean Sugar Industry." *The Geographical Review* 67, no. 2 (April 1977): 177–94.
"Northeast Brazil, 1700–1750: The Agricultural Crisis Reexamined." *Journal of Historical Geography* 1, no. 1 (1975): 21–38.
Genovese, Eugene D. *The World the Slaveowners Made.* New York, 1971.
Goes Calmon, Francisco Marques. *Vida econômico-financeira da Bahia.* Bahia, 1925; facsimile ed., Salvador, 1979.
Gonçalves de Mello, José Antônio. "Uma relação dos engenhos de Pernambuco em 1623." *Revista do Museu do Açúcar* 1 (198): 25–36.
Tempo dos flamengos. Rio de Janeiro, 1947.
Gorender, Jacob. *O escravismo colonial.* São Paulo, 1978.
Goulart, José Alípio. *Da fuga ao suicídio.* Rio de Janeiro, 1972.
Da palmatória ao patíbulo. Rio de Janeiro, 1971.
Goulart, Mauricio. *Escravidão africana no Brasil.* São Paulo, 1950.
Graham, Richard. "Slave Families on a Rural Estate in Colonial Brazil." *Journal of Social History* 9, no. 3 (1976): 382–402.
Gudeman, Stephen. "The *Compadrazgo* as a Reflection of the Natural and Spiritual Person." *Proceedings of the Royal Anthropological Institute* (1971): 45–71.
and Stuart B. Schwartz. "Baptismal Godparents in Slavery: Cleansing Original Sin in Eighteenth-Century Bahia." In Raymond Smith, ed., *Kinship Ideology and Practice in Latin America,* 35–58. Chapel Hill, N.C., 1984.

Hall, Douglas. "Incalculability as a Feature of Sugar Production During the Eighteenth Century." *Social and Economic Studies* 10. no. 3 (Sept. 1961): 340–52.

Hanson, Carl. *Economy and Society in Baroque Portugal, 1668–1703.* Minneapolis, 1981.

Higman, Barry W. "African and Creole Slave Family Patterns in Trinidad." In Margaret E. Crahan and Franklin W. Knight, eds., *Africa and the Caribbean,* 41–65. Baltimore, 1979.

"Household Structure and Fertility on Jamaican Slave Plantations: A Nineteenth-Century Example." *Population Studies* 27 (1973); 527–50.

"Slave Family and Household in the British West Indies, 1800–1834." *Journal of Interdisciplinary History* 6, no. 2 (1975): 261–87.

Slave Population and Economy in Jamaica, 1807–1834. Cambridge, 1976.

Hirschman, Albert O. "A Generalized Linkage Approach to Development With Special Reference to Staples." *Economic Development and Cultural Change,* supplement, 25 (1975): 67–98.

Hutchinson, Harry William. *Village and Plantation Life in Northeastern Brazil.* Seattle, 1957.

Ianni, Octavio. *Escravidão e racismo.* São Paulo, 1978.

Jasmins Pereira, Fernando. *O açúcar madeirense de 1500 a 1537. Produção e preços.* Lisbon, 1969.

Jobson de Andrade Arruda, José. *O Brasil no comércio colonial.* São Paulo, 1980.

Johnson, Harold B. "The Donatary Captaincy in Perspective: Portuguese Backgrounds to the Settlement of Brazil." *HAHR* 52, no. 2 (May 1972): 203–14.

Kennedy, John N. "Bahian Elites, 1750–1822." *HAHR* 53, no. 3 (1973): 415–39.

Kent. R. K. "African Revolt in Bahia: 24–25 January 1835." *Journal of Social History* 3, no. 4 (1970): 334–56.

Klein, Herbert. *The Middle Passage.* Princeton, 1978.

"Nineteenth-Century Brazil." In David Cohen and Jack P. Greene, eds., *Neither Slave Nor Free,* 309–34. Baltimore, 1973.

"The Portuguese Slave Trade from Angola in the Eighteenth Century." *Journal of Economic History* 32, no. 4 (Dec. 1972): 894–918.

Lahmeyer Lobo, Enalalia Maria. "As frotas do Brasil." *JGSWGLA* 4 (1967): 465–88.

Leite, Serafim. *História da Companhia de Jesus no Brasil.* 10 vols. Lisbon, 1938–50.

Lippmann, Edmund von. *História do açúcar.* 2 vols. Rio de Janeiro, 1942.

Lugar, Catherine. "The Portuguese Tobacco Trade and Tobacco Growers of Bahia in the Late Colonial Period." In Dauril Alden and Warren Dean, eds., *Essays Concerning the Socioeconomic History of Brazil and Portuguese India,* 26–70. Gainesville, Fla. 1977.

Maclachlan, Colin. "Slavery, Ideology and Institutional Change: The Impact of the Enlightenment on Slavery in Late Eighteenth-Century Maranhão." *Journal of Latin American Studies* 11, no. 1 (1979): 1–17.

Maeyama, T. "The Masters Versus the Slaves Under the Plantation Systems in Brazil." *Latin American Studies* (University of Tsukuba, Japan) 3 (1981): 115–41.

Magalhães, Basilio. *O açúcar nos primórdios do Brasil colonial.* Rio de Janeiro, 1953.

Magalhães Godinho, Vitorino. *Os descobrimentos e a economia mundial.* 2 vols. Lisbon, 1963–8.

A estrutura na antiga sociedade portuguesa. Lisbon, 1971.

"Portugal and Her Empire, 1680–1720." *New Cambridge Modern History* 6 (1970): 509–40.

"Portugal, as frotas do açúcar e as frotas do ouro 1670–1770." In *Ensaios,* vol. 2, 293–315. 3 vols. Lisbon, 1967–8.

Magre Mendes, Claudinei Magro. "No mundo do Quinguingo." *Anais da História* 8 (1976): 93–106.

Manning, Patrick. "The Slave Trade in the Bight of Benin, 1640–1890." In Henry A. Gemery and Jan S. Hogendorn, eds., *The Uncommon Market: Essays in the Economic History of the Atlantic Slave Trade,* 107–41. New York, 1979.

Marchant, Alexander. "Feudal and Capitalistic Elements in the Portuguese Settlement of Brasil." *HAHR* 22, no. 3 (1942): 493–512.

From Barter to Slavery: The Economic Relations of Portuguese and Indians in the Settlement of Brazil, 1500–1580. Johns Hopkins University Studies in Historical and Political Science, ser. ix, no. 1. Baltimore, 1942; reprinted Gloucester, Mass., 1966.

Marcilio, Maria Luiza. "Crescimento histórico da população brasileira até 1872." *Crescimento populacional* (Cuadernos de Centro Brasileiro de Analise e Planajamento [CEBRAP], São Paulo), 16 (1974): 1–26.

"Tendencias e estruturas dos domicílios na capitania de São Paulo segundo as listas nominativas de habitantes, 1765-1828." *Estudos Econômicos* 2 (1978): 131–44.

Mauro, Frédéric. "Contabilidade teórica e contabilidade prática na America portuguesa no século xvii." In *Nova história e novo mundo*, 135–48. São Paulo, 1969.

Études économiques sur l'expansion portugaise (1500–1900). Paris, 1970.

Le Portugal et l'Atlantique au xvii siècle. Paris, 1960.

Maxwell, Kenneth R. *Conflicts and Conspiracies: Brazil and Portugal 1750–1807.* Cambridge, 1973.

"The Generation of the 1790s and the Idea of Luso-Brazilian Empire." In Dauril Alden, ed., *Colonail Roots of Modern Brazil*, 107–44. Berkeley, 1973.

Menard, Russell R. "The Maryland Slave Population, 1658 to 1730: A Demographic Profile of Blacks in Four Counties." *William and Mary Quarterly*, 3d ser., 32, no. 1 (Jan. 1975): 29–54.

Merrick, Thomas W., and Douglas H. Graham. *Population and Economic Development in Brazil.* Baltimore, 1979.

Metraux, Alfred. "The Tupinambá." In Julian Steward, ed., *Handbook of South American Indians*, vol. 3, 95–135. 6 vols. Washington, 1948.

Miller, Joseph C. "The Slave Trade in Congo and Angola." In Martin Kilson and Robert I. Rotberg, eds., *The African Diaspora: Interpretive Essays*, 75–113. Cambridge, 1976.

Morgan, Philip D. "Work and Culture: The Task System and the Lowcountry Blacks, 1700–1880." *William and Mary Quarterly*, 3d ser., 39, no. 4 (1982): 563–99.

Morineau, M. "Or bresilien et gazettes hollandaises." *Revue d'histoire moderne et contemporaine* 25 (Jan.–March 1978): 3–59.

Morton, F. W. O. "The Military and Society in Bahia, 1800–1821." *Journal of Latin American Studies* 7, no. 1 (1975): 249–70.

Mota, Carlos Guilherme. *Nordeste, 1817.* São Paulo, 1972.

Mott, Luiz R. B. "Brancos, Pardos, Pretos, e Indios em Sergipe, 1825-1830." *Anais da História* 6 (1974): 139–84.

"Estrutura demográfica das fazendas de gado do Piauí-colonial: Um caso de povoamento rural centrífigo." *Ciência e cultura* 30 (1978): 1196–1210.

"Pardos e pretos em Sergipe 1774–1851." *Revista do Instituto de Estudos Brasileiros* 18 (1976): 7–37.

"A revolução dos negros de Haiti e o Brasil." *MAN* 13.1 (1982): 3–10.

"Violência e repressão em Sergipe: Notícias sobre revoltas de escravos (século xix)." *MAN* 5 (May 1980): 3–21.

Moura, Clovis. *Rebeliões da senzala.* 3d ed. São Paulo, 1981.

Nero da Costa, Iraci del. *Vila Rica: População (1719–1826).* São Paulo, 198.

Nizza da Silva, Maria Beatriz. *A primeira gazetta da Bahia: Idade d'Ouro do Brasil.* São Paulo, 1978.

"Os senhores de engenho e a cultura científica." *Ciência e cultura* 31, no. 4 (1979): 389–94.

Novais, Fernando A. *Portugal e Brasil na crise do antigo sistema colonial (1777–1808).* São Paulo, 1979.

Novinsky, Anita. *Cristãos novos na Bahia.* São Paulo, 1972.

"Fontes para a história econômica e social do Brasil. Inventários dos bens confiscados pela Inquisição." *Revista de História* 48, no. 98 (April–June 1974): 359–92.

Noya Pinto, Virgilio. *O ouro brasileiro e o comércio anglo-português*. São Paulo, 1979.

Oliveira França, Eduardo d'. "Engenhos, colonização, e cristãos-novos na Bahia colonial." *Anais. IV Simpósio Nacional dos Professores Universitários de História* (São Paulo) (1979): 182–241.

Oliveira Marques, António de. *History of Portugal*. 2 vols. New York, 1972–4.

Pares, Richard. "The London Sugar Market, 1740–1769." *Economic History Review* 9, no. 2 (1956): 254–70.

Patterson, Orlando. "Slavery." *Annual Review of Sociology* 3 (1977): 407–99.
Slavery and Social Death. Cambridge, Mass., 1982.

Pereira da Costa, F. A. *Anais Pernambucanos*. 7 vols. Recife, 1951.

Pinheiro da Silva, José. "A Capitania da Baía (Subsídios para a história da sua colonização na 2ª metade do século XVII)." *Revista Portuguêsa de História* 8 (1959): 44–284, and 9 (1960): 211–45.

Pinto de Aguiar, [Manoel,] ed. *Aspectos de economia colonial*. Salvador, 1957.

Queirós Mattoso, Katia M. de. *Bahia: A cidade do Salvador e seu mercado*. São Paulo, 1978.
"Conjuncture et société au Bresil a la fin du xviiiᵉ siècle." *Cahiers des Ameriques Latines* 5 (1970): 3–53.
"Os escravos da Bahia no alvorecer do século xix." *Revista de História* 97 (1974): 109–35.
"A Propósito de cartas da alforria na Bahia, 1779–1850." *Anais da História* 4 (1972): 23–52.
Ser Escravo no Brasil. São Paulo, 1982.
"Sociedade e conjuctura na Bahia nos anos da luta pela Independência." *Universitas* 15–16 (1973): 5–26.

Raffard, Henri. *A industria saccharifera no Brasil*. Rio de Janeiro, 1882.

Ramos, Donald. "Marriage and the Family on Colonial Vila Rica." *HAHR* 55, no. 2 (May 1975): 200–25.

Reis, João José. "A elite baiana face os movimentos sociais: Bahia 1824–1840." *Revista de História* 108 (1976): 341–84.
"Slave Resistance in Brazil, Bahia, 1887–1835." *Luso-Brazilian Review* (in press).

Ribeiro, José, Jr. *Colonização e monopólio no nordesto brasileiro*. São Paulo, 1976.

Robles Reis de Queiroz, Suely. "Algumas notas sobre a lavoura do açúcar em São Paulo no período colonial." *Anais do Museu Paulista* 21 (1967): 109–277.

Rodrigues, Nina. *Os africanos no Brasil*. 5th ed. São Paulo, 1977.

Romano, Ruggiero. "Tra xvi e xvii sécolo, una crisi economica: 1619–1622." *Revista storica italiana* 74, no. 3 (1962): 480–531.

Rubin, Vera, and Arthur Tuden. *Comparative Perspectives on Slavery in New World Plantation Societies*. New York, 1977.

Russell-Wood, A. J. R. "Class, Creed, and Colour in Colonial Bahia: A Study in Prejudice." *Race* 9, no. 2 (1967): 133–57.
Fidalgos and Philanthropists: The Santa Casa da Misericórdia da Bahia, 1550–1755. Berkeley, 1968.

Ruy, Afonso. *História da câmara municipal da cidade do Salvador*. Salvador, 1949.
A primeira revolução social Brasileira, 1798. Bahia, 1951.

Saunders, A. C. de C. M. *A Social History of Black Slaves and Freedmen in Portugal, 1441–1551*. Cambridge, 1982.

Schorer Petrone, Maria. *A lavoura canavieira em São Paulo*. São Paulo, 1968.

Schwartz, Stuart B. "Le Brésil: le royaume noir des mocambos." *L'Histoire* 41 (Jan. 1981): 38–48.
"Colonial Brazil: The Role of the State in a Slave Social Formation." In Karen Spaulding, ed., *Essays in the Political, Economic, and Social History of Colonial Latin America*, 1–24. Newark, Del., 1982.
"Elite Politics and the Growth of a Peasantry in Late Colonial Brazil." In A. J. R. Russell-Wood, ed., *From Colony to Nation*, 133–54. Baltimore, 1975.

"Free Labor in a Slave Economy: The Lavradores de Cana of Colonial Bahia." In Dauril Alden, ed., *Colonial Roots of Modern Brazil*, 197–98. Berkeley, 1973.

"Indian Labor and New World Plantations: European Demands and Indian Responses in Northeastern Brazil." *American Historical Review* 83, no. 3 (June 1978): 43–79.

"The Manumission of Slaves in Colonial Brazil, Bahia, 1684-1745." *HAHR* 54, no. 4 (Nov. 1974): 603–35.

"The Mocambo: Slave Resistance in Colonial Bahia." *Journal of Social History* 3, no. 4 (summer 1970): 313–33.

"Patterns of Slaveholding in the Americas: New Evidence From Brazil." *AHR* 87, no. 1 (Feb. 1982): 55–86.

"The Plantations of St. Benedict: The Benedictine Sugar Mills of Colonial Brazil." *The Americas* 39, no. 1 (July 1982): 1–22.

"Resistance and Accommodation in Eighteenth-Century Brazil: The Slaves' View of Slavery." *HAHR* 57, no. 1 (Feb. 1979): 69–81.

"Colonial Brazil: Plantations and Peripheries, 1580-1750." In Leslie Bethell, ed., *The Cambridge History of Latin America*, vol. 2, 423–99. 3 vols. to date. Cambridge, 1985.

Sovereignty and Society in Colonial Brazil. Berkeley, 1973.

Sheridan, Richard B. *Sugar and Slavery: An Economic History of the British West Indies, 1623–1775*. Baltimore, 1974.

Simonsen, Roberto. *História econômica do Brasil, 1500–1820*. 4th ed. São Paulo, 1962.

Tannenbaum, Frank. *Slave and Citizen: The Negro in the Americas*. New York, 1947.

Taylor, Kit Sims. "The Economics of Sugar and Slavery in Northeastern Brazil." *Agricultural History* 44, no. 3 (July 1970): 267–80.

Teixeira, Cid. *O morgado na Bahia*. Salvador, 1953.

Thomas, George. *Die portugiesische Indianerpolitik in Brasilien, 1500–1640*. Berlin, 1968.

Vanhagen, Francisco Adolfo de. *História geral do Brasil*. 5 vols. in 3. 7th complete ed. São Paulo, 1962.

Verger, Pierre. *Bahia and the West Coast Trade (1549–1851)*. Ibadan, 1964.

Flux et reflux de la traite des negres entre le golfe de Benin et Bahia de Todos os Santos. Paris, 1968.

Viotti da Costa, Emilia. "The Political Emancipation of Brazil." In A. J. R. Russell-Wood, ed., *From Colony to Nation*, 43–88. Baltimore, 1975.

Wanderley [Araújo] Pinho, [José]. *História de um engenho do Recôncavo*. Rio de Janeiro, 1946.

"Uma Partilha de Bens no Recôncavo da Bahia em 1779, com informações de caráter econômico, social e industrial." *ACCBTSGB* 1 (1966): 315–67.

Wetzel, Herbert Ewaldo. *Mem de Sá. Terceiro Governador geral*. Rio de Janeiro, 1972.

Wiznitzer. Arnold. *Jews in Colonial Brazil*. New York, 1960.

Theses and unpublished works

Alden, Dauril. "Commodity Price Movements in Brazil before, during, and after the Gold Boom, 1670–1769, The Salvador Market." 1983.

Amaral Ferlini, Vera Lucia. "O engenho Sergipe do Conde (1622–1653), Contar, Constatar, Questionar." M.A. thesis, University of São Paulo, 1980.

Aufderheide, Patricia. "Order and Violence: Social Deviance and Social Control in Brazil." Ph.D. thesis, University of Minnesota, 1976.

"Ships and Sugar: Quantitative Analysis of Shipping Records, 1595–1598, 1608–1617." University of Minnesota, 1973.

Barros de Castro, Antônio. "Escravos e Senhores nos engenhos do Brasil." Ph.D. thesis. State University of Campinas, 1976.

Bauss, Rudolph W. "Rio de Janeiro: The Rise of Late Colonial Brazil's Dominant Emporium, 1777–1808." Ph.D. thesis, Tulane University, 1977.

Burmeister, Stephen. "The Slave Population in Three Bahian Parishes: A Profile and Comparisons." University of Minnesota, 1980.

Cortes de Oliveira, Maria Inés. "O liberto: O seu mundo e os outros." M.A. thesis, Federal University of Bahia, 1979.

Denslow, David. "The First Brazilian Sugar Cycle, Growth and Maturity." Yale University, 1970.

Flory, Rae Jean. "Bahian Society in the Mid-Colonial Period: The Sugar Planters, Tobacco Growers, Merchants, and Artisans of Salvador and the Recôncavo, 1680–1725." Ph.D. thesis, University of Texas, 1978.

Harrison, W. F. "A Struggle for Land for Colonial Brazil: The Private Captaincy of Paraíba do Sul, 1533–1753." Ph.D. thesis, University of New Mexico, 1970.

Haskins, Edward. "An Economic Geography of the Bahian Recôncavo." Ph.D. thesis, University of Minnesota, 1956.

Joyce, Joseph Newcombe. "Spanish Influence on Portuguese Administration: A Study of the Conselho da Fazenda and Hapsburg Brazil, 1580–1640" (Ph.D. thesis, University of Southern California, 1974).

Kessler, Arnold. "Bahian Manumission Practices in the Early Nineteenth Century." American Historical Association, 1973.

Lasocki, Barbara Marie-Charlotte Wanda. "A Profile of Bahia (1820–1826), as Seen by Jacques Guinebaud, French Consul General." M.A. thesis, University of California, Los Angeles, 1967.

Lugar, Catherine. "The Merchant Community of Salvador, Bahia, 1780–1830." Ph.D. thesis, State University of New York, Stony Brook, 1980.

McCusker, John James, Jr. "The Rum Trade and the Balance of Payments of the Thirteen Continental Colonies, 1650–1775." 3 vols. Ph.D. thesis, University of Pittsburgh, 1970.

Monteiro, John. "A Study of Sugar Output in Seventeenth-Century Brazil." University of Chicago, 1979.

Morton, F. W. O. "The Conservative Revolution of Independence: Economy, Society and Politics in Bahia, 1790–1840." Ph.D. thesis, Oxford University, 1974.

Mott, Luiz. "A tortura dos escravos na Casa da Torre." Sociedade de Estudos da Cultura Negra, 1984.

Pondé de Sena, Consuelo. "Relações interétnicas através de casamentos realizados na freguesia do Inhambupe na segunda metade do século xviii." Salvador, 1974.

Prince, Howard. "Slave Rebellion in Bahia, 1807–1835." Ph.D. thesis, Columbia University, 1972.

Reis, João José. "Slave Rebellion in Brazil: The African Muslim Uprising in Bahia, 1835." Ph.D. thesis, University of Minnesota, 1982.

Silberstein, Paul. "Wage Earners in a Slave Economy: The Laborers of a Sugar Mill in Colonial Brazil." Berkeley, 1970.

Slenes, Robert. "The Demography and Economy of Brazilian Slavery." Ph.D. thesis, Stanford University, 1976.

Smith, David G. "The Mercantile Class of Portugal and Brazil in the Seventeenth Century: A Socio-Economic Study of the Merchants of Lisbon and Bahia, 1620–1690." Ph.D. thesis, University of Texas, 1975.

Soeiro, Susan, "A Baroque Nunnery: The Economic and Social Role of a Colonial Convent – Santa Clara do Desterro, Salvador, Bahia, 1677–1800." Ph.D. thesis, New York University, 1974.

SOURCES OF FIGURES

1-1. From Theodore De Bry, *Das VII Thiel America* (Frankfort, 1597).

2-1. From a painting by Frans Post.

3-1. From a painting by Albert Eckhout in the National Museum, Copenhagen.

3-2. From the *Reysboeck van het rijcke Brasilien, Rio de la Plata, Magalhanes* (1624).

4-1. Photograph by the author (1973).

4-2. Photography by the author (1973).

4-3. Photograph by the author (1974).

5-1. From a painting by Frans Post.

5-2. Based on information in the livro de safra 1650–1 published in *Documentos para a história do açúcar*, vol. 3, 495–536. Originally published in *CHLA*, II, 434.

5-3. Adapted from Hamilton Fernandes, *Açúcar e álcool: Ontem e hoje* (Rio de Janeiro, 1971).

5-4. Photograph by the author (1978).

5-5. ANTT, Junta do tabacco. Copied by Nancy Schwartz and redrawn by Brenda Quale.

5-6. From William Piso, *Historia naturalis Brasiliae* (Amsterdam, 1648).

6-1. Photography by David Bowe/Filmakers (Minneapolis). Taken in Pernambuco (1972).

6-2. From Willem Piso, *Historia naturalis Brasiliae* (Amsterdam, 1648).

6-3. (a) From Charles Ribeyrolles, *Brazil pittoresco* (Paris, 1861); (b) From a painting by Dirk Stoop in the Museum of the city of Lisbon.

7-1. Sources discussed in Appendix B.

7-2. Joseph Newcombe Joyce, Jr., "Spanish Influence on Portuguese Administration: A Study of the Conselho da Fazenda and Hapsburg Brazil, 1580–1640" (Ph.D. thesis, University of Southern California, 1974); AHU, Bahia pap. avul., caixa 4.

7-3. ANTT, Junta do Tabacco, maços 96A–106 passim; originally appeared in *CHLA*, II, 459.

7-4. Adapted from Stuart B. Schwartz, "Free farmers in a Slave Economy," in Dauril Alden, ed., *Colonial Roots of Modern Brazil* (Berkeley, 1973); Dauril Alden, "Commodity Price Movements in Brazil before, during, and after the Gold Boom, 1670–1769, The Salvador Market" (unpublished paper), 1983, Table 2.

7-5. Sources discussed in Appendix C.

11-1. From Zacarias Wagner, *Thierbuch* (1634–41?), reprinted in E. van den Boogaart, ed., *Johan Maurits van Nassau-Siegen (1604–1679)* (The Hague, 1979), 262.

12-1. Photograph courtesy of the Joaquim Nabuco Foundation (Pernambuco).

14-1. From Johann Moritz Rugendas, *Malerische Reise in Brasilien* (Paris, 1835).

15-1. Data drawn from José Jobson de Andrade Arruda, *O Brasil no comércio colonial* (São Paulo, 1981); Sebastião Ferreira Soares, *Notas estatísticas sobre a produção agrícola e carestia dos gêneros alimentícios no império do Brasil* (Rio de Janeiro, 1860).

15-2. AHU, Iconografia 28366/75.

17-1. From J. B. Debret, *Voyage pittoresque et historique au Brésil* (Paris, 1864).

INDEX

CAMBRIDGE LATIN AMERICAN STUDIES IN PRINT